U0932562

Economic Reform and Development the Chinese Way

汉英对照

中国经济改革发展之路

厉以宁 著　凌　原 译

外语教学与研究出版社
FOREIGN LANGUAGE TEACHING AND RESEARCH PRESS
北京 BEIJING

图书在版编目(CIP)数据

中国经济改革发展之路 = Economic Reform and Development the Chinese Way：汉英对照 / 厉以宁著；凌原译. — 北京：外语教学与研究出版社，2010.11（2016.11 重印）
ISBN 978-7-5135-0369-3

Ⅰ. ①中… Ⅱ. ①厉… ②凌… Ⅲ. ①经济体制改革—中国—文集—汉、英 Ⅳ. ①F121-53

中国版本图书馆 CIP 数据核字（2010）第 221101 号

出 版 人：蔡剑峰
系列策划：吴 浩
责任编辑：任小玫 彭 琳 仲志兰
装帧设计：视觉共振设计工作室
出版发行：外语教学与研究出版社
社　　址：北京市西三环北路 19 号（100089）
网　　址：http://www.fltrp.com
印　　刷：中国农业出版社印刷厂
开　　本：650×980 1/16
印　　张：40
版　　次：2010 年 11 月第 1 版 2016 年 11 月第 4 次印刷
书　　号：ISBN 978-7-5135-0369-3
定　　价：80.00 元

* * *

购书咨询：(010)88819926 **电子邮箱**：club@fltrp.com
外研书店：http://waiyants.tmall.com
凡印刷、装订质量问题，请联系我社印制部
联系电话：(010)61207896 **电子邮箱**：zhijian@fltrp.com
凡侵权、盗版书籍线索，请联系我社法律事务部
举报电话：(010)88817519 **电子邮箱**：banquan@fltrp.com
法律顾问：立方律师事务所 刘旭东律师
中咨律师事务所 殷 斌律师
物料号：203690001

“博雅双语名家名作”出版说明

1840 年鸦片战争以降，在深重的民族危机面前，中华民族精英“放眼看世界”，向世界寻求古老中国走向现代、走向世界的灵丹妙药，涌现出一大批中国主题的经典著述。我们今天阅读这些中文著述的时候，仍然深为字里行间所蕴藏的缜密的考据、深刻的学理、世界的视野和济世的情怀所感动，但往往会忽略：这些著述最初是用英文写就，我们耳熟能详的中文文本是原初英文文本的译本，这些英文作品在海外学术界和文化界同样享有崇高的声誉。

比如，林语堂的 *My Country and My People*（《吾国与吾民》）以幽默风趣的笔调和睿智流畅的语言，将中国人的道德精神、生活情趣和中国社会文化的方方面面娓娓道来，在美国引起巨大反响——林语堂也以其中国主题系列作品赢得世界文坛的尊重，并获得诺贝尔文学奖的提名。再比如，梁思成在抗战的烽火中写就的英文版《图像中国建筑史》文稿（*A Pictorial History of Chinese Architecture*），经其挚友费慰梅女士（Wilma C. Fairbank）等人多年的奔走和努力，于 1984 年由麻省理工学院出版社（MIT Press）出版，并获得美国出版联合会颁发的“专业暨学术书籍金奖”。又比如，1939 年，费孝通在伦敦政治经济学院的博士论文以 *Peasant Life in China—A Field Study of Country Life in the Yangtze Valley* 为名在英国劳特利奇书局（Routledge）出版，后以《江村经济》作为中译本书名——《江村经济》使得靠桑蚕为生的“开弦弓村”获得了世界性的声誉，成为国际社会学界研究中国农村的首选之地。

此外，一些中国主题的经典人文社科作品经海外汉学家和中国学者的如椽译笔，在英语世界也深受读者喜爱。比如，艾恺（Guy S. Alitto）将他 1980 年用中文访问梁漱溟的《这个世界会好吗——梁漱溟晚年口述》一书译成英文（*Has Man a Future?—Dialogues with the Last Confucian*），备受海内外读者关注；

此类作品还有徐中约英译的梁启超著作《清代学术概论》(*Intellectual Trends in the Ch'ing Period*)、狄百瑞(W. T. de Bary)英译的黄宗羲著作《明夷待访录》(*Waiting for the Dawn: A Plan for the Prince*),等等。

有鉴于此,外语教学与研究出版社推出“博雅双语名家名作”系列。

博雅,乃是该系列的出版立意。博雅教育(Liberal Education)早在古希腊时代就得以提倡,旨在培养具有广博知识和优雅气质的人,提高人文素质,培养健康人格,中国儒家六艺“礼、乐、射、御、书、数”亦有此功用。

双语,乃是该系列的出版形式。英汉双语对照的形式,既同时满足了英语学习者和汉语学习者通过阅读中国主题博雅读物提高英语和汉语能力的需求,又以中英双语思维、构架和写作的形式予后世学人以启迪——维特根斯坦有云:“语言的边界,乃是世界的边界”,诚哉斯言。

名家,乃是该系列的作者群体。涵盖文学、史学、哲学、政治学、经济学、考古学、人类学、建筑学等领域,皆海内外名家一时之选。

名作,乃是该系列的入选标准。系列中的各部作品都是经过时间的积淀、市场的检验和读者的鉴别而呈现的经典,正如卡尔维诺对“经典”的定义:经典并非你正在读的书,而是你正在重读的书。

胡适在《新思潮的意义》(1919年12月1日,《新青年》第7卷第1号)一文中提出了“研究问题、输入学理、整理国故、再造文明”的范式。秉着“记载人类文明、沟通世界文化”的出版理念,我们推出“博雅双语名家名作”系列,既希望能够在中国人创作的和以中国为主题的博雅英文文献领域“整理国故”,亦希望在和平发展、改革开放的新时代为“再造文明”、为“向世界说明中国”略尽绵薄之力。

外语教学与研究出版社
人文社科出版分社

中文自序

收集在《中国经济改革发展之路》这本论文选中的文章，是我在 1980 年到 1998 年之间发表的论文中的一部分。它们反映了我在这段时间内所思考的有关中国经济发展的问题。

例如，《论教育在经济增长中的作用》一文，发表于 1980 年。这时正值中国实行改革开放不久，拨乱反正，百废待兴。我感到 20 世纪 60 年代后期起，长达 10 年的“文化大革命”期间中国的教育事业不但没有任何发展，反而遭到十分严重的破坏，教育出现了大倒退，其原因之一在于从领导人到一般群众都轻视教育，轻视人才的培养。因此，必须把发展教育和重视人才视为当时最重要的工作。这篇文章就是在这样的背景下写成的。我指出，不重视教育，中国不仅会失去现在，更会失去未来。

《经济改革的基本思路》一文发表于 1986 年。中国的经济改革从 1979 年算起，至此已经进行了大约 7 年多。农村的家庭承包制已在全国范围内推广，农产品供给大量增加，人民生活已初步改善。这时面临的主要问题是如何在城市经济中推进改革。在这篇文章中，我提出了必须把国有企业改革放在首要地位，即必须把政企不分、产权不清晰的国有企业通过股份制改造为自负盈亏和自主经营的多元投资主体的企业。我认为这是中国经济改革取得成功的保证，也是今后中国经济顺利发展的制度前提。

接着，在 1987 年我发表了《社会主义所有制体系的探索》一文。这是一篇讨论今后长时期内中国经济发展的多元所有制格局的文章。在这篇文章中，我提出，中国今后的所有制体系将是一种二元经济体系：一方面是少数大型的企业集团，它们是多个投资主体投资形成的；另一方面是大量中小企业、个体工商户和承包制农户，它们中以个人投资或合作社投资为主。这种二元经济体系对中国经济发展中的经济增长、技术进步、缓解就业压力和提高居民收入等问题都会起到良好的作用。

《贫困地区经济与环境的协调发展》一文发表于 1991 年。这时，我兼任了国务院环境保护委员会的顾问，从事环境经济方面的研究。在调查中，我越来越感觉到发展贫困地区经济和保护环境、治理环境之间有非常密切的关系；如果单纯扶贫而不致力于贫困地区经济和环境协调发展，将事倍功半，不能使那里的人民真正脱贫致富。一年之后，中国政府成立了中国环境发展国际合作委员会，我被聘为中方委员兼环境经济专家工作组组长，继续这一领域内的研究和政策咨询工作。

1993 年，中国出现了投资过热现象，从而引发了严重的通货膨胀，怎样应对这一问题，成为中国经济学界当时普遍关注的问题。我发表了《非均衡条件下经济增长与波动的若干理论问题》一文，阐述了我对政府调控政策的观点。在这篇论文中，我提出了非均衡条件两条警戒线的分析思路。由于中国经济是非均衡的，因此无论是失业率还是通货膨胀率都大于零应该被认为是必然的，不可能把警戒线定在零失业率或零通货膨胀率的水平上。究竟多高的失业率或多高的通货膨胀率可以作为警戒线，可以根据具体情况再定。而且，应当设立两条警戒线，我把它们分别称作第一警戒线和第二警戒线。这样，根据零失业率线或零通货膨胀率线、第一警戒线和第二警戒线，整个经济运行空间被划分为四块：

1. 经济运行于零失业率线或零通货膨胀率线以下，是不正常的，这时或者形成劳动力不足，或者形成通货紧缩，这些都需要政府采取相应的宏观调控措施。

2. 零失业率线或零通货膨胀率线以上而没有突破第一警戒线的经济运行，是正常的。这时不需要进行政府的宏观调控。

3. 第一警戒线以上而没有突破第二警戒线的经济运行，属于轻度的非正常经济运行。这时需要采取适度的宏观调控措施。

4. 经济运行于第二警戒线以上，这属于严重的非正常经济运行，不仅需要政府加强宏观经济调控，甚至在必要时可以采取非常规的调节手段。

1997 年，东南亚金融危机已经开始，中国经济也受到一定影响。在这一背景下，我发表了《论财政政策与货币政策的配合使用》一文。这篇论文的基本论点是：无论是应对当时发生的东南亚金融危机，还是作为中国国内的经济政策，都应当学会如何配合使用财政政策与货币政策。“双紧”（指紧的财政政策和紧的货币政策）和“双松”（指松的财政政策和松的货币政策）都只是特殊情况下才能使用的宏观调控。一般情况下，财政政策和货币政策需要“松紧搭配”：即货币政策抽紧时，财政政策不妨宽松些；而财政政策抽紧时，货币政策不妨宽松些。这样才能获得较好的成效。

《论效率的双重基础》一文发表于1998年。写作这篇文章的背景是：随着市场化的进展，中国国内普遍对效率有了足够的重视，然而对于效率的基础却认识得不够清楚。本文指出，效率有两个基础：一是效率的物质技术基础，一是效率的道德基础。设备、厂房、原材料、职工的技术水平，都包括在效率的物质技术基础内。人们的信念、信心、文化和道德水平，则包括在效率的道德基础内。历史表明，仅仅有效率的物质技术基础，只能产生常规效率。那么，超常规的效率来自何处？来自道德基础。由此可以看出人们的信念、信心、文化和道德水平的重要性。针对中国的经济发展而言，当前的一项迫切任务是充实效率的道德基础，让人们的信念、信心、文化和道德水平在经济发展中发挥更大的作用。

以上所提到的，只是这本论文集中所收集的一部分文章的内容摘要。我相信读者在读完这本《中国经济改革发展之路》之后，将会了解我在20世纪80年代至90年代内有关中国经济发展的基本观点。

本书英文版的出版，得到郝平教授、凌原教授、蔡洪滨教授、周黎安教授的大力帮助。没有他们的帮助，本书不可能这么快就同读者见面。外研社社长于春迟、外研社总编辑蔡剑峰以及外研社人文社科分社吴浩、彭琳、任小玫、仲志兰等同志认真负责的精神，令我十分感动。在此双语版出版之际，我一并向他们致以衷心的感谢。

厉以宁

2010年10月16日

于北京大学光华管理学院

FOREWORD

The success of China's reform and development in the last thirty-two years has attracted global attention. The major steps which have led to China's success exhibit many Chinese characteristics. Of these the most striking is the ownership reform in the state and other nonprivate sectors. The theoretical and policy preparations for ownership reform took more than ten years. From being heterodox in the mid-1980s they had become mainstream thinking by the mid-1990s.

Professor Li Yining was arguably the most eminent figure in this process. His most influential public speech on ownership reform entitled, "Basic thoughts on economic restructuring" (Essay No. 3 in this selection), was delivered on April 25, 1986 in Peking University. His famous remark, "Economic restructuring may break down if price reform fails. The success of economic restructuring, however, hinges not on price reform, but on ownership reform, which entails revamping the corporate system," soon appeared in the headlines of a number of leading reformist newspapers and later on became a new proverb in the discourse of Chinese reforms.

In the mid-1980s, "market socialism," which was initially promoted by Oscar Lange and Abba Lerner, was the guiding principle of economic reform in China and Eastern European socialist countries. This principle advocated that the introduction of autonomy to state-owned enterprises (SOEs) would induce SOEs to behave like profit-maximizing firms. Once SOEs became sufficiently autonomous, comprehensive price reforms (i.e., price liberalization) would lead to the final success of the economic reform.[1] In line with this mainstream paradigm, Chinese leaders also endorsed the "big bang" approach and implemented a "one-shot" comprehensive price reform in the late 1980s, which, unfortunately, led to more problems than it solved.

At the other end of the spectrum of the reform debates, criticisms of the theory of market socialism and its reform practices in Eastern Europe since 1968, led by Professor János Kornai, became increasingly influential in the 1980s. Kornai's book *Economics of Shortage* became a bestseller in economics and Kornai himself an iconic figure among young intellectuals in China. His insightful analysis of state ownership and bureaucratic coordination led many young economists to believe that without ultimate private ownership, the expansion of enterprise autonomy and self-management under impersonalized state ownership would not be a medicine that would be effective in curing the soft budget constraint (SBC) syndrome. The SBC syndrome would continue to dull the price responsiveness of enterprises and thereby constrain the effects of price signals. Kornai himself later also concluded that unless state property was sold to private owners at a real market price, an attempt to reduce the percentage of state ownership gradually, i.e., to 95, 90, 85 percent and so on would not be able to make a difference.[2]

In sharp contrast to the above strands of thought, Professor Li had a keen observation of the *de facto* diverse property rights structure existing in SOEs in China. He argued that it was feasible and desirable to adopt the shareholding system in SOEs by quantifying interests among different public owners and then converting such quantified interests into shareholdings. With such a shareholding system in place, an individual public agency would have a measurable stake in the fortunes of a firm from which the agency would draw cash flow and control rights. As a result public agencies could more easily consolidate their material interests and assemble more consistent business strategies when facing market competition. They would find it in their best material interest to increase the value of the firm rather than to extend bureaucratic control over it. Furthermore, mixed ownership for a company as a result of joint investment by public, collective, and private partners and diverse forms of ownership in the economy would stimulate competition and induce further property rights reform (also see Essay No. 4 in this selection, first published in 1987).[3]

In the context of China in the mid-1980s, when the official ideology still viewed socialist state ownership as 100 percent ownership by the state on behalf of the whole people, it was analytically valuable, practically significant, and politically brave and skillful to highlight the *de facto* plural property rights structure of existing state ownership and then to link this structure to the feasibility and desirability of ownership reform.

Within academic circles in the West, Granick (1990) appears to have been the first person to analyze this plural structure.[4] Highlighting that Chinese SOEs were in fact agents with multiple principals exercising control over them, he asserted that these multiple principals acquired property rights through past investment in SOEs or traditional associations with individual SOEs. He cited a 1966 slogan "whoever builds and manages the enterprise has the use of its output." This slogan was regarded as epitomizing property rights relationships of the 1970s, i.e., instead of control rights being derived from ownership, *de facto* control rights now define ownership. In other words, this practical property rights arrangement is opposed to the usual textbook teaching in which the right to management is an attribute of ownership.

Rooted in the Chinese reality, the analytical work of Professor Li reveals that the conventional wisdom on state ownership in both the West and East is descriptively narrow. The claim that private investors should own the firm, despite its importance, is not the unique logical prerequisite of free markets and free enterprise. Diverse ownership and governance forms can emerge and evolve that are compatible with the evolutionary development of free market and free enterprise. The Chinese like to create a nickname for someone famous for a particular legacy and, not surprisingly, Professor Li is now known throughout China, as "Li Shareholding."

Another area to which Professor Li has made an important contribution is comparative economic history and the history of economic thought (cf., Essay No. 11 in this selection, published in 1993).[5] Integrating such comparative studies with his deep understanding of economic practices in China, he proposed an innovative augment on disequilibrium theory. As presented in Essays No. 5 (published in 1988) and No. 12 (published in 1993) of this selection,[6] he distinguishes two types of disequilibrium based on whether the majority of firms in the economy are viable profit-makers or not. The first type corresponds to the one dealt with in the existing disequilibrium theory, which features excessive demand or supply due to market friction, stickiness of prices and wages, and demand or supply constraints, rather than nonviability of firms. The second type is characterized not only by an underdeveloped market but also enterprises under various forms of bureaucratic control. He argues that China's economy has belonged to the second category throughout its transition process. To make the transition from the second type of disequilibrium to the first, the top priority is the reform of enterprise system with the aim of producing viable and profit-oriented enterprises.[7] This line of thinking provides a further support to his famous remark—"ownership restructuring holds key to the reform."

In addition to constructing this second analytical foundation for his ownership reform theory, Professor Li's work on the Chinese economy in disequilibrium also emphasizes the fundamental importance of achieving and maintaining healthy economic growth and social development in China under the conditions of the second type of disequilibrium. The majority of his essays in this selection discuss various coordination issues across economic reform, growth and development, and the urgency of finding solutions to immediate practical policy dilemmas. The central normative guideline has been that the reform and transition are means to serve economic growth and social development and, furthermore, that economic growth and social development are means to serve the well-being and happiness of ordinary citizens in society.

In dealing with the immediate policy dilemma, Professor Li has incorporated the methodology of "dialectical thought and synthetic analysis" of traditional Chinese medicine, which emphasizes holistic connections among many facets of human anatomy and physiology and examines the effect of the social and natural environment on the interrelations and conditioning of *yin* and *yang*. He pays particular attention to both the "treatment effect" and "side effect" of each policy pill, as well as its short-run and long-run effects. For instance, the first essay of this selection was published in June 1980 when the high urban unemployment rate was at the top of policy agenda. With a thorough and comprehensive analysis of the historical and structural roots of the high unemployment rate, Professor Li suggested that in the short and medium run, the solution would be to actively develop labor-intensive manufacturing industries and labor-intensive export processing to take advantage of China's abundant low-skilled labor force. However, in the long run, China has to develop human capital intensive manufacturing and services industries and actively promote human capital intensive exports so as to convert the persistent population pressure into an emerging comparative advantage. Therefore, it was strategically important to significantly increase investment in education in the 1980s so that China would no longer suffer high unemployment rates in the next two to three decades and become well prepared for the inevitable era of human capital intensive production and exports. Clearly, this vision is still valid today.

The publication of this *Economic Reform and Development the Chinese Way* enriches the literature in English that examines the past, present and future prospects of China's reforms, transition, and development. Although all the essays in this selection are well-known in China, they provide carefully examined alternative perspectives which scholars and students in the West may not be familiar with. I am honored to write the foreword for this excellent selection and commend it enthusiastically to scholars, policy makers, business professionals, as well as to more general readers, who are interested in the dynamics of China's transition and the growing importance of China in the world.

Academician, the Academy of Social Sciences, UK
Professor and Head, Department of Financial & Management Studies,
School of Oriental & African Studies, University of London,
August 9, 2010

THE ROLE OF EDUCATION IN ECONOMIC GROWTH (1980)

In my speech "Technology education and capitalist industrialization: a study of the rise of technological power in Western Europe and America,"[1] I dwelled on the relationship between education and economic growth in light of economic history. What I was driving at was that education is a major recourse for nations to groom technological personnel, and that only by putting a premium on education and the cultivation of talents can less developed nations boost their economic growth rates and catch up with and surpass the developed countries. As I put it in that speech, the role of education in economic growth has five aspects:

"First, education provides society with a supply of researchers and designers who can venture into the unknown, innovating in science, renovating and transforming productive technology. Without such contingents, the best a nation can do is to tag along after other nations, but in that way you cannot score major breakthroughs in science and technology.

"Second, education provides society with engineers and technicians who can master and apply advanced means of production. Without such technocrats, even if a nation has acquired sophisticated tools of production, it cannot put them to best use.

"Third, education brings forth production and technology managers well adapted to society's level of industrialization. Without teams of such managers, the production process can be prone to colossal waste in human, material and financial resources, making it impossible to benefit from the superiority of advanced productive technology.

"Fourth, education enhances society's scientific and cultural attainment, and sets the stage for promoting new products and disseminating and upgrading knowledge in science and technology. At the same time, education also lays the groundwork for the future growth of a nation's technological prowess, and guarantees the supply of a constant stream of high-caliber researchers, engineers and managers, and skilled workers.

"Fifth, education enables society to preserve and disseminate its accumulation of scientific knowledge and productive experience free from barriers of time and space and national boundaries. It is through education that such accumulated knowledge and experience are spread from one nation to another and from one generation to another as humanity's shared assets."

论教育在经济增长中的作用（1980）

两年前，我在《技术教育和资本主义工业化：西欧和美国技术力量形成问题研究》一文（1978 年北京大学“五四”科学讨论会上的报告，发表于《社会科学战线》1978 年第 4 期）中，曾从经济史的角度对教育同经济增长的关系作过一些分析。在那篇文章里，我所着重考察的是：教育是培养一国技术力量的主要途径；后进国家提高经济增长率以及在经济上赶上和超过先进国家的原因之一就是重视教育、重视人才的培养。关于教育在经济增长中的作用，在该文中归纳为以下五点：

“第一，它向社会提供一支能在科学上有发现、发明，在生产技术上有创新、变革的科学研究和设计队伍。如果没有这样一支队伍，在科学技术上至多只能步别国的后尘，很难取得重大的突破。

第二，它向社会提供一支能掌握和运用先进生产方法的技术队伍。如果没有这样一支队伍，即使有了先进的生产工具和生产方法，它们也不可能充分发挥作用。

第三，它向社会提供一支适应于工业化水平的生产和技术管理人员的队伍。如果没有这样一支队伍，就会造成生产过程中人力、物力、财力的巨大浪费，就不能发挥先进生产技术的优越性。

第四，它提高全社会的科学文化水平，为新产品的推广使用、为先进科学技术知识的普及和提高准备条件，同时也为今后技术力量的成长提供广阔的基础，为源源不断的高质量的科研人员、工程技术人员、管理人员和熟练工人的供给提供保证。

第五，它使社会积累起来的科学知识和生产经验得以保存和传播，这种传播可以不受国界的限制，也不受时间的限制。累积起来的科学知识和生产经验作为人类共同财富，通过教育从一个民族传播给另一个民族，从这一代传播给下一代。”

I would like to go on with my observation of the relationship between education and economic growth on the basis of the speech I made and published two years ago. However, this paper has a different focus. While in my previous speech I looked into the major role education plays in expanding the economy and raising its growth rate, this paper underlines education's important role in ensuring economic stability and sustained growth, and in providing effective solutions to problems that have occurred or may occur in the process of economic growth. In other words, my previous speech was about economic growth *per se*, whereas this paper is a study of employment, balance of international payments, income distribution, financial balance and other issues occurring in the process of stabilizing and sustaining economic growth. Furthermore, while my previous speech proceeded from the perspective of the economic history of Western Europe and America, this paper takes China's socialist economy as its focus and background.

This paper is delivered in four sections dealing respectively with education's relationship with employment, balance of international payments, income distribution, and fiscal balance, so as to illustrate education's role in guaranteeing economic stability and sustained growth.

I. The "structural" nature of the employment problem can be solved by developing and restructuring education

Theoretically speaking, any nation can grow its economy either by expanding its workforce or by investing more in machines and equipment and improving workers' technical knowhow and skills. The adoption of labor-saving technology and equipment may help cut down the material production sector's demand for workers in the course of economic growth. Consequently, given a constant population growth rate, economic growth itself cannot ensure full employment. The number of jobs to be created through output increase is determined not only by the rate of production expansion, but also by which approaches are adopted for such expansion. If a country develops its economy not by hiring more workers but by adopting new technology and equipment and improving workers' cultural and technical proficiency, then the ability of its material production sector to absorb the workforce will be limited.

本文以两年前发表的那篇文章为基础，继续考察教育同经济增长的关系。但这两篇文章的着重点有所不同。前一篇文章分析教育在促进一国经济增长和提高经济增长率方面的重要作用，本文分析教育在保证一国经济稳定、持续增长，以及有效地解决经济增长过程中发生的或可能发生的各种问题方面的重要作用。换言之，前一篇文章考察的范围在于经济增长本身，本文考察的范围在于稳定、持续经济增长过程中的社会就业、国际收支、收入分配、财政平衡等问题。此外，前一篇文章是从西欧和美国经济史的角度进行考察的，本文则以当前我国社会主义经济作为考察的对象。

本文分为四部分，分别考察教育与社会就业、国际收支、收入分配、财政平衡之间的关系，说明教育在保证经济稳定、持续增长中的作用。

一、我国当前社会就业问题的"结构性"。这种"结构性"就业问题要依靠发展教育和调整教育结构来解决

从理论上说，任何一个国家的经济增长既可以通过增加劳动力数量来实现，也可以不通过增加劳动力数量，而通过增加对机器设备的投资，并相应地提高劳动者的技术水平和熟练程度来实现。在经济增长过程中，由于物质生产部门采用节约劳动的新技术设备的结果，有可能减少对劳动力数量的需要。因此，在一定的人口增长率条件下，经济增长本身并不能保证充分就业。物质生产部门在增加生产量的过程中究竟能够吸收多少人就业，不仅取决于这些部门的增长速度，而且取决于这些部门采取什么样的经济增长途径。如果一国主要不是依靠增加劳动力数量，而是依靠新技术设备的采用和劳动力文化技术水平的提高来实现经济增长的话，物质生产部门本身能吸收的劳动力将是有限的。

On the other hand, economic growth also entails a process of change in a nation's economic structure. The inexorable law of material production is that some old manufacturing industries decline or are phased out while new ones rise and grow. The ratio between material and nonmaterial production in the national economy is changing as well. It is an irrevocable trend in economic growth for some nonmaterial production industries to grow in strength along with their shares in the national economy. With the national economic structure changing constantly, those working in languishing or failed industries need to find new jobs elsewhere. The rising industries in material production, and particularly the burgeoning industries in nonmaterial production, often run short of workforce. Thus in the long term, the emergence and growth of new industries in both material and nonmaterial production are major reasons why a nation can increase employment amidst economic growth.

The changing economic structure of a nation implies changes in both industrial and geo-economic structures. In China, underdeveloped regions may achieve a relatively higher economic growth rate, whereas developed regions may slow down, or grow at a relatively lower pace. Regions that either suffer a low growth rate or maintain a high growth rate mainly by spending more on technology and equipment will produce a glut of factory layoffs that will have to seek employment elsewhere, whereas regions with a high growth rate, those with a labor shortage in particular, are likely to accept the job-hunters.

These situations prove clearly that the employment problem confronting a country in the process of economic growth is mainly "structural." That is to say, the success or failure in tackling this problem hinges on whether the workforce structure—the makeup of workers of different trades, industries and locations in a region's total number of workers—is commensurate with local economic growth rates and economic structural changes, and whether the workforce itself can meet the technical needs of local economic growth. When the structure of a workforce does not match the local economic growth rate and the changing local economic structure, and when workers' technical proficiency level falls short of the needs of economic growth, unemployment will unavoidably exist alongside a surplus of unfilled job vacancies.

另一方面，一国经济增长过程也是一国经济结构变化的过程。在物质生产领域内，必然有些部门或行业衰落下去，甚至被淘汰，另一些部门或行业则不断兴起、发展。物质生产领域与非物质生产领域在国民经济中的比重也会发生变化，非物质生产领域的一些部门的发展及其在国民经济中所占比重的增大，是经济增长的不可避免的趋势。在衰落和被淘汰的部门就业的劳动者，随着国民经济结构的变化，需要另谋职业，转移工作部门。在新兴的物质生产部门中，尤其是在日益发展的非物质生产部门中，劳动力则往往是不足的。因此，一国经济增长过程之所以能够增加就业，从长期趋势来看，主要依靠新兴物质生产部门的发展和各种非物质生产部门的发展。

一国经济结构的变化不仅包括部门结构的变化，而且包括地区结构的变化。国内原来经济较不发达的地区在经济增长过程中可能以较快的速度增长，而原来经济比较发达的地区经济增长速度则可能减缓，或者以相对较慢的速度增长。这样，经济增长率较慢的地区，或者经济增长率虽高但主要依靠增加技术设备投资来实现经济增长的地区，劳动力将会过多，这些人也必须另找就业岗位。而经济增长率较高的地区，特别是原来劳动力不足的地区，则有可能吸收就业者。

从上述这些情况来分析，可以清楚地看到，一国经济增长过程中所遇到的社会就业问题，主要是“结构性”就业问题。这就是说，社会就业问题能否顺利地得到解决，要看劳动力的结构（不同技术水平的劳动力、不同工种的劳动力、不同地区的劳动力在劳动力总数中的构成）与经济增长速度是否适应，与经济结构的变化是否适应，要看劳动力本身在技术方面是否符合经济增长的要求。在劳动力结构与经济增长速度、经济结构变化不适应的情况下，在劳动者的技术水平不符合经济增长要求的情况下，经济增长过程中失业与职位空缺的并存将是不可避免的。

This paradoxical coexistence of unemployment and superfluous vacancies means that while people are looking frantically for jobs, many jobs are left unfilled. How is it that people lose jobs while the economy keeps growing? The answer is that if economic growth is achieved for the most part by raising labor productivity, while the population growth rate remains relatively high, those coming of employment age are likely to fail to land suitable jobs. Even if these people are a nonfactor, industries and regions with slow or stagnant growth lay off workers. This is particularly true of developing countries, where agriculture—known for its low labor productivity—often dominates the national economy. In the industrialization process, large numbers of villagers who have just quit farming may find it hard to land jobs. Unemployment—concealed unemployment[2] included—thus becomes unavoidable.

Why, then, are there vacancies that remain unoccupied? This is because, when the workforce structure does not tally with the prevailing economic growth rate and economic structure, the rising industries in both material and nonmaterial production cannot find what they want badly: skilled workers and competent engineers, technicians, researchers, and managers. The same labor shortage can also occur in established industries in material production that maintain growth by relying heavily on new technology and equipment, so much so that even workers on their payrolls cannot measure up to what such new technology and equipment require of them. Seemingly unwanted jobs may also occur in newly developed places where required workers are in short supply. This is an outstanding problem with developing countries, where, for historical reasons, skilled workers that can keep pace with industrialization are scarce.

Generally speaking, the number of the jobless can never match the number of jobs awaiting them in a national economy. The ratio between the two numbers differs with the changes and readjustments in a nation's economic growth rate and economic and workforce structure. However, even if the two numbers match each other, they cannot offset each other, because workers of different proficiency levels and fields of work are not interchangeable under modern production and technological conditions. In the long run, the coexistence of unemployment and unfilled job vacancies in a nation's economic growth is not temporary, but, most probably, perpetual. That is to say, job vacancies may disappear

失业与职位空缺并存，就是说，一方面是“人找事”，另一方面是“事找人”。经济增长过程中为什么会有失业？这是因为在经济增长主要靠提高劳动生产率来实现，而人口增长率又比较高时，新达到就业年龄的劳动力很可能找不到工作。即使不考虑新达到就业年龄的劳动力，那么增长率相对缓慢或停滞的部门和地区也会游离出一批劳动力。特别是对发展中国家来说，情况更为显著，因为在这样的国家中，农业一直在国民经济中占有重要地位，而农业中原来的劳动生产率一直是较低的。工业化过程中，从农业中游离出来的大量劳动力在社会上找不到可以容纳他们的工作岗位。因此，失业（包括隐蔽失业）是不可能避免的。

为什么同时又出现职位空缺？这主要是因为新兴的物质生产部门以及非物质生产领域内某些需要熟练劳动力的部门在劳动力结构与经济增长速度、经济结构不适应的情况下，找不到所需要的劳动者，例如技术工人、工程技术人员、科学研究人员、管理人员等。即使是原有的物质生产部门，如果它们的经济增长主要依靠采用新技术装备来实现，那么该部门内原来就业的劳动者也很可能不适合要求。因此这些部门也是缺少劳动力的。此外，职位空缺还可能出现于新发展的地区，因为这些地区本身无法提供所需要的劳动力。这种情况在发展中国家也是很突出的，因为这些国家中，由于历史的原因，适应于工业化要求的熟练劳动力尤其缺乏。

一般说来，国民经济中的失业人数与职位空缺额不可能恰好相符。二者之间的比率随一国经济增长率、经济结构变化情况和劳动力结构调整情况而异。但即使失业人数与职位空缺额基本上相符，它们也不可能彼此抵消，因为在现代生产技术条件下，不同技术水平和工种的劳动力往往不可能替代。所以从长期趋势来看，一国经济增长过程中，失业与职位空缺并存的现象不是暂时性的，而很可能是持久性的，即旧的失业人员就业了，职位空缺现象消失了，

when long-time job-seekers have found their jobs, but will occur again when new layoffs arrive on the scene. Unemployment, concealed unemployment included, is a waste of human resources, while job vacancies left unfilled are a waste of material resources—for them to exist at the same time is not only detrimental to economic growth, but also holds back the adoption and popularization of new technology and economic restructuring. The result is that the economy remains mired in low efficiency. Chronic joblessness can also be a major destabilizing factor for society.

In a nutshell, employment problems in a growing economy are attributable to the failure in reconciling the conflict between unemployment and unfilled job vacancies. Such is the "structural" nature of employment.

The employment problems confronting China are complicated. Some are universal to all economies, some are common to developing nations in economic development, but others are peculiarly China's own. These three categories of employment problems are intertwined. The universal ones stem from the fact that the increasing use of sophisticated machines and technological equipment has whittled down producers' need for workers, unskilled workers in particular. Those common to developing nations arise from the new job needs of large numbers of unskilled laborers that have just quit farming at the time of an agrarian society's transition to industrialization. The employment problems peculiarly of China's own are partly to be blamed on incompetent labor administration, but most of them are attributed to the lopsided economic development resulting from the ten-year chaos of the Cultural Revolution that considerably narrowed down people's job options. These problems were aggravated by the excessive population growth in the late 1950s and the early 1960s. Today, those born in those years are coming of age or will soon become eligible for jobs. If the employment problems for these people cannot be properly handled, both society and the economy will be in jeopardy. The situation is also complicated by a dire shortage of skilled workers and the low labor productivity of those in their jobs. The dilemma facing China today is that while many job-seeking youths are having trouble finding jobs, factories, too, find it hard to fill jobs with qualified workers. A nation's aggregate volume of labor resources are derived by multiplying the total number of workers with their average

但新的失业人员又出现了，新的职位空缺现象又产生了。失业（包括隐蔽失业）是人力资源的浪费，职位空缺是物质资源的浪费，失业与职位空缺的并存不仅不利于经济增长，而且将阻碍新技术的采用和推广，阻碍经济结构的必要调整，使一国经济停留在长期低效率的状态。特别是失业的长期化还会成为社会不稳定的一个重要因素。

总之，经济增长过程中的社会就业问题，很大程度上可以归结为经济增长过程中失业与职位空缺之间的矛盾无法得到解决。这就是社会就业的"结构性"。

我国的社会就业问题是复杂的。当前我们面临的社会就业问题，既有属于上述一般经济增长过程中带有普遍性的问题，又有作为发展中国家在经济发展过程中遇到的共同问题，还有我国所特有的问题。这三种问题是交织在一起的。属于一般经济增长过程中的问题，主要指先进机器使用和技术装备率提高后，物质生产部门中对劳动力的需求相对减少、对非熟练劳动力的需求甚至绝对减少。属于发展中国家经济发展中的共同问题，主要指在从农业社会转向工业社会的过程中，从农业中必然游离出大量非熟练劳动力，需要有就业岗位容纳他们。属于我国特有的问题，除了劳动管理体制不够完善以外，主要指十年动乱给国民经济造成了严重破坏，比例失调，使得劳动就业门路十分狭窄。加上 50 年代末、60 年代初人口增长过速，以致二十岁左右的青年人如今大批走上或即将走上工作岗位，如果就业问题不能妥善解决，对社会和经济增长都是非常不利的。但与此同时，我国当前也存在熟练劳动力供给不足、在职人员劳动生产率低的问题。一方面许多待业青年没有工作岗位，另一方面不少工作岗位找不到适合的工作人员。劳动力总资源等于劳动力数量与劳动者平均技术熟练水平（劳动力质量的主要标志）的乘积。

level of technical competency—the chief indicator of labor quality. In that sense, China's aggregate volume of labor resources is by no means abundant because its workers' average skill proficiency is low despite their sheer numbers.

The solution to our nation's employment problems, in the final analysis, is to create a constant supply of new jobs to keep pace with economic growth. If we cannot create new jobs, the need for labor will shrink with the adoption of new technology, even if population growth is kept at a low level. How to create new jobs? This involves the diverse economic sectors and forms of public ownership under the socialist system, as well as such factors as economic administration, various types of technical innovation, and the ratios between sectors and economic growth rate. These issues, however, are beyond the scope of this study. The topic at hand is this: Supposing substantial numbers of new jobs are created by readjusting and revamping the ownership structure, the economic system and the ratios between economic sectors, and by riding the nation's robust economic growth, can the nation come to grips with its employment problems? Given the "structural" nature of employment in our country, we can assert categorically that the disparity between the structure of the workforce and that of the national economy will never be eradicated without corresponding development in education and without restructuring the education system. The dilemma between "people hunting for jobs" and "jobs seeking takers," too, will remain for a long time to come. The important role of education in tackling employment problems rests precisely on its ability to deliver the nation from that dilemma.

Developing education and spending more on it can help dovetail the workforce structure with a growing economy's need for workers at different technical levels and in different fields of work. To achieve that end, we have got to adapt our educational structure to the changing economic growth rate and structure, and act on the long-term need of economic growth to readjust the categories of schools and the setup of academic programs, and to variegate the schooling terms. Long years of observation reveal two options in this regard. In the first option, when existing and prospective job-seekers are not outnumbered by anticipated unfilled job vacancies, the main thrust of our effort can be directed at

就这个意义上说，目前我国的劳动力总资源并不是十分丰富的，因为劳动力数量虽多，劳动者的平均技术熟练水平却比较低。

要使当前我国的社会就业问题得到妥善解决，归根到底有待于在经济增长过程中不断地创造出新的工作岗位。如果无法增加新的工作岗位，那么即使人口增长率很低，只要采用了新技术，对劳动力的需要仍会减少。但怎样才能增加新工作岗位呢？这里涉及社会主义制度下多种经济成分并存、社会主义公有制多种形式并存的问题，也涉及经济管理体制、技术创新类型、国民经济各部门比例关系以及经济增长速度等问题。这些方面的问题不是本文所要探讨的内容。本文所要讨论的是：假定通过所有制形式、体制、比例关系等方面的调整和改革，假定国民经济有较大幅度的增长，确实创造出相当多的新工作岗位，我国的社会就业问题能否得到解决呢？如果考虑到我国社会就业问题的"结构性"，那么可以断言，在教育事业没有相应的发展、教育结构未作相应的调整的条件下，劳动力结构与经济结构之间不相适应的情况是不会消除的。"人找事"和"事找人"的矛盾将会长期存在。教育对于解决就业问题的重要作用，正在于它有助于解决这一矛盾。

发展教育事业和增加对教育事业的支出，可以使劳动力的结构适合于经济增长对不同技术水平和不同工种的劳动力的需要。在这里，重要的问题是使教育的结构同经济增长速度、经济结构的变化相适应，根据长期经济增长的需要来调整各种类型学校的设置、各种专业的设置，以及作出各种不同学习期限的安排。从长期考察，不外乎以下两种可能性。一种可能性是：从长期看，待业人数和未来新达到就业年龄的人数之和可能小于预计的职位空缺额，那么调整的重点将放在进一步提高教育

further improving education and raising workforce quality, so that every worker that has been educated or trained can qualify for more demanding jobs, thereby enhancing labor productivity and further promoting the adoption of new technology. In this way, not only can the needs of economic growth be met, but the number of unfilled job vacancies can be curtailed as well. In the other option, when the total number of existing and prospective job-hunters outgrows the anticipated number of unfilled job vacancies, we can lay equal stress on improving and universalizing education, so that more high-caliber professionals can be cultivated for the national economy while legions of job-waiters are tooled with one kind of skill or another to qualify for suitable jobs. To achieve this end, apart from further restructuring the economy to increase job vacancies, attention should also be paid to developing secondary technical and vocational education so as to put more job-seekers through training. The school term for students can be lengthened so as to curtail the number of prospective job hunters and better prepare students culturally and technically for future economic growth needs. In other words, we would rather let our youngsters learn more knowledge and skill than keep them waiting for jobs when they are ill prepared in both skill and knowledge.

As things stand today, it is believed the second option is more workable for China for a long time to come. Thus, in education development and reform, we cannot go single-mindedly after improvement to the neglect of the role of education in tackling the "structural" employment problem.

We should also remember that education reform cannot be accomplished overnight. For one thing, economic growth itself demands that our schools supply large numbers of well-educated and skilled workers who measure up to its needs. Failing this, stable and sustainable economic growth will be out of the question. For another, the economy's ever-changing sectoral, regional and technological structures call for the adaptation of the education system. A certain level of national economic development is always consistent with a certain structure of education, with the latter changing in sync with the former. This fact should be considered when mapping out long-term national human resource plans.

水平、提高劳动力质量上，使每一个受过教育或训练的劳动力能发挥更大的作用，从而提高劳动生产率，进一步推动新技术的采用和推广。这样，既可以适应经济增长的需要，又可以减少职位的空缺额。另一种可能性是：从长期看，待业人数和未来新达到就业年龄的人数之和可能大于预计的职位空缺额，那么调整时应当是提高与普及并重，既为国民经济培养有较高水平的专家，又使大量待业者有一技之长，便于找到合适的工作。这时，除了有必要进一步调整经济结构，以便增加职位空缺额以外，特别应注意发展中等技术和职业教育，给待业者以就业训练。还可以适当地延长在校学生的学习期限，一方面减少准备加入就业者行列的人数，另一方面提高他们的文化技术水平，以适应今后经济增长的需要。换句话说，与其让青年人在无技术、少知识的情况下待业，不如让他们多学习些知识与技能。

在上述两种可能性中，从我国具体情况来看，可以认为在相当长的时间内后一种可能性更大，所以我国教育事业的发展和教育结构的调整不能只着眼于提高，而忽略教育在解决“结构性”社会就业问题上的作用。

在这里，还应当注意到，教育结构调整不是一劳永逸的。一方面，经济增长本身要求教育部门输送大批有一定技术文化水平的、适应经济增长需要的劳动者，否则经济增长很难稳定地、持续地进行下去；另一方面，随着经济的增长，部门结构和地区结构总是处在不断变动之中，技术构成状况也会不断发生变化，这就要求教育结构相应地与之配合。一定的国民经济发展水平是与一定的教育结构相适应的，前者变动了，后者必须随之变动。这也是我国在制定长期人力资源规划时应当考虑的一个方面。

So much for my analysis of the "structural" employment issue. The employment problems facing China today are "structural" in the main, but they do not stop merely at being "structural." "Individual occupation selectivity" is another social employment issue for present-day China. When job openings are available, people can still choose to stay jobless. They do not lack the needed education and skill, but they make this choice out of occupational considerations. The causes of this employment problem are manifold, but education can still play a role in tackling it. This is because the mission of educators is not limited to teaching cultural knowledge and technical expertise. Character building and education in revolutionary values are essential to students in this country.

II. Investment in education as a prerequisite for developing a knowledge-intensive economy; the gradual increase of knowledge-intensive exports as a strategic measure to improve China's balance of international payments amidst economic growth

As to the patterns of technological innovation for developing nations in the modernization process, I have voiced my opinions in my article "On the roles of capital-intensive and labor-intensive economies in the modernization process of developing nations" (*World Economy*, issue No. 6, 1979). Because what I wanted to drive at in that article was that developing countries are not going anywhere if they choose to develop a capital-intensive economy more than anything else, I made no mention of the differences between skilled and unskilled labor and of the developmental trends of a labor-intensive economy. In this study, however, to explain why investment in education is a boon to stable and sustained economic growth, I find it necessary to look further into the patterns of technological innovation, or, to be specific, the role a knowledge-intensive economy can play in economic growth.

Theoretically speaking, a nation out to seek economic growth must boost its financial savings and raise funds for investment purposes. If the supply of funds is in shortage at home, something can be done to procure foreign funds under appropriate credit conditions and in light of the situation of the world capital market. The plus side of the use of foreign capital is that it helps overcome immediate foreign exchange and capital shortfalls and brings in advanced technology from other lands. However, in the long run, the commitment to repaying both principal and interest

以上是就“结构性”社会就业问题进行分析。我国当前的社会就业问题主要是“结构性”的，但并不仅仅是“结构性”的。应当承认，我国目前还存在着“个人职业选择性”的社会就业问题。在这种情况下，某些工作岗位空闲着，需要劳动者，但劳动者不是由于缺乏必要的文化和技术，而是出于个人对职业的选择，宁肯待业，而不愿去工作。这种类型的就业问题产生的原因是多方面的。但教育对于这一类就业问题的解决也能起到一定的作用，因为教育的任务不仅是传授文化技术知识。政治思想教育、革命人生观教育，对于我国的青年学生说来，也始终是不可缺少的。

二、对教育的投资是发展知识密集型经济的前提。逐步增加知识密集型经济的产品出口是我国经济增长过程中改善国际收支状况的战略性措施

关于发展中国家现代化过程中的技术创新类型，我已经在《论资本密集型经济和劳动密集型经济在发展中国家现代化过程中的作用》（载《世界经济》，1979 年第 6 期）一文中发表过我的一些看法。由于那篇文章的中心思想在于说明“发展中国家首先发展资本密集型经济的做法是难以奏效的”，因此可以不涉及熟练劳动与非熟练劳动的区分，不涉及劳动密集型经济的发展趋势。而本文的中心思想在于说明对教育的投资如何有利于经济增长的稳定和持续，因此有必要对技术创新类型问题再作进一步的考察，即考察知识密集型经济在经济增长过程中的作用。

从理论上说，一国为了实现经济增长，必须增加积累，筹集可供投资使用的资金。在国内资金供给不足的条件下，可以根据国际资本市场的情况，按照适当的信贷条件，吸收国外资金。利用国外资金有助于克服短期内外汇不足和资金不足的困难，有助于引进国外先进技术，但从长期来考察，必然面临着还本付息问题。如果

will eventually become a problem for the borrower. If the nation cannot increase its foreign exchange revenue from exports or other sources, balance of payments deficit may become a major hindrance to sustaining its economic growth.

Let us imagine a nation that is before or at the beginning of industrialization and has an abundant workforce, whose wages are low, and whose traditional exports of labor-intensive products have a competitive edge on the world market. Such a nation can use its foreign exchange earnings from exports to meet its domestic demand for technology and commodity imports and improve its balance of international payments. However, when industrialization reaches a certain stage, labor-intensive exports will gradually lose their edge and put the nation at a disadvantage for the following reasons:

First, a growing economy inevitably boosts national income gradually. While per capita national income rises on a yearly basis, worker wages go up as well. As a result, the gap in average wage between the nation and the developed industrial nations is likely to narrow down, thus diminishing the benefits of the "entry ticket" the nation can get from its low wages to the world market. What merits particular attention here is that industrialization is a common trend for all nations. When industrialization arrives at a certain stage in the said nation, other less developed nations will follow suit and strive to expand exports and absorb advanced foreign technology. These "latecomers" are most probably in the possession of abundant workforce and even lower wages, and their exports of labor-intensive products are more competitive on the world market because they are made by workers with even lower pay. If the said nation goes on to depend on labor-intensive products for exports after it has increased workers' wages on the basis of economic growth and increased national income, it is bound to come across newer and tougher competitors on the world market, a situation that is obviously not in its favor.

Second, a considerable part of the products of a labor-intensive economy are primary ones. Economic growth is likely to boost the demand for primary products in nations pursuing industrialization. For instance, the demand for mineral products or farm and sideline produce

一国不可能扩大自己的出口或其他来源的外汇收入，那么经济增长过程中将会发生国际收支逆差增大的现象，从而经济的持续增长将遇到很大困难。

假定一国在工业化之前或工业化开始阶段是一个劳动力数量较多、工资水平相对较低的国家，它的传统出口品是劳动密集型经济的产品，这些产品在国际市场上有一定的竞争能力。出口这些产品可以使该国取得一定的外汇收入，以弥补进口技术和其他商品的需要，改善国际收支情况。但是，在该国的工业化进行到一定阶段之后，它在劳动密集型经济的产品出口方面的有利条件将会逐渐丧失，不利条件将会逐渐增多。这是因为：

第一，随着经济增长，国民收入将会逐年增长，平均每人的国民收入也会逐年增长，工人的实际工资也会有所提高。这样一来，该国的平均工资水平与其他工业发达国家的平均工资水平之间的差距有可能缩小，从而该国以前所拥有的依靠低工资水平而进入国际市场的有利性将会减少。特别应当注意的是，工业化是世界各国共同的趋势，在该国工业化进行到一定阶段之后，另一些原来未开始工业化的后进国家也会相继开始工业化，后者也力图扩大出口，吸收国外先进技术。这些更晚开始工业化的国家很可能也是劳动力数量很多、工资水平甚至还要低一些的国家。它们的出口品也可能是劳动密集型经济的产品。这些产品在国际市场上也许具有更大的竞争能力，因为它们是由工资水平相对更低的劳动力生产出来的。这样，如果该国在经济增长、国民收入增长、工人的实际工资有所提高之后继续以出口劳动密集型经济的产品为主，它在国际市场上将会遇到新的有力的竞争对手。这种情况对它显然是不利的。

第二，在劳动密集型经济的产品中，有相当大的一部分是初级产品。一国在进行工业化的过程中，随着经济的增长，国内对初级

tends to swell with the rise of new industries, urban development, development in communications and transport, and improvement in people's material and cultural lives. So the effort to sustain massive exports of primary products can be inhibited by economic growth and growing domestic demand for such products. If that happens, the nation's balance of international payments will be adversely affected.

Third, even though the output of labor-intensive products can grow in pace with a nation's economy, such a growth rate is generally low. Moreover, the effort to expand their supply is restrained by natural resources and productive technology. This is because living labor accounts for the lion's share of production costs, whereas materialized labor makes up a smaller portion of it. As a result, the growth of labor productivity is relatively slow. Supposing a nation in economic growth needs to import advanced technology constantly and repay the principal with interest on procured foreign capital, it must expand exports to meet that need. If that nation counts mainly on labor-intensive exports in return for foreign exchange earnings, it may not maintain its balance of international payments by expanding such exports because of their low growth rate and serious supply restraint. If the nation wants to expand its exports and maintain its balance of international payments, it can only have one of the three options. Option One: to export more non-labor-intensive products to pick up the slack in the slow growing supply of labor-intensive products. Option Two: to slash domestic demand for labor-intensive products and curtail its growth rate to guarantee exports. Option Three: to transform production technology for labor-intensive products and increase their labor productivity, so as to increase output and expand supply. Option One calls for changing the nation's traditional dependence on labor-intensive products for export revenue. Option Two is predicated on cutting home demand and restraining domestic growth rate, that is, to expand exports at the expense of domestic demand and economic growth. Option Three will bring down labor intensity in the nation's labor-intensive economy and gradually deprive it of its competitive edge. No matter what option is chosen, it is not only difficult but also against the law of economic growth for a nation to keep counting on labor-intensive products for export revenue when industrialization reaches a certain stage of development.

产品的需求可能逐步扩大（例如对矿产品的需求或对农副产品的需求，都将因新工业部门的建立、城市的发展、交通运输的发展、居民物质文化生活水平的提高而扩大）。于是，继续大量出口初级产品的做法要受到国内经济增长和国内对初级产品需求扩大的限制。如果出现了这种情况，这对于该国的国际收支状况的影响将是不利的。

第三，一国劳动密集型经济的生产量虽然可以随着该国国民经济的增长而增长，但其增长率一般是较小的。劳动密集型经济的产品供给的扩大不仅要受到自然资源的限制，而且还要受到生产技术方面的限制。这是因为：在劳动密集型经济的产品的生产成本中，活劳动部分所占比重较大，物化劳动部门所占比重较小，劳动密集型经济的劳动生产率的提高也就相对地缓慢些。假定一国在经济增长过程中需要不断引进国外先进技术，并且在吸引外资一定时间之后需要还本付息，那么出口额必须相应地扩大。假定该国一直主要依靠出口劳动密集型经济的产品来取得外汇收入，那么由于这些产品生产量的增长率较小，而供给的扩大又受到限制，该国将不可能采取扩大出口劳动密集型经济的产品的方式来保持国际收支的平衡。如果它想使出口额增大，保持国际收支平衡的话，那么只有从以下三种可供选择的增加出口的方式中任择其一：或者增加非劳动密集型经济的产品出口，以弥补劳动密集型经济的产品供给的较缓慢增长；或者压缩国内对劳动密集型经济的产品的需求，抑制这种需求的增长率，以保证继续有足够的劳动密集型经济的产品用于出口；或者对劳动密集型经济进行生产技术改造，提高其劳动生产率，以便增加劳动密集型经济的产品的生产量，使这些产品的供给增大。在这三种增加出口的方式中，如果按第一种方式去做，它本身就意味着依靠劳动密集型经济的产品出口这一传统做法的改变；如果按第二种方式去做，则要求以压缩国内的需求、限制国内的增长率作为前提，即牺牲国内需求和增长，以扩大出口；如果按第三种方式去做，那么劳动密集型经济中的劳动密集程度将会下降，依靠劳动密集型经济的优势将会逐渐消失。这也就说明，一国在工业化进行到一定阶段之后，要想继续保持以出口劳动密集型经济的产品为主，不仅是困难的，而且也是不符合经济增长规律的。

It should also be noted that even if a nation can still benefit from labor-intensive exports at a certain stage of industrialization (when, for example, its wages are low enough, there are still no tough competitors on the international market scene, domestic demand for primary products has not grown strong enough to affect exports, or its labor-intensive economy is still robust enough to stabilize such exports), it gets a raw deal if it goes on selling labor-intensive products in return for non-labor-intensive imports. This is because the history and system of the world economy have determined that trade between non-labor-intensive and labor-intensive products on the international market is an unequal exchange of value, a situation that is not going to change anytime soon. This being the case, why should nations stick to labor-intensive products as the major source of export revenue after they have gone through a certain stage of industrialization? Why can't they replace labor-intensive products with non-labor-intensive ones that can definitely stand them in good stead in world trade?

As shown previously, observed from whatever perspectives, heavy dependence on labor-intensive exports should definitely be relinquished when industrialization reaches a certain stage even though it is a necessity at the beginning. On no account should the practice of letting labor-intensive products take up the lion's share of exports become a long-term state policy.

This poses a problem: Since it is both difficult and inappropriate for a nation to allow labor-intensive products to go on dominating its exports at a certain stage of industrialization, what is to be done with its balance of payments deficit in the course of economic growth? Supposing that nation's international revenue from nontrade items is fixed, what should it do to increase exports so that it can boost imports and repay the principal and interest of foreign debts?

The way out rests in developing a capital-intensive economy, exporting capital-intensive products, or replacing home-made capital-intensive products with similar imports. Feasible though these options are, they are by no means simple. Some developed industrial nations in the world economy today have turned international trade to their advantage through long years of painstaking maneuvering. This, plus the

还应当指出的是，即使一国在工业化进行到一定阶段之后仍然享有出口劳动密集型经济的产品的有利性（比如，该国的工资水平仍然较低；在国际市场上暂时还未遇到有力的竞争对手；该国国内对初级产品的需求的增长还没有达到影响初级产品出口的程度；该国劳动密集型经济的产品的生产量增长率较高，从而这些产品的出口额未受影响，等等），但由于在国际市场上，非劳动密集型经济的产品与劳动密集型经济的产品的不等价交换是由国际经济中的历史和制度条件所造成的，并且，这种现象不可能在短期内改变，所以，靠劳动密集型经济的产品出口去换取非劳动密集型经济的产品的进口，在交换方面是不利的。既然如此，那么一国在工业化进行到一定阶段之后，为什么一定要坚持以劳动密集型经济的产品作为自己的主要出口品呢？为什么不设法以贸易条件对自己比较有利的非劳动密集型经济的产品的出口来代替劳动密集型经济的产品的出口呢？

这一点清楚地表明：无论从哪一个角度来看，以劳动密集型经济的产品出口为主的做法虽然在一国刚开始工业化时期是必要的，但在工业化进行到一定阶段之后，这种情况应当有所改变。以劳动密集型经济的产品作为主要出口品的做法，不宜于作为一国长期不变的方针。

这样就产生了一个问题：既然一国在工业化进行到一定阶段之后很难继续以劳动密集型经济的产品出口为主，而且也不适宜以这些产品出口为主，那么该国应当如何解决经济增长过程中的国际收支逆差问题？假定该国非贸易项目的国际收入为既定的，它应当如何增加自己的出口，以应付进口增加以及清偿外债（还本付息）的需要？

它可以发展本国的资本密集型经济，出口资本密集型经济的产品，或用本国的资本密集型经济的产品替代进口的同类产品。这当然是一种可行的办法，但这也不是容易实现的。在国际经济中，某些先进的工业国家通过长期的经营和历史上已经形成的有利的贸易

abundant capital in their hands, is of good service to them in exporting capital-intensive products. It is no mean task to compete with the capital-intensive products from these countries, let alone gain the upper hand in such a competition.

For this reason, developing nations that are latecomers to industrialization should spare no effort to develop and export something else after they arrive at a certain stage of industrialization, and that is the products of a knowledge-intensive economy.

The knowledge-intensive economy, observed from the perspective of labor quality and technological innovation, is actually a way of categorizing innovations, industries and products. As illustrated in the foregoing, the strength of a country's labor resources manifests itself in both the number and quality of laborers. Labor quality is not factored in when categorizing national economies into capital-intensive and labor-intensive types. Rather, economies are differentiated in this regard merely in terms of the ratio between labor and capital goods inputs in production by natural physical units. By contrast, in calculating the labor input by natural physical units, every person (or work hour) represents an equal amount of labor input; in calculating the input of capital goods, only their values are taken into account—the degree of sophistication of technology embodied in the capital goods and the technical proficiency of the workers using such goods are not factored in. However, an analysis in light of labor quality shows, firstly, labor input is naturally divided into skilled and unskilled labor input, and secondly, the input of capital goods is also naturally divided into those that, on one hand, embody technological sophistication and are applied by skilled labor, and on the other hand, do not embody the sophistication of technology used and are operated by unskilled labor. Thus national economies can also be categorized into skilled-labor-intensive ones and unskilled-labor-intensive ones. In a skilled-labor-intensive economy, labor is skilled, and the input of capital goods embodies mature technology in the hands of skilled labor. By the same token, products can also be classified as either skilled-labor-intensive or unskilled-labor-intensive. Knowledge-intensive products are exactly skilled-labor-intensive products.

条件，再加上它们拥有充足的资本，从而在资本密集型经济的产品的出口方面享有一定的优势。要同这些国家的资本密集型经济的产品相竞争，并在竞争中占上风，不是一件容易的事。

因此，对于稍后开始工业化的发展中国家来说，在工业化进行到一定阶段后应当大力发展并扩大出口的，应当是另一种类型的产品——知识密集型经济的产品。

所谓知识密集型经济，是从劳动力质量和技术创新的角度着眼的技术创新类型、产业部门与产品的一种分类方法。如前所述，一国劳动力资源的多少不仅表现为劳动力数量的多少，而且表现为劳动力质量的高低。在把国民经济按资本密集型和劳动密集型分类时，并未把劳动力质量因素包括在内。这里所说的资本密集型和劳动密集型，只是就生产中自然单位的劳动投入量与生产资料投入量之间的比例而言，而在计算自然单位的劳动投入量时，把每一个人（或每一工时）看成是等量的劳动的投入，在计算生产资料投入量时，也只是计算其价值额，而未把生产资料所体现的技术先进性同运用这些生产资料的劳动者的科学技术水平联系起来考察。但是，如果从劳动力质量的角度来分析，生产中所投入的劳动很自然地区分为熟练劳动的投入和非熟练劳动的投入，生产中所投入的生产资料也很自然地区分为体现技术先进性并由熟练劳动者运用的生产资料的投入和未体现技术先进性并由一般劳动者运用的生产资料的投入。于是就出现对于经济的另一种分类，即国民经济可以区分为熟练劳动密集型的与非熟练劳动密集型的两类，在熟练劳动密集型经济中，不仅所投入的劳动是熟练的劳动，而且所投入的生产资料是体现了技术先进性并由熟练劳动者所运用的。产品也可以相应地分为熟练劳动密集型经济的产品和非熟练劳动密集型经济的产品。所谓知识密集型，就是指熟练劳动密集型而言。

If a nation rich in workforce can not only keep upgrading workers' scientific and technical proficiency, imbue them with high labor productivity and enable them to innovate production technology, but can also employ skilled workers and use capital goods that embody the sophistication of technology in production, then its products will not customarily be labor-intensive but skilled-labor-intensive or knowledge-intensive. Such products are a crystallization of the latest science-and-technology achievements mastered by that nation's labor—workers, technicians, scientists and researchers included—and the advanced technical levels they have attained. They also epitomize the latest progress in production technology and the high labor productivity the nation has achieved. If that nation can export this kind of product in return for unskilled-labor-intensive imports, rather than sell labor-intensive products in exchange for capital-intensive products, it can still be competitive on the world market even though its wages are rising with economic growth, and it can also open up one market after another to promote sales. Furthermore, because the nation has stopped exporting labor-intensive products, it can steer clear of the extant terms of exchange in international trade that are detrimental to labor-intensive products, thereby forestalling economic losses that might be incurred by the system of unequal exchange.

Technological innovation knows no bounds; nor will improvement of labor productivity stop at a certain level. A developing nation striving for modernization enjoys broad prospects in both economic growth and balance of international payments so long as it sets its skilled-labor-intensive economy on a track of ceaseless development.

Thus the important role of educational investment becomes apparent in coordinating economic growth and the balance of international payments. Without steady follow-up investment in education, we can never achieve universal and remarkable development in the workforce's technical and work proficiency, bring forth high-caliber scientists and researchers, and revamp productive technology without letup. For this reason, investment in education is the prerequisite for developing a skilled-labor-intensive or knowledge-intensive economy, and for expanding export and balancing international payments amidst economic growth.

一个劳动力数量较多的国家，如果它不断提高本国劳动者的科学技术水平和熟练程度，使之具有高度的劳动生产率，使之能在生产技术方面不断地有所创新，能以熟练的劳动者和体现了技术先进性的生产资料进行生产，那么它所生产出来的产品就不是一般意义上的劳动密集型经济的产品，而是熟练劳动密集型或知识密集型经济的产品。这种产品中，凝聚了该国的劳动者（包括工人、技术人员、科学研究人员）所拥有的最新科学技术知识和已达到的先进技术水平，反映了该国在生产技术方面的最新成就，反映了该国所达到的高度劳动生产率。如果该国以这些产品出口来换取非熟练劳动密集型经济的产品，而不是用一般意义上的劳动密集型经济的产品来换取资本密集型经济的产品，那么即使国内的实际工资水平随着经济增长而上升，它仍然能够在国际市场的竞争中保持优势，而且还能够不断开辟新的市场，扩大销路。此外，由于它改变了以往那种出口一般意义上的劳动密集型经济的产品的做法，从而也就避免了在现存国际贸易结构中的不利于劳动密集型经济产品的交换条件，避免了不等价交换制度所带来的经济上的损失。

技术创新是无止境的。劳动生产率的提高不会停止在某一个限界之内。一个发展中国家在实现现代化的过程中，只要能使熟练劳动密集型经济不断得到发展，那么它在经济增长和改善国际收支状况这两个方面都将有广阔的前景。

这样就可以清楚地看出对教育的投资在协调经济增长与国际收支方面的重要作用了。没有连续的、追加的对教育的投资，就不可能普遍地、大幅度地提高劳动者的技术水平和熟练程度，就不可能培养出高质量的本国科学研究人员，就不可能使生产技术不断创新。因此，对教育的投资是发展熟练劳动密集型即知识密集型经济的前提，也是在经济增长过程中扩大出口、改善国际收支状况的前提。

To sum up, increasing investment in education is a strategic measure for improving the balance of international payments in the course of economic growth. Ours is a socialist nation. Where is our comparative strength in international trade? It lies in none other than the export of certain labor-intensive products. We have to make the most of this strength, and develop it unremittingly. However, we should never make it a long-term state policy for foreign trade, to say nothing of the inevitability that this strength of ours will most probably dwindle gradually with national economic growth. From a strategic point of view, we must heighten the skilled-labor intensity of every export commodity and the skilled-labor intensity of every exporting company. Our nation will stay competitive on the world market for a long time to come if our exports of farm products are no longer customarily labor-intensive, but improved strains and quality products that epitomize advanced science and technology and the latest research and development achievements; if our exports of industrial goods are no longer run-of-the-mill products of the labor-intensive processing industry, but quality goods that reflect the distinctively innovated Chinese technology and nascent research results; and if what we sell to the world market are no longer ores, coal, crude oil or other mineral products but a good variety of quality products that are fashioned out of mineral raw materials and that mirror China's new achievements in science and technology. Then the more productive our industrial and agricultural departments are, the more competitive our country will be on the world market. All these things, when done in due course, will put our nation's workforce at an advantage not only quantitatively but also qualitatively. With our "knowledge" crystallized in produce and labor service, we will remain invincible in the world market.

III. To increase wages and improve economic efficiency is the nation's cardinal mission that can be attained—to a certain extent—through investing in education

The topic of this section is the relationship between income distribution and economic efficiency. In a capitalist economy, the trade-off between "equality" and efficiency has special connotations. Under capitalist ownership of capital goods, "equality" is based on recognizing the capitalist hired-labor system, whereas efficiency is an outcome of

总之，增加对教育的投资是经济增长过程中改善国际收支状况的战略性措施。我国是发展中的社会主义国家。什么是当前我国在国际贸易中的优势？这就是在若干劳动密集型经济的产品的出口方面，我们相对地居于有利的地位。我们应当充分利用这一有利条件，发展这一优势。但这不宜于成为长期的对外贸易方针，而且我国目前享有的这一优势很可能随着经济的增长而逐渐减弱。从战略上考虑，我们应当加强每一种出口商品的熟练劳动密集程度，加强出口部门的熟练劳动密集程度。今后，如果我国输出的农产品不再是一般的劳动密集型农产品，而是体现了先进科学技术水平的农产品，即反映最新科研成果的、改良了品种的、高质量的农产品，如果我国输出的工业品不再是一般的劳动密集型加工制成品，而是体现了我国的技术创新特色、反映最新科研成果的、高质量的加工制成品，如果我们不再是出口矿砂、煤炭、原油等矿产品，而是出口利用这些矿产品作为原料进行加工、并反映我国科学技术新成就的各种优质产品，那么我国在国际市场上将能长期保持优势。我国的工业和农业越是成为具有高度劳动生产率的部门，我国在国际竞争中越能居于有利地位。如果做到了这一点，那么实际上我们拥有的就不只是劳动力数量上的优势，而且是劳动力质量上的优势。我们将以输出体现于产品和劳务上的“知识”而在国际市场上立于不败之地。

三、我国当前经济增长过程中的一个重要任务是提高广大职工的收入水平和提高经济效率。这个任务在一定程度上也可以通过对教育的投资来实现

这里所要讨论的是收入分配和经济效率之间的关系。在资本主义经济中，所谓“平等”和效率的交替有其特定的含义，因为在生产资料资本主义所有制条件下，“平等”是建立在承认资本主义雇佣劳动制度的基础之上的，效率则是资本主义竞争的产物。只要存在

capitalist competition. Fundamentally speaking, there will never be true equality so long as the capitalist hired-labor system remains, but this is irrelevant to the theme of this study. Nevertheless, the relationship between income distribution and economic efficiency is a major issue that merits attention.

To care for people and cultivate them is the purpose of socialist production. To develop production is to improve people's material and cultural wellbeing, and bring forth workers' talent. However, to develop production, we have got to be particular about efficiency and motivate our workers. Theoretically speaking, the principle of distributing to each according to one's work, if carried out to the letter along with sound social welfare measures, is conducive to the development of production and enhancement of efficiency, as well as a guarantee for workers' pay raise provided development in production is ensured. However, workers' average income in this nation is low, and the influence of egalitarianism on income distribution very much alive. Both facts hamper economic growth, sap people's enthusiasm, and render workers' pay rise all the more difficult. The egalitarian pattern of income distribution that has kept wages at a low level for a long time cannot be eradicated without painstaking efforts.

To illustrate this issue, and to explain the role education can play in readjusting the relationship between income distribution and economic efficiency, it is necessary to begin this study with the income distribution theory.

Generally speaking, in economic growth there may be two income distribution patterns. One is to pay workers entirely according to the quantity and quality of work done. Under the other pattern, the state takes steps to regulate people's income by making allowances for low-income earners and limiting or deducting from the income of those highly paid. Proponents of the first pattern argue that paying people entirely according to the quantity and quality of work done represents a fair and square evaluation of the labor or service provided by every member of society, and that this is the only way to duly reward those who work hard and sanction those who malinger or dillydally, and to motivate people to work to the best of their ability and talent. Supporters of the second pattern hold that to reward people entirely according to

资本主义雇佣劳动制度，从根本上说就不可能出现真正的平等。关于这一点，不准备在本文中分析。但在我国社会主义经济中，收入分配与经济效率之间的关系倒是值得研究的重要问题。

对人的关心和培养是社会主义生产的目的。发展生产，是为了提高人民的物质和文化生活水平，使劳动者充分发挥自己的才能。但要发展生产，就必须讲究效率，必须调动职工的积极性。从理论上说，如果认真贯彻按劳分配而又正确实行社会福利的措施，那么对生产的发展和效率的提高是有利的。对于劳动者来说，这也是保证在生产发展前提下提高收入水平的途径。然而在我国，职工平均收入水平偏低和收入分配中的平均主义的影响不可低估。收入分配中的平均主义严重阻碍经济增长，挫伤人们的积极性，从而使本来偏低的职工收入更难以提高。长时期内已经形成的平均主义的、职工平均收入偏低的收入分配格局，不是很容易改变的。要扭转这种格局，需做很大的努力。

为了更好地说明这个问题，并进而说明教育在调整收入分配和经济效率之间关系方面可能起到的作用，有必要从收入分配的理论谈起。

一般经济增长过程中，可能有两种不同的收入分配方式。一种收入分配方式是，在经济增长过程中，完全根据劳动者的劳动数量和质量给予报酬。另一种收入分配方式是，在经济增长过程中，国家对收入分配采取一定的调节措施，更多地照顾低收入者，并对高收入者的收入加以某种限制或扣除。主张前一种收入分配方式的人认为，经济增长过程中的这种收入分配方式是合理的，因为这是完全按照劳动者提供的劳动数量和质量给予报酬，每个劳动者所得到的收入的多少意味着社会对每个人提供的劳动或作出的贡献的评价。据说惟有这样，才能鼓励勤劳者，惩罚懒惰者，才能促使每个人尽量发挥自己的力量和才智，为经济增长多作贡献。主张后一种

the quantity and quality of work done is unfair because such quantity and quality are not entirely determined by whether people work hard or not. They argue that people differ in the ability to earn a living because there are broad differences in talent, intellectual attainment, physical strength, family background and education, and especially because people cannot choose the social and work environment and the capital goods they are supposed to use in production. For example, because some happen to be using highly productive machines while the others are not, someone may have worked hard, but the quantity and quality of work he does compare unfavorably with what is done by someone else who does not exert himself but has better talent and family background and works in a better environment. These factors embody the limits of the practice of rewarding people entirely according to the quantity and quality of work done, and are responsible for the fact that some people work harder than others but make less money while others do not work as hard but earn more. It thus stands to reason for the state to adopt regulating measures to give allowance to low-income people and limit the incomes of highly paid people.

Supporters of either income distribution pattern try to make their cases also by citing income distribution's beneficial effect on economic growth. Supporters of the first pattern believe that paying people entirely according to the quantity and quality of work done can inspire every worker to take the initiative into his hands and improve his expertise and skill, thereby promoting national economic growth. According to them, people's enthusiasm will be dampened, and their work efficiency reduced, if they are not paid according to the quantity and quality of work done, or if their incomes are evened up arbitrarily. Supporters of the second pattern believe that the first pattern tends to widen the income gap between members of society, thereby adversely affecting the mindset of some people, so that low-income people may become so frustrated and disappointed as to stifle their initiative, and hurt the national economy in turn.

The controversy surrounding these two income distribution patterns, however, makes little sense for capitalist economies. A capitalist society cannot possibly pay workers according to the quantity

收入分配方式的人认为：完全按照劳动者提供的劳动数量和质量给予报酬并不是一种合理的收入分配，因为一个劳动者提供的劳动数量和质量的多少并不仅仅取决于个人工作的勤劳与否。由于人与人之间有天赋的差别，智力与体力各不相等；各人的家庭条件和受教育的机会不同，从而获得收入的能力也不相等；特别是每个人都在一定的社会环境中工作，工作中所使用的生产资料状况不是自己所能决定的，有人有条件使用有较高生产率的设备，有人则不具备这种客观条件。因此，一个人可能已经竭尽了自己的最大力量，但他所提供的劳动数量和质量却不如一个并未使用最大力量，但天赋、家庭条件和工作环境比较有利的人。这就使得完全按照劳动者提供的劳动数量和质量来给予报酬的做法具有一定的局限性，使得社会上总有一部分人的收入与他们个人工作的努力程度相比是偏低的，并使得社会上还有一部分人的收入与他们个人工作的努力程度相比是偏高的。国家采取适当的收入分配调节措施，给收入低的人某些照顾，对收入高的人的收入进行某种限制，这才是合理的。

经济增长过程中的这两种收入分配方式的主张者还从收入分配对经济增长的效应来说明实行该种收入分配方法的必要性。前一种收入分配方式的主张者认为，如果完全根据劳动者提供的劳动数量和质量给予报酬，这将调动每一个劳动者工作的积极性、主动性，并将促使每一个劳动者不断提高自己的技术水平和熟练程度，其结果将会推动国民经济的增长。反之，如果不按照劳动者提供的劳动数量和质量来给予报酬，或者人为地拉平这种报酬，那就会挫伤劳动者工作的积极性，降低效率。后一种收入分配方式的主张者则认为，如果完全根据劳动者提供的劳动数量和质量给予报酬，社会成员的收入差距有可能扩大，收入差距的扩大将在一部分社会成员的心理上引起反响，某些低收入者会产生沮丧和失望的情绪，不利于调动他们的积极性，不利于经济增长。

一般经济增长过程中的这两种收入分配方式的争论对于资本主义经济而言，并没有实际的意义，因为资本主义社会中既不可能真正按照劳动者提供的劳动数量和质量给予报酬，而其国家政权的

and quality of work done, and its class nature determines that it cannot regulate the income of members of various classes in reasonable ways. The superior socialist system makes fair income distribution possible, as it can maximizes economic growth by dispensing income on a rational footing. The superiority of socialism, however, is yet to be brought to full fruition in China. Egalitarianism in income distribution and low average worker income are established facts in this country for a variety of reasons. Ambiguity in production goals compels people to produce for production's sake year in, year out. The belief that the more egalitarian it is, the better income distribution becomes makes it impossible to distribute income reasonably and motivate workers with it. As a result, the economy grows at a snail's pace, labor productivity remains penuriously low, and workers' disposable incomes cannot be increased, so much so that social stability and unity are affected. The situation has reached a point where something has to be done about it. But what exactly is to be done? In my opinion, when we discuss how to regulate the relationship between income distribution and economic efficiency, we must proceed from our nation's established income distribution pattern, from the egalitarianism that has been prevalent across the land for years, and from the current average income of workers. History cannot be reversed. It won't do to conjure up an income distribution pattern based on the assumption of "what we would have done if we were living in the pre-liberation year of 1949." Important though it is for us to explore such a pattern, it cannot solve real-world problems because the established wage standards make it easy to raise wages and hard to reduce them, and because the established welfare benchmarks make it easy to raise welfare and hard to reduce it.

Given the status quo in our nation, we are not getting anywhere if we stop paying people according to the quantity and quality of work done and increasing people's average income, and allow egalitarianism to go unchecked. It will not work, either, if our government acts impetuously, turns a blind eye to the real practices of income distribution and the welfare steps that have been taken, and carries to extremes the practice of paying people strictly according to the quantity and quality of work done. Considering the historical circumstances under which the current income distribution practice has come about, I believe the order of the day should be to gradually increase workers' pay in the process of

阶级实质又决定了它不可能真正按照合理的方式来调节各阶级的收入。社会主义制度的优越性，照理说应当为合理的收入分配创造出先决条件，并且能够通过合理分配收入来最大限度地促进经济增长。然而在我国，社会主义制度在这方面的优越性并未得到充分发挥。当前我国收入分配中的平均主义和职工平均收入水平偏低的形成原因是多方面的。多年来，由于社会主义生产目的不明确，为生产而生产的情形严重，加之，在越“平均”越好的思想支配下，已经造成了这样的局面：既不能合理分配收入，又不能调动职工积极性，结果是经济增长缓慢，劳动生产率低下，职工实际收入不能提高，同时，收入分配中的问题还影响安定团结。这种情况已到了非改变不可的地步。怎样改变呢？我认为，现在要讨论我国经济增长过程中收入分配与经济效率之间关系的协调，必须从客观上已经形成的收入分配格局出发，从长时期来社会上普遍存在的平均主义和职工现阶段平均收入水平出发。历史不能倒转。我们不可能设想一个“假如现在是 1949 年，我们应该如何如何”的模式。这种模式的探讨固然重要，但不能解决现实中的迫切问题。这是因为，在工资和福利方面存在着“非灵活性”：既定的工资标准，提高容易下降难；既定的福利标准，增加容易减少难。

因此，在我国目前情况下，如果在收入分配上不贯彻按劳动数量和质量给予报酬，不提高平均收入水平，听任平均主义为害，这是不行的。同时，国家如果操之过急，不从承认收入分配和福利措施的现状出发，过分强调完全以劳动数量和质量为标准给予报酬，也是不行的。平均主义的消除，需要有一个较长的过程，但消除它们是势在必行之事。考虑到我国收入分配格局形成的历史条件以及收入分配现状，在发展生产的过程中逐渐提高职工收入

developing production. Egalitarianism and low average worker income are the main causes behind low work efficiency; and low work efficiency is a major hindrance to economic growth. Our mission at hand is to root out egalitarianism and carry out the principle of distributing to each according to his work. That is to say, under the precondition of raising workers' actual income, we must do what we can to pay them in light of the quantity and quality of work done. If we keep doing this, workers' income is bound to grow considerably within a few years. However, a universal rise of average worker's pay may also result in the income of some people rising more quickly than others, thereby widening the income gap. If the growing income gap disgruntles some people, it will not be too late for the government to remedy the situation with regulatory steps, such as increasing the private income tax rate and levying an inheritance tax within the framework of a progressive tax system. In my opinion, we have got to foresee this potential trend and refrain from taking premature countermeasures. The problem will be taken care of sooner or later.

Coordination between income distribution and economic efficiency amidst economic growth involves not only the long-standing distribution pattern and the past and present wage and welfare systems, but also a number of ideological issues. For instance, such important ideological issues as workers' political awareness, social mores and values, and people's understanding of what "equality" and "happiness" really mean can affect, one way or another, people's enthusiasm, initiative and efficiency at work, and the balance between income distribution and economic efficiency. We must be careful about the countermeasures we are going to take against these ideological issues if we are to increase workers' pay without crippling their enthusiasm for work or hurting economic efficiency.

What, then, is the role of education in coordinating the relationship between income distribution and economic efficiency? Can education investment speed up the accomplishment of the abovementioned tasks? There is no doubt that education has a certain ideological impact on those being educated, thereby helping them foster a sound outlook on life, a sense of social responsibility and other values that should not be overlooked. It is also indisputable that this impact is not an issue. What is at issue is the content of such education and the approaches to it.

是迫切的任务。在收入分配方面，当前，平均主义和职工平均收入水平偏低是主要矛盾所在，从而低效率问题成为经济增长的主要障碍。所以，我们应当把逐步减少平均主义和贯彻按劳分配放在首位，在提高广大职工的实际收入水平的前提下，尽可能按劳动的数量和质量给予报酬。若干年后，职工的收入水平肯定要比目前有较大的提高，但也有可能在平均收入普遍提高的基础上，某些人的收入上升得更快，从而收入分配的差距有扩大的趋势。假定收入分配差距的扩大引起了社会上一部分人的不安，那么到那时再通过国家的适当调节（如提高累进制的个人所得税税率，征收遗产税）使收入分配差距缩小，也还为时不晚。我认为，我们需要预见到这一可能出现的趋势，但不必过早地采取收入限制措施。这个问题将来是可以解决的。

经济增长过程中收入分配与经济效率的协调，不仅与长期形成的收入分配格局、过去和目前的工资和福利制度等有关，而且还涉及意识形态领域内的若干问题。比如说，劳动者的政治思想状况、社会的风尚和评价标准、人们对“平等”和“幸福”的理解，都是意识形态领域内的重要问题，它们都能在某种程度上影响收入分配与经济效率之间的协调，影响在一定收入分配格局下人们的工作热情、主动性和效率。因此，要在我国经济增长过程中既提高广大职工的收入水平，而又不至于挫伤人们的工作积极性，不至于降低效率，必须重视意识形态领域内的措施。

那么，教育事业在协调经济增长过程中收入分配与经济效率之间的关系方面能起到何种作用呢？对教育的投资是否能促进上述任务的解决呢？毫无疑问，教育能使受教育者在意识形态方面受到某种影响，从而有助于使他们形成正确的人生观、产生社会责任感、建立新的评价标准。这种影响显然是不能忽视的。关于这一点，通常并没有什么争议，关键在于政治思想教育的内容和教育的方法。

In this study, however, I want to draw attention to the following four pertinent economic issues:

First, as education can improve people's money-making ability by raising their cultural and technical levels, an effective way to help low-income workers make more money is to put them through certain professional education or training. If the principle of distributing to each according to his work is followed in real earnest, a worker schooled in professional knowledge and technical expertise can earn more than those who lack such knowledge and expertise. Thus he is a beneficiary of the education he has received. Regular and spare-time education can both help individuals increase their private income. Therefore, those who have passed a certain level of academic or technical examinations should be issued a diploma or certificate and paid accordingly in the workplace. Developing education can upgrade the quality of the entire nation's workforce and boost the work efficiency of those who have been educated. This is particularly the case in this age of modern science and technology, where a growing economy badly needs quality workers who can never be replaced no matter how many low-quality workers there are. Low-income people will be stuck in the low income brackets, and their work quality will remain low if they do not receive professional training. It is thus clear that developing education helps bridge income disparity, increases efficiency, boosts the economy and increases workers' average income.

Second, the lack of labor mobility is detrimental to the effort to enhance economic efficiency and increase income. However, labor mobility is a complex issue that is beyond this study. What I want to say right now is this: Supposing the workforce in our nation has become somewhat more mobile through institutional and other reforms and readjustments, this leaves another important problem to be addressed, that is, there are people who, for lack of professional knowledge and skills, are not able to adapt themselves to the changing economic structure and ever-improving technology by changing their jobs. In the course of economic growth, large numbers of villagers quit farming as a result of raised productivity in agriculture, but their poor adaptability to new careers makes it hard for them to be absorbed by other sectors in need of workforce. Thus large numbers of them have stuck in agriculture, where

我在这里准备探讨的则是经济学方面的问题。我认为以下这四个问题是值得重视的：

第一，由于教育能使受教育者提高文化技术水平，从而提高未来取得收入的能力，所以要提高低收入职工的收入水平，有效措施之一就是使他们受到一定的专业教育和训练。这是因为，如果认真贯彻按劳分配，那么有专业知识和技术水平较高的人的工资收入与缺乏专业知识和技术水平较低的人的工资收入的差额，在其他条件相同的情况下，应当被看成是受一定的教育给个人所带来的收益。多受教育能增加个人取得收入的能力这一点，既适用于正规教育，也适用于业余教育。比如说，通过一定的考试制度，只要达到某一级水平的，就应当承认其学历，给予与其学历相称的报酬。另一方面，从全国范围来考察，发展教育将能提高我国的劳动力质量，使受教育者的工作效率有所提高。特别是在现代科学技术条件下，经济增长中迫切需要高质量的劳动力，质量较低的劳动力人数再多也不能替代他们。如果不发展教育，不使低收入职工受到专业训练，低收入职工的收入总是少的，他们的劳动质量也总是低的，对经济增长是不利的。这就清楚地说明发展教育事业既有利于缩小社会收入分配差距，又能普遍提高效率、促进经济增长，从而提高职工平均收入水平。

第二，劳动力缺乏流动性是不利于提高经济效率和增加收入的一个原因。我国当前劳动力缺乏流动性问题是一个相当复杂的问题。本文不准备讨论劳动力缺乏流动性的原因。这里所要考察的是：假定通过体制等方面的改革和调整，我国的劳动力流动状况有所改进了，那么就劳动力的流动而言，还存在一个重要的问题没有解决，即由于一部分人缺乏专业知识和技能，工作适应能力很差，在经济结构变动和技术不断进步的条件下，不能适应客观的需要而改变工作岗位。特别是，在经济增长过程中，即使农业生产率提高了，并且假定其他部门需要劳动力，但由于农业中大量劳动者工作适应能力差，仍然不能为

their labor cannot be fully utilized. Social efficiency suffers as a result. What merits particular attention is that, under these circumstances, low efficiency, lack of vocational adaptability, and low income are interrelated, and can also be addressed by relying on education development. Only through education can low-income people change their jobs when and where necessary, and get higher pay; only when their abilities and talents are brought into play in their new jobs can society reduce its loss in efficiency.

Third, generally speaking, low income not only affects its earners but also carries over to their younger generation. This is true everywhere, and socialist China is no exception. A socialist society is theoretically free from hereditary tenures, workplace discrimination and cliquishness, but owing to low incomes and the lack of adequate education facilities at home, children from low-income families have few schooling opportunities and even fewer opportunities to go to college. When they start work, they have fewer chances to get new jobs, let alone jobs with high pay. I think we should admit that their problem is caused by economic factors. A comparison of low-income families with high-income families shows that if income disparity has become a reality in the first generation, by the time of the second generation, a few low-income families may quit poverty, but most of them will remain poor or become even poorer. This is because, judging from the Chinese reality, among the generation of people in their forties and fifties, families with poor education generally have more children than others. In these families, few housewives hold jobs, a factor which keeps their per-family income at a low level. Low income leads to low level of education, and low level of education leads to low income, and the vicious cycle goes on and on. It goes without saying that the government may take steps to provide children of low-income families with more educational opportunities. But this way of doing things can backfire, because in an environment where higher education is underdeveloped while the remnant influence of feudalism lingers, government steps can degenerate into some people's tools for selfish gains. When that happens, there will be serious consequences: The efficiency of the national economy will be eroded, and a drain of precious human resources will occur. To break the

其他部门所吸收。大批劳动力被继续束缚在农业中而未能得到充分利用，对社会来说是一笔相当大的效率损失。值得注意的是，在这种情况下，低效率、缺乏职业上的适应性同低收入水平三者是联系在一起的。要解决这个问题，同样需要依靠教育事业的发展，即通过教育，使这些低收入者能在需要的时候变更个人的工作岗位，取得较多的收入，同时使他们的力量和才智在新的工作岗位上充分发挥出来，以减少社会的效率损失。

第三，就一般情况而言，低收入职工的收入水平不仅影响他们之中的这一代人，而且将影响他们的下一代。这种情况在我国社会主义条件下也仍然存在。从理论上说，社会主义社会是一个没有职业世袭制、职业歧视和排他性的社会，但由于低收入职工收入少、家庭缺少学习的条件，他们的子女受教育的机会一般比较少，接受较高等教育的机会可能更少，于是他们的子女改变职业的机会也相对地少一些，并且相对地较少有可能到有较高收入的工作岗位去就业。这主要是经济原因所造成的。我认为应当承认这一点。如果把低收入家庭与有较高收入的家庭拿来比较，假定第一代人的收入已经形成了差距，那么到了第二代，除了少数家庭有可能改变原来的收入状况而外，一般的情况则是收入差距的继续保持，甚至可能扩大。这是因为，就我国的实际状况而言，在四十多岁、五十多岁的一代人中，文化程度较低的职工家庭的子女较多，这些家庭的主妇参加工作的较少，从而家庭按人口平均的收入较低。这样，这些家庭将会遇到一个“受教育少—收入少”的恶性循环。当然，用行政措施也许可以增加低收入家庭子女的受教育机会，例如规定各种不同文化程度的人的子女升入高等学校的比率。但这种做法只会带来相反的效果，因为在高等教育不发达、而封建主义影响还不可忽视的环境中，这种做法只会成为某些人谋取私利的手段，它对社会造成的恶果将会更大，使国民经济的效率损失、人才损失更加严重。因此，要打破

vicious cycle suffered by low-income families without affecting economic efficiency and dashing talented people's hope for education, we must develop education. We must expand higher education and vocational education dramatically to increase the rate of school enrolment of low-income families' children and prepare them for high-income jobs in the future. At the same time, we should never do anything that might erode society's economic efficiency or deprive gifted people of the opportunity to continue their education and bring their talent into full play.

Fourth, with the whole picture of the national economy in mind, low-income people or families cannot be asked to improve their income level on their own. If our economy were still under the kind of turmoil and sabotage that we saw during the decade-long Cultural Revolution, or if it prows very slowly, little could be done to address the low-income levels as a social problem, no matter how hard these people worked to raise their incomes or improve their and their children's future money-making ability. The effective solution to income distribution problems in the course of economic growth comes down to national economic development, GDP growth, consistent technological innovation, and ever-increasing labor productivity. This is precisely where the role of education comes into play in regulating the relationship between income distribution and economic efficiency amidst economic growth. As I have stressed earlier, improving labor quality is a major guarantee for economic growth, while any achievements in innovating technology and raising labor productivity can be regarded as the accumulated results of investment in cducation.

Incidentally, I use the term "high-income" in this study as a reference to a certain group of individuals or families in the context of China's income distribution situation. It is relevant only to what happens in China, where the income levels of both workers and government functionaries are on the low side. This renders any comparison of China with the absolute statistics on average international income meaningless.

Instead, it makes a lot more sense to compare the consumer-goods structure (the percentage of food expenses in a family's income in particular) and the hourly wage's purchasing power (the exchange ratio between hourly wage and durable consumption goods in particular). For this reason, while riding economic growth to raise the income level of low-income families, we should also work to improve the income of all

低收入家庭所遇到的低收入和受教育少之间的恶性循环，而又不至于影响经济效率和挫伤一切有才能的人的学习积极性，应当从大力发展教育事业、扩大高等教育和职业教育着手，在整个教育事业发展的基础上提高低收入家庭子女的升学率，增加他们未来取得较多收入的能力，同时不致排斥一切有才能的人有深造和发挥才能的机会，不使社会的经济效率受到损失。

第四，从整个国民经济的观点来考察，低收入者的收入水平的提高不可能只依赖于低收入者本人或家庭的努力。如果我国经济仍像史无前例的十年那样动荡和遭受破坏，如果整个经济的增长速度十分缓慢，那么无论个人怎样努力增加自己的收入或提高本人和子女未来取得较多收入的能力，仍无助于改变低收入者收入低下这一社会现象。因此，经济增长过程中收入分配问题的有效解决途径，归根结底仍在于国民经济的发展和国民生产总值的增长，在于技术的不断创新、劳动生产率的不断提高。教育在协调经济增长过程中收入分配和经济效率之间关系方面的主要作用正在于此。因为正如前面一再提到的，劳动力质量的提高是我国今后经济增长的重要条件，而任何技术创新和劳动生产率的提高都可以看成是对教育的投资的累积性的成果。

还应当说明的是，虽然我在文中有时也用了“收入较高”的个人或家庭这样的字眼，但这仅仅是就国内收入分配格局而言的，它仅仅是在国内范围内具有相对的意义。如前所述，我国广大职工和干部的收入水平偏低。假定说各国间平均收入绝对数字的比较没有什么实际意义的话，那么无论如何，消费结构的比较（尤其是食物支出在家庭收入中所占比例的比较）、每小时工资购买力比较（尤其是每小时工资收入与耐用消费品的交换比率的比较）还是很可以说明问题的。因此，在我国经济增长过程中，除了要注意提高低收入

workers and government employees, so that every family can see changes in their consumption composition and the exchange ratio between hourly income and durables. Of course this arduous task cannot be accomplished without a whole package of government steps. To develop education and increase funding for it is one such significant step. This is because only with a quality workforce and robustly growing labor productivity is it possible for everyone to make enough money and for production costs to drop enough to bring down the prices of consumer goods, change every family's consumption structure, and raise everyone's hourly income higher enough to afford more consumer goods. These changes are interconnected and mutually promoting. Universal changes in family consumption structure and universal increases in worker wages can yield more jobs and make it easier to solve employment problems.

IV. Despite the conflict of rising educational funding with fiscal balance at the present stage of economic development, investing in education helps boost fiscal revenue amidst economic growth

Developing education calls for more funding. Where shall the money come from? The mere mention of this question arouses concern about an added burden on state treasury. That is why people are saying the need to develop education and increase the funding for it is in conflict with the effort to maintain fiscal balance.

At the present stage of China's economic development, government funding is crucial to education development. But is government the only source of funding for education? Of course not. To solve employment problems and create more jobs, we cannot count on direct government investment alone and turn a blind eye to nongovernmental fund-raising efforts. By the same token, we cannot set our eyes only on state coffers and relinquish social fund-raising efforts if we are to develop education and put more people through school. In this study, however, let us forget about raising funds for education from nongovernmental channels and suppose that government funding is the only financial resource for education in this country.

In that case, there is no lack of theoretical support for the concern that increasing educational funding will result in fiscal deficits. Supposing the financial revenue is fixed or its growth rate is rather low while the

家庭的收入水平而外，还应当提高全体职工、干部、劳动者的收入水平，使每个家庭的消费结构、每小时收入与耐用消费品的交换比率发生变化。这显然是一个艰巨的任务，必须采取多方面的措施才能逐步实现。在这些措施之中，发展教育事业、增加对教育的投资将是具有重要意义的措施之一，因为只有在劳动力质量较高、劳动生产率增长速度较快的前提下，才能使人们的收入普遍提高、使消费品的生产成本和价格下降，才能改变每个家庭的消费结构，才能使人们每小时的收入交换到更多的消费品。并且，所有这些变化都是联系在一起、互相促进的。家庭消费结构普遍发生变化，职工收入普遍增加，就能使社会增加更多的工作岗位，使就业问题较易于解决。

四、在我国经济发展的现阶段，较大幅度增加教育经费固然与维持财政平衡有矛盾；但从长期看，对教育的投资将有助于在经济增长过程中增加财政收入

要发展教育事业，就需要增加教育经费。增加的教育经费来自何处？很自然地会遇到一个尖锐的问题：这样一来，将会加重国家的财政负担。所以，人们经常说，发展教育事业、增加教育经费与维持财政平衡有矛盾。

在我国经济发展的现阶段，财政拨款对于发展我国的教育事业当然是重要的，但这是不是筹集教育经费的惟一途径呢？当然不是。我认为，正如在解决我国当前就业问题、广开就业门路时，不能只着眼于国家的直接投资，而忽视社会集资一样，在对待我国当前教育事业的发展、广开就学门路时，也不能只着眼于财政拨款，而忽视社会集资。但在这里，我们先把教育经费的筹集问题撇在一边，暂不讨论。我们可以暂时假定财政拨款是当前发展我国教育事业的惟一的经费来源。

如果确是如此，那么对于教育经费增加会造成财政赤字的顾虑，不是没有经济理论根据的。假定财政收入为既定，或财政收入增长率

growth rate of educational investment and spending on teachers' salaries are high, then financial deficits become unavoidable. Deficits increase money supply, which in turn causes prices to rise. Furthermore, if fiscal revenue is fixed while expenditure for national defense, administration and other purposes is curtailed to a maximum, increasing educational funding is likely to cut directly into investment in material production. This may reduce the economic returns from material production (or its profit growth rate), and inflate production costs (or bring down the cost reduction rate). In both scenarios, fiscal revenue and balance will be adversely affected, which may eventually trigger price increases.

However, we may see another possibility if we look a bit farther. Increasing educational investment is beneficial to both economic growth and the effort to maintain fiscal balance in the course of economic growth. Other things being equal, the source of increasing net revenues for an enterprise lies in its success in managing labor productivity to outgrow wage costs, expanding commodity production and reducing consumption of raw materials induced by improved labor productivity. As far as the entire national economy is concerned, increasing labor productivity to boost enterprise revenues is a reliable way to raise fiscal revenues and stabilize prices. In this light, the role of boosting educational investment speaks for itself. This is because, as I have said previously, increases in labor productivity can be regarded as an outcome of educational development.

This point of view can be further elaborated in three ways.

Firstly, insofar as its nature is concerned, education investment should be seen as a productive investment. Like investment in material production (such as building a factory or adding machinery and equipment), educational investment can also help increase the GDP. The difference between the two kinds of investment is that while investment in material production embodies itself in increasing the quantity and quality of material products, investment in education is reflected in workers' improved cultural and technical proficiency or in increasing the number of laborers who measure up to certain industrial or job requirements. The results of the former investment are plain for all to see, whereas the outcome of the latter can be easily overlooked, so much so that educational expenditure has for a long time been regarded as

较小，而为了发展教育，用于各种投资支出和教师工资支付的款项增长率较大，那么财政赤字将不可避免。财政赤字引起货币流通量增大，其结果将引起物价上涨。再者，如果财政收入为既定，而国防、行政等开支已经压缩到不能再压缩的地步，那么对教育拨款的增加将会直接减少对物质生产部门的投资，结果可能引起物质生产部门的收益下降（或收益增长率减少）和成本增大（或成本下降率变慢）。这样，物质生产部门企业收益的下降或较慢增长对国家财政收入的影响是不利的，从而也会不利于维持财政平衡，最终将引起物价上涨。

然而从较长期来考虑，我们还可以看到另一种可能性。增加教育投资不仅有利于经济增长，而且有利于在经济增长过程中维持财政的平衡。在其他条件不变的前提下，就一个企业范围而言，劳动生产率的提高超过工资成本的提高，依靠劳动生产率增长而实现的商品生产量的扩大和原材料消耗的降低，是企业收益增加的源泉。就整个国民经济而言，劳动生产率的提高以及由此实现的企业收益的增加，是增加财政收入，从而有利于维持物价稳定的可靠途径。只要从这个角度来进行分析，增加教育投资的作用就很清楚了，因为如前所述，劳动生产率的提高可以看成是教育事业的发展的结果。

关于这一点，可以从以下三个方面来作进一步的考虑。

第一，对教育的投资就其性质而言，应当被看成是一种生产性投资。对教育的投资同对物质生产部门的投资（如投资兴建一座工厂，添置一套设备）一样，其结果都将使国民收入增加。二者的区别主要在于，对物质生产部门的投资体现于物质产品数量的增加和质量的提高，对教育的投资体现于现有劳动者文化技术水平的提高，或达到一定规格和标准的劳动者人数的增加。前一种投资易于被察觉，后一种投资则很容易被忽视，以至于长期以来对教育的拨款被当成是非生产性的支出。因此，如果继续按照传统的看法，

nonproductive. If the role of education in promoting national economic development is still perceived in that old light, the inevitable conclusion is that adding educational funding can only upset fiscal balance. If, on the contrary, spending on education—an investment in human capital—is deemed conducive to heightening the cultural and technical proficiency of the workforce, thereby raising labor productivity and speeding up economic growth, then it is ultimately beneficial to fiscal balance.

Secondly, spending on education as a productive investment is characterized by a cycle that is longer than the construction cycle of the infrastructure, such as transportation and power supply. Of course there is no lack of cases in which educational spending brings quick economic returns, such as certain short-term training programs for technical workers. Generally speaking, however, it takes time to groom workers to a certain proficiency level in culture and technology, and it takes a much longer time to bring forth professionals of a certain caliber. Such facts give rise to the misunderstanding that education is like "distant water that cannot slake immediate thirst." As a matter of fact, that misunderstanding can be averted if people take a strategic point of view and regard education as a productive investment capable of yielding lasting economic returns, and if they can see the continuous role education can play in economic growth. To put it another way, if you are frustrated to see money being spent on education year in, year out, then you must be patient enough to wait until the number of laborers of a high cultural and technical caliber starts growing with each passing year. Just as education spending has about the same long harvesting cycle as infrastructure investment, so it can bring the same significant benefits to the national economy.

Thirdly, as a productive investment, education benefits society with its salubrious effect on the national economy as a whole. That effect can be easily neglected if we lose sight of the whole picture of society and the national economy, or if our vision is limited to a certain region, industry or firm. Of course, the direct effect of education investment can be felt in an individual region, industry or firm, especially in the case of certain types of local school or a factory's training school for technicians. This, however, is less important. Social gains from educational investment are a lot greater. Such gains are reflected, for one thing, in the fact that, by

看不到教育对国民经济发展的促进作用，那么就会认为教育经费的增加是不利于财政平衡的。反之，如果把对教育的支出（人力投资）看成是生产性投资，看成是通过劳动者文化技术水平的提高，从而通过劳动生产率提高而促成经济增长的一种投资，那么，从长期看，教育经费的增加将有利于维持财政平衡。

第二，教育作为一种生产性投资，它的周期较长，甚至比某些基础结构（运输、动力系统等）的建设周期还要长一些。当然，在经济生活中，有时也可以看到对教育的投资能较快地收到经济效果，例如开办某种技术工人短训班等等。但一般说来，培养有一定文化技术水平的劳动者，特别是培养达到一定规格、标准的专业人员，所需要的时间较长。这种情况很容易引起一种误解，即认为发展教育是"远水解不了近渴"。其实，如果具有战略的眼光，把教育作为一种能持久地带来收益的生产性投资，以及连续性地看待教育在经济增长中的作用，即不仅看到年复一年地对教育事业的拨款，而且更要看到过了一段时间之后，具有较高文化技术水平的劳动者人数年复一年地增多，我国的科学技术队伍年复一年地扩大，那么就会从根本上改变上述看法。正如对基础结构的投资一样，对教育投资的收获期较长，未来对国民经济的好处也是较大的。

第三，教育作为一项生产性投资，它的受益者是全社会。对教育投资的社会收益是指它给整个国民经济带来好处。因此，如果不从全社会和整个国民经济的角度来考察，而只着眼于某个局部地区、部门或生产单位，那就很容易忽略对教育投资的经济效果。当然，在某些场合，也可以察觉到对教育的投资给某个局部地区、部门或生产单位带来的好处，例如在本地区开办某种类型的学校，或为本部门或本生产单位培训某种技工，等等。但这是次要的。对教育投资的全社会收益要比它给个别地区、部门或生产单位带来的直接利益大得多。这一方面反映于受过一定训练和教育的劳动者通过

changing jobs or locations, educated workers will spread to all economic sectors and regions, and for another, in the improved scientific and cultural attainments of the entire population and the emergence of a rich crop of new inventions and innovations. Every invention or innovation is the fruit of long-accumulated investment in education, and, therefore, belongs to the entire society. With these inventions and creations, society is able to raise labor productivity, promote economic growth, improve workers' living standards and work conditions, create more jobs, and increase per capita national income. All these are the benefits society can reap from education. In all, if we shift our point of departure from a single region, industry or firm to take in the panorama of society, our judgment of the actual economic returns of education will not be limited to what a region, industry or firm has spent on education, nor shall our evaluation of the beneficial effect of education investment be restrained by the size of a partial investment. Clearly, even though increasing education spending in the course of economic growth may temporarily expand fiscal expenditure or curtail the income of some localities, from a long term point of view and by taking the overall situation into account, such spending is paramount to raising labor productivity, and effective in sustaining growth in national income and fiscal revenue.

Now that the benefits of developing education to the maintenance of fiscal balance in the long run are established, how should we look at the conflict between short-run increases in education spending and the need for fiscal balance? Let us return to the two hypotheses I have set at the beginning of this section.

Hypothesis One: Fiscal appropriation is, at present, the only source of funding for education. As a matter of fact, it is unnecessary to regard fiscal appropriation as the only source of funding for education, because nongovernmental fund-raising efforts hold great potential in this regard. How such potential should be tapped depends on the making and enforcement of government policy. We can save a huge amount of government spending on education as long as our policy allows nongovernment entities or individuals to run schools. Schools can be run effectively by involving nongovernment entities or collectives, and there is no lack of success in this field. I see nothing wrong with individuals running schools. Accomplished doctors, artists, accountants, translators and so on, are doing our nation and our youngsters a service

工作岗位的变换和工作地区的转移，将分布于国民经济各个部门和各个地区，另一方面，更重要地反映于全民族科学文化水平的提高和新的发明创造的涌现。任何发明创造都是长期对教育的投资的累积的成果，它属于整个社会。社会因这些发明创造而提高了劳动生产率，推进了经济增长，改善了一般劳动者的生活条件和劳动条件，扩大了就业机会，增加了平均每人的国民收入等等。这些都是社会的收益。总之，只要把着眼点从个别地区、部门和生产单位的收益转到全社会的收益，那就不会仅仅根据本地区、部门、生产部门用于教育方面的支出来判断这种投资的实际经济效果，也就不会用局部的教育投资收益大小来判断对教育投资的有利性了。由此可见，虽然在经济增长过程中因增加教育经费而有可能暂时扩大政府的财政支出或减少个别地区的收入，但从长期看，从整体看，对教育的投资是提高劳动生产率的重要途径，是促进一国国民收入和财政收入有保证地、持久地增长的有效方式。

发展教育从长期来说有利于维持财政平衡这一点，可能不会遭到人们的非议了。那么，我们究竟应当怎样看待短期内增加教育经费与维持财政平衡之间的矛盾呢？现在让我们回到本节开始部分进行分析时所作的两个假定上。

第一个假定是：财政拨款是当前发展我国教育事业的惟一的经费来源。实际上，不必把财政拨款当成教育经费的惟一来源，社会集资的潜力很大，这主要以政策的制定和贯彻为转移。只要我们实行容许社会办学、群众办学，甚至个人办学的政策，就可以在教育方面大大节省国家的开支。社会办学、群众办学、集体所有制单位办学，是行之有效的好办法，这方面不乏典型的经验。至于个人办学，这有什么不好？有专长的医师、艺术家、会计师、翻译家等等，个人或联合带一些徒弟，传授知识和技能，对国家有利，对青年人

by taking apprentices and teaching them knowledge or skills individually or by teamwork. These individuals are doing a lot of good to both the country and people when they run private vocational, technical or continuous education schools by tuition and cultivate talents for society without asking the government for a single penny. We would rather see young people in school than have them stay idle. As well as schools, an abundance of work-study programs are available for these people. To insist on running schools according to certain "rules" or "stereotypes" can do nothing but hold back development in education and put unwarranted burdens on the state treasury.

Hypothesis Two: Supposing fiscal revenue is fixed and defense and administrative expenditures have been pared down to a minimum, more spending on education can mean less investment in material production and result in fewer economic returns, to the jeopardy of fiscal revenue. Reality, however, has never been that simple. As we all know, investment in material production is just one condition for boosting aggregate production. There is at least another condition, and that is the economic returns from investment. If we can increase economic returns from investment in material production, speed up funds' turnover rate, and maximize the economic returns for every dollar spent, then we will see no reason why such investment cannot be downscaled. The former condition has been overestimated for a long time while the latter condition is overlooked, as if the more the investment is made, the higher the accumulation rate will become, with no consideration given to the economic returns of such investment. Astonishing waste is the inevitable result, and there is no lack of bitter lessons in this regard. Given a fixed fiscal revenue, why can't we do more to raise the turnover rate of funds and improve the efficiency of investment in material production? To speed up the training of technicians and managers is an effective way to enhance the economic returns of investment in material production. As long as we can find ways to raise the economic returns of such investment, it will not hurt the aggregate output, companies' economic returns, or government revenue to develop education with money saved from it under a fixed fiscal revenue.

V. Conclusion

In this study I have looked into the positive role education investment can play in tackling problems in employment, international payments,

也有利。个人办职业学校、文化补习学校，甚至专科学校，靠收学费来维持，替社会培养人才，不需要财政拨款，不也是利国利民的好事吗？与其让青年人闲着，上不了学，不如让他们进各类学校去学习。此外，勤工俭学、半工半读的途径也很多。那种强调“正规化”、“一个模式”的做法，结果如何呢？要么阻碍教育的发展，要么只好伸手向财政部门要经费，增加国家财政负担。

另一个假定是：假定财政收入为既定的，假定国防、行政等开支已经压缩到不能再压缩的地步，那么对教育拨款的增加将会减少对物质生产部门的投资，结果可能引起物质生产部门收益下降，不利于国家未来的财政收入。其实问题并不是如此简单。我们知道，对物质生产部门的投资只是总产值增长的一个条件，总产值增长的另一个条件是投资的经济效果的大小。如果能够提高物质生产部门投资的经济效果，让资金能周转得更快，让每一元投资能带来更大的产值，那么投资额不是不可以缩小的。长期以来，我们过分看重总产值增长的前一个条件，忽视后一个条件，似乎投资越多越好，积累率越高越好，投资经济效果却可以不计，结果浪费惊人。这方面的教训是很深刻的。为什么我们不能在既定的财政收入前提下，在加速资金周转、提高对物质生产部门的投资效果方面多做些文章呢？加速技术人员、管理人员的培养，恰恰是提高物质生产部门投资经济效果的有效途径。因此，只要我们设法提高投资的经济效果，那么在财政收入既定的条件下，为了发展教育而减少一些对物质生产部门的投资，既不至于影响总产值的增长，又不至于影响企业收益和国家未来的财政收入。

结束语

以上分别考察了对教育的投资在解决我国经济增长过程中的社会就业、国际收支、收入分配、长期财政平衡等方面所能够起到的

income distribution, and long-term fiscal balance in the course of China's economic growth. We have no alternative but to speed up educational development by spending more money on it, if we are to ensure stable and sustained economic growth, tackle the nation's "structural" employment issue and weaknesses in international trade, and coordinate the relationship between income distribution and economic efficiency. The economic history of other nations indicates that it is easy to achieve temporary economic growth, but difficult to gain stable and sustained economic growth on the basis of coordinated development in all fields of socioeconomic development.

In the West, class antagonism and other fundamental conflicts inherent in capitalism are worsening; and unemployment, inflation, international payment deficits and unequal income distribution are entangled with the need for economic growth in an insoluble mess. Even if these capitalist nations can increase investment in education, the best they can accomplish is to ease the situation temporarily—there is no way they can find real solutions to their problems. Despite that fact, since the 1960s Western economists have been emphasizing the role of education in economic growth and urging their governments to take human capital investment policy and human resource planning as important measures to ensure long-term economic growth.

Socialism is a superior system. Problems of one kind or another do occur in our economy, but these problems are not inherent in the socialist system. On the basis of eliminating private ownership of capital goods under capitalism and carrying out the distribution policy of "from each according to his ability, to each according to his work," it should be a great deal easier for our nation to coordinate diverse social and economic interests in the course of economic growth. Education definitely has a bigger role to play in this regard than under the capitalist system. How is it, then, that education has not played such a role in the past? This question merits careful thinking. In my opinion, apart from long years of interference from ultra-leftist ideology and the sabotage of the Lin Biao Clique and the Gang of Four, it also has a lot to do with our shortsightedness, our failure to consider socialist economic development from the viewpoint of national development strategy, and our lack of understanding of the role of education in long-term economic growth. To those who cannot see the nature and role of education in perspective,

积极作用。如果要使我国的经济稳定地、持续地增长，有计划地解决经济增长过程中出现的“结构性”就业问题和国际贸易中的优势减弱问题，协调收入分配和经济效率之间的关系，那就不能不加速发展教育事业，增加对教育的投资。从世界各国经济增长的历史可以看到，某段时间内的经济增长并不是难以实现的，难以实现的是经济稳定地、持续地增长，以及在经济增长过程中使社会经济各个方面保持协调。

在资本主义制度下，由于资本主义基本矛盾和阶级对抗关系的存在和激化，失业、通货膨胀、国际收支逆差、收入分配失调与经济增长之间的矛盾纠缠在一起。因此，即使加速发展教育事业，增加对教育的投资，至多也只能暂时缓和一下矛盾，而无法使上述这些问题真正得到解决。在那里，教育在经济增长过程中能够起到的协调社会经济各个方面的作用是有限的。但即使如此，60 年代以来西方资本主义国家的经济学家仍一再强调教育在经济增长中的作用，建议本国政府把人力投资政策和人力资源计划作为实现长期经济增长的重要措施之一。

社会主义制度是优越的。我国当前在经济方面出现的这些或那些问题，不是来自社会主义制度本身。在消灭生产资料资本主义私有制和贯彻“各尽所能，按劳分配”的基础上，我国经济增长过程中社会经济各方面的协调应当要比资本主义制度下容易得多。教育在这些方面所能起到的作用也肯定会比资本主义制度下大得多。但过去这些年，为什么实际上教育并未发挥这么大的作用呢？这是一个值得深思的问题。我想，除了长时期极“左”路线的干扰、林彪和“四人帮”的破坏以外，对社会主义经济建设缺少战略上的考虑，眼光过于短浅，对教育在长期经济增长中的作用认识不足，也是一个因素。在某些对教育的性质和作用缺乏认识的同志看来，教育是

education is a "soft" task that can be laid aside or delayed at will. Something is amiss, however, with that line of thinking. Therefore, I wrote this article with the same intention as when I wrote my thesis "Technical education and capitalist industrialization: a study of the rise of technological power in Western Europe and America" two years ago. That is, to send this message to our government policymakers: You have got to put a premium on education! When you mobilize society to raise money and open up schooling opportunities for our workforce, please make sure you will increase fiscal spending on education by a wide margin and thereby accelerate the development of education in our nation.

— *Journal of Peking University* (*Philosophy and Social Sciences*), issue No. 6, 1980

软任务，能挤一点就挤一点，能拖一拖就拖一拖。这种看法当然是错误的。因此，正如两年前我在写《技术教育和资本主义工业化》一文时的想法一样，我写这篇文章的目的仍是为了向国家的决策部门呼吁：必须重视教育，在动员社会集资广开就学门路的同时，较大幅度地增加国家对教育的投资，加速发展我国的教育事业。

（原载《北京大学学报（哲学社会科学版）》，1980 年第 6 期）

EFFECTIVE AND RATIONAL INVESTMENT UNDER SOCIALISM (1982)

What is effective investment? To put it simply, it is the kind of investment that works promptly in putting together production capacity, boosts the supply of aggregate social product, and stimulates economic growth. What is rational investment? In short, it is the kind of investment that maintains basic price stability, creates many job opportunities, and raises labor force income while spurring economic growth. Whether investment is effective or not is determined by whether it has increased aggregate social product; and the effectiveness of investment is measured by the growth rate of aggregate social product. In contrast, whether investment is rational or not is determined by whether it has met the following goals: (1) boosting the economy; (2) maintaining basic price stability; (3) creating more jobs; and (4) raising labor force income. And the rationality of investment is measured by its actual results in meeting these goals. Effective investment may or may not be rational investment. Under socialism, it is not enough for investment to be merely effective. No effort should be spared to turn effective investment into rational investment, and with the largest possible degree of rationality at that.

I. Investment—primary dynamo behind economic growth

Economic activity is a dynamic process in which one period of production, distribution, exchange and consumption circumscribes the next period. To allow production, distribution, exchange and consumption to take place on a larger scale in the next period, a certain amount of national income from the previous period must be spent in investment. The amount of investment determines the degree of changes in economic scale. Therefore, for a given return on investment, economic growth rate is always predicated on a given rate of investment, i.e., the percentage of national income spent on investment.

Investment always manifests itself as the primary driving force behind economic growth. The term "primary driving force" refers to the initial impetus that can set a stagnant economy on the track of growth. Without this initial impetus, no economy can be delivered from stagnation.

The relationship between supply and demand or between production and consumption may be thrown off balance in economic activity. The same can happen between economic sectors and between economic

论社会主义有效投资与合理投资（1982）

什么是有效投资？可以简单地把它归结为能够迅速形成生产能力，增加社会总产品的供给，促进经济增长的投资。什么是合理投资？可以简单地把它归结为既能促进经济增长，又能维持物价基本稳定，提供较多就业机会，提高劳动者实际收入水平的投资。投资是否有效，以它是否增加社会总产品供给为准，其有效程度则以社会总产品增长率来衡量；投资是否合理，以它是否兼顾经济增长、物价基本稳定、提供较多的就业机会、提高劳动者实际收入水平这四项目标来确定。投资的合理程度，则以它在实现这四项目标方面所取得的实际结果作为评价的尺度。有效投资可能是合理投资，但也有可能不是合理投资。社会主义投资仅仅成为有效投资还不够，应当使它们成为合理投资，而且应使其合理程度尽可能增大。

一、投资是经济增长的第一推动力量

经济活动是一个动态的过程。前一期的生产、分配、交换和消费，制约着后一期的生产、分配、交换和消费。要使后一期的生产、分配、交换和消费在更大的规模上进行，前一期的国民收入中必须有一定的数额作为投资。投资的多少，影响着经济规模的变动程度。因此，在投资效果为既定时，一定的经济增长率总是以一定的投资率（即投资在国民收入中的比例）为前提的。

在任何经济增长中，投资都表现为第一推动力量。第一推动力量是指使停滞的经济得以增长的最初的推动力。如果没有这种最初的推动力，经济就不能摆脱停滞的状态。

在经济活动过程中，由于人口的增长、居民需要的变化、外部竞争条件的变化以及其他情况的变化，供给与需求之间，即生产和消费之间可能出现不协调，各个经济部门和各个经济区域之间也

regions. If this lack of coordination is allowed to deteriorate further, it can bring down the economic growth rate or, worse, lead to zero or negative growth. Investment is indispensable if this situation is to be remedied and sustained economic growth ensured. Here, investment is still the primary driving force in adjusting economic structures, coordinating supply and demand, and maintaining economic relations in equilibrium.

Stagnant development of productive technology, worn-out equipment and outdated technological processes, misuse of equipment and raw materials, or failure to eliminate weak production links in good time in the course of economic activity can erode workforce productivity or inflict financial losses. If these conditions are allowed to continue, they will not only hold back economic growth but also adversely affect government revenue for the obvious reason that financial losses in enterprises invariably diminish government revenue. To reverse shrinking workforce productivity and compensate for enterprise losses, it is necessary to increase investment while adopting necessary management countermeasures. This is precisely where investment can be used as the primary driving force to renovate production technology, raise workforce productivity, and boost corporate profits and government revenue.

The reason why investment becomes the primary driving force on these occasions is that the significance of investment does not lie in the demand for it, but in the chain reactions it causes in economic activity. The demand arising from investment is, after all, limited, but the chain reactions it causes in economic activity can play a much larger role in national economy.

More investment means higher income, and higher income can stimulate investment. If this virtuous cycle can be made to last, a cumulative process will result in which investment brings along more investment, and income brings about still more income. This is how economic growth happens, how technology is upgraded and labor productivity grows, and how growth in corporate profit and government revenue are realized. By the same token, without the initial investment, there will be no subsequent investment; and without the income yielded by the initial investment, a constant flow of income will be out of the question.

This being the case, it is clearly unwise to underestimate or overlook the tremendous role investment can play as the primary dynamo behind economic growth.

可能出现不协调。这种不协调状态的加剧，将导致经济增长率下降，甚至导致零增长或负增长。为了改变这种不协调状态，保证经济增长的持续性，投资是不可缺少的。在这里，投资仍然表现为第一推动力量，它能促进经济结构的调整，使供给与需求相适应，使经济中各种比例关系相适应。

在经济活动过程中，由于生产技术的停滞、原有的生产设备或工艺的陈旧落后、对生产设备和原材料的利用不当，或由于生产中出现某些薄弱环节而未能及时予以改进，将会引起劳动生产率下降和亏损。这种情况如果迟迟未能改变，不仅经济无法增长，而且还会影响财政收入，因为企业的亏损必定导致财政收入的减少。要扭转劳动生产率下降和企业亏损的局面，除了从经营管理方面采取适当的措施以外，增加投资也是必要的。在这里，投资作为第一推动力量，将导致技术的创新、劳动生产率的提高、企业的赢利和财政收入的增加。

在所有这些场合，投资之所以成为第一推动力量，是因为投资的意义不在于投资本身所造成的需求，而在于投资在经济活动中所引起的一系列连锁反应。投资本身造成的需求毕竟是有限的，投资在经济活动中所引起的一系列连锁反应在国民经济中的作用要大得多。

增加投资能够增加收入，增加了的收入又能使投资增加，如此反复影响，就形成投资带动投资，收入带动收入的累积性过程。经济增长正是这样进行的；技术创新、劳动生产率增长正是这样实现的；企业的赢利、财政收入的增加也正是这样得到保证的。反之，没有最初的投资，也就不可能有后续的投资；没有最初的投资所带来的收入，也就不可能有此后的源源而来的收入。

因此，轻视或忽视投资作为第一推动力量的巨大作用，显然是不正确的。

My above analysis is, of course, built upon a given condition of management. It is not uncommon that mismanagement results in low labor productivity, sluggish economic growth, and financial losses. For this reason, this situation can be changed to a certain extent simply by improving management, without increasing investment.

My analysis is also based upon the initiative and motivation of the workforce. It is not uncommon that the lack of initiative or motivation, or the failure to motivate the workers and give full scope to their initiative limits workforce productivity to such a low level as to reduce the economic growth rate and incur corporate losses. In that scenario, we can also change the situation not by investing more but by taking proper steps to motivate workers and put the initiative into their hands.

II. Effective and ineffective investment

The effectiveness of investment rests with its ability to fuel economic growth, but not all kinds of investment have such ability. Investment may also be ineffective. Ineffective investment refers to the kind of investment that yields zero or negative growth.

Investment effectiveness or ineffectiveness has dual implications: microeconomic and macroeconomic. In microeconomic terms, investment becomes effective if it can boost the investor's output (that is, increase the investor's net output value). Otherwise, it is ineffective. In macroeconomic terms, investment becomes effective if it causes the national economy to grow (that is, increases national income); failing this, it is ineffective. Because all investment must go through certain processes from the start of the action to the yield of increases in production and national income, the time factor must be considered, that is, the length of interval from the beginning of investment to the date when output begins to grow and national income begins to rise. That duration varies in length with the situation in different sectors. However, no matter how long it takes, the effectiveness or ineffectiveness of investment hinges on whether the economic growth it has brought about is positive, zero or negative.

If the time factor is not considered, investment is ruled ineffective only if it cannot enhance production capacity or contribute to aggregate social product. Any investment can be ruled effective if it enhances production capacity or increases aggregate social product.

当然，上述这一切是以经营管理状况既定为前提。经济中常常存在这样的情形：经营管理方面的不善使得劳动生产率处于较低的水平，并引起经济增长率低下和企业亏损，因此，可以不必增加投资，只要改善经营管理，就能使状况有所改变。

上述这一切也是以劳动者主动性、积极性既定为前提。经济中也常常存在这样的情形：劳动者缺乏主动性、积极性，或劳动者主动性、积极性未被调动和未能充分发挥，使得劳动生产率处于较低的水平，并引起经济增长率低下和企业亏损。因此，也可以不必增加投资，只要采取适当的措施，调动和充分发挥劳动者的主动性、积极性，就能使状况有所改变。

二、有效投资和无效投资

投资的有效性在于它能促进经济增长，但并非任何投资都能起到促进经济增长的作用。投资可能是无效的。无效投资是指投资所引起的是零增长或负增长。

投资的有效性和无效性都有双重含义，即微观经济的含义和宏观经济的含义。就微观经济的含义而言，如果某项投资能使该投资单位的生产增长（即该投资单位的净产值增大），它就是有效的，否则就是无效的；就宏观经济的含义而言，如果某项投资能使国民经济增长（即国民收入增多），它就是有效的，否则就是无效的。由于任何投资从开始投资到生产增长和国民收入增加，总有一个过程，所以要考虑时间因素，即从开始投资到生产增长和国民收入增加之间的时间间隔的大小。各部门的具体情况不同，这种时间间隔的大小也不一样。但无论时间间隔大小，投资的有效性和无效性都是同经济增长（正增长、零增长或负增长）联系在一起的。

假定不考虑时间间隔的大小，那么，只有那些根本不能形成生产能力的、不能增加社会总产品的投资，才是无效投资。任何最终能形成生产能力和增加社会总产品的投资，都应被称为有效投资。

Thus the number of ineffective investment should be kept low, because most investment can yield production capacity and add to aggregate social product after a certain period of time, thereby contributing to economic growth one way or another.

However, it is far from enough to judge the effectiveness of investment or the lack of it this way. The time factor must be taken into account, that is, the length of time it takes from the onset of an investment action to the realization of output and national income increases. I have defined effective investment at the beginning of this article as something that is prompt in bringing about production capacity. In other words, no investment can be effective if it is overly time-consuming.

You may wonder why my definition of effective investment should contain the word "prompt." In what light should we understand that word? How can we tell whether investment is effective or ineffective based on our understanding of that word? As we all know, investment refers to the occupation of a certain amount of available capital for a certain period of time, whereas the available capital occupied by investment is part of the newly created value in the national economy that may be put to other uses in material production. Used properly, it can raise aggregate social product and elevate economic growth. Therefore, investment entails a certain degree of "probable" or "potential" increase in aggregate social product and economic growth rate. If this amount of money used as investment is prompt in bringing about production capacity, this "probable" or "potential" increase can be converted into an actual increase in aggregate social product. If this amount of money is left idle, i.e., it is used in no investment, it will never yield actual increase in aggregate social product. If an amount of money that can be invested to yield production capacity promptly is left idle, it obviously means losses in aggregate social product and national economic growth rate.

Supposing this amount of money is used as investment but takes a longer time than usual to enhance production capacity, it does absolutely nothing to boost aggregate social product or economic growth during that extra inactive period of time. Because, in this regard, inactivity is synonymous with losses in both aggregate social product and economic growth. During that extra time this amount of money should be regarded

这样，无效投资可能为数甚少，因为大多数投资，多多少少能在一定的时间间隔之后形成生产能力，使社会总产品有所增加，从而在经济增长中有某种程度的贡献。

如果仅仅从这样的角度来区分投资的有效性和无效性，那是远远不够的。必须考虑时间因素，即从开始投资到生产增长和国民收入增加之间的时间间隔的大小。本文在一开始就已规定了有效投资的定义，有效投资指能够迅速形成生产能力的投资。这就是说，迟迟未能形成生产能力的投资，不能称为有效投资。

这里需要讨论的是：为什么要在有效投资的定义中，加上“迅速”二字？如何理解“迅速”二字？如何根据对“迅速”的理解来区分投资的有效性和无效性？我们知道，任何投资都是在一定时期内对现有资金的占有，而投资所占有的现有资金是国民经济中新创造出来的价值的一部分。这笔现有资金在物质生产领域内可能有不同的用途，如果使用得当，它们能使社会总产品增加，使经济增长。因此，它们意味着一定数量的“可能的”或“潜在的”社会总产品增量，意味着一定程度的“可能的”或“潜在的”经济增长率。如果把这笔现有资金用来进行某种能够迅速形成生产能力的投资，那么，“可能的”或“潜在的”社会总产品增量可以转化为现实的社会总产品增量。如果这笔现有资金闲置不用，即不用于任何投资，那么就得不到这种现实的社会总产品增量。把迅速形成生产能力的投资同闲置不用的资金相比，后者显然表示一种损失，即社会总产品的损失、经济增长率的损失。

现在，假定利用这笔资金来进行某种迟迟未能形成生产能力的投资，以至于它们要比通常情形下形成生产能力所需要的时间多出一段相当长的时间。在这一段多出的时间内，所占用的资金意味着它们并未发挥作用，也就是未能被用于增加社会总产品和促进经济增长，这就等于社会总产品的损失、经济增长率的损失。如果说这笔投资在经过很长的时间之后才形成生产能力，那么在它形成生产

as ineffective investment. Moreover, even after it has yielded production capacity and begun to contribute to aggregate social product, it must make up for the losses it has caused previously to the national economy. Only after that can it qualify as effective investment.

This is why, in assessing investment effectiveness, due consideration should be given to the time needed for investment to put together production capacity.

How, then, should the word "prompt" in the wording "being prompt in yielding production capacity" be understood? Because of the differences in industries and investment projects, it is necessary to use the average time it takes for a specific industry or investment project to build production capacity as the benchmark. Investment that takes less than the average time to achieve the anticipated result can be regarded as being "prompt." The less time it takes to be effective, the "prompter" it becomes. Investment projects that take more than the average time to foster production capacity should be deemed "tardy in bringing about production capacity." The more time it takes in this process, the "tardier" it becomes.

With this benchmark, the effectiveness or ineffectiveness of investment can be defined as follows:

1. Investment that cannot yield production capacity or contribute to aggregate social product is ineffective investment;

2. Investment that takes less than the average time to yield production capacity is effective investment;

3. Investment that takes more than the average time to yield production capacity can be deemed effective only after it has reaped production capacity, contributed to aggregate social product, and made up for the losses it incurred during the extra time it took to yield such a production capacity. Before it has met these goals it should be regarded as ineffective investment.

III. Rational and irrational investment

No study of investment is complete if it focuses only on whether it has furthered economic growth or not. As the primary driving force behind economic growth, the positive role of investment lies not just in

能力之前比通常情形下所多占的时间内，它应当被看成是无效投资。而且，甚至在它已经形成生产能力，并且已经开始提供社会总产品时，它还需要把前一阶段作为无效投资给国民经济造成的损失弥补起来。只有当这些损失被补偿后，这笔投资才能名副其实地被称作有效投资。

这就是在分析投资的有效性时，有必要对形成生产能力所需要的时间长短加以考察的理由。

那么，应当怎样理解"迅速形成生产能力"这一表述中的"迅速"二字呢？由于各个部门、各个具体投资项目的情况不同，所以只能用特定部门、特定投资项目形成生产能力的平均时间作为标准。凡是在平均时间以下的，都可以理解为"迅速"形成生产能力。越低于平均时间，则越"迅速"。凡是超过平均时间的，都可以理解为"迟迟未能形成生产能力"。越高于平均时间，则越是"迟缓"。

按照这一标准来判断，投资的有效性和无效性的定义可以进一步明确地表述如下：

1. 根本不能形成生产能力，不能使社会总产品有所增加的投资，是无效投资。

2. 形成生产能力所需要的时间小于为形成该种生产能力所需要的平均时间的投资，是有效投资。

3. 形成生产能力所需要的时间大于为形成该种生产能力所需要的平均时间的投资，只有在它形成生产能力、提供社会总产品，并补偿了在超过形成该种生产能力所需要的平均时间的期间造成的损失之后，才成为有效投资。在这以前，它是无效投资。

三、合理投资和不合理投资

仅从促进经济增长这一个目标对投资进行分析，是不够的；投资作为经济增长的第一推动力量，它的积极作用既在于增加

boosting aggregate social product and economic growth rate, but also in coordinating economic relations and goals of development. In that sense, investment is actually a balancing force in an economy, or the driving force behind economic balance. Investment is deemed rational when it acts as such a balancing force.

Investment, however, may play an opposite role, that is, to disrupt the balances of economic relations and goals of economic development. Instead of keeping the economy on an even keel, it can throw the economy off balance or aggravate economic disequilibrium. Such is one of the attributes of irrational investment.

If investment is irrational, it may still help increase aggregate social product in the short run when it is effective. But in the long run, what appears briefly as effective investment can disturb economic relations and goals of economic development, and result in a stagnation or downturn in aggregate social product. This is where effective investment becomes ineffective investment.

Thus it is more important to see whether investment is rational or not than to judge if it is effective or ineffective. The concept of rational and irrational investment belongs in macroeconomic investment theory. When we talk about rationality or irrationality of investment, we do it in the context of macroeconomics.

Whether investment is rational or not depends on what role it plays in (1) economic growth, (2) price stability, (3) job creation, and (4) increase in labor income. Investment is considered irrational if it performs badly in one of these four fields, but it can be regarded as rational if it contributes to one field while the other three fields remain roughly constant. Investment becomes more rational if more such fields have improved while fewer of them remain constant.

Thus the definition of rational investment can be put more specifically:

As far as the role of investment in the aforementioned four fields is concerned, investment is rational if it has improved one of these fields while the others show no sign of decline.

社会总产品，提高经济增长率，还在于对经济中的各种比例关系起协调作用，对经济发展的各个目标起协调作用。从这个意义上说，投资实际上是经济中的一种平衡力量，或者称之为平衡的推动力量。如果投资能够起到这种平衡的推动力量的作用，那么投资是合理的。

但投资也可能表现出与此恰恰相反的作用：使得经济中的各种比例关系不相适应，使得经济发展的各个目标失调，顾此失彼，此长彼消，以致投资不仅不成为经济中的一种平衡力量，反而成为破坏平衡或加剧不平衡的力量。这样的投资是不合理的。

如果投资是不合理的，那么就短期而言，只要它是有效的投资，社会总产品的增加仍是可能的。但就较长的时期而言，由于经济中各种比例关系的不相适应和经济发展的各个目标的失调，社会总产品很可能停止增长，甚至还会下降。这样，有效投资就变成无效投资了。

由此可见，从投资的合理性和不合理性的角度来对投资进行分析，比从投资的有效性和无效性的角度来分析更为重要。合理投资和不合理投资概念，是宏观投资理论中的范畴。在谈到投资的合理性和不合理性时，投资只具有宏观经济的含义。

投资的合理与否，要根据投资对于经济增长、物价基本稳定、提供较多就业机会、提高劳动者实际收入水平这四方面的作用来判断。只要其中有一个方面的情况比投资以前恶化了，就不能称为合理投资。假定其中有一个方面的情况比投资以前好转了，而其余三个方面的情况维持与投资以前相同的水平而没有恶化，那么就可以称为合理投资。假定有较多方面的情况比投资以前好转了，较少方面的情况维持与投资以前相同的水平而没有恶化，那么投资的合理程度是增大的。

因此，可以把合理投资的定义进一步明确地表述如下：

就投资对于经济增长、物价基本稳定、提供较多就业机会、提高劳动者实际收入水平这四方面的作用而言，投资以后，至少其中有一个方面的情况比过去好转，而没有一个方面的情况比过去恶化，那么这样的投资就是合理投资。

If economic growth has picked up after investment is made, and the other three fields remain intact, that is, they have neither improved nor deteriorated, this is a typical case of effective investment also being rational, or to put it differently, effective investment and rational investment becoming the same thing. The minimum requirement for investment to be at once effective and rational is that it can at least promote economic growth while maintaining the status quo of the other three fields.

To combine effective investment with rational investment under that minimum requirement is just the starting point of arranging investment. We should try to improve all the four fields after investment is made. The more rational investment is, the more effective it becomes and the longer it can stay effective. The reason for this is clear: Without increasing aggregate social product, basic prices stability cannot be maintained, new job positions cannot be created in the national economy, and labor income will decline, and as a result, the national economy as a whole will deteriorate, and sustained economic growth becomes out of the question.

As much as the time factor should be taken into account when investment effectiveness or ineffectiveness is studied, the same should be done when investment rationality or irrationality is observed. This is because only by generating production capacity can investment play its role in coordinating economic relations, but it takes a period of time for that to happen. The length of this period is determined by the characteristics of the economic sector and the investment project in question.

What merits attention in this regard is that investment impacts price stability, the creation of jobs, and labor income in different ways. Before production capacity is generated, because there is only financial input and no output in aggregate social product, the amount of currency in circulation grows, which will have a negative impact on price stability. If, after production capacity is yielded, the growth rate of aggregate social product resulting from the investment is still lower than the growth rate of the amount of currency in circulation, it may still have a negative impact on price stability, a possibility that should not be overlooked. The situation, however, is different with the creation of new jobs. Investment may begin creating jobs immediately after it is made, because the investment action itself can absorb some workers. However, after investment has brought about production capacity, it may either increase employment (including the jobs created by this investment itself and the

如果在上述四个方面中，投资以后，经济增长了，但其余三个方面仍维持原状，即既没有比过去好转，也没有比过去恶化，那么在这种情况下，有效投资恰好是合理投资，或者说，有效投资与合理投资是同一回事。如果希望投资既具有有效性，又具有合理性，那么投资以后，经济的增长和其余三个方面的维持原状，就是最低限度的要求。

按照最低限度的要求来使有效投资与合理投资统一起来，只是安排投资的一个出发点。应当使得上述四个方面的情况在投资以后都有所好转。投资的合理性越大，不仅投资的有效性越能得到保证，而且还能使有效投资持续不断地进行下去。道理是很清楚的：社会总产品没有增加，物价不能维持基本稳定，国民经济中不能产生较多的就业机会，劳动者实际收入水平下降，其结果将使整个国民经济状况恶化，持续的经济增长也将成为不可能。

正如在考察投资的有效性和无效性时要把时间因素考虑在内一样，在考察投资的合理性和不合理性时，也应当考虑时间因素。这是因为：只有在投资形成生产能力之后，它们才能起到平衡经济的作用，而从开始投资到形成生产能力，将会有一段时间间隔。这段时间间隔的大小，以各个部门和各项投资的特点而定。

这里需要注意的一个问题是：物价稳定、提供较多就业机会、提高劳动者实际收入这三方面的情况是有所不同的。在开始投资与投资形成生产能力之间，由于只有资金的投入而没有社会总产品的产出，所以货币流通量是增长的，这就会对物价的稳定发生消极的影响。如果在投资形成生产能力之后，由于投资的结果而引起的社会总产品增长率仍然小于货币流通量的增长率，那么它仍然会对物价的稳定发生消极的影响。这一点是不容忽视的。以提供就业机会来说，情况则与此不同。从开始投资之时起，投资就有可能提供一定的就业机会，因为这些投资项目本身是吸收劳动力的。投资形成生产能力后，它可能对就业发生十分不同的影响：或者它有可能扩大就业（包括这些投资

jobs created by other industries or firms under its impact), or reduce employment (including fewer job opportunities in other industries or firms under the impact of this investment and fewer job opportunities directly caused by the termination of the investment project). With regard to real labor income, apart from the investment-induced changes in price level and employment that are likely to affect labor income, the investment-induced changes in labor productivity are a more important factor that inevitably affects changes in labor income. Before production capacity is realized, few significant changes will happen to labor productivity. Therefore, during the interval from the start of investment to the materialization of production capacity, changes in labor income are mainly related to changes in price level and employment, whereas after production capacity is created, changes in labor productivity will have an increasing impact on labor income.

Thus, to judge if investment is rational or not, not only its impact on price stability, job creation, and real labor income after it has brought about production capacity, but also its impact on these fields during the interval from the outset of the investment to the yield of production capacity should be observed. If the former impact is considered but the latter neglected, it is likely that the investment in question may have already had a negative impact, and a seriously negative impact at that, on the balance of national economy before it reaps production capacity. In that scenario, even if investment has generated new production capacity, its earlier negative impact on national economy may be so grave as to hold back the effectiveness of production capacity or offset its positive impact on balancing the national economy.

IV. Discrepancy between effective and rational investment

As I have pointed out in the foregoing, the criteria for judging effective investment are different from those for rational investment. The roles of effective investment and rational investment in the economy are different as well. Effective investment is not necessarily rational investment. Even if effective investment is also rational, it is not necessarily the most rational investment. On the other hand, although rational investment must also be effective, it may not be the most effective investment. The discrepancy between effective investment and rational investment is apparent.

项目本身增加的就业，也包括由此引起的其他部门和企业的就业的增加），或者它有可能引起就业的减少（包括由于投资引起的其他部门和企业的就业的减少，以及由于投资结束而引起的投资项目本身的就业的减少）。再以劳动者实际收入水平而言，除了因投资而引起的物价变动和就业变动这两方面可能引起劳动者实际收入水平变动以外，更重要的是由于投资而引起的劳动生产率的变化，劳动者实际收入水平的变化必然要受到劳动生产率变化的制约。在投资形成生产能力之前，劳动生产率一般并不发生重要的变化，因此从投资开始到投资形成生产能力之间的这段时间内，劳动者实际收入的变动主要同投资引起的物价变动和就业变动有关；而在投资形成生产能力之后，劳动生产率的变化将对劳动者实际收入水平发生越来越有力的影响。

由此可见，投资的合理与否，固然要看投资形成生产能力之后对物价稳定、提供就业机会和提高劳动者实际收入水平等方面的影响如何，也要看开始投资之后到形成生产能力之间这段时间内，投资对物价稳定、提供就业机会和提高劳动者实际收入水平方面的影响。如果只注意到前一种影响而忽视后一种影响，那就有可能造成这种情形，即在投资形成生产能力之前，投资已经给国民经济的平衡带来消极的影响，甚至严重的消极影响，这样，即使投资以后形成了生产能力，但由于在这以前投资给国民经济平衡带来的消极影响过大，以至于妨碍了生产能力的发挥，或抵消了生产能力形成后可以在国民经济平衡方面发生的积极作用。

四、有效投资与合理投资之间的矛盾

前面已经指出，判断有效投资的标准和判断合理投资的标准是不一样的，有效投资在经济中的作用和合理投资在经济中的作用也有所不同。因此，有效投资不一定是合理投资，或者说，有效投资即使是一种合理投资，但也不一定是合理程度最大的即最合理的投资；另一方面，合理投资虽然必须是一种有效投资，但它不一定就是有效程度最大的（即最有效的）投资。有效投资与合理投资之间显然存在着矛盾。

For instance, a specific investment project or investment in one certain field may be effective because it can raise aggregate social product, but it may have a negative impact on price stability by taking up so much funding for so long as to affect the amount of currency in circulation before it creates production capacity. After creating production capacity, the investment in question may also diminish the job positions it has created and cause other industries and firms to reduce their job positions. Even if it has created production capacity, the investment can still cause real labor income to dip due to price changes, job market fluctuations and declining labor productivity. Given these possibilities, and by taking its multiple goals and the balance of national economy into consideration, effective investment is likely to be irrational or have just a small degree of rationality at best.

Observed from the perspective of multiple goals and the balance of national economy, a certain investment is rational because it has improved at least one of the four fields—economic growth, basic price stability, job creation, and labor income—while the other fields have shown no sign of deterioration. However, because rational investment has to attain multiple goals, its capacity to boost aggregate social product may be lower than maximal (for instance, if the investment is not put into a highly sophisticated automated factory), although it can still boost aggregate social product to a certain extent. In this case, it cannot be counted as the most effective investment.

How, then, should we deal with the discrepancy between effective and rational investment? We may study the question from a normative or a positive approach.

A normative approach calls for realigning the goals of investment in the order of importance, urgency and priority of the multiple goals that the investment aims to attain. Then overall consideration should be given to the problems to be solved through this investment and the means of solving these problems, so as to find out to what extent effectiveness and rationality of this investment can be coordinated. According to the aforementioned definition, investment is rational if it has improved at least one of the four fields while the others show no sign of deterioration. The question now is which one of these four fields should be improved first. The answer must be based on a study of the actual situation to see

例如，某一项投资或某一方面的投资，单纯从增加社会总产品供给的角度来看，它是有效投资，但它有可能在形成生产能力之前因投资额较大，占用资金的时间较长，从而影响货币流通量，对物价稳定发生不利的影响；或者，它有可能在形成生产能力之后，本身吸收的就业和由此引起的其他部门、企业的就业反而减少了；或者，即使它形成了生产能力，但由于物价变动和就业变动的影响，或由于劳动生产率的下降，从而导致劳动者实际收入水平降低，等等。所以，从兼顾多种目标和平衡国民经济的角度来看，它却是不合理的投资，或合理程度较小的投资。

又如，某一项投资或某一方面的投资，从兼顾多种目标和平衡国民经济的角度来看，它是合理投资，因为它能使经济增长、物价基本稳定、提供较多就业机会、提高劳动者实际收入水平这四个方面的情况中至少有一方面的情况比过去好转，而没有任何一方面的情况比过去恶化。但是，正由于它要兼顾多种目标，因此它不一定是最能促进社会总产品增加的投资（比如说它不一定建成最新的自动化工厂），而可能是为了兼顾其他目标，并非购置最新设备，但仍能在某种程度上促进社会总产品增加的投资，从而它不是有效程度最大的（或最有效的）投资。

怎样对待有效投资与合理投资之间的这种矛盾呢？这个问题可以用规范方法来分析或用实证方法来分析。

用规范方法来分析，就是把投资所要兼顾的多种目标按照轻重缓急、先后次序进行排队，然后根据客观存在的实际条件，把通过投资所要解决的问题和可能解决的手段加以通盘考虑，再决定有效投资与合理投资究竟能在何种程度上协调一致。按照上面的定义，在投资所要解决的四个方面的问题中，只要其中至少有一个方面比过去好转，其余三个方面不比过去恶化，就是合理投资了。那么，应当首先让哪一个方面比过去好转呢？当然，这里涉及的是实现目标

which one of the four goals is most attainable. However, the answer also involves judgment of values, that is, which goal is more important and which goal is less important. To observe investment through normative analysis is to prioritize the four goals from judgment of values in order to make rational investment.

The positive approach follows established norms and rules, or is based on the assumption that all goals are equally important, to find ways to coordinate effective and rational investment. The solution to the discrepancy between effective and rational investment is related not only to the preconditions of a given investment but also to the methods of raising and operating the fund needed for this investment. The next chapter explores, from the viewpoint of positive study, the preconditions of investment and how to raise and operate the fund of investment.

V. Resource and marketability for effective and rational investment

The shared attributes of effective and rational investment are that, firstly, both can only take place where there are sufficient and usable economic resources, and secondly, there must be markets for the products of the production capacity they have created. In other words, economic resources and marketability are prerequisites for investment to be at once effective and rational.

Economic resources fall into two categories: material and human. Material resources, that is, means of production, include production equipment, raw materials, fuels and power, means of transportation, and storage facilities. Human resources encompass unskilled and skilled labor force, the latter including technical and management professionals. These resource conditions are indispensable for every investment project.

Now that effectiveness of investment hinges on its speed in putting together production capacity and boosting aggregate social product, it is difficult, or even impossible, to turn investment promptly into production capacity in the absence of means of production and human resources. Even if an investment project has been completed, it still cannot increase aggregate social product if it has no sufficient supply of means of production—such as raw materials, fuels, power, and spare parts for maintenance and repair purposes—and adequate labor force, or if transportation, storage and other factors fail to meet production needs.

的客观可能性问题，所以要根据条件来分析。但这里也有一个价值判断问题，即认为什么任务更重要，什么任务较次要。用规范方法来分析，就是从价值判断的角度来评定各个目标的先后次序，然后再设法使合理投资得以实现。

用实证方法来分析，是按照既定的规范准则，或假定所有目标都同样重要，再拟定使有效投资和合理投资协调一致的途径。有效投资和合理投资之间矛盾的解决，不仅与投资的前提条件有关，而且与投资资金的筹集和运用方式有关。下面，准备从实证分析的角度，对投资的前提条件和投资资金的筹集、运用方式进行一些探讨。

五、有效投资与合理投资的资源与市场条件

无论是有效投资还是合理投资，它们的共同点在于：二者都必须在有充足的、可利用的经济资源条件下进行，二者都必须使投资形成生产能力之后所生产的产品有市场。这就是说，资源条件和市场条件是投资有效性和投资合理性的共同前提。

经济资源包括物质资源和人力资源两大类。物质资源，也就是指生产资料，包括生产设备、原材料、燃料和动力、运输手段、仓储设备等。人力资源，包括非熟练劳动力和熟练劳动力，而熟练劳动力中，又包括技术、管理等方面的专业人员。这些资源条件是投资所不可缺少的。

以有效投资来说，既然投资的有效与否取决于它能否迅速形成生产能力，增加社会总产品的供给，所以不言而喻，如果缺乏生产资料和人力供给的保证，要迅速形成生产能力将是困难的，甚至是不可能的。否则，即使投资项目已经建成，但由于得不到充足的生产资料(包括原材料、燃料和动力、供修理和更换用的零部件等)，或者得不到适当的劳动力，或者运输和仓储等条件跟不上生产的需要，那么仍然无法增加社会总产品的供给。从这一点

In this regard, investment—the primary driving force behind economic growth—is based upon the adequacy of useful economic resources. Investment can put together production capacity rapidly where idle productive resources and a variety of idle workers are available. It can also quickly bring about production capacity where productive resources and labor force are unavailable but can be obtained through minor readjustments, or where economic resources are in short supply but there is an adequate foreign exchange reserve to be used to buy those deficient resources from foreign markets. However, in the latter scenario, things tend to be complicated because it involves the balance of foreign trade and of international payments. In the absence of all the abovementioned conditions, investment becomes ineffective because it cannot promptly create production capacity.

Given that the rationality of investment is determined by whether it can meet the four goals of economic growth, basic price stability, job creation, and real labor income, effectiveness—that is, promptness in creating production capacity—becomes the minimum requirement for rational investment. Because adequate supply of economic resources is a prerequisite for the speedy creation of production capacity, such supply must also be guaranteed for rational investment. Otherwise it cannot meet all four goals at the same time.

The next consideration is the market conditions for investment, that is, the product salability of an investment project. Whether such a product is made for production or consumption purposes, there must be people willing to buy it at a certain price. If production is carried out only for the purpose of meeting certain quotas for output or output value and the product cannot be sold out and has to be piled up in warehouses, the investment will not be able to contribute to economic growth. This conclusion is understandable, because investment can be rational only if it contributes to aggregate social product, maintains basic price stability, creates new jobs, and increases real labor income. Those roles can never be realized if nobody wants to buy the product of an investment project. Furthermore, investment may have a negative impact on prices and labor income if its product cannot be sold out. Such investment is irrational.

来看，投资作为经济增长的第一推动力量，以充足的、可以利用的经济资源的存在为前提。假定客观上存在着闲置的生产资料，又有闲置的各种劳动力可以利用，投资之后迅速形成生产能力是没有困难的。假定客观上暂时没有现成的、足够的闲置生产资料和劳动力，但只要稍加调整就可以保证生产资料和劳动力，那么投资之后也能迅速形成生产能力。或者，即使生产资料和劳动力都供应不足，但如果有足够的外汇储备，可以及时地转向国外市场去取得所缺少的经济资源，那么投资之后仍然有可能迅速形成生产能力，只不过在这种场合，情况会变得复杂些，因为这涉及外贸平衡和国际收支平衡的问题了。假定以上所说的这些条件全都不具备，投资就不可能迅速形成生产能力，它就成为无效投资。

以合理投资来说，既然投资的合理与否取决于它能否兼顾经济增长、物价基本稳定、提供较多就业机会、提高劳动者实际收入水平等多种目标，那么，投资合理性的最低限度要求就是它必须具有有效性，即能够迅速形成生产能力。由于充足的经济资源的供给是迅速形成生产能力的必要条件，所以合理投资也必须具备充足的经济资源供给这一前提，否则就无法对多种目标起到兼顾的作用。

再分析投资的市场条件。市场条件是指投资以后所生产出来的产品要适应市场的需要，要有销路。无论这些产品是供生产消费还是供个人消费，都需要有买主愿意在一定价格条件下购买它们。假定找不到买主，生产只是为某种产量指标或产值指标而生产，生产出来的产品只不过在仓库中积压起来，那就无法实现投资对经济的积极作用。这一点对合理投资来说，是完全可以理解的，因为投资之所以被称为合理的，正在于它能在增加社会总产品供给的同时，对维持物价基本稳定、增加就业机会和提高劳动者实际收入水平起作用，如果投资以后生产出来的产品没有销路，那么投资在所有这些方面本来可以起到的作用也就发挥不出来了。不仅如此，假定产品没有销路，投资对于物价和劳动者实际收入很可能发生消极的影响。这样的投资是不合理的投资。

Is product marketability also a prerequisite for effective investment? Because whether investment is effective or not is determined by whether it can bring about production capacity promptly and boost aggregate social product, people may argue that the effectiveness of investment is irrelevant to product marketability. They believe that investment is effective as long as it can produce a certain amount of products, regardless of product salability. In their eyes, investment becomes ineffective only if it cannot create production capacity or cannot do it fast enough—investment should not be deemed ineffective if it can bring about production capacity speedily even though its products are unwanted on the market. This idea, undoubtedly, is not correct.

This idea is wrong in that it only accepts the literal meaning of production capacity, and severs production capacity from product marketability. It is, therefore, a misunderstanding of production capacity. We know that the production capacity of a factory built with an amount of investment is only nominal if it does not produce and supply products. If the factory's products cannot meet market demand and only belong in warehouses, this factory is a nonfactor at best because of its failure to supply society with usable products. We would rather this kind of factory did not do anything, for the fuel, power, raw materials and so on it consumes could have been used for meaningful purposes. Therefore, production capacity created by investment should be real, rather than nominal. It should supply society with marketable products instead of things that cannot be sold out. If the effectiveness of investment and the creation of production capacity are understood in that light, product marketability must be regarded as a precondition for effective investment.

The argument that the effectiveness of investment is unrelated to the marketability of its product exactly mistakes nominal production capacity for real production capacity. The effectiveness of investment rests in real, rather than nominal, production capacity it creates.

VI. Profitability of effective and rational investment

Investment profitability is an important theoretical issue. Even if the product of an investment project can be sold out, what will be the consequences if it can only be sold out at a lower price than its production and interest costs?

那么，投资的市场条件这一前提对于有效投资来说，是不是也适用呢？也许会有这样一种看法：由于投资的有效与否取决于它能否迅速形成生产能力，能否增加社会总产品的供给，而迅速形成生产能力与否只是同资源条件有关，与市场条件没有直接的联系，所以，只要投资之后能生产出一定数量的产品，不管这些产品是否有销路，它们都可以被称为有效投资。按照这种看法，似乎只有那些根本不形成生产能力或未能迅速形成生产能力的投资才是无效投资，能迅速形成生产能力但产品与市场需要不相适应的投资则不算是无效投资。这种看法无疑是不正确的。

这种看法的错误在于：它仅仅从字面上理解生产能力的形成，而把生产能力同市场条件割裂开来。实际上，这是对生产能力的一种误解。我们知道，如果投资建成了一座工厂，但这座工厂建成后并不从事生产，不提供产品，那么仍然不等于具有实际生产能力，因为这只是一种名义生产能力；如果这座工厂建成后生产的产品不适合市场需要，只是积压在仓库内，那么这种情形至少同该工厂不从事生产一样，因为它同样没有为社会提供可供利用的产品；不仅如此，它甚至比该工厂不从事生产更坏，因为它消耗了其他工厂所生产出来的、本来可以安排其他用途的燃料、动力、原材料等。因此，投资以后形成的生产能力应当是实际生产能力，而不是名义生产能力，应当是为社会提供适应市场需要的产品，而不是生产出没有销路的产品。如果我们从这个意义上来理解有效投资和生产能力的形成，那么就必然把市场条件看作投资有效性的前提之一。

认为投资的有效与否与市场条件没有直接联系的想法，恰恰是混淆了实际生产能力与名义生产能力的区别，误把后者当作前者，而不了解投资的有效性在于它所形成的生产能力乃是实际生产能力，而并非名义生产能力。

六、有效投资与合理投资的赢利性问题

投资赢利性问题是一个重要的理论问题。即使投资以后生产出来的产品有销路，但如果它们只能以低于生产成本和利息费用的价格销售出去，那将会造成什么后果呢？

First of all, this kind of investment cannot be recouped in that case. Moreover, even after the investment project is completed, further expenses are needed to keep production going; otherwise even the original scale of production cannot be maintained. This kind of investment, even if it can bring about production capacity and its products are marketable, poses more losses than gains, and should never be allowed to happen.

Nevertheless, if we extend our vision from an individual investor to the entire national economy, different opinions may occur on investment profitability.

The national economy is an integrated entity, in which all sectors are organically connected. Some sectors or firms may have the needed economic resources and their products can meet market demand. But, for one reason or another, their products are priced equal to or lower than their production costs and interest expenses, and therefore, they cannot generate a profit. Should investment be made in such a sector or firm? Is profitability an overriding condition for investment? It seems that neither question can be answered with a simple yes or no, because both involve how the macroeconomic effectiveness of investment should be measured.

As illustrated in the previous chapter, effective investment has both macroeconomic and microeconomic implications, while rational investment belongs in the macroeconomic realm. Observed from a macroeconomic point of view, some kinds of investment in certain sectors or firms are unlikely to make a profit, but can contribute to faster growth in other sectors or firms and to the balance of national economy and coordination among investment goals. This kind of investment is still necessary, and can be regarded as both effective and rational.

Defenders of investment that is at once ineffective and irrational in practice may also cite the macroeconomic effectiveness of investment to back up their argument that this kind of investment should not be cancelled. They may accuse those who want to do so of lacking macroeconomic farsightedness. They can always find a "reason" to justify any investment project they like, arguing that it is so important to the national economy that it cannot be ditched even if it is not making money. Indeed, this issue can easily become controversial,

首先，对投资单位而言，这样的投资不仅不能回收上来，而且在投资以后，仍然需要追加一定的支出才能维持生产，否则它就连原来的生产规模也维持不下去了。这样的投资，即使形成了生产能力，并且形成的是产品有销路的实际生产能力，那么它只不过是一种对投资单位得不偿失的投资。一般说来，这样的投资是应当避免的。

然而，假定我们把视角由个别投资单位扩大到整个国民经济，那么我们对投资赢利性的问题可能会产生不同的看法。

国民经济是一个整体。国民经济各个部门有机地联系在一起。某些部门或某些企业，从它们本身的情况来分析，经济资源条件是具备的，产品也适应市场的需要，但由于某种原因，产品的价格只可能等于甚至低于生产成本和利息费用，从而是不赢利的。那么，是否应当在这些部门或企业进行投资呢？投资的赢利性是不是这些部门或企业的必不可少的投资前提呢？看来这个问题不可能简单地予以肯定或否定，因为这涉及投资的宏观经济效果的计量。

前面已经提到，有效投资有宏观经济的和微观经济的双重含义，合理投资则是宏观经济学范畴。从宏观经济的角度来看待投资，可能出现这样一种情况，即某些部门或某些企业的投资尽管其本身不具备赢利条件，但投资的结果却有助于其他部门或企业的生产有更大程度的增长，有助于国民经济的综合平衡，有助于协调各个目标之间的关系，那么这样的投资仍是十分必要的，这样的投资仍然可以称为有效投资和合理投资。

但投资的宏观经济效果也有可能成为替某些实际上无效的或不合理的投资进行辩护的借口，硬说这些投资项目不应当中止，否则就是缺乏宏观经济的考虑等等。甚至可以说，任何投资都能找到“合理的”根据，因为主张进行这种投资的人总可以提出“理由”，认为该项投资对国民经济如何如何重要，即使不赢利，也是不能取消的。的确，这是一个容易引起争论的问题。假定我们只承认投资

and can never be settled if we accept the existence and significance of the macroeconomic results of an investment project without setting benchmarks for its effectiveness and rationality in macroeconomic terms.

This is where econometrics comes in handy. Despite its limitations, the methods of econometrics are still useful for analyzing investment effectiveness and rationality in macroeconomic terms on certain occasions and under certain premises and presumptions.

The resource and market conditions for investment should be considered in the first place. Investment, no matter what kind it is, must be guaranteed with an ample supply of means of production and human resources, both of which are prerequisites for production capacity. The products invested in should also meet market demand, otherwise they can only become part of warehouse stockpiles and their production capacity is nominal at best. Various econometric methods can be employed when we analyze the resource and market conditions for an investment scheme. Generally speaking, the input-output analysis can be employed to determine the situation regarding resource supply and market demand.

The conditions for investment profitability come next. Investment profitability in microeconomic terms can be computed with cost-benefit analysis. Relationships in this regard are relatively simple. By factoring in the given output and price conditions, as well as production costs and interest expenses, we can clarify whether an invested project is making or losing money. Then the deadline for recouping the investment—normally a major benchmark for judging the microeconomic effectiveness of an invested project—can be set with reference to the production cycle.

The situation is a lot more complex when it comes to judging if an investment project is making a profit or not from a macroeconomic perspective. Investment rationality in the field of material production and investment effectiveness in macroeconomic terms cannot be studied without comparing various relations in the national economy and dissecting the input-output relationship between sectors in the national economy. If the product of Sector A is not only supplied directly to consumers but also needed by Sectors B, C and D for their production, while the products of Sectors B, C and D are also both supplied directly to consumers and needed by Sectors E, F, G and H for production purposes, and if that cycle goes on and on, then the results of follow-up investment in Sector A will be reflected not just in that sector's augmented income

的宏观经济效果的存在及其意义，而没有判断宏观经济意义上的投资有效性和投资合理性的标准，那么这个问题就无法解决。

在这种情况下，经济计量学方法是可以采用的。经济计量学方法本身固然有局限性，但在一定的场合，在一定的前提与假定之下，对于宏观经济意义上的投资有效性和投资合理性的分析仍有用处。

首先应当重视投资的资源条件和市场条件。任何投资都需要有充足的生产资料和人力供给的保证，因为这是形成生产能力的前提。投资以后生产出来的产品，也需要与市场需求相适应，否则生产出来的产品只能堆积在仓库里，投资所形成的生产能力只不过是名义生产能力而已。在分析投资的资源条件和市场条件时，可以采取各种计量方法。一般说来，可以采取投入产出分析方法来说明资源供给状况和市场需求状况。

再看投资的赢利性条件。微观经济意义上的投资赢利性，可以采取成本—收益分析方法来计算。在这里，关系是比较简单的。在一定产量和价格条件下，考虑到生产成本和利息费用，可以了解到投资单位的赢利与亏损状况，然后根据生产的时间可以了解到投资的回收期限。投资回收期的长短通常是判断投资单位的微观经济效果的重要尺度。

至于从宏观经济角度来考察投资的赢利与否，问题要复杂得多。物质生产领域内投资的合理性以及宏观经济意义上的投资的有效性，不能离开国民经济中各种比例关系的考察，不能回避国民经济各个部门之间投入产出关系的分析。如果甲部门所生产出来的产品除了直接供应消费者以外，还为乙、丙、丁等部门的生产消费所必需，而乙、丙、丁等部门所生产出来的产品除了直接供应消费者而外，还为戊、己、庚、辛等部门的生产消费所必需，如此等等，那么，对甲部门追加一定的投资的效果就不仅仅从甲部门本身所增加

but also in the augmented incomes of Sectors B, C, D, E, F, G and H. Suppose there is a certain ratio between income and employment, then the results of follow-up investment in Sector A will be reflected not just in its increased number of jobs but also in the changes that have taken place in the number of jobs in the other sectors. Using counterfactual analysis, we can compare the results of the following two approaches: first, to study total income, net income, employment and other variables before Sector A was invested in; second, to study the changes in the variables such as total income, net income, and employment in the other sectors after Sector A was invested in. From this comparison we can get to know the degree of profitability of investment in macroeconomic terms. Suppose that a certain investment project does not make money for itself, but contributes to the growth in total income, net income and employment in other economic sectors, and the benefits to the national economy from the growth in these sectors outweigh the losses caused to the national economy by the investment project's failure in making a profit, then the investment can still be considered as a gain to the national economy. As a matter of fact, there is an investment-recouping period for the project, but such a period is reflected in the national economy. If, on the contrary, a comparison of the two approaches indicates that the investment does make a profit for itself but has inflicted losses in total income, net income and employment on other sectors, or that the investment is losing money while these sectors' increases in gross income, net income and employment are negligible so that the benefits the investment has yielded for the national economy are barely enough to offset the losses it has inflicted on the national economy, such an investment is deemed detrimental to the national economy. If allowed to continue under the excuse of cherishing its macroeconomic results, the said investment becomes irrational, and—in macroeconomic terms—ineffective as well.

VII. Relationship between investment fund supply, public finance and investment

To make investment both effective and rational, due attention must be paid to the supply of funding. Suppose an investment project has favorable resource and market conditions and its product can be sold briskly enough to guarantee an after-sale profit, but it cannot continue or has to stop midway because of fund shortage, then it cannot put

的收入中反映出来，而且也从乙、丙、丁、戊、己、庚、辛等部门由此所增加的收入中反映出来。假定一定的收入量与一定的就业量之间存在某种比例关系，那么，对甲部门追加一定的投资的效果既反映于甲部门本身增加的就业量，也反映于其他各部门的就业量的变动。这样，如果采用反事实度量法，至少可以两种方案进行比较。一是不增加甲部门的投资时的各个部门的总收入、净收入、就业等变量的大小，二是增加对甲部门的一定量的投资后各个部门的总收入、净收入、就业等变量的变动率。两种方案进行对比的结果，可以了解到投资的宏观经济意义上的赢利性。假定某项投资本身不赢利，但确实能使各个部门的总收入、净收入、就业等有所增长，而增长的结果能使国民经济的收益大于该项投资本身不赢利给予国民经济造成的损失，那么该项投资仍是有利于国民经济的。该项投资实际上仍有一个投资回收期，只不过这种投资回收期反映于国民经济之中。反之，如果两个方案对比的结果，即使某项投资本身有所赢利，但却使各个部门的总收入、净收入、就业等有所减少，或者，某项投资本身有亏损，但各个部门的总收入、净收入、就业等增加甚微，以致国民经济的收益仍小于该项投资本身亏损给予国民经济造成的损失，那么，该项投资是不利于国民经济的。如果在这种情况下仍坚持以注意宏观经济效果的名义来从事该项投资，那么这种投资就是不合理的投资和宏观经济意义上的无效投资。

七、投资资金的供给、财政与投资的关系

要使投资成为有效投资和合理投资，必须重视投资资金的供给。如果某项投资具备了资源条件和市场条件，产品又有销路，并且预计销售后还有赢利，但由于资金供给不足，以至于投资无法进行，或者使在建项目中途停顿，那样就不可能迅速形成生产能力，

together production capacity in good time, and cannot become effective investment. Furthermore, this kind of investment is irrational because it is a loss to the national economy when the money spent fails to yield production capacity.

If, on the contrary, an investment scheme can yield production capacity promptly but spends too much to achieve the purpose, it may also disrupt public finance or money circulation, thereby exerting an adverse impact on price stability. Thus it can never become rational investment.

What can be done to avoid improper supply of funding and ensure effectiveness and rationality of investment? Let us begin answering this question by studying the relationship between investment and public finance.

Under socialism, fiscal appropriations are an important source of reinvestment. They generally have a direct impact on the volume and scale of investment and its effectiveness. More importantly, the impact of such appropriations also extends to the relationship between the multiple goals of investment and to investment rationality.

When we try to coordinate the relationship between economic growth and basic price stability, we face the urgent task of preventing the demand for monetary funds from running out of control, or, to put it another way, we must prevent the amount of currency in circulation from growing too fast. Inflation is eventually attributed to the failure of the growth in aggregate social product to outpace the growth in the amount of currency in circulation. Inflation can be prevented or erased only by boosting the growth rate of aggregate social product, reducing the growth rate of the amount of currency in circulation, or both.

Fast growth in the amount of currency in circulation is mainly an outcome of fiscal deficit or bank credit expansion. Therefore, when there is a serious fiscal deficit, especially when such a deficit has lingered for several years, fiscal appropriation designed to increase investment funding must be used cautiously. Otherwise the amount of currency in circulation may be further increased.

However, insofar as investment is the primary driving force behind economic growth, the lack of sufficient investment can neither boost aggregate social product nor change the situation where aggregate social product grows slower than the amount of currency in circulation. Tightening up investment alone can neither eliminate fiscal deficit nor

投资也不可能成为有效投资。不仅如此，由于已经投入但迟迟未能形成生产能力的资金是国民经济的一项损失，因此该项投资也只可能是一种不合理的投资。

另一方面，即使投资能迅速形成生产能力，但如果资金供给过度，投资也可能引起财政或货币流通方面的失调，从而对物价稳定发生不利的影响，这样，它同样不可能成为合理投资。

那么，怎样才能避免资金供给的不当，而使投资具有有效性和合理性呢？首先，让我们对投资与财政之间的关系进行一些探讨。

在社会主义条件下，增加投资所需要的资金的一个重要来源是财政拨款。一般情况下，国家的财政拨款直接影响着投资的数额和规模，影响着投资的有效程度。更重要的是，财政拨款影响着多种目标之间的关系，影响着投资的合理程度。

在协调经济增长与物价基本稳定这两个目标时，一个迫切的问题是如何防止对货币资金的需求量过大，也就是如何防止货币流通量的增长过快。通货膨胀之所以发生，其原因归根结底在于社会总产品的增长率小于货币流通量的增长率。而要防止和消除通货膨胀，或者依靠提高社会总产品的增长率，或者依靠降低货币流通量的增长率，或者双管齐下。

货币流通量之所以会有较大幅度的增长，主要是由财政赤字或银行信贷膨胀引起的。因此，在客观上已经出现较多的财政赤字时，特别是连年有财政赤字时，通过财政拨款方式来增加投资资金，是必须慎重的，否则很可能使货币流通量进一步增大。

但是，由于投资是经济增长的第一推动力量，缺乏必要的投资无法使社会总产品增加，甚至也无法扭转社会总产品增长率小于货币流通量增长率的局面。单纯地紧缩投资，既不能保证消灭财政赤字，

effectively keep inflation away from the door. This is because economic sectors are interlinked and only by constantly restructuring these sectors and their products can the proportional relationships in the national economy be coordinated. However, restructuring sectors and products calls for follow-up investment on most occasions. If investment is tightened up merely to eliminate deficits and forestall inflation, the national economy will fall further out of proportion and coordination. Worse, it can also land some industries or firms that may expand production and make a profit in financial loss, thereby doing a disservice to the effort to turn the fiscal situation around and eradicate inflation.

From the perspective of increasing aggregate social product, technical renovation and equipment upgrading are material conditions for labor productivity increases, but both call for follow-up investment. If investment is tightened up merely to wipe out deficits and forestall inflation, it is very difficult to boost labor productivity and aggregate social product by improving their material conditions. Furthermore, if other conditions remain unchanged but equipment cannot be upgraded for lack of necessary investment, workforce productivity will decline. As a result, the industries and firms that could have been producing and making a profit will lose money, and public finance and the effort to control inflation will be jeopardized as well.

To ascribe the rise of financial deficits or inflation merely to investment growth is to oversimplify a complex matter. Effective and rational investment is actually an important means by which to eliminate deficits and inflation, rather than to aggravate them. It is ineffective or irrational investment—investment that drags on and fails to yield production capacity, investment in unmarketable products, investment that is made in marketable products but incurs heavy losses or distorts economic relations—that should be held responsible for deficits and inflation.

This being the case, what merits the attention of the fiscal department is that they should curtail or cancel all the investment projects that lack resource and market conditions or fail to yield macroeconomic returns. However, investment projects that yield production capacities promptly, produce marketable products, make profit, and are conducive to the growth of total and net income of various sectors in the national economy, should not be curtailed or axed. Effective and rational investment is a dynamo behind a robust and booming national economy,

也不能保证不发生通货膨胀。这是因为：国民经济中各个部门是有机地联系在一起的，只有不断调整部门结构和产品结构，才能使国民经济的比例关系经常保持协调。但部门结构和产品结构的调整在大多数场合需要追加一定数量的投资。如果为了消灭财政赤字和防止通货膨胀而单纯采取紧缩投资的做法，只会使国民经济的比例不协调和进一步不协调，甚至会使某些本来可以增加产量和赢利的行业或企业因此转为亏损，而无助于财政状况的好转和通货膨胀的消失。

从增加社会总产品的角度来看，技术改造和设备更新是提高劳动生产率的物质条件，而技术改造和设备更新通常需要追加一定数量的投资。如果为了消灭财政赤字和防止通货膨胀而单纯采取紧缩投资的做法，那就很难从物质条件方面着手来提高劳动生产率和增加社会总产品。不仅如此，如果缺乏必要的投资，以致设备无法更新，在其他条件不变的情况下，劳动生产率将会下降，于是某些本来可以照常生产和赢利的行业或企业也会因此转为亏损，这样就会进一步不利于财政，不利于应付通货膨胀。

可见，不能简单地把投资增长看成是财政赤字或通货膨胀的起因。有效投资和合理投资不仅不会加剧财政赤字和通货膨胀，反而是用来消除财政赤字和通货膨胀的手段。只有那种无效的投资、不合理的投资，即迟迟未能形成生产能力的投资、产品无销路的投资，或者虽然产品有销路但却亏损累累的投资以及使国民经济各种比例关系不协调的投资，才应对财政赤字和通货膨胀负责。

因此，对财政部门来说，需要注意的是：必须紧缩或停止一切不具备资源条件和市场条件而又没有宏观经济效果的投资，而对于那些能够迅速形成生产能力、产品有销路、有赢利或有助于国民经济各部门总收入和净收入增长的投资，则不应当紧缩或停止。有效投资和合理投资是活跃、繁荣国民经济的推动力量，活跃、繁荣的

and a robust and booming national economy is the solid foundation of public finance and a guarantee for stable fiscal revenue. The financial department can avoid inappropriate supply of investment funding as long as it takes a scientific attitude toward investment, that is, to invest in what should be invested in and not to invest in what should not be invested in.

VIII. Choice of investment funding raising channels

Fiscal funding is a major financial source for investment, but certainly not the only source for it. Under socialism the money needed for investment purposes comes from at least four avenues: fiscal appropriations, nongovernmental fund-raisers, business reserve funds, and bank credits. Short-, medium- and long-term bank credits can be used as a source of money for all purposes of investment. Their strength lies in that they can urge investors to tighten up financial auditing and pay due attention to the microeconomic results of their investment projects. The bank, by screening investment plans and monitoring the spending, plays a definite role in enhancing the macroeconomic results of investment. Apart from money raised by way of savings and bond purchases, the funds from nongovernmental sources also include the money procured from people of all walks of life to run cooperative firms and boost domestic development. Business reserve funds refer to the portion of profit that firms are allowed to retain on the principle of autonomy to buy equipment, upgrade technology, expand production, reduce costs, and increase output.

Of the four major sources of funding, fiscal funding is not always the principal one. People can make their choices according to investment needs and financial situation. No matter what source is chosen, however, the aforementioned investment conditions should always be kept in mind. On no account should ineffective and irrational investment be made. Whenever an investment project gets off the ground, no effort should be spared to maximize its effectiveness and rationality.

A point that can be easily forgotten is that nongovernmental fundraisers are not only a substitute for government investment but also a method to withdraw money from circulation. The role of such fundraisers in substituting for government investment comes through when investment projects originally to be funded with fiscal appropriation revert to social fund-raising. However, investment is not just a supply

国民经济则是财政的坚实的基础，是源源不断的财政收入的保证。其实，只要财政部门对待投资持有这种科学的态度，即不该投资的不予投资，有必要投资的给予投资，就有可能避免投资资金供给的不当。

八、投资资金筹集方式的选择

财政拨款是社会主义投资资金的重要来源，但绝不是惟一来源。在社会主义条件下，投资所需要的资金至少有四个国内来源，即财政拨款、社会集资、企业保留资金、银行信贷。银行信贷（包括短期、中期和长期信贷）可以作为不同用途的投资所需要的资金。它的优点在于能够督促投资单位加强经济核算，注意投资的微观经济效果。而银行通过对投资方案的审查和监督资金的使用，还能从增加宏观经济效果方面对投资起一定的作用。社会集资，除了指社会通过储蓄和购买债券方式聚集的资金以外，还包括群众为创办合作企业而筹集的资金、社会各界人士为发展国内建设事业而筹集的资金等。企业保留资金则指企业根据自主权原则而保留的一部分利润。企业可以按照生产的需要，利用这些资金来增添设备，进行技术改造，扩大生产规模，降低成本，增加产量。

这四个国内资金来源中，财政拨款也不是在任何情况下都成为主要的资金筹集方式。由于投资项目的不同和客观经济条件的不同，可以在这些筹集资金的方式中作出适当的选择。但无论采取哪一种筹集资金的方式，前面一再提到的投资的条件都是必须考虑的。任何情况下都应避免无效投资和不合理投资。任何时候都应力求增加投资的有效性和合理性。

很容易被人们遗忘的是，社会集资这种筹集资金的方式不仅与国家的投资之间有一种替代作用，而且还可能成为货币回笼的一种方式。社会集资与国家投资的替代作用表现于：本来社会上的某些投资项目是由财政拨款来承办的，现在改由社会集资来进行了。但投资不只是货币资金的供给，物资的供给保证是不可缺少的。社会集资所

of money. Guaranteed material supply is indispensable, too. The money raised from nongovernmental channels needs to be spent on means of production. However, means of production needed for investment purposes are basically provided by the government department in charge of supplying them. If the government department does not possess sufficient means of production needed for an investment project, it means that the resource conditions for the project are not ripe. Just as I have said in my analysis of investment conditions, investment without adequate supply of means of production is ineffective and irrational and, therefore, should be abrogated. By the same token, if a nongovernment-funded investment project fails to get off the ground, it will not adversely affect the national economy. If the government department has sufficient means of production for an investment project, it means that the material conditions are ripe and that the project in question can be undertaken. In this case, the government department contributes to the national economy by supplying the needed means of production and withdrawing money from circulation. Otherwise, if nongovernmental funding is replaced with fiscal funding, it cannot withdraw money from circulation even though it could also be used for investment purposes.

From another point of view, in the absence of fund-raisers, what is the best use for money held in nongovernmental hands? This kind of money may end up in banks as saving deposits, or be spent on consumer goods. If it ends up as saving deposits, banks will have to think about how to put the money to good use. When there is investment demand, supply of money by bank credit plays the same role as nongovernmental money-raisers. However, if the money does not become saving deposits but is spent on consumer goods, especially on those in short supply, market supply will be strained. For this reason, if investment conditions are suitable and money can be raised from nongovernmental sources, such investment projects are more rational than others.

— *Finance & Trade Economics*, issue Nos. 1 & 3, 1982

聚集起来的货币资金，需要购买生产资料。为投资所需要的生产资料，基本上是国家的生产资料供应部门提供的。如果国家的生产资料供应部门所拥有的为该项投资所需要的生产资料不足，那么这表明该项投资的资源条件还不具备。根据前面在分析投资的条件时已经说明的，不具备充足生产资料供给的投资是无效投资和不合理投资，应当中止。于是此项以社会集资方式出现的投资未能实现，它并不会对国民经济造成不利的后果。如果国家的生产资料供应部门拥有为该项投资所需要的足够数量的生产资料，那么这表明该项投资的生产资料供给条件已经具备，投资可以进行。这时，国家的生产资料供应部门供应生产资料，收回社会上的货币资金，这对于国民经济显然是有利的。否则，如果由国家拨款代替社会集资，虽然也能同样实现该项投资，但却起不到促进货币回笼的作用。

从另一个角度看，如果不进行社会集资，那么保留于社会各界手中的这些货币的出路何在呢？它们可能以储蓄方式存入银行，也可能购买消费品。假定它们存入银行，银行也会遇到如何运用它们的问题，在社会需要进行某项投资时，银行的信贷方式提供资金，其作用与社会集资进行该项投资是一样的。但假定这些货币不存入银行，而转向购买消费品，特别是购买供不应求的消费品，结果将会使市场供应更加紧张。因此，在投资条件已经具备而社会集资又有可能的时候，选择社会集资方式的投资往往是一种更为合理的投资。

（原载《财贸经济》，1982 年第 1 期和第 3 期）

BASIC THOUGHTS ON ECONOMIC RESTRUCTURING (1986)

Years have passed since economic restructuring came under way in this nation. What is to be done next? Here I would like to share my thoughts, which come in twenty-eight points, and involve seven issues altogether. Some of these ideas may be controversial, but I see controversy as a good thing. Without discussion and debate, there will be no economic prosperity.

I. Ownership reform holds the key to economic restructuring

1. Economic restructuring may break down if price reform fails. The success of economic restructuring, however, hinges not on price reform, but on ownership reform, which entails revamping the corporate system. This is because price reform serves the main purpose of shaping an environment in favor of the growth of the market economy, but only ownership reform or corporate system reform can address such issues as interests, responsibility, motivation, and incentives.

2. The purpose of ownership reform is to build state firms truly liable for their own gains and losses. Being "truly liable for their own gains and losses" means that, for one thing, firms should bear all the consequences of financial losses, and for another, gains and losses must be symmetrically treated not only for firms but also for their leaders. The most crucial task of ownership reform is to make state firms really accountable for their successes and failures, and, even more so, to answer the question of what is to be done with firms in the red. Symmetrical treatment of gains and losses means that firms should enjoy their profits while absorbing their losses rather than passing the ball to the state, which is exactly what firms are doing today. Taking responsibility for their own losses will stimulate them to improve management. The reason why some nonstate firms can stay dynamic and motivated under pressure is because they can treat gains and losses symmetrically—meaning that they have all the economic gains to themselves while being totally liable to economic losses, bankruptcy

included. As things stand in this nation, the best that can be done with a failing state firm is to demote its general manager or shift him to another post. This way of doing things cannot be sustained. Gains and losses must be treated on a balanced footing. Mismanaged firms should go bankrupt, and bankrupt firm should be liquidated. There should be both a bankruptcy law and a social security act, and issues such as reemployment for layoffs should be tackled in real earnest.

经济改革的基本思路（1986）

我国经济体制改革已经进行好几年了，下一步经济体制改革应当怎样进行，我想谈一点个人的看法，一共七个问题，二十八点。其中有些看法可能引起争论。这是一件好事，没有争鸣，经济学就不可能繁荣。

一、所有制改革是改革的关键

1. 经济改革的失败可能是由于价格改革的失败，但经济改革的成功并不取决于价格改革，而取决于所有制的改革，也就是企业体制的改革。这是因为：价格改革主要是为经济改革创造一个适宜于商品经济发展的环境，而所有制的改革或企业体制改革才真正涉及到利益、责任、刺激、动力问题。

2. 所有制改革的目的是建立真正自负盈亏的全民所有制企业。"真正自负盈亏"主要是指：第一，企业必须负担亏损带来的一切后果；第二，盈亏必须是对称的。这里的"对称"，既对企业而言，也对企业负责人而言。所有制改革中最要紧的，就是真正使全民所有制企业自负盈亏，特别是要解决企业亏损后怎么办的问题。盈亏的对称性是指：盈利的好处归企业，亏损也应由企业承担，不能像现在这样，亏损归国家，这将成为改善企业经营的动力。有些集资兴办的企业之所以有活力，有动力，有压力，与盈亏的对称性有关。盈了归自己，亏也由自己负责，直到最后倾家荡产。目前在我国的全民所有制经济中，企业亏了以后，负责人只是换个工作或受降级的行政处分，这是不管用的。盈亏必须对称。因此，经营不善的企业，该破产的就破产，破产后就清理。要有破产法，还要有社会保障的规定，对工人的就业等问题要认真处理。

3. Collective firms may adopt the shareholding system. State firms may also be transformed into shareholding companies, holding companies, or socialist enterprise consortia.

The shareholding system talked about here is not about selling stock shares to workers or other individuals (although of course, some of the shares can be sold to workers and other individuals), but about distributing interests among public owners according to the number of shares they hold. There can be a variety of public shareholders. After a state firm has its current assets evaluated, its net assets should be counted as state shares because they come from state investment. The investment added by a local government to a state firm becomes locally owned state shares, while the shares in the firm's possession come from its own investment. In addition, investment made by other state enterprises also becomes shares owned by these enterprises. The positions of the stockholders on the board of directors are arranged according to how many shares they hold, but it is the board of directors that decides the policies and principles for a shareholding firm. Only in this way can the difficult problem of detaching government administration from business management be effectively addressed. The board of directors is established through the shareholders' congress. In this case, all shareholders are public owners. In such a structure, even if some shares are sold to individuals, they are unlikely to take up a large portion of the total stock. The holding company system is another option that works under public ownership. Once a state firm becomes a shareholding company, its shares can be put up for sale. In the West, a holder of less than 51% of the shares of a company can control it and turn it into his branch company. We can do the same. If, under the holding-company system, a powerful state company can turn itself into a socialist enterprise consortium by buying shares to control a number of companies, it can change the behavior of these companies, and shift their focus from short-run business to long-term operations with a broad strategic vision. In that position, the socialist company can adapt its policy decisions to long-term development goals. Whatever it does, an enterprise consortium must take the overall scheme of things into consideration. For instance, it can take the lead in oil development in northwest China. If it has foreseen a boom in the petroleum industry coming to that region in a few years, it may consider investing part of its profits there. To boost development, it may also engage in trans-sectoral or trans-regional business operations in

3. 集体所有制企业是可以实行股份制的。全民所有制企业体制改革的可行措施之一也是实行股份制、控股制，建立社会主义的公司财团（企业财团）。

这里所说的股份制，主要不是指把股票卖给职工或个人所有（当然也可卖点给职工、个人），主要指公有者之间按股取利。公股持有者是多种多样的：国营企业财产评估以后，这一部分股权归国家，等于国家投资在这里。地方增加投资，是地方的股权。企业扩大再生产部分的投资，是企业的股权。其他全民所有制企业进来投资，是其他全民所有制企业的股权。这样，根据股权的多少，在董事会中有适当的安排。建立董事会后，由董事会来决定这个股份制企业的大政方针。这样，才能真正解决政企职责分开的问题。不然，政企分开的问题总是不好解决的。必须建立董事会，由股东大会成立董事会。股东都是公方。假定股票可以卖点给私人，那么比重也不会很大。实行控股权，也是全民所有制可以采取的措施。控股制是可行的：既然实行股份制，公司企业的股票可以让大家认购，就可以实行控股制；西方国家中某个大股东掌握公司不到 51% 的股票，有可能控制这个企业，使之成为子公司。我们也可以这样做。可以假定：实行控股制后，一个强有力的社会主义大企业，通过层层控股，成为社会主义的公司财团。这个公司财团将能改变企业行为，使企业从只注意短期经营，变为也注意长期经营，因为它具有战略眼光。这时，它能根据今后公司的长期发展，制定决策。作为一个公司财团，要有全盘考虑。比如说，西北的石油开发，可以由公司财团出面搞，它注意到若干年后西北地区石油工业将兴起，就会考虑用一部分利润到西北投资。它可以跨部门、跨地区经营，

return for an average internal profit. China's western region should not be developed piecemeal by an assortment of small concerns, but should be handled by such giants as socialist consortia.

4. The tactics for ownership reform should differ depending on industry, locality, and business size. Firms may be categorized into industries according to their importance to the national economy and the scarcity degree of the resources they need, before deciding which industries should be shored up first and what kind of firms—public, collective or private—should be developed in the main. Such industries and enterprises should also be considered in the light of local conditions, and categorized according to their sizes. Large state firms in important industries or regions should be preserved, while other companies can be leased or subcontracted out; some of them can be sold to collectives or individuals. In this way, the state can let go of most small firms in order to keep those essential companies that form the backbone of the economy under socialist ownership. These "backbone" firms may be developed into competitive socialist enterprise consortia, or transformed into multinational corporations that will be a force to be reckoned with on the world market. At the end of the day, however, they will remain state owned. How about medium-sized and small firms? This depends on what industry is in question. Their shares can be sold to collectives and individuals to create companies under mixed ownership. This design of ownership reform holds the key to the success of economic restructuring. Once it is translated into reality, it will impart motivation, a sense of responsibility, incentive, and interest in our enterprises, and diversify ownership and management without sacrificing the leadership role and dominance of public ownership.

II. The need for a relatively complete market

5. Market can balance supply and demand with its self-regulatory function, but it also has limitations that can only be overcome with government regulation. However, this does not mean government can

do it all, or that market is needed only when government is weak. In my opinion, the relationship between government and market should be interpreted in this way: Market enables the economy to regulate itself and coordinate supply and demand, but needs government regulation to make up for its shortcomings, such as its limited resource supply and

自己内部可以取得一个平均利润。这样可以大大加速西北的开发。我们将来对西部的开发，不能像现在这样零敲碎打，而可以由社会主义的公司财团来开发、经营。

4. 所有制改革要因行业、地区、企业规模而异。对于企业，我们可以把各个企业按其在国民经济中的重要性，按其所需资源的稀缺程度，分成若干个行业。然后看看哪些行业应该发展？主要发展什么样的企业，是全民的、集体的，还是个体的？因地区而异，是指要按各个地区的特点来发展。因企业规模而异，是指企业要按不同大小来分类。假定这样的话，全民所有制企业将保留在重要的行业内，保留在一些地区。它们是较大规模的企业。其他的企业，该租赁的租赁，该承包的承包，有些还可卖给集体或个体。这样，把大部分小企业摆脱，国家则把一些全民所有制的骨干企业保留下来，让它们发育为社会主义的公司财团，让它们具有竞争能力，让它们成为中国的跨国公司，打入国际市场。它们仍是全民所有制企业。实现这样一种设想将是我们改革成功的关键。它将给企业带来动力、责任、刺激、利益。还有些中小企业要出卖股权，谁买？卖给谁？要看行业而定。集体、个人都可以买。这就可以形成一种新型的经济联合体：混合企业。这样，我们才能实行真正的多种所有制、多种经营形式。这绝不影响全民所有制的主导地位和公有制的统治地位。

二、我们需要一个比较完善的市场机制

5. 市场本身有一种自行调节的功能，它可以使需求和供给趋向平衡；它又有各种局限性，因此有必要进行政府调节。但绝不能反过来讲：政府能够包办一切，只是由于目前力量不足，才需要由市场来拾遗补阙。我们认为，政府调节与市场调节之间的关系是这样的：首先肯定市场本身有一种机制，能够使经济自动调节，能使供求趋向平衡；但因为它有各种局限性，如资源的有限供给、经济

incomplete economic information system. The bottom line for economic restructuring is that the socialist economy should be a market economy in the first place, and then a market economy supplemented by planning.

6. Market regulation coexists with government regulation. They supplement each other, but are not mutually interchangeable. They combine to form a dual mechanism, which, nevertheless, is not the combination of two separate elements. Government regulation must take market regulation as its starting point, and works merely to pick up the slack of market regulation. Market prices are greatly variable. Besides free prices resulting from complete competition, there can also be prices from incomplete competition; and state-regulated prices must be based on a wide variety of market prices although there can be discrepancies between planned prices and market prices. The causes and magnitudes of such discrepancies are subject to government regulation, which should still take market prices as its basis.

7. A relatively well-functioning market mechanism cannot be transplanted; it can only grow to completion by itself in an economy. In the past, it could not grow in this country because it lacked a salubrious environment, i.e., a socialist market economy. Today, it can grow and improve over time, as long as we are resolved to put a socialist market economy in place. Please note that I am using the term "relatively well-functioning" to describe my idea of a market mechanism. The market mechanism cannot become completely competitive the way things are in China under the current circumstances. We should be fully aware that our economy is limited by scarcity in resources, and that government regulation is needed to supplement market regulation.

8. A socialist market system should encompass four markets. First, a commodity market that entails a consumer goods market and a capital goods market. A real estate market should also be included, because commercial housing is an inevitable trend in our economic development. Second, a capital market which includes a securities market. Once

the shareholding system is introduced, a securities market is needed; otherwise, share flow and trading will be out of the question. The securities market can be regulated, and specialized securities markets set up. Where conditions are immature, banks may act as intermediaries to issue and deal in stock shares, or work as brokers to mortgage stock shares or discount them for cash. Third, a technology market for payable

信息系统不健全等等，所以需要政府调节。改革的基本思路是：社会主义经济首先是商品经济，然后才是有计划发展的商品经济。

6. 市场调节与政府调节是并存的、互补的，一方不能替代另一方。这就是二元机制。但二元机制绝不是板块结合。它的含义是：政府调节必须以市场调节作为出发点，它是为弥补市场调节的种种局限性而存在的。市场价格是多种多样的，只有在完全竞争的条件下才有自由价格；在其他条件下，将会形成不完全竞争的价格。而每一种市场都有自由价格与不完全竞争价格之分，计划价格必须以市场上的各种价格为依据。同时，计划价格与市场价格可以有上下出入。上下出入的原因和幅度，在于政府调节，但仍然必须以市场价格作为出发点。

7. 比较完善的市场机制不是靠引进的，而是自然发育的。过去，它之所以没有发育或发育不足，是由于缺乏发育的环境，缺乏社会主义商品经济的环境。只要发展社会主义商品经济，市场机制会自行趋于完善。我在这里使用了“比较完善”这四个字。市场不可能在现有条件下形成完全竞争的市场。应充分认识到我们的经济是资源供给有限的经济，而且还要考虑到政府调节的必要性。但我们可以使之“比较完善”。

8. 社会主义的市场体系应包括四大市场：一是商品市场。包括消费品市场、生产资料市场。房产市场也应包括在内，因为住宅商品化是我们经济发展的必然趋势。二是资金市场。包括证券市场在内。企业实行股份制后，假定允许企业买卖股票，假定允许个人购买股票，就应有一个证券市场来进行这样的交易。不然，这种证券将缺乏灵活性。但证券市场可以加以调节。或者存在专门的证券市场；在条件不成熟的情况下，也可以由银行代理发行股票、买卖股票，充当股票经纪人和实行股票的抵押、贴现。三是技术市场。

transfers of research and development results. Fourth, a labor market, or service market. Having never been opened to free competition, our labor market is fragmented and differs across localities. Given labor's limited lateral and vertical mobility, the labor market can only grow gradually. We have got to develop a unified commodity market in which nationwide circulation of consumer and capital goods is allowed. If such goods cannot be circulated nationwide, the reasons are more economic (such as high costs and low economic returns) than noneconomic. The capital market referred to here should be unified nationwide as well. If capital cannot circulate across the land, it should likewise be attributed to economic causes, rather than government interference and other noneconomic factors.

III. Raising government efficiency

9. Effective economic decisions, policy enforcement, and economic supervision are hallmarks of a highly efficient government. A government with little or no work efficiency is invariably crippled by legislation that is absent, bypassed, laxly enforced, or simply superseded by state power. An inefficient government plus an incomplete market can scuttle economic reform no matter how good the reform plan is. Therefore, to make economic restructuring a success, we must raise government efficiency without fail.

10. Government efficiency is more needed in economic regulation than in government intervention, more for indirect market control than for direct market control, and more for guidance planning than for central planning. We should be aware that managing the economy has become more challenging after economic restructuring came under way. The efficiency level of our economic administrators leaves a great deal to be desired. We must speed up training to raise their overall quality and proficiency, for only thus can government efficiency be boosted effectively.

11. We should relinquish planned management if it is arbitrary and unscientific, and dismantle economic regulation if it is ineffective and arbitrary. In either case, we would let the market mechanism run its course. Thus, the kind of government regulation that is paired with market regulation should be scientifically viable and highly efficient.

是指科技成果有偿转让的市场。四是劳动力非商品化条件下的劳动力市场，简称为劳务市场。考虑到劳动力市场从来不是完全竞争的市场，因而它是分层次的、因地而异的。由于人员的水平流动和垂直流动方面的局限性，它只可能逐渐趋向于完善。我们应该有一个统一的商品市场。这就是说，商品不管是消费品还是生产资料，可以在全国范围内流通。假定它不能流通，那仅仅是因为经济上的原因（如成本太高、收益太低），而绝不是由于经济以外的因素的干扰。资金市场也是指全国范围的资金市场。假定资金不能做到全国范围的融通，这仅仅是由于经济原因，而不是由于人为的、非经济因素的干扰。

三、提高政府部门的效率

9. 一个有高度效率的政府部门，表现为有效的经济决策、有效的政策执行、有效的经济监督。无法可依，有法不依，执法不严，以权代法，是政府无效率或低效率的标志。一个没有效率的政府部门，加上一个不完善的市场机制，那么我们的经济改革，即使方案再好，也不能实行。所以在改革的思路中，一个重要的方面是：必须提高政府部门的效率。

10. 经济调节比采取行政手段要求有更高的管理水平，间接控制比直接控制要求有更高的管理水平，指导性计划比指令性计划要求有更高的管理水平。应该认识到：改革以后，管理经济不是容易了，而是更难了。目前，我们经济管理干部的水平，大大落后于需要。所以要加速培养经济管理干部，提高干部素质。这是提高政府部门效率很重要的一个方面。

11. 与其是主观主义的、不科学的计划管理，不如不要计划管理；与其是无效率、瞎指挥的经济调节，不如不要经济调节。在这种情况下，不如索性让市场调节与商品经济来发挥作用。所以在二元机制中，与市场机制并存的那种政府调节，是指科学的、有高度

The dual mechanism does not mean market regulation and government regulation are both indispensable. Government regulation should be predicated on scientific feasibility and high efficiency. If we reject willful government intervention and bring the role of the market mechanism into play, at least we can boost the economy during fluctuations. The involvement of a bull-headed government can only inflict stagnation or setback on our economy—what happened in 1958 across this land was a typical case in point. We should learn to differentiate between sound and unsound government regulation. Sound government regulation is good in that it can overcome market failures; unsound government regulation can do nothing but nullify the self-regulatory function of the market mechanism. The market mechanism can strike a general balance between supply and demand and facilitate economic growth, even though it may take more time and is likely to cause major fluctuations in the course of it. If we can see the dual mechanism in such light, we are able to open up new horizons.

12. Administrative reform is a must if government efficiency is to be raised. The system whereby government officials are selected and appointed must be overhauled. We should evaluate the performance of civil servants within a framework that holds them accountable for the goals set for their tenures. It makes no sense that these people can only be promoted and not demoted. It makes little sense, either, that people can be both promoted and demoted. Of course, there should be both promotions and demotions, but only competent officials should be promoted and incompetent ones demoted—no exception should be made in this regard. Only thus can the government work efficiently, and institutional reform be speeded up.

IV. Entrepreneurship and socialist entrepreneurs

13. China needs legions of socialist entrepreneurs as much as it needs entrepreneurship. Our entrepreneurs should have strategic vision, dare to innovate and create, be pragmatic and imbued with organizational

and business acumen. In economic restructuring, socialist entrepreneurs should be protected, and their talent given full scope. Without entrepreneurs and entrepreneurship, the economy will be sluggish even if the ownership system is transformed, and even if shareholding firms, enterprise consortia, and new-type state firms are established. As argued above, ownership reform holds the key to economic restructuring. But the next question is: Who are to run the restructured state firms,

效率的政府调节。二元机制不是简单地说市场机制与政府调节都要有。政府调节以具有科学性与高效率为前提。假定我们不要瞎指挥的政府调节，只要市场调节，那么至少可以使经济在波动中增长。而瞎指挥的政府调节的加入，就有可能使经济停滞、倒退，1958 年的事例就很典型。应充分认识到这一点：对政府调节要有区别，看它是不是科学的。科学的政府调节是好事，它可以弥补市场的不足；不科学的政府调节，会使市场调节原有的优越性消失掉。因为市场机制大体上可以使供求趋于平衡，虽然时间和过程要长一些，波动要大一点，但经济还可以增长。所以，把二元机制提到这样的一个高度来认识，我们的思想就打开了。

12. 为了提高政府部门的效率，行政改革势在必行。干部选拔、任命制度必须改革。对干部应实行“任期目标责任制”，以便加以考核。干部“只上不下”，当然不对。干部“能上能下”的提法，也不一定妥当。应该是干部“有上有下”，该上就上，该下就下。应该是：干部当得好的就上，当不好就下。在干部任免上，没有照顾的问题。只有这样，我们的政府部门才会有效率，才会加速体制改革的进程。

四、企业家精神与社会主义企业家

13. 中国需要一大批社会主义企业家，需要企业家精神。企业家应该有战略眼光，有创新与实干精神，有组织能力与经营管理能力。在经济改革中，要保护社会主义企业家，让他们充分施展才能。没有企业家，没有企业家精神，即使改革了所有制，建立了股份制的企业，建立了公司财团，建立了新型的公有制企业，经济仍然缺乏生机。如前所述，所有制改革是关键。现在的问题是：谁来

and to use their talent to inject life into these firms? None other than entrepreneurs. Without entrepreneurs, ownership reform can get nowhere. Entrepreneurship is essential to ownership reform. In the years of reform, we should never lose sight of the importance of entrepreneurs and entrepreneurship.

14. Socialist entrepreneurs do not come forth by doing the government's bidding, nor can they be groomed in a "greenhouse." Their destiny is bound up with the development of the socialist market economy and with the economic activity of their enterprises, where they come to the fore through competition. We should keep an eye on businesses in adversity, rural firms included, for these are where socialist entrepreneurs are likely to emerge. We should go to medium-sized and small firms and those run by farmers if we are to find socialist entrepreneurs. Because those who can emerge unscathed from unfriendly territories at least have the makings of an entrepreneur. "Socialist entrepreneurs are born of pressure." That line sounds realistic to us all. Entrepreneurs born of adversity are the only people who can bring a competitive edge to our firms.

15. Entrepreneurs and entrepreneurship are fruits of the market economy. The farther the socialist market economy advances, the more entrepreneurs will turn up, and the more impact entrepreneurship will bring. The burgeoning socialist market economy can provide a constant supply of entrepreneurs—this is more effective than putting a lot of factory directors or managers through advanced training courses. Without a market economy we will not be able to produce so many socialist entrepreneurs. By the same token, our university economics departments cannot necessarily cultivate entrepreneurs even though they are doing a fair job of instilling basic economics knowledge in students.

16. Enterprises must be allowed to go through a "metabolic process" in which the new supersedes the old. Ill-managed enterprises should call it quits or be closed down, phased out, or liquidated. For a certain

percentage of enterprises to go bankrupt on a yearly basis is not the end of the world for the socialist economy. The platform for the socialist market economy should be preserved for emerging, dynamic, and competitive enterprises. Market competition is a whirlwind that can dispose of outdated and inefficient firms and preserve competitive ones. But more importantly, it can level the ground for more enterprises

主持这个新型的公有制企业？谁来施展才能，发挥企业的活力？那就是企业家。没有企业家，仅仅改革了所有制是不够的。所有制改革的内在的东西，就是企业家精神。我们在改革中要认识到企业家与企业家精神的重要性。

14. 社会主义企业家不是靠自上而下地指定产生的，也不是靠“温室”培养出来的。他们的命运与社会主义商品经济的发展联系在一起，与企业经济活动联系在一起。他们是在竞争的环境中拼搏出来的。我们要特别注意原来条件不好的企业，包括乡镇企业，那里是容易产生社会主义企业家的场所。要找社会主义的企业家，就应该到那些地方（中小企业、乡镇企业）去寻找。因为，那里条件差，能够从中拼杀出来的人，一定具有企业家精神。“社会主义企业家是环境逼出来的”，这句话对我们很有现实意义。这样产生的企业家，才能给企业带来竞争力。

15. 要认识到企业家与企业家精神是商品经济的产物。社会主义商品经济越发展，企业家将越多，企业家精神也越能发挥影响。因此，社会主义商品经济的发展，能培养出越来越多的企业家。这将胜过创办多少期厂长训练班、经理培训班。没有商品经济的环境，是培养不出社会主义企业家的。同样，大学里的经济系，可以使学生增长一些基本经济知识，不一定能培养出企业家。

16. 企业必须新陈代谢。办得不好的企业，该停产的停产，该关闭的关闭，该淘汰的淘汰，该清理的清理。社会主义经济中每年有百分之几的企业破产，不是坏事，而是好事。社会主义经济活动的大舞台，应该留给那些新兴的、有生命力的、有竞争能力的企业大显身手。市场竞争是一场旋风，它吹垮了那些落后的、没有效益的企业，保住了一批有竞争力的企业，但更重要的是：它清理了

to grow. Such is the process of innovation. Such is the way socialist consortia come to stay, and the way socialist multinational companies carve out a niche in the world market. Only in this way can our economy respond to the pressure of competition and brim over with vitality.

V. Economic norms based on socialist ethics

17. Social inequity spawns social instability, but social instability does not necessarily stem from social inequality. Income disparity may spur efficiency, but efficiency does not necessarily come from such disparity. In an objectively equal society, if the standard of living first rises and then drops, with increase outstripping decrease, the irreversible nature of consumption, income, and wages can also work psychologically to cause social unrest. In an objectively equal society, there are people who work harder and make more money than others, but there are also those who work less and are paid less. If those who make less money refuse to accept the fact that they do less than others and claim that they have been taken advantage of, they are likely to stir social instability. If the income gap exceeds a certain limit, it can affect efficiency and drive some people to despair and indolence. That is why in the socialist economy, the relationship between equality and efficiency should be handled properly. Equality, as we understand it, entails turning workers into owners of capital goods, equal opportunities for all and distribution according to work done. Efficiency, as we understand it, is also based on public ownership of capital goods, on equal opportunities, and on the principle of distribution according to work done. Only with this understanding in mind can the relationship between equality and efficiency be well handled.

18. From an economic point of view, despite its limitations, the market mechanism enables the economy to grow amidst fluctuations. From the perspective of social coordination, however, the limitations of the market mechanism are more pronounced, for the market itself cannot coordinate social development. We do not seek economic growth

for growth's own sake. Rather, economic growth should be consistent with coordinated social development. Efficient government regulation is needed because its impact is both economic and social. The social impact of government regulation manifests itself in regulating income distribution while ensuring economic growth, an impact that is mandated by the socialist goals for socioeconomic development. Thus, in the

场地，让更多的企业能够生长。这就是创新，这样才能有社会主义的财团，才能有打入国际市场的社会主义跨国公司。这样才能使我们的经济既有压力，更有活力。

五、符合社会主义伦理原则的经济行为规范

17. 社会不平等引起社会不安定，但社会不安定不一定来自社会不平等。收入分配的差距会增加效率，但效率不一定来自收入分配的差距。在一个客观上平等的社会中，假定人们的生活水平先上升，后下降，上升大，下降小，由于消费、收入、工资的不可逆性，也可造成社会的不安定。这是由于人们的心理造成的。另一种情况是：在一个客观上平等的社会中，有些人会自认为不平等。比如有人多劳多得，有人少劳少得，少劳少得的人不看自己少劳，只看少得，感觉自己吃亏了，这也会带来社会的不安定。如果收入分配的差距超过了一定限度，有可能影响效率，使一些人自暴自弃、消极怠工。所以在社会主义经济中必须处理好平等与效率的关系。我们所理解的平等，一是生产者成为生产资料的主人，二是机会的均等，三是现有生产力水平上的按劳分配。我们所理解的效率是在生产资料公有制基础上的效率，机会均等下的效率，符合按劳分配原则的效率。只有从这个角度来理解，我们才能妥善处理好平等与效率的关系。

18. 从经济上看，市场调节虽然有局限性，但它毕竟能使经济在波动中增长。从社会协调方面看，市场调节的局限性却要大得多。市场本身不能实现社会发展的协调。我们不是为增长而增长，经济发展与社会协调是统一的。我们之所以需要政府调节，是因为有效率的政府调节既表现在经济方面，也表现在社会方面。它表现在社会方面，是指在保证经济增长的前提下进行收入分配的调节。这种调节是另外一种意义的调节，与调节供求平衡不同，它是从社会

course of economic restructuring, progressive income tax, income-adjustment tax, and allowances for low-income families are needed, but should be kept within reasonable bounds to ensure economic growth and social harmony. At the same time, however, we have got to know that we cannot do without these taxes and allowances in securing economic growth and social harmony. This is exactly what economic reform is all about.

19. An important task of socialist cultural development is to foster new values. For instance, what is "equity"? What is "employment"? What attitude should we take toward the policy of "allowing some people to get rich first"? These questions should be considered in a new light, so that we can clarify the dos and don'ts in economic restructuring, and know what to strive for and what to give up. People tend to cling to things not worth their devotion. To change that habit calls for a change in values. We cannot make a sound judgment on economic restructuring without changing our values.

20. The concept of family and the small-time producers' belief in egalitarianism are at the core of the Eastern cultural tradition, whereas individualism is the nucleus of modern Western culture. The two are mutually conflicting. Those of us who live in a developing nation striving for modernization on the basis of traditional Eastern culture invariably find ourselves torn between these conflicting values. What we pursue is socialist modernization, and the problem confronting us is not so much to choose between the values of our traditional culture and the values of the modern Western culture as to go beyond these two cultures and explore new values that suit socialist ethics. This is a hard nut to crack, but we have to do it. In that sense, to change our values calls for an even more profound revolution than economic restructuring, a mission that cannot be fulfilled in just one generation's time. We have to be fully aware of the arduous and protracted nature of this mission.

VI. Immediate issues to be handled in real earnest

21. Extending lateral ties in the economy is a major immediate-term task for economic restructuring. Only by extending such ties can we unify our commodity market, gradually bring about a capital market, and lift the barriers resulting from the interference of central and local government boundaries. This task is of paramount importance.

意义上讲的。这种调节是符合社会主义的整个发展目标即社会经济发展目标的。因为，在经济改革中应注意到，累进制的所得税和调节税以及对低收入家庭生活的补助，一方面要有适当的限度，另一方面也是不可缺少的。它们既保证了经济增长，又保证了社会协调。我们整个改革要沿着这样一种方向前进。

19. 社会主义精神文明建设的重要内容之一是建立新的价值观念。比如说，什么是“公平”？什么是“就业”？怎样看待“一部分人先富起来”？这些问题值得我们重新思考。通过思考，我们可以明辨经济改革中的对与错、是与非，了解到什么是我们要争取的，什么是我们应该抛弃的。人们往往把不值得留恋的东西拼命地抱住不放，这就涉及到价值观念的转变。没有价值观念的转变，就不可能对经济改革作出正确的判断。

20. 传统东方文化的价值观念的核心是家族观念和小生产者的平均主义，近代西方文化的价值观念的核心是个人主义，二者是相冲突的。在传统东方文化基础上实行现代化的发展中国家，时时处处都会遇到两种价值观念的冲突。我们正在进行的是社会主义现代化，我们面临的问题不是在传统东方文化的价值观念和近代西方文化的价值观念之间作出选择，而是探索如何在两者之外，建立符合社会主义伦理原则的新价值观念。这是一个难题，但我们必须设法解决。从这种意义上说，价值观念的转变是比经济体制改革更深刻的一场革命。这不是一代人所能完成的，我们必须充分认识这个问题的艰巨性。

六、近期需要认真注意的问题

21. 扩大经济中的横向联系是近期改革的重要措施。只有扩大横向经济联系，才能使我们的商品市场趋于统一，使我们的资金市场逐步形成，才能打破条块分割。这一点非常重要。假定不搞企

If we cannot promote lateral economic ties between firms and let them collaborate and exchange with each other in capital, labor, and technology, and if we do not allow one company to sell its products on another company's turf, we can never build a workable market mechanism and break down the barriers between central and local government boundaries. This task is high on the agenda of the immediate round of economic restructuring. As we build on what we have accomplished so far to go on with economic reforms, the main thrust of our endeavor should be to extend lateral economic ties.

22. As things are today, excessive investment in infrastructure construction remains the number one headache in the Chinese economy. Overheated consumption funds can only take a second seat. This does not mean excessive increase in consumption funds should not be controlled, but that it is not our primary concern. Make no mistake about it, the consumers in our nation have money to spend in return for the material products and labor services they have provided. Income is always relevant to supply. If the control of consumption funds is overly tightened up, it can stifle supply and demand at the same time, and its side effects on economic development will be felt sooner or later. In regulating the economy, aggregate demand and supply should be properly controlled. On no account should we cut supply while curtailing demand. I believe premature consumption should be avoided, but there is no reason to say that China today is already in a period of premature consumption. Of course we should draw a lesson from other developing nations' experience and forestall the emergence of premature consumption. There are two telltale signs for premature consumption. One is an excessively low saving rate. By contrast, the saving rate in our nation is maintained at 30%, which is deemed a high level. The other is that the lion's share of scarce resources is overused by a new mode of consumption. For example, production will be affected if too much petroleum is consumed in everyday life. That scenario is yet to be experienced in this country.

Clearly, there is no trace of premature consumption in China today.

23. Equilibrium is part of an analytical approach, and the starting point of economic analysis. Equilibrium itself is not the goal. Our goal is to achieve the Four Modernizations. The socialist economy always swings around an equilibrium point as it moves along. In that sense, we are not seeking balance for balance *per se*. Fiscal balance and credit market equilibrium can mean nothing if the economy stagnates. We have

业的横向经济联系，不让企业之间在资金、人力、技术等方面互相协作交流，不让企业的产品打到对方的市场上去，那么，我们的市场机制是建立不了的，我们的条块分割是打不破的。这正是我们近期改革的重要内容。我们正在巩固已有的改革成果中前进，其中最重要的一条，就是扩大经济中的横向联系，这是改革在继续进行的证明。

22. 我国经济当前的首要问题仍然是基本建设投资过大，消费基金增长过快相形之下是次要的。这不是说消费基金不需要调节，而是说不能把这一点提到最突出的地位。要知道，我国消费者手中之所以有货币，是由于他们提供了物质产品和劳务。收入是与供给相联系的。如果对消费基金有过多的限制，往往在抑制需求的同时也抑制了供给，从而给将来的经济发展造成后遗症。经济调节中，既要调节需求，也要调节供给，绝不能在压低需求的同时把供给也压下去了。我们认为，消费早熟需要避免，但不能认为我国目前已进入早熟型消费阶段。我们应该汲取其他发展中国家的经验，防止早熟型消费的出现。早熟型消费有两个标志：一个是积累率过低，而我们的积累率保持在 30% 左右，是高水平的；另一个标志是稀缺生产资源中的大部分被新的消费方式所占用，比如石油，生活用油过多就会影响生产。我们没有出现这种情况，所以我们目前没有消费早熟。

23. 平衡是一种分析方法，是分析的出发点，平衡本身不是目的。我们的目的是实现四个现代化。社会主义经济在运动过程中，总是围绕着平衡点摆动，在一定范围的摆动中前进。从这一点来讲，我们不是为平衡而平衡。假定经济上不去，财政平衡是无意义的，

got to know that equilibrium can be maintained at a low or high level. Low-level equilibrium can be easily achieved by adopting a retrenchment policy. If, instead of going single-mindedly after curtailing demand, we do everything we can to stimulate supply, we can achieve high-level equilibrium, not to mention the fact that the economy always advances while hovering around an equilibrium point, which is a sign of basic equilibrium whether demand outgrows supply slightly or vice versa. In China today, for demand to outgrow supply slightly is a preferred and realistic option, whereas it is unrealistic to expect that supply can slightly outgrow demand. That is why we should adapt ourselves to the current situation and learn how to run the economy under such circumstances.

24. Government policy stability and continuity should be maintained to set people at ease, especially those in the thick of economic reform. Policy volatility can mar government policy. Major economic unrest often occurs when firms and individuals hasten to take countermeasures upon sensing an imminent major policy change. For this reason, if we can foster a settled sense of economic stability in firms and individuals and keep them confident in government policy, we can take the edge off the impact of the shock waves that might come from economic restructuring, and carry out reforms in a healthy social environment.

VII. Tentative projections of the Chinese economy

25. The leading position of the state sector in the national economy is not determined by its proportion of the nation's total number of firms or aggregate output value, still less by its shares in the key branches of the national economy. Rather, it is determined by its control of industries that are the lifeblood of the national economy, and by its shares in the output of crucial commodities. In the long run, there will not be many state firms, as most enterprises in this country will come under mixed or collective ownership. Moreover, the state firms referred to here are not the familiar old-fashioned type. Rather, they will be transformed into shareholding or holding companies that are publicly owned in the main,

and some of them will belong to a certain enterprise consortium.

26. From a long-term point of view, there is no reason why mandatory plans cannot be abolished to make way for guidance plans as the one and only form of planning. Of course, there must be certain conditions to

信贷平衡也是无意义的。我们要认识到，同样是平衡，有低水平与高水平之分。做到低水平平衡并不难，只需采取紧缩政策。如果我们不单纯抑制需求，而设法刺激供给，那是高水平的平衡。何况，经济总是在围绕着一个平衡点上下波动中不断前进的，“需求略大于供给”和“供给略大于需求”，都是基本平衡。按我国目前的情况看，“需求略大于供给”更具有现实性，而“供给略大于需求”是做不到的。所以我们当前必须学会如何适应这样的形势，学会在这样一种形势下进行经济建设。

24. 政策要保持稳定性和连续性。要让人们感到放心，让从事经济改革的人感到放心。政策的多变只会促使政策效力递减。经济中的重大震荡，往往发生于企业和个人估计到政策将会有显著的变化而纷纷采取预防性措施的时候。因此，使企业和个人对经济环境产生一种稳定感和对政策保持足够的信任，不仅可以在相当大的程度上减轻经济改革中可能发生的震荡，而且有利于保持一个促进经济改革的良好的社会环境。

七、我国经济前景的设想

25. 全民所有制经济在国民经济中的主导地位，不仅不依据全民所有制企业数目在全国企业数目中的比重，甚至也不依据产值所占的比重，而是依据它是否掌握着作为国民经济命脉的部门，是否在若干种关键商品产量中占有较大的比重。从长远来看，全民所有制企业不一定很多，大量的企业可能是混合经济的或者是集体的。而且，即使是全民所有制企业，也不是我们现在所认识的、传统意义上的全民所有制企业，而是一种新型的、股份制的、实行控股制的、属于某一个企业财团的以全民所有制为主的企业。

26. 从较长远的角度来看，指令性计划不是不可以取消的，指导性计划可以成为我国惟一的计划形式。当然，这要看我们的

make it happen. One such condition is that key resources are no longer in short supply and that the disparity between demand and supply has been reduced. Another condition is that the government is efficient enough in running the economy, because it is more difficult to carry out guidance planning than mandatory planning.

27. Of the four economic policy instruments in use today—fiscal policy, monetary policy, price control, and wages—the decision-making power to determine wages should be delegated to firms at the grass roots level. Central and local governments should use fiscal and monetary policies as chief economic regulatory means. Unless absolutely necessary, the use of price control as an economic lever should be minimized. Such is my idea of how to shape our long-term macroeconomic regulatory system. The State Planning Commission should take charge of drafting relevant long- and medium-term development plans.

28. The rural economy is probably where the Chinese economic landscape will change most dramatically. Farmland will devolve to the hands of skilled farmers. Farms will grow in size under a household responsibility system. Labor productivity will go up, and surplus labor force will be reallocated to rural firms. The countryside will be clustered with small towns, which will combine with large cities to form multilayered economic networks. Small towns will become cultural, educational, commercial, and recreational centers that also provide a complete array of community services. The improving Chinese standard of living will be benchmarked not by current cash-income growth but by increases in household wealth.

— A report to the Peking University "May Fourth"
Symposium on April 25, 1986

条件是否已经成熟。条件成熟的主要标志是某些资源已不像现在这样稀缺了，供求紧张程度已有所缓和。此外，还要考虑到国家在某些方面是否具有足够的经济管理能力，这是因为：实行指导性计划比指令性计划更难。

27. 在财政、金融、价格、工资四种调节手段中，今后，工资的调节下放到基层、企业；中央对经济的调节主要运用财政、金融两种手段，地方的调节也主要运用这两种手段。除非在十分必要的情况下，应尽量少采取价格调节手段。这就是我们长远的宏观经济调节政策。国家计委主要负责制定中长期计划。

28. 将来中国经济面貌的最明显的变化，可能反映在农村经济面貌的变化上。土地向耕作能手集中，家庭承包的农场规模扩大，劳动生产率提高，多余的劳动力主要进入乡镇企业，小城镇将普遍兴起，大城市、小城镇和农村形成多层次的经济网络。小城镇将成为生活服务、文化教育、文娱和商业中心。中国人民生活水平提高的标志，不是看现期的货币收入，而是看家庭财产存量的不断增加。

(1986年4月25日在北京大学“五四”科学讨论会上的报告)

A TENTATIVE STUDY OF SOCIALIST OWNERSHIP STRUCTURE (1987)

I

Ownership reform stems, in the final analysis, from the requirement for developing a commodity economy in this nation. It also arises from the unchangeable position of companies as commodity producers. Whatever its form, ownership structure should contribute to the promotion of production. A monomorphic ownership structure is detrimental to the growth of the commodity economy, to the motivation of firms as commodity producers, and to the effort to make the most of the superiority of socialism. All this gives rise to the mission of hammering out a post-reform ownership structure.

Will the post-reform ownership structure include public ownership? The answer is in the affirmative: Public ownership will be included. However, the reformed public ownership will no longer be the same as it is today. There will be differences between the two.

Under the influence of the traditional economic mode, people believed that the only workable way to run public companies was to put them directly into the hands of government institutions. In the reality of socialist economic development, however, the drawbacks of this practice were becoming pronounced. Companies became appendages of the government, which held all the power over human resources, finance and materials, and kept a tight rein on them. A company's performance thus had no direct bearing on its economic gains, nor was it held accountable for its own economic losses. Such was the inevitable outcome of the direct government intervention of business management, in which public ownership was synonymous with the direct involvement of government institutions in corporate activity. This is why the main thrust of ownership reform should be directed at public ownership.

We should know that in a public company, both capital goods and products belong to the public. The public attributes of such institutions represent the people's fundamental, overall and long-term interests. Recognition of the public ownership of such companies means that they are engaged in production and management in the common interest of the entire citizenry. The issue here is: How can public companies manifest their public nature in production and management, and go about their

社会主义所有制体系的探索（1987）

一

所有制改革归根结底是由商品经济发展的要求引起的，是由企业作为商品生产者这一不可改变的地位所引起的。至于改革后的所有制究竟具体采取什么样的形式，则应从有利于推动生产发展出发。单一的所有制不利于发展商品经济，不利于发挥企业作为商品生产者的积极性，也不利于使社会主义制度的优越性充分体现出来。于是出现了改革后所有制体系的设计问题。

改革后的所有制中是不是还包括全民所有制？对于这个问题，可以明确地回答：包括全民所有制在内。但改革后的全民所有制，并不等于现阶段的全民所有制。它们是有区别的。

在传统经济模式的影响下，人们曾经认为国家机构直接经营管理全民所有制企业是惟一可行的方式，甚至是惟一正确的方式。但实际上，在社会主义经济建设过程中，这种经营方式的弊端暴露得越来越充分。企业成为行政机构的附属物，企业的人权、财权、物权完全集中在国家手中，国家对企业管得太多太死，企业经营好坏与自身的经济利益没有联系，也不承担经济责任。这正是国家机构直接经营管理企业的必然结果，是把全民所有同国家机构直接经营企业混为一谈的必然结果。在所有制改革中，必须以改革全民所有制为重点。

要知道，既然是全民所有制企业，那么从本质上说，生产资料归全民所有，产品归全民所有。企业的全民性代表全体人民的根本利益、整体利益和长远利益。承认全民性是全民所有制的属性，意味着全民所有制企业是为了全体人民的共同利益而进行生产和经营的。问题在于：怎样才能使全民所有制企业在生产和经营中体现自己的全民性？怎样才能使它们真正为了全体人民的

economic activity truly in the interests of all the people? It should be noted that public companies are not an empty concept but entities in the thick of economic activity. Their public nature is embodied in the fact that both their managers and workers are responsible for the interest of the whole population in such activity. However, this responsibility does not mean that public companies can only be run by the government. Moreover, it should be noted unequivocally that, supposing the public nature of these companies could be manifested only under government management, those companies that are malfunctioning and riddled with malpractice cannot honor their commitment—rather, they can only betray the basic interest of the entire state and citizenry. Thus, in transforming public firms, we must understand their public nature in a new light. That is to say, their public nature should be reflected in the results of their economic activity rather than in being state-managed. To reform public ownership is neither to negate this form of ownership nor to change the nature of public companies. To reform public ownership is precisely to emphasize these firms' public nature through effective and fruitful economic activity.

II

An essential task of the socialist ownership structure is to meet the requirement of the developing socialist commodity economy that forms of ownership should be diversified. Ownership diversity means that a socialist society may have more than one form of ownership, both public and nonpublic. Moreover, capital goods need not come solely under public ownership but under a mixture of state, collective, and private ownership. In this mixed ownership system, public, collective, and private ownership are intertwined and infiltrate each other in a "you in me, me in you" situation. That is to say, the capital goods in a company may come under a mixture of ownership. The need for ownership diversity, including ownership mixtures, arises from the nature of labor in our nation at the present stage of development. Workers still care about their labor input—which differs in quality and quantity—and its economic returns out of the concern for their own interests. Furthermore, due to differences in working conditions, companies also vary in managerial performance and economic returns. Some may be more productive than

共同利益而进行经济活动？在这里，必须指出，全民所有制企业不是一个空泛的概念，它们是从事经济活动的实体。全民所有制企业的全民性体现在企业领导层和企业职工一起在经济活动中对全体人民的利益负责。但这种负责并不是指全民所有制企业必须由国家来经营管理。不仅如此，而且可以明确地指出，假定认为只有由国家来经营管理全民所有制企业才能体现这些企业的全民性的话，那么企业经营管理不善，弊端丛生，其结果恰恰不是对全体人民的利益负责，而是对全体人民的利益的损害。这样，在对全民所有制企业进行改革时，应该强调的是：必须对全民所有制企业的全民性有新的理解，即它们的全民性体现于经济活动的成果，而不是体现于国家对这些企业的经营管理。也就是说，改革全民所有制，不是要否定全民所有制，也不是要改变这些企业的全民性。改革全民所有制，正是为了使全民所有制企业的全民性通过它们的有效的经济活动而充分体现出来。

二

在社会主义所有制体系中，还包括一个主要的方面，这就是根据社会主义商品经济发展的要求，建立多种所有制，即实现所有制的多元化。所有制多元化是指：社会主义社会中可以存在多种所有制，包括公有制，也包括非公有制。此外，企业生产资料所有权也可以不是单一的，而是由全民、集体和个体按照多种方式交叉、渗透而形成的混合性质的。在这种混合性质的所有制中，全民所有、集体所有、个体所有相互渗透，你中有我，我中有你。这就是说，一个企业内部，可以有不同的生产资料所有权构成。所有制的多元化，包括混合性质的所有制的形成，首先与我国现阶段劳动的性质有关。企业中的劳动者的劳动存在着质与量的差异，他们仍然要用个人利益的眼光去看待自己的劳动及其劳动成果。而且，企业之间还存在着劳动条件的差异，这又会导致企业的经营成果和经济效益的差别。有些企业能够比一般的

others. The earnings from such extra output should be put at these firms' own disposal so as to spur their managers on to improve management. Diverse, mixed forms of ownership enable firms and workers to align themselves with production and management performance because this is where their own interests are at stake.

The existence of diverse and mixed forms of ownership is also relevant to our nation's present level of labor productivity. We know that a certain form of ownership of capital goods is determined by the development level of society's labor productivity. What forms of ownership should be adopted or allowed in a socialist commodity economy is circumscribed by the law governing labor productivity improvement. As things stand in our nation, productivity is relatively low and its development is uneven. This implies that, independent of man's will, diverse forms of ownership will be around for a long time to come while infiltrating or integrating each other inside a business.

In all, when designing a new national ownership structure, we should decide what kind of corporate ownership system is really needed. Such a decision cannot be detached from the requirements of the commodity economy and the restraints arising from the nature of labor and the level of productivity at the current stage of development. To advance the commodity economy, every company must organize its production and business as a producer, have the final say on production, supply and marketing, and strive to survive and grow through competition. The issue here is not so much "decentralizing power to companies" as "returning power to companies." Companies should have the decision-making autonomy that they deserve as commodity producers. The same is true with public companies. After ownership restructuring is completed, the government should put capital goods at these companies' disposal and allow them to handle the fruits of their economic activity. As to what form of ownership a company should adopt, it should be decided according to the merits of individual cases.

III

It is both necessary and workable to establish and develop shareholding companies in a socialist society. Socialist construction cannot do without colossal sums of money. Dispersed capital should be pooled, and the financial potential of all sectors tapped. To allow

企业生产出更多的劳动成果，这部分收入应归企业所有，以利于调动企业经营管理的积极性，促使企业经营活动改善。所有制的多元化和混合性质的所有制的存在，可以使企业和在企业中工作的劳动者更能从利益关系上使自己同生产经营成果统一起来。

再从我国现阶段的生产力水平来看，所有制的多元化和混合性质的所有制的存在也是与此有关的。我们知道，一定的生产资料所有制形式，取决于社会生产力的发展水平。社会主义商品经济中究竟采取什么形式以及在一定范围内存在哪些所有制，要受生产关系一定要适应生产力发展的规律的制约。现阶段我国生产力发展水平较低，发展也很不平衡，这种状况决定了在长时期内将是多种所有制的并存，决定了在一个企业内，完全可以使不同的所有制相互渗透或相互结合。这是不以任何人的主观意志为转移的。

总之，在设计我国所有制体系时，需要考虑我国究竟需要建立什么样的企业所有制关系。这一切不能离开发展商品经济的要求，不能离开现阶段劳动的性质和生产力水平的制约。为了发展商品经济，每个企业必须以商品生产者资格开展生产经营活动，企业有权自己决定其产供销活动，并且要在竞争中保存自己和发展自己。这不是什么“放权给企业”的问题，而是“还权给企业”的问题。企业作为商品生产者，应当拥有一个商品生产者所具有的自主经营权。即使是全民所有制企业，改革以后，国家必须把生产资料交由企业使用，并且让企业有权支配自己的经济活动的成果。至于每一个企业的所有制形式，则由具体的情况来决定。

三

在社会主义社会中，建立和发展股份企业不仅是必要的，而且也是可行的。社会主义建设需要大量资金。要改变资金分散的现象，必须集中资金，把社会资金潜力动员起来。因此，企业发行

companies to issue stock shares helps pool money and meet the funding needs of production expansion. Public ownership of capital goods is the foundation stone of the socialist economy. Shareholding companies should be built on the same foundation. If a collectively owned company sells shares to its workers, its collectiveness will remain intact because it is formed with money raised from and by its workers. The fact that the shareholding system can operate for collective companies should not be a cause of concern. The issue here, rather, is whether public firms should be allowed to issue stock shares, and whether doing so will change their public nature. We must see it in perspective. It is wrong to insist that only collective firms can issue shares and to forbid public companies from doing so. The adoption of the shareholding system by public companies should not be judged from a traditional viewpoint.

If a public firm becomes a shareholding company, its shareholders may fall into three categories judging from the current structure of capital goods ownership: central government agencies, local government agencies and the company itself. If all its shareholders are in the public category, the company's public nature will not be affected. If the public firm raises funds from all walks of life, its new shareholders will roughly fall into three categories, excluding foreign investors: other local government agencies and other public firms, collective firms and workers. If all the new shares are sold to the first category of shareholders, the firm's public nature remains. If the new shares are also sold to the second and third categories of shareholders, the firm's public nature will acquire a collective element. No matter what happens, the enterprise remains publicly owned.

To determine who controls the use of capital goods, it is necessary to find out who are running the shareholding company, because the right to own capital goods and the right to use them are separated. The operation of such a company is controlled by its managers. Given that the shareholders of a socialist shareholding enterprise are workers or organizations that represent the workers' interests, then the managers elected by shareholders' representatives should also be regarded as the workers' representatives. In a shareholding company under public ownership, if the second and third categories of new shareholders have contributed more money than the old shareholders and the first category

股票有助于使资金集中，以满足扩大生产的资金需要。由于社会主义经济制度的基础是生产资料的社会主义公有制，所以股份企业也将建立在这一基础之上。如果是集体经济的企业发行股票，由劳动者购买，那么从性质上说，这种由劳动者集资而组成的企业仍然是集体经济单位。看来，这类企业的股份化完全是可行的，也不会引起疑虑。问题是全民所有制企业能不能发行股票？全民所有制发行了股票后，性质会不会变？对这个问题，应有正确的理解，不能认为只有集体企业才能发行股票，而全民所有制企业不能发行股票。我们不能用关于全民所有制企业的传统的观点来看待全民所有制企业的股份化。

如果全民所有制企业成为股份企业，从现有的生产资料所有权来看，有三方面的入股者：一是中央政府部门；二是地方政府部门；三是全民所有制企业本身。这三类入股者都是全民所有制性质的。股份化不改变企业的全民性。如果全民所有制是向社会集资的，那么新的入股者又可以分为三类：大致有（这里不考虑外资入股）三种：一是其他的地方政府部门和其他的全民所有制企业；二是集体企业；三是劳动者个人。从新入股的构成看，如果只有第一类新入股者，企业的全民性没有变化。如果还有第二类和第三类新入股者，那么企业的全民性依然保留，但又增加了集体的成分。不管怎样，股份企业的生产资料仍然归劳动者所有的，这样的企业仍然是公有企业。

从生产资料使用权上看，由于股份企业的所有权与使用权是分离的，因此有必要考察谁真正在进行经营管理。经营管理归于企业的管理人员。既然社会主义股份企业的股东是劳动者或是代表劳动者利益的单位，那么通过股东代表选举的企业管理人员也就是劳动者利益的代表。以股份化的全民所有制企业来说，如果第二类和第三类新入股者的资金相对于原来的入股者和第一类新入股者的资金

of new shareholders, the company is still in the hands of those representing public ownership. If the second and third categories of newcomers have bought more shares than the others but such shares are scattered rather than concentrated, the company is still under public ownership. In all cases, the company's public nature remains basically unchanged.

Even if a shareholding company is controlled by the second and third categories of new shareholders who have contributed more money while the shares held by the second category of new shareholders are not scattered, isn't the enterprise still a public socialist enterprise? Isn't the management of the company still in the hands of those representing workers' interests? Is there anything to be concerned about?

Now, a look at the superiority of the enterprise shareholding system. As the best option available for invigorating our companies, the shareholding system has at least three advantages.

Firstly, the shareholding system can fundamentally change the situation in which government administration is confounded with business management, and thereby turn companies into purely economic entities. Under this system, the general manager is held accountable to the Board of Directors, and the Board of Directors is responsible to shareholders, and thus the company can no longer be an appendage to a government department. The shareholding company makes its own decisions in compliance with government policy and economic legislation. In other words, the government can no longer interfere in the company's business, but can influence its economic activity by holding its stock shares. The economic relationship between enterprises and the government becomes one between paying and levying taxes, and the enterprises will have no problem in making their own business decisions.

Secondly, a shareholding economy works relatively more effectively in meeting the need to allocate production factors efficiently. The profit level of such a company is a signal that guides the shift of capital to high-profit fields, thereby rationally allocating capital and workforce, and raising capital utilization efficiency. The shareholding company can find a foothold in market competition and develop itself only if it can put its capital to best use, utilize it sensibly, and avoid decision-making errors and waste of money. Government departments may, through legislative and compensatory measures, attract share capital to the national economy's weak links and backward sectors in a well-planned fashion, and promote the rational allocation of productive resources from a macroeconomic perspective.

而言是较少的，那么企业仍由全民所有制一方经营管理。即使第二类和第三类新入股者的资金相对说来较多，但只要它们是分散的，那么全民所有制一方也照样掌握了企业的经营管理权。这些都表明企业的全民性基本上没有变化。

退一步而言，即使第二类和第三类新入股者的资金较多，而且第二类新入股者的资金并不分散，从而掌握了企业的经营管理权的话，企业不仍然是社会主义公有制企业吗？企业的经营管理权不仍然掌握在劳动者利益的代表者手中吗？这又有什么值得顾虑的呢？

下面，让我们再分析一下企业股份化的优越性。股份化是现阶段可以采取的最有利于增强企业活力的措施，它的优越性表现于：

第一，建立股份企业将从根本上改变政企不分的状况，从而可以把企业办成一个完全经济性的实体。由于企业的负责人向董事会负责，董事会向股东负责，企业就不再是行政机关的附属物。股份企业在服从国家政策和经济法规的前提下，有独立决策的权利。换而言之，国家不能对股份企业直接进行干预，而只能通过股权，影响企业的经济活动。这样，企业与政府的关系，在经济上主要体现在纳税和收税的关系上，企业的经营决策权问题就会迎刃而解。

第二，股份经济可以比较有效地解决生产要素的合理流动问题。股份企业盈利高低是一个信号，可以引导资金转移到盈利高的部门，使资金和劳动力得到比较合理的配置，可以提高资金使用效率。在市场竞争的条件下，股份企业只有将资金投向最有发展前途的领域，合理使用资金，避免决策失误和资金浪费，才能立足，才能发展。至于政府部门，则可以通过各种调节和补偿措施，有计划地引导股份资金投向国民经济中的薄弱环节和落后部门，从宏观的角度来促进生产力合理布局。

Thirdly, raising funds by selling shares helps pool idle money from nongovernmental sources to meet financing purposes. Under the prerequisite that funds are raised from nongovernmental sources and workers are allowed to buy shares individually, the surplus of personal consumption fund comes in the form of newly added share capital that cannot be withdrawn arbitrarily. For this reason, after the surplus fund for personal consumption is absorbed to buy company shares, it is unlikely for such money to be withdrawn from a shareholding company and spent in the consumer goods market. Apart from allowing individuals to buy shares, the shareholding economy can also use part of the profit at a company's dispensation as a major fund-raising source. By pooling idle money from localities and companies and spending it on construction projects that have a close bearing on the immediate interest of these localities and companies, the shareholding economy can also speed up development, and effectively create jobs for society, rural areas in particular.

IV

The practice of companies buying each other's stocks gives rise to a corporate stock-holding system under socialism. As an inevitable result of economic development, this system, also known as "participatory system," originated in an economic organizational form that emerged from the monopolist stage of capitalism, when a big corporation infiltrated other companies by buying their majority shares and getting them under control. The control through stock-holding and penetration into multiple companies eventually brought about a corporate system in which the general company branched into one level of subsidiaries after another. Under capitalism, therefore, the corporate stock-holding system is a tool with which large capital controls and manipulates small capital.

As a form of business management in society's large-scale production, the stock-holding system can be made to work for the socialist shareholding economy on account of the dual attributes of business management: its natural attribute determined by society's large-scale production, and its social attribute determined by the social system. In terms of society's large-scale production, socialism is identical to capitalism; in terms of social system, socialism is categorically different from capitalism. Thus a socialist society can adopt the stock-holding system by retaining its natural attribute and altering its social attribute.

第三，入股集资有利于把社会上的闲散资金集中起来，实现融通资金的活动。在社会集资和劳动者个人入股的条件下，个人消费基金的结余部分表现为新增加的股金。个人是以投资者的身份出现的，入股后，不能任意抽回股金。因此，企业以集资入股方式吸收个人消费基金的多余部分之后，不存在股金退出企业而冲击消费品市场的可能性。除个人入股以外，股份经济还可以把企业拥有的留成资金作为集资的重要来源。由于各个地方和企业都拥有一定量的暂时闲置的资金，因此通过股份经济的途径，集中地方和企业的资金，承担与地方和企业利害关系密切的项目的建设，有利于加快建设的步伐，并且，这也是为社会提供更多就业机会（特别是对于开拓广大农村的就业门路而言）的有效途径。

四

各个不同的企业相互入股（即相互购买股票）的结果，产生了社会主义条件下的企业控股制。控股制又称参与制，它是股份经济发展的必然产物。控股制本是资本主义发展到垄断阶段时出现的一种经济组织形式，大资本通过控股，渗入其他企业之中，支配着这些企业。层层控股、层层渗透的结果，形成了总公司—子公司—孙公司这样的公司系统。因此，控股制在资本主义制度下，是大资本控制小资本、支配小资本的手段。

作为一种社会化大生产条件下的经济管理形式，控股制可以适用于社会主义股份经济之中。这是因为，管理具有二重性：一是由社会化大生产决定的自然属性；一是由社会制度决定的社会属性。就社会化大生产而言，社会主义与资本主义是相同的。就社会制度而言，社会主义与资本主义截然不同。因此，社会主义社会中可以采取控股制形式，即保留这一管理方式的自然属性，所改变的则是它的社会属性。

In a socialist economy, a competitive and highly efficient company may use its after-tax profit to buy another company's stock shares. When it has become the other company's majority shareholder and thus taken control of it, it will run or reshuffle that company according to its own will. Because of the role of equity and equity-related interests, the scramble between companies for majority holding rights is bound to intensify. When that happens, it is a boon, instead of a bane, for every shareholding company on the scene, because it gives them a good opportunity to improve their economic efficiency. When products become highly substitutable, when the prices of consumer goods show a large degree of elasticity, and when the profits from those products that are being upgraded become unstable, ill-managed businesses will be in danger of being "taken over" by others if they fail to cope with the situation. When such a business is taken over, the buying company may buy its stock in a large amount by taking advantage of its declining profit rate and its shareholders' hasty disposal of their shares. In this way the new CEO turns it into a subsidiary, and goes further to overhaul its production, management and technology. This happens even in a monopolistic industry, where failing companies are in danger of a "takeover."

A small business that does not perform well may be taken over by its employees. These employees are scattered stockholders with a shared desire for their business to make a profit and grow, and their personal interests are tied to its gains and losses. When and where possible, they may pool their equities and act collectively to take over the business and reshuffle its management. When this happens, it is definitely conducive to the future success of the business.

V

A powerful large socialist enterprise under the shareholding system may organize trans-sectoral and trans-regional business, and, through multilevel share-controlling actions, establish multiple layers of subsidiaries to form a socialist corporate consortium or enterprise group. Several large socialist enterprises can foster different economic ties and combine themselves into a consortium or enterprise group. At the center of a socialist corporate consortium is the decision-making

在社会主义经济中，一些有竞争能力的、经济效益高的企业可以利用自己的税后利润购买其他企业的股票。当它们在其他企业的股份中占到一定的比重，从而作为有影响的大股东而控制了那些企业，于是可以按照自己的经营方针来经营管理或进行企业改组。由于股权以及与股权联系在一起的股份利益在这里起着作用，所以一旦企业之间相互控股，企业之间的竞争必然激化。激化的市场竞争对于股份化的企业来说，不是坏事，而是好事，它促使每一个股份化企业必须提高经济效益。特别是在产品代替性强、消费品价格弹性大、产品更新期间利润不稳定的条件下，如果一个企业经营不善，它就面临被其他企业“接管”的威胁。这种“接管”意味着：其他企业作为新的股东利用这些企业利润率下降、原来的入股者急于想把股票脱手的形势，购买其大量股票，进而控制它们，先从组织上予以“接管”，使之变为自己的子公司，再从生产上、经营上、技术上加以改造。甚至在某些具有独占性的领域内，原来的企业如果经营不善，也是有可能被“接管”的。

至于一些较小的企业，在经营不善的条件下，也可能被本企业的职工“接管”。本企业的职工作为股东，虽然很分散，但他们对企业的要求是盈利、是发展，他们的个人利益同企业盈亏总额挂钩。因此，在必要的场合，他们可能集中股权，以集体代表的身份，对企业进行“接管”，重新经营。这对于企业的发展前景肯定是有利的。

五

实行控股制之后，一个强有力的社会主义大企业，实行跨部门、跨地区的生产经营，并通过层层控股，建立自己的子公司、孙公司。母公司同若干个子公司、孙公司集合在一起，就形成社会主义的公司财团（或称为企业集团）。若干个社会主义大企业通过各种方式的经济联系，也可以形成一些带有地方色彩的社会

matrix—or holding—company. Under the parent company there are first- and second-layer subsidiaries which, rather than being mere branches or appendages, do business independently, make their own decisions, and bear the responsibility for their losses and gains. The matrix company exerts its influence through its control of stock shares. That is to say, the parent company carries out its business principle through its equity, thereby fending off the drawbacks of administrative intervention. This corporate management system, in which rights are both centralized and decentralized, helps set a company's business activity on a rational and efficient footing.

Some giant socialist enterprises may rise, and some others may fall in market competition. To put it another way, one giant socialist corporate consortium may grow in strength while another may fall into a decline. There is nothing odd in this phenomenon. A giant enterprise can stay competitive and at the top of the ranking chart only with sensible and effective development strategies, wise leadership and fine workforce quality. Companies or consortia are doomed, no matter how large they are, if they are no longer competitive, if their development stratagems are wrong, or their leaders and workforce are low in quality and proficiency. The shareholding system and the controlling shareholder system compel a company to readjust and save itself. Without such readjustment and self-rejuvenation, a waning company can only watch helplessly as its stock dwindles in value and its property rights become vulnerable to a takeover. Such a takeover, however, may give the company a new lease of life and return it to the ranks of competent competitors.

Under the stock-holding system, the relationship between banks and enterprises may change in one of two ways. First, specialized banks may convert themselves into commercial corporations under shareholding management, and allow businesses to purchase their stock shares to become their shareholders. Judging from the prospects of ownership reform in this country, it is not unlikely that businesses will hold stock shares of specialized banks and join their management. Second, demutualized banks may also participate in managing other businesses; and, as things stand at the present stage of development, the relationship between banks and businesses is more likely to change this way. We can

主义公司财团，简称为地方财团（或地方企业集团）。社会主义公司财团的核心将是一个母公司，或称持股公司。它是本财团的经营管理方针的决策者。在母公司下面，有各个子公司、孙公司，这些公司并不是公司的分支机构或附属机构，它们都有自己的独立经营活动，自主经营，自负盈亏。母公司是通过股权的控制来施加影响的，也就是说，母公司的经营方针要通过股权的控制来贯彻。这就不会重犯行政干预的弊病。这样一种集中与分权相结合的公司管理体制，有利于促使企业经济活动合理化和高效率化。

由于市场竞争的开展，一些社会主义大企业兴起了，一些社会主义大企业衰落了，或者说，一些社会主义公司财团壮大了，一些社会主义公司财团的地位相对下降了，这完全是正常的现象。哪个大企业想保持上升的趋势，哪个公司财团想在排列名次上跃居前位，只能依靠自己的竞争能力，只能取决于自己的发展战略是否正确以及能否实现，只能寄希望于本企业、本财团的领导层和职工的素质。如果缺乏竞争能力，或者制定的发展战略错误，或者制定的正确的发展战略未能得到贯彻，或者领导层和职工的素质不高，那么即使是大企业、大财团，也会衰落下来。但企业的股份化和控股制本身，将给它们以内在调整力量，即自我更新的力量。衰落的企业如果不调整，不更新，它的股票价格不断下降，就有可能被“接管”。“接管”以后，企业也就可能以新的面貌登上市场竞争的舞台。

与此同时，在控股制的条件下，银行与企业之间的关系有可能发生变化。这种变化表现为两个方面。一是某些专业银行不仅实行了企业化，而且实行了股份企业化，于是企业可能购买银行的股票，成为它们的股东。从我国的所有制改革的前景来说，企业持有专业银行的股份并参与银行的经营管理的可能性不是不存在的。二是企业股份化之后，银行对企业实行参与。在现阶段，银行与企业之间关系的这一变化的可能性要更大一些。我们可以设想，银行不仅

assume that banks are not just loan providers. They are also stockholders of businesses and can run their own companies. After a bank gains control of a business' stock, the common interest resulting from this will bring the two sides closer. A bank that holds the stock of a large business can send representatives to join the latter in managing its funding, production and business operation.

Banks can also convert themselves into socialist banking consortia through their involvement in business. Such a banking consortium may work alongside a socialist corporate consortium to do business that transcends departmental and regional boundaries. At the core of this banking consortium is a central bank that functions as the holding company. The first and second tiers of subsidiaries to such a central bank are not its branches or affiliates; rather, they are economic entities that make their own business decisions and are liable for their own gains and losses. The holding central bank needs to influence the production and management of these subsidiaries by way of its equity. Moreover, the bank's involvement in business also helps improve its credit management because if a business applying for a loan has no idea about the risks involved, the bank providing the loan is liable for such risks. If the bank cannot recoup the loan it has issued in due time, or if the project invested with the loan falls through, the bank will bear the financial loss thus incurred. In a shareholding company established with a bank's participation, the outcome of business failures is borne by all partners, a fact that can galvanize the bank into improving its management.

VI

Mixed-ownership companies, as the name suggests, are economic entities invested jointly by public, collective, and private partners. Firms of this type allow for joint business activity under different types of ownership even in the absence of the shareholding system. However, demutualization of firms inevitably produces a large number of companies under mixed ownership. Enterprises under a single type of ownership will go on as usual, but the emergence of many mixed-ownership economic entities will be an inevitable trend in a socialist economy.

How to define the nature of such mixed-ownership companies in a socialist society? If a public or collective enterprise has increased its capital by raising funds through stock share sales, and thus obtained

是单纯的贷款提供者，而且也是投资者。银行可以直接从事企业投资活动，成为企业的股东之一，甚至银行还可以自己创办企业。在银行掌握企业的股权之后，银行与企业的关系就在股份利益的基础上联结在一起了。银行作为股权持有人，将派出自己的人进驻大企业，参与企业的管理，参加企业的会议。银行不仅仅参与管理企业资金的使用，也过问企业的生产和经营。

银行本身也可以通过对企业的参与而形成社会主义银行财团。社会主义银行财团同社会主义公司财团一起，实行跨部门、跨地区的经营。银行财团的核心仍然是持股公司性质的中心银行，它所控制的子公司、孙公司同样不是中心银行的分支机构或附属机构，而是自主经营和自负盈亏的经济实体。持股性质的中心银行同样需要通过对股权的控制来影响子公司、孙公司的生产经营。除此以外，银行对企业的参与还有利于银行自身的信贷工作的改进。这是因为，如果要求贷款的企业没有投资风险的观念，那将由提供贷款的银行承担一切投资风险。贷款收不回，项目建设失败了，其损失归于作为贷款提供者的银行。建立股份企业，特别是采取银行参与企业的做法，经营失败由股权人，即由参与企业的各方共同负责，这对于银行的经营的改进是可以起到积极作用的。

六

混合经济型企业是指由全民、集体、个体等多种所有制共同投资而组成的企业。即使不实现企业的股份化，只要容许不同所有制的企业联合经营，也可以产生一些混合经济型的企业。但企业的股份化的结果将导致混合经济型企业的大量出现。当然，纯粹的、单一所有制性质的企业也会继续存在，但应当认识到，大量混合经济型企业的出现是社会主义经济中的不可避免的局面。

社会主义社会中的混合经济型企业的性质应当如何确定呢？如果原来的全民所有制或原来的集体所有制以入股集资形式新增资金，

a certain portion of share capital from a mixed-ownership firm and controlled its management, this company should be regarded as a public enterprise. If such a mixed-ownership firm is not deemed public, what else should it be? Let us look into this matter more closely. If, say, an enterprise has been set up with funds raised by selling stock shares to both companies and individuals, such a mixed economic structure should be regarded as an economic conglomerate under a new form of public ownership, which is different from traditional types of public or collective ownership.

We regard this type of economic conglomerates as public enterprises because they are similar to collectives whose partners buy stock shares with capital goods or cash. They represent a brand-new type of public ownership enterprise, which not only identifies workers as masters of capital goods but also energizes itself by becoming an independent commodity producer that makes its own business decisions and bears responsibility for its own gains and losses. Such economic conglomerates are most likely to become the mainstay in China's future corporate ownership structure.

The emergence of mixed-ownership companies meets the demand to boost productivity in socialist economic development, corresponds with the reality of the country, and promotes the commodity economy. Such firms can grow in both rural and urban areas. Flexible in business operation, they can adjust their corporate sizes according to circumstances to accommodate the idle and the jobless and better connect rural and urban areas. The presence of such mixed-ownership firms challenges old public enterprises to improve their management and start ownership reform at an early date.

VII

Like mixed-ownership companies, small cooperatives represent another nascent form of ownership. Convenient and flexible, these small cooperatives differ from mixed-ownership firms in two ways:

First, the shareholders of a mixed-ownership company are enterprises and individuals, and state-owned companies may buy their way into it. By contrast, small cooperatives are formed entirely by individual shareholders.

Second, mixed-ownership companies vary in size, whereas cooperatives are generally small, even though it is possible for them to grow bigger and evolve into mixed-ownership companies. Nevertheless, cooperatives tend to remain small, at least in the formative stage.

并在混合经济型企业股金中占有一定份额，并且能够掌握企业经营管理权的话，那么这样的混合经济型企业无疑仍是公有制企业。但如果不是这样，那又如何确定其性质呢？对此，让我们作进一步的分析。比如说，如果一个企业是新创办的，其资金来自股票发行，而购买股票的，既有各种企业，又有个人，那么这样的混合经济型企业，是一种新的经济联合体，是传统的全民、集体所有制之外的一种新的公有制形式。

我们之所以把这种新型的经济联合体称为公有制企业，是因为它们在很大程度上类似于生产资料入股和资金入股的合作组织形式。它是新型的公有经济。这种经济组织形式既体现了劳动者群体作为生产资料主人这一特征，又最便于加强企业的活力，使企业成为独立的自主经营、自负盈亏的商品生产者。它在今后有可能成为我国新企业的所有制结构中的主体。

在社会主义经济建设中，混合经济型企业的出现正是适应了生产力发展的要求。它符合国情，促进了商品经济的发展。它既适合在乡村中成长，也适合在城市中发展。它方式灵活，可大可小，便于安置社会闲散人员，有利于密切城乡联系。新成立的混合经济型企业是原有的全民所有制企业的有力竞争者，可以迫使后者改善经营管理，或推动它们较快地走上所有制改革的道路。

七

与混合经济型企业一样，小型合作企业也是适合于我国国情、方便灵活的一种新的所有制形式。它和混合经济型企业的区别在于：

第一，混合经济型企业的入股者是各个企业和个人，并且可能有全民所有制单位投资入股，而小型合作企业则完全是由个人集资入股组成的。

Small cooperatives, being organized by individuals who buy their way into them, identify their workers as masters of capital goods. That is why they are seen as a new form of socialist public ownership. Their members own the capital goods, join in collective labor and management, and distribute their after-tax profit among themselves. Such earnings may be used to cover daily expenses or be converted into new stock shares. Members of such a small collective get paid for their labor as employees while earning a certain percentage of the tax-paid profit as shareholders.

Small cooperatives are especially suitable for businesses in retailing, handicrafts, community services and farm produce processing. Their members are engaged in collective labor, make economic decisions and share gains and losses. Whenever funds need to be raised, they put their heads together to decide the ceiling and floor for the money to be paid by every member according to a ratio between labor and fund. This way of doing things is entirely agreeable to the nature of small cooperatives.

It does not matter whether or not a small collective calls itself a "shareholding company." They represent the collective sector in the true sense of the term. They differ from shareholding companies precisely in that, instead of turning to society for financial help, they raise money exclusively among their members. They can become mixed-ownership firms if, someday, they start to raise money by issuing stock shares to the public.

To encourage individual workers to form their own small cooperatives by buying shares or converting their contribution of capital goods into shares, and to confirm the collective—i.e., public—nature of such cooperatives, is to respect both theory and practice. To accept the small cooperatives as public enterprises is for no other purpose than to recognize an established social fact that has to be accepted as such.

Small cooperative enterprises are often called "small collectives" or "collectives run by individuals." People may name such firms any way they want. However, when you choose to call them "small collectives," you are wrong if you think that small collectives are not as good as large collectives or that small collectives should be turned into large ones. When you choose to call them "collectives run by individuals," you are wrong if you believe that they are "informal collectives" or

第二，混合经济型的规模可大可小，而小型合作企业的规模一般说来是较小的。当然这并不否认小型合作企业以后可能发展、壮大，甚至也有可能逐渐演变为混合经济型企业，但至少就它们初创时期而论，它们是较小的。

小型合作企业由个人集资入股而组成，它们体现劳动者群体是生产资料主人这一特征，从而是社会主义公有化的一种形式。它的生产资料归参加合作者所有，合作者共同劳动，集体经营，税后利润分给参加合作的成员，这些成员可以把收入用于生活支出，也可以用于再入股。在小型合作企业中，参加合作的成员作为劳动队伍中的一员，取得劳动报酬，作为入股者，又取得一定的税后利润。

小型合作企业特别适合于零售商业、手工业、城镇服务业、农产品加工业。参加合作的成员以自己的劳动进行集体生产，自主经营、自负盈亏。集资时，每人最少要出多少资金，最多只能出多少资金，以及劳力同资金按什么比例分配，要民主商定。这一切完全体现了它作为合作经济组织的质的规定性。

从形式上看，小型合作企业也可能自称为"股份公司"。这是无关紧要的。实际上，小型合作企业是真正的、名副其实的合作经济。它不同于股份公司之处就在于它只由参加合作的成员集资入股，而不向外界集资。如果它以后采取发行股票的方式向外界集资，那么它就变为混合型企业了。

鼓励劳动者个人以集资入股（包括用生产资料折成股金）形式组成小型合作企业，并肯定它们的合作经济性质，即公有制性质，是对理论和实践的尊重。承认这样的企业是公有制企业，无非是承认本来早就应该承认的社会事实而已。

目前，小型合作企业往往被人们称为"小集体"或"民办集体"。当然，人们可以采用这种名称或那种名称。但应当注意的是，当人们称这类企业为"小集体"时，不能认为"小集体不如大集体"，"小集体要向大集体过渡"；当人们称这类企业为"民办集体"时，也不能认为"民办集体是非正式的集体"，"民办集体要过渡到公办

that they should be converted into public collectives. We must see cooperatives exactly as a form of collective economy as well as a form of socialist ownership that is highly flexible and adaptable to different levels of productivity and corporate scales. The cooperative economy does not necessarily need to develop itself into other forms of collective ownership, and there is absolutely no such inevitability either. The cooperative economy, other forms of collective economy, and the mixed-ownership economy each have their own strengths and applicable scopes, and should be allowed to exist side by side and develop together in the long run.

VIII

We may regard the adoption of the household responsibility system that links remuneration with output as the first step toward rural ownership reform. In this chapter, let me make some tentative study of the next stage of ownership reform in rural areas from the perspective of the national ownership structure.

Let us start with some background information about the next stage of rural ownership reform. We have to understand that, on the basis of initiating the household responsibility system, the rural economy is being restructured in transition to a large-scale commodity economy. Rural areas will adapt their production and processing undertakings to market demand, and provide large quantities of farm and sideline products. The advance of the commodity economy enables every farming household to enter the commodity market as both producers and business operators. Rural ownership reform should keep up with the burgeoning commodity economy.

According to the requirements of the commodity economy, the rural household responsibility system will be maintained for a long time in agriculture, forestry, fishery, and animal husbandry. However, rural production and businesses are bound to develop along specialized lines. That means some fields of production will operate independently and be specialized. On the basis of a division of labor and collaboration, farming households can freely collaborate with one another in different forms. The assets of such voluntary economic cooperation will be owned by the members, who will distribute the earnings among themselves according to work done. Part of such earnings, however, may also be distributed according to shares of capital or of capital goods. This will give rise to a large number of small cooperative farms (forest, fishing and

集体”。要知道，合作经济就是集体经济，它是灵活的社会主义所有制形式，可以适应不同的生产力状况，可以有不同的企业规模。合作经济不一定要向其他集体所有制形式过渡，而且也不存在这种过渡的必然性。合作经济形式，其他集体经济形式，混合经济形式，等等，各有优势和适用范围，应该长期共存，共同发展。

八

我们可以把农业中的联产承包责任制的实行看作农村所有制改革的第一步，现在，让我们从所有制体系的角度，对农村所有制的进一步改革加以探讨。

应当了解农村所有制进一步改革的背景，即这一改革是在什么条件下展开的。要知道，在实现联产承包责任制的基础上调整产业结构，农村经济将向大规模商品经济转化。农村将根据市场需要生产、加工、提供大量农副产品。商品经济的发展，使每个农民家庭作为商品生产者和经营者进入商品市场。因此，与蓬勃发展的商品经济相适应，农村的所有制将继续进行改革。

按照商品经济发展的要求，在农业、林业、渔业、畜牧业等生产活动中，家庭联产承包责任制的生产经营的形式会长期存在，但必将逐步走向专业化，甚至会把一些生产环节独立出来，形成某些生产环节的专业化。于是，在分工协作的基础上，农民家庭将采取不同形式的自由联合。这种自愿结合而组成的农民家庭的联合经营组织的财产，属于参加联合经营的农民家庭共同所有，按各自劳动成果的大小比例分配劳动收入。此外，收入的一部分也可以根据投入的资金和生产资料的多少按比例分配。这样就会产生一大批与上一节提到的小型合作企业相似

animal farms included) similar to the small cooperatives described in the previous chapter. A creation of the broad masses of farmers in their production activity, these cooperative farms will play a major role in the future development of the rural economy. They represent a new type of collective economy, and a breakthrough from the old agricultural collective economy in which capital goods and labor are centralized. On the basis of household management, these farms can bring farmers' funds and production factors under cooperative management. The emergence of such farms is nothing short of another round of rural ownership reform that can fire the enthusiasm of the rural population for production and development.

In the course of developing a commodity economy, the issue of revamping the ownership of old rural enterprises will be put on the agenda. These rural enterprises, according to common sense, represent a form of cooperative economy run by farmers (and townspeople) with their own money, labor and technology. Although many of them are dependent on loans, they are supposed to repay such loans with nothing but their profits. However, in actual fact, these enterprises have changed their collective economic nature and evolved, to a certain extent, into local government-run businesses. Some local officials, holding the power to appoint or dismiss the managers of these businesses, are given to interfering in their business activity. Farmers can hardly benefit from such businesses because their profits are often manipulated by these officials. Such problems with the old rural enterprises can only be redressed through ownership restructuring—that is, to put an end to government interference in them and let farmers be their true masters.

I do not here deny the fact that many rural enterprises are doing perfectly well and that, in many places, local farmers are benefiting from them. Rural enterprise ownership reform is not directed merely at mismanaged enterprises. Of course, enterprises that do not perform well should be straightened out, and the best way to do so is to restructure their ownership. However, well-run rural firms need ownership restructuring as well. Now that rural firms are collective economic entities, they should not become appendages to grass roots governments and muddle along under government administration that is entangled in business management. We have got to restore them to their true beings as collective firms. If we limit ownership reform to poorly run enterprises,

的小型合作农场（林场、渔场、牧场），它们是广大农民在实践中的创举，对未来农村经济的发展将起着十分重要的作用。这种小型合作农场（林场、渔场、牧场），是新型的集体经济，它们是对过去农业中集体经济统一生产资料和统一劳动的旧框框的突破。作为农民的自由联合的经营组织，它们是在家庭经营的基础上，采取集资形式集中各种生产要素的合作经营。它们是能够调动起广大群众的积极性的农村所有制的进一步改革。

在商品经济发展过程中，原来的乡镇企业的所有制改革问题必然被提上议事日程。乡镇企业的经济性质，照理说应当是农民（乡镇居民）的合作经济，它是农民靠自己的资金、劳力、技术建成的。不少企业尽管依靠贷款兴办，但贷款只能是农民用企业获得的利润偿还。然而在实际生活中，这些企业不是如上所述的合作经济性质的企业，而变成了（或在一定程度上变成了）官办企业。有些干部凭着对这些企业领导层的任免权，干涉企业的自主活动。一些企业即使获得较多的利润，但利润由干部支配，农民仍不能得到好处。因此，要改革乡镇企业的现状，就应当从所有制上解决问题，即打破目前实际存在的企业的官办模式，使农民成为名副其实的企业主人。

当然，这里并不否认现存的许多乡镇企业是办得很有成绩的，并且农民也确实能从乡镇企业得到利益，但我们所说的乡镇企业的所有制改革不是仅仅针对那些办得差的企业而言。办得差的企业无疑需要加以整顿，最有效的整顿方式就是进行所有制改革。即使是办得好的企业，也同样要改革所有制。这是因为，既然乡镇企业是集体所有制，那就不能使之成为基层政权的附属物，不能政企不分。“还这些企业以本来面目”，就是使之真正成为集体所有的企业。如果只对办得差的乡镇企业进行所有制改革，不对办得好的

we must answer the question: If, someday, a local government comes into the hands of a new leader who has changed the old way of doing things, will well-run enterprises start going downhill? Is there any way to prevent this scenario from materializing? Clearly, all rural firms, large or small, good or bad, should have their ownership restructured. Only by starting from ownership reform can these companies' business problems be fundamentally addressed. As to which enterprises should be the first to engage in such a reform, this should be decided in light of actual production and management situations.

How, then, should rural enterprise ownership be reformed? The guideline is to liquidate the assets and check the accounts, and to distribute the stock to every member household. In this way, farmers can become shareholders who can impose their will on their companies through voting in elections and exercising their management rights. Major issues on income distribution will be settled by consensus. Apart from getting paid for work done, shareholders are also entitled to dividends allotted according to shares. Township governments are not allowed to run enterprises, and their power should be limited to guiding and helping farmers in business activity. New rural firms and cooperatives established by rural workers with their own money, and mixed-ownership firms are, without exception, new types of public enterprises. Farming households should also be allowed to run wholly owned enterprises that belong in the private sector.

Rural supply and marketing cooperatives should have their ownership revamped in two ways. First, large numbers of rural supply and marketing cooperatives at the grass roots level should be converted into independent cooperative firms. Only thus can they truly become supply and marketing cooperatives that make their own business decisions, function as independent accounting units, and take responsibility for their gains and losses. Their after-tax profit will be dispensed among members according to shares after a certain amount has been set aside as public accumulation fund and welfare fund. Second, supply and marketing cooperatives at and above the county level, including specialized companies and industrial and commercial businesses, should be transformed into mixed-ownership, shareholding companies that make their own business decisions as independent accounting units and are accountable for their own gains and losses. They will have the same organizational setup as other shareholding companies.

乡镇企业进行所有制改革，那么不禁要问一句：假定将来有一天，基层政权的领导换人了，新上任的基层政权领导不再像过去那样考虑问题了，办得好的企业不就有可能变为办得差的企业吗？究竟有什么方法能避免这种情况的出现呢？可见，不管今天办得好还是办得差的乡镇企业，都应当一律进行所有制改革。从所有制上解决企业经营问题，是根本性的。至于哪些企业先改革所有制，哪些企业后改革所有制，则可以根据各个企业的生产和经营管理现状来安排。

那么，怎样从所有制方面改革乡镇企业呢？乡镇企业所有制改革的设想是：清产核资、折股到户。农民成为企业的股东，他们作为股东，通过选举实现自己的意志，行使管理企业的权利。在收益分配权利上，收益分配重大问题民主确定；股东除参加劳动领取报酬外，依其股金多少，按比例分享红利。今后，乡镇政权只负责指导和帮助农民经营，不要自己办企业。乡镇新办的企业，或者是乡镇劳动者自己集资兴办的合作企业，或者是有不同所有制混合的混合经济型企业。这两类企业都是新型的公有制企业。此外，如果农民家庭要独资办企业，这也是可以容许的，尽管它们属于个体经济性质。

农村中的供销社也有必要进行所有制改革。这一改革可以从两个方面着手：第一，大量分散于农村的基层供销社，应当转化为独立的合作企业，即成为名副其实的供销合作社，自主经营，独立核算，自负盈亏，税后利润除留作公积金、公益金的部分外，按社员的股金分配。第二，县以上的供销社，包括各个专业公司和工商企业，应当转化为混合经济型的企业，即有多种所有制混合的股份企业，也是自主经营、独立核算、自负盈亏的。它的组织管理与一般股份企业的组织管理相同。

By putting the rural ownership system through the abovementioned reform steps, the relationship between township governments and rural businesses will undergo another round of profound changes comparable to those taking place upon the adoption of the household responsibility system linking remuneration to output. The mode of rural economic activity born of the Movement of Agricultural Collectivization (1954-1955) and particularly of the Movement of the People's Communes that began in 1958, should be totally abolished. Grass roots governments will become pure administrative institutions detached from everyday production and business. Institutions that subject the broad masses of farmers to centralized administration, that allow a tiny number of township and town government officials to impose their will on people's economic activity, and that have hindered the growth of rural commodity economy and kept the monolithic rural economic structure unchanged for long years, will eventually be consigned to the dustpan of history.

The economic role of grass roots township governments will be limited to guiding the rural commodity economy. Land management is part of that role. The principle that land is public property shall never be changed, but it should not prevent land from being used with compensation. It is also the mission of grass roots governments to prevent arbitrary requisitioning of farmland and bar the selling and buying of land. These governments should also find ways and means to help local farmers beat poverty, organize them in running businesses, and help these businesses solve problems. They will also have a "matchmaking" role to play, that is, to bring enterprises together for technological and economic collaboration. "Serving the people" should be the motto for local governments in steering the advancement of the rural commodity economy. The purpose of their administration is specifically to serve farmers' business activities.

IX

Proprietorship over capital goods is at the core of ownership. However, to interpret ownership merely as proprietorship over capital goods is a narrow-minded understanding of the substance of ownership. In a broad sense, ownership also encompasses the organizational form of production and the administration and management of production, apart from proprietorship over capital goods. This being the case, the ownership reform discussed in the foregoing involves not only changes in ownership of capital goods before and after the reform, but also

通过上述农村所有制的进一步改革措施，继家庭联产承包责任制实行之后，乡镇的基层政权同经济活动之间的关系将发生更为显著的变化。农业合作化之后，特别是人民公社化之后的那种农村经济活动方式将彻底解体。乡镇的基层政权完全变为纯粹的政权组织，脱离具体的生产经营活动，从而以往那种把广大农民置于统一指挥、统一管理之下，使他们的经济活动被动地听命于少数乡镇干部的意志，限制广大农民积极性和创造性的发挥，阻碍农村商品经济的发展，并使农村产业结构长期单一不变的情况，将不再存在。

乡镇基层政权在经济上的作用主要体现于积极引导乡镇商品经济的发展。为此，它们要负责土地的管理。土地公有的原则不能改变，但土地应当是有偿使用的。要防止侵占耕地，严禁土地买卖。这是乡镇基层政权的职责所在。乡镇基层政权还要设法帮助农民寻找致富门路，组织农民兴办各种企业，并帮助这些企业解决发展中遇到的难题。乡镇基层政权还可以为企业的联营牵线搭桥，组织技术协作和经济协作。乡镇基层政权在引导农村商品经济发展的过程中，应当突出“服务”二字。它们的管理就是为农民的经济活动服务。

九

所有制的核心是生产资料所有权的归属。但把所有制理解为生产资料所有权的归属，仅仅是对所有制的狭义理解。对所有制的广义的理解是：除了生产资料所有权的归属以外，所有制还包括生产组织的形式和生产管理体制等。因此，以上所谈到的所有制改革，不仅涉及生产资料所有权的归属在改革前后的变化，而且也涉及生产组织的形式和

changes in the organizational form of administration over production. The new socialist ownership born of the reform effort refers precisely to proprietorship over capital goods, to new organizational forms of production, and to new administrative and managerial systems over production.

The reformed socialist ownership system will not be singular but plural. It will constitute multiple forms of ownership and can be understood from the following perspectives:

In terms of capital goods proprietorship, it will encompass diverse forms of nonpublic ownership in the service of the socialist economy, with socialist public ownership taking the lead. Under public ownership, there will be enterprises owned by all the people, enterprises under mixed ownership, and cooperatives. Under nonpublic ownership, there will be private firms, foreign-invested companies, and equity joint ventures with Chinese and foreign investment.

Concerning the organizational form of production and the administrative and managerial system over production, enterprises owned by all the people and enterprises under mixed ownership can be run on their own or rented or contracted out to cooperative enterprises or individuals. Likewise, cooperatives can also be run by themselves or rented or contracted out by individuals.

This socialist ownership system is born of the need of the burgeoning socialist commodity economy. In a shareholding company under public ownership, dividends are dispensed among shareholders according to their shares of capital (or money paid for stock shares), and shareholders are investors who contribute to production through the shares they have bought. The money they have spent on shares is similar in nature to bank savings, and therefore, they also deserve remuneration in the form of stock interest. The stock shares invested in the economy contribute a lot more to the growth and overall interest of the socialist economy than to the shareholder's individual interest. Leased and contracted management serves to adapt public enterprises to the demand for boosting productivity, allocating production factors effectively under the current circumstances, minimizing waste in human, material and financial resources, and promoting production.

I deem it unnecessary to say anything here about the presence of private economy that does not belong in the public sector of the socialist ownership system. This is because the private sector exists to supplement the socialist economy and help create jobs and tax revenues.

生产管理体制在改革前后的变化。改革后所建立的新的社会主义所有制，就是指新的生产资料所有权的归属、新的生产组织形式和新的生产管理体制。

改革后的社会主义所有制不是单一的，而是多元的。多种所有制构成了新的社会主义所有制体系。对这个体系可以这样理解：

从生产资料所有权的归属来看，这是一个以社会主义公有制为主体的、包括为社会主义经济服务的各种非公有制在内的所有制体系。公有制企业包括：全民所有制企业、混合经济型企业、合作企业。非公有制企业包括：个体企业、外资企业、中外合资企业。

从生产组织形式和生产管理体制来看，全民所有制企业、混合经济型企业可以自己经营，也可租赁、承包给合作经济或个人经营；合作企业同样可以自己经营或采取租赁、承包的方式，让个人来经营。

这样的社会主义所有制体系是根据社会主义商品经济发展的需要而产生的。在公有制企业中，虽然股份化的实行涉及按资金（或股金）分成，但投资入股对于投资者来说是对生产的贡献，其性质与在银行存款相似，应有一定的股息收入作为报酬。投资入股，发展社会主义经济，对社会主义经济的总体利益大于投资入股者的个别利益。而公有制企业的租赁、承包经营，则能够适应生产力发展的需要，使生产要素在现有条件下有效结合，减少人力、物力、财力的浪费，对生产的发展起到促进作用。

至于社会主义所有制体系中属于非公有制范畴的个体经济，它存在的必要性已经无需论述，因为个体经济是作为社会主义经济的必要补充而存在的，它为社会主义社会中的生产和生活服务，而且

Self-employed workers rely on themselves in business activity. It is only normal for them to make more money through diligence and shrewd management. Given correct government policy, effective administration, and sensible education and guidance, the private sector can grow in the course of serving socialism.

To sum up, ownership reform will bring about a dual economic system. On the one hand, the national economy will contain hundreds of large enterprises that will grow into corporate consortia (enterprise groups), which, through multilevel investment, will bring about a network of second- and third-tier subsidiaries. These consortia will point out the way for the national drive for industrialization and technological progress. On the other hand, the national economy will have numerous small enterprises under cooperative, private or mixed ownership, which will form a close-knit network of collaboration while competing with one another. Their shared mission will be to address the problems arising from the reallocation of surplus rural workforce, farm and sideline product production and processing, from the efforts to raise rural residents' income and build small towns, and from everyday services for urban and rural residents. These two groups of economic entities will each follow a different course of development and coexist in a mutually complementary relationship.

— *Hebei Academic Journal*, issue No. 1, 1987

还可以增加就业，增加税收。个体劳动者主要依靠自己的劳动从事经营。有些人辛勤劳动，经营有方，获得较多的收入，这是正常的。只要有正确的政策，加强管理，同时又善于教育和引导，就能保证个体经济沿着为社会主义服务的轨道发展。

总之，通过所有制改革，今后我国将形成如下的二元经济模式：一方面，是几百家最大的企业，它们通过层层控股，形成母公司、子公司、孙公司系统，形成公司财团（企业集团）。它们将决定我国工业化的方向、技术进步的方向。另一方面，是几十万家甚至上百万家小企业，包括合作经济的、个体的、混合所有制的小企业，它们形成紧密的协作网，同时又处于相互竞争之中。它们将着重解决农村劳动力的转移、农副产品生产和加工、农村居民收入水平的提高、小城镇建设、城乡居民生活服务等问题。二元经济的这两个不同的部分将各自按照自己的运动规律向前发展。二者是长期并存和互补的。

（原载《河北学刊》，1987 年第 1 期）

TWO TYPES OF DISEQUILIBRIUM, MAINSTREAM OF CURRENT ECONOMIC RESTRUCTURING (1988)

I. Differences of resource allocation in equilibrium and disequilibrium

In economics, disequilibrium is pertinent to Walrasian equilibrium. The latter is achieved under the assumption of a complete market and a flexible price system. Disequilibrium, which is a kind of equilibrium arrived at in the absence of a complete market and a flexible price system, is also dubbed "non-Walrasian equilibrium."

According to the theory of French economist Léon Walras (1834-1910), given that the market is complete and the price system flexible, given also that traders possess full information and prices adjust instantaneously with changes in supply and demand, then under a given price condition aggregate demand must equal aggregate supply, excess demand and excess supply do not exist, and the settlement of every transaction is guaranteed by an equilibrium price. No deals will be reached before equilibrium price is attained; only with equilibrium price can transactions take place. According to this theory, overproduction, unsalable products, chronic unemployment, and inflation associated with excess demand will never happen.

The analysis of Walrasian equilibrium, alien to economic reality, had long drawn acute criticism from dissentient Western economists. In *The General Theory of Employment, Interest, and Money* published in 1936, John Maynard Keynes (1883-1946) went out of his way to dissect the unemployment and other perennial problems in capitalist society. Nevertheless, up till the early 1960s Western economists' study of disequilibrium was partial and unsystematic at best. Their interpretations of Keynesian economic theory were categorically divided as well. Mainstream Keynes followers believe that Keynesian economics is still a theory based on equilibrium and that Keynes did not negate the Walrasian equilibrium theory despite the fact that he somewhat amended it. Some other interpreters maintain that Keynesian economics broke through the limits of the equilibrium theory and provided initial but systematic pronouncements on the disequilibrium theory. They back their argument by citing Keynes's belief that market mechanisms are not necessarily effective, and that market alone cannot totally coordinate trading activities,

论两种类型的非均衡经济和我国当前经济体制改革的主线（1988）

一、均衡条件下的资源配置与非均衡条件下的资源配置的区别

在经济学中，非均衡是相对于瓦尔拉均衡而言的。瓦尔拉均衡是假设存在着完善的市场和灵敏的价格体系条件下所达到的均衡。非均衡是指不存在完善的市场，不存在灵敏的价格体系条件下所达到的均衡。因此，非均衡又被称为非瓦尔拉均衡。

根据瓦尔拉的学说，既然市场是完善的，价格体系是灵敏的，交易者有充分信息，价格随供求的变化而随时进行调整，那么在任何一种价格条件下，需求总量必定等于供给总量，社会中的超额需求和超额供给都是不存在的，任何交易的实现，都以均衡价格为条件。没有达到均衡价格，不会成交；只有价格均衡了，才可能进行交易。根据这样的学说，生产的过剩、商品的滞销、经常性的失业，以及与超额需求有关的通货膨胀也就不会出现。

对于这种不符合经济实际的瓦尔拉均衡分析，虽然早就引起一些持有异议的西方经济学家的尖锐批评，而且凯恩斯在其 1936 年出版的《就业、利息和货币通论》一书中专就资本主义社会中经常性失业存在等问题进行了阐述，但直到 60 年代初，西方经济学界关于非均衡的研究仍是局部性的、非系统的。甚至对凯恩斯本人的经济理论的解释，也存在截然不同的观点。占主流地位的凯恩斯理论解释者认为，凯恩斯经济学仍然是一种均衡经济学，凯恩斯只是对瓦尔拉均衡学说作了一定的修改，基本上没有否定它。另一些凯恩斯理论的解释者则认为，凯恩斯经济学已经突破了均衡理论的界限，进行了非均衡理论的最初的、体系性的阐述。这具体表现于：凯恩斯认为市场机制不一定能充分发挥作用，市场难以把各种交易活动协调起来，无论是产量、就业量还是投资量都是波动的，

with the result that output, levels of employment and investment are subject to fluctuations, whereas overproduction, unemployment, and insufficient investment demand are commonplace under capitalism.

The disequilibrium theory has made substantial headway since the late 1960s. Studies of disequilibrium have indicated that under the condition of an incomplete market where prices fail to adjust demand and supply, economic forces will proceed from their respective circumstances to adjust themselves to the point where they are well adapted to each other and where equilibrium is achieved. Obviously, the equilibrium achieved by way of disequilibrium is not the equilibrium in a complete market but in an incomplete market; it is not the kind of equilibrium with zero unemployment and zero inflation rates, but with both unemployment and inflation in presence. In other words, disequilibrium is actually a form of equilibrium; but unlike the kind of equilibrium described in the Walrasian theory, it is the kind of equilibrium that exists in reality. Such is the connotation of disequilibrium.

If an economy is exactly in Walrasian equilibrium, the market will be highly self-restraining in resource allocation. The market's self-restraining role can be fulfilled smoothly through the changes in the actual and expected benefits of every microeconomic agent. When a microeconomic agent believes that a certain resource input will bring no benefit and decides to stop it, this microeconomic decision also measures up to the efficiency standard of society's resource allocation. If, on the contrary, the agent believes that a certain resource input is beneficial to itself and decides to increase it, its improved efficiency will also help boost social efficiency in resource allocation. Therefore, so long as the agent is sensitive to its own interests, its resource allocation will be adapted to market prices, and resources are bound to be channeled into efficient sectors, localities and enterprises and withdrawn from inefficient sectors, localities and enterprises. The market's self-restraining function in the process of resource allocation manifests itself in that it does not allow any ineffective resource input to last and enables resource allocation to automatically measure up to efficiency standards.

II. Two types of microeconomic agents and two types of disequilibrium

As my analysis of the market's self-restraining role in resource allocation indicates, the ability of the market to adjust and rectify

而在资本主义条件下，经常出现的是生产过剩、失业、投资需求的不足。

非均衡理论从60年代后期起有较大的进展。非均衡的研究表明：在市场不完善和价格不能起到自行调整供求的作用的条件下，各种经济力量将会根据各自的具体情况而被调整到彼此相适应的位置上，并在这个位置上达到均衡。显然，非均衡所达到的均衡，并非市场完善前提下的均衡，而是市场不完善前提下的均衡，并非与零失业率或零通货膨胀率同时存在的均衡，而是伴随着失业或通货膨胀的均衡。换言之，非均衡实际上也是一种均衡，只不过它不是瓦尔拉学说中所论述的那种均衡，而是存在于现实生活中的均衡。这就是非均衡的含义。

如果经济确实处于瓦尔拉均衡状态，那么市场在资源配置中的自我制约作用将是明显的。市场的这种自我制约作用可以顺利地通过每个微观经济单位的利益和预期利益的变化来实现。当微观经济单位认为某种资源投入对自己不利而决定停止资源投入时，这一决定也符合社会资源配置的效率标准。反之，当它认为资源投入有利而增加投入时，它的效率的提高同样有助于社会资源配置效率的提高。可见，只要微观经济单位对利益敏感，资源配置将受到市场价格的制约，资源必将被投入有效的部门、地区和企业，而从无效的部门、地区和企业流出。资源配置过程中的市场自我制约表现为：市场不可能使任何一种无效的资源投入持久化，市场将使资源配置自行符合效率标准。

二、两类不同的微观经济单位和两类不同的非均衡

从以上关于资源配置过程中市场自我制约的分析可以了解到，市场之所以能够在经济运行中对于过度扩张和过度收缩有自行调整

excessive expansions and recessions in economic practice is closely tied with the full vitality of microeconomic agents participating in market activity. Economic equilibrium is certainly on the premise of complete market and flexible prices, but the vitality on the part of microeconomic agents is a more important and fundamental prerequisite.

Thus microeconomic agents can be divided into two categories: those with full vitality, and those without full vitality or totally lacking it. A microeconomic agent can be brimming with vitality because it makes its own business decisions and takes full responsibility for its gains and losses. Such a firm can choose the best investment opportunities and patterns of production and management, distribute its after-tax profit according to its own interests, and take investment and management risks on its own. Such a firm is an independent commodity producer and manager. Such an individual, in economic terms, is a trader that takes part in market activity independently. Any microeconomic agent that does not have these attributes invariably lacks full vitality or lacks it totally.

In equilibrium, microeconomic agents are certainly brimming with vitality and, on this basis, form a complete market. This point need not be repeated here. What I want to find out is this: Is it true that microeconomic agents invariably lack full competitive vigor under economic disequilibrium? To find the answer, it is necessary to divide economic disequilibrium into two categories.

Economic disequilibrium in the first category is marked by an incomplete market, inflexible prices, presence of both excess demand and excess supply, and restraints on both demand and supply, while microeconomic agents in the market are independent commodity producers that make their own business decisions and take responsibility for their gains and losses, and that have the freedom to choose their investment opportunities and modes of management and bear investment and business risks.

Economic disequilibrium in the second category is characterized by an incomplete market and inflexible prices, and more importantly, by a market filled with microeconomic agents that, instead of being independent commodity producers making their own business decisions and bearing their own gains and losses, neither have the freedom to choose investment opportunities and management modes nor bear the responsibility for investment and management risks. Such microeconomic

和纠正的作用，是同参加市场活动的微观经济单位的充分活力紧密地联系在一起的。经济的均衡状态固然以市场的完善和价格的灵活为前提，但一个更为重要的或更为基本的前提则是微观经济单位的充分活力的存在。

由此可以把微观经济单位分为两类。一类是具有充分活力的微观经济单位，一类是不具有充分活力（直到完全缺乏活力）的微观经济单位。微观经济单位之所以具有充分活力，是因为它自主经营、自负盈亏，能够按照自己的利益进行各种投资机会的选择和生产经营方式的选择，能够按照自己的利益进行税后利润的分配，并且需要自己承担投资和经营的风险。这样的企业就是独立的商品生产者和经营者，这样的个人就是经济学意义上的、独立参加市场活动的交易者。如果微观经济单位不符合这些条件，它们必然不具有充分活力，直到完全缺乏活力。

在均衡条件下，微观经济单位无疑具有充分活力，并以此为基础形成完善的市场，这一点不必再重复了。这里需要分析的是，在非均衡条件下，微观经济单位是不是必然不具有充分活力呢？为了说明这个问题，有必要把经济的非均衡区分为两类。

第一类经济的非均衡是指：市场不完善、价格不灵活、超额需求或超额供给都是存在的，需求约束或供给约束也都存在着，但参加市场活动的微观经济单位却是自主经营、自负盈亏的独立商品生产者，它们有投资机会和经营方式的自由选择权，它们自行承担投资风险和经营风险。

第二类经济的非均衡是指：除了市场不完善、价格不灵活以外，更重要的是，参加市场活动的微观经济单位并非自主经营、自负盈亏的独立商品生产者，它们不具有投资机会和经营方式的自由选择权，它们也不自行承担投资风险和经营风险。这样的微观经济

agents have not shaken off their status as government subsidiaries or are bound hand and foot by their pre-capitalist ties.

If my division of economic disequilibrium stands, there is reason to believe that the disequilibrium in a capitalist economy belongs in the first category and that the disequilibrium in a pre-capitalist economy belongs in the second category. What happens in a socialist economy should be treated differently. Disequilibrium under a traditional and dual-track economic system falls into the second category because its enterprises have yet to shake off their status as government subsidiaries. Under the new economic system born of economic reform, enterprises become independent commodity producers that make their own investment and business decisions, and are liable for their gains, losses as well as investment and business risks. Thus the disequilibrium in the new economic system falls into the first category.

In the first category of disequilibrium, microeconomic agents are full of vitality. However, these microeconomic agents are in an economic disequilibrium. They make transactions in incomplete markets where prices are inflexible and information is incomplete and congested. Therefore, such vitality is limited by this environment. For instance, price rigidity makes it hard for these agents to adjust production in response to price signals, and wage rigidity also prevents them from optimizing their resource allocations. However, a microeconomic agent that has full vitality but is circumscribed by its environment is very different from a microeconomic agent that lacks full vitality. This is exactly the difference between the first and second categories of disequilibrium.

III. The market's self-restraint role in the first category of disequilibrium

The self-restraining role of the market in resource allocation can work effectively under economic equilibrium, that is, it may prevent any ineffective resource input from becoming protracted under two conditions. Firstly, the market is perfect and prices are flexible; and secondly, microeconomic agents can transact according to their own interests. The first category of disequilibrium furnishes the second condition because microeconomic units are already brimming with vitality. Its only problems are incomplete markets, inflexible prices, and

单位，或者没有摆脱行政机构附属物的地位，或者受到前资本主义关系的严重束缚。

如果经济的非均衡分为这样两类的话，那么可以认为：资本主义经济中所出现的非均衡属于上述第一类经济的非均衡，前资本主义经济中所出现的非均衡属于上述第二类经济的非均衡。至于社会主义经济中的情况，则需要区别对待：在传统的和双轨的经济体制之下，由于企业并没有摆脱行政机构附属物的地位，所以这种非均衡属于上述第二类经济的非均衡；通过经济体制改革，建立了新的经济体制，在这种新体制之下，企业成为自主经营、自负盈亏、有投资和经营的自主权并相应地承担投资风险和经营风险的独立商品生产者了，这时的经济的非均衡，就可以归人上述第一类经济的非均衡。

在第一类经济的非均衡条件下，从微观经济单位本身来看，它们是具有充分活力的，但由于这些具有充分活力的微观经济单位处于经济非均衡的环境之中，它们在不完善的市场上进行交易活动，而价格又不是灵活的，信息也不完备和通畅，这样，即使它们本身具有充分活力，这种活力的发挥却受到环境的限制。例如，价格有刚性，它们就不一定能完全根据价格信号来调整生产；工资有刚性，它们也就不一定能完全根据资源的最优组合方式来配置和组合资源，等等。当然，微观经济单位有充分活力而这种活力受到环境的限制，同它们不具有充分活力仍是很不一样的，这也就是第一类经济的非均衡与第二类经济的非均衡的区别。

三、第一类非均衡条件下市场的自我制约

在均衡条件下，资源配置过程中的市场自我制约之所以能够有效，即市场之所以有可能不让任何一种无效的资源投入持久化，归因于两个条件：第一，市场是完善的，价格是灵活的；第二，微观经济单位能够按照自身的利益进行交易活动。在第一类经济的非均衡状态中，第二个条件已经解决了，因为微观经济单位已经具有充分活力。问题只在于市场不完善，价格不灵活，经济中或者存在着

an economy in which restraints exist on resource supply and demand. However, we ought to regard microeconomic agents having full vitality as a more important condition than having a complete market. This is because a complete market and flexible prices serve mainly to provide a friendly environment for the development of a commodity economy, whereas encouraging microeconomic units to regain their competitive edge helps solve problems in market participants' interests, responsibilities, incentives and motivations. Even when market is complete and prices are flexible, its self-restraining role in resource allocations will be sharply limited if microeconomic agents do not have full vitality, cannot take advantage of complete market and flexible prices to make transactions, lack aggressiveness and enthusiasm to sensibly allocate resources and raise their resource utilization rate, and cannot bear the economic losses incurred from improper resource allocations.

All this indicates that the first category of economic disequilibrium possesses the more important one of the two conditions that enables the market to play its self-restraining role, that is, the existence of microeconomic agents with full vitality. This condition is beneficial for the market to fully play its self-restraining role. Because these kinds of microeconomic agents can act in their own interests to make deals, their instinct can prevent them from putting their resources into ineffective economic activity and enable them to refuse ineffective, efficiency-reducing approaches of allocating and utilizing resources. Consequently, even though the market is still incomplete and prices are inflexible, and even though there are still restraints on resource supply or demand, in the process of resource allocations, the market can still follow the efficiency standard to adjust the allocations and combinations of resources, thereby avoiding protracted ineffective resource input.

Nevertheless, the first category of disequilibrium is still a kind of disequilibrium, under which resource input is still different from that under equilibrium. The impact of this category of disequilibrium on microeconomic agents' market transactions and patterns of utilizing resources manifests itself in three ways:

First, with an incomplete market and imperfect and frictional information access, microeconomic agents cannot obtain adequate and timely information, and a lot of information they have obtained is incorrect. However, they have no alternative but to make resource input and combination decisions under the guidance of such limited or even

资源供给的约束，或者存在着需求的约束，或者二者同时存在。但应当把微观经济单位具有充分活力这个条件看成比市场完善这个条件更加重要。这是因为，市场的完善和价格的灵活，主要是为商品经济的发展创造一个良好的环境，而让微观经济单位具有充分活力，则是解决市场活动参加者的利益、责任、刺激、动力问题。即使市场完善了，价格灵活了，但如果微观经济单位没有充分活力，不能利用完善的市场和灵活的价格来进行交易，它们缺乏合理组合资源和提高资源利用效率的主动性、积极性，又不承担资源配置不当所造成的经济损失，那么市场在资源配置过程中的自我制约作用也就非常有限。

这意味着第一类经济的非均衡具有使市场自我制约的两个条件中的一个较重要的条件，即微观经济单位具有充分活力。这对于市场在资源配置中的自我制约作用的发挥是有利的。这时，尽管市场还不完善、价格还不灵活、资源供给约束或需求约束还存在，但由于微观经济单位能够根据自己的利益来从事交易，它们从本能上不会把资源投入无效的经济活动中去，也会拒绝无效的、促成效率下降的资源组合和利用方式。因此，市场在资源配置过程中实际上仍然按照效率标准来调整资源的投向和资源的组合，避免出现无效资源投入的持久化。

然而，即使是第一类非均衡，它仍是一种非均衡，这时的资源投入毕竟不同于均衡条件下的情况。第一类非均衡对于微观经济单位的交易活动和资源利用方式的影响，主要表现于以下三个方面：

第一，在市场不完善、信息不完备和不畅通的条件下，微观经济单位在市场上得不到足够的、及时的信息，甚至它们得到的信息中有不少是不正确的信息。这些微观经济单位不得不在有限的信息、甚至错误的信息的指引下进行资源投入和组合的决策，

erroneous information. This is likely to bring low economic efficiency and cause resources to be allocated in violation of efficiency standards.

Second, with inflexible or rigid prices, the adjustments of resource allocation by microeconomic agents will be restrained. This is because price rigidity cannot reflect the degree of resource scarcity and the results of resource input and, therefore, they find it hard to optimize their choices of needed resources. If, under rigid prices, the microeconomic agents are unable to follow optimized resource allocation approaches, the waste or idling of resources in allocation processes can hardly be avoided.

Third, because of the restraints on supply and demand, resources are allocated on a short-term basis where demand and supply are unbalanced. This entails tougher competition for microeconomic agents. In the case of supply restraints, the microeconomic agents on the demand side face the problem of limited supply sources and have to input more to secure supply. By the same token, in the case of demand restraints, the agents on the supply side face the problem of a limited market and have to input more to reach their sales goals. The extra resources spent by these agents for either supply or sales purposes are a manifestation of an abuse of social resources, which means more resources have been consumed than economic equilibrium allows. This is a clear example of improper resource allocation.

The above-mentioned impacts of the first category of disequilibrium on microeconomic agents' transactions and utilization of resources indicate that, even though the market can still play its self-restraining role, its effectiveness is whittled down.

IV. The market's self-restraining role in the second category of disequilibrium

The two conditions—a complete market with flexible prices and full vitality of microeconomic agents—for the market to play its self-restraining role effectively in resource allocation are absent in the second category of disequilibrium. Thus the market's self-restraining role is greatly restricted in the process of resource allocation. This may be analyzed in two ways.

On one hand, the reason why microeconomic agents lack vitality is that they have not truly become masters of their own interests, that the

其结果，很可能给经济带来较低的效率，并且使社会的资源配置不符合效率标准。

第二，在价格不灵活，即存在着价格刚性的条件下，微观经济单位的资源配置的调整要受到限制。这是因为，价格刚性并不能反映资源的稀缺程度和资源投入的效果，微观经济单位在组合资源时，不可能按照最优的方式来选择所需的资源。如果各个微观经济单位在价格刚性条件下不能从优化资源组合的角度来利用资源，那么就全社会的范围而言，资源配置过程中的浪费或闲置是不可避免的。

第三，由于资源供给约束和需求约束的存在，在供求不能平衡的场合要按照短线来配置资源。对微观经济单位来说，实际上是意味着竞争的加剧，即在供给约束的场合，微观经济单位作为需求一方，面临着货源有限的问题，从而不得不为获得供给而投入更多的力量；而在需求约束的场合，微观经济单位作为供给一方，面临着市场有限的问题，从而不得不为实现自己的销售而投入更多的力量。微观经济单位在供给约束和需求约束的场合，为争取货源和销路而投入的更多的力量，对社会而言，就是资源的超正常的使用，即资源的使用量要大于均衡条件下的情况，对资源的超正常使用，应当被看成是资源配置不当的一种表现。

第一类非均衡对于微观经济单位的交易活动和资源利用方式的上述影响，反映了市场的自我制约作用在第一类非均衡条件下虽然存在，但却受到了限制。

四、第二类非均衡条件下市场的自我制约

资源配置过程中市场自我制约取得效果的两个条件（市场完善和价格灵活，微观经济单位有充分活力），在第二类经济的非均衡状态中都不存在。这样，资源配置过程中的市场自我制约作用就受到了很大的限制。对市场自我制约作用所受到的限制，可以从以下两方面来进行分析：

一方面，微观经济单位之所以缺乏活力，主要是由于它并未成为真正的利益主体，生产经营的成果同它的利益没有直接的、必然的

fruits of their production are not directly and inevitably related to their interests, and that they are not held accountable for the economic losses resulting from their production, management or investment mistakes. In this way, they lack not only motivation and stimulus but also pressure and a sense of responsibility. They may become indifferent to opportunities that are obviously in their economic interests and help elevate their resource allocation efficiency. But at the same time they may willingly do things that are apparently detrimental to their own economic interests and that may aggravate their inefficiency in resource allocation. The market's self-restraining role is rendered ineffective when microeconomic agents are callous about boosting resource allocation efficiency, to say nothing of following efficiency standards to control the input and utilization of resources.

On the other hand, the reason why microeconomic agents lack vitality is not only that they do not care enough—or do not care at all—about their gains and losses in production and management, but also that their performance in production and business is subject to restrictions imposed by government departments—they have to do the government's bidding. For this reason, even if microeconomic agents care for their gains and losses in production and management and wish to readjust their input and use of resources, their status as government subsidiaries determines that they can not follow their own will, interests and principles. The market is thus stripped of its self-restraining role in resource allocation; there is nothing it can do no matter how unreasonably resources are allocated and how gravely efficiency is impaired.

The above analysis testifies that in the second category of economic disequilibrium, it is hard for the market to play a proper self-restraining role in resource allocation. This is exactly where the significant difference between the first and second categories of economic disequilibrium rests. In the first category of disequilibrium, the market's self-restraining role still works despite the constraints on it. By contrast, in the second category of disequilibrium, the market's restraints on ineffective resource input can hardly be made to work. Therefore, if efficiency in resource utilization declines due to insufficient resource input or inappropriate resource combinations, the market is unlikely to rectify it. Even if the market can send a warning signal about the widening gap between the demand for and supply of a certain resource, or about a drop in economic efficiency or a large price fluctuation, microeconomic agents are unable

联系，它也不为生产经营的失误或投资的失误而承担应有的经济损失。这样，微观经济单位既缺少动力和刺激，又缺少压力和责任感。明明是有利于自身经济利益的、从而也是有利于社会资源配置效率提高的，微观经济单位可能无动于衷，不屑去做；明明是不利于自身经济利益的、从而也是造成社会资源配置效率下降的，微观经济单位可能照常去做，甚至乐意去做。市场的自我制约作用在微观经济单位这种对资源配置的效率麻木不仁的态度面前显得无能为力，因此也就谈不到如何以效率标准来制约对资源的投入和利用。

另一方面，微观经济单位之所以缺乏活力，并不仅仅由于它对生产经营中的利益与损失关心不够或不予关心，而是由于它的一切生产经营都要受到行政部门的限制，微观经济单位必须按行政部门的命令行事。因此，即使某些微观经济单位关心生产经营的利益与损失，并且希望按照利益原则来调整自己的资源投向和资源使用方式，但它们作为行政机构附属物的地位决定了它们难以按照自己的意愿和利益原则去做。于是资源配置中市场的自我制约作用就无从发挥；哪怕资源配置再不合理，效率再低，市场也难以纠正。

以上两个方面充分说明，在第二类非均衡条件下，实际上很难使市场在资源配置过程中发挥其应有的自我制约作用。这正是第二类经济的非均衡与第一类经济的非均衡的显著区别。如果说在第一类非均衡条件下，资源配置过程中的市场自我制约作用虽然受到一定的限制，但毕竟存在并起作用的话，那么在第二类非均衡条件下，在资源配置过程中，市场机制几乎发挥不了它应有的制约无效投入的作用。比如说，如果资源投入不多，资源组合形式不合理，资源使用的效率下降等情况发生了，市场不可能纠正它们；或者，即使市场会发出警告的信号（某些资源供求缺口的扩大、社会的经济效益的降低、价格的较大幅度变动等等），但微观经济单位接收

to receive it. Even if they can receive it, they cannot—or do not want—to adjust the destinations or combinations of their resource input. Maladjustment in resource allocation will thus prevail, and grow from bad to worse, with one of the following three possible outcomes.

Possibility One: The economic disarray caused by increasingly disproportionate resource allocation forces the government to intervene with noneconomic means in an attempt to rectify it. Such nonmarket intervention, usually known as "rectification" or "policy readjustment," is not uncommon in the second category of disequilibrium. It should be noted that the government in this context refers to the supreme decision-making echelon. Only when this echelon has sensed the serious nature of such disproportionate resource allocation and resolves to "rectify" it or "readjust" its policy, can such noneconomic means of intervention be applied. However, by the time the supreme power has discovered the seriousness of the problem and resolves to do something about it, a lot of time has been wasted, and the delay inevitably causes considerable economic losses.

The issue, however, comes down to how the supreme policy-making echelon "rectifies" the situation. Only when the policy-makers have fully realized that the emergence and aggravation of disproportionate resource allocation are caused by the second category of economic disequilibrium (that is, incomplete market, inflexible prices and microeconomic agents lacking vitality), and only when they are determined to eradicate this category of disequilibrium, can the "rectification" effort reap real results. If the decision-makers' desire is to reverse the disproportionate resource allocation by noneconomic intervention while leaving this kind of disequilibrium intact, the strains on resource demand and supply can only be relaxed temporarily at best, and the disproportionate resource allocation will become so protracted and complicated as to involve another round of "rectification" or "policy readjustment" after a certain interval. The ultimate result is that unsolved problems grow in number, obstruction become more and more stubborn, the "rectification" effort becomes more and more difficult, and the situation goes from bad to worse.

Possibility Two: When disproportionate resource allocation occurs incessantly and hurts the economy badly, while the government decides not to intervene with noneconomic means, which means it will not work

不到这些信号，或在收到信号之后不可能调整自己的资源投向和资源组合形式，甚至不愿意调整自己的资源投向和资源组合形式。资源配置失调的状况将延续下去，并且越来越严重。那么，最终的结果又将是什么呢？不外乎以下三种情况中的一种：

第一种情况——由于资源配置失调的日趋严重而导致的经济恶化，迫使政府采取非经济的手段来干预经济，扭转资源配置的失调现象。这是一种非市场的制约方式，在第二类非均衡经济中，这种方式的干预（通常被称为"纠偏"、"政策调整"，等等）屡见不鲜。需要指出的是，这里所提到的政府，是指最高决策当局而言。只有在最高决策当局觉察到资源配置失调问题的严重性并且下决心"纠偏"、"调整政策"之后，这种非市场的扭转资源配置失调的方式才有可能被运用。从时间上看，等到最高决策当局觉察到问题的严重性并且下决心"纠偏"、"调整政策"，肯定已有较大的"滞后"，这给经济造成的损失也肯定是相当大的。

问题还在于最高决策当局如何"纠偏"。只有在最高决策当局真正认识到资源配置失调现象的产生及其日益严重的原因在于第二类经济的非均衡（即市场不完善、价格不灵活和微观经济单位缺乏充分活力），并且决心从消除第二类非均衡的措施着手时，这种"纠偏"才能取得真正的效果。否则，如果最高决策当局只是想用某种非经济的干预方式来扭转资源配置失调状况，而又继续保持第二类非均衡经济，那么至多只能暂时缓和一下资源供求的紧张状态，而使得资源配置失调的问题持久化、复杂化，以至于不得不在间隔一段时间之后，再次"纠偏"，再次"调整政策"。不仅如此，最终的结果必定是：问题越积越多，阻力越来越大，"纠偏"越来越困难，"纠偏"所取得的效果也越来越差。

第二种情况——在资源配置失调日趋严重和由此引起的经济恶化的情况下，政府不采取非经济的手段来干预经济，即政府不准备

to reverse the disproportionate resource allocation, the situation will keep worsening. When the problems have accumulated to a point where the conflict between resource demand and supply comes to a head, the economy will suffer from "stagnation," "inflation," or "stagflation," and, in the worst scenario, be pushed to the brink of collapse. Only then can the market's self-restraining role in resource allocation come into play. That is, when the economy is teetering on the verge of collapse, microeconomic agents will be forced to seek a way out. Confronted with a difficult and almost hopeless situation, they have no alternative but to seek a solution on their own through transactions that serve their own interests (or the interests of their workforce).

In this situation, many trading activities between microeconomic agents for their own interests are underground in the second category of disequilibrium. The rapid rise of such an underground market may force those microeconomic agents to pay more dearly for closing deals to their advantage, thus further changing the direction of resource allocation. Nevertheless, the underground market is still a kind of market, where sellers and buyers may bypass the intervention by noneconomic factors and allow transactions to be impacted by the scarcity of commodities and the prices determined by this scarcity (similar to the prices under incomplete competition). Under these circumstances, the market's self-restraining role in resource allocation can work so that sellers and buyers can reach deals under mutually acceptable conditions. In this way, the underground market contributes more or less to alleviating the difficult economic conditions and preventing disproportionate resource allocation from causing a total economic collapse. This seems ironical, but is most likely to happen in the second category of disequilibrium.

Possibility Three: When resource allocation grows increasingly more disproportionate and leads to economic deterioration, the government realizes that the problem is caused by economic disequilibrium and that such disequilibrium manifests itself not just in market incompleteness but, more importantly, in a lack of vitality among microeconomic agents.

Thus the government sets about overhauling the economy institutions while taking steps to revitalize these microeconomic agents and gradually improve market completeness. Meantime, in this reform process, the government also adopts macroeconomic regulatory steps, coordinates

着手扭转资源配置的失调现象。那么这种情况的继续发展，可能带来如下的结果：问题越积越多，当问题积累到一定程度以后，资源供求之间的矛盾充分暴露出来。这时，不仅经济中出现“滞”、“胀”或“滞胀”现象，而且严重的“滞”、“胀”或“滞胀”现象可能使经济处于濒临瘫痪的境地。到了这种场合，也只有到了这种场合，市场在资源配置过程中的自我制约作用才会比较明显地表现出来，这是指：经济的混乱和经济濒临于瘫痪的状况将迫使微观经济单位自谋出路，于是本来缺乏充分活力的微观经济单位在极度困难和几乎绝望的条件下，不得不为了自身的利益（甚至是为了本单位职工的利益），自行通过交易活动而谋求出路。

在第二类非均衡的经济中，这时所出现的微观经济单位之间为自身利益而进行的交易活动，有不少属于地下交易活动。也就是说，地下市场这时将迅速发展起来，地下市场可能使一些微观经济单位为了进行有利于自己的交易而付出昂贵得多的代价，还可能使资源配置的方向进一步扭转。但不管怎样，地下市场毕竟是一种“市场”。在这种“市场”上，供求双方的交易可能摆脱非经济因素的某些干扰，而由商品的稀缺程度以及由此决定的价格（类似于不完全竞争价格）来影响供求双方的交易。市场在资源配置过程中的自我制约作用，在这种“市场”上反而能够表现出来，使供求双方在双方都能接受的条件下成交。地下市场的活动在这种情况下多多少少起着缓解经济困境的作用，使资源配置的失调不至于严重到使整个经济陷于解体的地步。尽管这一切是带有讽刺意味的，但在第二类非均衡的经济中，这种现象却是有可能发生的。

第三种情况——在资源配置失调日趋严重和由此引起的经济恶化的情况下，政府认识到问题的根源在于经济的非均衡，而且认识到经济的非均衡不仅表现于市场的不完善，更重要的是表现于微观经济单位缺少活力，于是政府着手进行经济体制改革，从增加微观经济单位的活力和逐步使市场完善方面采取相应的措施；同时，在经济体制改革过程中，在宏观经济调节方面也采取一些措施，使政府

these steps with market regulations, and strives to ease the strains on resource allocation, thereby directing and combining social resources more appropriately.

Possibility Three is undoubtedly the least probable. When the economy is in the second category of disequilibrium, there is inertia in the economy that will push it closer to Possibility One. Possibility Two is usually not what the government hopes for in the second category of disequilibrium, but it is very probably the economy's spontaneous reaction when government intervention fails and there are no effective methods to control economic chaos. Meanwhile, if the economy moves towards Possibility Two, this may also be caused by the government's ineffectiveness in dealing with severe disproportion of resource allocation and underground trading activity. Possibility Three, however, may become reality only when:

—severely disproportionate resource allocation and economic aggravation awaken the government to the necessity of economic restructuring, especially the need to revive microeconomic agents through such restructuring;

—microeconomic agents, while gradually putting an end to their status as government appendages thanks to the government's effective economic restructuring steps, become motivated to care more about their own gains and losses in response to internal incentive and external pressure;

—at the same time, with the adoption of appropriate macroeconomic regulatory measures by the government, disproportionate resource allocation has been alleviated and the market's self-restraining role has been brought into play;

—and finally, on the basis of results achieved by the government in economic restructuring and regulation, the economy has come under the dual regulation of the market and government, causing a gradual improvement in resource allocation.

Obviously, none of these preconditions can materialize easily. However, under the second category of disequilibrium, of the aforementioned three possible outcomes of lopsided resource allocation, only Possibility Three is worth striving for. If Possibility Three becomes the reality, the second category of disequilibrium will be converted into the first category of disequilibrium. If economic equilibrium is an unrealistic proposition, to convert the second category of disequilibrium into the first category is nothing short of a second best choice.

调节与市场调节较好地结合起来，争取缓和资源配置中的矛盾，使社会的资源投向和资源组合逐渐趋于合理。

毫无疑问，第三种情况的出现并不是很容易的。当经济处于第二类非均衡状态之中时，经济的运动有一种惯性，使最终结果更接近于上述第一种情况。至于第二种情况，通常不是第二类经济的非均衡条件下政府所希望出现的，而很可能是在政府干预无效，对经济的混乱找不到有效的对策时，经济自发地趋向的结果。同时，如果经济趋向第二种情况，那么这也很可能是由于政府既在资源配置严重失调面前无能为力，而又对地下交易活动无能为力的缘故。但第三种情况的出现却需要有一系列前提:

首先，资源配置的严重失调和经济的恶化使政府认识到经济体制改革的必要性，特别是认识到通过经济体制改革，使微观经济单位具有充分活力的必要性。

其次，政府在经济体制改革方面采取了一些有效的措施，使微观经济单位逐渐摆脱原来的作为行政机构附属物的地位，有了内在的动力和外部的压力，关心自己的利益与损失。

再次，与此同时，政府采取适当的宏观经济调节措施，使资源配置的失调状况趋于缓解，使市场的自我制约的作用逐渐发挥出来。

最后，在经济体制改革和政府经济调节都取得成效的基础上，经济中逐渐形成了由市场调节与政府调节共同组成的二元机制，在二元机制起作用的情况下，资源配置状况将会逐渐好转。

可见，这一系列前提中的任何一个前提，都不是轻易能实现的。但在第二类经济的非均衡条件下，如果说资源配置的严重失调最终有三种可能的结果的话，那么惟有第三种结果才值得争取实现。而一旦实现了第三种情况，第二类经济的非均衡就转变为第一类经济的非均衡。如果说经济的均衡缺乏现实性，那么从第二类经济的非均衡过渡到第一类经济的非均衡，即第一类经济的非均衡的实现，仍不失为一种次优的选择。

V. Possible friction between dual mechanisms in the first category of disequilibrium

Market and government mechanisms may work in accord on one occasion and fall into disarray on another in the course of economic development. Inconsistency between the two may well be unavoidable.

The friction that may arise between the dual mechanisms is an issue pertinent to economic disequilibrium. Given the fact that disequilibrium falls into two categories, we should bear each category's attributes in mind when looking into such possible friction. Let us first consider what may happen in the first category of disequilibrium.

The inconsistency between market and government regulation in the first category of disequilibrium is apparent in two ways.

Firstly, if there are both market and government mechanisms in the economy in the first category of disequilibrium, with the former playing a basic regulating role and the latter assuming a regulating role at a higher level, friction may arise between them when supply is in disarray with demand. In this situation, because of market incompleteness, the rise or fall in prices can only slightly ease supply or demand shortfalls, and price changes cannot entirely reach the goals of market regulation. If, at this stage, the government steps in to make up for the deficiencies of market regulation but its regulating steps are at odds with the intention of market regulation, the shortfalls may be eradicated, but market mechanism will be damaged. This is a reflection of the friction between the two mechanisms. In other words, in this situation, government mechanism can work only at the expense of market mechanism—at least to a certain degree.

How should we evaluate the inconsistency or friction between the two mechanisms? We can only evaluate them from their regulatory results. Is it necessary, and worthwhile, for the market mechanism to be damaged, if only to a limited degree? Of course it is always better to rectify the situation in which supply falls short of demand or outstrips demand through government regulation without causing any damage to market mechanism. In that scenario, the two mechanisms are well coordinated and free from friction. But things do not necessarily go that way in reality. Therefore, the inconsistency between the two and the damage caused by government regulation to market mechanism can only

五、第一类非均衡条件下二元机制可能引起的摩擦

在经济运行过程中，市场机制和政府调节机制在某些场合可以保持协调，而在另一些场合，两种机制之间的不协调可能是难以避免的。

为什么在经济运行过程中二元机制的并存可能引起摩擦，这是一个与经济的非均衡状态有关的问题。考虑到经济的非均衡可以区分为第一类非均衡和第二类非均衡，因此在分析二元机制可能引起的摩擦问题时，也要从两类经济非均衡的特点着手。现在先考虑第一类非均衡条件下的情况。

第一类非均衡条件下市场机制与政府调节机制的不协调，主要表现于以下两个方面：

第一，在第一类非均衡条件下，如果经济中同时存在着市场调节和政府调节，并且市场调节作为基础性的调节起作用，政府调节作为高层次的调节起作用，那么两种机制之间可能出现如下的摩擦，即在经济中出现供给小于需求或供给大于需求时，由于市场不完善，所以价格上升或下降以后，货源缺口或市场缺口只是略有缓和，价格的变动不能完全符合市场调节的意图；假定这时进行政府调节，政府采取措施以弥补市场调节的不足，但政府的调节措施却可能同市场调节的意图相违背，这样，尽管货源缺口或市场缺口被消除了，但市场机制却遭到破坏。这就是两种机制的摩擦。换言之，在这种情况下，政府调节机制是以市场机制遭到破坏（至少是一定程度的破坏）作为代价而发挥作用的。

怎样看待两种机制之间的这种不协调或摩擦呢？这只有从调节的效果来评价。市场机制遭到破坏，哪怕只是一定程度的破坏，是不是必要？是不是值得？当然，最好是在不破坏市场机制的情况下，通过政府调节而消除经济中所出现的供给小于需求或供给大于需求的现象，如果那样，两种机制就协调了，就没有什么摩擦了，但现实情况不一定如此。所以说，两种机制之间的不协调以及由此而造成的政府调节对市场机制的某种程度的破坏，只有从调节的

be evaluated from the regulation results. Only by such evaluation can we see if such inconsistency is necessary and worthwhile. However, no matter what happens, friction between the two is highly probable.

Secondly, contrary to the above proposition, market mechanism may also hold back government regulation in the first category of disequilibrium, due directly to an incomplete market, incomplete and untimely information, the failure of prices in regulating supply and demand, and constraints on resource supply and demand. For instance, on certain occasions when the government takes steps to regulate the allocation of resources, these steps may not reach the expected goals because of factors such as incomplete market and incomplete and untimely information. In this scenario, the government hopes to inform market traders of what gains or losses are to be expected from its regulatory steps, in the hope that they will follow their own interests to readjust the allocation and input of their resources. In the meantime, however, the market is also conveying, through its own channels, its information on gains and losses to these traders. As a result of different information accesses and incomplete and delayed information, market mechanism may either accord with the intention of government regulation, which is, of course, the best scenario, or disturb or restrict government regulation. Both possibilities are also reflections on the inconsistency or friction between the dual mechanisms in the course of resource allocation or economic operation.

To sum up, in the first category of disequilibrium, market and government mechanisms may, in their coexistence, be locked in a state of inconsistency, and frictions between them are possible, and, sometimes, even unavoidable.

VI. Possible friction between dual mechanisms in the second category of disequilibrium

The second category of disequilibrium is more serious in degree than the first category. Therefore, the possible friction caused by the coexistence of market and government mechanisms may be more acute than in the first category of disequilibrium. This can be interpreted in three ways.

First, the fact that enterprises are not independent commodity producers or have not put an end to their status as government appendages

效果来评价，才能判断这样做是不是必要，是不是值得。但不管怎样，两种机制的摩擦仍是可能出现的。

第二，与上述情况相反，市场机制的作用的发挥在第一类非均衡条件下也有可能限制政府调节机制发挥其应有的作用。这也是同市场的不完善、信息的不完整和不及时、价格不能起充分调节供求的作用以及资源供给约束或需求约束的存在直接有关的。比如说，在政府采取某些措施对资源的配置进行调节的场合，由于市场不完善、信息不完整和不及时等原因，政府的调节措施不一定能达到预期的效果，在这里，市场调节对政府调节的限制也起着一定的作用。这是因为，政府通过自己的调节措施，把调节后的利益和损失等信息传递给参加市场活动的各个交易者，指望后者根据自己的利益原则来调整自己的资源组合方式和资源投向，而市场本身也从自己的渠道把利益和损失等信息传递给参加市场活动的各个交易者。信息的传递渠道不一致，信息又不是完整的和及时的，这样，市场机制的作用既可能同政府调节的意图相吻合（这当然是理想的），也可能成为对政府调节的一种干扰，从而成为对政府调节作用的一种限制。这同样是资源配置过程中或经济运行过程中两种机制之间的不协调或摩擦的反映。

总之，在第一类非均衡条件下，只要市场机制与政府调节机制并存，那么两种机制就有可能处于不协调状态，它们的摩擦的产生是可能的，有时甚至是难以避免的。

六、第二类非均衡条件下二元机制可能引起的摩擦

第二类非均衡经济的非均衡程度与第一类非均衡条件下的情况相比，是加重了，于是市场机制和政府调节机制共存可能引起的摩擦将大于第一类非均衡条件下可能引起的摩擦。这可以从以下三方面来说明。

第一，由于企业不是独立的商品生产者，企业没有摆脱行政机构

will hold up their efforts to organize production and input resources in compliance with the principle on market interest. Lack of market standards in evaluating enterprise performance inevitably corrodes the efficiency of these enterprises. In this situation, government regulation is unlikely to achieve its expected goals no matter what specific measures are adopted. The main reason for this is that market mechanism is distorted when enterprises are not functioning as independent commodity producers, and the friction between government regulation and the distorted market regulation thus becomes unavoidable.

Second, when enterprises remain government appendages, government regulation on the economy is distorted because the government, for lack of sufficient information on the economic interests of these enterprises, cannot guarantee that every regulation measure it takes is appropriate. Difficulties in coordinating distorted government regulation and distorted market mechanism is another cause of friction between the two.

Third, if supply and demand shortfalls associated with constraints on resource supply and demand occur in the second category of disequilibrium, what are such shortfalls' differences from those in the first category of disequilibrium? In the first category of disequilibrium, these shortfalls can be resolved by balancing the quotas through transactions in incomplete competition according to the market's priority or monopoly principle. The balance of quotas can also be realized through transactions in incomplete competition according to government principles of egalitarianism, goals, and history. No matter what friction this may cause between market and government mechanisms, it is still possible to balance the quotas so long as transactions are conducted in incomplete competition. However, the situation may change in the second category of disequilibrium. This is because enterprises are not independent commodity producers and cannot allocate and input their resources in light of their own economic interests. Thus both market principles regarding priority and monopoly and government principles concerning egalitarianism, goals and history will be distorted and lose their original meanings where enterprises are stripped of their independent interests and cannot transact to their own benefit. Transactions carried out in incomplete competition may not help balance the quotas, and supply or demand shortfalls may remain, or even aggravate. As a result, the friction

附属物的地位，所以要使企业按照市场的利益原则进行生产经营和资源投入，是有阻碍的。企业经营的好坏缺乏市场评价标准的结果，必然导致企业效率低下。这时，无论政府进行什么样的经济调节，都难以达到政府调节预定的效果，主要原因就在于在企业缺乏独立商品生产者地位的前提下，市场机制本身是扭曲的，政府调节与这种扭曲的市场机制之间的矛盾也就不可避免。

第二，不仅如此，假定企业没有摆脱行政机构附属物的地位，政府对企业的利益状况是缺乏了解的，政府所进行的各种经济调节很难建立在合理的基础之上，这样，政府所进行的经济调节也可能是一种扭曲的调节。扭曲了的政府调节与扭曲了的市场机制之间很难协调，这又是造成两种机制的摩擦的原因之一。

第三，假定在第二类非均衡条件下发生了与资源供给约束和需求约束有关的货源缺口和市场缺口，那么这与第一类非均衡条件下所发生的货源缺口和市场缺口有什么区别呢？在第一类非均衡条件下，这些缺口依靠按市场的优先原则、垄断原则等进行的不完全竞争下的交易来实现配额均衡，或者依靠按政府的平均原则、目标原则、历史原则等进行的不完全竞争下的交易来实现配额均衡。不管市场机制与政府调节机制之间存在着什么样的摩擦，只要进行不完全竞争下的交易活动，配额均衡仍是可能实现的。但在第二类非均衡条件下，情况会有所变化。这是因为，企业不是独立的商品生产者，它们不能根据自身的经济利益来组合资源和投入资源。于是市场的优先原则也好，垄断原则也好，或者政府的平均原则、目标原则、历史原则也好，在企业缺乏独立经济利益和不能按自己经济利益进行交易活动的场合，这些原则全都会被扭曲，而与它们本来的含义有较大出入。不完全竞争下的交易未必能实现配额均衡，从而货源缺口或市场缺口可能维持原状，甚至还会有所加剧。于是市场

between market and government mechanisms will be more acute in the second category of disequilibrium than in the first category of it.

VII. Implications of economic operation in the second category of disequilibrium

A clear message from the above analysis is that, on certain occasions, friction between market and government regulation mechanisms are unavoidable in the course of economic operation under either category of disequilibrium. Such is the limitation of the dual mechanisms.

In addition, the fact that friction exists to various degrees between the two mechanisms in the course of economic operation can only point to such a limitation, which means that under disequilibrium no economic operation can follow a perfect course. However, this is not to say the dual mechanisms are unnecessary.

It is worth noting that dual mechanisms will be unnecessary if the economy is in equilibrium and excess demand and supply are nonexistent. However, as we have seen, economic equilibrium is purely a theoretical assumption. In reality, the economy is always in disequilibrium of either the first or second category. The coexistence of dual mechanisms is no wishful thinking, but an objective reality in economic operation. Under economic disequilibrium, and when there are restraints on both resource supply and demand (that is, either supply or demand is in shortage), only by engaging both mechanisms can quotas be balanced through transactions in imperfect competition. Therefore, even though friction is unavoidable between the two mechanisms, the development of the socialist commodity economy will not be seriously held back so long as the dual mechanisms play their normal roles. Needless to say, the economy can run more smoothly in the first category of disequilibrium than in the second. In the second category of disequilibrium, if the friction between the two mechanisms is not handled properly but allowed to aggravate, the socialist commodity economy is bound to be seriously hindered. This further drives home the imminent importance of socialist economic reform to economic development, and the imminent importance of the full vitality of socialist enterprises to smooth economic operation. In other words, the less the economic disequilibrium is, the less serious the friction is between the two mechanisms. However, so long as the economic disequilibrium persists, such friction should never

机制与政府调节机制之间的摩擦就会大于第一类非均衡条件下两种机制可能引起的摩擦。

七、第二类非均衡经济运行分析的意义

通过以上的分析可以清楚地了解到，无论是在第一类非均衡条件下还是在第二类非均衡条件下，在某些场合，经济运行过程中市场机制与政府调节机制之间的摩擦是不可避免的。这可以看成是二元机制的局限性。

经济运行过程中两种机制之间存在着不同程度的摩擦这一事实，实际上也只能说明二元机制的局限性，说明在非均衡条件下经济运行过程不可能尽善尽美。但这并不能证明二元机制是不必要的。

要知道，如果经济处于均衡状态之中，过度需求和过度供给都不存在，那就不需要有二元机制。但正如我们都已经了解的，经济的均衡状态只是纯理论的假设，现实经济中存在着的是经济的非均衡状态（第一类非均衡或第二类非均衡）。二元机制不是我们主观愿望能决定其存在与否的，而是客观上必然存在的经济运行机制。在非均衡条件下，只有通过二元机制的发挥，才能在资源供给约束或需求约束存在（即货源缺口或市场缺口存在的场合，通过不完全竞争下的交易来实现配额均衡。因此，即使市场机制与政府调节机制之间的摩擦不可避免，只要二元机制正常地发挥作用，一般说来，社会主义商品经济的发展是不会受到严重阻碍的。当然，第一类非均衡条件下的经济运行要比第二类非均衡条件下的经济运行顺利得多；在第二类非均衡条件下，如果不善于处理二元机制之间的摩擦，使这种摩擦加剧，那么社会主义商品经济的发展必将受到严重阻碍。这就进一步说明了社会主义经济体制改革对于经济发展的迫切意义，说明了社会主义企业具有充分活力对于经济顺利运行的迫切意义。换言之，经济的非均衡程度越轻，两种机制之间的摩擦就越小，但只要存在经济的非均衡，这种摩擦即使无碍于经济发展

be overlooked even if they do not affect economic development and operation. We can minimize the negative impact of such friction if we see its existence in perspective and take steps to hold it in check.

In all, my analysis of the two categories of disequilibrium and the friction between the two mechanisms in the course of economic operations boils down to three conclusions on the current economic reforms in our country:

Conclusion One: We need to understand that our current economy is not in the first category of disequilibrium, characterized mainly by market incompleteness, but in the second category of disequilibrium, marked in the main by the fact that the market is incomplete and enterprises are yet to become fully vital. Therefore, enterprise reform should be the mainstream of the current economic restructuring, with top priority given to imbuing our enterprises with full vitality. Through this reform, the national economy should accomplish its transition from the second category of disequilibrium to the first category. As much as economic equilibrium is unattainable, it is feasible and worthwhile to shift the economy to the first category of disequilibrium.

Conclusion Two: If, instead of setting enterprise reform as the mainstream of the ongoing economic restructuring, we are bent on bringing the market to completion and decentralizing prices when the economy is still in the second category of disequilibrium and when our enterprises are yet to be fully energized, we will fail to achieve good results, the economy will be crippled, and the already imbalanced resource allocation will be even more imbalanced. The reasons are clear. Just as mentioned in the foregoing, the second category of disequilibrium tends to lock government and market mechanisms in acute friction. With distorted government regulation tangled with distorted market regulation, economic efficiency will be further eroded.

Conclusion Three: Based on the nature of economic disequilibrium, the second category of disequilibrium in particular, the macroeconomic administrative reform should, as part of the current economic restructuring, emphasize promoting the market's self-restraining role in resource allocation, and stress minimizing the friction between market and government regulation in the course of economic operation. If we fail to do these things in the macroeconomic administrative reform, the transition of the national economy from the second category of disequilibrium to the first category will be held back, and supply

和经济运行，也是不可忽略的。认识到它的存在，采取措施去缓和它，就可以减少它的消极作用。

总之，通过对两种类型的非均衡经济以及经济运行中二元机制的摩擦问题的分析，可以得出以下三点有关我国当前经济体制改革的论断。

第一，要认识到当前我国经济并非处于以市场不完善为主要特征的第一类非均衡状态中，而是处于以市场不完善和企业不具有充分活力为主要特征的第二类非均衡状态中。因此，经济体制改革必须以企业体制改革为主线，即以赋予企业充分活力的改革作为首要任务，并通过这一改革，使我国经济由第二类非均衡状态过渡到第一类非均衡状态。在不可能达到均衡状态的前提下，过渡到第一类非均衡状态是可行的、值得的。

第二，假定不以企业体制改革为当前我国经济体制改革的主线，总想在企业尚未具有充分活力的第二类非均衡条件下就进行完善市场和放开价格的改革，不仅不能收到良好的效果，反而会使经济恶化，使资源配置的失调状况加剧。理由是十分清楚的。正如前面所述，在第二类非均衡条件下，政府调节与市场调节之间存在尖锐的摩擦；扭曲了的政府调节和扭曲了的市场调节交织在一起，将使经济的效率进一步降低。

第三，根据经济的非均衡性质，特别是根据第二类经济非均衡的特点，在当前我国经济体制改革中，宏观经济管理体制改革的重点应当放在促进市场对资源配置的自我制约作用方面，以及缓和经济运行过程中市场调节与政府调节的摩擦方面。如果不是循着这些方面进行宏观经济管理体制的改革，结果必然会阻碍我国经济由第二类非均衡向第一类非均衡的过渡，必然会扩大经济中的货源缺口

or demand shortfalls are bound to be exacerbated. This is because the role of government regulation in eradicating supply or demand shortfalls is limited where enterprises cannot make their own business decisions and bear the responsibility for their gains and losses. When enterprises cannot readjust supply and demand according to their own interests the way they should as traders, the balance of quotas the government hopes for will never be achieved. If the government's administrative measures are detrimental to the effort to motivate enterprises in business activity and guide them in readjusting supply and demand in light of their own interests, and if such measures are designed to make up for supply shortfalls merely by reducing demand or to keep supply and demand in temporary balance merely by direct input or distribution, the Chinese economy will continue to languish in the extremely counterproductive second category of disequilibrium.

— *Economic Reference*, issue No. 128, 1988

或市场缺口。这是因为，在企业尚未实现自主经营、自负盈亏的场合，政府调节在消除货源缺口或市场缺口方面发挥作用的机制是受限制的：既然作为交易者的企业不可能按照自己的利益原则来调整自己的供给与需求，政府所希望达到的配额均衡也就难以实现。政府的经济管理措施如果不利于调动企业经营的主动性、积极性，不利于引导企业根据自己的利益来自行调整供给与需求，而只是单纯地用紧缩需求的方式来缩小货源缺口，或者只是单纯地用直接投入和直接分配的方式来实现供求的暂时平衡，那么我国的经济将会持续停留在极不合理的第二类非均衡状态之中。

（原载《经济研究参考资料》，
1988 年第 128 期）

RELATIONSHIP BETWEEN ECONOMIC REFORM, GROWTH AND INDUSTRIAL RESTRUCTURING (1988)

An unanswered question in our nation's economy is how to foster a congenial relationship in which economic reform, growth and industrial restructuring supplement each other, so that the economy can grow effectively in the course of economic reform, a new mechanism for resource allocation can be found through economic growth and industrial restructuring, and the traditional economic system can be converted into a brand new one.

This is no easy mission. The Chinese economy is in a state of disequilibrium. The market is incomplete. Resources are in shortage. Firms are yet to become commodity producers that are motivated by their own interests. Under these circumstances, if we rely mainly on market regulation to decide prices when our firms cannot pursue their own interests, and if the flow of production factors is still hampered by ambiguous property rights, we are courting two dire results. For one thing, prices will rise, market information will be distorted, and our industrial structure, instead of running on an even keel, will become even more lopsided to inhibit future economic growth. For another, if we count mainly on government regulation and allow the government to impose restrictions on prices and quotas on commodities, some industries may grow fast, but the development of other industries will be hindered. Economic growth may be maintained at a certain rate, but because firms are apathetic about improving their efficiency, the establishment of a new resource allocation mechanism will inevitably be delayed or encumbered. As a result, economic growth may only be achieved at the expense of efficiency, while the industrial structure will stay warped for lack of guidance from accurate market information. Such is the sixty-four dollar question for my fellow economists in this nation. This paper is a study of this question starting from a definition of the term "investment principal."

I

Firms are principals in economic growth and industrial restructuring. As the term "principal" is interpreted in the context of "investor," firms must be true interest principals before they can become efficient investors. To put it another way, they must possess independent interests and be concerned with such interests. They invest, and constrain

经济改革、经济增长与产业结构调整之间的关系（1988）

在当前我国的经济生活中，一个有待于解决的研究课题是如何在经济改革、经济增长与产业结构调整三者之间建立一种彼此推进的协调关系，以便既能在经济改革过程中实现有效的经济增长，又能通过经济增长和产业结构调整来建立资源配置的新机制，实现从传统经济体制向新经济体制的转变。

这一任务是艰巨的。当前我国经济处于非均衡状态，市场不完善，资源短缺，而企业还没有成为有真正的利益约束的商品生产者。在这种情况下，假定主要依赖市场机制的作用，让市场定价，那么在企业缺乏利益约束和生产要素的流动仍然受到产权关系不明确的限制的条件下，一方面会造成物价的迅速上涨，市场信号扭曲，从而产业结构不但难以朝着合理化的方向调整，甚至历史上形成的产业结构失调状况会加剧，并会阻碍今后的经济增长；另一方面，假定主要依赖政府调节的作用，即仍由政府实行价格限制和商品配额，那么，在一定程度上有可能促进某些产业部门的较快发展，抑制另一些产业部门产量的增加，并且也有可能维持一定的经济增长率，但由于企业的积极性受到束缚，企业的效率难以提高，因此势必推迟甚至阻碍资源配置新机制的建立，经济增长只可能以牺牲效率作为代价而实现，而产业结构最终不得不因缺少正确的市场信号引导而摆脱不了失调的困境。这就是摆在我国经济学界面前的一个难题。对这个难题，本文准备从投资主体的确定着手进行研究。

一

经济增长的主体是企业，产业结构调整的主体也是企业。这里所说的主体，是指投资主体而言。但要使企业成为有效益的投资主体，必须先使企业成为真正的利益主体。这就是说，企业必须具有自己独立的利益，企业要关心这种利益，企业进行投资是为了实现

themselves in so doing to achieve such interests. If, in formulating policies for economic growth and industrial restructuring, we regard firms as investment principals that have independent interests and are willing to be restrained by such interests, we can blaze a new trail in this field. If we take this as the starting point, corporate institutional reform will become the overriding issue, which entails establishing firms as interest and investment principals, and letting economic growth and industrial restructuring be conditioned and promoted by their investment choices, so as to attain the goal of coordinating economic reform, growth and industrial restructuring in simultaneous development.

Industrial restructuring entails reducing investment in some industries and increasing it in others. The industrial structure embodies both the output ratios and the input ratios between industries. Input circumscribes output, and the input-output ratio also conditions output. The proposition, "let firms become investment principals in industrial restructuring," means two things. First, we should permit firms to act in their own interests when choosing their investment destinations, or when deciding which departments need more investment and which departments need less, and thus to impact the output ratio between industries. Second, we should allow firms to act in their own interests when adjusting the input-output ratio, that is, controlling input and increasing output by raising efficiency. The second meaning is probably more important because only by turning firms into interest principals can they be highly motivated to boost output by improving efficiency. That is a more sensible way to overcome shortfalls in certain commodities when resources are in shortage and input is constrained by circumstances.

From another point of view, to convert firms into investment principals is to turn them into demanders for, or purchasers of, production factors. When a firm acts in its own interests to redirect its investment and modify the way it groups production factors, and influences the sales volumes of products supplied by other firms by adjusting its demand for production factors, it is actually impacting a certain industry's changes in output and scale and leading the way for industrial restructuring. For this reason, when a firm becomes an interest principal, it can in fact moderate industrial restructuring with both its input—resource input and input-output ratio included—and purchases from other firms. The rate of economic growth is ultimately decided

这种利益，企业在投资中自我约束也是为了实现这种利益。如果我们在制定经济增长政策和产 业结构调整政策时，把具有独立利益和接受利益约束的企业作为投资主体来看待，也许可以在这方面走出一条新路。假定以此为出发点，那么首要问题将是企业制度的改革，即赋予企业以利益主体和投资主体的地位，由企业的投资选择来制约经济增长和产业结构调整，促进经济增长和产业结构调整，从而达到经济改革、经济增长、产业结构调整三者协调并进的目标。

产业结构调整实际上就是压缩一些产业部门的投资和增加一些产业部门的投资，产业结构不仅体现于各个不同部门的产出比例，而且体现于各个不同部门的投入比例。投入制约着产出，投入与产出之比也制约着产出。“让企业成为产业结构调整的投资主体”这句话，具有两个含义：第一，企业根据自己的利益而选择投资方向，决定增加对哪些部门的投入，减少对哪些部门的投入，并由此影响产业部门之间的产出比例；第二，企业根据自己的利益而调整投入与产出之比，也就是通过效率的提高来制约投入，增加产出。这两个含义中，第二个含义可能更加重要。这是因为，只有让企业成为利益主体，企业通过提高效率来增加产出的积极性才能有较大幅度的提高。在资源短缺和投入受到客观限制的条件下，这将是克服某些商品短缺的更为合理的途径。

从另一个角度来看，企业作为投资主体，也就是意味着企业作为生产要素的需求主体或购买主体。当企业根据自己的利益调节投资方向和生产要素组合方式时，通过对生产要素的需求的调整而影响其他企业提供的产品的销售量，这样也就从客观上影响一些产业部门的产量和规模的变化，引导着产业结构的调整方向。因此，在企业成为利益主体时，企业既从自己的投入（包括投入的资源数量以及投入与产出之比）方面，又从自己对其他企业提供的产品的购买方面制约着产业结构调整。经济增长率归根到底是由每一个企业

by each firm's output growth rate. Economic growth and industrial restructuring are part of the same process once firms can maintain their output growth through industrial reform. When firms with independent interests become principals of economic growth, they also become principals of industrial restructuring.

II

When we regard firms as investment principals and put a premium on the role they can play in industrial restructuring through their investment and purchase choices, we must take into account the fact that they are engaged in economic activity under economic disequilibrium, and that the incomplete market and resource shortfalls invariably affect their investment and purchase decisions. In so doing, we will recognize the paramount role of the government in industrial restructuring. The greater the degree of economic disequilibrium, the more important the role of the government becomes in industrial restructuring.

The government is duty-bound to support nonprofit investment projects, a duty that is directly related to its nature. Under no circumstances should the government shun its responsibility for this field of investment. This point is self-evident, and no more proof is needed. The question to be discussed here is what, supposing the market is incomplete and resources are in short supply, the government should do as the economic regulator to influence firms' investment and purchase choices, and further impact industrial restructuring and put it on a sound footing. A fundamental answer to this question lies in the government's capacity to balance its quotas.

Balanced government quotas are achievable through the goals principle, the principle of averages, or the principle of historical ratios. Because each of these principles is limited in its scope of application and has its drawbacks, the government should choose between them on the basis of study and investigation.

The goals principle guides the government to allot quotas for the limited resources to be sold to industries in order of priority and urgency. This way of distributing resources helps implement government goals for economic growth and economic restructuring, boosts growth in some industries and restrains it in some other industries. But it also poses some questions. Is the alignment of the industries in order of priority and urgency scientifically viable? Can the ratios between the quotas on scarce

的产出增长率决定的，既然企业的产出增长率总是在产业结构调整过程中实现，所以经济增长与产业结构调整将是同一个过程。具有独立利益的企业在作为经济增长主体的同时，也就成为产业结构调整的主体。

二

当我们把企业看作投资主体并且重视企业的投资选择与购买选择在产业结构调整中的作用时，应当考虑到企业是在非均衡条件下进行经济活动的，市场的不完善和资源供给的短缺不可避免地会对企业的投资选择与购买选择发生有力的影响。这样，我们就不可能忽视政府在产业结构调整中的重要作用。经济的非均衡程度越大，政府在产业结构调整中所起的作用也越重要。

政府要对非盈利性的投资项目承担责任，这是与政府的性质直接有关的。在任何情况下，政府也不应当回避这方面的投资责任。关于这一点，几乎不需要再作论证了。现在需要探讨的是，假定市场不完善和资源供给短缺，政府作为经济调节者，究竟应当如何影响企业的投资选择与购买选择，进而影响产业结构的调整，使之趋向合理化？这主要是通过政府的配额均衡而实现的。

政府的配额均衡可以通过目标原则，或平均原则，或历史比例原则来实现，每一个原则都有一定的适用范围，每一个原则也都可能出现弊端，因此，政府在何种情况下采取何种原则，应当根据具体条件进行研究，然后作出决定。

目标原则是指政府根据产业部门的重要程度而制定轻重缓急的顺序，把有限的资源配售给各个有关的部门。这种分配资源的方式有利于贯彻政府预定的经济增长目标和产业结构调整目标，并且能够较快地促进某些产业部门的增长，限制另一些部门的增长。但问题是：产业部门发展的轻重缓急顺序的排列是否科学？能不能使

rescources be set in a way to make possible the simultaneous attainment of economic growth goals and those for industrial restructuring? Do the quotas measure up to benchmarks for resource utilization efficiency? Is there any way to prevent industries from putting the resources allotted to them to other uses or reselling them for a profit? In a sense, the side effect of the goals principle (even if it is scientifically viable) is that it may give preference to industries and firms with low efficiency, to the neglect of truly efficient industries and firms whose efficiency may be curbed by resource shortages. In this regard, the balance of government quotas under the goals principle (even if it is scientifically viable) is maintained at the expense of resource utilization efficiency unless measures are taken so that resources can be reallocated among industries, and firms can change their line of production.

The principle of averages directs the government to distribute resources equally among industries according to the aggregate demand of firms and the availability of such resources. This principle may become an impediment to achieving the government's industrial restructuring goals, as it serves basically to maintain the status quo of the industrial structure. However, from the perspective of sustaining economic growth, quota allocation under the principle of averages will not go so far as to cause dramatic fluctuations in the economic growth rate. Moreover, judging from the supply and demand of daily necessities, the principle of averages helps maintain social stability when limited resources are distributed according to it. Under this principle, resource utilization efficiency tends to drop, but such a drop is ascribed mainly to universal shortages in the supply of resources rather than to changes in the industrial structure (because, as a matter of fact, such a structure basically remains unchanged).

The historical ratios principle guides the government to allot resource quotas to be distributed among industries or firms in line with distribution ratios that have been followed for a long time in the past. This principle works in a way similar to the principle of averages, that is, by maintaining the status quo of the industrial structure and avoiding major fluctuations in the economic growth rate. However, it also poses some questions: Are the historical ratios—the cornerstone of this principle—reasonable or not? Is there any guarantee that the resources distributed to industries and firms are not put to other uses or resold for a profit? Now that it is impossible not to adapt historical quotas to reality,

有限资源配售的比例有助于经济增长目标与产业结构调整目标同时实现？这样的资源配额是否符合资源利用的效率标准？能不能保证配售到某一产业部门的资源不被挪作他用，不被转卖牟利？从某种意义上说，目标原则的副作用在于：它使某些部门和企业处于特殊照顾之下，而这些部门和企业却不一定是高效率的；至于另一些部门和企业，实际上被排除在资源供给以外了，尽管它们是高效率的，但由于资源不足而不得不使效率降低。因此，如果只有配额的目标原则（即使目标原则的确定是科学的），而没有促进部门间资源存量转移的措施和促进企业转产的措施，目标原则下的配额均衡将以社会的资源利用效率下降作为代价。

平均原则是指政府根据需求者所提出的需求数量和可供给的资源数量进行平均分配。从调整产业结构的角度来看，平均原则可能是阻碍政府预定的产业结构调整目标的实现的，因为这样做意味着基本上维持产业结构的现状；但从维持经济增长的角度来看，平均原则下的配额均衡不至于导致经济增长率的较大幅度的波动。加之，就居民生活必需品的供求而言，按平均原则来分配有限的资源仍然有着维持社会安定的作用。在平均原则之下，社会的资源利用效率也是会降低的，但这种降低应当主要归咎于资源供给的普遍不足，而不一定是改变产业部门结构所引起的（因为产业结构基本维持现状）。

历史比例原则是指政府根据历史上已经形成的或过去一贯沿用的资源分配比例来确定部门间或企业间的资源配额。用这种办法来分配有限的资源，其效应与采用平均原则相似，即基本上维持产业结构的现状，同时又可以避免经济增长率发生较大幅度的波动。但问题是：历史比例原则的确定既然以既成的资源分配比例为依据，那就涉及既成的资源分配比例的合理程度究竟如何。同样地，在这种情况下，能不能保证分配到一定的部门和企业中的资源不再被挪

how can distribution quotas be reset when and where such a need arises?

It is thus clear that when resource shortfalls necessitate distribution quotas, the government is faced with the arduous task of attaining both economic growth and industrial restructuring goals without discouraging firms in business activity and hurting resource utilization efficiency. Such quotas should be scientifically viable whether they are arranged in order of priority and importance, evened out, or according to established ratios. First of all, only with viable quotas can errors and conflicts be minimized while limited resources are dispensed. Then, no matter which principle is followed, everything should be done to forestall scarce resources leakage, i.e., the resale of scarce resources allotted from one industry or firm to another.

A compromise between these three principles may be reached to help balance distribution quotas under government regulation. Of the trio, the goals principle is relatively more conducive to the government's industrial restructuring goals; the historical ratios principle works better to sustain economic growth and minimize fluctuations in the economic growth rate; while the principle of averages helps more in reducing conflicts of interests and keeping firms motivated. To give full scope to the role of coordinated government quotas in industrial restructuring, we may as well take the goals principle as the guideline and draw on the historical ratios principle and the principle of averages when setting ratios for the distribution of scarce resources.

III

Economic growth amidst resource shortage is relevant to government quotas for distributing such resources between industries. If such resources are allotted according to the goals principle, economic growth is bound to take place in the course of industrial restructuring, whereas the economic growth achieved in the course of industrial restructuring is inevitably of a "tilting type," a byword for uneven economic growth.

The issue here involves judgment of the value of this type of uneven economic growth. Economic growth, whatever type it is, is attained in a real-world economic environment. We may regard this environment as the initial condition for economic growth. The economy invariably

作他用，不再被转卖给其他部门和企业而牟利？还有，历史比例不可能不根据实际情况而有所调整，如果要调整历史比例的话，那么怎样重新制定有限资源的配额？

由此看来，在资源供给不足从而有必要由政府采取配额的情况下，既要兼顾经济增长与产业结构调整目标，又要不挫伤企业经营的积极性，不使企业的资源利用效率下降，这的确是一个相当艰巨的任务。不管政府按照哪一种原则来实行配额，目标配额的制定（即产业部门重要程度顺序的排列）、平均配额的制定、历史比例配额的制定，首先，必须具有科学性，只有科学地制定这些配额，才能尽量减少政府配额过程中的差错和矛盾。其次，无论在哪一种原则之下，都应当防止短缺资源的渗漏现象的发生，也就是要防止被分配到一定部门和企业中的短缺资源转卖给其他的部门和企业。

一种折中的做法是兼取三种原则，实现政府调节下的配额均衡。三种原则之中，比较有利于达到政府预定产业结构调整目标的是目标原则；比较有利于维持经济增长，较少地导致经济增长率发生较大幅度波动的是历史比例原则；较少引起需求各方之间的摩擦，并且较少地挫伤所有企业的积极性的是平均原则。这样，要发挥非均衡条件下政府的配额均衡在产业结构调整中的作用，不妨以目标原则为主，兼顾历史比例原则和平均原则的特点，制定一种综合地确定短缺资源分配比例的办法。

三

资源短缺条件下的经济增长与短缺的资源在部门间的配额有关。假定在短缺资源的分配中主要依据的是目标原则，那么这时的经济增长必定是在产业结构调整过程中实现的，而产业结构调整过程中所实现的经济增长也必定是倾斜式的经济增长，即经济的不平衡增长。

这里涉及对于经济不平衡增长的价值判断问题。任何经济增长都是在一定的经济现实环境中出发的，我们可以把这种现实环境称作经济增长的初始状态。任何经济增长，在经历一定的时间之后，

reaches a certain anticipated economic level after a certain period of growth, and we may regard this anticipated economic level as the condition for end-of-period growth. Whether the economy is balanced or not, economic growth cannot be evaluated without taking its initial and end-of-period conditions into consideration. If the industrial structure is well coordinated at both stages of economic growth, then balanced economic growth is obviously the ideal. In this case, uneven economic growth is probably unnecessary or even detrimental to the attainment of the anticipated goals for coordinating the industrial structure. However, when the current Chinese economy is at the initial stage of disequilibrium and the industrial structure is already gravely lopsided, to strive for balanced economic growth not only is unrealistic but also contravenes the task of restoring economic equilibrium through optimal distribution of scarce resources. Therefore, our judgment of the merits or demerits of disequilibrium in economic growth should not be estranged from reality.

Whether the government's anticipated goals for economic growth and industrial restructuring can be reached as a result of imbalanced economic growth through quota rationing is determined, first of all, by whether the government industrial policy is scientifically viable or not, and secondly, by the determination with which this policy is carried out. If the government relinquishes its industrial policy and allows the market to run the economy completely, economic growth may be achieved and the industrial system restructured only when the market is relatively complete and firms are operating in accordance with their own interests. Even so, progress in industrial restructuring may be tardy because it always takes numerous transactions in which resources change hands numerous times before the market clears (that is, through spontaneous distribution of scarce resources or spontaneous division of the limited market). Given the current situation in our nation, an incomplete market and the failure of firms to assert their own interests make it hard for resources to be spontaneously redirected, and the results of market regulation of quotas are not necessarily in accord with prescribed government goals for economic growth and industrial restructuring. Thus the government needs to formulate its industry-prioritizing policy and proceed from this policy to achieve imbalanced economic growth under balanced government quotas.

This industry-prioritizing policy is, indeed, a tilted one. However, it should be noted that no leading industry can do without the assistance

总会达到某个预期的经济境界，我们可以把这种预期的境界称作经济增长的阶段终点。在评价经济的平衡增长与不平衡增长时，既不能脱离经济增长的初始状态，也不能脱离经济增长的阶段终点。假定初始状态是产业结构协调的，而预期的经济增长阶段终点也是产业结构协调的，那么经济的平衡增长显然是理想的增长途径。在这段时间内，经济的不平衡增长也许是不必要的，甚至还可能不利于预定的产业结构协调目标的实现。然而，在当前我国经济处于非均衡状态初始点上的产业结构已经出现严重失调的情况下，经济的平衡增长既缺乏可行性，又不符合短缺资源配额均衡经济增长的要求。因此，对于经济不平衡增长的是与非，不应当脱离实际而作出判断。

政府配额均衡条件下的经济不平衡增长的结果，究竟能否达到政府预定的经济增长目标与产业结构调整目标，与政府制定的主导产业政策的科学性有关，也与这一主导产业政策被贯彻的程度有关。假定政府不制定任何主导产业政策，一切听任市场调节来自发地形成经济中的主导产业，虽然其结果也有可能既实现经济增长，又调整了产业结构，但这通常以市场比较完善和企业具有利益约束为前提。即使如此，产业结构调整过程也可能相当缓慢，因为一旦出现了货源有限或市场有限等情况，通过市场自身的配额调节（短缺资源的自发分配或有限市场的自发分割）总是在无数次交易活动和资源转移之后才达到预期效果。就当前我国的实际情况来说，由于市场不完善和企业仍然缺乏利益约束，资源部门间的自发转移有困难，市场配额调节的结果不一定与政府预定的经济增长目标、产业结构调整目标相吻合，从而由政府制定主导产业政策，并根据这一政策来实现政府配额均衡下的经济不平衡增长，就显得十分必要。

主导产业政策是一种倾斜式的产业政策。但应当注意到，任何主导产业都需要有其他若干产业与之配合，而与主导产业直接有关

of several other industries that are themselves tied with even more industries. This being the case, if the government chooses to carry out such a tilted industrial policy, this policy can allot quotas for scarce resources among industries only according to how closely they are associated with the leading industry. Such a policy cannot be tipped in favor of only one or several industries to the neglect of the other related industries. That is to say, in economic disequilibrium, the bias of this tilted industrial policy should be kept within reasonable bounds if the government has no alternative but to count on quota rationing to bring about imbalanced economic growth and to concentrate resources on leading industries for industrial restructuring purposes. It should never be overdone. Otherwise, instead of spurring the leading industries, it may only sustain or aggravate the lopsided industrial structure.

As the above analysis indicates, the argument on economic growth is not about which is supposedly better, balanced growth or imbalanced growth. Given that the initial state of economic growth is characterized by a disproportionate industrial structure, the argument is unavoidably focused on the degree of imbalance in economic growth, that is, on the degree of bias of the tilted industrial policy. An over-tilted industrial policy is more harmful than an unbiased one in that it may exaggerate the already warped industrial structure. When the initial state of economic growth is characterized by a lopsided industrial structure, balanced economic growth may help maintain the status quo of the industrial structure and prevent it from further deterioration, even though it cannot completely redress its lopsidedness. This is a point the government should keep in mind when making its industry-prioritizing policy.

Now the issue comes down to how the government applies its industry-prioritizing policy and whether it can keep the prejudice of this policy within bounds. To find the answers, I deem it necessary to look into the roles of the corporate operational mechanism and price signals in the course of executing the policy.

IV

The industry-prioritizing policy is formulated and enacted by the government. Generally speaking, dystopian government behavior generates a disparity between this policy and the government's anticipated goals for economic growth and industrial restructuring. Because it is hard for the government to tilt this policy with absolute precision, something has to be done to restrain such a tilt. Such restraints

的其他若干产业又分别与更多的产业联系在一起。这样，即使政府实行的是倾斜式的产业政策，这种政策也只能按照与主导产业关系的密切程度来实行短缺资源的配额，而不可能倾斜到只顾某一个或少数几个产业而忽略其他有关产业的地步。这意味着，在非均衡条件下，如果说政府惟有通过配额均衡来实现经济的不平衡增长，集中较多的资源发展主导产业，以调整产业结构的话，那么产业政策的这种倾斜只能适度，而不应当过分，否则不仅不能加速主导产业的成长，反而有可能导致产业结构失调现象的延续或加剧。

通过以上的分析，可以清楚地了解到，关于经济增长的平衡与不平衡之争实际上并非如通常所说的，究竟是不平衡增长优越还是平衡增长优越。既然增长的初始状态是产业结构失调，那么争论的焦点就不可避免地成为经济增长的不平衡程度之争，也就是产业政策的倾斜度之争。过度倾斜的害处大于完全没有倾斜。经济的过分不平衡增长可能加剧产业结构的失调；而在经济增长的初始状态表现为产业结构已经失调时，经济的平衡增长虽然无助于产业结构失调现象的消除，但较为可能的是基本上维持产业结构现状，而不一定使之加剧、恶化。这正是在政府制定主导产业政策时需要注意的。

于是，问题归结为政府究竟如何运用主导产业政策，如何使产业政策的倾斜适度。为了说明这一点，有必要考察一下企业运行机制和价格信号在主导产业政策实施过程中的作用。

四

主导产业政策是由政府制定并由政府推行的。政府行为的非理想化使得政府所制定和推行的主导产业政策同政府预定要达到的经济增长与产业结构调整目标之间存在一定的差距。政府很难使得产业政策的倾斜恰到好处，这样就需要有一种力量对产业政策倾斜

do not come from the government itself but, in the main, from firms that are investment and interest principals.

If firms cannot put an end to their status as government appendages, and fail to base their investment choices on their immediate and anticipated interests, they can never react properly to changes in supply and demand if the government industrial policy becomes over-tilted. The lopsided industrial structure aggravated by an overly tilted industrial policy, as well as the growing deficiency in the supply of some commodities and the demand for other commodities, can be remedied only when the problems have come to a head and alerted the government. Enormous losses occur simply because the government cannot address the issues timely. And the consequence does not stop just there. Because the bias of the tilted industrial policy is related to the government's rationing of scarce resources, firms lacking constraints on their interests may profiteer by taking advantage of that policy. They may use the resources in short supply to produce commodities not badly needed on the market or engage in nonproductive profiteering activities. In that way, they can only exacerbate lopsided government rationing, instead of curbing it, thereby making scarce resources even scarcer.

If, contrary to the intention of the government industrial policy, the aforementioned phenomena occur, and if the government fails to pinpoint firms' lack of independent interests as the key to the problem, the government is likely to believe that all this was caused by unreasonable pricing or the double-track price system. That misjudgment may compel the government to abolish the double-track prices and decentralize them in an attempt to rectify the badly warped industrial structure and eradicate shortages in commodity supply and demand. Theoretically speaking, this way of doing things is not groundless, because correct price signals can direct the flow of resources to areas needed by the market, and firms' flexible reaction to such signals can lead them to shift production to commodities in short supply and their investment to weak links of the economy, thereby hastening the effort to balance the industrial structure. However, this behavior is totally disagreeable to an economy under disequilibrium. If the government chooses to do so, it can accomplish nothing but to further damage the industrial structure and drive the economy deeper into chaos. The central problem here is that firms that cannot make their own business decisions

过度进行制约。这种制约的力量不是来自政府本身，主要来自作为投资主体和利益主体的企业。

假定企业没有摆脱行政机构附属物的地位，依然缺乏利益的约束并且不能根据自己的现实利益和预期利益来选择投资机会，毫无疑问，当政府的产业政策严重倾斜（即过度倾斜）时，企业对于由此引起的市场供求比例的变化不可能作出反应。产业政策的过度倾斜所加剧了的产业结构失调，以及具体表现出来的某些商品供给缺口增大和另一些商品需求缺口增大，只有等到问题积累到一定程度，等到政府自己发现它们的严重性了，才有可能纠正过来。但这往往需要较长的滞后期，国民经济因此而受到的损失将是巨大的。不仅如此，由于产业政策的倾斜与政府对短缺资源的配额联系在一起，在企业缺乏利益约束的情况下，企业甚至有可能利用产业政策的倾斜过度来为自己牟利，如利用短缺资源去发展并非市场所急需的生产，或利用短缺资源进行非生产性的盈利活动。其结果，不但不是对产业政策倾斜过度的制约，反而会加剧不合理的产业政策的倾斜，加剧短缺资源的短缺程度。

如果客观上发生上述这些与政府在制定倾斜的产业政策时所预计的情况相违的现象，而政府又不把企业缺乏利益约束视为问题的症结所在，那么政府很可能作出一种错误的判断，即认为这一切主要是由价格的不合理或双轨价格的存在所引起的。于是政府试图以取消双轨价格制和放开价格来纠正产业结构的严重失调，消除商品供给缺口和需求缺口。从理论上说，这样做似乎是有根据的，因为价格信号的正确将导致资源流向市场所需要的领域，企业对价格信号的灵活反应将导致企业转而生产短缺商品，转而投资于经济中的薄弱环节，促进产业结构的合理化。但这与非均衡条件下的实际情况完全不符。假定政府这样做，所带来的恰恰是产业结构的进一步失调和经济的进一步混乱。关键仍在于：尚未自主经营、自负盈亏

and bear the responsibility for their gains and losses cannot become true interest principals to play a part in industrial restructuring.

As the above analysis illustrates, the lopsided industrial structure characterized by resource shortage in the initial stage of economic growth is an established fact, and so are the incomplete market and firms' lack of independent interests. With resources in shortage, rationing is imperative either by the government or the market. The double-track prices mean both government and market are rationing the scare resources. Government quotas are realized according to the goals principle, the principle of averages, or the principle of historical ratios. If the government decides to replace double-track prices with sole market prices, government quotas must be lifted, and scarce resources put at the mercy of the market. Then the market can allocate resources on a "first come, first served" basis or in line with the monopoly principle. No matter which principle the market chooses, the fact that the market is incomplete, that firm property rights remain ambiguous and that firms lack independent interests will curtail price elasticity in both supply and demand. The economy will end up with two new prices, i.e., open market prices and black market prices. The price gap between open and black markets inevitably sends prices on one round of hiking after another. This is exactly what happens in the Chinese economy under disequilibrium, a situation that does nothing but aggravate the lopsided industrial structure.

If the government takes into consideration the fact that the economy is in disequilibrium and that firms are yet to become independent commodity producers, and if the government is mindful of its goals for effective industrial restructuring, it should never decontrol prices and abolish the double-track prices. On the contrary, the government, while going on with quota rationing, should define firm property rights, transform their operational mechanism, and rely on their self-restraints to prevent the industrial policy from being overly tilted.

V

When firms become investment and interest principals, they will be able to restrain themselves in investment and operation. This self-restraining ability, once linked with firms' operational mechanisms, will help prevent the government industrial policy from becoming overly tilted. This is because firms will be capable of adjusting the direction and

的企业不可能成为真正起作用的产业结构调整的利益主体。

如上所述，资源短缺和初始状态中的产业结构失调是既成事实，市场不完善和企业缺乏利益约束也是既成事实。在资源短缺的前提下，配额均衡是不可避免的：不是由政府来实行配额，就是由市场来实行配额。价格双轨制意味着既有政府实行的配额，又有市场实行的配额，而政府实行的配额将根据目标原则（或平均原则，或历史比例原则）付诸实现。如果政府决定在这种形势下把价格双轨制转变为市场单一定价制，那就意味着取消政府的配额，而让短缺资源完全由市场来实行配额：市场或者按照“谁先来，谁先买”的优先原则分配，或者按照垄断原则分配。但无论市场按照什么原则来分配短缺资源，只要市场仍然是不完善的，企业产权关系仍然不明确和企业仍然缺乏利益约束，那么供给价格弹性较小和需求价格弹性较小的事实必然导致新的两种价格并存，即公开的市场价格与地下的市场价格（黑市价格）的并存。公开的市场价格与地下的市场价格你追我赶，始终保持某种差距，结果导致价格的轮番上涨。这正是我国经济处于非均衡状态下的实际情况。它不仅无助于缓和产业结构失调，而且只会使产业结构失调加剧。

政府如果考虑到经济的非均衡状态，考虑到企业尚未成为独立商品生产者这一客观事实，那么从有效地调整产业结构的目标着眼，绝不能在条件不成熟时放开价格和取消价格双轨制；而只能在保持政府配额的同时，确定企业的产权，改造企业运行机制，并依靠企业的自我约束来制约产业政策倾斜的过度。

五

企业作为投资主体和利益主体，将具有投资与经营的自我约束力；而这种与企业运行机制联系在一起的企业自我约束力，将成为对于政府的产业政策倾斜过度的一种制约。这是因为，企业是按照

amount of their investment under the guidance of their own interests. If the industrial policy is overly tilted towards a certain industry under the double-track price system, firms may react in two ways.

Firstly, they may accept market quotas, that is, to adopt market prices that are higher than government-mandated prices to produce commodities that accord with their interests and are in short market supply, thereby making up for supply shortages resulting from the government's excessively tilted industrial policy. Naturally, firms may run certain investment and business risks if they choose to react this way. As interest principals, however, they are not only entitled to do so but also willing to run such risks because risks accompany profits. Profits are enough of a motivation for them to take this course of action.

Secondly, firms may choose not to accept market quotas mainly because, proceeding from their own interests, they believe the market has so overpriced the resources as to expose them to excessive investment and business risks. Then the lack of government quotas invariably will prompt firms to change their business scale and scope by altering their line of production, stopping production, reducing output, seeking mergers, or setting up joint ventures. This will cause production factors to flow, and the resources to be regrouped, among industries or firms. As such flow and regrouping are driven by firms' own interests, it will help make up for product shortages resulting from the seriously tilted government industrial policy.

Both possible reactions to the government's tilted industrial policy help make up for product shortages resulting from that policy. Both reactions point to firms' intention to restrain themselves to curb resource misallocation caused by the overly tilted government industrial policy. Their self-restraining action can also restrain the tilted government policy in another fashion. That is, when they react in either way, the market situation will change to a certain extent, thereby forcing the government to stop tipping the industrial policy overly in favor of certain industries and revise its over-concentrated quota plans.

For example, if firms react in the first way, that is, if they purchase capital goods from the market at prices higher than government-mandated prices to produce certain commodities in short market supply,

自己的利益趋向而进行投资方向的变动和投资数量的调整的。如果政府产业政策的倾斜过度，在双轨价格条件下，企业将面临以下两种选择。

第一种选择是，企业宁肯接受市场配额，即利用高于固定价格的市场价格来生产既符合自己的利益，又适应市场需要的短缺产品。这样就可以弥补政府产业政策倾斜过度而导致的该种商品的短缺。当然，当企业作出这种选择时，企业要冒一定的投资风险和经营风险。但企业作为利益主体，它不仅有权这样做，并且也愿意承担这些风险。伴随着企业投资风险和经营风险而来的，将是企业的盈利。有了盈利的动力，企业是有可能作出这种选择的。

第二种选择是，由于政府的产业政策倾斜过度而导致政府配额过于集中，但企业又不愿接受市场配额（这主要是由于企业从自身利益出发，感觉到市场配额的价格过高，从而投资风险和经营风险过大）。这样，政府配额的不足必将导致企业改变生产规模和生产方向，包括企业转产、停产、减产、与其他企业合并或联营等等。由此涉及生产要素的流动和资源在部门间、企业间的重新组合。生产要素的流动和资源重新组合以企业自身的利益为指导，而企业的利益又以市场的实际需要为转移，于是也就有助于弥补政府的产业政策倾斜过度而导致的某些商品的短缺。有了盈利的动力，企业也会作出这种选择。

无论企业作出第一种选择还是第二种选择，其结果首先是有助于弥补政府产业政策倾斜过度而导致的某种短缺。这可以被看成是企业的自我约束对于产业政策倾斜过度的一种制约。除此以外，还存在着企业的自我约束对于产业政策倾斜过度的另一种制约。这就是在企业作出上述任何一种选择之后，市场形势都会发生一定的变化，从而促使政府改变原来的产业政策过度倾斜的做法，修正过于集中的配额方案。

比如说，假定企业作出第一种选择，从市场上用高于固定价格的价格来购买生产资料，生产市场所需要的短缺商品。这样，市场上该种生产资料的供给量将增加，而企业所生产出来的该种短缺

it will increase the supply of the related capital goods, and reduce the prices of the commodities being produced. The government will receive a certain signal from these firms when it allots quotas on the capital goods and commodities in question. Upon discovering that its original quota plans—that is, the over-concentrated plans made under the overly tilted industrial policy—can no longer work, the government is likely to adapt those plans to the new market situation.

If firms react in the second way, that is, if they cope with over-concentrated government quotas through the flow of production factors and the regrouping of resources, the supply of certain commodities in shortage will be increased, and the market situation will be changed. When the government has received such a signal, it is likely to readjust its quotas in response.

It is thus clear that balanced government quotas can help straighten out the industrial structure only when firms have ended their status as government appendages and become independent commodity producers that make their own business decisions and bear the responsibility for their gains and losses. Only thus can time-consuming delays be avoided in addressing an industrial structure warped by inappropriate distribution of government quotas. On the other hand, if the government counts on abolishing the double-track prices to improve the industrial structure without overhauling the nature and function of firms, the result will be contrary to its intentions.

All this illustrates the essential relationship between economic reform, growth and industrial restructuring under economic disequilibrium. In short, if effective corporate institutional reform cannot happen in the first place, it will be almost impossible for the nation to achieve present and future economic growth and industrial restructuring goals.

— *Quantitative & Technical Economics,* issue No. 12, 1988

商品的价格将下降。这将给予实行该种生产资料配额和该种短缺商品配额的政府以一定的信号，使政府感到自己原来制定的配额方案（即产业政策倾斜过度，配额过于集中的方案）已与新的市场形势不相适应了，于是政府就有可能调整配额来适应新的市场形势。

假定企业作出第二种选择，即企业通过生产要素的流动和资源的重新组合来应付政府原定的配额过于集中问题，那么生产要素流动和资源重新组合的结果将会导致市场上某些短缺商品供给量的增加，引起市场形势的变化。当政府接收到这种信号以后，也会重新考虑原来的配额方案，从而根据新的市场形势进行配额的调整。

由此可见，只有企业从作为行政附属物的地位转到自主经营、自负盈亏的独立商品生产者的地位，政府的配额均衡才有助于产业结构的合理化，才能避免因政府配额不当而造成产业结构失调迟迟不能解决的情况发生。反之，如果政府在企业体制未变的条件下，指望用取消双轨价格来协调产业结构，那就只能得到与政府的预定目标相反的结果。

这一切充分说明了非均衡状态中的经济改革、经济增长、产业结构调整三者之间的关系的实质。简言之，如果不首先进行有效的企业体制改革，经济增长与产业结构调整这两个目标不仅难以实现，而且会给以后的经济增长与产业结构调整造成困难。

（原载《数量经济技术经济研究》，1988 年第 12 期）

LAYING A SOLID FOUNDATION FOR NEW CULTURE (1989)

The topic of my speech today is the relationship between economic reform, new public ownership and a new culture. In my opinion, when we clarify the relationship between these three things, we will gain a better idea about the significance of and prospects for the economic reform that has been going on in our country for a whole decade, and find it a lot easier to understand the trials and tribulations our nation has gone through in the course of it.

I. The study of people

In studying economic issues we are obliged to face certain questions. What is the purpose of growing the economy? For whom do we provide products, labor, and service? Why should we turn out more and more products and provide more and more labor and service? These questions boil down to one: What is the purpose of production? Common sense tells us that production *per se* is not the purpose. Human beings do not live in the world merely as laborers. People do not come into this world to serve production—it is production that serves people. The purpose of production is for people to be better cared for and better educated. It defeats the purpose of production if we concentrate single-mindedly on offering more products while our standard of living and cultural and educational attainments remain the same, and if our people are not duly respected and cannot live up to their potentials.

Based on this plain and simple line of reasoning, we may define economics this way: Economics should not be limited to learning how to increase material wealth, but more importantly, it should study how to use the wealth created by people to meet their needs in their material and cultural lives. The highest level, or focus, of economic research is not material products, but people.

Based on this plain and simple line of reasoning, we can understand the meaning of the ongoing economic reform. Economic reform serves not merely to put the Chinese in possession of more products. More importantly, it is designed for them to achieve affluence and better cultural and educational endowment, and to be looked after, educated and respected as society's masters. From this perspective, it is clearly inadequate to argue for economic reform simply for the sake of economic reform.

为新文化创造经济基础（1989）

我今天演讲的主题就是经济改革、新公有制、新文化三者之间的关系。我想，把这三者之间的关系说清楚了，大家对中国经济改革的意义和前景的认识就清楚了，对中国经济改革中所遇到的各种艰难曲折也就较易理解了。

一、人的研究

在研究经济问题时，我们经常遇到一个问题：发展经济究竟是为了什么？我们是向谁提供产品和劳务？我们为什么要生产出越来越多的产品和劳务？这就是说：生产的目的究竟是什么？其实，这个道理应当是大家都懂的：生产本身不是目的，人不是单纯地作为劳动力而生活在世上的，人不是为了生产，生产是为了人。生产的目的是使人们得到更好的关心和培养。假定只顾提供越来越多的产品，而人们的生活水平没有提高，人们的文化教育水平没有提高，人们并没有得到尊重，人们的潜在能力发挥不出来，这些都不符合生产的目的。

根据这个朴素的道理，我们可以给经济学下这样一个定义：经济学不仅限于研究如何增加物质财富，更应当研究如何利用人们创造出来的财富来满足人们的物质和文化生活的需要。"物"并不是经济学研究的中心，经济学研究的最高层次是"人"，经济学研究的中心是"人"。

根据这个朴素的道理，我们可以了解中国目前正在进行的经济改革的意义：经济改革并不仅为了使我们将来能够拥有更多的产品，更重要的是如何使中国人能够过富裕的生活，使他们有更高的文化教育水平，使他们真正成为社会的主人，得到社会的关心、培养、尊重。从这个意义上说，就经济而论经济，就经济改革而谈经济改革，是远远不够的。

We must admit that in meeting people's material and cultural needs and in facilitating all-round human development, there is a yawning gap between reality and ideal. Therefore, we have to accelerate reform—economic, political, and institutional reforms included—and cultivate a new culture. I believe that not only will our per capita national income grow nonstop with rising labor productivity, but our civic character will also improve vastly with what has been accomplished in growing the economy and cultivating the new culture, so long as we can ensure essential progress in reform and development, motivate our workforce unswervingly, and give full scope to the wisdom and talent of our people. Reform is exactly where China's hope rests.

II. New culture holds people in due esteem

Prior to the liberation year of 1949, an old culture, in which people's position and role were disdained, dominated this nation for understandable reasons. But how is it that the old culture remains so powerful after 1949? It is because it has carved out a new form of existence under a new situation and in a new economic environment.

It goes without saying there is a certain correlation between the old cultures before and after 1949. The old culture is anti-scientific and antidemocratic, whereas science and democracy are salient features of the new culture. Our predecessors had studied this a long time ago. Today, it should be recapitulated further on the basis of previous studies. The old culture is centered on divinity, whereas the new culture is focused on people. The old culture emphasizes power, whereas the new culture stresses knowledge. Because of its emphasis on power, old culture is based on the official standard; for its stress on knowledge, new culture inevitably takes people and science as its starting point. Superstition is the shared attribute of pre- and post-1949 old cultures, which never hold people in center stage. In the old culture, power is worshipped religiously and pursued relentlessly, and science, knowledge, and people are never respected. The reason why the old culture of yesterday lingers on and a new form of the old culture came to the scene after 1949 is precisely because of the old culture's intricate foundation in the Chinese economy of yore and its deep roots in feudalism. That is to say, because the pre-1949 old culture escaped elimination, the post-1949 old culture has been allowed to rear its ugly head. If we call the pre-1949 old culture "standard

我们必须承认，在满足人们的物质文化需要方面，在人的全面发展方面，现状距离我们的要求或理想有不少差距，为此我们需要进行改革，包括经济体制改革、政治体制改革和新文化的建设。我们相信，只要这几方面的改革与建设取得实质的进展，劳动者的积极性被真正调动起来，人的聪明才智充分施展出来，不但我们的平均国民收入会在劳动生产率提高的基础上不断增长，而我们的国民素质也必定因经济发展和新文化建设的成就而大大提高。改革，正是中国的希望所在。

二、新文化尊重人

1949 年以前，忽视人的地位和作用的旧文化在中国占据主导地位，是可以理解的。为什么 1949 年以后，旧文化还是这样强大呢？这是因为，旧文化在新的形势和新的经济环境中找到了新的表现形式。

当然，1949 年前后的旧文化是有一定联系的。旧文化的特色是非科学和非民主，新文化的特色是科学和民主。关于这一点，前人早已作过分析。现在需要在这一分析的基础上再作进一步的概括。旧文化以神为中心，新文化以人为中心；旧文化强调的是权力，新文化强调的是知识。正因为旧文化强调权力，所以旧文化是一种官本位的文化；而由于新文化强调知识，所以新文化必然以人民为出发点，以科学为出发点。这样，无论是 1949 年前的旧文化还是 1949 年后以新形式出现的旧文化，其共同点就是迷信，而不以人为中心；就是对权力的崇拜和追求，而不是尊重科学、尊重知识、尊重人民。正由于旧文化在旧日中国经济中的基础非常坚固，旧文化在封建土壤中的根扎得太深了，所以 1949 年以后，除原来的旧文化照样存在外，又加上新形式下的旧文化。这就是说：在 1949 年前的旧文化未被清除的同时，又增添了 1949 年后的旧文化。如果我们把 1949 年前的旧文化称作“标准的旧文化”，把 1949 年后

old culture" and the post-1949 old culture "remodeled old culture," what existed from the 1950s through the 1980s were two kinds of old culture, the "standard old culture" and the "remodeled old culture," and the period from the late 1960s through the mid-1970s was one in which the two old cultures apparently got mixed. The "remodeled old culture" has been weakened considerably since the Third Plenary Session of the Eleventh Party Central Committee in 1979, but this has not happened to the "standard old culture." In fact, it has reappeared in such forms as construction sprees of temples and lavish tombs and the spread of wasteful weddings and funerals. This indicates that, on the one hand, the independent old culture won't beat a retreat anytime soon even with progress in economic restructuring and reform, and, on the other, once the old culture infiltrates lifestyles and habits, it becomes pegged to people's economic abilities. When people are having trouble making ends meet, there is little they can do even if they truly desire to build temples and lavish tombs or indulge in pomp and pageantry. Of course I am not saying they won't get these things done by falling into debt. Generally speaking, people become thrifty when they are hard up, but when they are better off, the "standard old culture" will penetrate their daily life and spread among them in no time.

Obviously, we can never eradicate the old culture, not even the "standard old culture," by raising people's income alone. The old culture totally denies people's status as masters of society and is steeped in benightedness and blind obedience. It can be rooted up and give way to new culture only by developing both the economy and education and raising people's scientific and cultural endowment. The kind of education I am talking about here is not simply the imparting of knowledge and expertise but, more importantly, the cardinal mission of "modernizing people."

Make no question about it, without the "modernization of people" there will be no modernization of society, the economy, or science and technology. Without the "emancipation of people" there will be no emancipation of productivity. New culture is connected with "modernization of people" and "emancipation of people." Only by grasping this point can we capture the profound meaning of the cultivation of a new culture.

出现的新形式下的旧文化称作"改装的旧文化"的话，那么从 50 年代到 80 年代这段时间内实际存在于中国的，是两种旧文化，即"标准的旧文化"与"改装的旧文化"的并存，60 年代末到 70 年代中期，是两种旧文化最明显地结合在一起的典型时期。中共十一届三中全会以后（1979 年以后），"改装的旧文化"已经有较大的减弱，而"标准的旧文化"的减弱程度则小得多，甚至在某些方面（如农村中的大修祠堂、大造坟墓、大讲婚丧排场等）还有所滋长。这一方面说明了旧文化存在的独立性，即并不随着经济结构的调整和经济改革的进展而立即消逝的独立性，另一方面还表明：只要旧文化已渗透到人们的生活方式之中和习惯之中，那么旧文化的表现就可能与人们的经济能力有关。家庭收入太低，连饭都吃不饱，即使人们想修祠堂、造坟墓、讲排场也会力不从心。当然，这不是说没有人用举债的方式来操办这些事，而是一般地说，人穷，这些自然会从简；有了钱，"标准的旧文化"很快就渗透到人们的生活之中，并滋长起来。

从这里，我们可以了解到，单纯依靠提高人民的收入水平，并不能消除旧文化，甚至连标准的旧文化也难以消除。由于旧文化处处是否定人作为社会主体的地位的，是以愚昧、盲从为特征的，所以在中国，要真正消除旧文化和促进新文化的发展，必须在发展经济的同时发展教育，提高国民的科学文化素质，而且这种教育，不是仅仅以传授知识和技术为主要内容，更重要的是把"人的现代化"作为主要内容。

要知道，没有"人的现代化"就谈不上社会经济的现代化和科学技术的现代化，没有"人的解放"就谈不到生产力的解放。新文化是同"人的现代化"、"人的解放"联系在一起的。了解了这一点，我们就能懂得新文化建设的深远意义。

III. The foundation of a new culture

Why is the old culture so powerful and the new culture so weak in China? Because the new culture has yet to build up its own economic base. The pre-1949 old culture was based on an old economic system, but, during the period from the late 1950s to the eve of the Third Plenary Session of the Eleventh Party Central Committee, another form of old culture, the "remodeled old culture," found its foundation in the ossified commodity economy and the traditional form of public ownership which confounded government administration with business management, made officials act like businesspeople, dampened producers' enthusiasm for production, and robbed the new culture of its corresponding economic foundation. The landmark significance of the Third Plenary Session lies in the fact that it unshackled people from long years of "Leftist" ideology, emancipated their minds, and pointed out the way for building a socialist system conducive to productivity development. After that meeting, we have not only transformed the old economic system into a new one, but also repudiated old culture, the "remodeled old culture" included, and built a socialist new culture. The socialist new culture has found its foundation in a planned socialist commodity economy that embraces a new type of public ownership whereby government administration is detached from everyday business management, officials no longer act like businesspeople, and producers are highly motivated.

Only by observing the mission for economic reform alongside the building of the socialist new culture can we fully comprehend the greatness of what our nation has been doing over the last decade and understand the adversities and trials involved in the cause of reform. It is hard to replace an old economic system with a new one, but it is even harder to replace an old culture with a new culture. Reform entails readjusting interests. Old culture and old habits hold sway over people's outlook on personal interests, labor productivity, education, and way of life, while the old economic system spawns egalitarianism and rigidity in such assertions of interests as wages, employment, and welfare. Reform is bound to touch upon everybody's established interests. If four of someone's five established interests have improved, he may still have complaints about the one interest that has suffered and go on to blame it on reform, because he takes the improvement in his established interests for granted and believes that something must have gone wrong if one of his interests has been impaired even if such an interest is unwarranted.

三、新文化的基础

就中国的情况而言，为什么旧文化的势力这样强大而新文化始终这样弱小呢？原因在于新文化没有自己的经济基础。1949 年以前的旧文化以旧的经济制度为基础。而从 50 年代末到中共十一届三中全会前，另一种形式的旧文化，即“改了装的旧文化”，也是有经济基础的。这就是僵化的产品经济体制，是政企不分、官商不分、抑制了生产者积极性的传统形式的公有制，所以新文化还是缺乏相应的经济基础。党的十一届三中全会的伟大意义在于冲破长期“左”倾思想的束缚，解放思想，为在中国建设适应生产力发展的社会主义体制指明了道路。党的十一届三中全会以来，我们不仅改革旧经济体制，建设新经济体制，而且也反对旧文化，包括那种“改了装的旧文化”，建设社会主义的新文化。社会主义新文化的经济基础就是社会主义有计划的商品经济，就是政企分开、官商分开、充分调动了生产者积极性的新型公有制。

只有把经济改革的任务同社会主义新文化建设的任务结合起来进行考察，我们才能懂得这 10 年来我们所做的工作之重大意义，也才能了解我们的改革事业之艰辛、困难。以新经济体制代替旧经济体制固然不易，以社会主义新文化代替旧文化尤其困难。改革中存在着利益调整问题。旧文化、旧习惯支配着人们对利益的看法、对发展生产力的看法、对教育和文化的看法，而旧经济体制又造成了平均主义和一系列利益刚性（如工资刚性、就业刚性、福利刚性等）。改革必然要触动每个人原有的利益。对一个人来说，如果他有五个方面的利益，哪怕有四个方面的利益增加了，只有一个方面的利益减少了，那么他很可能对改革有所不满，因为利益的增加在他看来是理所当然的，而利益（即使是不合理的利益）的减少，他则认为是不对的。

The result is that society abounds with complaints that stem from all sorts of conflicts of interests. It is thus apparent that without correcting people's outlooks on their interests, without loosening the rigidity of interests caused by egalitarianism and the old economic system, without breaking the bandwagon mentality concerning interests based on tradition, and without fostering new concepts of culture and interests, the road ahead for reform will bristle with impediments. If we have fully accepted this point, we can arrive at three conclusions:

First, "reform" contravenes not only a 30-year-old economic system but also three millennia of outdated culture and habits. Therefore, reform can never be a simple undertaking.

Second, reform has brought a lot of new interests to people, no question about it, but because it has broken or is ready to break the rigidity of interests under the old system, it has also deprived people of certain established interests. Thus reform is confronted with more impediments as people, oblivious to the new interests they have gained, are having misgivings about their lost established interests.

Third, rigidity in interests is uncalled-for, and some of the established interests born of such rigidity are detrimental to productivity growth. Both should be rectified, and reform should never be reined in because of it. We cannot afford to give up reform midway for fear of an unjustified rigidity in interests. Otherwise, our effort to develop productivity will be thwarted, and our hope for a prosperous economy dashed.

From a historical point of view, and from the perspective of our confrontation with the two- or three-millennium-old outmoded culture, ten years are just a twinkling of the eye. But what has been achieved in reform over those years has been breathtaking. History will pass a fair and honest judgment on it.

The new culture is bound to prevail once it acquires a sturdy economic foundation, that is, a socialist commodity economy and a new type of public ownership. The inexorable pace of socialist economic reform alongside the socialist new culture is unstoppable.

IV. The hope of China

I have just dwelled on the issue of confidence. I believe everyone present in this auditorium feels the same. True, the national economy has hit some snags—inflation, "official" and "nonofficial" smuggling, corruption, education crisis, and whatnot. We should admit these facts.

于是社会上存在着种种因利益摩擦而发生的不满。可见，人们不从利益观念上有较大的转变，不破除平均主义和旧经济体制造成的利益刚性，不破除利益本位的各种利益攀比，不建立与社会主义商品经济相适应的新文化观念、新利益观念，改革再往前深入，阻力会越来越大，改革所遇到的困难也就会相应增加。只要我们了解了这一点，我们就可以得出以下三个论点：

第一，"改革"不仅是同有 30 年历史的旧经济体制发生冲突，而且是同有两三千年历史的旧文化、旧习惯势力发生冲突。改革当然是不容易的。

第二，改革无疑给人们带来了不少新的利益，但由于改革打破了（或准备打破）旧体制下的利益刚性，又使人们失去了某种原有的利益，所以，当人们只注意原有利益的失去而不注意新利益的增加时，改革遇到的阻力就加大了。

第三，利益刚性是不合理的，由利益刚性所带来的原有利益中有些不利于生产力的发展，这些都非改不可。我们的改革绝不能就此止步，不能因为怕触动这些不合理的利益刚性而止步，否则我们的生产力发展不起来，中国经济无法繁荣。

从历史的角度看，从我们同有两三千年历史的旧文化的冲突的角度看，10 年只是历史长河中的一瞬间。10 年改革所取得的成就是惊人的。历史将会对此作出公正的评价。

一旦新文化有了自己的强大的经济基础（社会主义商品经济体制和新型公有制），新文化必将取得胜利。社会主义经济改革的进展与社会主义新文化的建立将是同步的、不可遏制的。

四、中国的希望

刚才谈到了信心问题。我想，在座的各位一定和我有同样的感觉。目前，中国的经济建设的确遇到了一些困难，什么通货膨胀啦，"官倒"、"私倒"啦，腐败现象啦，教育危机啦，等等等等。我们应当承认这些事实的存在。但是，埋怨，发牢骚，都无济于事。

Whining and griping gets us nowhere. Only by accepting the reality, knowing the challenges and hardships of reform, and getting to the root of the problems, can we understand why reform is irreversible and why problems can be redressed in the course of reform. Given that economic reform is challenged by the 30-year-old system plus three millennia of old culture, traditions and habits, we know that the old system will not crumble on its own and the old culture, traditions, and habits cannot vanish overnight. Nevertheless, we must recognize that our nation will be doomed if we lose heart and allow ourselves to descend into complaint and despair.

My career as a university teacher on the mainland has brought me in contact with members of the younger generations in and out of class. Take, for example, the young people in their thirties today. Unlike the college students of the 1950s, who had wallowed in idealism for a period of time before and after they started work, and who were somewhat belated in their awakening to the stubbornness of the prevailing old culture, these 30-somethings had taken part in the Cultural Revolution in the name of "casting away the Four Olds"—old ideas, old culture, old customs and old habits—during their middle-school or college days. Their tragedy is that in the adverse current of "annihilating old culture in name and maintaining old culture in practice," they had inadvertently become new culture's saboteurs. Superstition, blind faith, ignorance, and extremism had driven them to put on red armbands and hold aloft the Little Red Book—*Quotations of Mao Zedong*. When they sang the Song of Rebels and came to blows, wielding cudgels and belts, they saw themselves as faithful enforcers of the May Fourth Movement spirit[1]. However, it did not take long for them to come to their senses. "Re-education" in the countryside, loss of schooling opportunities, and joblessness eventually drove home to them the harms done by the old culture, especially to themselves. A considerable number of them were participants in or supporters of the Tian'anmen Incident of 1976[2].

History is at once merciless and dramatic. All of a sudden, those hoodwinked by the old culture became its intransigent foes. Their minds were racing. How should the new culture be fostered? How could the new culture prevail in its long-term combat against the old? Having mulled over these questions, some of them ardently joined the cause of fostering the new culture. However, as the majority of the people in their thirties today lost their schooling opportunities in the decade-long chaos, their

我们只有承认现实，理解改革过程中的困难和艰辛，找到问题之所在，才能知道为什么改革是不可逆转的，困难总可以在继续改革中得到解决。既然经济改革的对手不仅仅是30年的旧体制，而且也包括三千年的旧文化、旧传统、旧习惯势力，那么我们就可以了解到，如果大家只是埋怨、发牢骚、甚至泄气的话，旧体制不会自动瓦解，旧文化、旧传统、旧习惯势力也不会自行消失。这样一来，中国的前途不是更没有希望吗?

在国内，由于我一直在大学教书，课上课下，我接触到不少年轻人。譬如说，年龄大约三十多岁的这一代青年，他们不像50年代上大学的那一代人在参加工作前后有过一段理想主义的美好日子，也不像那一代人那样对旧文化统治的顽强性较晚才有所认识。这些年轻人在上中学或上大学时就以“破四旧”的名义参加了“文化大革命”。他们的悲剧在于：他们是被愚弄、被欺骗的一代，他们是在“名为破除旧文化，实为维护旧文化”的逆流中，不自觉地成为新文化的破坏者队伍中的一员的。迷信、盲从、无知、偏激，使他们在戴上红袖章、捧着小红书、唱着造反歌和手执棍棒、皮带到处冲杀时，还自认为是“五四”精神的忠实执行者。然而，他们很快就醒悟过来了。上山、下乡、失学、待业，这些使他们懂得了旧文化的危害，特别是对他们这一代人的危害。他们中的相当多的人成为1976年“天安门事件”的参加者和支持者。历史既是这样的无情，又是这样富有戏剧性，旧文化的蒙蔽对象转眼之间变成了最痛恨旧文化的一分子。但怎样建设新文化呢？怎样使新旧文化的长期战斗最终以新文化的胜利来结束呢？他们思考过这些问题，其中有些人现在也成为新文化建设的积极参加者。而从这一年龄的大多数人来看，由于他们在那些动荡的年代里失去了学习的机会，

attitude toward the new culture being fostered nowadays is based more on personal demands and expectations than on in-depth theoretical analyses and explorations. Nevertheless, there is one thing they share with people of other age groups, that is, they know from personal experience that it is no mean task to phase out the old culture and phase in the new culture.

The situation with the 20-somethings of today is somewhat different in comparison with the 30-somethings. A 22-year-old college graduate may have been born in 1966, the year the Cultural Revolution broke out. A 30-year-old lecturer, assistant researcher, engineer, or PhD candidate may have missed primary school because all manner of schools were closed and stopped enrolment in 1966. They have just a faint memory of the Cultural Revolution, or no memory of it at all. They started school in the wake of the Cultural Revolution, and their development has been associated with the sensible policies adopted since the Third Plenary Session of the Eleventh Party Central Committee. They have learned new knowledge, and have been fortunate to live in the reform and opening years. They are the new culture's born pursuers and aspirants. Frequent contacts with the outside world, and concerns about China's economic and technological underdevelopment, have combined with the on-campus academic atmosphere to convert this generation of undergraduates and graduate students, teachers, researchers, technicians and engineers into spirited builders of the new culture. Undeniably, however, they are not without their limits. Because they are too young to adequately understand the reality of Chinese society, they know little about the stubbornness and strength of the old culture, and tend to believe that the building of a new culture will be nothing but smooth sailing. They probably believe the old culture will step down the moment the new culture goes onstage. This oversimplified way of thinking turns them into a different type of idealists from the youngsters of the 1950s. The idealists of the 1950s believed their task was to build the new culture now that the older generation had basically fulfilled the mission to destroy the old culture. The idealists of the 1980s may not believe this mission has been basically accomplished, but they are convinced that, with their active participation, it will not take long for the new culture to triumph over the old. Unrealistic idealism is likely to fuel impetuosity, agitation, and, in time of setbacks, pessimism, and despair. Logically speaking, as a blessed generation, the 20-somethings of today should be less prone

他们对于新文化建设，更多的是感情上的要求和期待，而不是就这个问题的深入的理论分析和探讨。但是有一点，他们同其他年龄档次的人是相同的，这就是：他们从亲身的经历中懂得了旧文化的退出和新文化的建设都是很不容易的。

又譬如说，比他们更年轻的一代人，即大约二十多岁，不到三十岁左右的人，情况又有所不同。一个22岁的大学毕业生，可能出生于“文化大革命”爆发的那一年。一个30岁的讲师、助理研究员、工程师、博士生，在开始“文化大革命”的那一年，可能连小学还没有上，因为1966年，连小学都停课了，不招生了。“文化大革命”的印象，他们已经记不起了，或者他们根本没有这种印象。他们是在“文化大革命”结束以后开始自己正规的学习生活的，他们的成长同中共十一届三中全会以来的正确的方针和政策有关。他们学到了新的知识，他们赶上了改革与开放的时代。他们是新文化的天生的追求者和向往者。同外界交往的频繁，对中国经济和技术落后的不安，校园生活中的学术探讨气氛，这一切使这一大批年轻的大学生、研究生、教师、科学研究者、技术人员成为新时代的新文化建设的积极分子。然而，他们自身具有不可忽视的局限性，因为他们太年轻了，他们对中国的现实社会状况了解得很不够，他们不了解旧文化势力的顽固和有力，误以为新文化的建设是那么顺利，那么容易。他们也许会认为，只要新文化一出现，旧文化自然就会退出历史舞台。这种把问题看得过分简单的想法，使他们又成了另一种意义上的理想主义者，只是这种理想主义与50年代的那些年轻人的理想主义有所不同：50年代的理想主义者以为摧毁旧文化的任务已由上一代基本完成，因此留给他们的任务将是新文化的建设；80年代的理想主义者虽然并不认为摧毁旧文化的任务已经基本完成，但他们却认为，在他们的积极参与之下，新文化将很快地战胜旧文化。不切实际的理想主义可能带来的是急躁和激动，以及在遭到挫折以后的悲观、失望。照理说，他们是幸运的一代，埋怨

to dark moods than people a little older. In reality, however, that is not true. Why? It is partly because of their scanty knowledge of the trauma involved in the cause of reform and partly because they cannot beat the old culture merely with knowledge (they are a generation of knowledge) and passion (which they certainly do not lack). The new culture cannot succeed before it builds up its own economic base.

Thus they start whining and griping. But what good can complaining do? They are disappointed, but can disappointment change things? Confidence, as always, is of vital importance, and therefore, we should never lose heart. No matter how difficult reform is, we have got to brace ourselves and stick it out. We are ready to take chances no matter what. Our fate is bound up with reform. That is why I told my Hong Kong hosts just before this meeting, "The hope of China lies in our confidence in reform and in building the new culture. If everybody has lost heart, reform will be doomed."

I believe I made that remark for a reason. Many of you sitting in this auditorium have been to the mainland more than a decade ago and have returned there for visits recently. Did you see big changes out there? Of course you saw colossal changes. The changes will become even bigger ten years from now, no question about it. Every one of us, those who are not confident enough included, must see the world economic situation and future trend in perspective, and put our home situation into perspective too. The changes that have taken place over the last decade are by no means small. Ten years ago, it was impossible for us to talk openly about our backwardness and the gap between China and other countries. We would not have been able to speak our minds about our country's economic issues. More importantly, those unscientific "supreme directives" would have remained the only theoretical support for solutions to those issues. Therefore, of all the impediments to Chinese economic development, the old culture must never be disregarded. Never had its impact been so ferocious as it was a decade ago. Having seen the changes over the last decade, I believe we should remain firmly optimistic about our future.

V. Science and democracy can save China

When we see that the Chinese economy today is still trailing a long way behind many other economies in the world, an idea naturally comes to mind. Had we allowed the anti-scientific, anti-democratic old culture to prevail and manipulate our thoughts, we would have lost sight

情绪应当比年龄大一些的人少，但实际上并非如此。为什么呢？这一方面是由于他们对改革事业的艰辛了解得太少，另一方面则由于单单靠他们的知识（他们是有知识的一代人）和他们的热情（他们不乏热情）并不足以战胜旧文化。在新文化的经济基础尚未建立之时，新文化是不会胜利的。

于是他们埋怨起来了。但埋怨又有什么用呢？他们失望了，失望能改变现状吗？信心始终重要，信心不能丢掉。改革再困难，我们也要硬着头皮干下去。我们算是豁出去了，我们与改革共命运。因此，在今天的讲演会前，我同单志明、区树鸿两位先生谈过。我说："中国的希望在于我们大家对改革有信心，对新文化建设有信心。大家都没有信心，那么改革就真的没有希望了。"

我相信，我这么讲是有根据的。在座各位，不少人十多年前到过国内，不久前又故地重游。变化大不大？肯定可以看出巨大的变化。再过 10 年，变化还会大，这毫无疑问。我们大家，包括信心不足的人在内，要正确地认识世界经济形势和发展趋向，我们要正确地估计国情。10 年来的变化是不小的。10 年前，我们不可能公开讨论我们的落后和我们同世界其他国家的差距，我们不可能针对中国的经济问题畅所欲言地争辩，更重要的，那些不科学的最高指示成为惟一可以援引的解决中国经济问题的依据。因此，在阻碍中国经济发展的种种阻力之中，旧文化作为不可忽视的阻力之一，在 10 年前达到了无以复加的地步。看到了这 10 年的变化，我想我们对于前景应该是有信心的。

五、科学与民主可以救中国

当我们看到中国经济至今仍然大大落后于世界上许多国家时，我们很自然地会想到这样一个问题：如果听任非科学、非民主的旧文化继续统治着我们，支配着我们的思想，那么我们也许仍然不了解

of how underdeveloped we were. We cannot but owe this awakening to the outcry of the ideological, cultural, and academic circles, and to our growing exchanges and connections with other nations. Today, everybody, or at least most of us, have come to our senses. A major reason why reform is an irresistible trend is because ideas of science and democracy have been gradually engrained in people's hearts. We have every reason to believe that if the socialist new culture, for lack of a corresponding economic foundation, is too weak to compete with the old culture prior to the birth of a new type of public ownership, it will no longer be weak and at a disadvantage in competing with the old culture once the new type of ownership comes to stay and the economic foundation becomes an reality. The new type of public ownership under conditions of a socialist commodity economy will support the socialist new culture, which, for its part, is inevitably conducive to the consolidation of such ownership. This relationship of mutual support and promotion will have a major impact on future changes in the Chinese economy. With the support of the socialist new culture, the Chinese economy will enter a new period of historical development.

How is it that the socialist new culture can play such a role? Why is it that the Chinese economy cannot score major progress without the support of the socialist new culture? Why cannot the new culture grow on its own and be consolidated without its economic foundation in the socialist commodity economy under the new type of public ownership? In-depth analysis of these questions will touch upon the issue of science and democracy. We emphasize that science and democracy can save China not just because of their role in economic development, but more importantly, because of their role in modernizing and emancipating people. If our workers and farmers can truly understand the damage caused to the economy and our own long-term interests by egalitarianism, life-long tenures, the egalitarian practice of everyone eating from the same big pot regardless of work done, rigidity in interests and the bandwagon mentality concerning interests, will the impediments to reform not be minimized? If our government functionaries can truly see that only by shattering the old system that put the economy at the mercy of administrative directives can the Chinese economy take off, the income of government functionaries and their families grow in pace with the income of the rank-and-file in the course of economic growth,

自己的落后。这种觉醒不能不归功于最近 10 年来思想界、文化界、学术界的呐喊，也不能不归功于最近 10 年来我们同国外交往的增多和接触的频繁。现在，我们大家，至少国内的多数人，终于醒悟过来了。改革之所以成为不可阻挡的潮流，科学与民主思想的逐渐深入人心是一个重要的因素。我们完全有理由设想，如果说在社会主义商品经济条件下的新型公有制建立以前，缺乏相应经济基础的社会主义新文化由于相当弱小而不得不在同旧文化交锋时处于劣势地位的话，那么一旦建立了新型公有制，社会主义新文化有了自己的经济基础，社会主义新文化就不再是弱小的了，新文化在同旧文化的交锋时也就不再处于劣势了。社会主义商品经济条件下的新型公有制支持着社会主义新文化，而社会主义新文化也必将以全部力量来为新型公有制的巩固与发展服务。这种相互支持和相互促进的关系对今后中国经济的变化将产生重大的影响。在社会主义新文化的支持下，中国经济必定会进入一个新的历史阶段。

为什么社会主义新文化能够起着这样的作用？为什么中国经济的重大进展不可能没有社会主义新文化的支持？为什么新文化本身的发展和充实又不可能没有社会主义商品经济条件下的新型公有制作为自己的经济基础？对这些问题，可以作进一步的分析，这就涉及科学和民主的问题了。我们现在仍然强调科学与民主可以救中国，不仅仅着眼于科学与民主对经济发展的作用，更重要的是着眼于科学与民主在“人的现代化”、“人的解放”中的作用。大家不妨想想，如果我们的工人、农民能真正了解平均主义、“铁饭碗”、“大锅饭”、利益刚性和利益攀比对于经济的危害，以及对于自己长远利益的危害，改革的阻力是不是会大大缩小呢？如果我们的干部能真正了解只有彻底打破这种用行政命令的方式来领导经济的旧体制，中国经济才能起飞，干部及其家庭的收入水平才能在经济增长过程中同人民收入水平一样提高，而经济的管理才能更有效率，

and the administration of economy be more efficient, will the commodity economy and the new form of public ownership not be built a lot faster? If, more than anything, the broad masses of people truly regard themselves as the masters of society under the ideological guidance of science and democracy, will corruption not be considerably reduced? As I see it, all these questions can be answered in the positive. Herein lies the inseparable bond between the building of a new culture and economic and political reform. In the course of fruitful economic and political reform, a new culture commensurate with the new type of public ownership can definitely be translated into reality.

It takes a considerably lengthy process to raise the quality of the entire citizenry. Perhaps only after our economy has become truly well developed, our people's income has risen vastly, and our lives have become really affluent, can our culture, education, science and public health be provided with enough development funds and cherished by the entire public, and our national character—cultural, moral, etc.—be considerably improved. We are not here to overestimate the role of the economy. Rather, this conclusion is based on the historical experience of countries in economic and cultural development. Perhaps a well developed economy is the only way for the fine accomplishments of traditional culture to be truly cherished and carried forward. We have come to realize that on no account should a nation lose its fine cultural achievements. Outstanding cultural attainments should stand the sifting of history and the test of time. Is it not because of poverty, low per capita national income, and underdeveloped productivity that we do not have enough economic resources to maintain and carry forward our finest cultural accomplishments? Perhaps only when achievements in economic development have become an established fact can they become the best rebuff to the "remodeled old culture" and its foundation, the traditional economic system, and traditional public ownership. If we can say that many people today hate the "remodeled old culture" from the bottom of their hearts and are utterly disgusted by the anti-scientific and anti-democratic arguments advocated by it, such hatred and disgust are based mostly on theoretical and ideological understanding, or are felt mainly from their experience with the poor and backward Chinese economy manipulated by the "remodeled old culture." As to the questions of what will become of the Chinese economy after the commodity economy is developed and the new type of public ownership established, what will become of the people's income and livelihood,

商品经济体制的建立和新公有制的建立是不是会大大加快呢？特别是，如果广大人民群众能在科学与民主的思想指导下，把自己真正当成社会的主体，社会上的腐败现象是不是会大大减少呢？我想，我们是会得出肯定的答案的。这就是新文化建设与经济改革、政治改革之间的不可分割的关系。在经济体制改革和政治体制改革取得成就的过程中，与新型公有制相适应的新文化建设一定能成为事实。

整个国民素质的提高需要有一个较长的过程。也许，只有等到我们的经济真正发达了，等到我们广大人民的收入水平大大提高了，生活真的富裕了，我们的文化、教育、科学、卫生事业才能获得充足的发展资金，才能真正得到全社会的重视，而我们的国民素质（包括文化素质、道德素质等）才能大为改善。这并不是过分强调经济的作用，而是根据世界各国经济与文化发展的历史经验而得出的结论。也许，只有到那时，中国传统文化的优秀成果才能真正被重视和发扬光大。要知道，一个民族的优秀文化成果是不会被丢掉的。既然它们是优秀的文化成果，那就经得起历史的筛选，经得起时间的考验。当前我们之所以还没有足够的经济力量来维护它，发扬它，不正是因为穷，因为人均国民收入太少，因为生产力落后么？也许，只有到那时，旧文化，尤其是"改装的旧文化"，尽管还有一定的市场，有一定的影响，但经济发展成就这一事实本身就是对"改装的旧文化"及其立足的基础——传统经济体制和传统公有制——的最好的反驳。如果说今天已有不少人对"改装的旧文化"深恶痛绝，对"改装的旧文化"所鼓吹的那一套非科学、非民主的东西从内心感到厌恶，那么这主要是出于理论上、思想上的认识，或者主要是从"改装的旧文化"支配下中国经济的贫穷落后所体验到的。但商品经济发展以后和新型公有制建立以后的中国经济究竟如何，人民收入和生活状况究竟如何，

and what new social pattern and atmosphere can the economy bring once it becomes commensurate with the scientifically and democratically based new culture, our answers today are more imaginative than factual. However, once all this has become reality, a reality in which the benefits of economic growth, productivity development, and brand-new public ownership can be keenly felt by hundreds of millions of Chinese, our answers will no longer be empty or abstract. Rather, they will become concrete and solid, and bestow faith and spiritual strength on people. By that time, those who cherish science and democracy will no longer believe in the "remodeled old culture" no matter what high-sounding rhetoric it may employ.

VI. What entrepreneurs can do

Once, during a conversation on economic reform and the building of a new culture in the mainland, an entrepreneur asked me: "The building of a new culture is the task of the educational, cultural, and academic circles. What can a businessman do for it?" What the man did not know is that entrepreneurs have an irreplaceable part to play in building the new culture. I told him that new culture can never prevail over old culture by relying on intellectuals alone. The new culture can strike root in the Chinese soil only when entrepreneurs join workers and farmers under the new public ownership in contributing to the growth of the commodity economy and repudiating outdated traditions, culture, and habits in the course of it.

Generally speaking, our entrepreneurs today are not only doing their best to foster the new culture during the years of economic reform, but are also fostering a corporate culture. Given that corporate culture is a branch of new culture, let me talk at some length about how to foster it.

Corporate culture is the cultural concept and values of a company, and an embodiment of the collective faith and cohesion of its workforce. There will be no corporate culture to speak of if a firm remains a government appendage and has no independent interests, and if its workers' interests are irrelevant to its business performance. For this reason, company autonomy in business activity and company responsibility for gains and losses, combined with the unanimity of interest between the company and its workers are necessary internal economic conditions for corporate culture. Whether such a culture can be fostered also depends on the company's external economic conditions—meaning that at least it should find itself in a competitive commodity market.

与那种以科学与民主为内容的新文化相适应的经济究竟会使中国社会产生什么样的新格局、新气象，这些仍然是设想中的，它们还不曾成为事实。而一旦这些成了事实，数以亿计的人民真正感受到商品经济发展、生产力发展、新型公有制建立给自己带来利益了，对这一切的认识也就大不一样。认识不再是空泛的、抽象的，而成为具体和实在的。这就会给人们一种信念、一种精神力量。那时，“改装的旧文化”即使再以娓娓动听的辞藻来蒙蔽人们，崇尚科学与民主的人们也不会再相信了。

六、企业家能做些什么

在国内，当我谈到经济改革与新文化建设问题时，有些企业家问我:“新文化建设是教育界、文化界、学术界的事情，一个企业家能为新文化建设做些什么呢？”他们不知道企业界在新文化建设中的作用，是别人不能代替的。我对他们说:要使新文化对旧文化取得胜利，光靠知识界的努力是不够的。只有当企业家和新公有制之下的工人、农民参加到新文化建设中来，为商品经济的发展作出贡献，并在商品经济发展过程中共同摒弃传统文化、旧习惯势力的时候，新文化才能真正在中国的土地上生根。

综合起来说，企业家不仅在经济改革中为新文化建设而尽力，而且他们本身也在建设企业文化，即新文化的一种形态。这里特别需要说的是企业文化的建设问题。

企业文化是企业的一种文化观念和价值准则，是企业职工的信念和凝聚力的体现。如果企业仍然停留于行政机构附属物的地位，企业没有自己的独立利益，职工的利益与企业的经营状况缺乏联系，那就不可能形成企业文化。因此，企业的自主经营和自负盈亏、职工与企业利益的一致，就是企业文化建设的内部经济条件。企业文化的建设也有赖于企业的外部经济条件，即企业应当处于竞争性的商品市场环境中。

If no headway has been made in developing the socialist commodity economy, if a company fails to foster economic ties with the outside world through competition, and if its business deals are entirely controlled by a mandatory plan and the firm serves merely as a processing workshop, it will have no way of fostering, among its workers, the norms of conduct and values centered on efficiency, competition, risks and other concepts, and its relationship with its workers will be deprived of a foundation upon which risks and interests are shared. The building of corporate culture becomes empty talk under these circumstances.

Corporate culture cannot be built in the absence of two pivotal economic conditions. The first is corporate transformation, meaning that companies must be converted from the old type of public ownership in which government interferes in business management, and become a new type of public companies that are independent commodity producers, so that they and their workers can be internally adapted to the requirements of corporate culture. The second is transformation of the corporate environment, which means companies must be given a competitive economic environment in which transactions are conducted openly and contractually, and which provides both opportunities and pressure for them to readjust their relations of interest with their workers and foster a new and congenial relationship between themselves. Both conditions indicate that the socialist corporate culture is an outcome of socialist economic reform and a fruit of the endeavor to develop the socialist commodity economy and establish the new type public ownership under such an economy.

Corporate culture, being a major component of the new culture, cannot be detached from it to stand alone. Therefore, to understand the conditions that the socialist corporate culture cannot do without, we must study the new culture as the cultural background of corporate culture. Science and democracy are salient features of the socialist new culture. Holding people in great esteem, being solicitous for and cultivating them are attributes of the new culture that distinguish it from the old. Corporate culture is out of the question if, in its business activity and management, a modern company turns a blind eye to its people's corporate position, initiative, enterprising spirit and creativity. Nevertheless, businesses are, after all, microeconomic agents of society, and the relationship between a business and its workers, and the interpersonal relations of the workforce are microcosms of society's interpersonal relations. Exchanges between people cannot happen in companies without a social atmosphere. Corporate culture can never be

假定社会主义商品经济没有发展，企业同外界的经济关系不是通过竞争来实现的，企业的交易活动全都由指令性的计划所规定，企业只不过是一个加工车间，那么企业也就无法使职工树立以效益、竞争、风险等观念为中心的价值准则，职工与企业之间也就缺乏一种患难与共、利益均沾的适应关系存在的基础，这样，企业文化的建设必定是一句空话。

因此，企业文化的建设过程中，从经济上说最为重要的，一是企业自身的改革，即企业从传统的政企不分的公有制企业，转变为具有独立商品生产者地位的新型公有制企业，从内部解决企业与职工的适应问题；二是企业环境的改革，即企业所处的经济环境应当是竞争性的、交易活动公开化和合约化的环境，市场既给企业以机会，又给企业以压力，从而企业得以在这样的环境中重新调整自己与全体职工之间的利益关系，建立彼此适应的关系。这两个条件都表明，社会主义的企业文化是社会主义经济改革的产物，是社会主义商品经济发展以及建立了社会主义商品经济条件下的新型公有制的结果。

从文化上看，由于企业文化是新文化的重要组成部分，企业文化不可能脱离新文化而孤立地存在，因此要理解社会主义企业文化的产生条件，必须把新文化作为企业文化的整个文化背景来考察。社会主义新文化以科学与民主为特色。对人的重视、对人的关心和培养是新文化区别于旧文化的重要特征。就现代企业的经营与管理来说，如果忽视了人在企业中的地位，忽视了人的主动精神、积极进取精神、创造精神，那么企业文化也就无从谈起。然而，企业只是社会的一个微观经济单位，企业与职工的关系、企业中的人际关系是社会中的人与人之间的关系的一个缩影。企业中的人与人的交往是不可能脱离社会这个大环境而实现的。假定整个社会被旧文化

fostered or developed either, if society is still manipulated by the old culture, if anti-scientific, anti-democratic ideas that form the core of the old culture still hold sway, and if the practice of handling interpersonal relationships inside a firm in line with the interest principle is still being scorned.

In comparison with economic reform, it is a lot more difficult to transform the cultural sphere and allow the new culture to prevail. I am not saying economic reform can be free from obstacles and setbacks. Progress in establishing the new type of public ownership, for instance, is not smooth precisely because of a variety of impediments and difficulties in its way, not to mention the fact that the birth of this type of ownership calls for the repudiation of outdated values and the fostering of modern values, and involves revamping the relationships between company and government and between company and worker—in the latter relationship, workers are not nominal but actual owners. However, it is relatively easy to convince people of the fruitfulness of economic reform, as long as some progress has been made in developing the socialist commodity economy and fostering the new type of public ownership, and as long as economic efficiency has been improved and people's income raised. When such achievements become established facts, anyone wanting to gainsay the socialist commodity economy and the new public ownership will risk offending the masses of people who are beneficiaries of economic reform. By contrast, it is unrealistic to hope that a new culture—corporate culture included—will draw the same popular support. To build a new culture means to uproot outdated values, where the foothold of old culture is strong, and impediments come not only from society but also from people themselves. Although the positive results of corporate culture are apparent in a company's improved economic returns, people may still attribute them to economic reform rather than to cultural development. Furthermore, new concepts of employment, new principles for rewarding labor, new welfare standards, new interpersonal relationships, new consumer attitude, and new investment psychology are—because of their striking difference from old conventions—most likely to disconcert those deeply influenced by the old culture. Disharmony of this kind exists within and without any company. A clear message here is that cultural progress tends to encounter more obstacles than economic reform, and thus calls for more strenuous efforts.

所支配，假定作为旧文化的核心的非科学、非民主的思想仍然统治着社会，假定用利益原则来处理企业内部人际关系等做法仍然受到一些人的非议，那么也就谈不上企业文化的建设与发展。

与经济改革的情况有所不同的是，在文化领域内要进行变革并且使新文化占据支配地位，相形之下要困难得多。当然，这并不是说经济改革不会遇到阻力，不会发生波折。就以新型公有制的建立来说，由于存在着各种不同的阻力和困难，这方面的进展远不是那么容易的。何况新型公有制的建立，包括企业与政府之间关系的改变，企业与职工之间关系的改变，特别是职工不再以名义的所有者身份出现而以实际的、具体的所有者身份出现，也需要涉及传统价值观念被抛弃和现代价值观念的树立等问题。但不管怎样，在经济改革过程中，只要朝着社会主义商品经济的发展和新型公有制的建立等方向前进了，经济效益的提高和人民收入的增长以及随之而来的人民生活水平的上升就具有最大的说服力，以证明经济改革是有成效的。这时，无论什么人对社会主义商品经济和新型公有制进行非难，都会在得到经济改革实惠的群众面前被冷落。但包括企业文化在内的新文化的建设却不可能有这样的反响。新文化建设意味着旧的价值观念的转变。旧文化在这方面的统治是牢固的，阻力不仅来自社会，而且来自人们自己。企业文化的成果固然可以直接反映于企业经济效益的提高上，但人们往往不把这种效益的提高归结为文化建设的成就，而仅仅把它们看成是经济改革的产物。相反地，新的就业观念、新的劳动报酬原则、新的福利标准、新的人际关系、新的消费态度和投资心理等等，很可能引起在不同程度上受到旧文化深刻影响的人们的不安，因为这一切都与传统的看法不一致。企业内部存在着这种不协调情况，企业外部也存在这种不协调情况，这一切清楚地说明了在文化方面所遇到的阻力要比在经济方面所遇到的阻力更大，清除这些阻力的文化建设工作也就必定更艰巨。

Specifically, fostering corporate culture will promote economic growth in at least three ways.

Firstly, any firm that has come a long way in fostering its corporate culture invariably becomes a pacesetter for counterparts and gives them food for thought: How is that company able to cultivate an interpersonal relationship based on camaraderie among workers and mutual trust between workers and managers? How is that company capable of raising its economic efficiency so dramatically? Why can't we do what that company is capable of doing? Does the discrepancy between companies in fostering corporate culture reflect their discrepancy in institutional reform? While searching for answers to these questions, companies will set about exploring ways and means to speed up their own transformation. The pacesetter's diffusing impact will be spread to managers and workers. Once these people have seen the need for it, their institutional reform and their effort to build their own corporate culture will naturally pick up speed.

Secondly, the impact on the government of what a company has achieved in fostering corporate culture cannot be underestimated either. The government judges a firm's accomplishments in fostering corporate culture by searching for signs of improvements, such as whether corporate income and government revenue have increased simultaneously, whether its products are popular or not with the public, whether the strain on supply and demand has been eased, and whether the workers are happy with their jobs and motivated. If the government is impressed by what the firm has accomplished in fostering corporate culture, it will willingly summarize and disseminate the firm's experience. When and where necessary, the government will go on to study the causes behind that firm's accomplishments and, by comparing it with other firms, try to answer the question of why that firm can foster its corporate culture but the others cannot. Isn't it because that firm is successful in corporate institutional reform in the first place? If the government does not want to stop at merely summarizing that firm's success and experience, it will set the firm up as a model to advance institutional reform in other firms. The importance of the progress made by that firm will not be lost on the government, but it is more important for the government to disseminate its experience and encourage more firms to follow suit in corporate institutional reform. Only thus can a few firms' success in cultural cultivation be used to drive the corporate

具体说来，企业文化建设将从以下这些方面推动经济发展:

第一，企业文化的建设在某个具体的企业中取得了成绩，必然会对其他企业起着示范作用。其他企业会考虑这样一些问题: 为什么在那个企业中出现了新的人际关系，职工与企业之间的关系会变得如此适应，经济效益会有如此显著的提高? 在那个企业中能够实现的，为什么在自己这里还不可能实现? 企业文化建设方面的差距是否反映了企业本身在体制改革方面的差距? 于是这些企业将由此寻找差距存在的原因，并在社会经济等方面探索加速改革的途径。这种示范效应不仅会在企业领导人中间产生，而且也会在企业职工之间产生。而一旦其他企业的领导人和职工们都感到了加速体制改革的必要性和建设企业文化的必要性，企业体制改革的进程和企业文化建设的进程都会加快。

第二，企业文化的建设在某个具体的企业中取得成绩所给予政府部门的影响，同样是不可低估的。政府无非是从企业收入的增加和政府从企业所得到的收入的增加，从企业产品受到社会的欢迎和社会供求矛盾的趋于缓和，以及企业职工情绪的稳定、职工积极性的增加等方面来考察企业文化建设的效果。由此，政府部门将会对这些企业在企业文化建设方面所作出的成绩感兴趣，愿意总结经验，进行推广。只要政府部门认识到有这些需要，它就会进一步考虑这些企业取得成绩的原因，并把这些企业同另一些企业进行比较: 为什么这些企业在企业文化建设中能够取得成绩而另一些企业做不到这些? 是不是这些企业在体制改革中有某些重大的进展，才使它们具备发展企业文化的条件? 政府部门将不再局限于总结这些企业取得成绩的经验，而必然会以此作为例证来推动其他企业的体制改革。个别企业取得成绩，对政府部门来说固然是重要的，但对政府来说更重要的是推广这种经验，让更多的企业通过体制改革而取得同样的成绩。这样，个别企业的企业文化建设成就必定会推进

institutional reform as a whole. This role of government cannot be replaced by individual firms.

Thirdly, from a cultural point of view, the impact of a company's success in fostering corporate culture is by no means limited to the company itself, its workers, and their families. In other words, the "corporate spirit" that embodies the corporate culture of a successful and influential company can shake old cultural traditions to the core. For instance, a company can send shockwaves through a system where egalitarianism still holds sway by boldly replacing absolute equality with a system whereby income is distributed according to effective work done or economic efficiency. Initially, those who believe in egalitarianism will be taken aback, but then they will gradually come to their senses. The established facts—such as the company's improved economic efficiency and workers' pay rises—will eventually change their attitude. By the same token, a company can also shock the public with a new interpersonal relationship that eschews traditional hierarchy and the established pecking order in the course of overhauling business management and fostering corporate culture. Such a shockwave will spill over the remnant influence of the hierarchical concept in society and further disseminate the new culture. The impact of the achievements in fostering corporate culture on social culture and values may be intangible, but should never be underestimated.

— A speech to Hong Kong Chinese Importers' and
Exporters' Association on January 1, 1989

整个企业体制改革的进程。政府部门的这种作用是个别企业所无法替代的。

第三，企业文化的建设在某个具体的企业中取得了成绩，从文化的角度来看，其影响绝不会仅限于企业本身或仅限于本企业职工及其家属这一较小的范围。这就是说，以某个有成就、有影响力的企业的“企业精神”体现出来的企业文化，会对社会文化中的旧传统产生冲击。比如说，当社会上还流行着平均主义的分配思想的时候，如果某一个企业大胆地进行了分配制度的改革，破除了平均主义的分配方式，实行按有效劳动分配或按效益分配，那就很可能在社会上引起震动，使社会上那些有平均主义分配思想的人先是惊讶，然后通过企业效益增长和职工收入普遍上升的事实的教育而逐渐明白了道理。又如，假定与旧文化紧密联系的等级观念至今仍有相当大的影响，那么一旦某个企业进行了改革，并在企业文化建设过程中建立了新的人际关系，破坏了传统的等级制度和等级观念，那么这也将引起社会的震动，这种震动最终必将冲击社会上存在的等级观念，从而推动着新文化的传播。尽管企业文化建设的成就对社会文化和价值观念的影响是无形的，但这种无形的影响是绝不能低估的。

（1989 年 1 月 12 日在香港中华出入口商会的演讲）

CULTURAL ECONOMICS: A TENTATIVE STUDY (1990)

I. Peculiarities of cultural and art products

Cultural economics is not concerned with the process by which cultural and art products are produced but with the economic issues pertinent to the production and reproduction of such products. Thus something has to be said about the attributes of cultural and art products. In terms of economics, they fall into two categories: those in the form of physical commodity, like audiovisual products, fine arts, books and periodicals; and those in the form of service, that is, labor services provided by cultural and art organizations, such as performance art. In comparison with material production, the production of cultural and art products is unique in that it is more individualistic and creative. Looking back, we may find nothing inappropriate with the way we categorize cultural and art products and interpret their peculiar attributes. However, if we probe the issue of cultural economics more deeply, we will know where the problems are.

If, for instance, a novelist or playwright comes up with a novel or a drama script, the first material form of his brainchild is a manuscript instead of a published book. This manuscript must be recognized and accepted by editors of a press or a journal before it turns into the book form and is sold on the market. Thus the material forms of cultural and art products we see on the market are a kind of "collective" product, that is, products brought into being "collectively" not only by authors but also by editors, printers, and the like. If we regard cultural and art products as commodities, and their supply-and-demand relationship as a market relationship, two "trading" processes will take place in reality: (1) trading between authors and publishers; (2) trading between publishers and buyers (readers and distributors included). The former trading process, in which cultural and art products are not ordinary commodities but special ones, is different not only from transactions over raw materials in the course of material production, but also from purchases of household handicrafts or farm and sideline produce by modern processing companies. This difference is one of the peculiarities of cultural and art products.

文化经济学的探索（1990）

一、关于文化艺术品的特殊性质

文化经济学所要考察的不是文化艺术品的生产过程本身，而是与文化艺术品的生产和再生产有关的各种经济问题。这样就不可能不涉及文化艺术品的性质。从经济学的角度来考察，文化艺术品大致上可以划分为两类：一类是可以用物化形态表现出来的，如音像制品、美术作品、书刊等；另一类是精神服务产品，也就是文化艺术部门和单位为社会提供的劳务，如表演艺术等。文化艺术品的生产与物质资料的生产相比，其特殊性反映于它们更具有个体性和创造性。当然，这种分类方法和对于文化艺术品的特殊性质的表述并无不妥之处，但如果再深入地推敲一下，也许我们会感觉到文化经济学中关于这一问题的研究的真正困难所在。

比如说，一个小说家或戏剧作家，他为社会创作了一部小说或一部戏剧，但具体地以物化形态表现出来的，首先是一部书稿，而不是一部现成的书。这个书稿首先需要被出版社或杂志社的编辑所承认，被他们接受，然后才由出版社或杂志社付印成书刊，在市场上销售。因此，我们在市场上所看到的以物化形态表现出来的文化艺术品，是指“集体”的产品而言，而这里所说的“集体”不仅包括作家本人，而且包括编辑人员、印刷工人等等。由此可见，如果把文化艺术品视为商品，把文化艺术品的供给与需求关系当做市场关系来看待的话，那么这里实际上存在两个“交易”过程：一是作家同出版社、杂志社之间的“交易”；二是出版社、杂志社同购买书刊的人（包括读者和书刊中间商）之间的“交易”。在前一个“交易”过程中，文化艺术品并不是一般意义上的商品，而是特殊意义的商品。这种“交易”既不同于物质资料生产过程中的原材料交易，也不同于现代加工企业对家庭手工业者或农副产品生产者的产品收购。不能不认为这是文化艺术产品的特殊性之一。

As to the labor services provided by cultural workers and artists, they are likewise a lot more complicated than those provided by ordinary workers or organizations in other fields. For example, if a cultural worker or artist renders his labor or service as directly as a street performer does to his audience, the issue becomes as simple as what happens between a labor supplier and a labor demander—a deal between the two parties concerned in any supply-and-demand relationship. Nevertheless, this is not the dominant way for cultural workers or artists to offer labor service today. As things are nowadays, an author sends his manuscript to a publisher first, and then the publisher publishes the book and sells it on the market. An actor, a singer, or a dancer has to be hired by a troupe or sign a performance contract with it, before the latter puts on singing or dancing performances and pays the performer a portion of the box revenue. In that sense, this form of "trading" takes place only once, not twice. This is to say, only when a performer is brought in front of his audience can his service be really delivered. When he is hired by, or signs a contract with, a troupe, he is yet to deliver his "commodity" (i.e., his service), while the troupe hires him or signs a contract with him based merely on his previous experiences or evaluation reports. However, even this manner of transaction in labor and service is different from usual, because the "buyer" of cultural and art products (or the labor and service in performing art) is not an individual but all the audience, and the supplier is in fact also a "collective," even though one main performer (i.e., singer or dancer) plays a pivotal role in it. This is another special attribute of cultural and art products.

Judging from the two "trading" processes or either one of them, cultural and art products are commodities of a special nature. But the issue does not stop then and there. Let us take another look from the social evaluation perspective of the use value of cultural and art products.

II. Social assessment of the use value of cultural and art products

Normative economics comes to mind at the mere mention of the social evaluation of a commodity's use value. We must accept that in material production, the use value of a commodity *per se* does not have an ethical attribute. Opium and morphine have some use value because, when used as commodities, they serve certain human needs—they

再以劳务的提供来说，文化艺术工作者提供的劳务同样地要比一般的劳务部门或劳务供给者提供的劳务复杂得多。不妨举一个例子：假定文化艺术工作者都像街头艺人那样直接面对观众，以表演艺术取得报酬，那么问题显然比较简单，即一方是劳务供给者，另一方则是劳务需求者，"交易"就在供求双方之间进行。但这不是文化艺术工作者当前提供劳务的主要方式。在目前的条件下，文化艺术工作者提供的劳务有可能采取下述形式，即类似于作家提供书稿给出版社，再由出版社销售书籍；一个演员、歌唱家或舞蹈家先受聘于演出团体或同演出单位订立合同，由演出团体或单位组织歌唱会或舞蹈表演，取得票房收入，然后付出一定的报酬给表演者，但在这里，文化艺术产品的"交易"只有一次，而不是两次。这就是说，只有在表演者面对观众时，他才提供了劳务，而在他受聘于演出团体或同演出单位订立合同时，并未提供具有商品性质的劳务，演出团体或单位是根据表演者以前的表演经历或根据考核而聘任他或同他订立合同的。然而，即使这样的劳务"交易"，也不同于一般劳务的交易，这是因为，文化艺术产品（表演艺术劳务）的购买者是所有的观众，而不是某一个买主，而供给者实际上也是一个"集体"，尽管某个主要的表演者（歌手或舞蹈家）在这个"集体"中可能起着最重要的作用。这也可以被看成是文化艺术产品的又一个特殊性。

以上，无论是从两个"交易"过程的角度还是从一个"交易"过程的角度，都可以了解到文化艺术品作为一种商品是具有自己的特殊性质的。但问题还不仅限于此。让我们再从文化艺术品的使用价值的社会评价方面来进行探讨。

二、关于文化艺术品使用价值的社会评价

一谈到商品使用价值的社会评价，问题必然转入了规范经济学的领域。要知道，在物质生产领域内，一件商品的使用价值本身，并不具有伦理的性质。鸦片、吗啡作为商品，由于能够满足人的某种

may be either used in the pharmaceutical industry or bought by drug addicts. The production, sale, and use of commodities such as opium and morphine are strictly controlled because they are a potential bane to society and humanity. The same can be said of weapons and certain chemicals, such as cyanides: the problem here is not so much related to their use value but rather to the way people use them. To tighten up the control of the production and sales of weapons and certain chemicals is precisely to prevent them from being used for improper purposes.

As commodities, cultural and art products are at once similar to and different from the aforementioned material products. For instance, books, movies and audiovisual products about reactionary politics, pornography, murder or violence may have some buyers in the marketplace, but they are definitely poisonous to society.

Nevertheless, these cultural and art products are different in some ways from opium, morphine, weapons and certain chemicals. Opium and morphine are generally harmless when employed as raw materials for anesthetics—they become a public hazard only when abused by drug dealers and addicts. The same can be said of weapons and certain chemicals falling into the hands of criminals. It is thus apparent that the problem does not arise from these commodities' use value *per se* but from who uses them and what they are used for. As to books, movies and audiovisual products about reactionary politics, pornography, murder, or violence, however, the problem is not as simple as who uses them or what they are used for, because their use value is suspicious in itself—they should not have been produced in the first place. Once they are produced, their pernicious social impact becomes immediately evident. We can hardly believe they can be put to "normal use," unless they are used for special purposes by the public security bureau or the judiciary. But even in that case, there is no need for these departments to organize the production of these products. Therefore, there is no need, either, to subject this kind of cultural and art products to "restricted production and sales."

This is another peculiarity of cultural and art products based on a social assessment of their use value. Such products are different from material products in that, born of people's spiritual needs, they have normative connotations peculiarly of their own. These products are the

需要，所以它们就具有使用价值：既可以在医药工业中使用它们，也有可能被吸毒者所购买。对鸦片、吗啡之类商品的生产、销售和使用之所以要实行严格的管制措施，正因为它们有可能成为毒害社会、毒害人们的商品。同样的道理也适用于武器和某些化学制品（如氰化物）等等，问题在于使用者如何使用它们，而不在于它们的使用价值本身。对武器和某些化学制品的生产和销售进行严格管制，也是从防止其不正当使用的角度来考虑的。

文化艺术品作为商品，既有与此相类似之处，又有不同之处，例如，宣传政治反动、淫秽色情、凶杀暴力的书籍、电影、录像带等，尽管它们被投入市场后会有购买者，但它们却在明显地毒害社会。

然而与上面举例时所提到的鸦片、吗啡、武器、某些化学制品有所不同，鸦片、吗啡在被医药工业用作麻醉药品的原料时，一般不会造成危害，而只有当它们被滥用时，特别是鸦片、吗啡被贩毒者和吸毒者购买，或武器和某些化学制品流入不法之徒手中时，它们才危害社会。可见，关键不在于这些商品的使用价值本身，而在于谁使用它们，怎样使用它们。文化艺术产品中的那些宣传政治反动、淫秽色情、凶杀暴力的书籍、电影、录像带等，一般说来，问题不仅仅在于谁使用它们和怎样使用它们，甚至可以认为，它们的使用价值本身就是值得怀疑的。它们本来就不该被生产出来，而它们一旦被生产出来，就会产生有害的社会影响。很难认为对它们有所谓“正当使用”的问题，除非公安、司法等部门对它们有特殊的用途，但即使如此，这些部门也完全不需要为此目的而组织生产它们。因此，对这类文化艺术产品也就不存在所谓“严格管制下的生产和销售”问题。

这就是根据文化艺术品使用价值的社会评价而得出的文化艺术品的特殊性质的另一种表现。换句话说，文化艺术品之所以不同于物质资料生产的产品，是由于文化艺术品作为人们的精神生产的产物，本身有规范的含义。文化艺术品是它们的创作者的劳动的

brainchildren of those who created them. To become commodities, they also need the labor input of related people—editors and printers in the case of books, and producers in the case of audiovisual products—other than those who created them. They also need an intermediary "trading" process, so that they can be delivered to consumers. Their normative attribute is reflected in society's appraisal of their use value. The reason why the production and sale of books, movies, and audiovisual products about reactionary politics, pornography, murder, or violence should be banned under all circumstances is precisely based on their normative attribute, that is, public assessment of their use value. This is precisely why not only their publishers and editors but also their authors should be held accountable.

III. Economic returns of cultural and art commodity production

Let me devote this section to another issue, the economic returns of the production of cultural and art commodities. Please note the concept I dwell on here is the "economic returns of the production of cultural and art commodities," not the "economic returns" of all cultural and art products and creative works. These are two different concepts. When someone composes a poem or creates a painting or sculpture but does not market it, does it have economic returns? I would say it has no economic returns at all. (It does have its social returns as far as it is appreciated or read widely. Such social returns can be big or small, positive or negative, depending on its merits or demerits, which I will deal with in another section.) That is why this section is focused on the economic returns of cultural and art products that have become commodities. Where there are commodities, there must be suppliers (sellers) and demanders (buyers), prices and markets. On the part of the supplier, it is about costs, net returns, and the motivation and conditions for reproduction. On the part of the buyer, it is about the degree to which such a commodity satisfies his purchase intention and its actual effects. On the part of an organizer or a manager of such economic activity, consideration should be given to a series of issues such as the adjustment of resource allocation caused by the production and sales of these commodities, the margin of growth in GNP and national income, and fluctuations in fiscal revenues and expenditures. None of these factors can be ignored when the economic returns of cultural and art commodity production is studied.

成果。它们要成为商品，除了有创作者本人投入的劳动以外，还包括其他有关的人员（如书刊的编辑人员、印刷工人、音像制品的制作人员等等）所投入的劳动，并且需要通过“交易”这一中间环节，到达消费者手中。这类商品的规范性质反映于它们的使用价值的社会评价方面。宣扬政治反动、淫秽色情、凶杀暴力的书刊和音像制品之所以必须被取缔，之所以在任何条件下都不允许其生产和销售，正是从规范的意义上，也就是从社会评价的意义上来考虑的。也正是从这个意义上，不仅应当追究其出版者、编辑者的责任，而且更应当追究其创作者的责任。

三、关于文化艺术商品生产的经济效益

下面，让我们转而探讨另一个问题，即文化艺术商品生产的经济效益。请注意，我在这里使用的是“文化艺术商品生产的经济效益”概念，而不是泛指一切文化艺术品或文化艺术创作物的“经济效益”。这是有区别的。假定一个人创作了一首诗、一幅画、一件雕塑，而并未投入市场，那么这种创作物不成为商品。它有没有经济效益呢？可以说，经济效益的概念这里并不存在（至于社会效益，那是会有的。只要它被人们所观赏或传诵，社会效益也就会产生。当然，社会效益有大有小，有正有负，这都要由具体情况来决定。关于这些，后面再进行探讨），所以我在这里指的只是那些成为商品的文化艺术创作物的经济效益。既然是商品，那么必然有商品供给者（卖方）、商品需求者（买方）、价格、市场。对商品供给者来说，还有成本、净收益、再生产的动力与条件等问题。对商品需求者来说，则有购买意愿的满足程度、使用所购买的商品的实际效果之类的问题。而对于经济活动的组织者、管理者而言，需要考虑的是通过这类商品的生产和销售而引起的资源配置格局的调整、国民生产总值和国民收入的增长幅度、财政收支的变动问题等等。所有这些，在研究文化艺术商品生产的经济效益时都是不可回避的。

This field of study thus takes on a vast scope that is not limited to the costs and returns of commodity producers or the growth rate of GNP or national income. Simply put, the economic returns of cultural and art commodity production can be analyzed from at least six different angles:

1. Comparing the labor and earnings of authors of cultural and art products. Designed to observe an individual's economic returns by taking into account the peculiarities of cultural and art commodities, this is a rather laborious research topic. What an author—writer, painter, or actor—puts into a cultural or art commodity is undoubtedly complex labor, but its degree of complexity cannot be easily measured. Because of this, it is hard to set an objective benchmark for such complex labor, and even harder to quantify and gauge its quality and to pay for it properly.

2. The cost-benefit ratio of suppliers—publishing houses, per-forming troupes, audiovisual workshops, etc. Supposing the supplier lists his pay to an author in his wage cost, which also includes his pay to the staff members involved, this wage cost plus depreciation expenses and consumption of raw materials makes up the total cost. The supplier's economic returns are determined by the margin between the total cost and the returns, i.e., the sales income.

3. The economic returns of the buyers (users) of cultural and art commodities. This refers to such a commodity's end-consumers, not including intermediate buyers. The more a cultural or art commodity meets a buyer's need, the more satisfied he becomes, and the more he is convinced that the deal has brought considerable economic returns. It is true that people normally do not regard the degree of their satisfaction as a benchmark for economic returns. In fact, there is no criterion to measure such satisfaction. Nevertheless, so long as we regard economic returns as synonymous to "maximum gain at a certain expense" or "minimum expense in return for a certain amount of gain," we cannot deny that the "minimum cost principle" and the "maximum returns principle" are being followed by both suppliers and buyers in judging their economic returns.

The reason why a buyer considers where to spend his money before he buys a commodity, chooses a seller when he is buying it, and appraises the results of the purchase after he has bought it, is because all these behaviors are directly related to his concern with economic returns.

这样，文化艺术商品生产的经济效益的研究领域就相当广泛，而不仅限于对于商品生产者的成本与效益的考虑，或对于国民生产总值和国民收入增长率的分析。简单地说，对文化艺术商品生产的经济效益，至少可以从六个不同的方面来考察。

1. 文化艺术商品创作者投入的劳动与其所得的收入的比较。这是从文化艺术商品的特殊性出发所考虑的个人经济效益问题，但这又是一个艰巨性较大的研究课题。文化艺术商品创作者（例如作家、画家、演员）所投入的劳动无疑是复杂劳动，但这种劳动的复杂程度却是不易衡量的。由此也难以给这种复杂劳动制定一个客观标准，难以判断投入劳动的数量与质量同所获得的收入的相符程度。

2. 文化艺术商品的供给单位（如出版社、演出团体、音像制作企业）的成本与收益之比。假定这些供给单位把付给文化艺术商品创作者的报酬列入工资成本之内（工资成本中还包括付给其他有关工作人员的报酬），并且再计算折旧费、原材料消耗等，那就构成了供给者的全部成本。供给者的经济效益大小取决于成本与效益（销售收入）之间差距的多少。

3. 文化艺术商品的购买者（使用者）的经济效益。这里排除了中间购买者的情况，而把文化艺术商品的购买者定义为最终消费者。购买者认为所买到的文化艺术商品越能符合自己的购买意愿，他们越会感到满足，他们也应认为这样的购买（交易）是有较大经济效益的。尽管人们通常不把这种满足程度视为经济效益的尺度，而且事实上对这种满足程度也缺乏衡量的标准，但只要我们把经济效益看成是“以一定的支出取得尽可能多的收获”或“以尽可能少的支出取得一定的收获”的同义语，那么不可否认，标志着经济效益高低的“最小成本原则”或“最大效益原则”无论在文化艺术商品的供给者那里，还是在文化艺术商品需求者那里，都是存在的。文化艺术商品的购买者之所以会在购买前进行支出方向的比较，在购买中会对购买对象进行选择，在购买行为完成后会对这项购买行为作出评价，是因为与他们对经济效益的考虑直接有关。

4. From the perspective of government finance, the production and sales of a commodity or of a particular industry can change fiscal revenues and expenditures. The larger the growth in net fiscal revenues such production and sales can bring, the better its economic returns is believed to be; the smaller such growth is, the poorer its economic returns is believed to be. The same is true with the economic returns of cultural and art commodities.

5. Contribution to the economic growth rate is another benchmark for judging the economic returns of the production and sales of a single commodity or a certain industry. Economic growth rate is usually computed on the basis of the annual rate of changes in GNP or national income, a method that also applies to the economic returns of cultural and art commodity production. For example, the press and publication industry, whose output value is part of GNP, is in a check-and-balance relationship with other sectors of the national economy. We have reason to believe the press and publication industry has contributed a great deal to economic growth if its growing output value has led to considerable growth in the output value of related industries.

Of the above five perspectives, only the second, and the fourth are relatively easy for analysts, and the first, third and fifth are relatively difficult. Nevertheless, none of them is more difficult than the sixth perspective that follows.

6. From the perspective of resource allocation, the production of a commodity, or the commodity production of a certain industry, calls for an input of resources, while the results of production can change the aggregate quantum and structure of resources. This is true with both material production and the production of cultural and art commodities. Supposing the aggregate quantum of resources is limited and the resource allocation pattern fixed, adjustment can be made only through incremental changes in resources. Thus society must answer the following question when appraising economic returns: Is the production

of a commodity or the commodity production of an industry improving or deteriorating resource allocation? Improvement and deterioration are benchmarks by which to judge whether economic returns is positive or negative. The degree of improvement or deterioration is the benchmark for determining the degree of positive or negative returns. Such a conclusion is derived from theoretical analysis.

4. 从国家财政的角度来看，某一商品的生产和销售，以及某一行业的商品生产和销售，都会使财政收支状况发生变动。通过这些生产和销售而使财政收入净增加额越大的，可以被认为是经济效益越好，反之则被认为是经济效益越差。对文化艺术商品的生产和销售，同样可以采用这种方式来衡量其经济效益。

5. 对经济增长率的贡献大小也是衡量某一具体商品的生产和销售以及某一行业的商品生产和销售的经济效益高低的标准。经济增长率通常是以国民生产总值或国民收入的年变动率计算的。对于文化艺术商品生产的经济效益的衡量，这一方法同样适用。比如说，新闻出版的产值是国民生产总值的组成部分，它们同国民经济其他部门之间存在着相互制约的关系。如果新闻出版业产值的增长能导致与之有关的其他行业的产值有较大程度的增长，我们就可以认为新闻出版业对经济增长的贡献较大，从而认为新闻出版业的经济效益是较好的。

以上五个方面中，只有第二和第四这两方面较易于分析，而第一、第三、第五这几个方面都是难度较大的。然而，更难以分析的是下面所要讨论的第六个方面。

6. 从资源配置的角度来考察，某一具体商品的生产以及某一行业的商品生产总是需要资源投入的，而生产的成果则又会使社会的资源总量和结构发生变动。物质资料的生产是这样，文化艺术商品的生产也是这样。假定社会的资源总量是有限的，并且资源配置的格局已经形成，唯有通过资源增量的变动才能予以调整。于是在衡量经济效益时社会面临如下的问题：某一具体商品的生产以及某一行业的商品生产究竟是导致资源配置状况的改善，还是导致资源配置状况的恶化？资源配置状况的改善或恶化，是衡量该项生产的经济效益正负的标准，而改善或恶化的程度则是衡量该项生产的正值经济效益或负值经济效益大小的尺度。理论分析所得出的结论就是如此。

The snag lies apparently in evaluating the current pattern of resource allocation and in measuring the degree of changes in resource allocation. People may suggest that the disparity between aggregate demand and supply—or, to probe more deeply, the extent of shortage or overstock of some key commodities—could be employed as the criterion for appraising the pattern of resource allocation and the degree of changes in it. However, this criterion can be applied only to short-term economic returns, but far from enough for long-term returns. That is to say, the allocation of a certain resource may not be problematic in the short run, but may cause a lot of problems in the long run. Some of the problems are latent or obscure and seemingly harmless to the economy for the time being. But if the problems remain unsolved, they will emerge and become so acute as to hurt the economy sometime in the future. Only by perceiving the economic returns of the production of a commodity or the commodity production of a certain industry in this light, can we gain a relatively comprehensive understanding of the concept "economic returns." Despite the aforementioned snag, resource allocation can never be factored out when studying the economic returns of the production of either physical materials or cultural and art commodities.

When we gradually shift our study to resource allocation, especially to its long-term economic returns, we are bound to come across the most difficult issue, that is, how to measure social returns. This issue is particularly critical to cultural and art commodities. We have already touched upon this topic in our previous discussion about the social appraisal of the use value of cultural and art products.

IV. Social returns of cultural and art commodity production

In a certain sense, the long-term economic returns of the production of a commodity or the commodity production of an industry are consistent with its social returns. But social returns usually entail a broader meaning than economic returns, and can be directly linked with socioeconomic development goals. If the production of a commodity or the commodity production of an industry is conducive to socioeconomic development goals, we can presume that its social returns are high; if it is detrimental to socioeconomic development goals, we can presume that

难点显然在于对既定的资源配置格局的评价以及对资源配置状况变动程度的衡量。也许有人会提出，用社会总需求与社会总供给的差距大小，或者更深入一层，用关键性产品的短缺程度或积压程度，未尝不可以作为对资源配置格局评价和资源配置状况变动程度的判断标准。但要知道，这通常只适用于近期经济效益的分析，而对于长期经济效益的分析则是远远不够的。也就是说，从近期看，某种资源配置状况不一定反映出什么问题，但从长期看，这种资源配置状况所暴露出来的问题则比较多。有些问题至今仍是潜伏的、不明显的，它们对经济似乎不构成危害，而如果持续下去，那么到一定时刻，潜伏的问题会公开化，不明显的问题会变得突出，而对经济的危害也就暴露出来了。只有从这样的高度来认识某一商品生产的经济效益和某一行业的商品生产的经济效益，才能对经济效益概念有较完整的理解。不管是对物质资料的生产还是对文化艺术商品的生产，都不应该忽略从资源配置角度对经济效益的考察，虽然在衡量这种经济效益方面存在着以上所说的困难。

当我们把研究的重点逐渐转移到资源配置方面，特别是关于资源配置的长期经济效益方面时，我们必然会遇到一个最为困难的问题，这就是社会效益的衡量。这个问题对于文化艺术商品来说尤其重要。前面在讨论文化艺术品使用价值的社会评价时，我们实际上已经接触到这个问题了。

四、关于文化艺术商品生产的社会效益

在一定的意义上，某种商品生产以及某一行业的商品生产的长期经济效益与它们的社会效益是一致的。但社会效益通常要比经济效益具有更广的含义。可以把社会效益直接同社会经济发展目标联结在一起。假定某种商品以及某一行业的商品生产有助于社会经济发展目标的实现，那么可以认为该项商品生产的社会效益较大；反之，假定某种商品以及某一行业的商品生产不利于社会经济发展目标的实现，那么可以认为该项商品生产

it has no social returns at all. Therefore, when analyzing the social returns of commodity production, we have to clarify what are the socioeconomic development goals and what benchmark should be employed to judge if such production is a boon or a bane to such goals.

Socioeconomic development goals are multiple, rather than single. For instance, we should raise people's income, but at the same time, we must avoid widening the income gap; we should meet people's growing demand for a better material life, but their demand for a better spiritual life should also be taken care of; and we should improve both the social environment and the natural environment at the same time. Multiple socioeconomic development goals indicate that it is not enough to develop material production alone—the production of cultural and art commodities also matters. When we talk about the social returns of cultural and art commodity production, we can never overlook the role such production should and can play in attaining multiple socioeconomic development goals.

Every socioeconomic development goal can be divided into sub-goals to be attained in different stages. The goal of meeting people's spiritual need, for example, should comprise a variety of specific goals for different periods. When evaluating the social returns of the production of a certain art product in a certain stage, we may do it in comparison with the degree of people's satisfaction with that product in meeting their demand for spiritual life during that stage. Only thus can we see if its social returns are positive or negative and determine the margin of changes in such positive or negative social returns.

In the case of a socioeconomic development goal for bettering the quality of people's lives, after that goal has been divided into sub-goals for different stages, we can also compare the social returns of a given cultural and art commodity with the projected sub-goal for a better life quality in a specific stage. I think we can be sure about the applicability of this approach to assessing the social returns of the production of such commodities. Of course many details in this approach need to be hammered out through the concerted efforts of those interested in cultural economics.

缺乏社会效益。可见，在对一定的商品生产的社会效益进行分析时，有必要先明确究竟什么是社会经济发展目标，以及用什么来判断一定的商品生产究竟是有利于社会经济发展目标的实现还是不利于社会经济发展目标的实现。

社会经济发展目标不是单一的，而是多元的，比如说，既要提高居民的收入，又要避免收入分配的差距过大；既要满足居民在物质生活方面不断增长的需要，又要满足居民在精神生活方面不断增长的需要；既要改善居民生活的社会环境，又要改善居民生活的自然环境，等等。多元的社会经济发展目标表明，单一发展物质资料的生产是不够的，文化艺术商品生产的发展起着同样重要的作用。我们在讨论文化艺术商品生产的社会效益时，绝不能忽视文化艺术商品生产的发展在实现社会经济发展的多元目标中应该和可以起到的作用。

社会经济发展目标中的任何一个目标都可以分解为各个不同的阶段性目标。以满足居民在精神生活方面的需要来说，这一目标可以分解为若干个不同的阶段性目标，每个阶段性目标是比较具体的。因此，在衡量一定阶段内的艺术商品生产的社会效益时，可以把文化艺术商品生产的社会效益同相应阶段内要达到的居民精神生活方面的需要的满足情况进行比较，以确定社会效益究竟是正值还是负值，确定正值或负值的社会效益的变动幅度。

就提高居民的生活质量这一社会经济发展目标而言，在把它分解为若干不同的阶段性目标之后，也可以采取同样的方法把文化艺术商品的社会效益同相应阶段内要达到的提高居民生活质量的情况进行比较。这种方法对于衡量文化艺术商品生产的社会效益的适用性，我认为是可以肯定的，当然，许多细节还应作进一步的研究，这将有待于关心文化经济学的同志们的共同努力。

In observing the social returns of cultural and art commodity production, the most complex issue is perhaps how to evaluate its role in enhancing people's ideological awareness or in corrupting their minds. Theoretically speaking, it is the same as the aforementioned social appraisal of the use value of cultural and art products. However, insofar as social returns are concerned, such a role needs to be evaluated. Nobody can deny that cultural and art commodities are playing such a role, but it is difficult to measure it. The difficulty lies in particular in the fact that people's minds can be nourished or corrupted by a host of factors—the production, marketing and utilization of these products are just a few of them. In evaluating the social returns of cultural and art products, we have yet to find a way to strip these products from the other factors that are playing the same role for an exclusive study. It is, indeed, another hard nut to crack awaiting future researchers.

— *Economics & Culture*, issue No. 4, 1990

在考察文化艺术商品生产的社会效益时，最为复杂的问题也许是对文化艺术商品在提高人们的思想觉悟或腐蚀人们心灵方面的作用的估计。从理论上说，这与前面讨论过的文化艺术品使用价值的社会评价具有相同的含义，但从社会效益的角度来看，则存在对文化艺术商品的作用的估计问题。我们可以明确地说，这种作用无疑是存在的，也是人们所不能否认的，但作用大小的估计却非常困难。特别是，提高人们的思想觉悟或腐蚀人们的心灵的因素很多，文化艺术商品的生产、销售和使用只不过是众多因素中的一项。迄今为止，在估计文化艺术商品生产的社会效益时还找不到一条可以把文化艺术商品在这方面的作用同其他因素的作用分离出来而单独予以估计的途径。这个难题只有留待今后的研究者来解决。

（原载《经济文化》，1990 年第 4 期）

ENVIRONMENTAL PROTECTION AND COMPENSATION TO VICTIMS OF ENVIRONMENTAL DAMAGE (1990)

I. Two kinds of victims

Compensating victims is a major theoretical and policy issue in the economics of environmental protection. It is, therefore, necessary to clarify the definition of "victims" before looking into the issue. As a matter of fact, victims fall into two categories: (1) those victimized in the course of environmental damage; and (2) those victimized in the course of environmental treatment. There are both direct and indirect victims in each category.

Direct victims of environmental damage are individuals who lose health, property and the means to earn a living, make less money, whose lives are disturbed, or whose family relationships are upset because of the damage done to their living environment. They also include businesses that suffer losses in output, product quality, revenue and property due to environmental damage.

Indirect victims of environmental damage comprise mainly those individuals and businesses whose economic interests have been impaired by the financial and other losses incurred by the aforementioned direct victims—individuals or businesses—with whom they maintain close economic ties.

Direct victims of environmental treatment include businesses that are forced to close down, reduce output or relocate, and individuals working in such businesses. These businesses and individuals make less money as a result. Such direct victims also include families that are relocated due to the needs of environmental treatment—their property may be impaired, their income may drop, and their daily lives may become disturbed or disorganized.

Indirect victims of environmental treatment comprise mainly those individuals and businesses who suffer economic losses due to their close economic ties with the direct victims (individuals or businesses) of environmental treatment who make less money because of it.

People and businesses become direct or indirect victims for different reasons. They are victimized directly or indirectly because of the behavior of those causing environmental damage or those involved in environmental protection. The damage done to them differs in degree

环境保护与受害者的补偿问题（1990）

一、环境破坏和环境治理过程中两种不同性质的受害者

对受害者的补偿是环境保护经济学中的一个重要的理论和政策问题。在分析这个问题时，首先有必要对“受害者”概念加以说明。实际上，这里有两种不同性质的受害者：一是环境破坏过程中的受害者，一是环境治理过程中的受害者。并且，每一种受害者又可以分为直接受害者和间接受害者。

环境破坏过程中的直接受害者，主要是指因环境受到破坏而使生命财产受到损失的个人，如身体受损害、财产受损失、失去谋生的手段、减少收入、生活变得不安定或不协调等。因环境受到破坏而使产量下降、产品质量下降、收入减少、财产受损失的企业，也应包括在环境破坏过程中的直接受害者之列。

环境破坏过程中的间接受害者，主要是指同环境破坏过程中的直接受害者（个人或企业）在经济上有较密切的联系，从而因直接受害者收入减少等情况而在经济上受到损失的个人和企业。

环境治理过程中的直接受害者，主要是指因治理环境的需要而停业、减产、迁移的企业，以及在这些企业中工作的个人，这些企业的收入和个人的收入将因此而减少。环境治理过程中的直接受害者还包括因治理环境的需要而迁移的家庭，他们的财产可能受到损失，收入可能下降，生活也可能变得不安定、不协调等。

环境治理过程中的间接受害者，主要是指同环境治理过程中的直接受害者（个人或企业）在经济上有较密切的联系，从而因直接受害者收入减少等情况而在经济上受到损失的个人和企业。

这两类受害者（包括直接受害者和间接受害者）受害的原因是不同的：环境破坏过程中的受害者是因环境破坏者的行为而受害，而环境治理过程中的受害者则是因治理环境的行为而受害。同时，这两类受害者受害的程度可能有差别：环境破坏过程中的受害者

as well. Victims of environmental damage bear both economic and physical losses, and in extreme cases, their lives may be at risk. Victims of environmental treatment suffer mainly from losses in income or assets, and their lives may be disarrayed by a changed living environment, although few of them are physically impaired or have their lives threatened.

Victims (individuals or businesses) feel differently about their miseries, too. Victims of environmental treatment may demand compensation because they have either felt or foreseen its adverse impact on their income. Victims of environmental damage may have found out either after damage was done to them or after they were told about it. Some of them may have been oblivious to such damage for a considerable length of time and thus failed to raise compensation demands.

To distinguish the two categories of victims helps research into the issue of compensating victims of environmental protection in the following ways:

Firstly, it helps clarify the nature of such compensation and the rationale behind it. Individuals and businesses must be compensated properly for the damage done to them either in environmental damage or in environmental treatment. However, the nature of compensation and the rationale behind it may differ with the causes of the damage done. The harm done to victims of environmental damage is caused by is perpetrators, and, theoretical speaking, should be compensated by the same perpetrators—they may pay victims themselves or through the government. Although the damage done to victims of environmental treatment should be blamed ultimately on the party that has caused it in the first place, the victims, out of personal feelings, or by tracing such damage to its immediate cause, tend to blame the party—government agencies, businesses, social organizations or individuals—that undertakes to repair such damage through environmental treatment, and demand compensation from that party. Double compensation, which occurs when the party treating the damage demands compensation from someone who caused the damage, is out of the question if the environmental damage was done by the same party that treats it; otherwise, double compensation becomes the issue. Theoretically speaking, there are ample reasons to demand twofold compensation. However, whether or not such compensation can occur in reality depends on the circumstances.

不仅在经济上遭受损失，而且可能在身体上受到损害，甚至生命受到威胁；环境治理过程中的受害者则主要是收入或财产遭受损失，可能也包括因生活环境改变而使生活变得不安定、不协调，但不会有身体上受损害和生命受威胁之类的情况发生。

从受害者（个人或企业）自身对受害的感受来说，情况也有所不同。只要进行环境的治理，那么在经济上受不利影响的受害者就会感觉到或预感到自己的收入的变动，他们将因此提出补偿的要求。至于环境破坏过程中的受害者，他们或者在事后才发现自己在某些方面受到了损害，或者在实际上受损害之后经过他人的告知才了解到自己已经受到损害，甚至有可能在较长时间内察觉不到所受的损害，从而没有补偿的要求。

区别两种不同性质的受害者，对于环境保护中的补偿问题的探讨有以下重要意义。

第一，有助于确定补偿的性质和受补偿的理由。个人或企业无论是在环境破坏过程中受到损害，还是在环境治理过程中受到损害，都有必要给予相应的补偿，但由于受害的性质不同，因此补偿的性质和受补偿的理由也不一样。环境破坏过程中的受害者所遭受的损害，是由环境破坏责任者造成的，从理论上说，应当由环境破坏责任者给予补偿。这既可以由环境破坏责任者直接支付给受害者，也可以由环境破坏责任者付款给政府有关部门，而由政府有关部门给受害者补偿。而环境治理过程中的受害者所遭受的损害，虽然追根溯源仍由环境破坏责任者造成，但从受害者的感受来说，或从事件发生的直接原因来说，则是由于治理环境的主体（政府有关部门、企业、社会团体或个人）治理环境的行为所导致的，从而要由治理环境的主体给受害者补偿。治理环境的主体有可能就是当初破坏该环境的责任者，如果是这样的话，那就不存在再补偿的问题（即治理环境一方向当初破坏环境的一方要求补偿），否则就会产生再补偿的问题。从理论上说，再补偿是有充足理由的，至于在实际经济生活中能否实现，则要取决于各种具体的情况。

Secondly, the distinction helps determine the way compensation is made. Once direct and indirect victims of either environmental damage or treatment are distinguished, it is easy to choose a proper way to compensate them. Those victimized in the course of environmental damage should be compensated by the responsible party, with compensation money dispensed directly and in full. Where double compensation is not considered, victims of environmental treatment should be compensated directly, indirectly or in both ways by the party responsible for the treatment. Such compensation may be paid entirely, partially or in both ways in the light of the actual situation.

Thirdly, it helps bring the role of the government into play in compensation, a role that is associated with the government's commitment to protecting the people's interests and the environment. That is to say, whether the damage is attributed to environmental destruction or environmental treatment, the government is duty-bound to do its level best to compensate victims. However, it should be noted that even though governmental decision-making mistakes may cause environmental damage, the real perpetrators are mostly businesses or residents, who are naturally accountable for compensation. In that case, the government's major task is to see to it that victims are properly compensated by the perpetrators. The situation with environmental treatment is somewhat different. The government may either be the decision-maker for environmental treatment or its executor. Thus it may become the party either to directly compensate victims or to demand recompensation from those who caused the damage in the first place. If the party engaged in environmental treatment is not the government but businesses, social organizations or individuals, the government may handle compensation in one of three ways: (1) The government may guarantee that victims are duly compensated by the party engaged in environmental treatment. (2) When the party engaged in environmental treatment demands recompensation from the perpetrator of the environmental damage being treated, the government will make sure such a demand is met fully or partially according to the circumstances.

(3) When the party responsible for environmental treatment can compensate victims only partially, and thereby fails to meet the victims' demand, the government will decide, according to the circumstances, whether the victims' demand should be met, and to what degree.

第二，有助于确定补偿的方式。在区分了两种不同性质的受害者，以及进一步区分了直接受害者和间接受害者之后，所采取的补偿方式也就易于被确定下来。这主要是指：对环境破坏过程中的受害者应当由环境破坏责任者给予补偿，而且应以直接补偿和充分补偿为主；在不考虑上述再补偿问题的条件下，对环境治理过程中的受害者应当由治理环境的主体给予补偿，其补偿方式可以是直接补偿，也可以是间接补偿，或二者兼用，并且可以根据具体情况采用充分补偿或部分补偿。

第三，有助于确定政府在补偿方面所发挥的作用。政府在补偿方面所发挥的作用，是与政府负有保护人民利益、保护环境的责任分不开的。因此，无论是因环境破坏而造成的受害，还是因环境治理而造成的受害，政府都有责任为受害者得到相应的补偿而尽力。但这里需要说明的是，在环境破坏方面，虽然政府有可能因决策的失误而导致环境的破坏，但造成某一具体地区的环境破坏的直接责任者，则多半是某些企业或居民个人，后者也就自然地成为向受害者支付补偿的一方。这样，在对环境破坏过程中的受害者进行补偿时，政府的主要作用是如何保证受害者能从环境破坏责任者那里得到相应的补偿。在环境治理方面，情形有所不同。政府既可能是环境治理的决策者，也可能是环境治理的执行者。因此，政府既有可能成为直接向受害者进行补偿的一方，也有可能成为要求当初造成环境破坏的责任者再补偿的一方。假定环境治理的主体不是政府，而是某些企业、社会团体或个人，那么政府在补偿方面可能发挥以下三种作用：（1）政府保证受害者能从环境治理一方得到相应的补偿；（2）在环境治理一方要求当初造成环境破坏的责任者再补偿时，政府可以根据具体情况使环境治理一方的要求得到全部或部分满足；（3）在环境治理一方只可能给予环境治理过程中的受害者部分的补偿，从而受害者的要求还不能满足时，政府将根据具体情况决定是否满足受害者的要求或在多大程度上满足受害者的要求。

Fourthly, the distinction helps probe further into the issue of compensation in environmental protection. As is to be illustrated in a later section in this study, many difficult issues concerning compensation for victims of environmental protection remain unsolved in theory and in government policy. To address these problems, the two categories of victims should be distinguished in the first place.

II. Principles and approaches for compensating victims of environmental damage

As mentioned above, environmental damage is done by those held responsible for it, and should therefore be compensated for by them. But this is true merely in theory. In reality, the situation is a lot more complex.

First of all, who should be held responsible for environmental damage can be a controversial decision. Such a decision can only be made according to the actual situation. Take, for example, the waste water discharged by a paper mill situated in the upper reaches of a river which impairs the interests of dwellers in the lower reaches. In this case, it is easy to pinpoint the paper mill as the culprit and ask it to pay dwellers for the damages done. If in the upper reaches of the river there are several factories whose waste water discharges have hurt the townspeople living in the lower reaches, not only must the total responsibility for environmental damage be clarified, but the responsibility to be shared by all those factories should also be decided according to the amount of waste water each factory has discharged, thereby making it possible to address the compensation problem properly. Nevertheless, we may also find ourselves dealing with the following scenario, in which acid rain has impaired the interests of the businesses and individuals of a certain place. Can we ascertain who caused such environmental damage? If the answer is yes, can we settle the amount of compensation money to be paid by the perpetrator? The same dilemma may occur again in another scenario, in which long years of soil erosion and vegetation destruction have drastically changed a region's climate, and resulted in alternating drought and flood that eventually hurt the interests of local residents. In this case, it is also difficult to identify the perpetrator and quantify the money to be paid as compensation. Clearly, only when both the responsibility of the perpetrator and the losses inflicted on the victims are clarified can the aforementioned compensation principle be followed. Otherwise, another way must be found to compensate the victims.

第四，有助于对环境保护中补偿问题的进一步探讨。正如本文将会提到的，环境保护中的补偿问题在理论上和政策上还有许多难点问题有待于进一步探讨。然而，要使这些问题得到较好的解决，首先必须把两种不同性质的受害者区分开来，这是深入探讨的出发点。

二、对环境破坏过程中的受害者的补偿原则和补偿方式

前面已经指出，环境破坏过程中受害者所受损害，是由环境破坏责任者造成的，应当由后者给予补偿。但要知道，这是单纯从补偿理论的角度说的，现实中的问题显然比这复杂得多。

首先，环境破坏责任者的确定可能存在着争议。这要根据具体情况而定。比如说，一条河流的上游有一家造纸厂，它排放的污水使下游居民的利益受到损害。这种情况下的环境破坏责任易于被确定。由造纸厂给受损害的居民以补偿，也是没有疑问的。即使一条河流的上游有若干家排放污水的工厂，下游若干城镇的居民的利益受到了损害，那么，不仅环境破坏的总的责任可以被确定下来，而且每家工厂具体的责任也可以通过排污量的计算而大体上被确定下来，从而补偿问题也就有实现的可能。然而我们在现实生活中还会遇到这样的情形，比如说，一个地区受到了酸雨的危害而使企业和个人的利益遭受损失，能确定环境破坏责任者是谁吗？能由此确定环境破坏责任者应付的补偿数额吗？又如，由于多年造成的水土流失和植被破坏而使得某一地区气候异常，旱涝洪灾不断，使居民利益受损，这也无法确定具体的环境破坏责任者，从而无法确定环境破坏责任者应付的补偿数额。由此可见，只有在能够确定环境破坏责任者的具体责任，并且确定环境破坏受害者的损失的情况下，才能按上述的补偿原则进行补偿。如果不是这样，那就需要另外探讨补偿的途径。

Then, in our study of compensating victims of environmental damage, we may also be faced with the complicated task of how to clarify the degree of damage and quantify the losses inflicted. In the previous section I dwelt on how to differentiate between direct and indirect victims. It should be noted, however, the economic losses inflicted on direct victims of environmental damage are not necessarily higher than the losses of those victimized indirectly by such damage. If, in that case, the perpetrator of environmental damage can only compensate direct victims, it raises the highly controversial question: Should the indirect victims be compensated for their losses too? If the answer is yes, who is to compensate them?

Next, when it comes to victims of environmental damage, only businesses and individuals are counted as victims that deserve compensation. Looking deeper into the issue, however, it is not hard to see that the state or local community is also a victim of such damage. This is because when an environment is destroyed, it means a loss in national assets and in the local community's stock of resources. This means those responsible for environmental damage, once verified, should compensate two groups of victims: (1) businesses and individuals whose interests are directly impaired; and (2) the government or the local community.

Based on the above analysis, and by taking into account the complex situation in reality, we propose four principles for compensating victims of environmental damage:

1. Those responsible for environmental damage should, once their responsibility is settled, compensate the direct victims appropriately; such compensation should be delivered directly and in full to make up for the victims' losses.

2. Apart from compensating the direct victims, those responsible for environmental damage should, once their responsibility is fixed, also compensate the state or the local community for the losses they have caused to national assets and to the local community's stock of resources.

3. If, after damage is done to the environment, for one reason or

another the responsibility for it cannot be allotted to the businesses or individuals that have perpetrated it, and, as a result, if direct victims of such damage cannot be compensated directly, the direct victims may be handled with social compensation, an approach that will be dwelt upon a few paragraphs later.

其次，在分析对环境破坏过程中的受害者的补偿问题时，还会遇到一个复杂的情况，即如何确定受害者的受害程度和损失的大小。前面在谈到直接受害者与间接受害者的区别时已经涉及这个问题，但应当注意的是，直接受害者固然是直接因环境破坏而受损害的，但从经济方面来看，其损失的大小不一定高于某些间接受害者间接地遭受的损失。因此，即使在确定了环境破坏责任者之后，环境破坏责任者所能给予补偿的也只可能是直接受害者。至于间接受害者所遭受的损失，是不是也应当得到补偿呢？如果应当得到补偿，那么又应当由谁来支付呢？这些问题同样是有争议的。

再次，以上在讨论环境破坏过程中的受害者时，都把企业和个人作为环境破坏的受害对象来看待，补偿的对象也就是受害的对象。但如果对这个问题作深入一步的分析，不难发现，环境破坏的受害对象实际上还包括国家或社会。这是因为，环境破坏的同时也就是国民财富的损失，是社会所拥有的资源存量的损失。这样就产生了一个新的问题：在确定了环境破坏责任者之后，环境破坏责任者应当支付两类补偿费用，一类是给直接受到损害的企业和个人的，一类是给国家或社会的。

根据以上的分析，并把现实生活中的各种复杂的情况考虑在内，我们可以把环境破坏过程中的受害者的补偿原则表述如下：

1. 在确定环境破坏责任者对环境破坏应负的责任的条件下，环境破坏责任者应当对直接受害者给予相应的补偿，补偿应当是直接的和充分的，以弥补后者所遭受的损失。

2. 在确定环境破坏责任者对环境破坏应负的责任的条件下，环境破坏责任者除了应当对直接受害者给予相应的补偿外，还应当给国家或社会相应的补偿，以补偿国民财富的损失、社会所拥有的资源存量的损失。

3. 尽管环境遭到了破坏，但由于各种原因，使得环境破坏的责任无法明确到具体责任者（企业和个人），从而对环境破坏的直接受害者的直接补偿也就难以实现。在这种情况下，对直接受害者的补偿可以通过社会补偿的方式进行。关于社会补偿，将在下面论述。

4. If indirect victims of environmental damage fail to receive the compensation that they deserve after direct victims have been compensated by the perpetrator, the social compensation approach should also be employed.

After laying down these principles for compensating victims of environmental damage, we need to define the approaches to such compensation. If businesses and individuals are direct victims, they may be compensated in one of two ways: (1) they may be directly compensated by those responsible for the environmental damage; or (2) those responsible for the environmental damage may be asked to deliver compensation money to the government and the government then pays the direct victims. Furthermore, compensation for the government or the local community shall be paid in money by those held responsible for the damage done. If perpetrators of environmental damage who choose to compensate victims through the government are also obliged to compensate the government, the government, upon receiving all the compensation money, shall divide the money into two according to a certain ratio, retain one portion, and dispense the other portion among direct victims.

Now let us consider social compensation. As a kind of indirect compensation, it is administered to victims of environmental damage with funds raised from all walks of life. Social compensation can be dispensed in the following ways: (1) preferential loans that help victims boost production and thereby raise their income, or that help stricken areas restore and develop local economy so as to increase their per capita income; (2) employment guidance and assistance to victims or residents of stricken areas; and (3) technical assistance to victims or stricken areas. In other words, social compensation as an indirect way of atonement is not given directly to victims, but is delivered in such forms as loans, employment guidance and assistance and technical assistance to enable victims to earn more and thus make up for their losses incurred in the course of environmental damage.

The organization in charge of social compensation raises the money needed from all quarters, including fees paid by firms, donations from businesses, individuals and nongovernmental organizations, as well as

4. 即使确定了环境破坏责任者并由该责任者向直接受害者支付了补偿，环境破坏过程中的间接受害者的补偿问题仍无法因此得到解决。但间接受害者既然也是环境破坏过程中的受害者，他们的损失就应当得到相应的补偿。这种补偿也可以通过社会补偿的方式进行。

在明确了环境破坏过程中对受害者的补偿原则之后，接着需要探讨的是对受害者的补偿方式。如果企业和个人是直接受害者，那么环境破坏责任者可以按以下两种方式之一支付补偿费用：一是由环境破坏责任者直接支付给直接受害者；二是由环境破坏责任者付款给政府有关部门，而由政府有关部门给直接受害者补偿。此外，环境破坏责任者对国家或社会的补偿方式，是向国家或社会直接支付一定的补偿费用。假定环境破坏责任者采取的是向政府有关部门付款，再由政府有关部门向直接受害者付款的补偿方式；同时，环境破坏责任者还必须向政府支付补偿费用的话，那么政府有关部门在得到环境破坏责任者缴纳的一笔总的补偿费用之后，将会按一定的比例进行分配：一部分留下，一部分支付给环境破坏过程中的直接受害者。

现在我们来分析社会补偿方式。社会补偿是一种间接的补偿，是由社会各方通过多种方式筹集资金而形成的基金组织对环境破坏过程中的受害者进行的补偿。这里所说的间接补偿，是指以下这样一些补偿方式：例如，向受害者或受害地区提供优惠的贷款，以帮助受害者增加产量，从而增加收入，或帮助受害地区恢复和发展经济，提高当地的人均收入水平；指导和协助受害者或受害地区的劳动者就业；向受害者或受害地区提供技术援助，等等。换言之，与直接补偿不同，社会补偿作为一种间接补偿，并不是把补偿费用直接交给受害者本人，而是通过信贷、就业指导和帮助、技术援助等方式使受害者得以增加收入，以弥补在环境破坏过程中所遭受的损失。

社会补偿的基金组织是从事这种补偿的机构，它所需要的资金是多方面筹集而来的。其中，既有企业的缴纳、企业和个人的

government funding. The scope and amount of such compensation are decided in light of the organization's financial ability and compensation plans. Given that it is theoretically viable to compensate all victims of environmental damage, this form of social compensation is a wise choice. It goes without saying that many details for such compensation need to be further discussed and clarified.

III. Principles and approaches for compensating victims of environmental treatment

The term "environmental treatment" in this study refers to the treatment of an environment that has been damaged to various degrees, for the purpose of mitigating the damage done or restoring the environment in the best possible way. This kind of environmental treatment calls for certain economic and technical measures, and will have a certain impact on the industrial, technological, employment and consumption structures in the areas concerned. The losses in income or other fields inflicted by environmental treatment on businesses or individuals are contingent upon adjustments made in the course of environmental treatment to local industrial, technological, employment and consumption structures. Therefore, our study of compensation to victims of environmental treatment cannot but be linked with these readjustments.

As pointed out in the previous section, compensation to victims should be paid by the party responsible for environmental treatment. This, however, is just the starting point of such compensation. There are more complicated issues to be addressed as well. It is, therefore, necessary to proceed from the starting point to look further into the whole picture.

Firstly, the state or local community should be regarded as the beneficiary of environmental treatment. If the losses incurred in the course of environmental damage to national assets and to a local community's stock of resources are the reason why the state or local society should be compensated by those held accountable for such damage, in the course of treating such damage the state may benefit from increases or mitigated losses in national assets, and the local community may benefit from increases or mitigated losses in its resources. Therefore, the government should pay a proper portion of compensation money to victims whether or not it is the party engaged in the environmental treatment.

捐赠、社会团体的捐赠，也有政府拨款。对受害者补偿数额的多少是不易确定的，这只能根据社会补偿基金组织的财力大小和其制定的社会补偿规划来确定补偿的范围和数额。但不管怎样，既然从理论上已经确认有必要对一切环境破坏过程中的受害者进行补偿，那么选择社会补偿这种方式将是比较恰当的。当然，社会补偿方面的许多细节仍有待于关心这个问题的人们去进一步研究。

三、对环境治理过程中的受害者的补偿原则和补偿方式

环境治理是指对已经遭到不同程度破坏的环境进行治理，以减少破坏程度，或使其尽可能得到恢复。环境治理过程中需要采取一定的经济和技术措施，并且会对所治理的区域内的产业结构、技术结构、就业结构、消费结构等发生某些影响。因环境治理行为而在收入等方面遭受损失的企业和个人之所以会有这样的损失，与环境治理过程中产业结构、技术结构、就业结构、消费结构的调整有关。因此，在讨论环境治理过程中对受害者的补偿问题时，不能不联系到这些结构的调整。

前面已经指出，给予受害者的补偿要由治理环境的主体支付。但这只是关于环境治理过程中对受害者补偿问题的初步的考虑。事实上，这方面的补偿问题同样是相当复杂的。我们有必要在初步考虑的基础上再进行一些探讨。

首先，应当认为，国家或社会是环境治理的受益者。如果说环境破坏过程中因国民财富的损失、社会所拥有的资源存量的损失而使国家或社会有理由从环境破坏责任者那里得到一定的补偿的话，那么在环境治理过程中，国家或社会将因国民财富的增加或损失的减少、社会所拥有的资源存量的增加或损失的减少而受益。因此，不管政府是否作为治理环境的主体出现，政府对于环境治理过程中的受害者都应当承担一定的补偿费用。

Secondly, in the course of environmental treatment, on the one hand, some firms and individuals may suffer an income loss while others may enjoy an income rise through industrial, technological, employment and consumption restructuring—the former are victims of environmental treatment, and the latter beneficiaries of it. On the other hand, the income of some businesses and individuals will grow in a repaired or treated environment; thus they become beneficiaries of environmental treatment even without restructuring local industry, technology, employment, and consumption. The businesses and individuals that are beneficiaries of environmental treatment are duty-bound to pay a proper part of the compensation money to victims of environmental treatment.

Thirdly, as illustrated above, the environment needs treatment because it has been damaged. Perpetrators of this damage have the obligation to pay a certain amount of compensation money for a second time, this time to those victimized in the course of repairing the environmental damage. Such is the recompensation demanded of the perpetrators of environmental damage by the party engaged in environment treatment. Obviously, such recompensation can be realized only after the perpetrators of environmental damage are verified.

Lastly, it is necessary to take a close look at institutions that may engage in this kind of remedial environmental treatment, such as government institutions, businesses, and nongovernmental organizations. The environmental treatment conducted by government institutions is generally in the national or public interest through such forms as homeland management and treatment, natural resource preservation, economic development, and living standard betterment in a certain area. For this reason, these institutions usually regard compensating victims of environmental treatment as part of the cost. For instance, when the government evacuates families from an area for environmental treatment purposes, it routinely pays a relocation grant to compensate these families. Such a grant naturally becomes part of the environmental treatment cost. The environmental treatment conducted by a nongovernmental organization is often relevant to its public welfare goals. Thus the amount of money it pays fully or partially to compensate those victimized in the course of environmental treatment is in keeping with its welfare goals in the same way as its other environmental protection expenses. The environmental treatment carried out by businesses is somewhat

其次，在环境治理过程中，一方面，通过产业结构、技术结构、就业结构、消费结构的调整，有些企业和个人的收入会减少，有些企业和个人的收入会增加，前者被称为环境治理过程中的受害者，后者则是环境治理过程中的受益者；另一方面，即使不通过产业结构、技术结构、就业结构、消费结构的调整，由于环境条件的改善，有些企业和个人的收入也会增加，他们同样成为环境治理过程中的受益者。这样，无论从哪一个方面看，在环境治理过程中收入有所增加的企业和个人，作为受益者，对于环境治理过程中的受害者也应当承担一定的补偿费用。

再次，正如前面已经指出的，环境之所以需要治理，是由于环境遭到了破坏，因此，当初破坏环境的责任者有责任为环境治理过程中的受害者承担一定的补偿费用。这就是治理环境的一方向当初破坏环境的一方所要求的再补偿。显然，这只有在环境破坏的责任者被明确的条件下才能实现。

最后，还应当对治理环境的一方进行分析。政府有关部门、企业或社会团体都有可能从事治理环境的活动，但各自的活动是有特点的。政府有关部门从事治理环境的活动，主要是从国土整治、改善环境质量、保护资源、发展经济、提高当地居民生活水准等方面考虑，即更多地从国家利益或社会利益的角度着眼。因此，政府有关部门通常把给予环境治理过程中的受害者的补偿费用，作为环境治理的整个费用的一个组成部分。一个常见的例子是：政府有关部门为了治理某一流域的环境，需要从该地区迁出若干户居民。为了补偿迁出者的损失，按情况给予安置费，这些安置费包括在整个治理费用之内。社会团体从事治理环境的活动往往与该社会团体的公益目标相联系。这样，给予环境治理过程中的受害者的补偿费用同用于环境治理的其他费用一起，都符合于该社会团体的公益目标，并由该社会团体自己承担或部分承担。比较复杂的和特殊的是企业

complicated by two possibilities. Firstly, a business sets about improving the environment of a certain place in order to expand production or upgrade technology; secondly, some businesses have caused certain damage to the environment of a certain place, and, because they are held responsible for such damage, they must treat it in compliance with law or government ordinance. A business may also have both the responsibility for repairing the environment of a place and the need to expand production and upgrade technology. There is a difference between these two possibilities no matter what the causes. In the latter possibility, no recompensation is needed in the course of environmental treatment; in the former possibility, recompensation is a necessity. It is not impossible for that demand to be met as long as the responsibility for the environmental damage done previously can be clarified; otherwise, the business must take it upon itself to compensate victims of environmental treatment.

Moreover, compensation to be made to victims of environmental treatment is not handled the same way as that to victims of environmental damage. A party responsible for environmental treatment can only compensate direct victims—businesses and individuals that have lost part of their income because of environmental treatment. The funding for environmental treatment—compensation money included—is so limited that indirect victims, who tend to be large in number and wide in scope, must be omitted from the compensation list. This is because, unlike environmental damage, environmental treatment itself entails goals for improving environmental quality, restoring the economy of the area concerned and enabling it to grow. That is to say, while direct victims are compensated to a certain extent, indirect victims may benefit from local economic rehabilitation and growth resulting from environmental treatment, and increase their income even though they are not compensated directly by the party engaged in environmental treatment. It can be said that the compensation for indirect victims of environmental treatment is subsumed in the use and result of the environmental treatment funding.

Based on these observations, the principles for compensating victims of environmental treatment may be spelled out as follows:

1. The organization engaged in environmental treatment shall, in the course of it, compensate direct victims appropriately for their losses. Because environmental treatment can increase national assets or mitigate losses, and boost the local community's stock of resources or reduce its losses, the government should bear part of the compensation cost.

作为治理环境一方所进行的活动。客观上存在着两种可能性：一是某些企业为了扩大生产规模和技术改造的目的，着手对一定地区的环境进行治理；二是某些企业过去曾经对一定地区的环境有所破坏，它们是该地区的环境破坏责任者，后来根据法律或政府的决定，它们有责任对这一地区的环境进行治理。某些企业也可能既有治理某一地区的环境的责任，又有扩大生产规模和技术改造的任务。但不管怎样，这两种情况仍是有区别的。在后一种情况下，不存在治理环境过程中要求再补偿的问题；而在前一种情况下，企业将会提出再补偿的要求，而只要具体的环境破坏的责任是明确的，这种再补偿的要求并非不可能实现，否则对环境治理过程中受害者的补偿只能由作为环境治理一方的企业来承担。

此外，在对受害者的补偿方面，环境治理过程也反映了不同于环境破坏过程的特点。环境治理一方能够给予补偿的，是直接受害者，即因环境的治理而直接减少收入的企业和个人。至于间接受害者，由于范围广、涉及的人数多、环境治理一方的治理费用（其中包括补偿费用）有限，因此可以不列入补偿之列。这是因为，环境治理与环境破坏不同，环境治理本身就包含了改善环境质量、恢复受治理地区的经济并使之得到发展的内容。这样，在直接受害者得到一定的补偿的同时，间接受害者即使不能从环境治理一方得到补偿，也能从环境治理的效果，即地区经济的恢复和发展中得到好处，从而增加收入。这就是说，对环境治理过程中的间接受害者实际上也是有所补偿的，只是这种补偿并不以人们易于察觉到的补偿形式出现，而是隐含在环境治理费用的使用及其效果上。

根据以上的分析，可以把环境治理过程中对受害者的补偿原则表述如下：

1. 在环境治理过程中，环境治理的主体应对直接受害者所遭受的损失给予相应的补偿。由于环境的治理可以使国民财富增加或损失减少，使社会所拥有的资源存量增加或损失减少，因此，无论政府是否作为环境治理的主体出现，政府都应当承担一定的补偿费用。

2. As environmental treatment is in itself a process of restoring and developing the economy of a given area, its indirect victims will benefit from it in due course. Therefore, they may not be compensated where the funding for environmental treatment—compensation money included—is limited and the compensation scope is too wide.

3. Compensation occurring in the course of environmental treatment is part of the cost, and the compensation money is raised in different ways, including the money paid by the government and other beneficiaries, and the money paid by the verified perpetrators of the environmental damage being treated. This kind of compensation money will be paid only to direct victims of environmental treatment.

Now that the principles are laid down, what should be discussed next is the way compensation money is to be paid. Compensation to victims of environmental treatment can be paid directly, indirectly or in both ways. It can also be paid in full or partially. Of course, such compensation is meant for direct victims.

Then, to be specific, how to go about direct and indirect compensation? Generally speaking, direct compensation is designed to make up for residents' property and income losses incurred in the course of resettlement, and may be paid by the government or the party engaged in environmental treatment. The other losses caused to direct victims of environmental treatment may be indirectly made up for. If workers will lose their income because their factories have to stop production or are shut down in the course of environmental treatment, it is better to compensate them indirectly (such as by shifting the factories to other fields of production or the workers to other jobs) than directly (such as by granting a living allowance to them). The workers of a factory that has stopped production or closed down may also get paid by insurance so that their living standards will not drop too much, but this form of help belongs under social insurance and therefore has nothing to do with compensation from environmental treatment. As to the term "partial compensation," it means that the losses incurred by victims of environmental treatment may be partially compensated for—they can be fully compensated for only when there is enough money to cover it. The reason for it is the same: environmental treatment itself is a course of restoring and developing the economy of the area involved, which is an intangible form of compensation for victims.

2. 环境治理过程本身就是使所治理的地区经济恢复和发展的过程，环境治理过程中的间接受害者可以从这个过程中得到好处。因此在环境治理费用（其中包括补偿费用）有限而涉及面又较广泛的条件下，可以不对环境治理过程中的间接受害者另给补偿。

3. 环境治理过程中的补偿费用，是整个治理费用的一个组成部分。它是通过多种方式筹集的，其中既有环境治理一方所提供的，也有政府作为受益者以及环境治理的其他受益者所提供的，还有在当初环境破坏的责任者已经明确的前提下由该责任者所提供的。所筹集的补偿费用将用于对环境治理过程中的直接受害者的补偿。

在确定了这些原则之后，接着需要讨论的是补偿方式。给环境治理过程中受害者的补偿可以是直接补偿，也可以是间接补偿，或者二者兼有；并且这种补偿可以是充分的补偿，也可以是部分的补偿。当然，这都是指对直接受害者的补偿。

那么，具体地说，直接补偿和间接补偿如何进行呢？一般说来，直接补偿主要用于在环境治理过程中因居民迁移而发生的财产、收入的减少的补偿。这种补偿可以由政府有关部门或环境治理主体支付给居民个人。对于在环境治理过程中直接受害者的其他方面的损失，则可以通过间接补偿方式进行。如果说在环境治理过程中有些企业停产或关闭，从而职工将失去收入的话，那么对这些职工的损失的补偿，以间接补偿的方式进行（如协助企业转产、协助职工转业）要比以直接补偿的方式进行（由环境治理主体发给生活津贴）更好一些。停产或关闭的企业的职工，在一定的社会保障制度之下也有可能得到某些收入，这可以使他们的生活水平不致下降得过多；但这属于社会保障的范围，不属于环境治理的补偿，从而不由环境治理费用中的补偿费用来支付。对于这里所提到的可以“部分补偿”的问题，则应作如下的理解，即对环境治理过程中的受害者所遭受的损失，在财力许可的条件下，可以充分补偿，否则也可以实行部分补偿。理由同样在于：环境治理过程本身就是所治理地区的经济恢复和发展过程，环境治理本身包含了对受害者的补偿。

IV. A closer observation of certain issues

i. Ultimate bearers of direct compensation costs

Those held accountable for environmental damage may be producers or consumers. If consumers are liable for such damage, they have no way of shifting their direct compensation responsibility to any other people—in other words, they are the ultimate bearers of direct compensation costs. Whether or not producers can shift such payment to others is determined by the nature of their products, market conditions, and their own financial situation. If the supply of their products outstrips the demand, or supply and demand are balanced while their products are in complete market competition and they must bear the responsibility for their own gains and losses, the producers must eventually pay direct compensation whether such payment is listed as production cost or not—they pay for it at the expense of their profit. That is to say, they cannot but be obliged to swallow the bitter pill of environmental damage.

In reality, however, the producers that are supposed to pay for direct compensation are mainly large and medium-sized state businesses that do not take responsibility for their gains and losses. Their profits inevitably shrink once direct compensation payments are listed as their production costs, even if their products are in complete market competition, their supply outstrips demand, or their supply and demand are in balance. However, such losses are not borne by these producers, but by the state. The absurdity here is that businesses are the culprits of environmental damage, but it is the government that foots the bill.

If a product is in short supply and the market competition for it is incomplete, and if there is no rigidity in its price, the direct compensation to be delivered by its producer, once listed as a production cost, is incorporated into the product's price. Buyers of such a product end up as the ultimate bearers of the direct compensation cost. If the buyers are consumers, they cannot shift such a burden to others; if the producer is the buyer of his own product, the issue returns to such premises as whether the supply of his product is in excess of demand or in balance with it, whether market competition for it is complete or not, and whether the producer is responsible for his gains and losses. At the end of the day, the likelihood is that consumers and the state will find themselves paying for such direct compensation.

四、对若干问题的进一步探讨

（一）直接补偿费用的最终负担问题

环境破坏的责任者既可能是生产者，也可能是消费者。由消费者支付直接补偿费用，是无法转嫁给其他人的，消费者作为环境破坏的责任者，就是直接补偿费用的最终负担者。至于生产者所支付的直接补偿费用能否转嫁出去，则取决于生产者的产品的性质、市场条件以及生产者的经济体制状况。假定生产者所生产的产品是供大于求或供求平衡的，市场上的竞争是充分的，而生产者又自负盈亏，那么生产者所支付的直接补偿费用不管是否列入生产成本，它们最终仍然由生产者自己负担。生产者以盈利的减少作为支付直接补偿费用的代价，也就是作为破坏环境的苦果而由生产者自己承受。

然而在现实生活中，支付直接补偿费用的生产者主要是公有制大中型企业，它们还没有成为自负盈亏的利益主体。这样，即使它们的产品在市场上遇到充分的竞争，并且产品供大于求或供求平衡，直接补偿费用列入生产成本之后，生产者的盈利将会减少。这种损失也不是由生产者自己负担的，而是落在国家身上。于是出现了一种不合理的现象：环境破坏的责任者是企业，为此而支付的直接补偿费用的最终负担者却是国家。

假定生产者的产品是供不应求的，市场竞争不充分，价格是非刚性的，那么直接补偿费用在进入生产成本之后就会在提高了的产品价格中体现出来，于是这些产品的购买者就负担了这些直接补偿费用。假定购买者是消费者，消费者不可能再把所负担的直接补偿费用转嫁给其他人；假定购买者是生产者，那么问题又回到了前面已经提到的产品是否供大于求、市场竞争是否充分、生产者是否自负盈亏等条件。这样，归根到底，消费者和国家最终承担着直接补偿费用的可能性始终是存在的。

As illustrated above, to deepen corporate reform and establish a corporate system that holds businesses accountable for their gains and losses is a must if producers held liable for environmental damage are to be made to compensate. It is also imperative to improve the market and bridge the gap between supply and demand. If we fail in this, it will be impossible to prevent consumers and the state from unwarrantedly becoming the ultimate payers of direct compensation.

Who, then, are the legitimate ultimate cost bearers of direct compensation to victims of environmental treatment? The answer is the government and those engaged in environmental treatment. Where recompensation is not an issue, the direct compensation paid by the government or nongovernmental organizations is listed as part of the treatment cost in expenditure—it cannot be shifted to consumers because it is not part of production costs. However, the situation is complicated when it comes to businesses engaged in environmental treatment. If a business improves the environment in order to expand production or upgrade technology, it tends to lump direct compensation payment with its environmental treatment cost as part of its production expansion investment. This investment is to be recouped over a length of time determined by its economic efficiency. But no matter how long the recouping period, the direct compensation payment will be eventually factored into the business's production cost. The situation thus returns to what has been discussed previously, where such cost is eventually borne by the state and the consumer if the business is not liable for its gains and losses, if its product is in short supply and market competition is incomplete, and if there is no price rigidity. If the business is liable for environmental damage and if its environmental treatment is designed to remedy such damage, in the natural course of events its compensation payment becomes part of its total environmental treatment cost. As a matter of fact, however, the business will seek to shift this payment, whenever possible, to the state and the consumer, a possibility that justifies the necessity to deepen corporate reform, straighten out the market and mitigate supply shortfalls.

ii. Judging full and partial compensation

The term "partial compensation" refers to the kind of compensation that falls short of making good the losses inflicted on victims of environmental damage or treatment. It is relevant by and large to the losses suffered by direct victims. Because the indirect victims of either

以上分析表明：为了使作为环境破坏责任者的生产者最终承担这些费用，深化企业改革和建立自负盈亏的企业体制是不可回避的，使市场逐步完善并缩小需求大于供给的缺口也是不可回避的。否则，由消费者和国家最终负担直接补偿费用这种不合理的现象将难以消失。

下面，再考虑环境治理过程中对受害者的直接补偿费用的最终负担情况。这种直接补偿费用由政府和环境治理一方支付。假定不考虑再补偿问题，那么由政府有关部门和社会团体所支付的直接补偿费用，作为环境治理费用的一部分，列入政府有关部门和社会团体的一定项目的支出。它们不列入生产成本，从而不能转嫁给消费者。但企业从事环境治理活动时，情况就比较复杂。如果企业出于扩大生产规模和技术改造的需要而投资改造环境、治理环境，这时的直接补偿费用包括在整个治理费用之内，是作为扩大再生产的投资的一部分而出现的。这些投资将被回收，回收期的长短视企业从事的该项投资的经济效益而定。然而，不管回收期多长，这些投资迟早会摊入企业的生产成本。于是问题同前面讨论的情况相似，即在企业不能自负盈亏、产品供不应求、市场竞争不充分、价格非刚性等条件下，最终仍是国家和消费者承担这笔费用。如果企业本身就是环境破坏的责任者，企业对环境的治理是以恢复已被自己破坏的环境为目的的，直接补偿费用作为环境治理费用的一部分，照理说应当由企业自己承担，但实际上企业在条件许可时仍然把它们转嫁出去而由国家和消费者来承担。这也表明了深化企业改革、促进市场完善、缩小需求大于供给的缺口的必要性。

（二）充分补偿与不充分补偿的判断问题

这里所说的不充分补偿，是指在环境破坏和环境治理过程中给予受害者的补偿不能弥补受害者所受的损失。这种不充分补偿主要是针对直接受害者损失的补偿而言。这是因为，无论是在环境破坏还是在

environment damage or treatment are always scattered over a large area, their number and their losses cannot be quantified easily, whereas the amount of money available is too limited to meet their demand for "full compensation," even with the money raised by the local community counted in. Therefore, the compensation to indirect victims, if delivered, is considered partial.

Although direct victims, by contrast, may be compensated directly or indirectly, it should be noted that it is no easier to ascertain if an indirect compensation to direct victims is full or not. Indirect compensation is marked by two characteristics. For one thing, victims have to wait for a certain time to be convinced that they have been compensated; for another, its effect hinges on the work efficiency of those who make such payment and the approach they take—the same amount of indirect compensation payment may have different effects on different beneficiaries. These two distinctive characteristics indicate that whether indirect compensation is paid fully or partially is not determined merely by its amount.

This is exactly why I have focused my study of partial compensation on direct compensation to direct victims of environmental damage or treatment. Whether a direct compensation payment is full or partial can be calculated by comparing the amount of property and income losses inflicted on a direct victim with the amount of compensation money he receives from the perpetrator of environmental damage or the party engaged in environmental treatment. Compensation is deemed full if the two amounts match, and deemed inadequate or partial if the victim is underpaid for his losses. In this regard, it is easier to figure out the property loss than the income loss. Property loss can be pinpointed if its value is properly estimated, whereas income loss is somewhat complicated. Apart from wages and other fixed income, earnings from sales, rents and other activities should also be included; when all these figures are computed, the anticipated changes in output and price, depreciation rate benchmark, and the number of years involved should also be factored into the depreciation category. Because it is not uncommon for income losses to be over- or under-estimated, compensation may be inadequate where payment cannot cover the total losses, or overgenerous where payment outstrips the total value of losses. Only with appropriate methods can such errors be avoided when evaluating a victim's property and income losses.

环境治理过程中，间接受害者的范围都是相当广泛的，他们所遭受的损失不易被计算出来；而能够用来补偿这些间接受害者的资金又比较有限，因此很难按“充分补偿”的要求来补偿间接受害者。即使采用前面提到过的社会补偿的方式来进行补偿，“充分补偿”仍然不易实现。可以认为，如果要对间接受害者进行补偿的话，那么这种补偿通常是不充分的。

对直接受害者既可以采用直接补偿方式，也可以采用间接补偿方式。应当注意到，对直接受害者的间接补偿究竟是充分补偿还是不充分补偿的判断，同样是不易做出的。间接补偿的两个显著特点是：第一，它的效应逐渐发生，从实行补偿到受害者感受到自己得到补偿有一个过程，时间或长或短；第二，它究竟能够产生多大的效应，与运用间接补偿费的机构和工作人员的效率高低有密切联系，与运用的方式恰当与否也有密切联系。从而同样数额的一笔间接补偿费会产生不同的效应，给予受害者的实际好处也不一样。根据间接补偿的这两个显著特点可以了解到，对受害者的间接补偿的充分与否，不单纯取决于间接补偿费数额的多少。

正因为如此，所以我们把有关不充分补偿的考察集中于环境破坏和环境治理过程中对直接受害者的直接补偿上。判断这种补偿是否充分的标准就在于直接受害者在财产、收入方面遭受的损失数额与直接受害者从环境破坏责任者那里或从环境治理的主体那里得到的补偿费数额的比较。二者相符的是充分补偿；损失数额大于所得数额的则是不充分补偿，或称部分补偿。在这里，对财产损失的估算相对来说要比对收入损失的估算容易一些，只要财产的估价恰当就可以比较准确地算出；而收入损失的估算涉及面较广，除固定的工资等收入外，还有生产销售收入、财产租赁收入、其他收入，并且所有这些收入在计算时还有贴现问题。这里包括预期的产量变化、价格变化、贴现率的标准、应计入的收入年限等。收入损失估算得偏高、偏低是常见的。这样，在直接补偿方面，不仅有可能出现不充分补偿（补偿额小于损失额），而且有可能出现过度补偿（补偿额大于损失额）。为了避免这种情况，对于直接受害者财产、收入损失的估算，应有一套较合理的方法。

Because it takes time for indirect compensation to take effect, its benefit seems to be delivered to victims in a constant stream. Thus indirect compensation may also be regarded as something paid in installments. Direct compensation is different in that it is paid in a lump. If that lump sum payment is commensurate with the victim's property and income losses, it is full and the case is closed. If that lump sum is partial, the direct compensation in question can become full with follow-up installments of payment. Given that full compensation is the guideline for dealing with direct victims of environmental damage, payment in installments is feasible where the starting payment is not enough to cover a victim's losses. Following the same guideline above, compensation to direct victims of environmental treatment can be paid directly or indirectly, in full or partially. Full compensation may also be paid in installments.

iii. Compensation for irreparable losses

What is covered by the full and partial compensations that have just been discussed is victims' property and income losses. However, victims' losses are often not limited to property and income. For instance, environmental damage may also impair its victims' health and blight their lives, and environmental treatment may also destroy its victims' lives and jobs. Full compensation payment can only make up for their property and income losses, leaving their other losses unaddressed.

The losses inflicted on victims can also be classified as reparable or irreparable ones. Generally speaking, property and income losses can be made good through full compensation. The damage done to victims' lives and health may or may not be compensable. This is because of the incomparability of people's grievances in daily life even if the degree of damage done to their health can be defined. Victims vary in lifestyle. Some prefer the idyllic country life of farming to dwelling in an urban apartment building; some like living with family members and dislike separation from their children. Even if they have been compensated in some ways for the changes of lifestyle caused by environmental damage or treatment, they may still see such changes as an irreparable loss.

People's impaired health can be cured or incurable, but no amount of compensation is enough to make up for badly impaired health or lost life.

由于间接补偿是逐渐产生效应的，受害者在间接补偿逐渐产生效应的过程中陆续得到实际的好处，所以间接补偿可以被视为多次补偿、分期补偿。直接补偿与此不同，它是以补偿费的形式支付给受害者的。假定一次性支付的补偿费与受害者的财产、收入损失额相当，那么这种一次性支付的补偿就是充分补偿，支付一次就够了。假定一次补偿是不充分补偿，那么直接补偿也可以采取多次补偿、分期补偿的方式，使累计的补偿额与损失额相当，使不充分补偿成为充分补偿。由环境破坏引起的对直接受害者的补偿既然以充分补偿为原则，所以在一次补偿不足以弥补损失时，多次补偿、分期补偿的做法是可行的。至于在环境治理过程中对直接受害者的补偿，根据前面已经论述过的补偿原则，可以按不同的情况给予直接补偿或间接补偿、充分补偿或部分补偿。如果采用充分补偿的做法，那么也可以实行多次补偿、分期补偿。

（三）对不可挽回的损失的补偿问题

以上在讨论充分补偿与不充分补偿时，所提到的损失都是指财产和收入的损失。然而受害者的损失不限于财产和收入的损失。例如，在环境破坏过程中，受害者的损失还包括身体受损害、生活变得不安定或不协调等。在环境治理过程中，受害者的损失也包括生活变得不安定或不协调等。因此，即使用充分补偿的方式来弥补受害者的损失，那也只意味着补偿额同受害者的财产和收入损失额相当，其余的损失并未得到补偿。

从另一个角度来看待受害者的损失，这种损失还可以分为可以挽回（或可以弥补）的损失与不可挽回（或不可弥补）的损失。一般而论，受害者在财产、收入方面的损失，通过充分补偿是可以挽回的。受害者的生活不安定、不协调或受害者的身体遭到损害，既可能通过某种补偿而得到弥补，也可能难以弥补。这是因为在生活安定或不安定方面往往具有不可比性，而在身体受损害方面，则要看受损害的程度而定。假定受害者本人对生活方式有自己的评价标准，例如喜欢田园式的乡居生活而不喜欢城市公寓的生活，喜欢家人团聚而不喜欢与子女分居，那么在环境破坏或环境治理的过程中，即使因生活方式的变更而得到了某种补偿，这仍然会被受害者本人看成是一种不可挽回的损失。以身体的受损害而言，在环境破坏后，受害者身体受损，有些是可以复原的，有些则不能复原。如果因环境破坏而使受害者的身体遭到严重损害，甚至丧失生命，那么无论得到多少补偿费，也很难弥补损失。

The situation becomes complicated once the compensation issue involves losses other than those in property and income. To start with, victims whose health has been impaired by environmental damage do have every reason to deserve the same—direct as well as full—compensation payment that they receive for their property and income losses. But this poses two questions. First, what kind of compensation for impaired health can qualify as being full? The answer remains elusive to this day. For the time being, we can only make do by referring to the way work-related injuries and deaths and traffic accidents are handled. Precisely because of the irreparable nature of serious damage to people's health, we have to enhance our awareness of environmental protection in the first place. Second, how should victims be compensated for their impaired health when and where the perpetrator of environmental damage is yet to be identified? Impaired health may be compensated for through the social compensation fund. But can such welfare fund be used as direct compensation in such cases? In other words, apart from indirectly compensating victims for their property and income losses in the form of credit and assistance in employment and technology, can the social compensation fund also incorporate the money raised from various quarters as direct compensation to pay victims for their impaired health? This is probably a feasible solution, provided such social compensation fund can reach a considerable financial scale and have secured steady fund-raising sources.

The mental disorder and discomfort caused to residents by lifestyle changes resulting from environmental damage or treatment can hardly be converted into economic losses. Therefore, this kind of loss cannot be covered with the full or partial compensation payments for property and income losses, nor is there a legitimate reason for these residents to demand the same full compensation as for impaired health. Changed lifestyle, indeed, is a hard nut to crack in this regard. Pending an effective solution, we may just leave the issue aside for the time being under the supposition that after being fully compensated for their property and income losses, residents will be gradually acclimatized to their changed living environment.

Furthermore, while racking our brains over how to compensate for irreparable losses, we should lose no time in finding ways and means to compensate for the irreparable losses inflicted on the state or society by the damage done to natural resources or the ecological environment. Let me call attention to three issues:

由此可见，对受害者的补偿问题，一旦涉及财产、收入以外的损失，就会变得复杂起来。首先应当肯定，因环境破坏而导致身体受损害的受害者，有理由得到环境破坏责任者的充分补偿。这种充分补偿与对环境破坏过程中受害者财产、收入损失的补偿一样，应以直接补偿费形式支付给个人。但这里还存在两个问题。第一，对身体受损害的补偿怎样才能被称为充分补偿？这是一个学术界至今未能解决的难题。对此，只能参照工伤事故、交通事故等的处理情况而定。正因为身体所遭受的严重损害是不可挽回的损失，所以我们必须增强环境保护意识。第二，在环境破坏责任者不明确的条件下，如何补偿身体遭受损害的受害者的损失？前面曾经提到，这种补偿可以采用社会补偿的方式。但社会补偿在这方面能否以直接补偿方式出现呢？比如说，假定通过多种渠道筹集了社会补偿基金，那么基金除了采取信贷、就业指导和帮助、技术援助等方式给受害者在财产、收入上的损失予以间接补偿外，还可以用支付直接补偿费的方式给那些身体遭受损害的受害者予以相应的补偿。可以设想，只要社会补偿基金达到一定的规模，并且资金有稳定的来源，这也许是一个可行的办法。

在环境破坏和环境治理过程中，居民个人因生活方式的改变而感到的不安定、不协调等等，是难以折算为经济上的损失的。这种损失既不能像财产、收入方面的损失那样得到充分补偿或部分补偿，也不能像身体受损害那样有充足的要求补偿的理由。因此这是一个不易处理的问题。只能这样认为，在目前关于环境保护中的补偿问题的研究水平的限制下，可以不考虑居民个人因生活方式改变而产生的上述损失，而假定居民个人在财产、收入方面的损失得到充分补偿之后将会逐渐适应新的生活环境。

此外，在讨论对不可挽回的损失的补偿问题时，还需要研究国家或社会因资源破坏、生态环境破坏等等而遭到的同样是不可挽回的损失的补偿方式。这里有三个问题值得注意。

Issue One, if liability for environmental damage remains unidentified, there is no way for the state or society to be compensated for this kind of loss. This is a bitter pill, indeed, for the state or society to swallow. The entire population will have to bear such losses ultimately.

Issue Two, even if liability for environmental damage has been defined and the perpetrator has compensated, the amount of money the government receives will most likely be a pittance in comparison with the actual damage done to resources and the environment. Thus the losses, too, will eventually be borne by the entire population.

Issue Three, even if the compensation paid by the perpetrator to the government can offset the estimated amount of losses inflicted by environmental damage, it is still not enough to make up for all the losses incurred by the state or society, because some of the damaged resources are not renewable and part of the damaged eco-environment can never be restored. Such losses will ultimately be borne by the entire population as well.

My observation of these issues drives home, from another angle, the need to tighten up environmental protection.

iv. Compensation for environmental damage resulting from wrong government policy decisions

Businesses and individuals have been the subjects of my analysis so far in this study when it comes to defining the liability for environmental damage. No mention has been made of the environmental damage resulting from wrong government policy decisions and the resultant issue of compensation to victims. As a matter of fact, there is no lack of cases in which faulty government policy decisions are to blame for environmental damage.

That may happen in two scenarios: In the first scenario, economic growth goals are on the top of government agenda while environmental protection fails to get equal attention. The result is that environmental damage occurs and inflicts losses on its victims in the course of economic growth. In the second scenario, the government, having seen the need to restore the destroyed environment of a certain region, makes a wrong policy decision, such as adopting unworkable treatment approaches and attending to one thing to the neglect of another. Thus new damage is done in the course of treating the damage, and local people and businesses are victimized as a result.

第一，如果环境破坏责任者不明确，国家或社会因资源破坏、生态环境破坏等而遭到的损失将不可能从其他地方得到补偿，而只能由国家或社会承担。这种损失归根到底由全民承担。

第二，如果环境破坏的后果是严重的，即使在环境破坏责任者明确的条件下，由后者向政府有关部门支付了一定的补偿费用，但由于已经造成的资源破坏、生态环境破坏的损失很大，补偿数额与损失数额相比微乎其微。这种损失归根到底也仍然由全民承担。

第三，即使在环境破坏责任者明确的条件下，其向政府有关部门支付的补偿费用与所估算出来的损失数额相当，但由于被破坏的资源中有些是不可再生的资源，被破坏的生态环境中有些是不可能复原的，这样，环境破坏责任者所支付的补偿费用仍然难以弥补国家或社会在这方面的损失。这种损失归根到底也由全民承担。

对这些问题的考察，从另一个角度向人们说明了加强环境保护的必要性。

（四）政府决策失误导致的环境破坏的补偿问题

前面在讨论环境破坏的责任者的确定时，一直把企业和个人作为分析的对象。在那里，把政府决策失误所导致的环境破坏以及对受害者的补偿问题排除在外了。但实际上，政府的决策失误在环境破坏方面是有责任的。

可以按以下两种不同的情况来讨论。第一种情况是：政府的决策单纯从经济增长目标出发，而没有把环境保护作为同样应受重视的目标。结果在经济增长过程中出现了环境的破坏，使受害者遭受了损失。第二种情况是：在环境已经破坏而政府感到有必要对环境进行治理的前提下，政府在环境治理工作中做了错误的决策，如采用了不科学的治理方案，实行了顾此失彼的环境治理措施。结果在环境治理过程中又出现了新的环境破坏，使受害者遭受了损失。这两种情况都表明了政府决策失误所导致的环境破坏是客观存在的。在讨论补偿问题时，有必要对这两种情况加以区别。

Let me dwell on the second scenario first, in which the government makes a decision on environmental treatment and goes on to carry it out. If it takes a policy misstep whose dire consequence becomes swiftly apparent, it may use its fund for environmental treatment—compensation payments included—to pay for the losses inflicted on victims. But if it takes a long time for the consequence to be discovered and for victims to become aware of the damage done, the fund will no longer be available by then to pay for the losses.

Now, about the first scenario, which may occur in the process of economic growth, where a faulty policy decision arises from the government's obsession with economic growth and neglect of environmental protection. The losses inflicted by this policy misstep may or may not be compensated for in the course of economic growth. Even if victims are compensated to a certain extent, such compensation tends to be belated and indirect, and limited to property or income losses. Whether such compensation is full or not is determined by the margin of economic growth and by how long it takes to pay it. In addition, this kind of belated, indirect compensation for property or income losses is often delivered to collectives rather than individuals. That is to say, the benefits—in the form of, say, income increase—of economic growth are there for all to share, but the fact that people's losses through environmental damage are different in degree can result in a discrepancy in income increase from economic growth. Those getting the highest increase in income are not necessarily the same people whose losses are the heaviest, while those suffered the most may end up getting the lowest pay rise. Therefore, collective compensation in the course of economic growth is limited to a point where it can only address part of the compensation problem arising from environmental damage caused by government errors. Furthermore, if environmental damage has hurt people's health, compensation cannot be delivered collectively.

Likewise, the state and society should be compensated for losses resulting from destruction of resources and the environment. Government decision-making mistakes committed in either economic growth or environmental treatment can inflict losses on national assets and local community's stock of resources. These kinds of losses—some of which are irreparable—can be borne only by the state or society, that is, by the entire population.

先谈第二种情况。在这种情况下，政府作为环境治理的决策者，通常是以环境治理主体的身份从事环境治理的活动。如果政府在环境治理的决策方面有失误，并且这种失误很快地反映出来，那么因此而造成的受害者的损失可以用环境治理费用（其中包括了补偿费用）来补偿。但如果政府决策失误在一段较长的时间以后才被人们察觉，并且受害者的损失在较长时间才被受害者感受到，那么这样的补偿问题就不可能依靠环境治理费用来解决。

再谈第一种情况。这种情况是在经济增长过程中出现的。政府决策的失误表现为片面地注意经济增长而忽视环境保护。在这种决策失误之下造成的受害者的损失，可能会在经济增长过程中得到某种补偿，但也可能得不到补偿。而且，即使受害者得到某种补偿，那也只是一种滞后的和间接的补偿、一种仅限于财产或收入方面的补偿。至于补偿是否充分，那就要视经济增长的成果、时间的长短等因素而定。加之，经济增长过程中所给予的这种滞后的、间接的财产或收入方面的补偿往往是集体意义上的补偿，而不是个别的、有针对性的补偿。这就是说，在经济增长过程中，许多人都得到好处（如收入增加），但这些人在环境破坏过程中受到的损失程度不一，他们在经济增长过程中所增加的收入也多少不等。收入增加最多的不一定是当初受损失最大的，而受损失较大的可能增加的收入较少。因此，经济增长所导致的集体意义上的补偿固然也是一种补偿，但却是具有较大局限性的补偿。这种集体意义上的补偿，只能被看成是政府决策失误造成的环境破坏的补偿问题的部分解决。不仅如此，由于环境破坏而使受害者的身体遭受损害，这样的损失也无法依靠上述集体意义上的补偿来弥补。

再从资源破坏、生态环境破坏给国家或社会造成的损失来看，补偿问题同样是存在的。无论政府在经济增长过程中有决策的失误还是在环境治理过程中有决策的失误，都会带来国民财富的损失，带来社会所拥有的资源存量的损失。而在这种情况下，损失（其中有些是不可挽回的损失）只可能由国家或社会承担，也就是由全民承担。

Wrong government policy decisions on environmental protection, and the consequent damage and compensation merit public concern not only because such damage often covers a vast area and its consequences tend to be grave and multitudinous, but also because it takes more time and effort to correct such mistakes. However, because the government is often not the actual perpetrator of environmental damage and the actual bearer of the compensation payment for it, the serious nature of the government's decision-making mistakes tends to elude public attention. This is why it is essential to step up the effort to put government decision making on economic growth and environmental protection on a democratic and scientific footing, and to attach equal importance to both economic growth and environmental protection goals.

— *Social Sciences in China,* issue No. 4, 1990

政府在环境保护工作中的决策失误及其引起的环境破坏和补偿问题之所以应当引起人们的重视，还同其后果的严重性有关。政府在环境保护工作中的错误决策导致环境破坏的范围广，后果严重，纠正这种错误决策所需要的时间较长，费力较大；而由于政府往往不是具体的环境破坏责任者，不具体承担环境破坏的补偿费用，因此政府在环境工作中的错误决策的严重性不易被人们所认识。这就告诉我们，加强政府在经济增长过程中和环境治理过程中决策的民主化和科学化，努力做到经济增长目标与环境保护目标兼顾，具有特别重要的意义。

（原载《中国社会科学》，1990年第4期）

COORDINATING ECONOMY AND ENVIRONMENT IN LESS DEVELOPED REGIONS (1991)

An old argument claims that the poorer a place is, the less mindful the locals are of the ecosystem, the more indiscriminate they are in land reclamation, logging, and mining, while having less money to treat the damaged environment and thus sinking deeper into poverty. Another oft-heard opinion puts it this way: When a place is poor, water, soil and air pollution are rare; but when the local economy is booming and the local standard of living is improving, the local rivers, soil and air are polluted too. Which argument holds water? Or are both of them reasonable? If both hold water, does it mean that the cause of environmental protection is helpless whether a place is rich or poor, or that it can be helped only when the place is neither poor nor rich?

In fact, both environmental economics and development economics are confronted with the same baffling paradox concerning the economic operational mechanisms for environmental preservation and for the development of less developed regions. Only by beginning our study from these mechanisms can these questions be answered.

I. Economic operational mechanisms associated with environmental preservation and developing less developed regions

Society, whatever its type, invariably relies on an inherent impetus and employs the resources at hand to keep the economy going in the direction of certain goals. Defying all sorts of interference, it strives to reach these goals or approach them as closely as it can. The "economic operational mechanisms" is a general term for all the relationships society employs to go through this process. These relationships are inherent in society, rather than emanating from outside. Generally speaking, there are four operational mechanisms at work in the course of socioeconomic development:

1. Goals mechanism. How do goals and the system of goals come about? How are these goals aligned in such a system? The issues that should be studied pertinent to economic development are: What are the goals of development? What are the starting point and basis for these goals? Do the environment and ecological equilibrium belong in the goals system; and if yes, what are their positions in it?

贫困地区经济与环境的协调发展（1991）

我们经常听到这样一种说法：一个地区越穷，就越不重视生态环境（比如滥开荒，滥砍树，滥挖矿），也越没有财力来治理被破坏的环境，结果越来越穷。我们还经常听到另一种说法：某个地区过去虽然穷，但当地水污染少，土壤污染少，空气污染也少，后来，经济发展了，人民生活水平提高了，反而河流被污染了，土壤被污染了，空气也被污染了。这两种说法之中哪一种说法有道理，还是两种说法都有道理呢？如果说两种说法都有道理的话，那么，对生态环境的保护来说，似乎穷也不好，不穷也不好，难道只有处在“穷与不穷”之间才好吗？

实际上，我们所接触到的是环境经济学与发展经济学二者共同遇到的一个难题：环境保护和贫困区开发的经济运行机制问题。只有从经济运行机制方面着手研究，才能对上述问题有比较正确的回答。

一、与环境保护、贫困区开发有关的经济运行机制

任何一种社会，总是在一定的目标的指引下，依靠某种动力，使用各种资源，使经济运转起来，并在运转中排除各式各样的干扰，达到预定目标或尽可能接近预定的目标。社会的经济运行机制就是社会借以实现上述过程的一系列关系的总称，这些关系产生自这个社会的内部，而不是来自外界。概括地说，在社会经济发展中，经济运行机制包括以下四方面的机制。

1. 目标机制。目标和目标体系是如何形成的？目标顺序是如何排列的？从经济发展来说，需要研究的问题包括：发展的目标是什么？确定这些目标的出发点和依据有哪些？环境与生态平衡是不是被列入发展目标体系以及它们在这一目标体系中的位置如何？

2. Impetus mechanism. What are the sources of impetus? How is impetus produced? In what ways can impetus be obtained? If the ecosystem and ecological equilibrium are listed in the goals system, how can people be motivated to take the environment and ecological equilibrium seriously in the course of pursuing development and acquiring the impetus to do so? In other words, what is to be done to motivate people to be concerned with the environment and ecological equilibrium? How can the impetus for this motivation be made to last?

3. Resource allocation mechanism. What principle is to be followed in allocating resources? In what way should resources be allocated? How do self-restraints and restraints for and between resource allocation principals come about? How do these two kinds of restraints work? How are resources allocated in the course of economic growth or environmental protection in the context of the relationship between the two? What conflicts will occur between economic growth and environmental protection in the course of resource allocation? What is to be done to reconcile such conflicts? How should resource-allocating principles restrain themselves and each other in economic growth and environmental protection?

4. Interference elimination mechanism. How should we identify interference in the course of economic operation? How might we eliminate such interference? If economic growth and environmental protection are mutually interfering, how can such interference be identified? How can we estimate the seriousness of such interference? Can it be disposed of spontaneously in the course of economic growth? What is to be done if economic growth itself cannot overcome such interference?

Each mechanism has its distinct attributes. The topic of this study is the socialist economy's operational mechanisms in relation to environmental protection and the development of less developed regions, but the focus is on how these come about under the old operational mechanisms compared with their progress under the new ones being established. The purpose is to prove that the question of whether the economic operational mechanisms are old or new can make a difference in environmental protection and the process and results of developing underdeveloped regions.

2. 动力机制。动力的源泉是什么？动力是怎样产生的？以什么方式取得动力？假定生态环境与生态平衡被列入了发展目标体系之中，那么怎样才能在发展过程中形成认真对待环境与生态平衡的动力？怎样得到这种动力？换句话说，怎样激励人们关心环境，关心生态平衡？怎样才能使这种动力长久维持？

3. 资源配置机制。资源按何种原则配置？以何种方式配置？资源配置主体在这一过程中的自我约束和相互约束是如何形成的？这两种约束怎样发挥作用？从经济发展与环境保护二者的相互关系来分析，经济发展过程中的资源是怎样配置的，环境保护过程中的资源又是怎样配置的？经济发展过程中的资源配置方式与环境保护过程中的资源配置方式之间有哪些矛盾？这些矛盾如何得到解决？经济发展与环境保护中的资源配置主体在资源配置方面如何自我约束与相互约束？

4. 排除干扰机制。怎样识别经济运行中的干扰？怎样排除这些干扰？假定经济发展与环境保护过程分别受到了来自各种因素的干扰，那么这些干扰是怎样被认识到的？怎样估计这些干扰的严重程度？经济发展过程中能否自行排除这些干扰？如果不能自行排除这些干扰，那么干扰将如何被排除？

不同的运行机制，在目标、动力、资源配置、排除干扰这四个方面是各有特点的。现在，我们需要研究的是社会主义经济中与环境保护、贫困区开发有关的经济运行机制问题，考察的重点放在社会主义社会的两种不同的经济运行机制（传统的经济运行机制与建立中的新经济运行机制）之下环境保护与贫困区开发过程的比较上，以便说明经济运行机制的不同决定了环境保护状况与贫困区开发过程及其效果的不同。

When we study and analyze these four mechanisms, we find differences between the old and new goals mechanisms and between the old and new impetus mechanisms, but such differences are not pronounced. Because both mechanisms are based on the same system of socialist ownership, it is impossible for categorical differences to arise from their old and new forms, despite the fact that the goals are aligned and prescribed somewhat differently and that there are differences in how the source for impetus should be understood and in the way such impetus is obtained. However, our analyses and comparisons do reveal striking differences between the new and old resource allocation mechanism and the new and old interference elimination mechanism. It is the differences in these two mechanisms that are the principal factors behind the differences between old and new socialist economic operational mechanisms in the state of environmental protection and the course and results of developing impoverished regions.

II. Environmental damage under old economic operational mechanisms

Dynamically speaking, a less developed region may encounter two kinds of environmental damage in the course of development. One such damage may have already existed in the early stage of development, in the form of damaged forests, grassland, and vegetation, depleted mineral ores and soil erosion resulting from predatory exploitation of natural resources by local residents in a hasty bid to beat poverty. Generally, this is the only kind of environmental damage that less developed regions suffered before they began to develop industry. The other kind of environmental damage occurs in industrial development and in the form of water, soil and air pollution caused by the emergence of factories. Of course, the first kind of environmental damage may exist alongside the second kind in the stage of industrial development.

What is the relationship between these two kinds of environmental damage and the old socialist economic operational mechanisms? Let us begin our discussion with a study of the supply and demand in less developed regions.

Such a region is usually an entirely or basically closed economy. Its scanty or zero external connection indicates that it has little or no input and output exchanges with other regions, and that local demand basically matches local supply at a fairly low level.

根据前面提及的经济运行机制所包括的四个方面，即目标、动力、资源配置、干扰的排除，在对以社会主义所有制为基础的两种不同经济运行机制进行分析、比较时，我们可以清楚地看到，它们在第一和第二方面的差别虽然存在，但并不十分显著。这是因为，由于两种不同的经济运行机制都建立在社会主义所有制的基础上，目标机制与动力机制的差别不可能达到目标截然不同与动力截然不同的地步，尽管在目标顺序和目标制定方式上存在着某些差别，以及在对动力源泉的认识和取得动力的方式上也存在着某些差别。但是，资源配置机制与排除干扰机制在社会主义传统经济运行机制与新经济运行机制之下则有很大的差别。正是资源配置机制与排除干扰机制的不同，成为决定两种不同的社会主义经济运行机制之下环境保护状况与贫困区开发过程及其效果不同的主要因素。

二、传统经济运行机制下贫困地区的环境破坏

动态地看，一个贫困地区在发展过程中有可能遭到两类不同的环境破坏。一类破坏是在发展初期就可能存在的，即当地居民为了使自己早日摆脱贫困状态，掠夺性地对待自然资源，致使森林、草原、矿产资源、植被遭到破坏，水土流失。这时由于工业还没有发展，一般只有这一类破坏。另一类破坏是在工业逐渐发展的过程中才出现的，即随着工厂的建立，水源被污染，土壤被污染，空气也被污染。当然，第一类破坏即使在工业发展以后也仍可能继续存在，因此工业发展后两类不同的环境破坏是可能并存的。

这两类环境破坏同传统的社会主义经济运行机制有什么关系呢？让我们先从一个贫困地区的供给与需求两方面分析谈起。

一个贫困地区通常是一个封闭的或基本上封闭的经济体系，它或者同外界没有经济联系，或者联系很少。假定它同外界联系很少，那么这表明该地区与其他地区之间的投入产出联系很少，本地区的需求基本上与当地的供给在很低的水平上是相适应的。

Such a region is not immune to the first kind of environmental damage even if it is basically in seclusion. For instance, cooking fuel shortage may compel local people to fell trees indiscriminately. Shortfalls in grain supply resulting from low-yielding farmland may precipitate wanton land reclamation. Nevertheless, it should be noted that even if the first kind of environmental damage happens in a secluded region, its consequences may be limited. This is one of the characteristics of a closed economy. Of course, the first kind of environmental damage will not cease in such a secluded region because of poverty. If the local economy is under old socialist economic operational mechanisms, and if a shortage in basic means of living has prompted behaviors that are damaging to resources and environment, such behaviors can only be intervened with administrative steps because the region has no internal mechanisms to coordinate its economic growth and ecological equilibrium.

Nevertheless, regional seclusion is bound to give way in the course of economic growth. The input-output ties between a secluded place and the outside world will grow gradually even if old operational mechanisms are still at work. The development of one place not only boosts its own supply and demand but also is impelled by the supply and demand of other places. Disparity between places in the margin of supply and demand growth will compel them to restructure their economies and readjust their spatial distribution of human, material, and financial resources, thereby causing local resident income to rise to varying degrees. This unevenness between places in economic growth and resident income increase stems mainly from geographical locations, natural endowment, population density and resources, and is not decided by differences in economic operational mechanisms. In other words, in places where old economic operational mechanisms still hold sway in local economic life, local economic structural changes are not circumscribed by economic operational mechanisms, but by noneconomic operational mechanisms.

Under the impact of disequilibrium between regions in economic and resident income increases, the first kind of environmental damage may go from bad to worse in less developed regions where the state of seclusion is collapsing and economic ties with other regions are growing. Such environmental deterioration can not be checked by merely relying on administrative intervention under old economic operational mechanisms. Undeniably, the officials and citizens of such regions care about developing local economies and increasing local income, and are doing

一个贫困地区，即使在基本封闭的状态中，也不是不会发生上述第一类环境破坏的。比如说，由于缺乏燃料，人们可能滥砍树；由于土地贫瘠、亩产量低、粮食供给不足，人们可能滥开荒。但应当注意到，处于基本封闭状态的贫困地区，即使发生第一类环境破坏，其破坏的程度也有可能受到某种限制。这正是封闭型经济的一个特点。当然，封闭条件下，由于该地区处于贫困状态，所以第一类环境破坏不会中止。如果这时客观上存在的是传统的社会主义经济运行机制，并且假定发生了由于基本生活资料供给不足而造成破坏资源、破坏环境的行为，则只能采取行政性措施进行干预，而缺乏内在的协调经济发展与生态平衡的机制。

然而，在经济发展过程中，地区的封闭状态肯定要被逐步打破。这时，就算传统经济运行机制仍在起作用，地区同外界的投入产出联系也会逐渐增加。一个地区经济的发展不仅引起本地区的供给增长和需求增长，而且也会被其他地区的供给和需求增长所带动。各个地区的供给和需求增长幅度的不一致，会使各个地区的经济结构进行某种程度的调整，使原来的人力、物力、财力的空间分布进行某种程度的调整，而不同地区居民收入水平提高的程度也会因此而很不一样。这时，各地区经济发展和居民收入提高的这种不平衡性，主要是由于地理位置、自然条件、人口密度、资源状况的影响，而并非是经济运行机制的不同起着决定性的作用。制约着地区经济结构变化的基本因素不是在经济运行机制方面，而是在非经济运行机制方面，假定传统经济运行机制继续支配着经济生活的话。

贫困地区的封闭状态被打破以及在同其他地区经济联系增多的情况下，在受到地区之间经济发展与居民收入提高不平衡的影响之下，上述第一类环境破坏的程度就有可能加剧。单靠传统经济运行机制之下的行政干预措施很难予以制止。不可否认，有些贫困地区的干部和群众是关心本地经济发展和收入水平提高的。他们动脑筋，想办法，

their best to deliver themselves from the quagmire of underdevelopment and destitution. But what should they do to quit poverty and achieve prosperity fast? Development hinges on industry, but industry calls for capital. Where shall the needed capital come from? Industry can be developed with state investment, but not every less developed region can procure state investment in local industry. If a region cannot count on industry to grow its economy and accumulate its capital, where else can it turn to for help? Under old economic operational mechanisms, it is rather difficult for a poor region to go from rags to riches. This gives rise to two possibilities. One is that even though the region's external economic ties are growing, it may find it hard to develop its industry for lack of capital; and even though its agriculture may grow to a certain extent, it cannot grow enough to obtain the capital it badly needs. Thus the region finds it impossible to overcome poverty, while its per capita income gap with other regions widens gradually as a result of its slow economic growth. In the other possibility, the local residents may, of their own accord or in an organized way, resort to excessive tapping of local resources and selling them to boost income, but despite their hard work, they cannot gain what they want, and become even poorer. Their efforts may have an adverse impact on their region and those of others and on both their present and future. There is no lack of such examples in the course of China's economic development.

III. Changing economic operational mechanisms more important than formulating incentive policies for poverty-stricken regions

We should admit that in a less developed region, the speed of economic growth, the margin of increase in local resident income, and the degree of seriousness of damage done to the local environment and resources are closely associated with economic policy for a given period of time. However, these problems have more to do with economic operational mechanisms than with economic policy.

As illustrated above, "economic operational mechanisms" is a general term for the series of relationships an economy relies upon for development. Some of these relationships are defined in legislation and statutes; the others are instituted in economic rules and regulations. Under a given economic operational mechanism, the promulgation and effective enforcement of a major economic policy will impact the

不辞辛苦，力求改变本地区的落后和贫困状态。那么，怎样才能迅速致富呢？发展要靠工业，工业需要资金，资金来自何处？假定国家进行投资，工业可以发展起来，但绝不是每一个贫困地区都有条件吸引国家在本地区进行工业投资的。如果一开始无法依靠工业来发展本地经济和依靠工业来积累资金，那么依靠发展工业来实现致富的目的将如何实现呢？在传统经济运行机制之下，这是很困难的。于是出现了两种可能性：一是，尽管贫困地区同外界的经济联系增多了，但本地的工业由于缺乏资金难以发展，本地的农业虽然有可能发展，但农业却难以为本地区积累资金，从而难以达到致富的目的，于是本地区同其他地区的人均收入差距将因发展速度的不同而逐渐扩大；另一种可能性是，为了积累资金，居民自发地或有组织地过度开采当地的资源，靠出卖资源来增加收入，在这种情况下，即使人们辛辛苦苦，也不会取得应有的成果，甚至会变得愈加贫困。由此造成的恶果，不但影响本地区，而且也影响其他有关地区，不但影响现在，还会影响到将来。在经济发展过程中，这样的例子是屡见不鲜的。

三、转换贫困地区的经济运行机制比制定优惠政策更为重要

应当承认，一个贫困地区经济发展的快慢，居民收入提高幅度的大小，以及资源或环境破坏的严重程度，同一定时期的经济政策有密切的关系。但是更为重要的不是经济政策问题，而是经济运行机制问题。

正如前面已指出的，经济运行机制是指经济借以运行的一系列关系的总称。这些关系有些是以法律、法规确定的，有些依赖于经济政策的规定。在经济运行机制既定的条件下，公布一项重要的经济政策并有效地推行之，会对既定的经济运行条件和运行过程发生这样的

condition and progress of economic operation one way or another, and thus yield economic and social returns. Such is the way government policy works. The impact of economic policy on a given economic operational mechanism alters the condition and orbit of economic operation to a certain extent, and goes on to affect demand and supply, and input and output, causing changes in local economic and income levels. However, it is economic operational mechanisms, rather than policy, that play a more profound part in the development of a less developed region. They determine the course of economic operation. By contrast, if government policy is to play a role, it must influence these mechanisms and change them in certain ways. For instance, the government may grant tax exemption or reduction, financial subsidy, and low-interest or interest-free loans to a rather poor region, hoping to help it beat poverty at an early date. However, the beneficial effects of these incentives can be restricted if the prevailing economic operational mechanisms are detrimental to local economic development. This is because the financial subsidy, interest-free or local-interest loans granted to the poor region through preferential government policy are often not used as start-up fund for local development. Instead, they are frequently spent to cope with immediate financial woes, and are not enough to generate a local economic boom. That is why people often say it is essential to endow less developed regions with the "blood-making" function. "Blood transfusion," whether sporadic or long-term, can never put any population or region on the road to prosperity.

Given that the economic growth of less developed regions is predicated on the soundness of economic operational mechanisms, environmental protection and ecological equilibrium, by reason of their close relevance to economic growth, are also determined by such mechanisms rather than by economic policy. Economic policy alone is not enough to help poor regions overcome poverty. By the same token, it is not enough to rely on economic policy alone to help these regions maintain ecological equilibrium in the course of development. This being the case, we need to learn what kind of economic operational mechanisms are detrimental to the economic growth and ecological equilibrium of poverty-stricken regions, and what kind of economic operational mechanisms can help these regions address these issues. Once we have found the answers to both questions, we will know what policy to take to curtail the economic operational mechanisms that do

或那样的影响，从而产生经济和社会效应。政策的作用就是这样发挥出来的。经济政策通过对既定的经济运行机制的影响，在一定程度上改变了运行条件和运行过程，然后影响需求与供给、投入与产出，使地区经济和收入水平发生某种变化。但是，在贫困地区经济发展中，在深层次起作用的是经济运行机制，而不是政策。经济运行机制决定着经济运行过程，而政策要发挥作用，则必须对经济运行机制产生影响，使经济运行机制发生某种变化。比如说，某一地区是相当贫困的，为了促使该地区摆脱贫困状态，政府制定了优惠政策，包括减免税收、给予财政补贴、发放无息或低息贷款等。可是如果经济运行机制仍然不利于地区经济的发展，这些优惠政策的作用将是有限的。这是因为，尽管通过政府的优惠政策，该地区得到了财政补贴，得到了无息或低息贷款，但这些资金不会成为该地区经济发展的启动资金，政府给予的财政补贴和无息或低息贷款往往被用于缓和眼前的困难，不足以使该地区的经济繁荣兴旺。所以人们常说，对于贫困地区来说，更重要的是使它们有“造血”的机能，光靠“输血”甚至长期“输血”都无法使它们脱贫致富。

既然贫困地区的经济发展主要取决于经济运行机制是否合适，那么与贫困地区经济发展有关的环境与生态平衡问题也同样取决于经济运行机制，而并非取决于经济政策。正如仅仅依靠经济政策不足以使贫困地区摆脱贫困状态一样，仅仅依靠经济政策也不足以使贫困地区在经济发展过程中解决环境与生态平衡问题。这样，我们就必须进一步探讨：究竟什么样的经济运行机制不利于贫困地区的经济发展和生态平衡？什么样的经济运行机制有利于解决这些问题？假定这个问题明确了，那么政策的导向也就可以确定下来，即需要制定的是哪些政策，以便从某些方面限制不利于贫困地区经济

not work and promote the role of the workable mechanisms. Once sound economic operational mechanisms are chosen, less developed regions will be able to increase their internal accumulation and reinvestment, and limit environmental damage. On the contrary, if they allow old economic operational mechanisms to go on dominating local economic life, they can never beat poverty no matter how much external input or "blood transfusion" they can receive. In that sense, a less developed region can be likened to either a funnel or a reservoir, and investment from the outside can be compared to water. If such a region works like a funnel, it will remain in poverty because all the "water" it receives will drain away sooner or later. If, however, the region works like a reservoir in which all the "water" it receives is retained, and the "fish" raised in it thrive, then the local economy will keep changing for the better. In that case, even if investment arrives in one installment from the outside, it will have such a start-up effect that the entire "reservoir" will be energized. Thus, to develop the economy of a less developed region, the first thing to do is not to turn the region into a "funnel" but to prevent incoming investment from going down the drain. For this purpose, we have to replace old economic operational mechanisms with new ones, and turn local economies from "funnels" to "reservoirs."

IV. Less developed regions' internal accumulation mechanism

Capital investment is pivotal to the development of less developed regions. The issue entails (1) the source of capital, (2) the direction or structure of the capital, and (3) the efficiency with which such capital is used. In a socialist economy, the differences between old and new economic operational mechanisms in capital investment are striking in all three aspects.

Insofar as the source of capital is concerned, a region's internal accumulation comes from the accumulations of local businesses and residents. If the region is perennially poor, it may have no industry to speak of. Even if it has a few industrial firms, their accumulations won't amount to a lot, and the low-income local residents will not have large savings. This is a realistic problem, but what I want to prove here is that, no matter how much local firms and residents may have in their bank savings, it is imperative to procure their reinvestment. This is where a

发展和生态平衡的经济运行机制的作用，促进有利于这些问题的解决的经济运行机制发挥作用。只要经济运行机制转换了，贫困地区内部积累与再投入将会增加，环境破坏将受到内在的制约。反之，如果传统经济运行机制继续起着支配经济生活的作用，外部投入（也就是所谓“输血”）再多也不能迅速改变贫困地区的面貌。贫困地区既可能是一个漏斗，也可能是一个蓄水塘。外部投入好比向这里注水。如果贫困地区是漏斗，那么注入的水再多，迟早也要流完，结果，贫困地区依然是贫困地区。如果贫困地区是一个蓄水塘，外部注入的水不会流失，而会蓄积在塘里，于是在塘里养鱼，鱼就会繁殖，那里的经济面貌就会发生变化。这时，哪怕外部的投入只是一次性的，但却是启动性的，这个水塘也就活起来了。所以说，要发展贫困地区经济，首要的问题是不让贫困地区成为漏斗，不让外部投入流失。为此就需要把传统经济运行机制转换为新的经济运行机制，把“漏斗”型的地区经济改变为“蓄水塘”型的地区经济。

四、贫困地区的内部积累机制

贫困地区经济发展中的一个关键性问题是资金投入问题。这个问题包括三个方面：一是资金来源；二是资金投入的方向或资金投入的结构；三是资金使用效率。在社会主义经济中，传统的经济运行机制与新的经济运行机制的区别在资金投入问题的三个方面极为明显。

就资金来源而言，一个地区内部积累的来源是企业的积累和居民的积累。假定这个地区一直处于贫困状态，那么正如前面已经指出的，或者本地没有什么工业，或者，即使有少数工业企业，这些企业也不会有很多积累；同时，本地居民的收入也少，他们或者没有积累，或者只有很少量的积累。这是一个现实问题。然而在这里要探讨的是，不管企业和居民的积累多么少，关键是要吸引他们再投入，

kind of internal mechanism is needed to attract local reinvestment in such a region. In my previous brief introduction to economic operational mechanisms, I have pointed out that we need to approach the issue from the perspectives of goals, impetus, resource allocation, and elimination of interference. I have also mentioned that between the two kinds of economic operational mechanisms based on socialist ownership, the differences between old and new goals and impetus mechanisms are not as important as those between old and new resource allocation and interference elimination mechanisms. The differences between the old and new internal accumulation mechanisms are actually those between the principle for resource allocation and the approach to it. Thus it is safe to say that the internal accumulation mechanism for a region is an integral part of the resource allocation mechanism for the entire society.

There are three reasons why the internal accumulation mechanism can work in less developed regions under the new economic operational framework but cannot do so under the traditional framework.

Firstly, resource allocation is realized through capital investment and reinvestment. The pattern of resource allocation is readjusted repeatedly due to structural differences between such investment and reinvestment. But how can capital investment and reinvestment be guaranteed? The answer is apparent: We must convince such investors that they can benefit from such investment and reinvestment. Herein lies the role of capital investment and reinvestment in guiding interests. It goes without saying that the benefits in question refer to relative benefits. As both investment and reinvestment inevitably flow to where gains are high, this gives rise to the price issue. Under old economic operational mechanisms, the price ratio is irrational. All a less developed region can provide are primary products. As the prices for resources are on the low side, the prices for these primary products are kept low as well, whereas the production and trading costs (transportation included) for the less developed region's products are on the high side. Not only will the region end up with a negligible surplus in hand, it will also be deprived of its fountainhead of capital for investment and reinvestment. Such a situation can hardly attract capital investment and reinvestment from within the region. If, however, new socialist economic operational mechanisms are set up, the price ratio will be rectified and the prices for resources will rise to an appropriate level while production and trading costs drop relatively, so that internal investment and reinvestment become an attractive

于是就需要形成一种能够吸引本地区内部再投入的机制，即内部积累机制。前面在概述经济运行机制时，曾指出需要从目标、动力、资源配置、排除干扰这样四个方面来考察；而且，前面还曾提到，在同一种社会主义所有制基础上的两种不同的经济运行机制之间，目标与动力方面的差别不是主要的，差别主要在资源配置和排除干扰方面。这里所说的在两种不同经济运行机制之下地区内部积累机制的区别，实际上就是资源配置原则、资源配置方式之间的区别。因此可以这样认为：地区内部积累机制是社会的资源配置机制的一个组成部分。

在传统经济运行机制之下，贫困地区内部积累机制之所以难以形成，新的经济运行机制之下这一内部积累机制之所以存在，可从以下三个角度作出解释。

第一，资源配置是通过资金投入和再投入实现的。由于资金投入和再投入的结构不同，从而不断出现资源配置格局的调整。但是，怎样才能保证资金的投入和再投入呢？很明显，必须使得投入的主体认为这种投入和再投入有好处。这就是资金投入和再投入的利益导向，当然这里所说的利益大小是就相对利益而言的。投入和再投入必定趋向于相对利益较高的领域，于是就涉及价格问题。传统经济运行机制之下，价格比例不合理，贫困地区所能够提供的是初级产品，但由于资源价格偏低，初级产品价格也偏低，加之贫困地区产品的生产成本和交易成本（运输成本包括在交易成本之内）偏高，于是一方面，贫困地区自身不可能有多少剩余，投入与再投入的资金没有来源；另一方面，这种场合也很难对贫困地区内部的投入和再投入有吸引力。如果今后实现了新的社会主义经济运行机制，那么价格比例将趋于合理，资源价格将上升到应有的水平，生产成本和交易成本则会相对下降，这样内部投入和再投入的吸引力

prospect. A major lesson to be drawn from this is that if macroeconomic decision-makers are really resolved to help less developed regions to prosper, they should, rather than choose the "blood transfusion" method, focus on changing their economic operational mechanisms and gradually address their low resource prices and high production and trading costs. Only in this way can these regions be helped to formulate an effective internal accumulation mechanism.

Secondly, capital investment and reinvestment come from a surplus fund that can be broken down into consumption fund and savings, or consumption fund and investment fund converted from savings. Therefore, from the perspective of resource allocation, the issue involves the distribution of the surplus fund in the very beginning. An underdeveloped economy with low labor productivity, combined with inappropriate pricing of the primary products such an economy provides, results in a scanty surplus fund at the disposal of such regions. If, under these circumstances, a considerable part of the surplus fund is spent on consumption, what is left for investment can be negligible. If less developed regions are to be developed in real earnest, everything should be done to prevent irrational consumption expenses from eroding the internal accumulation fund that can otherwise be used for investment and reinvestment purposes. The term "irrational consumption" points mainly to consumer expenses not on daily necessities but on outmoded conventions and customs, as well as consumer expenses that go way above local productivity and resident income levels. Under old economic operational mechanisms, such "irrational consumption" can only be controlled by administrative means. This kind of control may be effective on the surface, but it can bring a problem: For lack of motivation for internal investment and reinvestment, potential investors—namely, businesses, urban residents, rural firms, and farming households—may choose to bypass administrative orders, thus forcing local government to tighten its control time and again. What is more, even if administrative control succeeds under old economic operational mechanisms in coordinating prices and costs by raising resource prices and reducing production and trading costs, such a balance may still be eroded by irrational consumer expenses, and the hopes of internal capital investment will still be dashed if businesses and people are not motivated to invest and reinvest. After new socialist economic operational mechanisms are established, businesses and people will have

就必然会增大。从这里可以得到一个重要的启示：如果宏观经济决策部门决心帮助贫困地区脱贫致富的话，那么与其用“输血”的方式来帮助贫困地区，不如把转换经济运行机制作为重点，逐步解决资源价格偏低以及生产成本和交易成本偏高的问题，这才真正有助于贫困地区形成有效的内部积累机制。

第二，资金投入和再投入来自剩余，剩余又分解为消费与储蓄，或消费与投资（投资来自储蓄的转化）。因此，就资源配置而言，一开始就涉及剩余的分配问题。贫困地区的经济落后，劳动生产率低，它所提供的初级产品价格又不合理，因此剩余本来就很少。如果在这种情况下，剩余中有较多部分被用于消费，那么可供投资的部分就非常微薄了。为了开发贫困地区，一定要防止不合理的消费支出侵蚀本来可以用于投入和再投入的内部积累。这里所说的不合理消费，主要是指与民间的陈规陋习有关的各种非生活必需的消费支出，此外也包括某些与现有生产力水平和居民收入水平不相适应的消费支出。然而在传统经济运行机制之下，这只能依靠行政措施来加以控制。行政措施的控制从表面上看是有效的，但却会带来一个问题，即资金投入的主体（包括企业、城镇居民、农村生产单位、农民家庭）缺乏来自内部的资金投入和再投入的热情，因而不能很好地同行政措施相配合，结果政府不得不一再强化行政干预。况且，在传统经济运行机制下，即使依靠某种行政措施，使资源价格上升了，生产成本和交易成本降低了，价格与成本之间有了一定正值的差额，但如果资金投入的主体依然缺乏资金投入和再投入的热情，这个差额仍会被不合理的消费支出侵蚀，内部再投入依旧落空。新的社会主义经济运行机制建立后，资金投入和再投入主体

both initiative and motivation to invest and reinvest, and, with internal constraints in place to hold back irrational consumer expenses, internal accumulation will grow. Local governments, on their part, can make more use of economic regulatory means—tax rate and interest rate readjustments — that work a lot better than hard and fast administrative rules.

Thirdly, resource allocation includes investment and reinvestment, as well as grouping such investment and reinvestment. Given that investment and reinvestment are embodied in both value and material, when they come in material forms, they give rise to such issues as ratios and approaches for regrouping human, material and financial resources. Furthermore, taking the input-output relationship and the flow of resources between regions into account, investment and reinvestment also entail how to effectively integrate the resources of one region with those of another region so that their value and material forms can be well coordinated. We have to put less developed regions on the track of fast economic growth in a way that enables the resources of one region to be integrated with those of another region in the most effective way possible, and through such integration, to yield more internal accumulations. Of course, if a less developed region must rely entirely on the inflow of resources—financial resources in particular—to grow its economy, such reliance cannot help the region formulate its internal investment and reinvestment mechanisms, nor is it realistic in the current stage of Chinese development. However, as things are in this nation, less developed regions can find it very difficult to jump-start their economies without the inflow of outside resources. The issue here is how internal resources can be integrated with external resources. Under old economic operational mechanisms, local and inter-regional groupings of resources are seriously constrained by the lack of autonomy and flexibility on the part of investors and reinvestors. If, under these circumstances, the resources of one place can still be integrated with the resources of another place, this is most likely to happen through administrative intervention, but such integration can be both ineffective and short-lived. If new socialist economic operational mechanisms are permanently instituted, investors, endowed with autonomy and flexibility, can act in their own immediate and long-term economic interests to choose ways that work for such integration. Whether a less developed region can

既有自主性，又有资金投入和再投入的热情，它们就有内在的限制不合理消费支出的倾向，内部积累就会增多。至于政府的调节，也可以更多地采取经济调节（如调整税率、利率）的形式，调节效果也会比单纯依靠行政措施好得多。

第三，资源配置不仅包括了资金投入和再投入，而且包括了投入和再投入的组合。要知道，资金投入和再投入既以价值形式表现，也以实物形式表现，而在以实物形式表现时，就有人力、物力、财力资源的组合比例和组合方式等问题。此外，由于地区之间存在着投入产出关系，存在着资源的流动，因此，资金投入和再投入也包括了一个地区的资源如何与其他地区的资源有效结合，以便在价值形式和实物形式上相一致的问题。这样，为了使贫困地区的经济有较快的发展，应当尽可能地创造本地资源同外地资源的有效结合方式，并通过这种结合来提供较多的内部积累。当然，一个贫困地区要完全依赖于外部资源（尤其是外部的财力资源）流入来发展经济，既无助于本地区自身内部投入与再投入机制的形成，而且在我国经济的现阶段也缺乏现实性。但从一个贫困地区的具体条件出发，如果完全没有外部资源的流入，地区经济的启动有时会遇到很大困难。因此，重要的是在于本地资源同外地资源究竟以何种方式结合。在传统经济运行机制之下，由于资金投入和再投入的主体缺乏自主性和机动性，本地资源的组合方式以及本地与外地资源的结合方式都受到很大限制。这时，如果说仍然有本地资源与外地资源结合的话，那么也主要是通过行政性措施来实现的，既难以有效结合，又难以长期结合。如果建立了新的社会主义经济运行机制，资金投入的主体有了自主性和机动性，它们就会从经济利益（包括近期利益和长期利益）出发，选择有效的结合方式。由于贫困地区

integrate its resources effectively with those of other places determines whether it can acquire a sizeable internal accumulation and speed up increases in local residents' income. Therefore, in order to bring about such an efficient integration in resources, it is imperative to change the economic operational mechanisms through reform.

V. Capital investment structure and coordination between development and environment

According to the analysis made above, the second aspect of the regional capital investment issue involves the direction and structure of this kind of investment. The capital invested is known as "capital inflow," while the sectoral structure of such capital manifests itself in the form of capital stock that is accumulated over a long period of time. Under old economic operational mechanisms, it is the government that decides the direction of capital investment. An irrational capital sectoral structure makes stock readjustment very difficult. A feasible way to cope with the problem is to regulate the capital flow, the amount of money to be spent on capital investment. However, for one thing, the capital flow is limited, and for another, once the capital flow is invested, such amount of money will become part of the stock. We may as well liken capital flow to "flowing water" and the stock to "still water." To turn capital flow into capital stock is like turning "flowing water" into "still water." If that happens, the capital's sectoral structure in a less developed regions will become lopsided, a lopsidedness that cannot be rectified, thereby making it hard to bring about a workable mechanism to facilitate internal accumulation and internal investment and reinvestment.

Moreover, given the continuous process it takes to boost development and improve local resident income in less developed regions, it is imperative to maintain stability in investment and reinvestment from within these regions. Such stability is unreachable under old economic operational mechanisms, because the reliance on administrative steps alone can deprive capital investment and reinvestment of the guidance of interests and make lasting integration of resources between regions impossible. As a result, investment proceeds in fits and starts and fails to ensure steady and efficient growth. What, then, will happen under new socialist economic operational mechanisms? We need to ensure that the initiative for internal investment and reinvestment is in the hands of companies with internal accumulations and of urban and rural residents with bank savings. It should not be in government hands. Only when companies and individuals are willing to invest in local economic undertakings can we be convinced that an internal

本地资源同外地资源能否有效结合是关系到该地区经济能否产生较多的内部积累、能否加速居民收入水平提高的重要条件，所以单从资源结合方式来看，也有必要通过改革来转换经济运行机制。

五、贫困地区资金投入的结构与经济发展—环境的协调

根据以上分析，地区的资金投入问题的第二个方面是资金投入的方向或资金投入的结构。资金投入量是流量，现有的资金部门结构表现为资金的存量，它们是长期形成的。在传统经济运行机制之下，资金投入的方向是由政府部门决定的。如果资金的部门结构不合理，那么存量调整的难度很大。可行的办法只是调节流量，即调节资金投入量。然而，一方面流量有限，另一方面，流量一旦投入就会变为存量。不妨把流量比喻为“活水”，存量比喻为“死水”。流量变为存量，也就等于“活水”变成了“死水”。于是贫困地区的资金部门结构不仅失调，而且失调状况不易改变，内部积累机制难以形成，内部投入和再投入也难以顺利进行。

此外，考虑到贫困地区经济的发展和居民收入水平的提高是一个持续的过程，就资金投入和再投入而言，应当设法使这种来自内部的投入和再投入保持稳定性。传统经济运行机制之下，是实现不了稳定的投入和再投入的。这是因为，仅仅依靠行政措施，资金投入和再投入缺乏利益导向，地区的资源结合又不可能持久，这样，势必会形成“热一阵”、“冷一阵”的状况。那么，新的社会主义经济运行机制之下，又将如何呢？要知道，内部投入和再投入的主动权在形成内部积累的企业和有了储蓄的城乡居民手中，而不在政府手中。只有企业和城乡居民愿意把手中的货币投入本地区经济

accumulation mechanism has taken shape. However, it is naïve to believe that an internal accumulation mechanism will become permanent simply because an old economic operational mechanism has given way to a new one. If, under new economic operational mechanisms, firms begin to make their own business decisions and urban residents are keen on investing and reinvesting, their investment direction becomes an issue. Where do they want to invest, in their own region, or in other regions with better conditions? If, under the guidance of their interests, they choose to invest somewhere else instead of their own region, less developed regions will have no guaranteed money for investment and reinvestment in development despite the fact that they have adopted new economic operational mechanisms. This is where government regulation can help. Financial authorities at various levels may set aside a certain amount of construction fund to maintain investment and reinvestment in less developed regions on a certain scale. Local governments may also set preferential tax rates so that funds can be drawn from nongovernmental channels to less developed regions to make up for their investment and reinvestment shortfalls. On the basis of raising funds from the state, regions, businesses and various walks of social life, a development fund may be established, and its money can be deployed according to a region's internal investment and reinvestment needs.

At this point, we need to consider how to enhance equilibrium between economic growth and the environment in less developed regions by putting capital investment where it is most needed in the course of development. If invested capital is structurally flawed and results in disequilibrium in the capital sectoral structure, how effectively can changing economic operational mechanisms work in coordinating development and environment?

It should be conceded that old economic operational mechanisms cannot solve these problems for reasons already explained in a previous chapter. Given that old economic operational mechanisms can neither foster internal investment and reinvestment mechanisms in less developed regions, nor remedy the lopsided capital sectoral structure through readjusting capital stock, their limits are apparent in tackling problems in coordinating development and the environment. Can the problems be addressed under new socialist economic operational mechanisms? This is a complex issue that merits in-depth study.

的发展事业，内部积累机制才能被认为已经形成。因此，不能认为只要经济运行机制一转轨，贫困地区的内部积累机制就会形成。比如说，在新的经济运行机制之下，企业有了自主性，城市居民有了投入、再投入的积极性，但他们究竟把资源投入何处呢？是投入本地区还是投入其他条件的地区呢？如果利益导向其他地区而并非本地区，那么，即使建立了新的经济运行机制，贫困地区经济发展的投入和再投入也仍然缺乏保证。在这种情况下，政府的调节是必要的。各级财政部门可以根据具体情况，规定一定比例的贫困地区建设资金，作为对贫困地区投入和再投入规模的某种保证；又如，政府还可以通过优惠的税率，动员社会资金，吸引它们投入贫困地区的开发，以补充这些地区内部投入和再投入之不足；在国家、地方、企业，社会各界广泛集资的基础上，还可以建立某一地区的开发基金，按照内部投入和再投入的实际状况而适当运用。

下面，我们需要着重研究的是，在贫困地区经济发展的过程中，如何才能通过资金的合理投向来促进经济发展与环境的协调？如果客观上已经存在着资金投入结构的不当从而存在着资金部门结构的失调的话，那么，从协调经济发展与环境的角度来看，转换经济运行机制在这些方面究竟能够起多大作用？

应当承认，传统经济运行机制不可能解决这些方面的问题，其理由已经在前面作了说明。关键在于：在传统经济运行机制之下，既然难以形成贫困地区的内部投入和再投入机制，又难以通过资金存量的调整来改变资金部门结构不合理的现状，因此，传统经济运行机制在解决贫困地区的经济发展与环境协调方面的局限性就是不言自明的。那么，在新的社会主义经济运行机制之下，能否解决这些问题呢？这是一个比较复杂的问题，需要较深入地探讨。

Theoretically speaking, the establishment of new economic operational mechanisms does not guarantee adequate market information, nor does it indicate that capital investment principals are assured of access to adequate and timely information. A good part of the information they obtain may still be incorrect and misleading when they make resource input decisions. As a result, resource allocation can hardly meet the demand for equilibrium between development and the environment. Furthermore, capital investors, whose economic behavior cannot be restrained by such a demand because of resource supply shortfalls, may most probably step up their exploitation of natural resources to make up for such shortfalls, thus making it even more difficult to coordinate development and environmental issues.

Obviously, the establishment of new socialist economic operational mechanisms does not mean that problems in between economic growth and environmental protection can be automatically addressed. In comparison with the situation under old economic operational mechanisms, internal investment and reinvestment are bound to increase considerably under new mechanisms. However, the questions of which region or industry should be invested with such internal capital, and particularly, whether it can be invested in environmental protection, and if so, how much can be invested in it—these cannot be determined merely by changing economic operational mechanisms. Two points are worth noting no matter what happens:

Firstly, more capital will flow into internal investment and re-investment under new economic operational mechanisms than under old ones. For that matter, even though the establishment of new mechanisms cannot spontaneously bring about a balance between development and environment in less developed regions, it at least sets the financial stage for such a balance.

Secondly, under old mechanisms, because businesses were government appendages that could not make their own decisions and be responsible for their own gains and losses, their indifference to government steps to coordinate development with environmental protection often derailed such attempts. By contrast, new economic operational mechanisms can turn businesses into independent commodity producers that are mindful of their own interests and willing to adapt their behavior to government intentions when they assess the impact of government steps on themselves and seek advantages and avoid risks from these steps.

从理论上说，即使建立了新的经济运行机制，并不意味着市场信息必定是充分的，也不意味着资金投入的主体必定得到足够的、及时的信息，它们得到的信息中也许有不少是不正确的信息，从而它们不得不在有限的信息、甚至错误信息的指引下进行资源投入的决策，其结果将使社会的资源配置不符合经济发展与环境协调的要求。加之，由于资源供给不足，资金投入的主体不可能以经济发展与环境的协调作为自己的经济行为的约束，而很可能以加紧开采自然资源来应付短缺资源的供给不足。这就进一步加剧了经济发展与环境协调的困难。

由此可以认识到，新的社会主义经济运行机制的建立并不能自然而然地解决贫困地区的经济发展与环境之间的协调问题。同传统的经济运行机制之下的情形相比，在新的经济运行机制之下，内部投入和再投入肯定要大大增多，但这些内部资金究竟投入什么地区，投入什么部门，特别是它们能否投入环境保护领域或究竟有多少数额投入环境保护领域，并非仅仅取决于经济运行机制的转换。但无论如何，有两点是值得指出的：

第一，在新经济运行机制之下要比传统经济运行机制之下有较多的内部投入和再投入，这样，即使新机制的建立不等于贫困地区经济发展与环境间可以自行趋于协调，也毕竟为推动这种协调准备了财力方面的前提。

第二，在传统经济运行机制之下，由于企业没有摆脱对行政机构的依附地位，不能自主经营和自负盈亏，因此，即使政府采取了旨在协调经济发展与环境调节的措施，企业也可能对此无动于衷，从而使这些调节措施不能取得很好的效果。而在新的经济运行机制之下，企业作为独立的商品生产者，会从自身的利益出发考虑政府采取的措施对自己的影响，趋利避害，使自己的行为符合政府调节的意图。

Thus we can arrive at the conclusion that even though a shift in economic operational mechanisms does not mean that capital investment will be automatically directed rationally and that environmental protection will receive more investment because of it, the new economic operational mechanisms can bring more internal investment and reinvestment, and enable businesses to act on their own interests to adapt their behavior to government regulation intentions. Thus it is more likely for development and environment to be balanced under new economic operational mechanisms than under old ones. From the perspective of capital investment or capital investment structure, this drives home the close connection between environmental protection, development of less developed regions, and changing the economic operational mechanisms.

VI. Resource utilization efficiency in less developed regions

Efficiency in capital utilization is the third issue pertinent to local capital investment. With a given amount of capital investment and a given direction or structure for it, capital utilization efficiency is the foremost factor in determining the level of regional development and of increases in resident income. Furthermore, capital utilization efficiency also has a direct bearing on the level of ecosystem damage, the development of the environmental protection sector, and the level of balance between development and environment.

Capital utilization efficiency is an identical concept to resource utilization efficiency. The economic resources put into development can be converted into capital if they come in money form. Therefore, the level of capital utilization efficiency is the same as the level of resource utilization efficiency. Resource utilization efficiency also represents the level of effectiveness at which resources are used. Effective use of resources means that: (1) all sorts of resources have been put to full use, without being left idle or to waste; (2) various groupings of resources are working efficiently, that is, they can yield the highest possible efficiency under the assumption that the other conditions remain unchanged; and (3) the results of using resources are exactly what is needed by society, or, in other words, the products, labor and services provided by grouped resources have become effective supply. In short, effective utilization of resources entails three aspects: full use of resources, efficient resource grouping, and results of such grouping that are welcomed by society. Only by taking these three aspects into overall consideration is it possible to judge if resources have been put to effective use and—if the answer is yes—how effectively they have been used.

因此，我们可以得出这样的结论：尽管经济运行机制转换本身并不等于资金的投入方向趋于合理，不等于环境保护领域的投资由此增多，不等于经济发展与环境之间日益协调，但由于前面提到的这两点（新经济运行机制之下有较多的内部投入和再投入，以及企业将会根据自己的利益而按政府的调节意图改变经济行为），经济发展与环境协调的可能性要比在传统经济运行机制之下大得多。这就从资金投入方面或资金投入结构方面说明了环境保护、贫困地区发展、经济运行机制转换三者是紧密地联系在一起的。

六、贫困地区的资源利用效率

地区资金投入的第三个问题是资金利用效率。在资金投入数量和资金投入方向或结构为既定的条件下，资金利用效率的高低便成为决定地区经济发展和居民收入水平提高程度的最重要因素。此外，资金利用效率的高低还直接关系到生态破坏程度，关系到环境保护部门的发展状况，关系到经济发展与环境的协调程度。

资金利用效率与资源利用效率是同一个概念。经济发展中所投入的经济资源，如果以货币形式来表现的话，那么都可以折算为资金。因此，资金利用效率的高低也就是资源利用效率的高低。资源利用效率也被称为资源的有效利用程度。资源有效利用是指：（1）各种资源都得到充分利用而没有闲置、浪费；（2）各种资源的组合是有效率的，即能在其他条件不变的情况下产生尽可能高的效率；（3）资源利用的结果，即资源组合所提供的产品和劳务，是社会所需要的，它们成为有效供给。简言之，资源有效利用包括资源充分利用、资源组合有效率、资源组合的成果为社会所需要三个内容。只有从这三个方面进行综合分析，才能判断资源是否得到了有效利用，以及在多大程度上得到了有效利用。

Under old economic operational mechanisms, the effectiveness of resource utilization is seriously handicapped. An incomplete market, coupled with lethargic company performance, inevitably keeps resource utilization efficiency low, and ineffective supply of resources cannot be remedied with the economy's internal strength alone. In both scenarios, intervention in the economy can be effected only through noneconomic government means. However, if economic operational mechanisms remain intact, problems will keep snowballing even if the government can reconcile the conflicts resulting from low resource utilization efficiency through noneconomic means. When the problems come to a head, the conflict between resource supply and demand will be fully exposed. An economy in disarray invariably forces firms to seek the way out through underground transactions in an attempt to protect their interests (as well as the interests of their workers). This may enable a few firms to somewhat improve their resource utilization efficiency, but for society as a whole, such efficiency will remain low and tend to be aggravated by such underground transactions. This is because the underground market may force firms to pay a high price if they want to turn such transactions to their favor, thereby steering resource allocation further from the right course.

Under new economic operational mechanisms, and with newly gained decision-making autonomy and flexibility, firms will become keener than before in pursuing the highest possible resource utilization efficiency because it is directly relevant to their immediate interests. The gradually improved market works alongside government macroeconomic regulatory steps not only to furnish favorable conditions for placing resources where they are needed and grouping them as reasonably as possible, but also to set the stage for universal improvements in resource utilization efficiency. Insofar as resource utilization efficiency is raised, it is both necessary and urgent to shift the socialist economy to new operational mechanisms.

VII. Putting an end to the "low income—ecosystem damage—low income" vicious cycle

From the angles of capital investment sources, the direction of such investment, and capital utilization efficiency, I have just probed into the development of less developed regions and the balance between such development and environmental protection under old and new economic operational mechanisms. As a matter of fact, these three facets of capital investment are closely interrelated. Pivotal to these facets, moreover, is

在传统经济运行机制之下，资源的有效利用受到严重的限制。市场不完善和企业缺乏活力，不可避免地造成资源的低效率利用，无效供给难以依靠经济内在的力量来加以制止。这时，只有依赖政府采取非经济的手段来干预经济。但经济运行机制不转换，即使政府以非经济的手段来暂时缓和因资源利用效率低下而造成的矛盾，问题也只会越积越多。当问题积累到一定程度以后，资源供求之间的矛盾便充分暴露出来。经济的混乱迫使企业不得不为了自身的利益（甚至是为了本单位职工的利益），通过地下交易活动而谋求出路。对个别企业来说，资源利用效率也许有所提高，但对全社会而言，资源利用效率仍然是低下的，甚至还会因地下交易活动而变得更差。这是因为地下市场可能使一些企业为了进行有利于自己的交易而付出昂贵得多的代价，还可能使资源配置的方向进一步扭偏。

建立新的经济运行机制之后，由于企业有了自主性和机动性，由于企业的资源利用效率高低直接同自身的利益有关，提高资源利用效率便成为企业最关心的目标。而市场的逐渐完善与政府采取的宏观经济调节措施，不仅为社会的资源投向和资源组合趋于合理创造了条件，而且为资源利用效率的普遍提高提供了良好的环境。因此，从提高资源利用效率这一角度来说，及早使社会主义经济运行机制转轨，也是非常必要和迫切的。

七、重要的是及早摆脱"低收入—生态破坏—低收入"循环

以上从资金投入的来源、资金投入的方向、资金利用效率三方面探讨了两种不同的经济运行机制下的贫困地区开发问题以及经济发展与环境的协调问题。实际上，资金投入的这三个方面是紧密地联系在一起的；而且，这三个方面中，具有关键性意义的是如何

the question of how to establish an internal accumulation mechanism in less developed regions. Such a mechanism is the foremost precondition for speeding up balanced development in these regions. As long as these regions can establish their own internal accumulation mechanisms and secure a constant flow of capital to invest and reinvest in local economies, they will find it easier to tackle their other problems. To put it another way, if the economy of a less developed region is like a funnel that cannot retain any water, using and distributing such water is out of the question.

In the course of balanced economic development in less developed regions, effective use of resources is predicated on the formation of local internal accumulation mechanisms. One of the reasons why residents of these regions do not value their resources and are given to tapping them wantonly is because in their effort to develop local economies and raise their income, they have no alternative but to consume local resources as much as they can. Only when they have developed their internal investment and reinvestment mechanisms can they cherish their resources and economize on them. Only then can these regions put improving their efficiency in utilizing local resources on the agenda. The same is true of integrating local resources with those of other regions. It is true that all the input of resources, local or otherwise, should be put to best use and grouped as effectively as possible, and that every effort must be made to put the fruits of such grouping on the market (in the form of products and services). However, nothing is more important to these regions than putting an internal accumulation mechanism in place. Only with such a mechanism can developed regions be motivated for economic collaboration with less developed regions, can sustained integration of local and outside resources happen steadily, and can actual benefits be reaped from the economies of less developed regions. In the absence of such a mechanism, interregional economic collaboration cannot be made to last—in extreme cases, once happened, it can never happen again.

In developing less developed regions, particularly in coordinating their development and environment, we must not lose sight of the salient features of the issue of effective resource utilization. After an internal accumulation mechanism has been set up in such a region, the effort to put resources to effective use and to keep raising the resource utilization efficiency should never be slackened. That is to say, the arrival of the internal accumulation mechanism does not mean utilization of resources can become immediately effective. If effectiveness is overlooked in this

及早建立贫困地区的内部积累机制，这是加速贫困地区经济协调发展的首要条件。只要贫困地区形成了内部积累机制，不断地有资金投入和再投入本地的经济之中，其他一切问题就比较容易处理了。换言之，如果一个贫困地区的经济始终像一个“漏斗”，蓄不住水，那也就谈不上如何利用这些水、如何分配水源等等了。

在贫困地区经济协调发展过程中，资源的有效利用正是以本地区内部积累机制的形成为前提的。贫困地区的居民为什么不珍惜自己的资源而过度采伐，原因之一就在于他们要发展本地区经济和提高居民收入水平，除了尽量消耗本地资源之外，没有其他的途径。只有在本地区内部形成投入与再投入机制之后，资源才会被珍惜，才会被有节制地利用；也只有在这时，贫困地区才会认真考虑如何提高本地资源的利用效率问题。在贫困地区本地资源同外地资源相结合的问题上，情况同样如此。虽然无论是对本地资源还是对外地资源而言，都要使投入的资源能得到充分利用，都要尽可能实现资源的有效组合，并且都力求使这些资源组合的成果（产品和劳务）得以在市场上实现，但对贫困地区来说形成内部积累机制是最为重要的。只有这样，与贫困地区进行经济合作的地区才会对此有持久的热情，两地资源的结合才能持续地进行下去，也才能给贫困地区经济带来实际的好处。否则，即使两地进行了经济合作，这种合作也不可能持久，甚至只是一次性的。

当然，在贫困地区开发过程中，尤其是在协调贫困地区的经济发展与环境之间的关系的过程中，资源有效利用问题仍有其本身的特点。在贫困地区内部积累机制形成之后，仍要时刻注意资源的有效利用，使资源利用效率不断提高。这就是说，不能认为内部积累机制的形成等同于资源的有效利用。如果不注意资源的有效利用，

regard, the accumulation rate will fluctuate even in the presence of the internal accumulation mechanism. If the accumulation rate is on the low side, it can do little to boost economic development in less developed regions. Therefore, these regions must do their level best to increase resource utilization efficiency when fostering internal accumulation mechanisms, so that their internal investment and reinvestment can yield more output and surplus. It must be pointed out that effective utilization of resources is not only connected with the economic operational mechanism but also affected by production technology. Efficiency in resource utilization varies with technical conditions. Under a given economic system, improved technology can boost such efficiency, increase the output of per-unit input, and put available resources to more uses. It can even help discover and utilize more resources. Such is the importance of steady improvement of production technology in less developed regions.

The cultivation of internal accumulation mechanism and the increase of resource utilization efficiency in less developed regions are subject to the enthusiasm of local businesses and residents (workers included). The cultivation of the internal accumulation mechanism, in particular, hinges on motivating capital-supplying businesses and individuals. For instance, the motivation of businesses as investors helps them reinvest more; the enthusiasm of residents (workers and farmers included) as bank creditors helps boost the savings rate and furnishes favorable conditions to convert bank savings into investment. In boosting resource utilization efficiency, it is essential to motivate every supplier of production factors, including capital and labor suppliers—managers, technicians, workers and farmers. Furthermore, the enthusiasm of those on the demand side is also indispensible to efficient utilization of resources, because the marketing of the fruits of resource grouping cannot do without them. Otherwise, the products may be stockpiled or become unsalable. Of course I am not saying that demand should be stimulated artificially, but that demand is elastic, and that if properly guided, rational demand often has room to expand. To motivate those who need capital is in fact to guide them to expand purchases properly while turning the supply from poor regions into effective supply. In this regard we have to see the fact that the demand of less developed regions for manufactured goods is

那么即使形成了内部积累机制，积累率却有高有低；如果内部积累率偏低，这对贫困地区的经济发展依然起不了什么作用。因此，贫困地区必须在形成内部积累机制的同时，尽可能提高资源利用效率，以便使来自内部的投入和再投入有更多的产出，从而有更多的剩余。此外，资源有效利用既是一个经济运行机制问题（即经济体制问题），也是一个生产技术问题。在不同的技术条件下，资源有效利用程度必定有所差异。如果经济体制为既定，提高技术水平不仅可以提高资源有效利用程度，增加单位投入的产出，还可以使现有的资源具有更多的用途，甚至发现更多的资源，利用更多的资源。这说明了在贫困地区不断提高生产技术水平的重要性。

在贫困地区形成内部积累机制和提高资源利用效率，都同调动企业的积极性、居民（包括职工）的积极性有关。对于内部积累机制的形成来说，重要的是调动企业和居民（包括职工）作为资金供给一方的积极性。例如，调动作为投资者的企业的积极性，有助于企业增加再投入；调动作为储蓄者的居民（包括职工和农民）的积极性，有利于提高储蓄率，并为储蓄转化为投资创造条件。在资源有效利用方面，重要的是调动所有生产要素供给者的积极性，既包括资金供给者的积极性，也包括劳动供给者的积极性。在劳动供给者之中，包括了管理人员、技术人员、工人、农民等等。不仅如此，需求一方的积极性的调动对于资源有效利用也是不可忽视的。这是因为，要使得资源组合的成果在市场上实现，需求一方的积极性同样重要，否则生产出来的某些商品就会积压、滞销。当然，这并不是说要人为地刺激需求，而是说需求是有某种伸缩性的，如果加以引导合理的需求仍有扩大的余地。调动需求一方的积极性，实际上是指对需求者进行引导，以适当扩大他们的购买行为，并使贫困地区的供给成为有效供给。在这里，有一个重要的问题需要说明，这就是贫困地区由于人均收入少，市场狭小，对各种工业品的

circumscribed by their per capita income and small markets. Therefore, to put demand under proper guidance can help improve the resource utilization efficiency on both sides of the supply-demand relationship.

As efficient utilization of resources also calls for protecting resources and the environment, we should, in the course of opening up less developed regions, focus our attention not only on whether resources are fully utilized (so that none of them is left idle) and grouped efficiently, and whether the products of such grouping are needed by society, but also on the protection of resources and the environment. From a long-term point of view, negligence in resource and environmental protection inevitably leads to overheated development and damaged resources. This is a pivotal issue to the development of less developed regions, for it has a close bearing on whether these regions can be released from the "low income—ecological damage—low income" vicious cycle that can be overcome only by replacing "ecosystem destruction" with "ecosystem preservation." If this fundamental change can be effected, low income can be gradually turned into middle-level income and further to high income.

During a recent fact-finding tour of Fengning and Weichang counties in Chengde Prefecture, Hebei Province, I told my hosts that I often heard the old refrain about developing mountain economies: "You'd better live off the mountains if you live there." There is nothing wrong with that saying, because mountainous regions cannot be developed without tapping local resources. It can be very difficult to jump-start the economy in such regions if local resources are left unused. However, the old refrain can also be misunderstood by those who think: "We have nothing to fear, now that we can live off the mountains." If that philosophy is taken for granted, then everything in the mountains will be used up before you have realized it. That is, when mountain resources are used up or ruined, the mountains will become so uninhabitable that folk living on them will have nowhere else to turn to for sustenance. For this reason, that old refrain may be reworded like this: "Nourish the mountains to eat off them." To make the mountains "eatable," you have to "nourish" them. This means to cherish mountain resources and tap them in a restrained way while conserving them and building up their stock. Nobody can succeed in developing a mountain economy if they are given to "eating off" the mountains and do not care to "nourish" them. Chengde Prefecture happens to be a mountainous region, but my remarks apply not just to mountainous regions but to every less developed region as well.

需求也有限。因此，对需求的引导，是既有利于从供给方面提高资源利用效率，又有利于从需求方面提高资源利用效率的。

由于资源有效利用还意味着对资源的保护和对环境的保护，所以在贫困地区开发过程中，不能只注意到资源是否被充分利用（没有闲置的资源），资源组合是否有效率，资源组合的成果是否为社会所需要，而且还应注意资源保护和环境保护问题。从较长时期来考察，不保护资源和环境，必定会导致资源的过度开发和资源的破坏。对于贫困地区经济发展来说，这是非常重要的问题。贫困地区的经济究竟能不能最终摆脱“低收入—生态破坏—低收入”的困境，与此有着十分密切的关系。要突破“低收入—生态破坏—低收入”这一恶性循环，关键在于把“生态破坏”变为“生态保护”。只要这一环节发生了根本性的变化，低收入就可以逐步变为中等收入，然后再变为高收入。

不久前，我在河北承德地区丰宁、围场两县考察时曾针对当地的情况谈到，在发展山区经济的过程中，经常听到这样四个字：“靠山吃山”。这句话的本意并不错，因为山区的经济发展离不开山区资源的优势，如果抛开了山区资源的优势，山区经济的起步确实是困难重重的。但这句话也可能被某些人所误解，即认为既然“有山可吃”，那还怕什么呢？如果那样的话，结果就会“坐吃山空”，直到把山区资源耗竭了，山区资源破坏了，山既“不可靠”，“吃也无处可吃”了。所以，正确的说法应当是“养山吃山”。要使得山有“可吃之处”，必须“养山”。“养山”就是珍惜山区资源，合理开发，并且不断维护山区资源，使山区资源存量日益增多。在发展山区经济时，不“养山”而“吃山”，没有不失败的。河北省承德地区是山区，我的这些话，不仅对山区，实际上对所有的贫困地区都是适用的。

Only by "nourishing" the "mountains" can they become a source of wealth. Only by "nourishing" the "water" can the "water" become a depository of wealth. A great deal can be accomplished when you are devoted to nourishing something. This is not merely about technicalities, but more than anything else, about economic operational mechanisms. For a less developed region to escape poverty and embark on the road toward prosperity, the only way out lies in coordinating economic development with environment protection, and in reversing the vicious cycle of "low income—environmental damage—low income" into the virtuous circle of "income increase—ecosystem protection—income increase." Both conversion and coordination can happen after old economic operation mechanisms have given way to new ones. Such is my conclusion.

— *Social Sciences in China*, issue No. 4, 1991

只有“养山”才能把“山”视为财源，只有“养水”才能把“水”视为聚宝盆。“养”字大有文章可做。这不单纯是技术性问题，首要的是经济运行机制问题。贫困地区要真正脱贫致富，唯有走经济与环境相互协调发展的道路，变“低收入—破坏生态—低收入”循环为“提高收入—保护生态—提高收入”循环。在转换了经济运行机制之后，从前一循环向后一循环的转变就有了前提，贫困地区经济与环境的协调发展也才有了可能性。这就是我们所得出的结论。

（原载《中国社会科学》，1991 年第 4 期）

COMPARATIVE ECONOMIC HISTORY AND THE MODERNIZATION OF CHINA (1993)

I. Economic history: an overview (prelude)

Economic history, as an academic discipline, studies the historical process of economic activity that involves the evolution of the economic system, the development of productivity as well as the interaction between the two. It is a hybrid of economics and history, as its name suggests. From the viewpoint of the history of economics, a lot has been said and written about past economic phenomena and issues, and many ideas have been put forth on the relationship between economics and history from perspectives ranging from mercantilism to classical economics. These efforts, however, were not systematic enough to give rise to economic history as an academic discipline. It was not until the late 19th century that economic history emerged in Western Europe as an independent discipline, thanks to contributions from numerous prominent European scholars. These included representatives of the German history of economics such as Gustav von Schmoller, Albert Eberhard Fridrich Schaffle and Karl Wilhelm Bücher, as well as their contemporaries James Edwin Thorold Rogers, Henry de Beltgens Gibbins, Arnold Toynbee and William James Ashley of Great Britain, Emile Levasseur of France, and Charles Franklin Dunbar, Henry Walcott Farnam, Gerald C. Gross and Richard Theodore Ely of the United States. Economic history came a long way in Europe and America in the first half of the 20th century. Scholars like Werner Sombart and Ernst Wagemann of Germany, John Harold Clapham, Michael Moissey Postan and Richard Henry Tawney of Great Britain, Henri Sée of France, Eli Filip Heckscher of Sweden, Alfons Dopsch of Austria, Henri Pirenne of Belgium, James Walter Thompson, Mikhail Ivanovich Rostovtzeff and Abbott Payson Usher of the United States distinguished themselves with important works in their respective areas of this discipline.

Under the influence of various philosophical, historical, and economic thoughts, economists are divided in their outlook on such major issues as the relationship between theory and history, on the roles of geographical environment, population, and government in economic development, and on whether socioeconomic development is single-

比较经济史研究与中国的现代化（1993）

一、从经济史学谈起

经济史学是以人类经济活动的历史过程，即以经济制度的演变、生产力的发展以及二者之间相互作用的历史过程作为研究对象的学科。它是经济学和历史学的交叉学科。从经济学说史上看，虽然从重商主义者到古典经济学家，曾经有不少人论述过历史上的经济现象和经济问题，提出过有关经济和历史的相互关系的观点，但这些非系统的论述还不构成经济史学。作为一门独立学科的经济史学，于 19 世纪晚期产生于西欧。德国新历史学派的代表人物，如施莫勒（G. von Schmoller）、谢夫莱（A. E. P. Schaffle）、毕歇尔（K. Bücher），以及同一时期英国的罗杰斯（J. E. T. Rogers）、吉宾斯（H. de B. Gibbins）、阿诺德 · 汤因比（Arnold Toynbee）、艾希利（W. J. Ashley），法国的勒瓦瑟尔（P. E. Levasseur），美国的登巴（C. F. Dunbar）、法尔南（H. W. Farnam）、格罗斯（G. Gross）、伊利（R. T. Ely）等人，都为西方经济史学的建立做出了成绩。在 20 世纪前半期，在欧洲和美国，经济史学有较大的发展。德国的桑巴特（W. Sombart）、瓦格曼（E. Wagemann），英国的克拉潘（J. H. Clapham）、波士坦（M. Postan）、托尼（R. H. Tawney），法国的亨利 · 瑟（Henri Sée），瑞典的赫克歇尔（E. F. Heckscher），奥地利的道布希（A. Dopsch），比利时的皮朗（H. Pirenne），美国的汤普逊（J. W. Thompson）、罗斯托夫采夫（M. I. Rostovtzeff）、阿歇尔（A. P. Usher）等人，都是在经济史学的一定领域内有重要著作问世的知名学者。

在经济史学的发展过程中，不同的研究者由于受到不同的哲学思想、史学思想和经济学思想的影响，在理论与历史之间的关系、地理环境或人口因素在经济发展过程中的作用、政府在经济发展过程中的作用、人类社会经济的发展是单线的还是复线的、人类社会

or multi-tracked, progressive, or radical. Many of their opinions on the history of humanity's economic activity, the metamorphosis of economic systems and the development of productivity may be blinkered or Eurocentric in their global overview of economic history, yet it has to be admitted that their achievements are valuable for later researchers, both in the collection and collation of historical archives on economics and in textual research on specific facts in economic history.

Comparative economic history as a branch of economic history mainly dwells on the similarities and differences between the economic processes of countries and regions in the world, and analyzes their causes and effects for a deeper understanding of the historical process of socioeconomic activity. In both genesis and development it is something of a latecomer in comparison with economic history. For a considerably long period of time after economic history was established as a field of study, many scholars—such as G. Schmoller, K. Bücher, W. J. Ashley, H. Sée, H. Pirenne, E. F. Heckscher and J. H. Clapham—made comparative studies of the economic history of different countries, yet their efforts were hardly systematic. Moreover, because of their research focus on the establishment of a certain theoretical model for economic history, they tended to sort out and arrange the economic historical facts and figures of different countries in compliance with this established model. In other words, limited by the circumstances of the time, none of these European economists lived to see comparative economic history maturing into an independent discipline—it was a branch of economic history at best.

II. The rise of comparative economic history

It was not until the end of the Second World War, particularly after the mid-1960s, that the importance of comparative economic history came to be recognized by the academic world. This had something to do with the postwar world political and economic situation. Following the disintegration of the old world political order, and with many less developed nations embarking on the road of modernization, comparative studies of economic systems, economic growth, and economic policies caught on widely among scholars, thereby paving the way for the birth of comparative economic history as an academic discipline. Ragnar Nurkse, Simon Smith Kuznets, Walt Whitman Rostow, Alber Otto

经济的发展是渐进的还是突变的这样一些重大问题上，存在着意见分歧。他们对人类经济活动的历史、经济制度演变的历史甚至生产力发展的历史都有自己的看法，尽管其中不少看法可能是较片面的，或者是以西方世界作为中心来概述全世界的经济史的，但应当承认，无论在经济史料的收集与整理方面，或在某一具体经济史事实的考证与辨析方面，他们的研究成果值得以后的研究者们重视与参考。

比较经济史学是经济史学的一个分支，它考察世界上各个不同国家和地区经济史过程的差异和共同点，分析这些差异和共同点的原因与后果，以加深对人类社会经济活动的历史过程的认识。比较经济史学产生与发展的时间要比经济史学晚得多。要知道，在经济史学产生以后的较长时期内，虽然像施莫勒、毕歇尔、艾希利、亨利·瑟、皮朗、赫克歇尔、克拉潘等人都曾对不同国家的经济史进行过比较研究，但这些比较研究并不是系统的。并且，由于他们研究的重点主要放在某种经济史理论模式的建立上，因此对不同国家的经济史资料的编排、整理往往服从于他们固有的经济史理论模式。换言之，在当时的条件下，比较经济史学还没有成为一门独立的学科，经济史的比较研究附属于一般经济史研究。

二、比较经济史学的形成

比较经济史学的形成和经济史比较研究的重要性被学术界所认识，主要是在第二次世界大战结束以后，尤其是在 20 世纪年代中期以后。这是与当时的世界政治经济形势分不开的。第二次世界大战结束后，随着旧的世界政治体制的解体和不少后进国家先后走上现代化的道路，关于经济制度、经济发展、经济政策的历史比较成为学术界广泛感兴趣的课题，这方面的研究为比较经济史学的形成创造了重要的条件。像讷克斯（R. Nurkse）、库兹涅茨（S. Kuznets）、罗斯托（W. W. Rostow）、赫尔希曼（A. O. Hirschman）

Hirschman, and other scholars who had made a name for themselves in their studies of economic growth, delved into comparative economic history and came up with groundbreaking discoveries and enunciations. Although these people, with the exception of W. W. Rostow, are not considered as economic historians, the important position of their works in comparative economic history can never be ignored. The advent and development of theories on human capital, institutional and technological innovation, political cycles, the long wave, the political market and public choices, either have provided new theoretical backing for the study of comparative economic history, or become vivid research topics.

The rise of econometric history, also known as cliometrics or new economic history, was yet another major factor that contributed to comparative economic history in its formative years. Econometric history first appeared in the late 1950s, and progressed swiftly after the mid-1960s. American economic historians Robert William Fogel, Douglass Cecil North and Stanley Lewis Engerman are its major representatives. These economic historians label past studies in this field "traditional economic history" for the reason that they have stopped at the level of historiography, fallen short of integrating economic theories with economic history, and failed to apply modern quantitative analysis in studying past historical events and economic development processes. Accordingly, they believe they have remedied all these deficiencies with their brand of new economic history. During the period from the 1960s to the 1980s, the new economic history caught the attention of the academic world and gave a major impetus to comparative economic history by coming up with a series of works on the histories of technological innovation, institutional innovation, railways, the southern US economy, the Western European medieval manorial system, historical calculations of GNP and labor productivity, and the historiography of business cycles. This great impetus manifested itself mainly in improvements in research methodology. As R. W. Fogel and S. L. Engerman point out in

The Reinterpretation of American Economic History (1971), "When the data are very good, simple statistical procedures will usually suffice. The poorer the data, the more powerful are the methods which have to be employed. Nevertheless, it is often true that the volume of data available is frequently below the minimum required for standard statistical procedures. In such instances the crucial determinant of success is the

这样一些以研究经济成长著称的经济学家，都在比较经济史学领域内进行了专门的论述。尽管除了罗斯托以外，其他几位学者都不被归入经济史学家范畴，但他们的著作在比较经济史研究中的地位却是不容忽视的。此外，诸如人力资本理论、制度创新理论、技术创新理论、政治周期理论、长波理论、政治市场与公共选择理论等等的产生和发展，也使得比较经济史研究有了新的理论依据或更为生动的研究内容。

在比较经济史学形成过程中，另一个起着重要作用的因素就是计量经济史学（econometrichistory）或历史计量学（cliometrics）的兴起。计量经济史学有时也被称作新经济史学（new economic history），它出现于 20 世纪 50 年代末期，自 60 年代中期以后有较大的发展。福格尔（R. W. Fogel）、诺思（D. C. North）、恩格尔曼（S. L. Engerman）等美国经济史学家是主要代表人物。他们把以往的经济史学称作传统经济史学，认为后者停留于历史编纂学的水平，而未能把经济理论同经济史结合在一起，以及未能运用现代数量分析方法来研究历史上的重要事件、经济的发展过程。他们认为新经济史学弥补了传统经济史学的上述缺陷。60 年代至 80 年代，新经济史学在技术创新史、制度创新史、铁路史、美国南部经济史、西欧中世纪庄园制、历史上国民收入与劳动生产率的计算、经济周期史等领域内所发表的若干论著，引起了学术界的注意，并给比较经济史研究有力的推动。这种推动主要是在研究方法上。正如福格尔和恩格尔曼在 1971 年出版的《美国经济史的重新解释》一书中所指出的："如果资料十分完备，简单的统计方法通常就够用了。资料越是贫乏，就越需要使用高深的统计方法。但无论如何，可以利用的资料的确总是低于标准统计方法所要求的最低限度。在这种情况下，如果要获得成就，关键就在于研究者

ability of the investigator to devise methods that are exceedingly efficient in the utilization of data—that is, to find a method that will permit one to achieve a solution with the limited data that are available."[1] Besides the support from certain theories, improved research methods, quantitative methods in particular, are also *sine qua non* for the achievements made in comparative studies of the economic development processes of different countries and regions.

From a methodological point of view, both vertical and lateral comparative approaches can be applied in comparative economic history. Vertical comparative analysis refers to a study of changes that have taken place in different periods in one or several countries along the historical course of economic development, so as to discover the norms governing economic development. Lateral comparative analysis refers to a comparison of the economic situations in different areas of a country or in several countries over a certain period or at a given time, so as to illustrate the distinctive economic features of the areas or countries being compared. Choices of economic indicators and of years are pivotal to the success of vertical comparison. The older the indicators, the more fragmented the statistical data tend to be, and the more difficult the comparison becomes. Moreover, such a comparison can make sense only when different statistics are converted into something that can be measured with the same benchmark. As to the choice of years, arbitrariness must be avoided—the years chosen to represent certain turning points or historical periods in economic development should be solidly grounded. Only thus can convincing conclusions be derived from such a vertical comparison. As to lateral comparative analysis, apart from the above-mentioned caution in the choice of economic indicators and years (as well as the comparability of such indicators), due attention should be paid to the connection between lateral and vertical comparisons. This is because only by putting the two kinds of comparison together can the regular pattern of the economy's historical development be seen more clearly, and only thus can the deficiencies of statistics concerning a certain historical period in a certain country be made up for with an approximate value derived from corresponding data available for the same historical period in another country. This drives further home the significance of quantitative analysis to the rise of comparative economic history.

要能够设计出在利用资料方面特别有效的方法，也就是说，研究者要能够发现一种可以靠有限的有用资料来解决问题的方法。"[1]比较经济史学研究除了有赖于一定的理论作为依据以外，研究方法特别是数量研究方法的进展也是使不同国家、不同地区经济发展过程的比较研究取得成就的一个不可忽视的原因。

从方法论的角度看，比较经济史研究中既可以采取纵向比较分析，又可以采取横向比较分析。纵向比较分析是指按照经济发展的历史过程分析一国不同历史时期或若干国家不同历史时期的变化，以探求经济发展的历史规律性。横向比较分析是指对一定时期内或一定时点上一国国内不同地区或若干国家的经济状况进行比较，以说明待比较的各国或各个地区的历史上的经济特色。在纵向比较分析时，重要的问题一是指标的选择，一是年代的选择。在指标方面，越是往前推，统计资料越不完整，从而比较越困难，并且不同的统计资料还必须经过换算，口径取得一致，然后才能使比较具有意义。在年代的选择上，主要的考虑在于防止选择的随意性，用来标志历史时期的年份或用来说明经济发展转折点的年份应当具有充足的依据，只有这样，才能通过纵向比较分析而得出较为可信的结论。再就横向比较分析而言，除了同纵向比较分析一样要注意指标的选择（以及指标的可比性）与年代的选择而外，横向比较分析同纵向比较分析之间的联系也是必须重视的。这是因为，只有使横向比较分析与纵向比较分析相结合，才能更清楚地说明经济的历史发展的规律性，并能在某种程度上弥补一些国家的某个历史时期内统计资料的不足，而用另一些国家相应历史时期内已有的统计资料进行推算，得出近似值，作为参考。这也就进一步说明了数量研究方法的进展对于比较经济史学形成的意义。

III. Comparative economic history and studies of modernization

The modernization issue has been drawing the attention of international academia as a major research topic since the end of the Second World War. Both development economics and comparative economic history have studied it, but the former has distinguished itself by approaching the topic more from the perspective of economic history, that is, by comparing the historical processes of socioeconomic development. To put it more exactly, development economics studies the mode and policy of economic development by leaning heavily on the allocation and flow of production factors, the relationship between saving and consumption, the roles of market mechanism and government functionaries, the relationship between sectoral and regional economic structures as well as between economic development and technological innovation, and the internal-external balance in the development process. Although development economics also links the modernization issue with the roles of institutional, cultural and other factors, it puts a premium on the present situation instead of on historical summary. By comparison, comparative economic history has a different focus in modernization studies.

As a branch of economic history, comparative economic history not only is devoted to historical economic development, but also explores issues with more extensity and profundity. To name just a few: How important are the roles of traditional culture, religion and ethics in the historical process of socioeconomic development of different countries or regions? To what extent can the differences in socioeconomic history between countries (and regions) be interpreted in light of their differences in traditional culture, religion and ethics? Both questions, however, fall into the category of comparative economic history rather than development economics. To cite another group of questions: What are the implications of the Asian mode of production? What is the economic difference between Eastern and Western pre-capitalist societies? How did such a difference come about, and what is its relationship with the later capitalist economic development? What conclusions can be arrived at if the role of geographic environment in economic development is belittled or exaggerated? Can such conclusions stand the test of science? These questions are, likewise, concerns of comparative economic historians, and rarely dwelt on by development economists.

三、比较经济史学与现代化问题研究

第二次世界大战结束以后，有关现代化问题的研究日益成为国际学术界注意的重大课题。发展经济学与比较经济史学都把现代化作为自己的研究任务，但发展经济史学在研究现代化问题时有着自己的特色。它更多地从经济史方面，也就是从人类社会经济的历史过程的比较方面来研究这一问题。较确切地说，在有关现代化的研究中，发展经济学侧重于从生产要素配置与流动、储蓄与消费之间的关系、市场机制与政府职能的作用、部门结构与地区经济结构、经济发展与技术创新、发展过程中的内外均衡等方面来研究经济发展的模式与政策。发展经济学虽然也把现代化问题同制度、文化等因素的作用结合在一起，但它的重点是放在当前，而不是放在历史的总结上。比较经济史学对现代化问题的研究的重点与此是有所不同的。

比较经济史学作为经济史学的一个分支，它不仅侧重于研究经济的历史发展，而且通常探讨一些更为广泛、更为深刻的问题。例如，传统文化、宗教、伦理观念在不同国家、不同地区的社会经济发展的历史过程中曾经起过多大的作用？不同国家、不同地区的社会经济史的差异在多大的程度上可以用传统文化、宗教、伦理观念的差异来加以解释？这些问题是比较经济史学考察的内容，而并非发展经济学的研究者们注意的焦点。又如，亚细亚生产方式的真正含义是什么？东方的前资本主义社会在经济上与西方的前资本主义社会的区别何在？这种区别是怎样形成的，它同此后的资本主义经济发展有着什么样的关系？如果不重视地理环境在这方面的作用，或者，过分渲染地理环境在这方面的作用，将会导致什么样的结论？这些结论是否经得起科学的检验？这些问题同样是比较经济史研究者关心的，而发展经济学则较少涉及这一类问题。

Modernization entails a process of sustained economic, social, political and cultural development, with economic development as the driving force behind it. The academic world is widely divided as to when worldwide modernization was started. It is dated back variously to the scientific revolution of the 16th and 17th centuries, to the industrial revolution towards the end of the 18th century, or to a more recent date. The consensus, nevertheless, is that the hundred years beginning from the late 19th century constituted the modernization stage in the socioeconomic development of human history. Therefore, no research into modernization can be complete without summarizing the experiences and lessons of all nations in their economic development during those years. It goes without saying that modernized nations need to sum up their historical experiences so that they can address, with appropriate countermeasures, the socioeconomic problems arising from economic development. Nations that are striving for modernization, too, find it necessary to summarize their own experiences and those of others in economic development over the years. Without such summary, they may go astray or repeat other nations' mistakes in their modernization drive. In that sense, the study of modernization is synonymous with comparative economic history. More than that, because comparative economic history can prepare conditions for in-depth modernization studies, it is, indeed, an indispensable branch of foundational research for the latter.

In a comparative study of the relationship between tradition and modernization featured in the book *The Modernization of Japan and Russia* (Cyril Edwin Black et al, New York, 1975), I have discovered a typical example to illustrate the collaboration between comparative economic history and modernization research. C. E. Black and his co-authors chose to compare the Japanese modernization process with that of Russia precisely because the two nations, each with a heritage different from that of Western Europe, were seeking modernization and adapting it to their respective traditions. According to the authors' observations of modern economic history, Japan and Russia share a distinguished feature in their modernization processes in that they have both succeeded in preserving their traditions. However, such traditions are no longer the same as they were—they have been adapted to modernization. What the authors are saying is that, firstly, modernization is not the same as

现代化是一个经济、社会、政治、文化的持续发展的过程，而以经济发展过程作为其主要的内容。尽管学术界对世界的现代化的开始日期有不同的看法，如有人认为应当从 16 世纪和 17 世纪的科学革命算起，有人认为应当从 18 世纪末的工业革命算起，也有人认为应当从更近一些算起，但不管怎样，至少从 19 世纪晚期以来的 100 年的历史，都被承认是人类社会经济发展中的现代化阶段，因此对现代化的研究无疑包含了对世界上各个国家最近 100 年经济发展的经验与教训的总结。已经实现现代化的国家固然需要总结自身经济发展的历史经验，以便正确对待经济发展所遗留下来的社会经济问题，寻求妥善的对策；而目前正在进行现代化的国家则更加需要总结本国和其他国家这些年来经济发展的经验和教训：如果没有这种总结，现代化过程中就会走弯路，就会重复自己走过的和别人走过的错误道路。从这个意义上说，不仅现代化的研究与比较经济史的研究是一致的，而且比较经济史研究还为现代化研究的深入准备了条件，比较经济史研究甚至可以被看成是现代化研究的一项不可替代的基础性研究。

在这里，不妨以布莱克（C. E. Black）等人合著的《日本和俄国的现代化》（1975 年纽约版）一书中关于传统与现代化之间关系的比较研究为例，以说明比较经济史研究与现代化研究的结合。布莱克等人之所以选择日本和俄国的现代化过程进行比较，正因为这两个国家有着不同于西欧的传统，而同时又力求在适应过去传统的基础上实现现代化。关于传统与现代化的关系，根据布莱克等人对日本和俄国近代经济史的考察，日本和俄国现代化过程的一个显著特点是传统的东西在现代化过程中被保存下来，并且同现代化相适应，但这种传统已经不再是原来的传统了，它们变成了同现代化适应的传统。布莱克等人得出的一个重要结论是：现代化不等于

"Westernization" or "Europeanization"; secondly, these two terms imply that Western or European institutions and values are indispensable elements of modernization, as if other nations could only adopt Western or European values and institutions at the expense of their own heritages; and thirdly, as the Japanese and Russian experiences indicate, modernization can in fact be realized only when it is adapted to local traditions. Only by making the most of its past accumulations of wealth can a nation achieve success in its modernization effort and choose the best modernization strategies. Otherwise, all such effort will prove worthless.

This comparative research in economic history by C. E. Black and others tells us that the present cannot be torn away from tradition and that any type of successful modernization is necessarily the unification of tradition with modernization.

IV. Why comparative economic history catches the fancy of Chinese academia

Since the 1980s, a wide spectrum of Chinese society has shown great interest in the issue of modernization, an interest that manifests itself in its concern not only for the approach to Chinese modernization and its prospects, but also for the modernization processes of many other countries and regions. The reason why studies of socioeconomic development strategies—or modernization strategies—have deeply interested Chinese academia is because such strategic studies are of paramount importance in that they take place against the background of summarizing the experiences and lessons of other countries' modernization drives, and that their successes and failures are closely related to China's future development and the institutional and development modes the nation is going to adopt. Many scholars have joined in such studies since the beginning of the 1980s. We have every reason to believe that these scholars' ever-increasing attention to comparative economic history is inseparable from the tangential and circumferential research on socioeconomic development strategy at that time, an inclusive summary of empirical results from the modernization process in fellow countries.

A thought of far-reaching influence has run through Chinese research into comparative economic history: What matters for socioeconomic development is not economic growth alone, but—at least mainly—coordinated economic and social development. For a long period of

"西方化"和"欧洲化";"西方化"和"欧洲化"的含义在于:西方或欧洲的制度本身和价值观念本身被看成是现代化的主要内容,似乎其他社会可以忘掉自己的历史传统而采纳西方的或欧洲的价值标准与制度;但事实上,日本和俄国的现代化表明,现代化总是在传统与现代化相适应的基础上实现的。一个国家只有最大限度地利用过去遗留下来的财富,才能使现代化的努力富有成效,也才能对现代化的战略作出有益的选择,否则现代化可能是徒劳的。

应当承认,布莱克等人的比较经济史研究可以给人们这样一种启示,即现实与传统不可能割裂,任何一种成功的现代化必然是传统与现代化的统一。

四、为什么比较经济史研究引起了中国学术界的浓厚兴趣

进入80年代以后,中国社会各阶层都对现代化问题产生了浓厚兴趣。这种兴趣不仅反映于对中国现代化的途径和前景的关切,而且反映于对世界上其他许多国家和地区的现代化过程的注意。关于社会经济发展战略也就是现代化战略的研究之所以成为中国学术界深感兴趣的课题,正由于这种战略的研究是以其他国家现代化经验和教训的总结作为背景,而这些战略研究总结的是非得失又紧密地联系到中国今后的发展前途,联系到中国未来的体制模式和发展模式,从而具有十分重要的意义。不少学者从80年代一开始就参加了这方面的讨论。可以认为,比较经济史研究在80年代日益被中国的学术界所重视,与当时对社会经济发展战略的研究,即对其他国家现代化过程中经验和教训的总结是分不开的。

在中国学术界的比较经济史研究中,一种有深远意义的思路是:对人类社会经济发展而言,重要的不是经济增长,或者不仅仅是经济增长,而是经济与社会发展的协调,或主要是这种协调。

historical development, the role of industrialization has been overestimated. That is why the traditional development strategy adopted since the late 18th century always emphasized the growth of gross national product to the neglect of the costs involved; stressed industry, heavy industry in particular, to the neglect of agricultural development; favored investment in technical equipment over investment in human resources; and went blindly after abundant supply of consumer goods while ignoring the uncertain aftermath of such an abundance and the resultant changing lifestyles. In a word, coordinated socioeconomic development is more important—and worth the effort of less developed countries—than single-minded pursuit of economic growth.

Such a thought naturally gives rise to the following statement when evaluating the Industrial Revolution: the industrialization that swept across the West from the late 18th century through the 19th century was about revolutionizing production technology rather than about emancipating and developing intellectual resources. It was not until the 20th century, or as late as the mid-20th century, that this resource gained the attention it deserves. In other words, it was not until very late that investment in education was given proper consideration in association with modernization. This is a good lesson for all developing nations in pursuit of modernization. If China ignored this lesson drawn from comparative economic history and followed the example of some countries in the 18th-19th centuries in regarding human beings merely as tools and appendages to machines and came tardily to emancipate and develop its intellectual resources, its modernization process would definitely be delayed, and the widening gap between the economy and culture would become a heavy price to be paid for modernization.

It need be pointed out that China was not immune to the worldwide "Weber fever" of the 1980s, when some scholars in this nation were drawn to the German sociologist and economic historian Max Weber's theories in their studies of the crux of the modernization issue from a comparative research perspective. The spread of Weber's theories in China stemmed from the problems the nation had come across in its modernization drive and from the Chinese desire to learn from other nations' experiences and lessons in this regard. Comparative economic history posed the following questions: Why did the Industrial Revolution follow different courses in different countries and regions? Which factors

以往，在长期的历史发展过程中，工业化往往被抬高到不适当的位置上，所以 18 世纪末期以来的传统发展战略是片面强调国民收入的增长，忽视为这种增长所付出的代价；片面强调工业，尤其是重工业，忽视农业的发展；片面强调对技术装备的投资，忽视对人力开发的投资；片面强调消费品的丰裕，忽视消费品丰裕和生活方式变化以后可能带来的不确定的后果，等等。总之，经济与社会发展的协调要比单纯的经济增长更加重要，更加值得后进的国家去追求。

根据这样一种思路，在对西方国家的工业革命进行评价时，十分自然地出现了如下的看法，这就是：18 世纪末和整个 19 世纪内所经历的工业化主要以生产技术的革命作为特征，而不曾把智力的解放、智力资源的开发作为特征，后一方面的问题只是到了 20 世纪，甚至是到了 20 世纪中期以后才被重视。也就是说，与现代化有关的教育投资问题到很晚才被摆到恰当的位置上，这正是后进国家在现代化过程中必须吸取的教训。中国的现代化如果忽略了这一根据比较经济史研究所得出的经验、教训，仍然像 19 世纪某些国家的做法那样，开始时把人仅仅看成工具，看成机器设备的附属物，直到后来才重视智力的解放、智力资源的开发，那就会拖延现代化的进程，并会以经济与文化差距的扩大作为现代化的沉重代价。

需要指出，在 80 年代内，中国学术界的一些人从比较经济史研究的角度考察现代化问题时，对德国社会学家、经济史学家马克斯 · 韦伯（Max Weber）的理论感兴趣，于是世界范围内的“韦伯热”也就对中国有所影响。为什么会有这种影响？这仍然要从中国现代化过程中所遇到的问题以及中国对世界上其他国家现代化的经验和教训的总结谈起。通过比较经济史研究，不难提出下列问题：为什么工业革命在不同的国家和地区有不同的进程？是哪些因素

precipitated the industrial revolution in one country after another? What was the most important of all these factors? Scholars of comparative economic history may list a host of factors that might have facilitated or hampered the industrial revolution in a given nation, such as the formation of capital, market, labor and its quality, technological progress and government policy. However, one may doubt if industrial revolution could take place by way of capital, market, labor, technology and policy alone. True, these factors are indispensable, but they are not sufficient to bring about industrial revolution. We have to delve into social structure, culture and ethics and look for the other factors that might have stimulated or hindered industrial revolution. In his works Weber made a point of integrating economic history with cultural and institutional histories. That is a basic reason why his theses have drawn the attention of scholars studying the issues pertinent to modernization.

Weber's ideas are, without doubt, controversial, but even his detractors have to concede that his ideas are quite illuminating. One of his revelations is that industrial revolution cannot take place in a nation that, despite having prepared the essential production factors, is ill prepared ideologically and ethically—meaning that the nation still lacks the social environment and mental driving force that are essential to industrial revolution or economic progress. In other words, there is a subtle spiritual force behind the industrial revolution that drives people to explore the unknown and run businesses in return for economic results. Furthermore, in Weber's own words, industrial development is also a process in which interpersonal relationships are readjusted, for the interpersonal relationships prior to the industrial society—such as the hereditary hierarchy, clannish rule and vassalage fealty—are detrimental to industrial development. For example, even though the Roman Empire in its heyday had no lack of needed capital and labor and its market was wide enough, industrial revolution in the modern sense of the term did not take place in that empire because its social structure, institutional scope and the interpersonal relations based on it were hostile to industrial development. Take Italy for another example. That country had acquired adequate capital and developed a wide market during the 14th-16th centuries, but its social structure, institutional environment and interpersonal relations rendered an industrial revolution improbable

促成了这个国家或那个国家的工业革命？在促成工业革命的若干因素中，最重要的因素是什么？当然，经济史的研究者们可以列出资本形成、市场、劳动力及其素质、技术进步、政府的有关政策等因素在促成或阻碍某一国家的工业革命方面的作用。但在研究中也会产生问题：难道仅仅有了资本、市场、劳动力、技术或政策，就一定能够实现工业革命吗？毫无疑问，这些因素都是不可缺少的，但仅有这些，还不足以实现工业革命，需要从更深的层次上去发现促成或阻碍工业革命的因素，也就是需要从社会结构、文化、伦理等方面去寻找工业革命的原因。马克斯·韦伯在他的著作中，把经济史的研究同文化史、制度史的研究结合在一起，这就是他的论点引起目前研究现代化问题的学者们注意的基本理由。

关于马克斯·韦伯的论点，无疑是有争议的。但即使不同意韦伯论点的人，也并不否认这些论点有某种启发性。从韦伯的论述中可以得到的启发是：一个民族，虽然在某个发展阶段具备了生产要素条件，但如果不具备意识形态、伦理道理观念的条件，即缺乏产生工业革命或经济进步的社会环境和精神动力，那么工业革命仍然难以发生。换言之，在工业革命的背后，存在着一种不易被人们察觉的精神力量，它引导人们去为经济的成果孜孜不倦地开拓、经营、获取利润。此外，按照韦伯的说法，工业发展过程同时也是人际关系的调整过程，前工业社会的人际关系（如世袭关系、家族统治、人身依附等）是不利于工业发展的。例如，在罗马帝国最盛时期，不是没有为工业发展所需要的资本和劳动力，市场的范围也不可谓不广，但当时的社会结构、制度的范围以及在此基础上形成的人际关系却不利于工业的发展，所以在罗马帝国不可能发生近代意义上的工业革命。又如，14～16 世纪的意大利，资本相当充足，市场范围也相当宽广，那么，为什么这时的意大利不会发生工业革命，这同样只有从社会结构、制度环境和人际关系方面来解释。当时

on its land. In those years, the Italian economy was not matched with a compatible social enterprising spirit, and as a result, the nation's accumulated wealth was channeled into nonproductive undertakings and failed to fuel technological and industrial growth. Weber's expositions in this regard drive home not only what comparative economic history means for modernization research, but also that society, culture and ethics must be studied extensively if we are to deepen our study of the modernization issue. Hence it is justifiable for Weber's Chinese followers to believe that his revelations pertinent to China's modernization lie in his methodological approach rather than in his theories *per se*.

V. A historical comparison of economic fluctuations

A nation is likely to suffer economic fluctuations in its pre-modernization period. Such fluctuations, however, are either caused by noneconomic factors such as war, natural adversity, pestilence, or influences from the outside world. This being the case, pre-modernization economic fluctuations tend to evade the attention of comparative economic history researchers. But this is not the case when a nation has entered its modernization period. In the modernization process, economic fluctuations may be caused by internal and economic factors and show certain regularity. For this reason, the historical comparison of economic fluctuations has become a new topic for studies of the Chinese style of modernization.

British economist John Hicks's work *A Theory of Economic History* (1969) is of great utility for its reference value to Chinese researchers in this field. Like American economist and political scientist Joseph Alois Schumpeter, Hicks is interested in mounting a descriptive theory of socioeconomic history rather than specific elaborations on a certain period involved in a certain research topic about economic history.[2] In Hicks's view, it is understandable that quantitative changes in gold and silver can lead to fluctuations in prices within a secluded economy (for example, what it was prior to the Industrial Revolution). Even under the gold standard system, quantitative changes in a currency can still be counted as a reason for fluctuations in prices and the economy. However, in the 20th century, because the metallic basis of the currency was weakened, economic fluctuations could no longer be interpreted according to the amount of the currency, nor could it be simply ascribed to the adoption of a certain currency policy. The issue had to be seen in a

意大利的经济与社会进取精神并不是吻合的，结果在意大利已积累的财富转化为非生产性的事业，而没有成为发展技术、发展工业的动力。韦伯的这些论述不仅表明了比较经济史研究对于现代化研究的意义，而且也表明对现代化问题的深入研究要求在社会、文化、伦理等领域内广泛开展研究。中国学术界中一些对韦伯理论感兴趣的人，认为韦伯著作所给予中国现代化研究者的启发，与其说是韦伯的理论本身，不如说是韦伯所提供的一种可以用于观察现代化过程的方法。

五、经济波动的历史比较

一个国家，在实现现代化以前，经济也可能有波动，但这种波动或者是由非经济原因（如战争、自然灾害、瘟疫）造成的，或者是外界传递而来的，因此这种经济波动一般并不引起比较经济史研究者的注意。进入现代化之后，情况便有所不同。现代化过程中，很可能由于内部原因、经济原因而发生经济的波动，波动带有一定的规律性。正因为如此，所以在中国现代化的研究中，对经济波动进行历史比较也成为一个新的课题。

约翰·希克斯（John Hicks）1969 年所著《经济史理论》一书对中国的研究者在这个领域的探讨有参考价值。和熊彼特（J. A. Schumpeter）一样，希克斯感兴趣的是提出一种解释人类社会经济史的理论，而不是专门去研究某一时期的某一类具体的经济史课题。[2] 在希克斯看来，当经济还是一个封闭体系的时候（例如工业革命以前），金银数量的变化引起物价的升降和经济的波动，是可以理解的。甚至在金本位制度下，货币数量的变化仍然可以作为物价升降和经济波动的一个原因。然而到了 20 世纪，由于货币的金属基础削弱了，对经济波动的原因必须寻找另外的解释方式。这时，经济的波动既不可能再用货币数量来解释，也不能单纯归因于某种货币政策的

new light. The cycle of economic growth and recession had to be probed from the perspective of the interaction between internal investment, savings and consumption. Moreover, the process of economic fluctuations could be illustrated by reference to the role of commerce, the supply of and demand for labor as well as the scope of market. That is to say, different research methods had to be applied to the history of economic fluctuations in the pre-industrialized society, during the Industrial Revolution and after the mid-20th century because each of these periods had its own peculiarities. According to Hicks's pronouncements in *A Theory of Economic History* and other works like *A Contribution to the Theory of the Trade Cycle, Journal of Economic Perspectives* and *Crisis in Keynesian Economics*, economic fluctuations are not uncommon in a modernization process, and pose no hindrance to economic growth—fluctuations are merely a temporary setback or slack in the historical course.

Obviously, researchers of China's modernization will not rest contented with Hicks's theoretical presentation of economic fluctuations. But so far as methodology is concerned, historical comparison (Hicks's cycle analysis included) is still useful. In the 1980s, despite a divergence in opinions, scholars were basically unanimous on two basic conclusions in their analyses of the process and causes of the cyclical fluctuation of the Chinese economy over the previous 40 years. Firstly, economic fluctuations are unavoidable in China because, like other economies that are modernized or being modernized, the Chinese economy will never be in a rectilinear motion. Secondly, the causes of economic fluctuations in China's modernization drive are internal in the main, while the impact of the world market is secondary. However, scholars are strikingly divided on the causes of the fluctuations, the duration of each fluctuation, and the intervals between them. For example: Which is a more important cause of the fluctuations, the amount of currency or commodity demand and supply? Should the modernization drive be focused on investment or attach equal importance to investment and consumption? Which sector is more accountable for causing fluctuations, the agricultural sector or the construction industry? Which is more of a factor in the changing process of fluctuation: finance or banking, planning or market? With their own distinctive features, the economic fluctuations in China's modernization process can be analogized neither to those in Western and Southeast

实施，而必须从经济内部投资、储蓄、消费的相互关系的角度，探讨经济增长与衰退的更替，并且还应当从商业的作用、劳动力的供求、市场规模等方面来说明经济波动的过程。这就是说，前工业社会的经济波动史、工业革命时期的经济波动史、20 世纪中期以后的经济波动史，在性质上是不一样的，在研究方法上也应当有所不同。按照希克斯在《经济史理论》和他的其他一些著作（如《经济周期理论》、《经济学展望》、《凯恩斯经济学的危机》）中所表述的观点，现代化进程中的经济波动不仅是正常的，而且波动并不会阻碍经济增长，波动只是历史过程中的某种曲折或间歇而已。

中国现代化的研究者显然不会以希克斯对经济波动的理论解释为满足。但从方法上看，历史比较研究方法（包括希克斯的周期分析方法在内）依然是一种有用的工具。80 年代内，有关近四十年来的中国经济周期波动的过程和原因的分析，尽管观点不一致，但仍有两个基本结论是大体上接近的。一个基本结论是：中国和其他已经实现现代化或正在进行现代化的国家一样，在经济发展的道路上不可能是直线上升的，经济的波动在所难免；另一个基本结论是：同其他国家一样，中国在现代化过程中发生经济波动的原因应当主要从内部去寻找，来自国际市场的影响虽然存在，但却是次要的。至于造成波动的因素和波动时间的长短、间隔时间的大小，观点的分歧也相当明显。例如，究竟是货币数量重要还是商品供求状况重要；究竟是以投资因素为主还是投资与消费并重；在历次引起波动的部门中，究竟是农业起的作用大些还是建筑业起的作用大些；还有，波动过程中的变化，应当更多地归因于财政还是应当更多地归因于金融，应当更多地归因于计划还是应当更多地归因于市场，等等。肯定地说，中国现代化过程中的经济波动具有自身的特殊性，不仅不能用西方国家、东南亚国家的情况来类比，甚至也不能用

Asian countries, nor to those in the former Soviet Union and Eastern European countries. All this merits continued and in-depth study, for which comparative economic history may offer more support.

In historical comparative research, economic fluctuations are invariably connected with the economic system. If changes in the volume of investment or the growth rate of investment are regarded as a major cause for economic fluctuations in the modernization drive, this poses another question: Are changes in investment not related to a certain economic system? By the same token, if changes in the volume or supply of money are regarded as a major cause for fluctuations, are not these changes, too, an outcome of a certain economic system? From a macroeconomic point of view, changes in investment and money supply have different causes and effects under different economic systems, a fact that has a great deal to do with fiscal, monetary, and planning systems and market structure. From a microeconomic point of view, changes in investment and money supply are also directly linked with the corporate system. For example, whether a business is a true investor and stakeholder that makes its own decisions, whether it is sensitive to changes in credit and interest rate, and whether it is motivated by its own interests to seek technological progress and reduce its share of the money flow are inseparable from the changes in investment and money supply. All these indicate that comparative studies of economic fluctuations are, as a matter of fact, concerned with comparing the causes and effects of fluctuations under different economic systems.

When it comes to comparative research on economic systems, Chinese modernization scholars tend to hold one of two opinions:

—Opinion 1: China's economic system is highly comparable with those of the former Soviet Union and Eastern European countries, historically so with the former Soviet economic system in particular. The analogy between the Soviet economic system over the 70 or so years since the Russian Revolution of 1917 and the Chinese economic system over the last 40 years is quite manifest in some historical periods. Thus the historical relationship between the economic systems of the former Soviet Union and Eastern European countries and their respective economic fluctuations can serve as a reference for studies of the economic fluctuations that have occurred in the modernization process of China.

前苏联、东欧国家的情况来类比，这一切都有赖于研究的继续深入。比较经济史研究可以为此提供较多的依据。

实际上，关于经济波动的历史比较研究必然同经济体制的历史比较研究联系在一起。这是因为，如果说投资数额或投资增长率的变动是导致现代化过程中经济波动的一个重要因素，那就会出现另一个问题：投资方面的变动难道不同一定的经济体制有关吗？同样的道理，如果说货币数量或货币供应增长率的变动是导致现代化过程中经济波动的一个重要因素，难道这些变动不是一定的经济体制下的产物吗？从宏观经济体制来考察，投资和货币供应量的变动在不同的经济体制之下有不同的原因和效应，这同财政体制、金融体制、计划体制和市场结构有密切关系。从微观经济体制来考察，投资和货币供应量的变动又同企业体制直接有关。例如，企业是不是真正的、有自主权的投资主体和利益主体，企业对于信贷和利率变动的反应是否灵敏，企业有没有技术进步和降低流动资金占有额的利益动机等等，都同投资和货币供应量的变动有着不可分割的联系。这样，对经济波动的比较研究实际上也就是对不同经济体制下经济波动原因和效应的比较研究。

在谈到经济体制的比较研究时，中国的现代化研究者们倾向于两种看法。一种看法是：中国的经济体制与前苏联、东欧国家的经济体制有较大的可比性，特别是与前苏联的经济体制在历史上有较大的可比性。如果把 1917 年以后七十余年内苏联各个历史阶段的经济体制拿来同中国四十年来各个历史阶段的经济体制对应地进行比较，那么在某些历史阶段，这种相似性是相当明显的。所以，在分析中国现代化过程中的经济波动时，可以以前苏联、东欧国家的经济体制同各自国家的经济波动之间的历史关系作为参考。

—Opinion 2: In terms of GNP per capita and the percentage of agricultural population in the total population, the Chinese economic system is more akin to, and considerably more comparable with, some other developing countries insofar as socioeconomic structure, market organization and price system are concerned. These developing countries are susceptible to economic fluctuations on their road to modernization due to lopsided industrial structures and shortfalls in resource supply, or due to the unsalability of primary products and decreases in residents' income. Because these countries' fluctuations are relevant to a great extent to the problems existing in their economic systems, it is necessary to make historical comparisons between the Chinese economy and those of the developing countries if economic fluctuations in the course of modernization are studied in the context of economic systems.

The above two opinions are both reasonable and not incompatible to each other. As seen from the perspective of its economic system, fluctuations in China's modernization process are similar not only to those in the former Soviet Union and Eastern European countries but also to some other developing countries.

VI. Deep-seated issue: traditional social structure as a brake

Historical comparison of economic systems brings to light a deep-seated issue, that is, whether or not the traditional social structure acts as a brake on the modernization process. If the answer is yes, how serious is that role? And how can it be mitigated? It is precisely because Alexander Gerschenkron and Umberto Melotti have dwelt on all these questions and come up with unique explanations that Chinese economists are drawn to the former's works on comparative economic history and find the latter's study of the Third World and multi-linear mode of growth enlightening.

Gerschenkron's view is that the retarding role of traditional social structure is reflected in its constraints on the supply of production factors, which is a major hindrance to the progress of underdeveloped countries. He thinks that large-scale industrial development in Russia and Balkan countries has been shackled by traditional social structure in comparison with Western Europe. But it is noteworthy that while Gerschenkron acknowledges the existence of the braking effect of traditional social structure in modernization, he also stresses that

另一种看法是：按人均国民收入和农业人口在总人口中所占比例来看，中国的经济体制（就社会经济结构、市场组织、价格体系等方面而言）可能更类似于现代化程度较低的某些发展中国家，中国同它们之间有较大的可比性。这些发展中国家在现代化过程中，或者由于产业结构失调和资源供给不足，或者由于初级产品滞销和居民收入减少，都会引起经济波动。这种经济波动在很大程度上是同经济体制方面存在的问题有关的。因此，如果要联系经济体制来研究现代化过程中的经济波动，更需要把中国同某些发展中国家作一番经济的历史比较。

显然，以上两种看法都是有道理的，而且它们之间也没有什么不能相容之处。中国现代化过程中的经济波动，从经济体制上看，也许既有同前苏联、东欧国家的情况相似之处，又有同某些发展中国家相似之处。

六、一个深层次的问题：传统社会结构制动作用的评价

从经济体制的历史比较必然导致一个深层次的问题，这就是：一国在现代化过程中，传统的社会结构对于现代化是否存在制动作用（或阻滞作用）？如果存在这种作用的话，那么制动阻滞的程度有多大？如何才能减少这种制动的作用？格辛克隆（A. Gerschenkron）的比较经济史论著之所以引起了中国学术界的注意，梅洛蒂（U. Melotti）关于第三世界与多线发展模式的研究之所以对中国学术界有所启发，都因为他们涉及了上述这个深层次的问题，并提出了自己的独特的见解。

格辛克隆的论点是：传统社会结构对于现代化的制动作用主要反映于生产要素供给的约束上，这正是许多后进国家在发展中所遇到的严重障碍。与西欧国家相比，俄国和巴尔干半岛各国都表现出传统社会结构对于大工业发展的束缚和牵制。但值得注意的是，格辛克隆一方面承认传统社会结构对现代化的制动作用的存在，另一

underdeveloped countries may find themselves at a relative advantage once they are resolved to achieve modernization. In this regard, he employs two terms: the "advantages of a latecomer," such as the traditional social structure's low labor cost; and the "disadvantages of a latecomer," such as the yawning gap in technology between underdeveloped and developed countries. He also points out that the advantages and disadvantages are coexistent and mutually convertible. An underdeveloped country can overcome its disadvantage if it can make the most of its advantages, including low wages. If an underdeveloped country lets the opportunity slip through its fingers, its latecomer advantage may fail to play a role and its modernization process may be delayed, just like a man who, having missed a bus, has to wait for a long time before catching the next one. Because good opportunities are rare, a "major outburst" in economic development—akin to a sprint at the finish line of the industrial revolution race—is not only necessary but also beneficial to nations under the heavy influence of a deep-rooted traditional social structure.

For his part, Melotti elaborates from different perspectives on the retarding role a traditional structure plays in the modernization of underdeveloped countries. As he sees it, the vast land area of these countries (mainly in Asia, Africa and Latin America) is studded with numerous village-sized economies that have evolved into a stable but self-enclosed and self-sufficient economic setup that ties producers down to the narrow activity scope of their lands. The economic development and social structural changes are seriously held back as a result. But how is it that Japan, of all Asian countries, made its modernization drive a success after the Meiji Restoration? Is the political factor alone enough of an answer to that question? In answer to it, Melotti points out that despite its distinctive Asian characteristics and its differences from European countries, in its pre-Restoration years Japanese society did not attempt to nip capitalism in the bud the way the other Asian countries did socioeconomically. The reason why post-Restoration Japan wasted no time in embarking on the capitalist track of development was not because of any external factors but because of the salient features of its innate traditional social structure.

方面又强调后进国家一旦决心实现现代化，也可能有着比较有利的条件。他使用了这样两个概念，即“后发性优势”与“后发性劣势”。比如说，传统社会结构之下的劳动力价格低廉，就是“后发性优势”之一；后进国家在技术上同先进国家的差距的扩大，则是“后发性劣势”之一。他指出，“后发性优势”往往与“后发性劣势”同时存在，并且二者可以相互转化。只要后进国家充分利用自己的优势（如工资低），那么劣势是可以克服的。反之，如果这些国家错过了机会，那就好像赶班车一样，错过了这一趟班车，就必须等很久才能搭上下一班车，“后发性优势”也就发挥不了作用，现代化也会延误。正是由于机会难得，所以经济发展中的“大突发”（指工业革命中的“猛烈的冲刺”）对传统社会结构有较大影响的国家说来是必要的，也是有利的。

梅洛蒂从不同的角度探讨了后进国家的传统社会结构对现代化的制动作用。他认为后进国家（主要指亚洲、非洲、拉丁美洲国家）辽阔土地上无数分散的村落经济成为一种特殊的稳定机制，它是封闭的、自给自足的，生产者被牢固地拴在土地上，拴在狭小的活动范围内，从而阻碍这些国家的经济发展以及与经济发展联系在一起的社会结构的变更。那么，为什么亚洲的日本能够在明治维新之后成功地实现了现代化呢？难道单纯用政治因素就能说明这一问题吗？梅洛蒂指出，不可否认，日本的社会结构和意识形态具有明显的亚洲特点，与西欧国家有一些差异，但重要的是，日本即使在明治维新之前，仍不像亚洲其他国家那样从社会经济上扼杀资本主义经济因素的产生。明治维新后日本之所以能够迅速转入资本主义发展轨道，主要不是取决于外部力量，而是由日本传统社会结构的特点决定的。

For researchers of the Chinese way of modernization, Gerschenkron and Melotti have provided valuable references to the retarding role of traditional Chinese social structure in modernization. As a matter of fact, research on that role is highly relevant to the design and progress of the nation's economic restructuring and political reform. In this regard at least two views are prevalent among Chinese researchers: one view holds that haste makes waste, given the nature of the fabric of traditional society and the difficulties it poses, and that only by pushing political and economic reforms one step at a time and coordinating reform with development can progress be made in the modernization drive and gradual changes brought to the traditional social structure. The other view maintains that, bearing in mind the retarding impact of traditional social structure, modernization cannot be sustained without breaking up this structure or at least blunting its impact considerably, and that economic and political reforms should be sped up, since slowly progressing reforms can only prolong the survival of the traditional social structure and allow it to go on holding back the modernization process. A compromise between these two views suggests that economic restructuring should be accelerated and political institutional reform conducted in a progressive way. In other words, once economic restructuring and economic development make some headway, political reform will go more smoothly and become more acceptable to the public because it helps minimize the shock wave emanating from the ensuing reshuffling of the traditional social structure.

Although divided in their opinions on the relationship between development and traditional social structure in the modernization process of different countries, Chinese scholars of comparative economic history see eye to eye on the fact that the traditional social structure does have a retardant impact on the nation's modernization drive. They see this as something that cannot be tampered with carelessly, and unanimously suggest that prudence be applied when countermeasures are chosen.

Ours is socialist modernization. Therefore, improving and developing the socialist system should be the ultimate goal for economic restructuring and political reform, and the steps to be taken should be socialism-oriented as well. In their modernization studies Chinese scholars of comparative economic history are, indeed, sober-minded on this issue.

无论是格辛克隆的研究还是梅洛蒂的研究，对于研究中国现代化问题的人来说，都可以作为研究中国传统社会结构对现代化的制动作用的一种参考。实际上，对中国传统社会结构的上述作用的研究具有十分深刻的意义，它不仅与中国的经济体制改革的设计与进程有关，而且与中国的政治体制改革的设计与进程有关。在学术界有两种影响较为广泛的意见。一种意见是：根据中国传统社会结构的特点，中国在现代化过程中的政治体制改革和经济体制改革的难度很大，因此改革应当是渐进的，欲速则不达；改革与发展必须相互配合，稳步推进，这样才能既促进中国的现代化，又促成传统社会结构的逐渐转变。另一种意见是：由于传统社会结构对中国的现代化有很大的制动作用，如果不首先使传统社会结构解体，使其影响大大减弱，中国的现代化将难以获得进展。为此，不仅中国的经济体制改革要加快，而且政治体制改革也要加快。渐进的改革只可能延续传统社会结构的存在，使得传统社会结构对现代化的制动作用依然是强有力的。介于这两种意见之间有下述这种折中见解，即认为经济体制改革应当加快，政治体制改革不妨以渐进的方式进行。也就是说，在经济体制改革取得一定的进展，经济发展取得一定的成就之后，政治体制改革的实行将较为顺利，传统社会结构变更过程中所带来的社会震荡也就相对地小一些，从而易于被社会所承受。中国的比较经济史研究者在分析各国现代化过程中发展与传统社会结构之间的关系时得出了不同的论点，虽然见仁见智，各持一端，但有一点是一致的，这就是：承认传统社会结构对中国现代化事业有着不可忽视的制动作用，因此必须正视这一问题，慎重地选择对策。由于中国的现代化是社会主义现代化，中国的经济体制改革和政治体制改革以社会主义制度的完善与发展作为目标，所以对策的选择应当以社会主义为方向，中国的比较经济史研究者探讨现代化问题时对这一点是有清醒认识的。

VII. Concluding remark: global diversity in the modernization process

Comparative research on the relationship between traditional social structure and modernization inevitably leads to another major issue as to whether modernization is single-or multi-tracked on a global scale. Historical materials on economic history have indicated that the Western European model of social development and its approaches to industrial revolution are not necessarily appropriate to the modernization process of developing countries. This issue can be traced back to some other questions: What did a typical feudal society look like? Where did it occur, in Western Europe, the East, or China specifically? The assumption that all Western European, Eastern and Chinese feudal societies were, without exception, typical ones may not be incorrect. In a word, there are a host of topics that are open for discussion, and the divergence of opinions can never evaporate into thin air overnight.

Shortly after the end of the First World War, Oswald Spengler pointed out in his book *The Decline of the West* that human history was about none other than the spontaneous rise and fall of civilizations, and that every civilization runs its own course, emerging and perishing on its own. His study of the rise and fall of civilizations convinced him that there is no cause-and-effect relationship in history, and Western civilization will eventually meet its demise along the same course followed by ancient Egyptian, Babylonian and Mayan civilizations. Spengler was able to broaden the vista of comparative history by eschewing the unilinear theory regarding Western Europe and embracing diversity in historical development, although his denial of the norms of historical development, his neglect of the successive and continuous nature of history, and his indifference to the intrinsic relationship between civilizations are open to question. Later, in his work *A Study of History*, Toynbee developed the theory on diversity in historical progress, believing that all civilizations are parallel in their development but each follows its own course of rise and fall. He maintained that civilizations are not isolated but interrelated: If a demised civilization can give birth to—or influence the rise of—a second generation of lasting civilization, it is evidence that one civilization's fall is probably the starting point of another. True, Toynbee somewhat exaggerated the role of religion in his dissertations on human

七、比较经济史研究的另一结论：世界现代化过程的多样性

从有关传统社会结构与现代化之间的关系的比较研究，必然导致另一个重要问题的探讨，即就全世界范围而言，现代化过程是单线的还是多线的？经济史资料充分说明，西欧的社会发展模式和工业革命的途径不一定适用于发展中国家的现代化。再往上推，究竟什么是典型的封建社会，它究竟存在于西欧，还是存在于东方，或者存在于东方的中国？甚至可以假定，西欧的、东方的、中国的封建社会都是典型的封建社会，这种观点也不一定就不正确。总之，在这个领域内，供讨论的问题还有很多，意见的分歧不可能在短期内消失。

早在第一次世界大战结束后不久，施本格勒（O. Spengler）在所著《西方的没落》一书中就曾指出，人类历史无非是各种不同的文明自行生长和衰亡的历史，这些文明彼此自成体系，自生自灭。施本格勒在研究了文明兴衰史之后认为，历史发展中因果关系是不存在的，因此西方文明同其他文明一样，也面临着衰亡的命运，这种衰亡仅仅是重复以往的一些文明（如埃及文明、巴比伦文明、玛雅文明等）经历过的路程而已。施本格勒对历史规律性的否定、对历史继承性和连续性的忽略以及对不同文明之间内在联系的漠视，尽管都有争论之必要，但他能够突破西欧单线论，提出历史发展多样性的观点，无疑开拓了比较历史研究的视野。此后，阿诺德·汤因比在所著《历史研究》中，进一步发展了历史进程多样性的学说，认为各种文明的发展是平行的，一切文明都有自己的成长与衰亡的过程。而且，他不把每一种文明看成是孤立的、封闭的体系，而认为文明之间是相互联系的：即使历史上一种文明衰亡了，但如果由它所创造的或在它影响之下产生的下一代文明能够成长，那么一种文明的衰亡可能就是另一种文明产生的起点。汤因比对人类历史的发展和文明的兴衰的论述中，确有

development and the rise and fall of civilizations; but like Spengler, he also stressed the multi-linear development of history and maintained that civilization is multi-centered instead of having only one center. Such a proposition was accepted by most of his fellow history researchers.

Nevertheless, Spengler and Toynbee were general historians and historical philosophers, not economic history scholars. Though they touched upon many issues pertinent to economic history in their works, they never delved into the historical process of economic development and changes. As Hicks commented in *A Theory of Economic History*, "... the grand designs of a Toynbee or a Spengler, the makers of historical patterns which have more aesthetic than scientific appeal."[3] However, there is no denying the inspiration of comparative studies of civilizations to comparative economic history as an approach to historical philosophy or historical research. We may not accept Spengler's historical pessimism or condone Toynbee's belief in religion as the driving force behind the rise and development of civilizations. Nevertheless, we are obliged to admit that the influence of traditional social structures and concepts is comprehensive, and works on a civilization or a regional economy in many ways, resulting in differences in civilizations, regional economic activity and development modes.

Studies of diversity in socioeconomic development and modernization often put scholars of comparative economic history in mind of two questions: Would Eastern traditional social structures have crumbled without the invasion of the Western forces? Can Eastern nations accomplish industrial revolution and embark on modernization by their own bootstraps? The traditional social structure in Eastern countries was a powerful constraint on their economic development, and no amount of war, social unrest and dynasty substitutions in ancient and medieval times could change it substantially. Economic booms, long or staggered, did occur in the East in those times, but they stood no comparison with the economic development or industrial revolution of modern times. On the surface, Western inroads are directly related to the disintegration of traditional social structures in the East, as if without the former, the latter would not have happened, or without the latter, there would not have been industrial revolution or modernization. Though some people accept this deduction, the issue remains unsettled, and the dispute continues.

过分夸大宗教的作用之处，但他同斯本格勒一样，也强调历史发展的多线论，即以文明的多中心替代文明的单一中心。这一论点已被当代的比较历史研究者中的多数人所认可。

施本格勒和汤因比都是历史学家、历史哲学家，他们不是经济史学家。尽管他们在自己的著作中涉及了不少经济史问题，但他们并没有专门研究经济发展和经济变更的历史过程。希克斯在《经济史理论》中写道："汤因比和施本格勒创制的历史模式，就其艺术感染力而言，在其科学吸引力之上。"[3] 然而，不可否认的是，文明的比较研究作为一种历史哲学或作为一种历史研究方法，对经济史的比较研究是有启示的。虽然人们不一定接受施本格勒的历史悲观主义，也不一定赞同汤因比那种把宗教视为文明产生和发展的推动力量的观点，但仍应当承认，传统社会结构和传统观念的影响是综合的影响，它们从若干不同的方面对一种文明或一个区域的经济发生影响，从而形成文明之间的差异或不同区域经济活动方式、经济发展途径的差异。

在分析人类社会经济发展的多样性、现代化过程的多样性时，比较经济史的研究者时常考虑到：如果没有西方势力对东方社会的侵入，东方传统的社会结构是不是会自行解体呢？东方社会是不是会凭借自己的内部力量实现工业革命，走上现代化的道路呢？的确，在东方国家，传统的社会结构是强大的经济发展制约因素，古代和中古历史上的战争、社会动荡、朝代更迭等等并没有使社会结构发生实质性变化。古代和中古的东方也曾出现过较长时期的、阶段性的经济昌盛，但这与近代意义上的经济发展或工业革命不是一回事。因此，从表面上看，西方势力的入侵同东方传统社会结构的解体是直接有关的，似乎没有前者就没有后者，而没有后者也就没有工业革命和现代化了。尽管有些人同意这种推论，但这个问题仍然没有解决，争议继续存在。

Scholastic opinions vary as to whether the disintegration of traditional social structure resulted from external forces or not. One opinion that may be of high reference value for studies of the Chinese modernization process has this to say: the inroads of external forces could only destroy the surface of the traditional social structure—its collapse was caused by internal forces alone. An early case in point in this regard is Latin America, where Spanish invasion and occupation did not cause the local socioeconomic structures to crumble. A more recent example is India, whose deep-rooted social structure survived the invasion of British economic forces till the mid-1940s. In that country, cities and rural areas were two different worlds. If capitalism was able to make some headway in cities, the traditional social structure remained intact in the vast rural areas. A third case in point is South Korea: Why was the South Korean economy able to grow rapidly, beginning from the 1960s when the disintegration of its traditional social structure picked up speed, while its economy had lagged behind for a long time earlier as it kept its original social structure under Japanese rule before the Second World War? Is it not the case that the destructive factor came mainly from within the country? These examples show that it is prejudiced and superficial to assume that without foreign invasion there would not be the collapse of traditional social structure and the advent of industrial revolution and modernization in the East. Without dissecting the deep-seated structure of traditional society or putting a premium on studying the role of internal forces within that society, there will be no way to account for the actual disintegration of traditional social structures in the East and the diversity in both world history and the modernization process. Of course, this is not to deny the role of the invading forces from the West in the collapse of the traditional social structures of the East. Instead, it is to say that the role of internal forces should be given center stage in studies of the modernization issue, including the relationship between the disintegration of traditional social structure and the process of modernization.

VIII. Disequilibrium in the modernization process within a country

The imbalanced nature of the modernization process has come to the attention of almost all researchers of comparative economic history in their study of different countries. This valuable finding virtually gainsays the assertion that countries follow a unified mode of modernization.

关于传统社会结构是否由外部力量所破坏的讨论，研究者们表述过不同的看法。一种对中国现代化进程的研究可能有较大借鉴意义的见解是：外部力量的侵入所能破坏的只是传统社会结构的表层，传统社会深层结构的瓦解则是内部力量作用的结果。拉丁美洲是较早的例证：西班牙的入侵和占领并不曾摧毁当地的社会经济结构。印度是较后的例证：直到 20 世纪 40 年代中期为止，印度的传统社会深层结构也未被英国经济力量所破坏，城市和乡村是两个不同的世界，如果说城市中的资本主义有一定程度的发展的话，那么广大农村却仍旧维持传统的社会结构。再一个例证是韩国：为什么它在第二次世界大战前的长时期内经济是落后的，日本的统治并没有破坏其传统社会结构，而从 60 年代以来，韩国的经济却有较快的发展，传统社会结构解体的速度大大加快了？难道这种促成传统社会结构解体速度加快的力量不是主要来自社会内部吗？从这些例证可以看出，所谓没有外来入侵就没有东方传统社会结构的解体，从而也就没有东方的工业革命和现代化的论点，是片面的、肤浅的。不从传统社会的深层结构进行分析，不对社会内部力量的作用进行研究并给予足够的重视，既说明不了东方传统社会结构解体的实际过程，也说明不了世界历史的多样性和现代化过程的多样性。当然，这并不否认西方势力入侵在东方传统社会结构解体过程中的应有的作用。这只不过是表明在现代化问题的研究中，包括在传统社会结构解体与现代化进程之间关系的研究中，要把社会内部力量的作用放在主要的位置上。

八、一国内部现代化进展的不平衡性

在研究各国现代化进程时，比较经济史的研究者几乎都注意到各国现代化进展的不平衡性。这一结论是很有价值的，它实际上等于

In this respect, Sidney Pollard's hypothesis has attracted the notice of comparative history researchers in China.

Pollard points out that the study of European industrialization should be based on the innate laws of industrial development instead of on country-specific modes, and that the industrialization process looks like an outbreak of a skin rash epidemic. At the very beginning, new industrial cities emerge in a country like a rash of clustered spots in the human skin in varied quantity and density, some of which grow more densely clustered into an inflamed patch while others remain sparsely scattered after a certain period of time. Therefore he believes that studies of the industrialization process should not be based on countries but on regions, that is, by regarding the distribution and proliferation of the "red spots" as signals of the industrialization progress. As he puts it, "It is the argument of this article that the industrialization of 19th century Europe was a single process and had an economic logic of its own. Like an epidemic, it took little note of frontiers, crossing them with ease while leaving neighboring home territories untouched."[4]

Pollard's "red spots" hypothesis helps decode the imbalance in the modernization process between countries and in a given country. It also indicates that such imbalance does not impede the efforts of countries or of regions inside a country to form an economic body. According to him, during its period of industrialization Europe was an integral community and so was the European market, and no European country could do without this community in industrial development. The industrialization of one region often has a major impact on other regions with its capital, labor, technology and import and export commodities. But the impact of the latter on the former cannot be overlooked either. When one region makes the first step toward industrialization, it brings development opportunities to other regions. Although these regions are a step later, such opportunities still put them at an advantage over the neighboring regions that are relatively more backward.

Modernization researchers may draw inspiration from Pollard's assumption. For instance, at a certain point of time, China has a number of industrialized cities and towns scattered in various provinces. They look like "red spots" on the Map of China, but at the same time, every

否定了各国现代化按统一的模式进行的论点。在这方面，悉尼·波拉德（Sidney Pollard）的假设引起了中国的比较经济史研究者的兴趣。

波拉德指出，欧洲的工业化不应当按国别模式研究，而应当从工业发展本身的规律来考察。工业化过程好像"发疹"的过程：新兴工业城市好像一个个小红点，起初各国都有红点出现，但有稀有密；隔了一段时间之后，有些地方的红点增多了，红点更密了，红点与红点之间连成片了，而另一些地方的红点仍然是稀疏的、点缀性的。因此，波拉德认为，对工业化过程的研究不能采用国别研究方法，而只能采用区域研究方法，即用红点的分布和红点的扩散作为工业化进展的标志。波拉德写道："19世纪欧洲的工业化是单一的过程，它有自己的经济逻辑。它像一场瘟疫，不受边界的限制；它轻而易举地越过了边界，但却使相邻的国内领土未受瘟疫的波及。"[4]

波拉德的"发疹"假设不仅有助于说明各国现代化进程的不平衡性，而且也有助于说明一国内部现代化进程的不平衡性。但波拉德的假设还包含了这样一个内容，即上述发展的不平衡性并不妨碍各国共同构成一个经济的整体，以及一国国内各个发展不平衡的区域共同构成一个经济的整体。他认为，在工业化时期，全欧洲是一个整体，欧洲市场也是一个整体，任何一个欧洲国家发展工业时都离不开这个整体，一个地区所实现的工业化从资本、劳动力、技术、进出口商品等方面对另一些地区的影响固然是重要的，但反过来，周围各个地区对这个工业化地区的影响同样不可忽视。一个地区在工业化方面先走一步之后，它往往给另一些后进的地区带来发展的机会，而后进地区的工业化虽然开始得较晚，但它们的周围还有一些更落后的地区，所以它们仍然有利可得，仍然有相对的优势可以利用。

在进行现代化的比较研究时，从波拉德的假设可以得到一些有益的启示。比如说，在一定时点上，中国各个不同的地区或不同的省份）都存在若干工业发展程度较高的城镇。它们好像是"红点"，

province still has large areas in which not a single "red spot" can be seen. Thus, the differences between the provinces—or rather, the disequilibrium between them in industrial development—find expression in their differences in the number, density and size of the "red spots." In modernization studies, we should figure out the reasons behind these differences in those regions, the diffusion trend of the "red spots" as well as the relationship between them in different provinces.

Pollard's assumption and regional research method are valuable to studies of Chinese modernization and unbalanced regional development in economic history. For example, they may help ward off over-simplified conclusions in studying the regional distribution of large handicraft workshops with hired labor in the Ming and Qing dynasties and modern factories of the late 19th and early 20th centuries.

IX. Comparative research on economic history yet to be deepened and widened

As mentioned earlier, comparative economic history is a relatively young academic discipline. In China, it did not begin to gain the importance it deserves until recently. It is drawing more and more researchers in this nation, but that is not reason enough to say that comparative economic history has come a long way in this nation. As things stand here, studies in comparative economic history are mainly centered on modernization, leaving many other important issues untouched or merely briefly mentioned. Insofar as methodology is concerned, the new economic history methodology has not had any influence on China so far. A few scholars have employed the econometric approach in their historical studies into recent decades; but their results have been obviously restricted by the lack of historical data for one thing, and by the institutional hindrance to Chinese economic development for another. But this does not mean that the econometric approach is not applicable to the study of Chinese economic history at all. With economic history and comparative economic history gaining steady ground and depth, the prospects of econometrics are becoming brighter in this nation. We have got to be patient, for it takes time to explore how to incorporate the institutional factor into the econometric study of Chinese economic history.

分散在不同的地区，但与此同时，在任何一个地区，即使是工业发展程度较高的地区，仍会有大块空白，其中一个“红点”也不存在。不同的地区之间的区别表现为“红点”多少不等、“红点”分布的稀密程度不等以及“红点”本身的大小不等。这就是国内发展的不平衡。在研究时需要弄清楚的是：不同地区的上述区别是怎样形成的？各个地区的“红点”的扩散趋势如何？各个地区的“红点”之间有什么样的联系？

其实，波拉德的假设和他的区域研究方法不仅对中国的研究者在分析现代化进程时有参考之处，而且也可以用于对经济史上的地区发展不平衡性的探讨。例如，在研究明清两代带有工场手工业性质的、较大型的雇工企业的地区分布状况时，在研究 19 世纪末和 20 世纪初的近代工厂的地区分布状况时，都可以参考波拉德的假设，避免得出简单化的论断。

九、中国的比较经济史研究还有待于继续深入和拓宽

正如前面已经提到的，比较经济史学作为一门独立的学科形成较晚。而在中国，只能认为比较经济史方面的研究近年来开始受到重视，对它感兴趣的学者逐渐增多，但还不能认为比较经济史研究在中国已经有较大的发展。加之，在现阶段的中国，关于比较经济史领域内的研究，主要围绕着现代化问题而进行。这个问题以外的许多重要的问题，或者尚未被研究者所涉及，或者只是在探讨现代化问题时才被提到。从方法上看，新经济史学的方法整个说来在中国还没有产生影响，个别的研究者在研究现代化问题时，曾使用经济计量方法来研究近几十年的历史过程，但这一方面由于经济史资料的限制，另一方面由于在中国经济发展过程中制度因素起的作用相当大，从而历史的计量研究的局限性是很明显的。当然，这并不等于说在研究中国经济史问题时不可能采取计量方法。可以认为，随着中国的经济史和比较经济史研究的深入与研究范围的拓宽，随着经济史资料整理工作的进展，历史计量研究是有前途的，研究的开展必然是渐进的。并且，在计量研究中，如何结合影响中国经济史的制度因素进行分析，也会有一个探索的过程。在这方面不能急于求成。

Discussing the relationship between economic history and economics in 1985, Robert M. Solow wrote in the *American Economic Review*: "A modern economy is a very complicated system. Since we cannot conduct controlled experiments on its smaller parts, or even observe them in isolation, the classical hard-science devices for discriminating between competing hypotheses are closed to us. The main alternative device is the statistical analysis of historical time-series."[5] His statement is reasonable in that the historical statistics method would be the best choice wherever other physical and chemical types of scientific experiments failed in the study of socioeconomic events. But queries on its effectiveness arise. Supposing the process of economic development and many historical facts are yet to be clarified, to what extent can a historical statistics method account for the issues even if it can be made to work? In the face of fragmented historical data and inaccurate figures concerning certain years, how can we guarantee the effectiveness of this method? We have no intention to play down the value of this method. We just want to point out that in quantitative studies of the Chinese economic history, only by collecting and collating historical data, and by weeding through falsehoods to fill in the blanks with nothing but authentic data, can full scope be given to quantitative analysis in studies of Chinese economic history.

As to the relationship between economic history and economics, Solow also points out: "So the economic historian can use the tools provided by the economist but will need, in addition, the ability to imagine how things might have been before they became as they now are."[6] His mention of "imagination" in this context is quite thought-provoking. It turns out that this view is shared by many other new economic historians. Thus a hypothesis is turned into a tool in the hands of analysts of economic history. For example, R. W. Fogel studied the historical role of the American economy by assuming that the American continental railway did not exist at all in 1890. R. W. Fogel and

S. L. Engerman also began their research on the slave economy in the southern United States under the assumption that there was no Civil War in 1861-1865, and then went on to discuss the prospects of plantation economy. No wonder in a journal review of Frederic C. Lane's thesis "Role of government in economic growth in early modern times," Douglass Cecil North and Robert Paul Thomas make this statement together: "The

1985 年，罗伯特·索洛（Robert M. Solow）在《美国经济评论》上谈到经济史与经济学的关系时，曾经这样写道："现代的经济是十分复杂的体系。既然我们不能在其规模较小的一些局部进行有控制的试验，或者哪怕对它们作孤立的观察，我们就无法使用经典的、硬科学的手段来甄别相互挑战的那些假设。可供选择的另一种基本手段，就是按历史顺序进行统计分析。"[5] 索洛的这番话是有一定道理的。这表明，既然不可能用物理或化学的实验方法来验证社会经济现象，于是历史统计方法就成为可供选择的一种替代了。但人们会进一步思考：假定经济的发展过程还不明朗，历史本身的许多事实还不清楚，那么历史统计方法即使可以被应用，但这又能在多大程度上说明问题呢？假定历史资料残缺不全，而某些年份的统计数字并不准确，那么历史统计方法又怎能得到有效的利用呢？我们丝毫没有贬低历史统计方法的意思，我们想指出的只是：在中国经济史的计量研究中，更为基本的工作应当以整理历史统计资料、去伪存真、填补某些空白为先，在这个基础上计量研究才有用武之地。

索洛在谈到经济史与经济学的关系时还说过："经济史学家能够使用经济学家提供的工具，但除此以外还需要有想像力，想像事物变为如今这种状况以前，可能是怎样的。"[6] 索洛在这里提到的"经济史学家在研究中需要有想像力"，很耐人寻味。其实，不仅索洛一个人有这种看法。在新经济史学的作品中，这已经不是一种设想，而且已被用于经济史分析之中了。例如，福格尔在研究美国经济在历史上所起过的作用时，可以假定 1890 年的美国不存在铁路，然后进行考察；福格尔和恩格尔曼在研究美国南部奴隶制经济史时，可以假定 1861～1865 年的南北战争不曾发生，并由此出发来探讨种植园经济的前景。无怪乎诺思和托马斯（Robert Paul Thomas）在评论莱恩（Frederic C. Lane）的《政府在近代初期经济增长中所起的

most crucial ingredient in comparative economic history, or any other economic history for that matter, is the development of imaginative theory."[7] By the term "imagination," we do not mean groundless or wild guesses, but academic inferences based on facts and achievements in comparative research on economic history. Only this kind of "imagination" can be academically valuable.

Why so much ado about "imagination" in economic history research and its relevance to comparative economic history? The reason is apparent: Combining vertical and lateral comparisons in economic history makes it possible to use the development process and socioeconomic problems of one country to speculate on what problems another country might encountered in about the same stage of development. Such is one of the ways in which economic historians may bring their imagination into play. "History may not repeat itself, but it does rhyme a lot," as Mark Twain puts it. As to a particular economic period in a certain country or region, speculations based on comparative research into economic history are bound to be more accurate than mere wild guesswork. In this regard, researchers in this nation have a great deal of work ahead of them. The more solid the studies in comparative economic history are, the more fruitful such studies become, and the more convincing the inference from an economic process—the estimation and evaluation of problems to be confronted in the modernization process included—tends to be. (*Translated by Ren Xiaomei*)

— *Social Sciences Front* bimonthly, issue No. 1, 1993

作用》时这样写道："对比较经济史或任何其他经济史来说，最重要的是提出富于想像力的理论。"[7]我们不应把经济史研究中的"想像"理解为毫无根据的、漫无边际的臆测。经济史学家的"想像"——如果我们同意采用这一概念的话——必须以比较经济史的事实和研究成果为基础，这样的"想像"才是有学术价值的。

为什么在这里强调比较经济史研究同经济史学家的"想像"之间的关系？理由是很清楚的。通过经济史的纵向比较与横向比较的结合，可以用历史上其他国家或地区在相似的阶段所经历的发展过程和当时面临的经济、社会问题来推测另一个国家在某一时期可能经历的发展过程和可能遇到的问题。这就是经济史学家想像力的一种应用。虽然历史不会简单地重复，但建立在比较经济史研究基础上的对一定阶段、一定国家或地区的经济演进过程的推断，要比纯粹主观的臆测具有大得多的可信性。从这个意义上说，中国的比较经济史研究者还有大量的工作需要去做。比较经济史的研究越扎实，越有成效，对经济演进的推断（包括对现代化过程中将会遇到的各种问题的估计和评价）就越有说服力。

（原载《社会科学战线》，1993年第1期）

GROWTH AND FLUCTUATIONS IN ECONOMIC DISEQUILIBRIUM (1993)

I. Restraints of disequilibrium on growth and fluctuations

The late 1960s witnessed a great stride made in disequilibrium theory. In his two papers, "The Keynesian counter-revolution: a theoretical appraisal"[1] and "A reconsideration of the micro-foundations of monetary theory,"[2] American economist Robert Wayne Clower came up with a notable argument on disequilibrium theory: Economic instability comes not from a specific market but from discordance between markets, a discordance that stems from the incompleteness of these markets and of the information transmission mechanism between them. If this argument on disequilibrium is applied to analysis of economic growth and fluctuations, the result will be obvious: Not only will the equilibrium equation of growth predicated on the complete conversion of savings into investment and the full utilization of the production capacities thus yielded become void, but the supposition about fluctuations that lists the restrictions of income and its changes on effective demand as a major destabilizing factor in an economic system will also be considered as having major limitations.

Shortly afterwards, Swedish economist Axel Leijonhufvud published *On Keynesian Economics and the Economics of Keynes*[3] among other books. Like Clower, Leijonhufvud reinterpreted the Keynesian economic theory with a disequilibrium approach, and made his own analysis of the causes behind economic stability and instability. He maintains that between labor supply and commodity sales on the economic chain in real life, there are intermediary links, including employers hiring workers, workers producing commodities, employers paying workers, workers buying commodities with their wages, and employers selling commodities. Nevertheless, price rigidity, incomplete markets, clogged information and flawed transmission mechanism may disconnect any one of these links, thereby severing the economic chain and inevitably destabilizing the economy. This is precisely a manifestation of economic disequilibrium. If this analytical method based on disequilibrium is

非均衡条件下经济增长与波动的若干理论问题（1993）

一、经济的非均衡对于经济增长与波动的制约

经济非均衡理论从 20 世纪 60 年代后期起有较大的发展。克劳威尔（Robert Wayne Clower）于 1965 年发表的《凯恩斯派反革命：理论上的再评价》（载于哈恩与布雷克林编《利率理论》，1965 年伦敦版）和 1967 年发表的《货币理论的微观基础的再考虑》（载于《西方经济学杂志》，1967 年 6 月）两篇重要论文中，就非均衡理论提出了一个与经济增长、经济波动有关的值得注意的论点，这就是：经济的不稳定并非来源于某一市场本身，而来源于包括各个市场之间的不协调。至于各个市场之间的不协调的存在，则又应当从各个市场的不完善性和信息传递机制的不健全方面来寻找原因。如果把这种非均衡分析方法运用于经济增长与波动分析的领域内，那么显而易见，不仅以储蓄全部转化为投资和已形成的生产能力得到充分利用为前提的均衡增长公式将失去作用，而且以有效需求受到收入及其变动的限制作为经济体系内在不稳定的主要因素的经济波动假设也将被看成是具有很大局限性的。

紧接着，莱荣霍夫德（Axel Leijonhufvud）出版了《论凯恩斯派经济学和凯恩斯的经济学》（1968 年牛津版）一书和其他一些作品。他同克劳威尔一样，也以非均衡的分析方法来重新解释凯恩斯经济理论，并就经济稳定与不稳定的原因作了如下的分析。他认为，经济生活中，以劳动的供给为一端，以商品的销售为另一端，这两端之间有若干中间环节，如雇主雇用工人、雇工生产商品、雇主付给雇工工资、雇工用工资购买商品、雇主使商品销出等等。但由于价格刚性的存在、市场的不完善、信息的不通畅、传导机制的缺陷等原因，上述各个中间环节中只要有一处未能衔接，这个经济的链条就会中断，经济的不稳定也就难以避免。这正是经济非均衡的一种表现。如果把这种非均衡分析方法运用于经济增长与波动的分析

applied to economic growth and fluctuations, it can likewise prove that it is neither possible for the economy to follow the road of balanced growth as designed by those who subscribe to the equilibrium theory of growth, nor can economic fluctuations be overcome by negotiating the balance between aggregate demand and aggregate supply on the basis of the equilibrium equation for national income.

From the 1970s onward, French economist Jean-Pascal Benassy and Hungarian economist János Kornai probed deeply into the theory of disequilibrium from different points of view. They have made quite a few breakthroughs in disequilibrium studies, which is evident in Benassy's *The Economics of Market Disequilibrium, Macroeconomics and Imperfect Competition* and *Macroeconomics: An Introduction to the Non-Walrasian Approach*[4], and Kornai's *Anti-Equilibrium, Economics of Shortage* and *Growth, Shortage and Efficiency*[5]. Their studies on macroeconomic operation contribute greatly to studies of economic growth and fluctuations.

Benassy's contribution to the theoretical study of disequilibrium lies mainly in his analyses of the restraining factors in economic disequilibrium and of the effects of quantitative quotas. According to him, when prices are rigid, traders ought to adjust demand and supply according to both market price and quantity signals. That is to say, traders are restrained by both prices and quantity. The quantity constraint is embodied in quantitative quotas of various forms. That is to say, the market rations the limited supply among demanders when supply falls short of demand, and apportions the limited demand among suppliers when supply outstrips demand. The equilibrium achieved through quantitative quotas is called "rationed equilibrium," which is actually a kind of disequilibrium or, in a certain sense, temporary, ex post equilibrium. The position of this kind of equilibrium is determined by the shortest side in demand and supply. Benassy maintains that, when observing an economy in disequilibrium, not only should the presumption of price flexibility be abandoned, but price rigidity and asymmetric price elasticity should be taken into consideration as well. Although price rigidity is somewhat relevant to asymmetry in price elasticity, the two factors are different in their impact on actual economic activity. Asymmetry in price elasticity tends to complicate resource allocation in economic disequilibrium, and to further hold back the

领域内，那就同样可以证实经济增长不可能按均衡增长论者所设想的那种均衡增长途径进行，经济波动也不是遵照国民收入均衡公式所要求的调节总需求与总供给之间的平衡关系的做法就能克服的。

70 年代以来，贝纳西（Jean-Pascal Benassy）和科尔内（János Kornai）分别从不同的角度对非均衡理论作了深入的探讨。贝纳西的《市场非均衡经济学》（1982 年纽约版）、《宏观经济学与非均衡理论》（1984 年巴黎版）、《宏观经济学：非瓦尔拉分析方法导论》（1986 年纽约版）等书，以及科尔内的《反均衡》（1971 年阿姆斯特丹版）、《短缺经济学》（1980 年阿姆斯特丹版）、《增长、短缺与效率》（1982 年牛津版）等书，都在非均衡分析方面有不少突破。他们关于宏观经济运行的研究对于经济增长与波动的研究有着重要的意义。

贝纳西在非均衡理论分析中的主要贡献是在对于非均衡条件下的限制因素的分析方面以及数量配额的效应分析方面。按照贝纳西的观点，在价格不灵活时，交易者既要根据市场的价格信号来调整需求量和供给量，又要根据市场的数量信号来调整需求量和供给量，于是交易者受到双重限制，即价格限制和数量限制。数量限制的具体形式就是不同形式的数量配额，也就是：在供给小于需求时，如何把有限的供给分配给需求者们；而在供给大于需求时，如何把有限的需求分配给供给者们。通过数量配额而实现的均衡，称为配额均衡。它是一种非均衡，又是一种特定意义下的、暂时的、事后的均衡。这种均衡的位置是由供给或需求中的短线（短边）决定的。贝纳西认为，在考察非均衡经济时，不仅应当摒弃均衡假设中关于价格灵活性的前提，而且必须引入价格刚性与价格伸缩的不对称性。价格刚性与价格伸缩的不对称性固然有某种联系，但在实际经济生活中的效应则是有区别的。价格伸缩的不对称性使非均衡条件下的资源配置更为复杂，政策的作用也更加受到限制。如果

effectiveness of government policy. If the concept of expectation—that is, individual traders' expectations of uncertain behaviors in economic disequilibrium—is factored in, to stabilize the economy in disequilibrium will become a tougher proposition.

Kornai's analytical approach to the disequilibrium theory is distinctly his own. His study is focused on economic disequilibrium under repressed inflation, that is, disequilibrium characterized by supply shortfalls, where limited commodity supplies are rationed out to demanders by way of quantitative quotas. In that scenario, any increase in fiscal expenditure can further boost the demand on the commodity market, and further strain the distribution of the already limited supplies, thereby worsening the repressed inflation. If, on the contrary, the government attempts to curtail demand by tightening up expenditure, supply and demand will shrink simultaneously, thereby defeating the purpose of making up for supply shortages. Kornai's study of economic disequilibrium is valuable in that he focuses discussions on both hard and soft budget restraints, because the existence of firms' soft budget constraint can keep the economy in long-run disequilibrium and make it hard to eradicate supply shortfalls.

The studies by Western economists drive home clearly that both economic growth and fluctuation are inevitably restrained by economic disequilibrium.

The influence of the equilibrium theory runs deeply in the economic growth theories represented by the Harrod-Domar model, Neo-classical model and Neo-Cambridge model that came in vogue in the 1950s and 1960s. What sets the Neo-Cambridge model far apart from the other two models is that it incorporates two different kinds of income and the restraints of income distribution on economic growth. However, even with this legitimate contribution to growth theories, the Neo-Cambridge model still fails to eschew explicit or implicit assumptions of a complete market, flexible prices, and smooth information transmission. As a result, this model ascribes the difficulties encountered in the process of economic growth mainly to income distribution problems rather than to market imperfections and the incompatibilities between markets. In this way, the Neo-Cambridge model falls short of accounting for the restraining impact of persistent supply shortages on economic growth.

再引入预期概念，即交易者对非均衡条件下的不规则的经济行为的个人预期，那么非均衡的经济更不易趋于稳定。

科尔内的非均衡理论分析另有特色。他着重考察的是抑制性通货膨胀条件下的经济非均衡，也就是以短缺作为特征的经济非均衡。这时，有限的商品供给通过数量配额而给予需求各方。在这种情况下，如果增加财政支出，那么商品市场上的需求会进一步扩大，有限的商品供给的分配会更加紧张、更加困难，抑制性的通货膨胀也会更加严重。反之，如果试图用紧缩财政支出的手段来减少商品市场上的需求，那么在需求减少的同时供给量也将减少，其结果仍然没有解决供给缺口问题。科尔内在研究非均衡经济时，把企业的预算硬约束与软约束作为讨论的重点之一。他的这些观点是很有价值的，因为企业的预算软约束的存在将使经济长期处于非均衡状态，也就是使经济中的短缺现象难以消除。

从国外经济学界对于非均衡经济的研究可以清楚地了解到，无论是经济增长还是经济波动，都必然受到经济的非均衡的制约。

在以哈罗德—多马模型、新古典模型甚至新剑桥模型作为代表的流行于 50 ~ 60 年代的经济增长论中，经济均衡论的影响是很深的。这种影响不仅反映于哈罗德—多马模型和新古典模型内，而且也反映于新剑桥模型内。新剑桥模型与哈罗德—多马模型、新古典模型的一个重大的区别，是在模型中引入了两类不同的收入以及收入分配对经济增长的制约作用。这当然应当被承认为新剑桥模型的贡献。然而，即使是新剑桥模型，也没有摆脱市场完善、价格灵活、信息传递通畅等公开的或暗含的假设；新剑桥模型所反映的经济增长过程中遇到的困难，主要来自收入分配方面的矛盾，而不是主要来自市场机制的不完善以及各个不同市场之间的不协调。这样，新剑桥模型依然解释不了经济增长过程中供求缺口的持续存在对于经济增长的制约作用。

One thing that should be noted is that Joan Robinson and other major advocates of the Neo-Cambridge model were, theoretically speaking, against assumptions of economic equilibrium. Proceeding from Keynes's viewpoints on economic disequilibrium, they raised a series of arguments against mainstream post-Keynesian theorists. But why was it that they could not shake off the influence of the equilibrium theory in their analysis of economic growth? It was because their microeconomic theory was inadequate and weak, and because their neglect of analyses of market transaction behaviors, corporate operational mechanisms, and information transmission mechanisms determined the inherent drawbacks in their model of economic growth.

In economic fluctuation studies, the relevant theory represented by the IS-LM (investment · savings—liquidity preference · money supply) and Multiplier-Accelerator models that were popular in the 1950s and 1960s is preconditioned by equilibrium and equilibrium growth assumptions. According to these models, economic fluctuations are caused by overinvestment, over-saving, over-supply, or inefficient money supply, and by the inherent law of technology and equipment upgrading, and are not directly associated with market imperfections, price rigidity, and informational frictions. What is more, the IS-LM model also ignores the analysis of the microeconomic basis of the macroeconomy, while the Multiplier-Accelerator model does the same by leaning heavily on the economy's technical factors. Such oversight determines the serious flaw in the fluctuation theories that were current in the 1950s and 1960s.

The progress made in the late 1960s in researches on the disequilibrium theory provided no small inspiration for studies of economic growth and fluctuations. And the restraining effects of the imbalanced nature of the economy on growth and fluctuations were increasingly accepted in academic and economic circles thanks to constructive explorations made by researchers in the disequilibrium theory. These explorations were made without totally disallowing the significance and reference value of either the Harrod-Domar, Neo-classical and Neo-Cambridge models in the realm of theoretical research on economic growth, or the IS-LM and Multiplier-Accelerator models in their studies of the fluctuation theory. Such explorations were important in that they

需要说明的是，新剑桥经济增长理论的主要代表人物如琼·罗宾逊等人，从经济理论上说，是反对经济均衡假设的。他们从凯恩斯的著作中找到了经济非均衡的论点，并由此提出了一系列不同意后凯恩斯主流经济学派的论点。但为什么在经济增长分析中却未能摆脱经济均衡论的影响呢？原因在于他们的微观经济理论是不足的、有弱点的。他们忽略了对市场交易行为的分析、企业运行机制的分析、信息传递机制的分析。这就决定了他们的经济增长模型的内在缺陷。

在经济波动的研究中，流行于 50～60 年代的经济波动论以 IS—LM 分析（投资·储蓄—流动偏好·货币供给分析）、乘数—加速原理分析为代表的学说，是以经济均衡假设和经济的均衡增长假设为前提的。根据这些分析，如果说经济中产生波动的话，那么这只是由于经济运行中出现的投资偏多或储蓄偏多，货币供给过多或货币供给过少，以及技术设备更新的自身规律所致，而与市场机制的缺陷、价格的不灵活、信息传递的不通畅等等没有直接的关系。再说，IS—LM 分析还忽略了宏观经济的微观经济基础的分析，乘数—加速原理分析则偏重于经济中的技术性因素的考察，它们同样不考虑宏观经济的微观经济基础。这也就决定了这些流行于 50～60 年代的经济波动论的严重不足。

60 年代后期起关于经济的非均衡理论分析的进展，对于经济增长与经济波动的研究有重要的启示。经济的非均衡性质对于经济增长与经济波动的制约作用，经过非均衡理论的研究者的探讨，已经日益被学术界与经济界所承认。这些探讨并不是一概否定哈罗德—多马模型、新古典模型、新剑桥模型在经济增长理论研究领域内的意义及其在某些方面的可借鉴性，也并不是一概否定 IS—LM 分析、乘数—加速原理在经济波动理论研究领域内的意义及其在某些方面的可借鉴性。这些探讨的重要性在于：它们

approached growth and fluctuations from a unique perspective, thereby putting their studies on a new and more realistic footing. That is why some of their conclusions are closer to reality than those derived from the theories popular in the 1950s and 1960s.

The studies of disequilibrium analyses of growth and fluctuations so far can be summarized in the following four major conclusions:

First, with incomplete markets, inflexible prices and inefficient information transmission, the conversion of savings into investment will be held back, and the imbalance between supply and demand, once it occurs, cannot be easily corrected. Shortages in supply and demand can be mitigated by the function of market to a certain extent, but will not disappear totally. The equilibrium thus achieved under a nonzero unemployment rate or a nonzero inflation rate can restrain economic growth or cause major fluctuations.

Second, disequilibrium makes it harder for markets (commodity market, capital market, labor market, etc.) to function in a coordinative way. Once supply or demand shortages occur in one market, they cannot possibly disappear and will go on to cause new shortages and exacerbate existing ones in other markets. This may become a restraint on growth or an importance cause behind major fluctuations.

Third, disequilibrium is characterized by price rigidity. The major impact of price rigidity on growth and fluctuations is manifested in that economic agents have to make supply-demand decisions based on imprecise signals. However, price rigidity does not mean that a price will hold forever. On the contrary, it may entail sudden, large-scale, and asymmetric price changes. This is detrimental to economic growth, to be sure, and more importantly, it may cause or aggravate fluctuations.

Fourth, the presence of disequilibrium or equilibrium under nonzero rates of unemployment and inflation is bound to alter the expectations of market participants, which in turn gives rise to irregular and shortsighted economic behaviors. Such behaviors are likely to become not only a major cause behind intensified fluctuations, but also a stubborn retardant on steady and sustained economic growth.

从另一个角度来分析经济增长与经济波动，从而使经济增长与经济波动的分析具有一个新的、与现实状况联系更紧的立足点；它们所得出的某些结论，比流行于 50 ~ 60 年代的有关理论分析更为符合实际。

经济非均衡分析在经济增长与波动方面所得出的主要结论可以归纳为以下四点：

1. 如果市场不完善、价格不灵活、信息传递不通畅，那么投资与储蓄之间的转化将受到阻碍，供给与需求之间的不平衡一旦出现，就不易消失。市场只可能使供给缺口或需求缺口有所缩小，但这些缺口仍将继续存在。于是将出现非零失业率条件下的均衡或非零通货膨胀率条件下的均衡，这就制约了经济增长或导致经济的较大波动。

2. 经济的非均衡使得不同市场（商品市场、资金市场、劳动力市场等）之间的协调更为困难。一旦一个市场出现了供给缺口或需求缺口，不仅这个市场上的缺口难以消除，而且必将引起其他市场上的缺口的产生与扩大。这种情况成为经济增长的制约因素或成为经济较大波动的重要原因之一。

3. 经济的非均衡以价格刚性的存在作为特征。价格刚性对于经济增长与经济波动的主要影响表现于交易者根据经济生活中的假象来制定供给与需求的决策。但价格刚性并不一定意味着价格永远不变，而很可能意味着价格的突然的、较大幅度的变动，而且是不对称的变动。这对于经济增长固然不利；更重要的是，这可能引发较大的经济波动或使波动加剧。

4. 经济的非均衡以及非零失业率与非零通货膨胀率条件下均衡的存在，必将改变市场交易双方的预期。预期的不稳定或预期的紊乱，将导致经济行为的不规则，导致经济行为的短期化。这不仅是加剧经济波动的一个重要原因，而且也是阻碍经济稳定增长与持续增长的有力因素。

II. Telling two kinds of disequilibrium apart and a study of growth and fluctuations

Using disequilibrium analysis, and combining it with the country's actual economic situation, we will be able to get a better understanding of the guidelines for the ongoing economic reform and the way the economy develops.

Given that disequilibrium is caused by incomplete markets, inflexible prices and inefficient information transmission, either of the following arguments will make sense in theory:

Argument A: To avoid volatile fluctuations and stabilize the growth rate, it is necessary to remove price restraints and improve market conditions, and to put economic agents on equal competitive footings. Economic growth will be realized in a relatively complete market with flexible prices.

Argument B: With market mechanism flaws such as incomplete markets, inflexible prices and inefficient information transmission, it is necessary to tighten up macroeconomic management to make up for market deficiencies and rectify economic deviations with government regulation of quotas and prices. Steady and sustainable economic growth will be achieved mainly by allocating capital, labor, and production materials via quantitative quota. To put it another way, economic growth under disequilibrium can be achieved mainly through quantitative quota implementation.

Both arguments stem from analyses of economic disequilibrium. In fact, Argument A is a succinct interpretation of the theory on "price reform as the centerpiece of economic reform," while Argument B emphasizes "macroeconomic stabilization as the centerpiece of economic reform." Insofar as economic growth and fluctuations are concerned, Argument A attributes economic fluctuations in disequilibrium to incomplete markets and inflexible prices, so that flexible prices and better market conditions are the first steps to take to avoid fluctuations or maintain stable economic growth; while Argument B ascribes fluctuations to incomplete markets or limitations in the market mechanism itself, so the inevitable reform step is to strengthen macroeconomic management through government quota and price regulation.

二、两类非均衡的区分与经济增长、经济波动的分析

按照非均衡理论的分析，并且结合我国的实际经济情况进行考察，我们可以对当前经济体制改革的思路以及经济增长的途径有较深入的认识。

要知道，既然经济的非均衡状态来自市场的不完善、价格的不灵活、信息传递的不通畅等，那么按照这样的逻辑，从理论上必定得出下列两个论断中的一个：

甲：由于经济的非均衡来自市场的不完善、价格的不灵活、信息传递的不通畅，因此，要使非均衡条件下的经济避免较大的波动，使经济有比较稳定的增长率，在经济体制改革中首先要实现的是放开对价格的限制和完善市场，使经济生活中的交易各方都处于平等竞争的位置上。经济增长将在市场完善和价格放开的环境中实现。

乙：由于经济的非均衡来自市场的不完善、价格的不灵活、信息传递的不通畅，这些都反映了市场机制的局限性。因此，在经济体制改革中的首要任务应当是加强宏观经济管理，以政府的数量配额与价格调节来弥补市场机制之不足，纠正市场不完善所造成的经济中的偏差。在经济增长方面，为了维持较稳定的经济，政府的数量配额（包括资金配额、劳动力配额、生产资料配额等）将起着主要的作用。这就是说，非均衡条件下的经济增长应当是以政府的数量配额为主的经济增长。

以上所指出的甲、乙两种论断，都来自对经济的非均衡分析。论断甲是经济改革中的“价格改革主线论”的简要表述，论断乙是经济改革中的“宏观调控主线论”的简要表述。就经济增长与经济波动的分析而言，按照论断甲的说法，非均衡条件下的经济波动主要归因于市场不完善和价格不灵活，避免经济波动的主要改革措施或维持经济较稳定增长的主要改革措施就必然是放开价格和完善市场。按照论断乙的说法，非均衡条件下的经济波动主要归因于市场不完善或市场机制本身的局限性，避免经济波动的主要改革措施或维持经济较稳定增长的主要改革措施就必然是加强宏观经济管理，把政府的数量配额和价格调节放在主要地位。

However, a study of the actual performance of the Chinese economy proves that neither price reform nor macroeconomic stabilization, if chosen as the centerpiece of economic reform, can ensure the smooth development of reform and ward off wild fluctuations or maintain steady economic growth. This means that neither Argument A nor Argument B tallies with the current Chinese economic situation.

Given that both arguments are based on studies of disequilibrium assumptions and therefore inappropriate, one may wonder what really went wrong. Isn't it that the disequilibrium theory itself is wrong, or that analysis of this theory is not thorough enough to account for such complex issues as economic restructuring, growth, and fluctuations in this country?

In comparison with the equilibrium theory, the disequilibrium theory is, without a doubt, an advance in economics. Equilibrium assumptions are unwarranted in the absence of complete markets, flexible prices, and efficient information transmission. In reality, however, economies are always in disequilibrium; therefore, they can be observed only with disequilibrium analytical methods. For this reason, we cannot make light of the disequilibrium theory simply because the above two arguments do not fit. The problem does not lie in disequilibrium analysis itself.

What really went wrong? The problem dwells in the flaws of general disequilibrium analysis, so much so that it falls short of explaining such complicated issues as economic restructuring, growth, and fluctuations in China.

What merits attention is that general disequilibrium analysis does not take into account the dynamics of firms as microeconomic units. Instead, its assumption is that firms are dynamic enough. It thus follows that analysts attribute disequilibrium to incomplete markets, inflexible prices, and inefficient information transmission. This is how Arguments A and B are drawn, and why disequilibrium analysis is flawed. In my book *Disequilibrium in the Chinese Economy*[6], I propose to divide disequilibrium into two categories, one with incomplete markets, and the other with both incomplete markets and enfeebled firms. The current Chinese economy falls into the second category. This being the case,

然而，对我国的实际经济情况进行研究后却发现，无论是在经济体制改革中按照“价格改革主线论”的主张去做，还是按照“宏观调控主线论”的主张去做，都不可能顺利地推进我国的经济体制改革，也不可能避免我国经济的较大波动或维持我国经济的较稳定的增长。换言之，“价格改革主线论”或“宏观调控主线论”都是不符合我国经济的实际状况的。

这样就产生了一个新的问题。要知道，经济改革中的“价格改革主线论”与“宏观调控主线论”都来自对经济的非均衡分析。既然这两种论点都不妥当，那么将会引起人们的进一步思考：究竟是非均衡理论错了呢，还是一般的非均衡理论分析不够完善，从而解释不了像我国经济体制改革、经济增长与波动这样复杂的问题呢?

非均衡理论相对于均衡理论而言，确实是经济理论的一种进展。经济均衡的假设依存于市场完善、价格灵活、信息畅通等前提。如果不具备这样一些前提，那么经济均衡的假设就不能成立，而现实经济必定是非均衡的经济，从而只能运用非均衡分析方法来进行分析。可见，我们不能由于“价格改革主线论”与“宏观调控主线论”不适合我国当前的经济现实而认为非均衡分析是错误的。问题不在于非均衡分析本身。

那么，问题究竟何在? 问题在于一般的非均衡理论分析不够完善，以至于解释不了像我国经济体制改革、经济增长与波动这样复杂的问题。

需要指出的是：一般的非均衡理论分析并未把微观经济单位企业是否具有充分活力考虑在内，而是暗含了这样一个假定，即企业作为微观经济单位已经具有充分活力；因此，经济非均衡现象主要来自市场的不完善、价格的不灵活、信息传递的不通畅等。正因为如此，所以由此推出的结论或者是以价格改革为经济改革的主线，或者是以加强宏观经济管理为经济改革的主线。这就是一般的非均衡理论分析的不完善之处。我在《非均衡的中国经济》（1990 年经济日报出版社版）一书中，就这一问题提出了如下的看法：经济的非均衡分为两种类型，第一类经济非均衡是指市场不完善条件下的非均衡，第二类经济非均衡是指市场不完善和企业缺乏活力条件下的非均衡。现阶段的中国经济处于第二类非均衡状态，中国的经济体制改革应当相应地分为两个阶段，即应当以深化

economic restructuring in this nation should proceed in two stages: Firstly, to transform firms more deeply until they become dynamic and profit-maximizing entities that enjoy decision-making autonomy and are liable for their profits and losses, so that the Chinese economy can complete its transition from the second category of disequilibrium to the first category of it; and secondly, to center economic restructuring on building a complete market and decentralizing prices, so that the economy can edge its way toward equilibrium. My book differs from the general studies of the disequilibrium theory in that I have differentiated between two categories of economic disequilibrium and observed the attributes of the second category of disequilibrium.

It makes sense to distinguish between these two kinds of disequilibrium, because it helps analyze Chinese economic growth and fluctuations. Economic growth is restricted to a larger extent and more vulnerable to fluctuations in the second category of disequilibrium. In the same vein, it is more difficult to maintain steady economic growth and avoid wild fluctuations under the second category of disequilibrium than under the first category of it. Without clarifying the difference between the two categories of disequilibrium, we may mistake incomplete markets, inflexible prices and inefficient information transmission for the main restraints on economic growth and the basic causes behind fluctuations. We will miss the point or only take ineffective measures if we adopt economic policies in light of these judgments. It is like a doctor who, acting on a false diagnosis, writes out an inappropriate prescription and leaves an illness untreated or even aggravated.

If, instead of telling the two kinds of economic disequilibrium apart and seeing that China is in the second kind of it, we set improving market conditions and decentralizing prices or intensifying macroeconomic management as our major policy decisions to stabilize economic growth and avert fluctuations, we are ignoring the most forceful restraints on economic growth and fluctuations imposed by weak firms that, as investors and consumption fund issuers, are not responsible for their management decisions, profits and losses. Under the second category of disequilibrium, firms are yet to become independent commodity producers liable for their management

企业改革为主线，使企业从缺乏活力转为具有充分活力，从不自主经营和不自负盈亏转为自主经营和自负盈亏，以便使中国经济由第二类非均衡状态过渡到第一类非均衡状态。然后，以完善市场和放开价格作为经济体制改革的主线，以便使中国经济由第一类非均衡状态逐渐向均衡状态靠拢。对两类经济非均衡的区分，以及针对第二类经济非均衡的特征进行研究，就是我所著《非均衡的中国经济》一书的基本论点，也是我在非均衡分析中不同于一般的非均衡理论分析的地方。

区分两类不同的经济非均衡，对于研究中国的经济增长与波动是有意义的。经济增长在第二类非均衡条件下所受到的制约，要比在第一类非均衡条件下多得多；导致经济波动的因素在第二类非均衡条件下也要比在第一类非均衡条件下多得多。同样的道理，与在第一类非均衡条件下的情形相比，在第二类非均衡条件下，维持经济的较稳定增长或避免经济出现较大的波动要困难得多。如果我们不了解第二类非均衡状态与第一类非均衡状态的区别，只把市场的不完善、价格的不灵活、信息传递的不通畅看成是对于经济增长的主要制约因素，看成是引起经济产生较大波动的基本原因，从而根据这些判断来选择维持经济稳定增长的对策或制定防止、消除经济较大波动的对策，那么很可能不得要领，以至于选择的对策收不到应有的成效。正如医生在给病人治疗时，如果对病情的诊断有错误，对病因判断错了，那么就会开出不恰当的处方，不但医不好病，反会延误病情。

假定不区分两类不同的经济非均衡，不了解当前的中国经济正处于第二类非均衡状态，而是把完善市场和放开价格作为维持经济稳定增长与防止经济较大波动的主要对策，或者把加强宏观经济管理作为这样的对策，那就忽略了企业作为投资主体和消费基金发放主体的不自主经营、不自负盈亏对经济增长与波动的最有力的制约作用。在第二类非均衡条件下，企业还没有成为自主经营、自负盈亏的

decisions, profits and losses, so their status as investors and consumption fund issuers is nominal and unrestrained. In that scenario, the following problems will occur:

1. Owing to their lack of autonomy, firms may not be able to make investment even when it is profitable to do so, thus making it hard to keep overall economic growth in pace with these firms' increasing economic returns.

2. Having no self-restraints on investment and bearing no investment, production and management risks, firms in the process of expanding investment will be susceptible to repetitive construction and fail to realize economies of scale. In that case, economic growth is likely to be a process of ballooning overstock and financial losses for such firms.

3. Myopic economic decisions such as allocating the consumption fund to serve immediate interests will impair firms' growth potentials and leave them with outdated equipment and technology. Economic growth will be held back as a result.

4. Firms with no self-restraints may issue more consumption fund than is allowed by their economic returns, and such economic returns are often adulterated even though they are pegged to wages and bonuses. Under these circumstances, the more tightly wages and bonuses are pegged to economic returns, the bigger the losses will become for firms and the state. Economic growth will invariably be held back as a result.

5. The negative macroeconomic impact of the lack of self-restraints on investment and consumption fund cannot be underestimated. Overinvestment and runaway growth in consumption fund are one of the manifestations of this negative impact. In that case, even if the economic growth rate is increased, such an increase will be short lived and sow the seed for future economic disorder. Extended losses on firms and stressed fiscal balance are another manifestation of this negative impact, with stressed fiscal balance becoming a major cause behind economic instability and a huge obstacle to sustained economic growth.

6. The fact that firms take no responsibility for their own profits and losses and, in particular, cannot stop production or be closed down, merged or transferred because of government-business collusion, deprives the flow of corporate capital stock of proper channels and makes it impossible to optimize the reallocation of production factors. With

独立商品生产者；企业的投资主体、消费基金发放主体的地位，或者是虚的，或者不受约束，其结果必然造成以下的问题：

1. 企业想投资，但由于缺乏这方面的自主权，投资意愿未能实现，从而经济增长难以与企业经济效益的增长同步。

2. 企业不具有投资的自我约束机制，也不承担投资风险、生产经营风险，以至于在投资增长过程中，重复建设难以避免，规模效益无法实现，从而经济增长的过程可能同时就是库存品积压数量增长的过程、企业亏损额扩大的过程。

3. 企业的行为是短期化的，消费基金的发放是为了企业眼前利益，企业的经济增长后劲遭到破坏，设备老化，技术陈旧，经济增长将因此受到限制。

4. 企业缺乏内在约束机制，消费基金的发放可以不受本企业经济效益的限制，或者，工资奖金虽然同企业经济效益“挂钩”，但企业经济效益却是掺了水的、虚假的。这样，工资奖金越是同企业经济效益挂钩（也就是不合理的挂钩），企业的实际损失就越大，国家因此遭受的实际损失也越大，这不能不限制经济增长。

5. 企业在投资方面缺乏自我约束以及在消费基金发放方面缺乏自我约束，对宏观经济的消极影响是不可低估的。消极影响之一是导致投资膨胀与消费基金增长过快。这时，即使经济增长率可能高一些，但经济增长却是依靠投资膨胀与消费基金增长过快支撑的。这样的经济增长不可能持久，而且很可能为此后的经济巨大震荡种下了根源。消极影响之二是企业的亏损面增加和财政收支的紧张，而财政收支的紧张又成为经济不稳定的重要原因和经济持续增长的巨大障碍。

6. 企业的不自负盈亏，特别是政企不分的事实，使得企业的关、停、并、转十分困难，企业资产存量的流动缺乏途径，生产要素也无法在社会范围内优化组合。其结果，产业结构的调整迟迟不能

bottlenecks like these, industrial restructuring can never go smoothly, and sustained economic growth is hamstrung as well.

7. When firms have no decision-making autonomy and bear no responsibility for their profits and losses, neither can their capital stock be made to flow, nor can the purpose of industrial restructuring through reinvestment be served. Increases in investment are limited, and limited increases in investment can hardly put an end to the disproportionate industrial structure. The problem, however, does not stop here. If we liken corporate capital stock to a pool of stagnant water, and reinvestment to flowing water, the real problem is that when year's increased amount of investment is reinvested in a firm, it becomes part of the firm's capital stock the next year. If this cycle is made to last, it is tantamount to constantly turning running water into stagnant water—no amount of running water can put an end to the situation. Consequently, bottlenecks persist and economic growth is greatly held back.

8. Under the second category of economic disequilibrium, because firms, as microeconomic units, remain as government appendages, whenever the government takes macroeconomic regulation steps, they either find it difficult to adapt their business activity to macroeconomic changes or cannot respond properly for lack of self-restraints. As a result, the government regulation steps fail to yield the desired results. The lack of elasticity—in the investment interest rate, the import-and-export exchange rate, and output prices—is exactly a telltale sign of the undesirable results of government regulation steps. In the absence of stability-oriented internal adjustment mechanisms, once economic fluctuations occur, the situation can only be tackled with government intervention. However, under the second category of disequilibrium, government intervention from top on down to the grassroots level often comes seriously belatedly. The higher-up leadership (or decision-making authorities) will not take action until problems become serious enough. Furthermore, the negative impact of inappropriate government intervention on economy stability should never be overlooked.

These eight problems illustrate what is so unique about the growth and fluctuations in the Chinese economy in the second category of disequilibrium. Therefore, our studies of Chinese economic growth and fluctuations should proceed from the relevant factors, with the second category of disequilibrium as the precondition.

顺利进行，“瓶颈”现象也迟迟不能消除。这样就制约了持续的经济增长。

7. 在企业不自主经营、不自负盈亏的条件下，不仅企业资产存量难以流动，从而通过企业资产存量的流动来调整产业结构的意图不易实现，而且通过投资增量来调整产业结构的意图也是很难实现的。投资增量是有限的，有限的投资增量是不容易扭转整个产业结构失调的局面的。但问题不限于此。问题在于：企业资产存量好比一潭死水，投资增量好比活水，今年的投资增量一投入企业后，就转化为来年的企业资产存量。这就等于不断地把活水变为死水，活水再多也无济于事。其结果是“瓶颈”依然存在，经济增长依然受到巨大的限制。

8. 在第二类非均衡条件下，由于作为微观经济单位的企业往往同政府部门没有分开，在政府采取宏观经济调节手段时，企业或者难以通过调整自己的经济活动来适应宏观经济形势的变化，或者因缺乏自我约束机制而对宏观经济调节手段作不出适当的反应，于是宏观经济调节手段收不到应有的效果。诸如投资缺乏利息弹性、进出口缺乏汇率弹性、产量缺乏价格弹性等等，就是宏观经济调节手段效果差的反映。这样，一旦发生经济波动，经济内部就缺乏内在调节以趋向稳定的机制，而不得不依靠自上而下的行政干预措施来缓和矛盾。在第二类非均衡条件下，自上而下的行政干预措施往往是严重滞后的，即必须等到下面的问题已经相当尖锐了，上级（甚至是最高决策当局）才会下决心采取调整措施。加之，行政干预措施的不当给经济的稳定所带来的消极性后果，也是不容忽视的。

以上所说的这些，足以说明处于第二类非均衡条件下中国经济增长与经济波动的特殊性质。因此，在对现阶段中国的经济增长与波动问题进行研究时，不仅需要从经济增长与波动本身的有关因素来分析，而且需要以第二类非均衡作为整个分析的前提。

III. Understanding the wooden barrel principle in disequilibrium

An important principle in the disequilibrium theory is the "law of the shortest side," which is believed to be the key restraint on economic growth and the essential cause behind fluctuations. The "law of the shortest side" is tenable in this regard. This is because in a disequilibrium economy, the market cannot play a complete role in regulating the relationship between supply and demand, and therefore the existence of the shortest side becomes an inevitability, which forces production factors to be reallocated in compliance with the minimum demand. This is like a barrel composed of planks of different lengths. The capacity of the barrel is determined by the shortest plank rather than the longest one. If more water than the shortest plank allows is poured into the barrel, the water will spill out. This is what the "law of the shortest side" entails.

When applying the "law of the shortest side" to the study of growth and fluctuations in economic disequilibrium, the following problems are worth our further consideration:

1. Why can the shortest side persist for a long time? Despite years of economic growth, the shortest side of previous years remains to this day or becomes even shorter. That is, the shortest plank of the barrel becomes still shorter. What has gone wrong?

2. In theory, production factors are mutually replaceable and supplementary to a certain extent. This means that the shortest side could be replaced or made up for by certain longer sides. In reality, however, the ability of longer-side production factors to replace or supplement shorter ones is very limited, a fact that has a considerable influence on economic growth and fluctuations. The issue here is: Why mutual replacement and complementation between production factors can be so difficult as to allow the "law of the shortest side" to become the key factor in inhibiting economic growth and causing fluctuations?

3. Reallocation of production factors can address economic problems caused by shortest-side factors, boost economic growth and curtail

fluctuations. Take, again, the barrel for example. Since how much water a barrel can contain is determined by its shortest plank, the situation can be remedied in two ways. One is to saw a certain length off the longest

三、对非均衡理论中的“短线决定原则”的理解

在非均衡理论中，一个重要的原则是“短线决定原则”（或称“短边原则”）。这被认为是制约经济增长与经济波动的关键所在。“短线决定原则”之所以成立，是因为在非均衡经济中，由于市场不可能起着充分地协调供求关系的作用，短线的存在是不可避免的，而短线的存在则使得生产要素只可能按低限的要求进行组合。这种情况正如一个由若干块木板条所组装成的木桶一样：如果这些木板条长短不一，那么组装成的木桶究竟能够盛多少水不取决于较长的那些木板条，而惟一地取决于最短的那块木板条。把水注入这样的木桶后，只要水高于最短的那块木板条的长度，水就向外漏出了。这就是“短线决定原则”的含义。

研究非均衡经济中的经济增长与经济波动时，从“短线决定原则”来理解，至少有三个问题值得我们作进一步思考，这三个问题是：

1. 为什么短线会长期存在？若干年以前的短线，经过这些年的经济增长，至今仍然是短线，甚至短线更短了，即木桶的最短的那块木板条又缩短了，这是什么缘故呢？

2. 照理说，生产要素之间存在着一定程度的可替代性或互补性，也就是说，即使存在着短线，但短线不是不可以靠某些长线来替代和补充的。然而事实却表明，在非均衡经济中，长线的生产要素对短线的生产要素的替代和补充却是十分有限的，这对经济增长与经济波动有较大的影响。需要研究的是，为什么生产要素之间的替代与互补受到严重限制，从而使“短线决定原则”一直起着制约经济增长与经济波动的关键作用？

3. 为了缓和短线所造成的经济困难，在通常情况下，还可以采取生产要素重新组合的办法，以促进经济增长，减少经济波动。不妨仍以木桶为例。虽然木桶盛水量的多少取决于组装成木桶的最短的那块木板条，但未尝不可以采取下述两个办法之一作为补救措施。

plank and nail it onto the shortest one, so that the two new planks are level with each other. This can happen only when production factors are mutually supplementary. The other is to dismantle the barrel and put the old planks together to make a new one, hopefully a larger one. This is tantamount to the aforementioned reallocation of production factors. Nevertheless, in reality, such reallocation is an unrealistic proposition probably because the barrel is too solid to be torn apart for reassembling. Then we should ask: Why is the barrel so solid? Why can't we break it apart? Is it really difficult to reallocate production factors?

All these problems are relevant to the characteristics of growth and fluctuations under economic disequilibrium. Bearing in mind the differentiation between the two types of disequilibrium, and combing it with the fact that the Chinese economy is in the second category of disequilibrium, let us proceed from the "law of the shortest side" to observe these three problems, so as to better understand the "law of the shortest side."

i. Problem 1: the shortest-side syndrome in the second category of disequilibrium

The shortest-side syndrome refers to the situation where shortest-side factors remain, or are growing even shorter in spite of years of economic growth and restructuring. Where is the problem? In economic equilibrium, shortest-side factors will disappear when the market mechanism promotes the free flow of production factors and resources are reallocated in response to price signals. In this way, even if new shortest-side factors emerge in the process of economic growth, the economy is immune to the shortest-side syndrome. Apparently, the shortest-side syndrome tends to occur when production-factor is stagnant and resources cannot be reallocated smoothly.

Supposing our economy is in the first category of disequilibrium, which is characterized by incomplete markets, inflexible prices and incomplete information, production factors can flow more freely by improving the markets and decentralizing the prices, and resource reallocation can take place in response to price signals. In this way, the shortest-side syndrome may disappear gradually. Though scarcity in some resources may make it difficult to reallocate resources and overcome the

一是把长的木板条锯下一段，钉在最短的木板条之上。这就相当于上面提到的各种不同的生产要素之间的互补，即以长线补短线、长线代短线的做法。二是把这个木桶拆开，用原有的各块木板条重新组装成一个容器，也许这个新组装成的容器可以盛较多的水。这就相当于这里所提到的生产要素的重新组合。然而事实同样表明，生产要素难以重新组合。也许是由于这个长短边不等的木桶组装得太牢了，难以拆开它，因此也就无法把各块木板条重新组装为一个新的容器。于是就应当思考：为什么原有的木桶组装得这么牢？难道就找不到把它拆开的办法吗？难道生产要素真的那么难以重新组合吗？

这三个问题都与非均衡条件下的经济增长与经济波动的特点有关。在研究中，我们必须结合两类非均衡的区分，结合我国当前正处于第二类非均衡状态这一事实，分别考察这三个问题，以便进一步理解“短线决定原则”。

（一）第二类非均衡经济中的“短线顽症”

这里所说的“短线顽症”，就是指经过多年的经济增长与结构调整而未能消除久已存在的短线甚至短线更为严重的状况。原因究竟何在？要知道，如果经济处于均衡状态，市场机制的作用将促进生产要素自由流动，资源将在价格信号指引之下重新配置，从而使短线消失。这种情况下，即使在经济增长过程中仍会出现新的短线，但“短线顽症”则是不存在的。可见，“短线顽症”的存在同生产要素不能自由流动有关，同资源难以重新配置有关。

假定经济处于第一类非均衡状态，即非均衡的根源在于市场不完善、价格不灵活、信息传递不通畅，那么通过完善市场和放开价格等措施，生产要素的流动性将显然增大，价格信号将对资源的重新配置发挥指引作用，“短线顽症”也就有可能逐渐被克服。某些资源的稀缺也许会给资源的重新配置带来困难，使得短线不容易迅速

shortest sides, the syndrome can be avoided if this scarcity can be eased with replacements or imports.

However, the situation is more complicated in the second category of disequilibrium, which is peculiarly prone to the shortest-side syndrome. In this category of economic disequilibrium, clogged production-factor flow and troubles in industrial restructuring and resource reallocation can be imputed respectively to the "lack of information, incentive and channel."

"Lack of information" means that when faltering firms operate in an incomplete market, their access to price signals is bound to be inappropriate, untimely and incomplete. At the same time, because these firms, as microeconomic units, are under the strict control of their leadership authorities, the government cannot obtain timely and accurate information from both the market and these firms. Therefore, government quota adjustments are often at odds with market needs, and resources can only be reallocated in the absence of accurate information. As a result, shortest-side factors are mistaken for longest-side ones, and vice versa; and ineffective supply is regarded as being effective.

"Lack of incentive" means that the lopsided industrial structure is a solid fact, and firms have obtained adequate information about shortest-and longest-side factors and can respond accordingly, but they are not motivated enough to take action and run the risks. This is because, as government appendages that have not the final say in management and are not liable for profits, losses and production and management risks, these forms are neither motivated to restructure their products and nor willing to run such risks.

"Lack of channels" means that even if firms as microeconomic units and the government as macroeconomic authorities have both received adequate information about shortest-and longest-side factors and are willing to restructure the economy, there are no channels to facilitate the free flow of production factors. This is because firms are mere government appendages while the economy has been sectioned by a labyrinth of ownership boundaries, making it difficult to reallocate resources, let alone optimize them. All this bears out the unavoidability of the shortest-side syndrome.

消失。但稀缺资源在相当大的程度上是可以通过资源的相互替代或国外资源的利用来加以缓和的，所以不至于形成“短线顽症”。

然而，正如前面所指出的，第二类非均衡下的情况远比第一类非均衡下的情况复杂。“短线顽症”是第二类非均衡状态中所特有的病症。生产要素流动的受阻、产业结构调整的困难、资源重新配置设想的难以落实，在第二类非均衡条件下，可以归结为“无信息、无动力、无渠道”所致。

“无信息”是指：由于缺乏活力的企业在不完善的市场上进行活动，价格方面的信息必然是不准确、不及时、不通畅的。由于作为微观经济单位的企业受到行政主管部门的严格控制，政府既无法从市场及时地获得准确的信息，又不能从企业那里及时地获得准确的信息。因此，政府的数量调节也往往同市场实际有所出入。其结果，资源的配置只好在缺乏信息的条件下进行。短线被误认为非短线，长线被误认为非长线，无效供给被误认为有效供给等现象也就屡见不鲜。

“无动力”是指：尽管客观上确凿地存在产业结构失调的状况，企业也得到了有关短线与长线的确切信息，但由于企业不自主经营与不自负盈亏，不承担生产经营的风险，因而也就缺乏调整产品结构的动力，不愿冒结构调整的风险。

“无渠道”是指：即使作为微观经济单位的企业和作为宏观经济管理部门的政府都得到了有关短线与长线的确切信息，并且都有结构调整的意愿，但在政企不分、企业附属于行政主管部门、经济被不合理地分割为“条条所有”、“块块所有”等条件下，生产要素的流动（姑且不谈自由流动）是没有渠道的，资源的重新配置（姑且不谈优化配置）也是难以落实的。这一切充分说明了“短线顽症”的不可避免性。

ii. Problem 2: difficulties in mutual replacement between production factors in the second category of disequilibrium

As mentioned above, as long as production factors are able to replace each other, shortest-side factors can be eased with the help of longest side ones. This is not to say, however, that such replacement is absolute; rather, it is relative, and cannot work under all circumstances. Moreover, the replacement of one factor by another can either improve or reduce efficiency. Only when the margin of drop in efficiency caused by such replacement is narrower than that caused by the scarcity of the factors in question can such replacement be deemed feasible.

In an economy in equilibrium, whenever production factor replacement is possible, the price and cost-benefit ratio will motivate firms to alleviate the shortest-side syndrome by choosing effective methods for such replacement. In the first category of economic disequilibrium, replacement difficulties caused by inflexible prices and distorted price signals can be overcome by improving the market conditions and decontrolling the prices. However, the situation is worlds apart in the second category of economic disequilibrium, where the problem is not limited to the incomplete production-factor market. The fact that production factor suppliers and demanders are government appendages is more of a problem. For instance, when human resources are controlled by government quotas and sectioned to different departments, localities and firms, they are unable to make up for capital shortages even if replacement is possible. It is also necessary to make reinvestment and upgrade technology and equipment when there is a possibility of replacement between material production factors. On the one hand, because material production factors are supplied by some departments and localities, and demanded by others, it is hard to achieve supply-demand balance under intersected government administration. On the other, reinvestment involves problems concerning the investment system. If the old system continues, production factor replacement cannot take place. In a word, it is not easy for production factor replacement to be realized.

iii. Problem 3: hindrance to production factor reallocation in the second category of disequilibrium

We have noted that shortest-side factors can be compensated for through reallocating production factors. However, why is it so difficult to

（二）第二类非均衡经济中生产要素替代的困难

前面曾指出，如果经济中存在着短线，那么只要存在着生产要素的可替代性，以长线补短线，那么短线便可以缓和下来。当然，生产要素的可替代，并不是绝对的，而是有条件的，即唯有在一定条件下才能实现生产要素的替代。此外，生产要素替代的结果，既有可能使效率不受损失，也有可能使效率下降。假定生产要素的替代使效率下降的幅度小于因缺乏某种生产要素而导致的效率下降幅度，那么替代仍是可行的。

在经济均衡状态中，凡有可能实现生产要素替代的场合，价格因素以及由此决定的成本与收益比较将促使企业选择生产要素替代的有效方式，从而缓和短线问题。假定经济处于第一类非均衡状态，那么尽管生产要素的替代会因价格的不灵活与价格信号的扭曲而遇到困难，但通过市场的完善化与价格的放开，生产要素替代中的障碍是可以克服的。然而，在第二类非均衡条件下，情况便大不相同了。问题不仅在于生产要素市场的不完善，而主要在于一些生产要素的供给与需求同生产要素供给者与需求者依附于行政主管部门的状况联系在一起。比如说，在资金短缺而又可能以人力资源替代资金的场合，由于人力资源是被政府的数量配额所制约的，人力资源是被分割为部门持有、地方持有、单位持有的，于是生产要素替代便被置于难以实现的境地。又如，在某些物质的生产要素可以彼此替代的场合，往往需要追加投资、改造技术设备才能实现这种替代。但一方面，即使是物质的生产要素，由于它们分别由不同的部门和地方所提供，又被不同的部门和地方所需要，在条条块块分割的条件下，供求之间往往不易协调；另一方面，追加投资又必然涉及投资体制方面的问题，如果传统的投资体制不改革，生产要素的替代仍然难以实现。

（三）第二类非均衡经济中生产要素重组的障碍

前面也已经指出，经济中的短线问题还可以通过生产要素的重新组合来加以缓和。但问题在于：在第二类非均衡经济中，为什么生产

reallocate production factors in the second category of disequilibrium? Take the barrel again. Why is it so sturdy that it refuses to be torn apart and reassembled? Herein lays the key to studies in the ongoing Chinese economic growth and fluctuations.

Production factor reallocation calls for at least three conditions: first, well-defined property rights; second, smooth flow of production factors; and third, competence of the organizer of such reallocation.

The biggest reason why reallocation of production factors under the second category of disequilibrium is so difficult is that the first two conditions are not available. To be more specific, the second kind of disequilibrium is subject to ill-defined property rights under public ownership, business-government collusion, lack of responsibility for management, gains and losses, and lack of internal and external restraints on the part of firms. All these result in inefficient production factor flow, indeterminate beneficiaries of reallocation gains, and undefined risk bearers in such reallocation. These obstacles to reallocation arise when the first two conditions are not satisfied.

Judging from the third condition, the success of production factor reallocation lies in the organizer's proficiency for the task and ability to secure potential benefit from it. Who, then, is the eligible organizer in the second category of economic disequilibrium? As government appendages, firms have yet to become autonomous commodity producers, and are therefore not qualified. If firms cannot organize the reallocation of production factors, how about the government? It is not that the government cannot to do the job, but that it may not be able to fulfill the task in the absence of the first two conditions. Let me explain. If what is referred to here is the central government, it is powerful enough and in the possession of the means for such reallocation, but, as a macroeconomic regulatory institution, it cannot possibly be directly engaged in reallocating production factors. In fact, the government here refers to local authorities. Supposing a local government has difficulty in reallocating production factors due to institutional obstacles, to what extent can it break through those obstacles? Is it authoritative enough to overcome those obstacles? What's more, can a local government be highly efficient in directly organizing the reallocation of production factors? In

要素的重新组合如此困难？以木桶为例，为什么长短边不等的那个旧木桶如此牢固而不易拆开和重新组装？这正是在研究现阶段中国经济增长与经济波动时不能忽略的。

要实现生产要素的重新组合，至少需要三个条件：一是生产要素的产权十分明确；二是生产要素可以流动；三是生产要素的重新组合者是胜任此项工作的。

第二类非均衡经济中生产要素重新组合之所以困难，首先是由于上述第一个条件和第二个条件尚未具备。具体地说，第二类非均衡经济的特征是公有制的产权不够明确，政企不分，从而企业不能自主经营和自负盈亏，缺乏内在约束与外在约束。其结果，生产要素不易流动，生产要素重新组合后的收益归属不确定，生产要素重新组合过程中的风险承担责任不明确，这就是由于上述第一个条件和第二个条件不具备而导致的生产要素重新组合的困难。

再从上述第三个条件来看。生产要素重新组合的实现有赖于能够胜任生产要素重新组合工作并能因此获取潜在利益的生产要素重新组合者的存在。在第二类非均衡经济中，谁充任生产要素重新组合者？由于政企没有分开，企业尚未成为自主经营、自负盈亏的商品生产者，企业难以胜任生产要素重新组合者的工作。如果不由企业来重新组合生产要素，而由政府来重新组合生产要素，结果又将如何？当然，不是说不能由政府充当生产要素的重新组合者，而是说，在上述第一个条件和第二个条件未具备时，即使由政府来重新组合生产要素，也未必能实现这一任务。这是因为，如果这里所说的政府是中央政府，那么中央政府虽然有很大权威性，也有相应的重新组合生产要素的手段，但中央政府毕竟是中央政府，它起着宏观经济管理者的作用，不可能从事直接的生产要素重新组合工作。实际上，这里所说的政府主要是指各级地方政府。试问：地方政府在遇到体制上的种种障碍而难以重新组合生产要素时，究竟能在多大程度上打破这些障碍？地方政府的权威性是否足以打破这些障碍？再者，由地方政府来直接从事生产要素的重新组合工作是否

any case, it is difficult for any local government to be fully competent in the second category of economic disequilibrium. Thus, the third condition is not available either. Furthermore, whether the organizer is a firm or a government, reallocation of production factors can succeed only when it is handled by someone who is highly innovative and capable of organizing modern production. In fact, innovators and organizers of this type are rare, a fact that also accounts for what a difficult task allocating production factors can be in this nation.

IV. Production and circulation in economic growth

The relationship between production and circulation merits due attention. In analyzing economic growth factors, some authors tend to emphasize elements in the production field, such as investment quantity and its proportion in national income, the input-output ratio, the contribution of production factors (technology and human resources included) to economic growth, different combinations of production factors and their impact on corporate and macroeconomic returns. They tend to give a second seat to the circulation factor in economic growth in general and sustainable economic growth in particular. Three reasons may account for this analytical approach. First, they stress the decisive role of production in circulation to the neglect of the reaction of circulation to production. Second, they base their calculation of the economic growth rate on output value, as if increases in output value are equal to economic growth, regardless of the fact that the percentage of ineffective supply in output value cannot be counted as part of real economic growth. Third, insufficient attention to circulation and misunderstanding in the role of markets lead to inadequate understanding of circulation. Small wonder that circulation is held in a secondary seat in economic growth in these authors' analyses of economic fluctuations.

In the Chinese economy, however, the importance of circulation and consumption to production and distribution is becoming increasingly more pronounced in the traditional economic system's transition to a new one. It is because people's freedom and motivation in economic life are growing steadily. They are engaged in production to meet their needs. Those needs are satisfied on a daily basis through market transactions,

有效率？更重要的是，地方政府能否保证新的生产要素组合方式产生较高的效率？在第二类非均衡经济中，很难认为地方政府就一定能胜任生产要素重新组合工作。因此，这些情况说明了上述第三个条件同样是不具备的。加之，无论是企业充当生产要素的重新组合者还是政府充当生产要素的重新组合者，都需要有富于创新意识和现代生产组织能力的人来从事这项活动。而在中国的现实情况下，这样的创新者、组织者是远远不够的。这也可以从另一个侧面说明生产要素重新组合的困难。

四、经济增长过程中生产与流通之间的关系

在经济生活中，生产与流通之间的关系是值得研究的。一些著作在分析经济增长因素时，往往侧重于生产领域内的考察。这里包括：对投入的资金数量及其在国民收入中比例的考察，对投入与产出之间的比例的考察，对各种生产要素（包括技术、人力等）在经济增长中的贡献大小的考察，对生产要素组合方式及其对企业经济效益与宏观经济效益的作用等等。至于流通因素对经济增长，特别是对经济持续增长的影响，通常被置于较为次要的地位。造成这种情况的原因主要有三点。第一，只是片面地看到生产对流通的决定作用，而忽视了流通对生产的反作用。第二，以产值作为经济增长率计算的依据，似乎只要产值多了，就等于经济增长了，而不考虑产值中有多少是属于无效供给，而无效供给的增长是不能代表经济的实际增长的。第三，对流通因素的不重视与对市场作用的不理解，使得对流通的作用不认识或只有片面的认识。于是在经济增长与经济波动的分析中，流通因素的分析被置于次要地位就不足为奇了。

然而，在我国经济中，特别是在从传统经济体制向新的经济体制过渡的过程中，流通与消费对于生产与分配的重要性已经越来越明显。这是因为，在走向新的经济体制的道路上，人们在经济生活中的自主性、积极性不断增长。人从事生产，而生产是为了满足人的需要。人的需要日益靠市场上的交易行为得到满足，生产出来的

and more and more commodities are reaching people through the market. Commerce promotes production, coordinates distribution, ensures circulation and guides consumption. As to all the consumer goods, most of the public goods and a fair quantity of capital goods, the effectiveness of their supplies hinges on whether circulation can go smoothly. Poor circulation leads to ineffective supply, and goes further to hold back economic growth and give rise to major fluctuations.

The importance of circulation to economic growth is also evident in the flow and reallocation of production factors. Production factors fall into two categories: real ones and latent ones. The production factors that flow and reallocate through circulation are, first and foremost, real ones. And they are bound to activate latent ones. For instance, the full employment, free flow and reallocation of real labor resources will inevitably bring latent labor resources to the market to augment the real labor resources. The same is true with capital. If real capital is put to full use of and flows freely to effectively combine with other production factors, more latent capital will be brought forth. This is the way latent production factors are converted into real ones, to the benefit of economic growth. The role of circulation figures prominently in this regard in the current period of development in the Chinese economy. To maintain sustained economic growth in this country, which abounds in latent production factors but falls short in the supply of absolutely and relatively real ones, it is necessary to turn latent production factors into real ones through reform and hard work on circulation.

So much for the paramount importance of circulation to the Chinese economic life. In recent years, however, there has appeared an abnormal "debt chain" in circulation. Although this "debt chain" is directly related to economic austerity, overstocked inventory, shortage in capital investment and the ensuing overdue obligations to suppliers, however, we can understand it more profoundly and in a new light if we turn our attention to economic disequilibrium, the second category of it in particular.

The "debt chain" is not to be perceived merely as a result of an inordinate industrial or product structure. It is understood that this inordinateness can lead to sluggish sales, overstocked inventory and

各种商品将越来越多地通过市场来实现。商业起着促进生产、协调分配、保证流通、指导消费的作用。就所有的个人消费品、绝大多数公共消费品以及相当数量的生产资料而言，供给的有效性与流通领域内的工作是否顺利展开有密切的关系。流通渠道的不通畅，必定把本来可以成为有效供给的供给变成无效供给，进而阻碍着经济的增长，导致经济的较大波动。

流通对于经济增长的重要意义还可以从生产要素的流动和重新组合方面进行分析。要知道，生产要素分为现实的生产要素和潜在的生产要素两类。流通所促成的生产要素的流动和重新组合，首先是指现实的生产要素的流动和重新组合而言。但毫无疑问，现实的生产要素的流动和重新组合必将促使潜在的生产要素被动员出来。比如说，对现实的劳动力资源的充分利用，以及现实的劳动力资源得以在较大范围内自由流动和重新组合，必将导致潜在的劳动力资源投入市场，以增加现实的劳动力资源。资金的状况亦复如此。如果现实的资金得以充分利用，并得以自由流动，得以在效率增长的基础上同其他生产要素相结合，那么就会有更多的资金被动员出来。这些就是潜在的生产要素向现实的生产要素的转化，这种转化对经济增长是有利的。在我国现阶段，流通在这方面的作用尤其重要。由于我国存在着大量潜在的生产要素，于是在现实的生产要素不足（包括绝对意义上的不足和相对意义上的不足）的条件下，通过流通领域内的改革与努力开展工作，把潜在的生产要素转化为现实的生产要素，可以使经济持续增长。

关于流通问题在我国经济生活中的重要性，已如上述。但近年来，我们却在经济生活中发现了一种反常的现象，即"债务链"的存在。"债务链"虽然与经济紧缩、企业产成品积压、国家投资资金缺口的出现以及由此引起的企业之间的相互拖延货款有直接的关系，但如果我们把分析的重点转向经济的非均衡，特别是转向第二类非均衡，那么对流通领域出现的这一问题将会有新的、较深刻的认识。

不能把"债务链"仅仅看成是由于产业结构的不协调或产品结构的不协调所致。当然，产业结构、产品结构的不协调会使得一些企业的产成品滞销、积压，从而无法按期向交易的另一方支付货款。

overdue obligations to suppliers, but it is unfair to regard it as the fundamental cause behind the "debt chain." Inordinate industrial or product structure is nothing new, but why this "debt chain" has surfaced only in the last couple of years? What is more, why haven't we done anything about it? What has thrown the industrial or product structures off balance, or, in other words, what is the deep-seated cause behind the "debt chain"? Obviously, the answers cannot be found from structural inordinateness alone.

It is equally superficial to impute the "debt chain" to economic austerity. Austerity is nothing but a government policy, whereas the "debt chain" is deeply rooted in the economic system. It is thus unfair to blame the "debt chain" on a certain government policy, not to mention the fact that after this chain appeared, government policy has never stopped its move from austerity to relaxation, such as major increases in credit and loan grants. However, the loans issued to undo the "debt chain" never worked. It is all too obvious that austerity is not the culprit for the "debt chain."

In light of a study of the attributes of the second category of economic disequilibrium, the "debt chain" may be explained in this way: The development of a commodity economy is in direct conflict with government business collusion, which is a hallmark of this category of disequilibrium. Therefore, the "debt chain" was born of the contradiction between government-business collusion and the burgeoning commodity economy. To be more exact, without the commodity economy, government-business collusion would not have resulted in overdue obligations to suppliers, let alone a "debt chain." If government were detached from business, the "debt chain" would not appear no matter how fast the economic economy grows, not even when a temporary slump appeared. This is because when a creditor asks for repayment according to law, the debtor may liquidate his assets to honor the debt until he files for bankruptcy. However, this is not the case with present-day China. On the one hand, a commodity economy is emerging; and on the other, the second category of disequilibrium persists. That is to say, the long-standing government-business collusion is yet to give way. When transactions between firms are taking place in increased frequency, if A is overdue in payment to B, and B to C, the debtor-creditor relationship

但这绝不是造成“债务链”的基本原因。产业结构或产品结构的不协调已经好多年了，为什么以往不曾导致“债务链”而只是在近两年才出现“债务链”呢？再说，即使产业结构与产品结构不协调，那么为什么不能采取有效措施予以调整呢？造成产业结构与产品结构不协调的原因，也就是造成“债务链”的深层次原因是什么呢？可见，对这个问题的分析不能仅限于结构不协调的分析。

假定认为“债务链”主要是由经济紧缩引起的，那么这种看法同样较为肤浅。这是因为，经济的紧缩是一种政策措施，“债务链”有其深刻的经济体制背景，并非因某种政策措施而出现。何况，在出现“债务链”之后，政策就不断由“紧”向“松”转变，例如信贷投放大量增加。然而，为解开“债务链”而注入的贷款并没有起到预期的作用，“债务链”依然存在。这不恰好说明紧的经济政策不是形成“债务链”的主要原因么？

根据对第二类非均衡的特征的分析，应当对“债务链”问题作如下的解释：政企不分是第二类非均衡的基本特征，而商品经济的发展又是同政企不分这种状况直接冲突的，因此，“债务链”的根源在于政企不分与商品经济发展之间的矛盾。具体地说，假定商品经济不发展，这时即使政企没有分开，但不会引起企业与企业之间的债务拖欠，“债务链”也不会出现。假定政企已经分开了，那么即使商品经济发展很快，甚至出现了经济的暂时不景气，“债务链”也不会出现。债权的一方可以根据法律向欠债的一方索债；欠债的一方还不起债，就以资产清偿债务，直到破产还债。现阶段中国经济的特点则是：一方面，商品经济与过去相比已有较大的发展；另一方面，第二类非均衡依然存在。换言之，在现阶段的中国，由于商品经济已经有较迅速的发展，而政企不分则依然成为经济生活中的现象。于是在企业之间的交易日趋频繁的情况下，一旦由于某种原因而出现了甲企业对乙企业的货款拖欠、乙企业对丙企业的货款拖欠，欠债的企业与债权者之间的关系就复杂了。所有欠债的企业

can be very complicated. In government-business collusion, debtors are always backed by the government, so that creditors are not in a position to ask for due repayment, let alone demand for liquidating the assets. It is another story when a debtor is responsible for its own benefits and losses. This indicates that liability disputes between firms come down to disputes between government departments when the "debt chain" involves firms that are government appendages. Because such disputes cannot be settled by bankruptcies, the debts will be piled up, and the chain will grow in length with each passing day. Fundamentally speaking, the "debt chain" can never be eradicated if we fail to deepen corporate reform, detach government from business, and turn firms into commodity producers making their own business decisions and bearing their own profits and losses. In other words, the transition from the second category of disequilibrium to the first category of it must be accomplished at an early date to get rid of the "debt chain."

The nature of economic disequilibrium also sheds light on another major issue in the field of circulation, the issue of the outsourcing of circulation. Stable and sustained economic growth is determined not only by production, but also by circulation. Production bottlenecks, clogged circulation channels and ineffective supply all play a part in volatile economic fluctuations. Therefore, the outsourcing of circulation should become an indispensable part in our study of economic growth and fluctuations, the growth and fluctuations in the Chinese economy in particular.

At the first glance, clogged circulation channels bring about an overstock of some commodities and shortages of others, and strain supply. These problems merit attention, but they cannot be addressed by improving circulation alone. The outsourcing of circulation takes on a different meaning in economic disequilibrium from in economic equilibrium: In economic equilibrium, where the market is complete, prices are flexible, information transmission is smooth and firms are liable for their management decisions, benefits and losses, the outsourcing of circulation is inevitably characterized by free circulation of commodities at flexible prices and by production and sales in the interest of firms. In the first category of disequilibrium, firms are responsible for their own business management, benefits and losses. However, the market is incomplete, prices are inflexible, and information transmission is clogged.

的后台都是政府部门，债权者无法要求欠债的企业如期清偿债务，也无法实现以欠债的企业的资产来抵债。这种情况与欠债的一方是自负盈亏的企业是很不一样的。可见，只要“债务链”的各个环节上的企业是政企不分的企业，这些企业的后台都是政府部门，那么企业之间的债务纠纷实际上就是政府部门之间的一种纠纷，这种纠纷是不能靠破产还债的方式来解决的。于是债务越拖越多，“债务链”越拉越长。可见，这种债务无非是政企不分的企业欠政企不分的企业的债。要消除“债务链”，从根本上说，必须深化企业改革，使政企真正分开，使企业成为自主经营、自负盈亏的商品生产者，也就是使经济及早从第二类非均衡状态过渡到第一类非均衡状态。

从经济的非均衡性质可以进一步了解流通领域内的另一个重要问题，即流通的社会化问题。由于经济增长的持续与稳定不仅取决于生产因素，而且也取决于流通因素；由于经济的较大波动不仅来自生产领域内“瓶颈”的制约，而且也来自流通渠道的阻塞，来自供给的无效性，因此，对流通社会化问题的考察应当被视为经济增长与波动研究的一个不可缺少的组成部分。对当前中国经济增长与波动的研究尤其如此。

从现象上看，流通渠道不畅，某些商品的库存量过大而另一些商品的货源不足和供应紧张都值得注意，但不可能仅仅从流通渠道方面解决这些问题。在非均衡条件下，流通社会化的含义与均衡条件下是不相同的。如果经济处于均衡状态，市场完善，价格灵活，信息通畅，企业又是自主经营与自负盈亏的商品生产者，于是流通的社会化必然表现为价格放开条件下的自由流通与生产企业的自产自销。如果经济处于第一类非均衡状态，企业自主经营与自负盈亏，但市场不完善、价格不灵活、信息传递不通畅，这时，自由流通

As a result, free circulation will run up against obstacles. Firms will find it hard to organize production and sell their products on their own. In addition, supply or demand shortfalls will make it hard for market prices to play a due role in economic adjustment, so much so that such shortfalls must be eased, to some extent, with quantitative adjustment either by the government or by the market. The situation is much more complicated in the second category of disequilibrium. Apart from an incomplete market, inflexible prices, and clogged information transmission, firms are failing and yet to become autonomous. The disparity between supply and demand is more acute in capital goods than in consumption goods, and therefore, it is more pressing to develop capital goods than to procure more consumer goods. According to this interpretation, the outsourcing of circulation in the second category of disequilibrium should be interpreted in this way: We should develop all sorts of markets, capital goods markets in particular, while combining quantity regulation with price regulation in relevant markets, particularly in the markets for pivotal capital goods. Only thus can obstacles to circulation be lifted, and the effective combination of production factors optimized nationwide. The percentage of quantity quotas and that of price regulation should be decided in light of the degree of economic disequilibrium, because we can always make do with the second best choice where and when the first best choice is hard to come by. It is in accord with the principle of the second best choice to understand the outsourcing of circulation in economic disequilibrium from the perspective of combining quantity and price regulation. What merits attention here is that the replacement of price regulation with quantity regulation in economic disequilibrium is not the same as replacing complete competition with incomplete competition. Rather, it is the replacement of one kind of incomplete competition with another. In economic disequilibrium, there will never be a complete market, and therefore the effort to improve the market is invariably in conflict with quantity regulation. It is unrealistic to deny the existence of such a conflict and its effect on economic growth and fluctuations. In the current stage of economic development, what we should and can do is to improve the management of circulation as much as possible, dredge up the circulation channels, further the commercial reform to minimize obstacles to the outsourcing of circulation. In the meantime, we should also mitigate economic disequilibrium in multiple ways to ease the conflict between market improvement and quantity regulation.

将受到阻碍，生产企业的自产自销在客观上会遇到困难，供给缺口或需求缺口的存在使得市场的价格调节发挥不了应有的作用，从而必须在一定程度上依赖数量调节，包括政府的数量调节或市场自发的数量调节。如果经济处于第二类非均衡状态，情况便更加复杂。这时，除了市场不完善、价格不灵活、信息传递不通畅而外，企业也并非自主经营和自负盈亏的企业，企业活力是远远不足的，生产资料的供求矛盾通常比消费品的供求矛盾更为尖锐，发展生产资料市场也比发展消费品市场更为迫切。按照这种观点，在第二类非均衡条件下，流通社会化应当被理解为：发展各类市场，尤其是生产资料市场，在有关市场上尤其是在关键性的生产资料市场上采取数量调节与价格调节相结合的调节措施，以减少流通中的阻碍，促进社会范围内生产要素的有效组合。至于数量调节与价格调节各自所占的比重，则依据经济的非均衡程度来确定。这是因为，在没有条件实现最优选择的场合，次优选择将是可行的。在非均衡经济中，按数量调节与价格调节相结合的方式来理解流通的社会化，符合次优选择原则。在这里，一个应当注意的问题是：经济非均衡中数量调节对价格调节的替代并不是不完全竞争对完全竞争的替代，而是一种不完全竞争对另一种不完全竞争的替代。既然非均衡条件下的市场不可能是完全竞争的市场，那么市场的完善化同数量调节之间肯定存在一些矛盾，否认这些矛盾的存在及其对经济增长与经济波动的影响是不现实的。现阶段我们应该做到的和能够做到的，是尽量提高流通领域的管理水平，减少流通渠道中的阻塞，深化商业改革来缩小流通社会化的阻力，以及从多方面着手以减少经济的非均衡程度，从而达到缓解市场的完善化同数量调节之间的冲突。

We have elaborated on the restraining impact of circulation on economic growth and fluctuations, probed into the deep-seated causes behind the "debt chain," and elucidated the need to outsource circulation in economic disequilibrium. Thus, we are able to better understand the economic growth and fluctuations in China in two ways:

Firstly, observed from the viewpoint of circulation alone, the profound impact of the second category of disequilibrium on the realm of circulation has clearly become a potent restraint on economic growth and an essential cause behind fluctuations. Only by taking into consideration the effect of the second category of disequilibrium on both production and circulation can the economic growth and fluctuations in this country be better interpreted.

Secondly, from our observations of circulation we can arrive at this conclusion: If, instead of proceeding from invigorating our companies to push economic restructuring, we allow government-business collusion to persist in the long run, sustained economic growth will be out of the question, and major fluctuations will become unavoidable. This fully bears out what economic restructuring is all about in the second category of disequilibrium.

V. Thoughts on normal and abnormal fluctuations

The topic of this study being fluctuations in economic disequilibrium rather than in equilibrium, we are confronted with the issue of normal and abnormal fluctuations. Fluctuations are always deemed abnormal in economic equilibrium, where normal fluctuations are nonexistent. However, it is the other way round in disequilibrium, where gaps in either supply or demand are a common occurrence, and the market can bridge such gaps but cannot root them out. That is to say, disequilibrium is essentially balance with nonzero unemployment rate and nonzero inflation rate. To put it differently, disequilibrium is a kind of equilibrium that is accompanied by a certain unemployment rate or a certain inflation rate (or a balance with certain demand shortfalls and certain supply shortfalls).

Any economic gap can be interpreted as "shortage." For instance, a rise in prices, which means that excess money is chasing commodities that are in short supply, can be termed as "commodity shortage." Unemployment, which indicates that many workers are hunting for a few

以上我们着重探讨了非均衡条件下流通对经济增长与经济波动的制约，对我国近年来出现的"债务链"的深层次原因进行了分析，并对非均衡经济中的流通社会化问题作了解释。通过这些论述，我们对当前我国的经济增长与经济波动问题有了进一步的认识:

第一，即使单独从流通的角度来考察，我国经济所处的第二类非均衡的性质对流通领域的深刻影响也已成为制约经济增长与经济波动的有力因素。而只有把第二类非均衡的性质对生产领域的影响与对流通领域的影响综合起来考察，才能更好地说明我国经济增长与波动的特征。

第二，从流通领域的考察可以得出如下的结论，即如果不从增强企业活力着手进行经济体制改革，而听任政企不分的状况长期存在，那么不仅无法导致经济的持续增长，而且也无法避免经济的较大波动。这充分说明了第二类非均衡条件下经济体制改革的特点。

五、关于正常波动与非正常波动的思考

由于我们所要研究的是非均衡条件下的经济波动，而不是均衡条件下的经济波动，因此，我们不得不涉及正常波动与非正常波动的问题。这是因为，在均衡条件下，一切经济波动都可以被认为是非正常的，正常波动实际上并不存在。然而，在非均衡条件下，情况与此显然不同。非均衡条件下，或者存在着经常性的供给缺口，或者存在着经常性的需求缺口，市场的作用只表现为使缺口有所缩小，而不能使缺口消失。也就是，非均衡实质上是一种非零失业率与非零通货膨胀的均衡，即非均衡实质上是伴随着一定的失业率或一定的通货膨胀的均衡（伴随着一定的需求缺口或一定的供给缺口的均衡）。

我们可以把经济中的任何缺口都用"短缺"二字来表示。如果经济中出现的是物价上涨，那么这表明有过多的货币在追求较少的商品，从而可以用商品短缺来表示。如果经济中出现的是失业，

jobs, can be expressed as "job shortage." Similarly, undercapitalization denotes a "fund shortage," while overcapitalization points to "shortage in investment outlets." A bottleneck in resource supply indicates "shortage of a certain resource," while idle resources indicate "shortage of resource users." Since any gap can be regarded as a shortage, there must be two kinds of shortages in economic disequilibrium—normal shortages and abnormal shortages.

As stated above, normal shortages are common and inevitable in economic disequilibrium. However, it does not mean that a certain shortage cannot be eliminated by any means, but that one shortage can be eliminated probably at the cost of another shortage that causes even a greater loss in efficiency. For instance, a 2 percent unemployment rate is an indicator of a normal shortage of jobs, but someone insists to eliminate this normal unemployment rate. We are not saying that he has no way of accomplishing it, but that in doing so, some firms may be overstaffed and suffer major efficiency losses. In other words, the normal job shortage is eradicated in return for a higher disguised unemployment rate and a greater loss in efficiency.

We may follow a similar line of thinking to prove how a visible inflation rate that is within a normal range of shortage in economic disequilibrium is made to disappear in return for an increased disguised inflation rate and a major efficiency loss. From this analysis, we can see that the alert line for macroeconomic operation in disequilibrium cannot be marked with zero shortages (zero unemployment rate, zero inflation rate, etc.). The alert line in question is designed to guide government regulation. When the economy runs below this line, there is no need to take action. Only when the economy surges above the line should the government take appropriate steps to regulate it. Under disequilibrium, the position of the alert line is directly relevant to the extent of normal shortages. Assuming there is a zero shortage level in the economy (zero unemployment rate, zero inflation rate, etc.), the alert line must be somewhere above this level. The space between the two lines represents normal shortage; the space above the alert line is abnormal shortage, as is shown in Figure 1:

那么这表明有过多的劳动者在追求较少的工作岗位，从而可以用工作岗位短缺表示。同样的道理，资金不足意味着资金的短缺，而资金过剩则意味着投资场所的短缺；资源供给中“瓶颈”的存在意味着相应的资源的短缺，而经济中的资源闲置则意味着相应的资源使用单位（资源用户）的短缺等等。既然任何缺口都可以用短缺来表示，那么在非均衡条件下，必然存在着两种短缺，一是正常短缺，一是非正常短缺。

如上所述，在非均衡条件下，正常短缺是不足为奇的，也是难以避免的。当然，这并不是说无法以任何手段来消除某一种短缺；而是说，假定要消除非均衡经济中的正常短缺，那么很可能要为此作出较大的牺牲，即必须以另一种效率损失更大的短缺作为代价，才能使某一种正常短缺消失。比如说，假定经济中的正常工作岗位短缺表现为失业率 2%，这一失业率（2%）就是正常的工作岗位短缺度。如果硬要采取措施来消除这 2% 的失业率，即让失业者全部就业，那并不是说无法做到这一点，但要这样做，就可能造成一些工作场所的人浮于事，从而造成效率的较大损失。换言之，在上述情况下，正常短缺度之内的公开失业率的消失，是以隐蔽失业率的增长、效率的较大损失作为代价的。

我们也可以按类似的方式来分析非均衡条件下属于正常短缺度之内的公开通货膨胀率的消失如何以隐蔽通货膨胀率的增长、效率的较大损失作为代价。根据以上的分析，非均衡条件下宏观经济运行的“警戒线”不可能是一条以零短缺度（零失业率、零通货膨胀率等）为界的“警戒线”。这里所说的“警戒线”是指政府调节所依据的线。如果经济运行在“警戒线”以下，政府不需要调节；只有经济运行在“警戒线”以上时，政府才需要按照具体的情况采取适当的调节措施，对经济的运行进行协调。非均衡条件下的“警戒线”的位置与正常短缺度的大小直接有关。假定在经济中有一条零短缺度（零失业率、零通货膨胀率等）的线，这条线并不是非均衡条件下的警戒线。“警戒线”在这条零短缺度的线之上，二者之间有一段距离，这就是正常短缺度。“警戒线”之上，则是非正常短缺度。可以用下面的简图来表示（见图 1）。

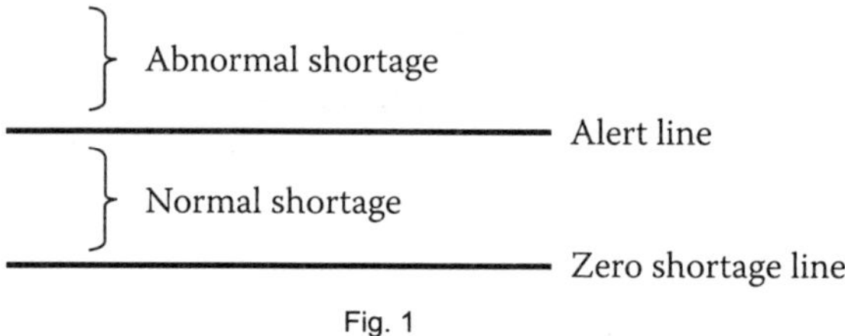

Fig. 1

In the book *Strategic Choice for Prosperity* by Li Yining and others, the concept of "alert line" is explained in Chapter 8, "The integration of planning and market mechanism in resource allocation": There are two alert lines—the first alert line and the second alert line. The first line sets the boundary between market regulation and government-planned regulation. The second line runs above the first one. Whether the government should give priority to direct regulation or indirect regulation depends on the space above the first alert line. When the economy operates between the two lines, it comes mainly under indirect government regulation. When it runs above the second alert line, it is evidence that indirect regulation has not achieved desired results and, therefore, it is time to shift the emphasis to direct regulation in place.[7]

With a second alert line added to Figure 1, Figure 2 is drawn. The alert line featured in Figure 1 is presented as the "first alert line" in Figure 2:

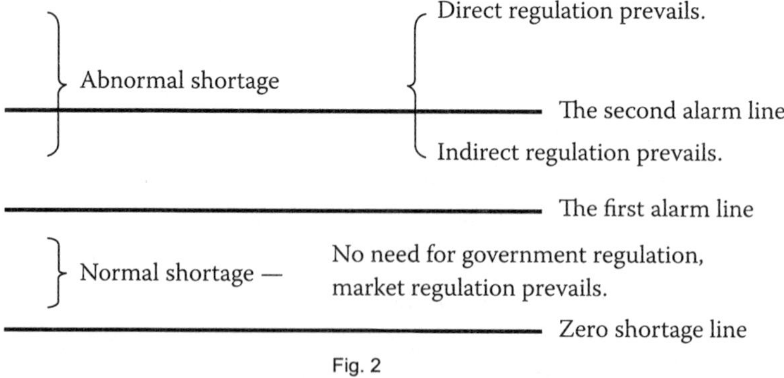

Fig. 2

In *Strategic Choice for Prosperity*, an additional explanation is made: "Whether it is indirect regulation or direct regulation that prevails, the adoption of planned quotas should not be excluded when restraints on resource become strong and shortages run high, and changes in market prices and supply and demand must be followed."[8]

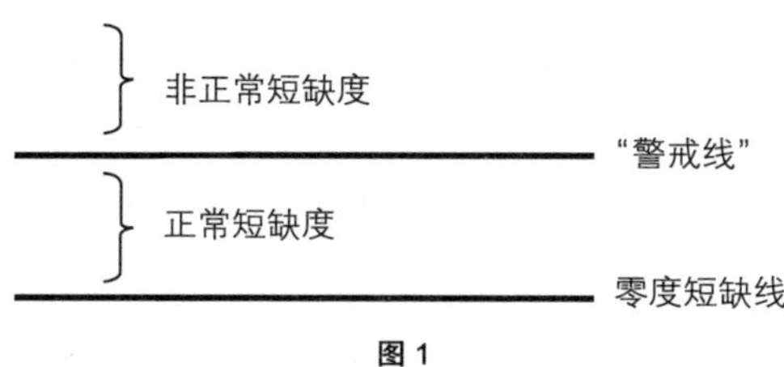

图 1

在厉以宁等所著《走向繁荣的战略选择》一书第八章"计划与市场在资源配置中的结合"中，对"警戒线"概念作了如下的表述：有两条"警戒线"，即"第一警戒线"与"第二警戒线"。"第一警戒线"是用以表明市场调节与计划调节之间的界限的，"第二警戒线"是在"第一警戒线"之上的又一条"警戒线"。究竟政府的计划调节是以直接调节为主还是以间接调节为主，则需要视超出"第一警戒线"的情况而定。在"第一警戒线"与"第二警戒线"之间，政府的计划调节以间接调节为主，而当"第二警戒线"被突破后，这表明以间接为主的调节方式未能达到预定的调节目标，所以有必要转为以直接调节为主。[7]

图 1 中所标出的"警戒线"，相当于这里所提到的"第一警戒线"。这里，在加上"第二警戒线"之后，将得出下面这个简图（见图 2）。

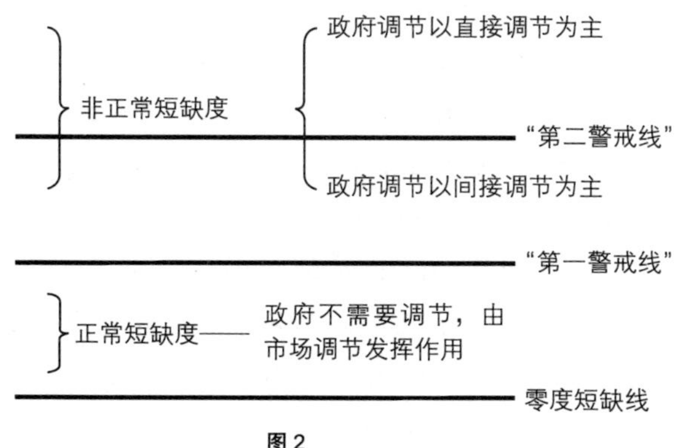

图 2

在《走向繁荣的战略选择》一书中，对此曾说明如下："这里所说的间接调节为主或直接调节为主时，都不排除少数产品在资源约束程度较强而短缺度较高时，需要采取计划配额；也不排除在进行间接调节和直接调节时，需要参照市场价格和市场供求的变动情况。"[8]

As shown in Figure 2, the second alert line divides abnormal shortages into two sections. Let us call the section between the second and the first alert lines "abnormal shortage I," where the government gives priority to indirect regulation. The section above the second alert line is dubbed "abnormal shortage II," where the government gives priority to direct regulation. If abnormal shortage in the economy is serious enough to necessitate forceful intervention, the government can turn to the "last resort," unconventional intervention in the economy. The reservation of this "last resort" testifies to the government's resolve and strength to regulate the economy—it will never look on with folded arms as the economy goes from bad to worse.[9]

This can be shown in Figure 3:

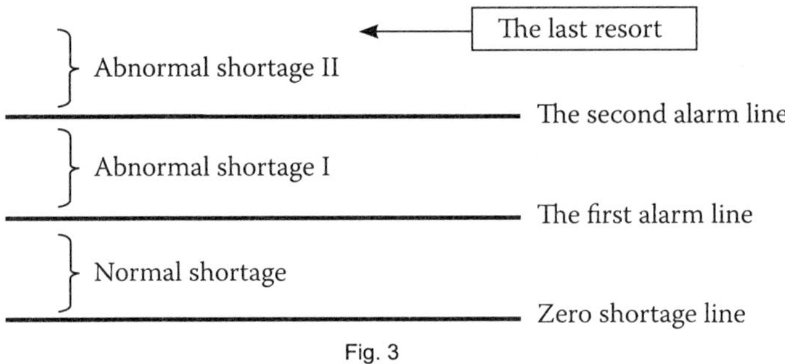

Fig. 3

With these concepts in mind—zero shortage line, normal shortage, abnormal shortage I, abnormal shortage II, the first alert line and the second alert line—we gain a better understanding of what normal fluctuations and abnormal fluctuations are all about.

What are normal fluctuations in economic disequilibrium? We can reach this preliminary conclusion: When the economy operates above the zero shortage line and below the first alert line—that is, within the scope of normal shortage—fluctuations are normal.

What about abnormal fluctuations in economic disequilibrium? We can also arrive at the following preliminary conclusion: When the economy operates above the second alert line but is still within the scope of abnormal shortage II, fluctuations are abnormal.

Figure 3 indicates that the section between the zero shortage line and the first alert line represents normal shortage. When the economy runs

以上，“第二警戒线”把非正常短缺度分为两部分。“第二警戒线”与“第一警戒线”之间的非正常短缺度，可以称为“非正常短缺度 I”。这时，政府的调节以间接调节为主。“第二警戒线”以上的非正常短缺度，可以称为“非正常短缺度 II”。这时，政府的调节以直接调节为主。如果经济中的非正常短缺度达到了非常严重的地步，以至于政府必须采取更强有力的干预措施，那么，政府可以动用“最后手段”，也就是非常规的干预经济的手段。“最后手段”的存在及备用，表明了政府调节经济的决心和力量，表明了政府绝不会听任经济无休止地恶化下去。[9]

于是可以得出下面的简图（见图 3）。

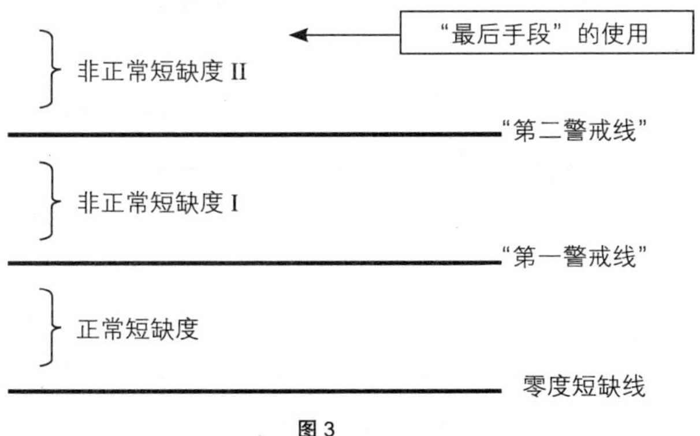

图 3

现在，我们在明确了零短缺度线、正常短缺度、非正常短缺度 I、非正常短缺度 II、“第一警戒线”与“第二警戒线”等概念之后，就可进而理解正常波动与非正常波动了。

什么是非均衡条件下经济的正常波动？我们可以初步做出这样的判断：尽管经济运行离开了零短缺度线，但只要经济运行仍然在正常短缺度的范围内波动，而没有突破“第一警戒线”，那么这样的经济波动可以被视为正常波动。

什么是非均衡条件下经济的非正常波动？我们也可以初步做出这样的判断：经济运行突破了“第二警戒线”，而在非正常短缺度 II 的范围内波动，那么这样的经济波动可以被视为非正常波动。

如图 3 所示，零短缺度线与“第一警戒线”之间是正常短缺度，

within this range, normal fluctuations in economic disequilibrium occur; what happens in the section above the second alert line is abnormal shortage II, in which abnormal fluctuations in disequilibrium take place. This poses the question: Are fluctuations normal or abnormal when the economy operates between the first and second alert lines? Further analysis is needed to give a reasonable answer.

Fluctuations are usually indicated with changes in the economic growth rate. However, the economic growth rate cannot accurately reflect shortages. A high growth rate can be achieved under both normal and abnormal shortages, and so can a low growth rate. Therefore, when studying the economy's performance in a specific year or a period of years, we find it hard to discover the close ties between economic growth rate and the degree of shortages. In addition, changes in the degree of shortages are concealed when fluctuations are measured by economic growth rate. Therefore, if we judge whether fluctuations are normal or not merely by changes in economic growth rate, we are courting two mistakes.

First, fluctuations seem to have nothing to do with economic disequilibrium. The difference between normal and abnormal fluctuations under disequilibrium conditions is concealed in the changes of economic growth rate. Thus we cannot see through fluctuations and predict their future course of development.

Second, a high economic growth rate can be achieved in the presence of abnormal shortages, whereas a low growth rate may happen amidst normal shortages. This being the case, if we judge fluctuations on the basis of growth rate changes, we will probably go astray in attempting to maintain a high economic growth rate by expanding abnormal shortages instead of maintaining a low growth rate by curtailing such shortages.

Obviously, we cannot jump to a conclusion on normal or abnormal fluctuations in economic disequilibrium simply according to changes in economic growth rate. Rather, we should base our observation on changes in the degree of shortages.

We will get a clearer picture of this if we observe the economy for a longer period of time. This is because, supposing the economy operates

经济运行在这个范围内，呈现着非均衡条件下经济的正常波动；"第二警戒线"以上是非正常短缺度 II，经济运行在非正常短缺度 II 的范围内，波动是非均衡条件下经济的非正常波动。那么，当经济运行在"第一警戒线"与"第二警戒线"之间时，这样的经济波动是非均衡条件下的正常波动还是非正常波动？这个问题需要进一步分析，而不能简单地认定是正常波动还是非正常波动。

我们知道，经济波动通常按经济增长率的变动来表示。经济增长率与经济生活中的短缺度并不是同一个概念。经济增长率大小并不能准确地反映短缺度。比如说，经济增长率高，既可能是在正常短缺的范围内实现的，也可能是在非正常短缺的范围内实现的。与此相似，低的经济增长率既可能在非正常短缺的范围内实现，也可能在正常短缺的范围内实现。因此，当我们就个别年份或少数年份进行考察时，我们通常难以发现经济增长率与短缺度之间的紧密联系，而且使用经济增长率的大小作为衡量经济波动的依据还掩盖了短缺度的变动率。如果我们简单地以经济增长率变动的状况作为经济正常波动与非正常波动的判断标志，那么不可避免地会导致两个错误。

第一，这一切似乎与经济的非均衡性质无关。非均衡条件下的正常短缺与非正常短缺之间的区别在经济增长率变动的形式下被掩盖了，于是既说明不了波动的真相，更看不出波动的趋势。

第二，由于经济增长率高有可能在非正常短缺的范围内实现，而经济增长率低却有可能在正常短缺的范围内实现，因此，在依据经济增长率变动来判断经济波动时，特别是在制定消除经济波动的对策时，有可能把人们引入错误的途径，即宁肯以非正常短缺度的增大来维持较高的经济增长率，而不愿以非正常短缺度的缩小来维持较低的经济增长率。

由此可见，在判断非均衡条件下经济的正常波动与非正常波动时，不能简单地以经济增长率的变动情况或经济增长率的大小作为依据，而应当以短缺度的变动情况或短缺的多少作为依据。

如果按较长一段时间来分析，对这一点会有更清楚的认识。这是因为，在非均衡条件下，假定经济持续在非正常短缺度的

within the range of abnormal shortages under disequilibrium conditions, problems caused by such shortages will definitely affect economic growth rate and betray themselves in the form of marked fluctuations.

Now let us return to the previous question: Is it normal or abnormal fluctuation under disequilibrium when the economy operates between the first and second alert lines? The answer should be based on changes in shortages during an extended period of economic growth. There are two scenarios:

The first scenario: The economy has been operating within a normal shortage range, and economic growth has been achieved on this basis. If the economy runs above the first alert line and fluctuates between the two alert lines, such fluctuations are deemed abnormal.

The second scenario: The economy has been operating within abnormal shortage II, that is, above the second alert line, and economic growth has been achieved on that basis. If the economy operates between the two alert lines and fluctuates within abnormal shortage I, it is considered a normal fluctuation, because compared to the previous period, the economic fluctuations are moving towards normalcy. (*Translated by Zhong Zhilan*)

— A speech at a meeting to summarize the "Growth Theories and Mathematical Models of the Chinese Economy," a National Natural Science Foundation of China research project, on March 21, 1993

范围内运行，因非正常短缺而造成的困难必定使经济增长率受到影响，经济增长必定会有较大的起落，经济的波动也就必定明显地表现出来。

现在让我们回到前面提出的问题上来，即经济运行在“第一警戒线”与“第二警戒线”之间时，究竟是非均衡条件下的正常波动还是非正常波动？这就需要根据较长时间经济增长过程中短缺度的大小来判断。有两种不同的情形：

一种情形是：前一时期的经济运行于正常短缺度的范围内，经济增长一直是在正常短缺度的基础上实现的。这时，如果经济运行突破了“第一警戒线”，并且在“第一警戒线”与“第二警戒线”之间波动，那么可以认为这是一种非正常的波动。

另一种情形是：前一时期的经济运行于非正常短缺度 II 的范围内，即运行于“第二警戒线”之上，经济增长一直是在非正常短缺度 II 的基础上实现的。这时，如果经济运行落到了“第一警戒线与”与“第二警戒线”之间，即在非正常短缺度 I 的范围内波动，那么可以认为这是一种正常的波动，因为相对于前一时期而言，经济波动已逐渐趋向于正常了。

（1993 年 3 月 21 日在国家自然科学基金项目“中国经济增长理论及数学模型”总结会上的报告）

PROPERTY RIGHTS REFORM OF RURAL ENTERPRISES (1994)

I

More and more people are coming to terms with the importance of rural enterprises to the Chinese economy, an importance that has been borne out by reality. The reform of large and medium-sized state enterprises and the development of rural enterprises are part and parcel of the effort to reshape the microeconomic foundation of the socialist market economy being developed in this nation. Academic discussions are elaborate and thorough concerning the property rights reform of large and medium-sized state enterprises, but somewhat lacking on the significance of similar reform of rural enterprises and the approaches to it. Indeed, discussions about the latter have merely touched upon the development of the "joint-stock cooperative system." In truth, the property rights reform of rural enterprises is no less important and difficult than that of state enterprises. Moreover, the term "joint-stock cooperative system" is yet to be clarified. All this necessitates some in-depth study.

To begin with, we should not take the burgeoning development of rural enterprises over the recent years for granted. Rather, we should contemplate the role of the market in the survival and development of these enterprises, and look at the question of what is to be done to adapt them further to the market.

Rural enterprises have no lack of competitors. On the home market, they compete with each other, but their competition comes mainly from state enterprises, large urban collectives[1], private businesses, equity joint ventures with Chinese and foreign investment, and imported commodities. After a rural enterprise is built or expanded, its managers must think about where its market is, how to carve out a niche in the market for its products, and how to expand its market shares.

Rural enterprises cannot count on local governments for incentives or fringe benefits. They are mistaken if they believe that local governments can help them secure local markets, bar the entry of outsiders, monopolize local supply of raw materials, and prevent local raw materials from being shipped to other areas. This is because local protectionism runs counter to market economy principles, and, judging from the

论乡镇企业的产权改革（1994）

一

在当前的中国经济中，乡镇企业的重要性已经越来越被实践所证实，也已经越来越被人们所认识。在建立社会主义市场经济的过程中，改造原有的国有大中型企业和发展乡镇企业都是重新塑造社会主义市场经济微观基础的基本内容。关于国有大中型企业产权改革的意义，学术界讨论得比较充分，也比较具体。相比之下，对乡镇企业产权改革的意义与做法，就不那么充分，或者只提及发展“股份合作制”。其实，乡镇企业产权改革的重要性和这一改革中可能遇到的困难，并不亚于国有大中型企业的产权改革；而且，“股份合作制”一词的含义也不很明确，所以在这个领域内有深入研讨的必要。

首先，我们不能只注意近年来乡镇企业迅速发展的事实，而应该考虑市场环境对乡镇企业存在与发展的作用，考虑乡镇企业如何进一步适应市场的问题。

乡镇企业有不少竞争对手。在国内市场上，其竞争对手主要是国有企业、原来的城市“大集体”企业、中外合资企业、私营企业以及其他乡镇企业。此外，进口的商品也同乡镇企业的商品有竞争关系。乡镇企业建立和扩大生产规模后，必须考虑到自己的市场究竟在哪里，怎样才能使自己的产品在市场上占有一席之地，并使自己的产品在市场中所占的份额越来越大。

乡镇企业不能指望地方政府的特殊照顾、额外的优惠。如果乡镇企业把希望寄托于地方政府用行政干预的方式来保证本地的市场，排斥外地的企业进入本地的市场，或垄断本地的原材料供应，限制本地的原材料输往外地，那么，一方面，地方政府的这种保护本地乡镇企业的做法是与市场经济的原则相悖的。这种做法无论

requirements of either the planned economy or the market economy, is bound to be ditched. From the perspective of the planned economy, the practice of monopolizing the supply of raw materials and carving up local markets among local businesses flies in the face of the principle of centralization and of quota-based distribution. From the perspective of the market economy, local protectionism violates the principle of fair and square market competition and market unification. In the short run, this protectionist practice may benefit rural enterprises, but in the long run, it is wrong in that it protects backwardness, strangles businesses, and can backfire on rural enterprises themselves. Enterprises must grow in strength through market competition, because their survival hinges on product quality, profitability, and creativity.

If flexible business mechanisms can stand rural enterprises in good stead when competing with enterprises under the planned economy (state enterprises and big urban collectives), that competitive edge can do them little good when they are pitted against equity joint ventures and private enterprises. Competition between rural enterprises themselves can be tough, too, as their competitiveness is neutralized by the common business mechanisms they employ and the common incentives they receive from local governments. Market competition is merciless; its result is always the same: In the course of it, some rural enterprises collapse, some grow in strength, and new ones keep appearing.

Therefore, it is reasonable to conclude that market conditions are the test of rural enterprises. Today, such enterprises are burgeoning everywhere in the country. Will this robust development grow to disastrous proportions? Under central planning, fast proliferation of rural enterprises would have been the undoing of the national economy. However, that was then, this is now. The rural enterprises we have today are worlds apart from their predecessors in that they must face the market and be tested by it. The underdogs in market competition are doomed. Their predecessors might have still been muddling along under central planning and gone on consuming all sorts of resources no matter how inefficient they were and how deeply they sank into debt. The test of the market was always there, but under central planning, businesses could ignore such a test or stay impervious to it. Not so for the rural

按计划经济体制的要求来看，还是按市场经济体制的要求来看，都必定受到抵制，必定行不通。这是因为，从计划经济体制的角度看，地方垄断原材料供应和分割市场的做法不符合计划经济的高度集中原则、计划配额原则；而从市场经济体制的角度看，这种做法违背了市场公平竞争原则，违背了市场统一化的原则。另一方面，地方政府的这种保护本地乡镇企业的做法即使有可能在短时间内给这些乡镇企业带来某种好处。但从长期看，从根本利益上看，这种做法是不利于乡镇企业的发展的，因为这是一种保护落后和扼杀企业生命力的错误做法。乡镇企业应当在市场竞争中成长、壮大，企业的真正生命力在于自己的产品质量，在于自己的经济效益，在于自己的创新能力。

如果说乡镇企业在同计划经济体制下的企业（如国有企业、城市“大集体”企业）竞争时，可以凭借自己的机制灵活而占有一定优势的话，那么在同中外合资企业、私营企业竞争时，这种优势就不存在了。特别是乡镇企业之间相互竞争时，由于彼此都有相同的经营机制，而且也都能得到本地政府部门的优惠政策的照顾，任何一家乡镇企业的优势也就无法显示出来。市场竞争是无情的。竞争的结果，总会有一批乡镇企业垮掉，有一批乡镇企业发展壮大，还会出现一批新的乡镇企业。

由此可以断言，市场是乡镇企业的检验者。各地都兴建了乡镇企业，乡镇企业的数量越来越多。乡镇企业的数量这么多，发展速度这么快，会不会给国民经济带来灾难呢？对这个问题，可以这样看：假定处于计划经济体制之下，企业数量过多，发展速度过快，肯定使得国民经济承受不了；然而，目前的乡镇企业与计划经济体制下的企业是不一样的，乡镇企业必须面向市场，经受市场的检验。如果在竞争中失败，乡镇企业就会垮掉。而计划经济体制下的企业则不然，即使效益差，亏损累累，企业照样可以存在，照样消耗各种资源。因此，市场的检验固然是客观存在的，但计划经济体制下的企业却不在乎市场的这种检验，甚至可以说它们不惧怕市场

enterprises of today. They are sensitive to the test of the market because their survival is on the line. They must strive to raise economic efficiency and produce nothing but what the market needs. In other words, under central planning, the existence of too many losing companies was a disaster to the national economy because they could be established but were not allowed to die, they were allowed to hang around but not allowed to disappear. By contrast, rural enterprises today are allowed to rise or fall of their own accord; those doing poorly are phased out without mercy; the national economy is immune to fluctuations caused by drastic increases in the number of rural enterprises; and society is in no danger of turmoil when large numbers of such enterprises collapse. This being the case, if people are saying there are too many enterprises, that is because too many ill-managed enterprises are still dragging along under old-fashioned central planning and because too few enterprises can measure up to market requirements and stand the test of the market. If people are saying enterprises are growing too fast, we know they are complaining about the unbridled development of enterprises that are insensitive to market changes and never bother to cater their production to market demand, while enterprises that produce only for the market and whose products sell briskly on the market are not growing fast enough. Rural enterprises of today belong in the latter category.

II

I deem it necessary to say something about repetitious construction. Should repetitious construction be discontinued? Generally speaking, it should be disallowed. This is because with a given supply of resources, repetitious production is synonymous with waste, or unwarranted use of resources that serves nothing but to aggravate the already strained supply. With a given level of market purchase power, repetitious construction or production often means that, for lack of demand, some products become a drag on the market or are stockpiled, which again is tantamount to wasting or abusing resources. This double waste or abuse of resources is a cost or a menace that repetitious construction poses for the economy.

When censuring repetitious production, people tend to lump rural enterprises in with it, as if there were an indissoluble bond between the rise and expansion of these enterprises and repetitious production. Yet they have forgotten what really matters with such production is not whether an enterprise is rural or state-owned, but whether it has changed

的检验，它们对于市场的检验是麻木不仁、无动于衷的。而乡镇企业对于市场的检验却十分敏感，经不起市场检验的将被淘汰，这就迫使乡镇企业努力提高经济效益，努力生产市场所需要的产品。换句话说，计划经济体制之下，企业多了而企业效益又不佳，那就必定给国民经济带来灾难；因为企业只能生，不能死，只能存，不能亡。而乡镇企业则既能生，又能死，既能存，又能亡。效益差的乡镇企业将被无情地淘汰，国民经济就不会因乡镇企业数目增加而波动，社会也不会因乡镇企业中一批效益差的企业的倒闭而发生较大的震荡。从这一角度来看，我们不能不得出这样的结论：如果说企业多了，那是指计划经济体制下的无效益企业多了，而适应市场经济要求和经得起市场检验的企业还不够多；如果说企业发展快了，那是指对市场不敏感，从而不面向市场而进行生产的企业的发展过快，而那些面向市场进行生产并受到市场欢迎的企业的发展速度还不够快。乡镇企业就属于后一类企业。

二

这里，需要对重复建设一词做一些分析。重复建设是不是必须取缔呢？一般说来，不应该从事重复建设，不容许重复建设的现象发生。这是因为，在资源供给为既定的条件下，重复建设意味着资源的浪费、资源的不合理利用，从而使本来就紧张的资源供给更加紧张。此外，在市场购买力为既定的条件下，重复建设意味着总有一些产品因缺乏市场而滞销积压，这同样是资源的浪费、资源的不合理利用。资源的双重浪费、双重不合理使用，这就是重复建设的代价或重复建设对经济的危害。

人们有时在谴责重复建设时，把乡镇企业同重复建设挂上钩，似乎乡镇企业的建立和扩大生产规模同重复建设之间结下了不解之缘；而忘却了同重复建设有着最密切关系的不在于企业是属于乡镇

its operational mechanisms and whether its investment system is new or old. Rural enterprises are flexible in management, and they make their own business decisions while bearing their own gains and losses. Common sense tells us that repetitious production is a losing cause because it inevitably strains resource supply, inflates production costs, and inhibits sales because of the market's limited purchasing power. Rural enterprises do not meddle in repetitious production in the same way that a man never bangs his head against a wall, knowing perfectly well that such an action spells nothing but headache. By contrast, enterprises that do not have to bear the consequence of investment risks under central planning may willingly go after large production scales and as many production projects as possible at all costs, even if such investment brings no returns at all. The crux of the issue is precisely whether an investing enterprise is accountable for the investment risks it chooses to run. Rural enterprises do not embrace redundant production because they can, of their own accord, shun investment and redundant production projects that bring no economic returns.

From a macroeconomic point of view, we should go a little further in our observation of what people really want out of repetitious production. The term generally refers to building a new factory to make a product that someone else is already making. It is a typical behavior of waste. But the question here is: Does banning repetitious production protect monopoly and backwardness? Is repetitious construction detrimental to the national economy on all occasions? Should competition be allowed between manufacturers of the same product? Take, for instance, a certain product being manufactured by a factory, which is in short supply and leaves a considerable market share to be filled. The dilemma here is whether to allow the factory to expand production or to build a new one to make up for the shortage. In this case, construction of a new factory should obviously not be regarded as repetitious. Again, if the factory already in existence can meet market demand for the product in question but its price is too high and its quality leaves something to be desired, whereas the same product to be made by the factory to be built will be better in quality and lower in price, is it wise to allow the existing factory to monopolize the product and bar the participation of the new factory? It simply does not make sense to tolerate one factory making an inferior product and reject another factory that can offer the same product with a

企业还是国有企业，而是企业的经营机制是否转换了，投资体制是新的还是旧的。乡镇企业有着自己的灵活机制，既自主经营，又自负盈亏。如果明知是重复建设的项目，资源供应紧张就必定导致生产成本的上升，市场购买力有限就必定导致销售困难，结果必定是得不偿失，那么谁会硬往重复建设的墙壁上撞呢？乡镇企业是不会往这堵墙上撞的，因为它们知道硬撞的后果是自己的倒闭。但那些不承担投资风险的计划经济体制下的企业却有可能不顾重复建设的后果，铺摊子、上项目，即使投资无效益也在所不惜。可见，问题恰恰在于企业作为投资主体是否承担着投资风险。乡镇企业之所以会避免无效益的投资，避免重复建设，原因正在于此。

从宏观经济的角度来看，对重复建设还需要做进一步的探讨。一般所说的重复建设，是指某种类型的产品已经有某家企业进行生产，如果再建设一家企业，生产同种类型的产品，那就是重复建设，就是资源的浪费。但需要研究的是：禁止重复建设是不是会造成保护垄断、保护落后的现象？重复建设是不是一律损害国民经济？同类产品生产者之间是否容许竞争？比如说，某种类型的产品已经由某家企业进行生产，但产品数量不符合社会的需求，市场仍有较大的份额有待于企业去占据。在这种情况下，是只容许该家企业扩大生产规模呢，还是容许建立新的企业，由新建的企业的产品来填补市场的空缺？显然，新建的企业的加入不应当被认为是重复建设。再说，假定原来生产某种类型产品的企业尽管能够提供市场所需要的足够多的产品，但价格比较高昂，产品质量仍有改进之必要；而新建的企业所生产出来的同类产品，却能以较低的价格供应给需求者或产品质量比较好。那么在这种情况下，难道只容许原来生产该种类型产品的企业垄断该类产品的生产，而不容许新企业的加入？难道宁肯要价格较高、质量较低的产品而拒绝新企业生产价格

lower price and better quality. In all, repetitious construction should not be used as an excuse to justify protecting monopoly and backwardness.

Now, a look at the waste of resources associated with repetitious construction. It should be pointed out in the first place that it is a waste or abuse of resources to allow a factory to go on making a product at high price and with poor quality while banning the construction of a new factory to produce the same product more competitively. If, under the pretext of sanctioning repetitious construction, we choose to ban the construction of the new factory that can use the same amount of resources to produce a superior product, and tolerate the existing factory's poor performance, isn't that an abuse of resources? Moreover, it should be reiterated that the market is the test of all enterprises, rural enterprises included. As long as the principle of "survival of the fittest" is followed in economic affairs, those making expensive and shabby products will be eliminated and those making cheaper and better products will survive even if both the amount of capital goods and the market purchasing power are limited. The limited supply of capital goods and market share should be awarded to the latter and denied to the former. Through a period of competition, the fittest survive, and the least fit are phased out. The waste of resources is naturally taken care of through market competition. Isn't there any reason for us to insist that repetitious production is bad? Overlapping production of expensive and shabby commodities should be banned, and so should the overlapping construction of factories producing such commodities, whether the factories involved are owned by the state or farmers.

A profound lesson to be drawn from practice is that rural enterprises can never measure up to the requirements of the market economy if they fail to speed up property rights reform, organize production according to market needs, give precedence to profitability, and establish a managerial system that fuses incentives with restraints. We dare say that the good days are numbered for those rural enterprises that are doing well despite their ill-defined property rights. The market economy is pressing them to overhaul and transform themselves before it is too late.

较低、质量较高的产品？这无疑是不合理的。这种情况下的新建企业的加入也不应当被认为是重复建设。总之，重复建设不应当被当成是保护垄断、保护落后的挡箭牌。

再看一看与重复建设有关的资源浪费问题。首先要指出，假定只容许原有的企业生产出价格较高、质量较低的产品，而不容许新建的企业去生产价格较低、质量较高的产品，这同样是一种资源的浪费、资源的不合理使用。一定数量的资源，既然有可能被某家新企业用于生产价格较低、质量较高的产品，但却以禁止重复建设为借口而不准这家新企业成立，宁肯让原有的某家企业用来生产价格较高、质量较低的产品，这不是资源的不合理使用又是什么？其次，需要说明的是：市场是企业（包括乡镇企业）的检验者，即使生产资料的供应有限，市场购买力为既定，只要经济中遵循的是“适者生存”原则，那么生产价格较高、质量较低的产品的企业将被淘汰，生产价格较低、质量较高的产品的企业将继续生存下来。有限的生产资料供应将属于后者而不属于前者，既定的市场份额将被后者所取得而把前者排除在外。这样，经过一定时间的较量之后，适者生存，不适者被淘汰，资源浪费问题也就自然而然地通过市场竞争而解决了。我们有什么理由认为重复建设一定是坏事呢？只有重复生产价格高和质量低的产品，才是必须取缔的；只有重复建立那些生产价格高和质量低的产品的企业，才是必须禁止的，才是名副其实的重复建设。不能看投资主体是国有资产管理部门还是乡镇企业。

从这里，我们有一个深切的体会：如果不加快产权改革，不能真正按照市场需求自主组织生产经营，不能真正把经济效益放在首位，不能真正建立激励和约束相结合的管理体制，乡镇企业是适应不了市场经济的要求的。我们甚至可以说，对某些现在虽然产权尚未明晰但仍能取得成绩的乡镇企业来说，它们的“好日子”可能不会太长了。市场经济的形势逼得它们非改革不可，非抓紧改革不可。

III

This justifies the need to elaborate on the importance of rural enterprise property rights reform. This reform is designed to standardize the organization and behavior of market participants. At the present stage of development in this nation, its mission is to revamp those enterprises in which government administration is entangled with business management and property rights are ill defined, and which cannot make their own management decisions and bear responsibility for their gains and losses. Only when management is free from government intervention and property rights well defined can enterprises have the final say in economic activity, and account for their own profits and losses. The property rights reform entails transforming old enterprises and establishing new ones. According to the reform guideline, new enterprises should, from day one, have their management detached from government patronage and their property rights clarified, make their own decisions and be liable for their own gains and losses.

As is mentioned above, the market is the test for enterprises, and "survival of the fittest" the rule of market competition. To root out repetitious production, enterprises must be overhauled and new ones set up according to the guidelines for property rights reform. Only thus can they restructure their products in light of market changes, phase out unneeded products and turn out products that are needed and can elbow out competitors' high-priced shabby products. More importantly, property rights reform puts all enterprises on the same scratch line and detaches their management from government administration. Abiding by law and paying taxes according to rules, they are not directly under government administration and their production and business activity are immune from direct government intervention. Through property rights reform, every company bears investment risks and is liable for their gains and losses, instead of living off the government's egalitarian system of distribution and preferential treatments. The significance of property rights reform as a fundamental step towards a modern market economy is self-evident.

People are still wondering if property rights reform is as much needed by rural enterprises as by state enterprises or large urban collectives. The answer is in the positive: Rural enterprises need property rights reform. Such enterprises' survival and further growth are predicated on changing their operational mechanisms, making independent business decisions, bearing responsibility for their gains and losses, and ceasing to

三

由此我们可以对乡镇企业产权改革的重要意义进行较详细的分析。产权改革涉及的是市场主体的组织规范化和行为规范化的问题。在我国现阶段，产权改革是指如何把那些政企不分、产权不明、不自主经营、不自负盈亏的企业改造成为政企分开、产权明确、自主经营、自负盈亏的企业。产权改革既与改造原有企业有关，也与建立新企业有关，因为根据产权改革的思想，新建的企业从一开始就应当按照政企分开、产权明确、自主经营、自负盈亏的模式来建立。

前面已经指出，市场对企业进行检验，市场竞争中盛行的是“适者生存”原则。要制止真正的重复建设，企业必须按照产权改革的思想改造或新建，以便它们既可以适应市场的变化而调整产品结构，避免生产社会所不需要、不欢迎的产品，而是生产社会需要、欢迎的产品；又可以用自己的价格较低、质量较高的产品去排挤竞争对手所生产的价格较高、质量较低的产品。更重要的是，通过产权改革，一切企业都处在平等的起跑线上，都同政府机构分开，都只是“遵守法律，照章纳税”，既不受政府机构的直接管辖，又不接受政府机构对自身的生产经营活动的直接干预。此外，通过产权改革，一切企业都承担投资风险，自负盈亏，而不再躺在国家身上吃大锅饭，也不受政府的偏爱和特殊照顾。产权改革是建设现代市场经济体制的基础性改革，其必要性与重要性是不言自明的。

至今依然有人怀疑，乡镇企业是不是同国有企业或原来的城市“大集体”企业一样需要进行产权改革？回答是明确的：乡镇企业同样需要产权改革。要知道，乡镇企业的继续存在和进一步发展是以乡镇企业转换经营机制，自主经营和自负盈亏，并且已经不再成为政府

be government appendages. If they do not have the final say on business decisions and cannot take responsibility for their own profits and losses, how can it be said they have stood the test of the market and followed the "survival of the fittest" rule to compete for all their worth? If they are still subject to stringent government restrictions and intervention the way state enterprises and large urban collectives used to be, how can it be said they are a force powerful enough to breach the dyke of central planning? The saying that rural enterprises are following a different property rights system than the state enterprises and urban collectives is a vague statement. It does not tally with reality in two ways.

On the one hand, only a fraction of rural enterprises have radically changed their business mechanisms to qualify as independent commodity producers. Many others are not qualified as such because they are still following the beaten track of central planning—they are rural enterprises in name but "rural-owned" or "town-owned" enterprises in reality. In other words, they are still appendages of local governments at the grass roots level. For them, property rights reform is yet to begin, and local rural or town governments are yet to come to terms with the necessity and importance of such reform. That is why it is absolutely wrong to believe property rights reform is not a requisite for rural enterprises.

On the other hand, even those rural enterprises said to have changed their operational mechanisms have, in fact, only begun to do so. Their property rights structure is yet to be standardized, and their relationship with rural governments is yet to be readjusted before they can qualify as one hundred percent independent commodity producers.

Therefore, the pressing task for rural enterprises today is to push property rights reform, standardize their property rights configurations, and put their property rights structure on a sound footing. To believe their immediate task is expanding production and increasing investment is to overlook the key to their development. It matters, of course, for rural enterprises to expand production and increase investment. But that should come as an inevitable result of property rights reform rather than a substitute for such reform.

The impact of rural enterprise property rights reform does not stop just there. There are other aspects where its impact is apparent. Firstly, it

部门的附属物为前提的。这是因为，假定乡镇企业同国有企业、原来的城市“大集体”企业一样不能实现自主经营和自负盈亏，那又怎么谈得上乡镇企业经得起市场的检验，并能按照市场的“适者生存”原则在市场大海中拼搏、竞争呢？假定乡镇企业同国有企业、原有的城市“大集体”企业一样受到政府部门的严格限制和干预，那又怎么谈得上乡镇企业的建立和存在本身是对计划经济体制的有力冲击并使计划经济体制大堤的缺口越来越大？也就是说，不能笼统地认为乡镇企业在产权制度上不同于国有企业和原来的城市“大集体”企业。事实并不完全如此。这可以从两方面来解释：

一方面，在所有的乡镇企业中，只有一部分乡镇企业实现了经营机制的转换，符合独立商品生产者的条件；还有一部分乡镇企业则尚未实现经营机制的转换，不符合独立商品生产者的条件。它们名为乡镇企业，实际上应当被称为“乡有企业”、“乡营企业”、“镇有企业”、“镇营企业”，即最基层的政权机构所拥有与直接经营的企业。对这部分乡镇企业而言，产权改革还没有开始，甚至当地的乡政府、镇政府还不懂得在乡镇企业中进行产权改革的必要性和重要性。正因为如此，所以绝不能认为乡镇企业已不需要产权改革了。

另一方面，即使以那些已经实现了经营机制转换的乡镇企业来说，它们的经营机制的转换也还只是初步的，它们的产权设置还有待于规范化，它们同乡镇政府之间的关系也还需要进一步调整，以符合乡镇企业作为独立商品生产者的要求。

当前，摆在乡镇企业面前的一项迫切任务应是大力推进产权改革，使乡镇企业的产权设置规范化，使乡镇企业的产权结构合理化。如果以为乡镇企业当前的迫切任务只是扩大生产规模和增加投入，那就是忽略了乡镇企业发展的关键所在。扩大乡镇企业的生产规模和增加投入当然也是很重要的，但这更可能是进行了认真的产权改革之后的必然结果，而不是对产权改革的取代。

乡镇企业产权改革的意义远远不止于此。关于乡镇企业产权改革的深远意义，可以从以下四方面来做进一步分析：（1）有利于

enhances farmers' awareness of their status as owners of their enterprises and thereby fortifies their resolve to boost production and transform their homeland; secondly, it improves farmers' cultural endowment and business acumen and puts rural socioeconomic development on a fast track; thirdly, it promotes rural government reform and shores up the nation's political power at the grass roots level; and fourthly, it improves farmer income and livelihood and furnishes beneficial conditions for the achievement of common prosperity in rural areas. The following is a further elaboration of the impact of rural enterprise property rights reform in these four aspects.

1. Enhancing farmers' awareness of their status as owners of rural enterprises.

It should be noted that without genuine property rights reform, the property rights of rural enterprises can remain vague and ill defined, and farmers' self-respect as owners—even if they are just partial owners—of rural enterprises will be hurt, and this will further shake their commitment to production and investment. If, on the contrary, property rights reform has been carried out in all seriousness so that every farmer-investor in such an enterprise becomes clear about his or her share of property rights, their awareness of themselves as owners of their enterprise will be vastly enhanced. They will become more attentive to the incremental value of the assets in their enterprise, and be personally concerned with their business performance and more enthusiastic for production and investment. When rural enterprises are energized by property rights reform to increase their profits and output, they can open the eyes of their farmer-owners and investors to the prospects of rural development and the impact of their economic growth on rural development. Their resolve to turn their villages into brand-new ones will be greatly fortified as a result. It is often reported that, bored or disheartened by village life, able-bodied farmers are quitting farming and leaving their country homes, causing a drain on the rural workforce.

True, this is what happens in some rural areas. However, it is equally true that in areas where rural enterprises have grown to a sizeable scale, and particularly where such enterprises are using part of their profits to improve rural cultural and living conditions, farmers are in a peaceful frame of mind and live a contented life. Not only are local

大大提高农民作为乡镇企业所有者的主体意识，增加农民的生产积极性和建设新农村的决心；（2）有利于大大提高农民的文化技术与管理水平，使农村的社会经济得到迅速发展；（3）有利于推进乡镇基层政权机构的改革，加强乡镇基层政权建设；（4）有利于提高农民的收入，提高农村的生活水平，为农村的共同富裕创造条件。现具体论述如下：

第一，关于农民作为乡镇企业所有者的主体意识的增强问题。

要知道，如果乡镇企业不进行认真的产权改革，产权依然处于不清晰、不明确的状态，那么农民尽管作为乡镇企业的所有者（即使是部分所有者），但他们对乡镇企业的资产的关心程度必然受到很大的限制，他们对乡镇企业资产的较差的关心程度又必然挫伤他们的生产积极性和投资积极性。这是未进行产权改革的乡镇企业的严重缺陷。反之，只要认真地进行乡镇企业的产权改革，明确了产权，使每个投资者都在企业的产权中有清晰的、确定的份额；这样，即使农民只是乡镇企业的资产的一部分所有者，他们作为所有者主体、投资主体的意识必将大大增强。农民将关心本企业的资产及其保值增值状况，将把企业的经营好坏视为自己所关心的主要问题之一。农民的生产积极性和投资积极性将大大提高。同时，只要乡镇企业通过产权改革后增加了活力，增加了盈利，扩大了生产规模，作为所有者、投资者的农民就可以由此看清农村建设的前景，看清乡镇企业经济力量的成长与壮大对于农村建设的意义，他们建设新农村的决心也会大大加强。经常听到有人说，农民不安心在农村中生活、工作，农村的人力纷纷外流，农村的健壮劳力都走了等等。不错，在一些农村确实存在这种情况。但我们同样可以看到，在乡镇企业发达的地区，特别是在乡镇企业发展后把自己的一部分盈利用于改善农村文化和生活设施的地区，农民的情绪则是较为稳定的。

able-bodied farmers staying put, but farmers are coming from elsewhere to join them as well. Therefore, there is every reason to believe that once property rights reform has boosted farmers' awareness as owners of rural enterprises and vastly energized their enterprises, tremendous changes are bound to take place in the rural economic and cultural landscape, and local farmers will become more committed to building up their homeland than ever before.

2. Improving farmers' cultural and technical proficiency and management acumen.

Farmers' cultural and technical proficiency and business acumen can be improved in many ways. An important way is property rights reform of rural enterprises, which is meant to turn farmers into true owners and investors of such enterprises, give them the opportunity to attend enterprise meetings, and open up new avenues for them to improve their cultural endowment, skills, and business acumen. This is because without such a reform, farmers are just nominal owners of their enterprises, and have no opportunities to attend these enterprises' meetings and make their voice heard, to say nothing of improving themselves through the activities of these enterprises. Under these circumstances, farmers' relationship with their rural enterprise is reduced to the point where they are mere workers or people who have spent some money on them—no enterprise would regard them as its masters. That situation can change dramatically through property rights reform, which serves to clarify farmers' status as owners and investors as well as their share of property rights to rural enterprises. As owners and investors, they can take part in the decision-making process or send representatives to meetings. In this way they gain a gradual understanding of their enterprise's business and financial situation, and get to know the causes for their successes or failures behind the rise and fall of the value of their assets. If a farmer happens to be working in the enterprise he owns or invests in, he is entitled to participate, directly or indirectly, in the making of production and business decisions. If several rural enterprises are presented to him as investment options, he may compare them, and upgrade his technological and economic know-how through such comparisons. The market economy is often said to be a great school in which people can learn a lot of things that cannot be learned from books. However, farmers

这些地区不但留住了本地的农民、本地的健壮劳力，而且还吸引外地的健壮劳力前来做工。因此，完全有理由认为，在通过产权改革而大大增强了农民作为所有者的主体意识，大大提高了乡镇企业活力之后，农村的面貌必将呈现巨大的变化，农民建设自己的家乡的热情也必将大为高涨。

第二，关于农民文化技术与管理水平的提高问题。

要提高农民的文化技术与管理水平，可以通过好多途径；但不能忽略的是，通过乡镇企业的产权改革，使农民成为名副其实的所有者主体、投资主体，使农民有机会参与乡镇企业的各种会议，也是提高农民文化技术与管理水平的一个重要途径。这是因为，在未明确乡镇企业的产权时，尽管农民是名义上的乡镇企业主人，但这是虚的，而不是实的。他们既没有机会参与乡镇企业的各种会议，也没有机会表达自己对乡镇企业发展业务的意见。这样，也就谈不上农民通过乡镇企业的活动而提高自身的文化技术与管理水平。这种情况下的农民与乡镇企业之间的关系，或者是农民入厂做工，农民单纯充当劳动力，或者是农民单纯出钱，但乡镇企业却没有把农民当成是真正的主人。乡镇企业产权改革以后，情况将发生重大变化。这时，农民作为所有者、投资者的地位明确了，农民投资所形成的产权份额也清晰了。相应地，农民作为所有者、投资者将直接参与或选出代表参与乡镇企业的有关决策和参加有关会议，他们将逐渐懂得企业的经营和财务状况，进而对企业的兴衰和资产的增减原因有所了解。如果农民是企业的职工，他们在这里就不单纯充当劳动力，而且也直接或间接地参与生产经营决策。如果农民不是仅有一家乡镇企业作为投资对象，而是有可供选择的投资机会，他们就会对各个投资机会进行比较，并从比较中增进自己的技术与经济知识。人们常说市场经济是一所大学校，从这里可以学习到许多书本上学不到的东西。但作为乡镇企业中的劳动力，农民真正从市场中

can learn a lot more from the market economy as rural business owners and investors than if they are mere workers. The more they come to know the market economy, the more smoothly the market economy can grow. To help farmers understand the market economy deeply, it is necessary for them to participate not just as consumers, workers, or bank-savings depositors but as investors and managers as well.

3. Bolstering up rural governments at the grass roots level.

The building of governments at the township level involves a number of issues, such as promotion of democracy in rural government elections, the building of Party organizations at the grass roots level, and the character building of rural government officials. It also involves readjusting the relationship between grass roots governments and rural enterprises. Rural government reform is intimately related to the property rights reform of rural enterprises, and the key to the success of both reforms lies in unfettering businesses from government intervention and turning rural enterprises into independent commodity producers with well-defined property rights and decision-making autonomy and bearing their own gains and losses. When rural enterprises cease to be government appendages, rural governments can no longer regard them as their own businesses, let alone turn them into their slush funds. This is something that can never be achieved without genuine property rights reform. As a matter of fact, there is no lack of local governments which, by capitalizing on rural enterprises' ill-defined property rights, put these enterprises under their control and turn them into their slush funds even if they are not making a profit. This inevitably saps the energy of these enterprises and dampens their farmer-owners' ardor for production and investment. As a hotbed for corruption among rural government officials, these illegal "off-book coffers" also spoil the image of grass roots political power, rob local governments of popular support, and destabilize local political and economic life. The dire consequences of the wanton behaviors of rural government officials in this regard have been borne out by a series of legal cases that have been cracked in recent years. As *de facto* bosses of some rural enterprises with political and economic power in their control, these people have wantonly violated the norms of the market economy by willfully withdrawing money, extorting reimbursement for personal expenses, and practicing nepotism in

所学到的并不多；而农民如果作为乡镇企业的所有者、投资者，并且真地能够参与决策，那么农民从市场经济中所学到的就多得多。农民越懂得市场经济，市场经济就越能顺利地发展；而要农民比较深刻地了解市场经济，就应使农民不再局限于以消费者、劳动者、储蓄者的身份参加市场经济，而且也以投资者、经营者的身份参加市场经济。

第三，关于乡镇基层政权的建设问题。

乡镇基层政权的建设所涉及的问题较多，包括乡镇基层政权机构选举的民主化、乡镇基层的党组织自身的建设、乡镇基层政府工作人员素质的提高等等，也包括乡镇基层政权机构与乡镇企业之间关系的调整。乡镇基层政权机构的改革与乡镇企业的产权改革是密切相关的，关键在于乡镇企业应当成为政企分开、产权明确、自主经营、自负盈亏的独立商品生产者；乡镇企业不再是乡镇基层政权机构的附属物，乡镇基层政权机构不再把乡镇企业当做自己的直辖企业，不再把乡镇企业当做自己的“小金库”。如果不进行认真的产权改革，是做不到这一点的。不可否认，在某些地区，在乡镇企业产权不明确、不清晰的条件下，一些盈利的（甚至也有一些不盈利的）乡镇企业被当地的乡镇基层政权机构牢牢掌握在自己的手中，视为乡镇基层政权机构的“小金库”。于是，一方面乡镇企业的活力受到极大限制，农民的生产积极性和投资积极性大受挫折；另一方面，这也成为某些乡镇基层政府工作人员腐败的原因之一。而乡镇基层政府工作人员的腐败又破坏了乡镇基层政权的形象，失去群众对他们的信任，并使得乡镇的政治生活、经济生活不正常，使得当地社会难以安定。迄今为止，已有一些被揭露的乡镇干部胡作非为并造成严重后果的案件，他们的胡作非为往往同他们成为乡镇企业的实际主管人有关。他们把政治权力、经济权力集中于自己身上，从乡镇企业那里随意支取货币，或把各种开销拿到乡镇企业

enrolling workers. Shouldn't these behaviors be sternly sanctioned in the course of reforming the property rights of rural enterprises? Obviously, it is not just a paramount economic issue, but also a political issue with a close bearing on whether rural political power can be consolidated and whether rural social stability can be maintained. We have got to follow the principle of defining property rights and separating administration from management when we readjust the relationship of rural enterprises with grass roots governments and turn them into independent commodity producers that enjoy well defined property rights and decision making autonomy, and bear their own gains and losses. On no account should this task be taken lightly.

4. Raising farmer income and striving for common prosperity in rural areas.

Improved rural livelihood is a fruit of increased farmer income. The issue here is how farmers can increase their income quickly. Simply put, there are two ways to achieve this. First, developing farm production (animal husbandry, fishery, forestry, sideline occupations included), and boosting labor productivity by a large margin. Second, striving for fast growth in rural enterprises in the primary, secondary, and tertiary industries and for major growth in labor productivity, so that farmers can make more money immediately as laborers and investors. In addition, rural enterprises may also use part of their profits to support agriculture, improve rural cultural and living facilities and ameliorate farmers' livelihood. Some farmers have left their home villages for somewhere else, but many of them end up working in rural enterprises away from home. It is thus clear that the property rights reform of rural enterprises and the effort to revive rural enterprises for further development are conducive to increasing farmer income and improving rural material and cultural lives. What is to be done to help the rural poor to beat poverty? What is the relationship between the development of rural enterprises and the drive to help the rural poor? First of all, helping the rural poor is a social issue that can be addressed only by the concerted efforts of the entire society. This calls for special policies addressed to impoverished areas and households, aid from urban businesses and institutions for economic, technological, and educational and medicare development of underdeveloped areas, as well as help from families that have become affluent earlier than others to poor families. Another method that works

报账，或把持乡镇企业招工用人的大权。所有这些都是与市场经济的要求相背离的。难道不该在乡镇企业产权改革的过程中对这些现象来一番清理、整顿吗？由此可见，按照乡镇企业产权明确化的原则来调整乡镇基层政权机构与乡镇企业之间的关系，使乡镇企业成为政企分开、产权明确、自主经营、自负盈亏的独立商品生产者，并不单纯是一个至关重要的经济问题，而且是一个关系到今后能否巩固乡镇政权和保证乡镇社会安定的政治问题。我们决不能轻视这一问题。

第四，关于农民收入的提高与农村共同富裕问题。

农民收入增长所带来的结果是生活水平的提高。问题在于农民怎样才能较迅速地增加收入？简单地说，主要有两条途径。一是农业（包括畜牧业、渔业、林业、副业）生产以较快的速度发展，劳动生产率有较大幅度提高，农民可以由此提高收入。二是乡镇企业（包括第一、二、三次产业中的乡镇企业）以较快的速度发展，劳动生产率有较大幅度提高，农民作为劳动者和作为投资者都可以由此提高收入。此外，乡镇企业还可以利用自己的一部分利润来支援农业或用于改善农村的文化与生活设施，提高农民的生活水平。即使农民外出做工，其中也有相当一部分是到外地的乡镇企业去工作。可见，乡镇企业的产权改革以及由此引起的乡镇企业活力的增强和乡镇企业的进一步发展，有利于提高农民的收入和改善农村的物质文化生活。那么，农村中的扶贫问题又将如何解决呢？乡镇企业的发展同农村中的扶贫有什么联系呢？在这里，首先需要指出，农村扶贫是一个社会问题，有赖于全社会的共同努力才能解决，包括各级政府对贫困地区和贫困户采取特殊的政策，城市各个企事业单位以不同方式支持贫困地区发展经济、技术、文化、教育、医疗卫生等，也包括农村中的先富裕农户对贫困户的帮助。乡镇企业

is to enlist help from rural enterprises for poverty-stricken areas and underprivileged households. For instance, enrolling workers from poor areas and investing in these areas for developmental purposes helps tap local resources and boost local income. Rural enterprises in relatively more developed regions may pair up with counterparts in less developed regions. In all, the enthusiastic participation of rural enterprises can vastly accelerate increases in the income level of households and regions in financial difficulties. Such actions are an embodiment of the fruits of property rights reform.

IV

Now look at the target models for rural enterprise property rights reform. That the contract responsibility system cannot become a target model for enterprises under the market economy is a foregone conclusion among many accomplished economists, and therefore does not need further elaboration. Instead, what target model should be set for this field of property rights reform merits further study.

The cooperative system can be a target model for rural enterprise property rights reform, as it defines the economic nature and organizational form of enterprise properties. What this goal can achieve can be summarized in four points.

First, when adopted to establish or transform rural enterprises, the cooperative system helps separate government administration from business management, clarify property rights and enable enterprises to enjoy business autonomy and handle gains and losses on their own.

Second, when employed to establish or transform rural enterprises, the cooperative system helps combine farmer-investors and farmer-workers into one, thereby motivating farmers as both investors and workers.

Third, when used to establish or transform rural enterprises, the cooperative system can foster a congenial internal environment, thereby enhancing internal cohesion, and promoting labor productivity.

Fourth, when applied to establish or transform rural enterprises, the cooperative system enables them to tighten up their management system under a standard corporate constitution, restrain their leaders and protect the lawful rights of workers and investors, thereby paving the way for their smooth development.

对贫困地区和贫困户的扶植、帮助同样是扶贫的有效途径之一。比如说，乡镇企业从贫困地区招工；有较好效益的乡镇企业到贫困地区投资开发，既可利用当地的资源，又能增加贫困地区的收入；发达地区的乡镇企业同贫困地区的乡镇企业加强经济联系等。总之，有乡镇企业的积极参与，贫困户和贫困地区收入水平的提高将会大大加快。这也反映了产权改革后乡镇企业的发展对社会所做的贡献。

四

现在让我们来探讨乡镇企业产权改革的目标模式问题。承包制不能成为市场经济体制下的企业目标模式，这在经济学界已成定论，并且被许多有造诣的经济学家所公认，因此用不着再赘述了。那么乡镇企业产权改革的目标模式是什么？这倒是可以进一步研究的课题。

乡镇企业合作制是乡镇企业产权改革的目标模式之一。合作制既表明企业的经济性质，也表明企业的财产组织形式。合作制的优点可以简略地归结为：

1. 以合作制的形式组建或改造乡镇企业，能达到政企分开、产权明确、自主经营、自负盈亏的目的。

2. 以合作制的形式组建或改造乡镇企业，能把企业的投资者与企业的劳动者合为一体，从而调动农民作为企业投资者与企业劳动者的积极性。

3. 以合作制的形式组建或改造乡镇企业，能在企业内部造成一种比较协调的环境，从而有利于增强企业内部的凝聚力，促进生产力的发展。

4. 以合作制的形式组建或改造乡镇企业，能以规范的合作制企业章程来健全企业的管理制度，并对企业领导层进行约束，对企业职工和投资者的合法权益进行保护，从而有利于企业的顺利发展。

With the aforementioned strengths, the cooperative system for rural enterprises should not be overlooked as an organizational form for corporate properties. The notion that cooperative enterprises are outdated does not tally with reality. It needs be stressed that the rural enterprises established or transformed according to a standard principle are different from their counterparts that existed under central planning or still exist nowadays. Ill-defined property rights make it hard for those rural enterprises that are known as collectives in name only to identify who their investors are. Some of these firms are established with money raised by individuals, but they do not treat their investors as owners, and the investors themselves do not regard themselves as owners, either. By contrast, the rural enterprises that have adopted the cooperative system take on a new look that distinguishes themselves categorically from firms under collective ownership. The cooperative system may also be a form of collective ownership, but it is a new form of collective ownership adapted to the socialist market economic system.

The cooperative system, nevertheless, is just one of the target models for rural enterprise property rights reform. Compared with joint-stock rural enterprises, cooperative rural enterprises have five limits.

First, the cooperative system works smoothly when rural enterprises are small, but it falls somewhat short when they grow larger. When it is adopted to set up or transform a small rural enterprise, its investors are also its workers, thereby creating a congenial corporate atmosphere in which the "one man, one vote" decision-making system—the slogan of the cooperative system—works perfectly. But if the enterprise is big and has a lot of people on its payroll, the same decision-making system is likely to dwindle into a mere formality if it is put in place, for it cannot work as effectively in coordinating the enterprise's internal relationships as it does in a small enterprise.

Second, from a financing and fund-raising point of view, a cooperative rural enterprise compares unfavorably with a joint-stock one. A joint-stock rural enterprise can raise funds from a wide spectrum of public avenues, whereas a cooperative rural enterprise may have trouble raising more money than its internal fund-raising mechanism allows, especially under its "one man, one vote" decision-making system. This limit of the

乡镇企业合作制的上述优点是明显的。因此在乡镇企业产权改革时，不应该忽视合作制这种企业财产组织形式。那种所谓合作制企业已经过时的说法，不符合实际。要知道，按照规范的原则组建或改造而成的乡镇企业不同于计划经济体制下曾经存在或至今仍然存在的集体所有制企业。那种集体所有制企业名为集体所有，实际上依旧是产权不明确、不清晰的企业，究竟是谁投资的，任何人也说不清楚。即使有些集体所有制企业当初由个人集资（或一部分由个人集资）而产生，但出了资的个人不仅没有被看成是企业的实际的主人，甚至他们本人也不认为自己是企业的实际的主人。然而，以合作制形式组建或改造的乡镇企业则使得乡镇企业的面貌一新，截然不同于以往那种集体所有制企业。合作制也可以称作集体所有制，但这是一种与社会主义市场经济体制相适应的新的集体所有制。

但乡镇企业合作制只是乡镇企业产权改革的目标模式之一，而不是乡镇企业产权改革的惟一模式。与股份制的乡镇企业相比，合作制的乡镇企业的不足主要有以下五点：

第一，在企业规模不大时，乡镇企业合作制的上述优点可以明显地表现出来；而当企业规模较大时，乡镇企业合作制就显得不够了。比如说，企业规模不大，以合作制形式组建或改造乡镇企业，可以把企业的投资者与企业的劳动者合为一体，在企业内部造成一种比较协调的环境，作为合作制特色的"一人一票制"也容易实现。但如果企业规模较大，人数较多，就不一定能发挥合作制的长处。"一人一票制"即使推行，也易于流于形式，而难以把企业内部的关系协调得如职工人数较少时那样。

第二，从融资集资的角度来看，合作制的乡镇企业是明显地不如股份制的乡镇企业的。股份制的乡镇企业可以从社会广泛地筹集资金；而合作制的乡镇企业则受到从职工内部集资，特别是"一人一票制"的限制，难以筹集更多的资金。乡镇企业合作制的这一

cooperative rural enterprise becomes more pronounced when it grows in size or when it lets a major profit-making opportunity slip through its fingers because of lack of money.

Third, when a rural enterprise sets about redefining its property rights, it is often harassed by the issue of converting its capital stock into stock shares. The same problem can be easily addressed under the joint-stock system. Yet under the cooperative system, it can be solved only by selling the capital stock evenly among members, something that is easy for a small enterprise but becomes unwieldy for a large one.

Fourth, an enterprise in the course of development sometimes needs to acquire another enterprise's stock, or take control of it through such acquisition. Sometimes it needs to sell its stock shares to other enterprises. It may also grow into an enterprise group through mergers. These normal economic behaviors can go smoothly if rural enterprises are regrouped or transformed under the joint-stock system, but may hit some snags under the cooperative system.

Fifth, the cooperative system differs from the joint-stock system in that the stock shares of such a rural firm can be withdrawn freely, which can be a destabilizing factor for its production and business scale, whereas in a joint-stock rural enterprise, shares can change hands only among colleagues, which helps maintain its production and business scale. Moreover, under the joint-stock system, stock shares are transferred at the current price instead of the original price, which puts investors at a relative advantage. Under the cooperative system, it is hard to price the withdrawn shares—if the original price is applied, the man withdrawing his stock will find himself at the losing end of the deal, but if a higher price is set on the basis of reevaluating the assets, it may trigger off an exodus of stockholders. If that happens, how can the enterprise go on with its production? However, if a cooperative rural enterprise bans such withdrawal altogether, doesn't this violate the cooperative principle? Herein are some operational snags for such an enterprise in dealing with voluntary withdrawal of stock shares. Cooperative rural enterprises are also confronted with the quandary of whether or not to admit new participants. If they do not accept new members while allowing those on the payroll to withdraw freely, won't they shrink in size constantly?

局限性在企业规模增大或在有盈利机会存在但由于缺乏资金而难以如愿时更为突出。

第三，从原有的乡镇企业改制为产权明确的乡镇企业时，经常会遇到资产存量折股问题。在股份制条件下，资产存量的折股问题比较容易解决；而在合作制条件下，通常只有把资产存量平均出售给每一个社员才能解决。如果企业规模不大，让全体社员买下资产存量仍是可行的；如果企业规模较大，全体社员买下资产存量这种做法的可行性较小。

第四，在企业发展过程中，有时需要对外参股、控投，有时需要吸收其他企业的参股，有时企业有可能成长为企业集团。这些经济行为完全是正常的。如果按照股份制形式来组建或改造乡镇企业，这些经济行为可以顺利地进行。如果按合作制形式来组建或改造乡镇企业，这些经济行为的实现就会困难得多。

第五，合作制与股份制的另一不同之处在于：当人们参加合作制的乡镇企业后，退出是自愿的，也是自由的；而当人们参加股份制的乡镇企业后，退股是不容许的，股份只能转让给另一人。因此，股份制有利于企业的生产经营规模的稳定，合作制则不利于企业的生产经营规模的稳定。此外，在股份制之下，股份转让时不是按参加时的价格转让，而是按照现行的价格转让，这对于投资者比较有利；而在合作制之下，退出时究竟按什么价格计算是一个难以解决的问题。如果退出时仍按入社时的价格计算，退出者岂不是吃亏？如果退出时按资产重估后的折价计算，那就有可能引发更多的人要求退出，生产又如何继续进行下去？假如合作制的乡镇企业不容许退出，不就与合作制的原则不符了吗？所以合作制乡镇企业在“自愿退出”问题上会遇到操作的困难。同样的道理，在对待新加入者方面，合作制的乡镇企业也会遇到类似的难处。允不允许新加入者进入？如果不允许新加入者进入而只允许原来的加入者退出，那么合作制的乡镇企业岂不是会越来越小，至少是社员人数越来越少？

At least their membership will keep diminishing. If new participants are welcome, what price should they pay for admittance? If the original price is used, it will do a great favor to newcomers and attract more new arrivals, leaving old members to feel cheated. Thus the conflict between old and new members will go from bad to worse. If newcomers are asked to pay at a price based on a reevaluation of the assets, the going will be tough for the enterprise. For joint-stock rural enterprises, where stock can only be transferred internally, the problem becomes a lot simpler.

V

Despite all that has been said, the beauty of the cooperative system for rural enterprises can hardly be gainsaid. It works as effectively as the joint-stock system in helping rural enterprises meet their goals by reforming their business mechanisms, keeping government administration from interfering in business management, defining their property rights, making their own business decisions and bearing responsibility for their gains and losses. The problem, however, is that the cooperative system works perfectly in small rural enterprises, but not as effectively as the joint-stock system in large rural enterprises, particularly where large and medium-sized enterprises are established or transformed. In other words, the cooperative system is appropriate for the property rights reform of small rural enterprises, while the joint-stock system should be pursued where the property rights of large and medium-sized enterprises are reformed.

This brings forth another topic for our discussion: the joint-stock cooperative system. What is the "joint-stock cooperative system" all about? Most of the rural enterprises that claim to be under this system are small companies under joint partnership. The others are irregular joint-stock enterprises. Rural enterprises that follow the textbook perfect cooperative system or joint-stock system are few and far between. For this reason, not just those rural enterprises that have not reformed their property rights should carry out such reform—those already passing themselves off as "joint-stock cooperative" enterprises should also undertake this reform in earnest, so as to standardize their operational system. They may either be transformed into cooperatives or joint-stock firms, or, in the light of their property rights situations, become private firms under either single ownership or partnership.

如果允许新加入者进入，那么新加入者按什么价格出资入社？按原来加入者所支付的价格，原加入者肯定吃亏，新加入者肯定占便宜。那又会促使更多的新加入者进入，原加入者与新加入者之间的矛盾必然加剧。新加入者按资产重估后的价格加入，则也会遇到操作的困难。在股份制的乡镇企业中，由于不得退股而只能转让股份，问题会简单得多。

五

以上所说的这一切并不等于否认乡镇企业合作制的优点。从转换企业经营机制，实现政企分开、产权明确、自主经营、自负盈亏的角度来考察，乡镇企业合作制与乡镇企业股份制一样，都可以达到原定的目标。问题主要在于：乡镇企业规模不大时，合作制是较为适合的；而在乡镇企业规模扩大后，尤其是在新组建的大中型乡镇企业和原有的大中型乡镇企业改制时，合作制的不足之处将突出地暴露出来，所以它不如股份制。换言之，小型乡镇企业的产权改革适宜以合作制作为目标模式，而大中型乡镇企业的产权改革则以股份制作为目标模式为宜。

在这里，还有一个问题需要提出来进行讨论，这就是关于乡镇企业的"股份合作制"问题。究竟什么是"股份合作制"？从目前已经采取"股份合作制"的乡镇企业来看，其中多数是一种合伙制的小企业，还有一部分是不规范的股份制企业。真正实行规范的合作制的或规范的股份制的乡镇企业是少数。因此，不仅尚未进行产权改革的乡镇企业需要进行产权改革，而且已经被称为"股份合作制企业"的那些乡镇企业，也需要通过认真的产权改革使之规范化：或者向合作制的模式规范化；或者向股份制的模式规范化；或者按其本来的产权组成状况，名副其实地正名为私营企业，包括独资企业和合伙企业。

The term "joint-stock cooperative system" is somewhat off the mark. The cooperative system and the joint-stock system entail different organizational forms of corporate assets. An enterprise may or may not choose either system. It is impossible for a firm to adopt both at the same time, or combine them in one. Nevertheless, the "joint-stock cooperative system" catches the fancy of many a rural enterprise out of three probable considerations.

First, concern over being dubbed "capitalist," a term that may cause some raised eyebrows in socialist China. Out of the belief that the cooperative system is socialist and the joint-stock system capitalist, some enterprises choose to call themselves a "joint-stock cooperative enterprise" when regrouping or transforming themselves to measure up to the requirements of the joint-stock system. They do this to avoid unnecessary controversy and enhance their sense of security even though the name bears little meaning for a joint-stock company. Such concern is uncalled for today. The joint-stock system is, if anything, an organizational form of corporate assets. It is therefore contentious to call it either socialist or capitalist. The joint-stock system can stand on its own. There is no need to pass it off under the ill-fitting title of "joint-stock cooperative system."

Second, the belief that the adjective "cooperative" can help attract government policy incentives. This again is unnecessary. Government policy incentives may be granted in two ways. Firstly, an enterprise that meets national or local policy requirements for industrial restructuring naturally qualifies for such incentives whether or not its name contains the word "cooperative." It is the industrial nature of the enterprise's investment and production that counts. Secondly, cooperative enterprises deserve certain policy incentives in compliance with relevant national and local legislation. An enterprise must be regrouped or transformed under the cooperative system to qualify for such incentives. It won't do to add "cooperative" to the name of an enterprise that is not really a cooperative one. If a "joint-stock cooperative" is truly cooperative, why don't they simply call themselves "cooperative"? It is useless to gild the lily.

Third, mistaking the "joint-stock cooperative" system for a corporate property organizational form with Chinese characteristics, which is different from both the cooperative system and the joint-stock system.

"股份合作制"这个名称并不科学。从企业财产组织形式上看，合作制与股份制是两种不同的企业财产组织形式。一个企业或者实行合作制，或者实行股份制，或者既不实行合作制又不实行股份制，而不可能同时实行合作制与股份制，也不可能把合作制与股份制合为一体。目前，不少乡镇企业喜欢采用"股份合作制"这种名称，可能有以下三个原因：

一是害怕被说成是资本主义性质的。这是因为，在过去较长时间内，一谈到合作制，就认为这是社会主义性质的；一谈到股份制，则被看成是资本主义性质的。因此，明明是按照股份制的方向来组建或改造乡镇企业（尽管组成的是不规范的股份制企业），但由于怕别人说三道四，就使用了"股份合作制"这个名称，以增加安全感。现在看来，这种顾虑是不必要的。股份制无非是企业财产组织形式的一种，它本身并不表明姓"社"还是姓"资"。是股份制就是股份制，不必硬套上"股份合作制"这样一个不科学的帽子。

二是以为使用"合作"一词在政策上可以得到某些优惠，因此就在股份制之上加上"合作"一词。其实，这也是多余的。政策的优惠可能来自两个方面。一方面，如果符合国家或地区的产业结构调整的要求，那么从产业政策上考虑，政府是会给予优惠的。这时加不加上"合作"一词无关紧要，重要的是投资与生产的产业特征。另一方面，如果是真正的合作制企业，那么根据国家或地区对合作制企业的扶植的规定，企业可以得到一定的优惠。但这时必须确实把企业组建或改造为合作制企业，而不能只从表面上看是否加上"合作"一词。假定有些"股份合作制"的乡镇企业真的是合作制企业，何必不直接使用合作制的名义，而要用"股份合作制"名义呢？

三是把"股份合作制"看成是有中国特色的一种企业财产组织形式，即这类企业既不同于真正的合作制企业，又不同于规范的

It so happens that some enterprises have divided their stock into "collective shares" and "corporate shares." Believing that this division does not accord with the standard joint-stock system, and that "collective shares" and "corporate shares" smack of the cooperative system, they have renamed themselves "joint-stock cooperative enterprises." It also happened that some people—on the ground that the cooperative system allows investors to withdraw their shares but the joint-stock system does not, and that in a cooperative enterprise under the "one man, one vote" decision-making system, votes are decided by the number of stock shares—have coined the term "joint-stock cooperative" system in the hope of incorporating the strengths of both systems, so that old investors can withdraw their shares while new investors, individuals and legal entities included, can be attracted. They assert this "joint-stock cooperative system" is distinctively Chinese. This way of thinking, however, is misleading. For their tremendous role in Chinese economic development, rural enterprises are "distinctively Chinese" enough. There is absolutely no need to concoct an ill-fitting joint-stock or cooperative system. Such irregular systems, if allowed to exist, can only hold back the growth of rural enterprises.

VI

Property rights reform is under way among rural enterprises. The rise of the "joint-stock cooperative" rural enterprises are a nascent phenomenon no matter how you look at them. They deserve help and guidance to meet established business norms. They should not be discriminated against, still less rebuked or disbanded. Their rise is spontaneous to a large extent. Rural government officials and local farmers have embraced them with great gusto. Some of these enterprises, though looking somewhat outlandish, are the brainchild of local people. If the rise and development of rural enterprises had played a positive role in the development of China in the 1980s, part of that contribution came from the "joint-stock cooperatives." If, with their presence and growth, rural enterprises are a powerful onslaught on central planning, the contributions of "joint-stock cooperative" rural enterprises cannot be denied. Practice proves that in comparison with the "orthodox" enterprises which are collective in name but centralized in deed, the "joint-stock cooperative" rural enterprises may well qualify

股份制企业。比如说，在股权设置中，有"集体股"、"企业股"这样的股份，这当然与规范的股份制不符。所以，有人认为不如改称"股份合作制"，因为"集体股"、"企业股"之类似乎带有合作制的成分。又如，有人认为，在合作制之下，出资人可以申请退股，在股份制之下，退股是不容许的。在合作制之下，一人一票；在股份制之下，按股份多少决定票数多少。假定采取"股份合作制"，那么既可以容许出资人退股，又可以按"一股一票"的原则吸收有实力的投资者（包括自然人和法人）加入，岂不是兼有合作制与股份制的特色？这样的企业财产组织形式——"股份合作制"——难道不就反映了"中国特色"吗？应当指出，以这种方式来理解"有中国特色的"乡镇企业财产组织形式，是不准确的。毫无疑问，乡镇企业的成长及其在中国经济建设中的巨大作用这一事实本身就已经具有"中国特色"了，有什么必要硬要从企业财产组织形式上去制造不规范的股份制或不规范的合作制呢？不规范的合作制或股份制只能阻碍乡镇企业的进一步发展，它们算不上什么"中国特色"。

六

乡镇企业的产权改革正在进行之中。已经存在的"股份合作制"的乡镇企业，不管怎么说，都应当被认为是近年来中国经济生活中出现的新事物。对于它们的不规范性，要予以指出，切切实实地给以帮助和指导，使它们走向规范化。不应当歧视它们，更不应当指责它们或取缔它们。它们在很大程度上是自发地产生的。乡镇干部、群众的热情很高，有些做法（尽管不规范）来自群众的创造。如果说乡镇企业的兴起与发展对 80 年代的中国起过重要作用的话，那么其中也包括了"股份合作制"乡镇企业所起的作用。如果说乡镇企业的存在与成长是对计划经济体制的有力冲击的话，那么"股份合作制"乡镇企业的功劳也不可磨灭。实践已经充分证明，同以往那种名为集体所有的计划经济体制下的"正统"企业相比，

as "heterodoxy." However, to unshackle the national economy from central planning, we would do better to have more of such "heterodoxy." Property rights reform should be carried out variously in light of specific circumstances, and different measures are called for to institutionalize the property rights configuration of rural enterprises. Such reform should also be allowed to go at different speeds. The general trend is that the cooperative system will be the target model for property rights reform in small rural enterprises, and the joint-stock system for this reform in large and medium-sized rural enterprises. Having made this point previously, I will not labor it further.

Joint-stock rural enterprises need not be listed on the stock market. Under the joint-stock system, only a few companies eventually become listed. Someday, however, some rural enterprises may qualify for it, a likelihood that should never be excluded. Most joint-stock rural enterprises, however, may be converted into limited liability companies, which I believe is a property organizational form universally applicable for rural enterprises. A certain number of them may be transformed into limited liability companies with internal stock shares. It should be noted that the joint-stock system cannot be divided into "urban enterprise joint-stock system" or "rural enterprise joint-stock system," nor can it be split into "joint-stock system for regrouped state enterprises" or "joint-stock system for regrouped rural enterprises." The joint-stock system applies to all manner of shareholding companies.

Some enterprises, out of one consideration or another, choose to stay with the name "joint-stock cooperative enterprise." What is to be done about this? In this case, impetuosity gets us nowhere. The goal of property rights reform is to prevent the government from interfering in business management, to define property rights, and delegate enterprises with autonomy to make business decisions and handle their own gains and losses. A rural enterprise may still be known as a "joint-stock cooperative enterprise" provided it has reached the goals of property rights reform, adopted effective business operational mechanisms, and has already been organized and operated under a standard joint-stock or cooperative system. Someday, it may awaken to the need to change its name to "joint-stock enterprise" or "cooperative enterprise."

The "joint-stock cooperative system" is a transitional corporate property organization form. The "rural enterprise" is transitional, too, and many firms have stuck to this name since its debut for two reasons:

"股份合作制"的乡镇企业可称作是"异端"。为了打破计划经济体制的严重束缚，多一些"异端"是好事。乡镇企业的产权改革可以因地制宜，采取不同的步骤来促进乡镇企业产权设置的规范化，而且在速度上必定有差别。总的趋势将是：小型乡镇企业产权改革的目标模式是合作制，大中型乡镇企业产权改革的目标模式是股份制。关于这一点，前面已经谈过，不再赘述了。

股份制的乡镇企业不是指一定要公开上市。在股份制条件下，公开上市的股份有限公司是极少数。乡镇企业中，够条件公开上市的，当然不排除这种可能性。大多数股份制的乡镇企业可以改为有限责任公司，这是一种普遍适用的乡镇企业财产组织形式。还有一定数量的股份制乡镇企业可以改为内部持股的股份有限公司。要知道，股份制就是股份制，它不分什么"城市企业股份制"和"乡镇企业股份制"，也不分什么"由国有企业改组的股份制"和"由原乡镇企业改组的股份制"。规范化是一个统一的标准，凡是股份制企业都适用。

有些企业由于种种考虑而宁肯保留"股份合作制"的名称，怎么办？对此不必操之过急。产权改革的目的是为了实现企业的政企分开、产权明确、自主经营、自负盈亏。只要乡镇企业通过产权改革达到了这一目的，有效地转换了企业经营机制，实际上已经按照规范的股份制或规范的合作制组建和运作了。它们愿意采取"股份合作制"这一名称，就听之任之，不要干涉。等到将来某一天，它们自己感到有必要正名为股份制企业或合作制企业之时，它们自己会不再使用"股份合作制"这一名称的。

不仅"股份合作制"这种企业财产组织形式是过渡性的，甚至可以认为，"乡镇企业"这种提法也具有过渡性质。在乡镇企业刚刚

first, to differentiate them from enterprises under the dominant central planning, such as state enterprises and large urban collectives; and second, to take into consideration the fact that they are located in villages and towns, with their workforce coming mainly from among local villagers. What will become of these "rural enterprises" in the future? Will there be any more "urban enterprises" in contrast with "rural enterprises"? Can "rural enterprises" be established only in villages or towns, and can their workforce come only from local villages? If, in these early days, it is necessary to use the term "rural enterprise" to highlight their differences in business operational mechanisms from those under central planning and their identity as "above-norm" commodity producers, is there any need to differentiate "above-norm" commodity producers from "planned" commodity producers in a future market economic environment? As mentioned in the foregoing, enterprises are enterprises, joint-stock enterprises are joint-stock enterprises. There is absolutely no need to divide them into "urban" and "rural" enterprises, still less "urban" and "rural" joint-stock enterprises. "Rural enterprise," as a transitional name, will disappear at last, and so will "rural joint-stock enterprise."

This, however, will not happen anytime soon. Returning to reality, we should pursue joint-stock reform among rural enterprises and devise proper ways and means to establish and operate them. Moreover, to repeat once again, even though the notion of "joint-stock cooperative system" is inaccurate, and the establishment and operation of such enterprises can be very difficult, we may as well let such a title stay, considering the fact that it has been widely accepted by rural officials and farmers. The use of the name "joint-stock cooperative system", or simply the "joint-stock system," represents a departure from the status quo. In property rights reform, instead of haggling over names endlessly, we should set our eyes on the essence of things. If an enterprise is traveling down the road of property rights reform, it will not reach its goal in just a single leap. A more realistic approach is to go step by step toward the final destination.

— *Study & Exploration* bimonthly, issue No. 3, 1994

出现的时候，这些企业之所以被称为“乡镇企业”，一来是为了同当时占支配地位的计划经济体制下的企业（如国有企业、原来的城市“大集体”企业等）相区别。二来考虑这些企业设置于乡镇，而且劳动力也主要来自附近农村。那么今后呢？难道还有与“乡镇企业”相对而言的“城市企业”吗？难道“乡镇企业”只可能设置于乡镇之中，企业所需要的劳动力仅限于农村吗？假定当初成立乡镇企业时，考虑到这些企业与计划经济体制下的企业的运作方式不同，即这些企业是“计划外的”商品生产者，所以要用“乡镇企业”来表示其运作方式的特点。那么今后在市场经济大环境中，还需要分什么“计划外的”商品生产者与“计划内的”商品生产者吗？正如前面已经指出的，企业就是企业，股份制企业就是股份制企业，用不着分什么“城市企业”与“乡镇企业”、“城市股份制企业”与“乡镇股份制企业”。迟早有这么一天，“乡镇企业”这一过渡性的称呼将不再存在，“乡镇股份制企业”这一说法也将消失。

这可能是若干年之后的事情，距现在还有一大段时间。因此，立足于现实，我们仍有必要着手乡镇企业的股份制改革，研讨乡镇股份制企业的组建与运行问题。而且，需要再重复一遍：尽管从理论上说“股份合作制”这种提法是不确切的，在组建与运行中也会碰到各种各样的困难，但考虑到“股份合作制”的名称已经在相当广的范围内被农村干部和农民接受，因此可以不必取消它。用“股份合作制”的名称也好，改用“股份制”的名称也好，都是在现有起点上的前进。可以这么说，在产权改革工作中，不要在名称上争论不休，而要看实质，即是否循着产权改革的道路往前走。“一步到位”是做不到的，“分步到位”更有现实意义。

（原载《学习与探索》，1994 年第 3 期）

RATIONALITY AND PROPORTIONALITY IN INCOME DISTRIBUTION (1994)

What does an equitable income distribution entail? Is rationality a better benchmark than equity for income distribution? These are major questions pertinent to the theory of income distribution. My answer is that the term "equitable income distribution" is vague and smacks of a rehash of the old idea of egalitarianism, so the word "equitable" does not make as much sense as the word "rational" in this regard. This being the case, it is probably appropriate to replace "equitable income distribution" with "rational income distribution."

What kind of income distribution can be considered as being rational? Let us start this topic from the double meanings of rational income distribution.

I. Double meanings of rational income distribution

The term "rational income distribution" means two things: the rationality of income *per se*, and the rationality of income disparity among people. These two meanings, though closely related, are different. For instance, both Mr. A and Mr. B have taken part in market activity as production-factor suppliers with A earning n yuan and B making m yuan in return. The first meaning of rational income distribution poses the following questions: Is the distribution rational for A to make n yuan and for B to make m yuan? Should they be paid higher than n yuan and m yuan, or lower? If they should be paid higher than n yuan and m yuan respectively, how higher should it be for their income to be called rational? If they should be paid lower, how lower for it to be called rational? Such questions pertain to the first meaning of the term "income distribution rationality." The second meaning of the term poses the following questions: Supposing A earns n yuan and B earns m yuan, how little should the disparity between n and m be for it to be called rational? How wide should the disparity between n and m be for it to be called irrational? Mr. A and Mr. B are of course not the only production-factor suppliers and market participants, and there are income gaps among them. We may divide all production-factor suppliers and market participants into groups according to their incomes, to make it convenient to study the meanings of income distribution rationality by looking into the income disparities among these groups in the light of the second meaning of rational income distribution, or "income distribution rationality."

收入分配的合理性与协调（1994）

究竟什么是收入的公平分配？收入分配的合理是不是比收入分配的公平更为合适？这是收入分配理论中的一个重要问题。我的观点是：收入分配的公平是说不清楚的，而且容易导致平均主义分配方式的复归，因此"收入公平分配"的提法不如"收入合理分配"的提法。用"收入分配合理"一词作为"收入分配公平"的替代语也许更为恰当。

那么，究竟什么是收入的合理分配呢？让我们从收入分配合理性的两种含义谈起。

一、收入分配合理性的两种含义

收入分配的合理性有两种含义：一是指收入本身是否合理；二是指人与人之间的收入差距是否合理。两种含义虽然有密切联系，但并不一样。比如说，甲、乙二人都作为生产要素供给者参加了市场活动，某甲得到 n 元，某乙得到 m 元。收入分配合理的第一种含义是指，某甲得到 n 元，某乙得到 m 元，这是否合理？他们应当得到比 n 元、m 元更多的收入呢，还是只应得到少于 n 元、m 元的收入？如果说他们得到的收入应当高于 n 元或 m 元，那么高多少是合理的？如果说应当低于 n 元或 m 元，那么低多少是合理的？这就是第一种意义上的收入合理问题。再说，假定某甲得到 n 元，某乙得到 m 元，那么 n 元与 m 元之间的差距究竟多大为合理，否则就是不合理？社会上不只是某甲、某乙两人，而是有众多的生产要素供给者、市场参与者，他们之间的收入是有差距的。可以在众多的生产要素供给者、市场参与者中，按照收入状况划分为若干组。这样就便于通过对组与组之间收入差距的研究，进而说明社会收入分配的合理与否。这是第二种意义上的收入合理问题。

There are both differences and correlations between the two meanings of income distribution rationality. Studies of the first meaning should serve as the basis for studies of the second meaning. If Mr. A's earning of *n* yuan is rational and Mr. B's earning of *m* yuan is also rational, then the income gap between A and B, or the income disparity between *n* and *m* may also be deemed as rational. However, if A's earning of *n* yuan is irrational, it is hard to believe that the income gap between them, or the income disparity between *n* and *m* is rational no matter how rational B's earning of *m* yuan may be; and vice versa.

People may argue that income distribution in China's recent past under central planning could still be regarded as being well coordinated because despite the meagerness of people's income, the income disparity among them was not so glaring. Does that argument hold water? The question can only be answered after we have understood the double meanings of income distribution rationality. We have to acknowledge that in those years under central planning, when income distribution was dominated by egalitarianism, everyone was underpaid as production-factor suppliers. Given that the earnings of all people were irrational, their income disparity was irrational as well. When income distribution is irrational in either meaning of income rationality, well coordinated income distribution is out of the question in principle.

II. What is meant by income distribution proportionality

Having clarified the double meanings of the rationality of income distribution in the previous section, let me explain what income distribution proportionality means.

Income distribution proportionality is based on both the first and second meanings of income distribution rationality. As was pointed out in the previous section, without the first meaning of income distribution rationality, there can be no income distribution rationality in its second meaning. Well proportioned income distribution is impossible without matching income distribution rationality's double meanings. This being the case, we cannot talk about income distribution proportionality in the absence of income distribution rationality.

第一种意义上的收入合理问题与第二种意义上的收入合理问题有联系，也有区别。对第一种意义上的收入合理问题的研究，应成为研究第二种意义上的收入合理问题的基础。比如说，如果某甲得到 n 元收入具有合理性，某乙得到 m 元收入也具有合理性，那么某甲与某乙的收入差距（n 与 m 的差距）可以被认为是合理的。但是，如果某甲得到的 n 元的收入是不合理的，那么不管某乙得到的 m 元的收入是否合理，都难以认为某甲与某乙的收入差距（n 与 m 的差距）具有合理性。反之，如果某乙得到的 m 元收入是不合理的，那么不管某甲得到的 n 元收入是否合理，也都难以认为某甲与某乙的收入差距（n 与 m 的差距）具有合理性。

也许有人会提出：以前，在计划经济体制下，尽管人们的收入水平都很低，但彼此之间的收入差距不大，所以这仍应当被看成是收入分配的协调，即使是低收入条件下的收入分配的协调。能不能这样看问题呢？只要我们懂得了收入分配合理性的两种含义，这个问题就不言自明了。要知道，在计划经济体制下，在平均主义分配方式占支配地位的条件下，人们的收入都低于他们作为生产要素供给者本应得到的收入。既然彼此的收入都不合理，那么他们之间的收入差距也就不具有合理性。收入分配不合理（包括第一种意义上的收入分配不合理和第二种意义上的收入分配不合理），那还怎么谈得上收入分配的协调呢？

二、收入分配协调的含义

下面，让我们在弄清楚收入分配合理性两种含义的基础上，再就收入分配协调的含义进行阐释。

收入分配协调是以第一种意义上的收入合理分配和第二种意义上的收入合理分配为前提的。这就是如前面已指出的，没有第一种意义上的收入合理分配，第二种意义上的收入合理分配就无从谈起。而如果没有这两种意义上的收入合理分配，收入分配协调也就没有可能性。因此，我们不可能脱离收入分配的合理性来讨论收入分配的协调。

It was also mentioned in the previous section that if income distribution is well-proportioned at a low income level for every market participant, it is proportionality in a false, disguised form. This point can be understood only from the perspective of egalitarian income distribution. Egalitarianism is associated with low efficiency, low productivity, and low income level. A seemingly moderate income disparity under egalitarianism should never be interpreted as evidence of near-perfect income distribution proportionality. Well-coordinated income distribution can only be realized when income is distributed according to people's production efficiency so that every production-factor supplier can receive a rational income. Only then can we say that income disparity among people is rational as well. When everybody's income is low regardless of productivity level, income distribution proportionality is an improbable proposition no matter how income is distributed.

Talking about whether income distribution is well-coordinated or not, people usually refer to the proportionality not only of income distribution among individuals, but also of income distribution among regions. Regional income distribution is another topic of income distribution. We should see that although the effort to guarantee proportionality in income distribution among individuals may run up against some difficulties, it can still be handled with relative ease in comparison with the effort to achieve balanced regional income distribution. This is because whether income distribution among individuals is balanced or not is directly related to whether income distribution is rational or not. The evaluation of the rationality of income distribution among individuals can be relatively easy once the degree of income distribution rationality is measured (even though such measurement is somewhat difficult, a point that I will elaborate on later). By comparison, it is far more difficult to determine whether regional income distribution is well-coordinated or not for the following two reasons.

First, although individual income distribution rationality can be benchmarked by the amount of income individuals earn according to their production efficiency, such a benchmark does not apply to the rationality of regional income distribution. Individual income rationality means individuals earn on the basis of their productivity as production-factor suppliers. However, regional income distribution rationality is not well defined. Regional income may refer to a region's GNP and national income. If that is what regional income is all about, then it is hard to

前面还指出，低收入水平上的收入分配协调，不可能是真正的收入分配协调，而是一种虚假的、真相被掩盖了的、所谓的"收入分配协调"。对这个问题的认识，必须同对平均主义分配方式的认识联系在一起。在平均主义分配方式之下，效率低，生产力水平低，收入水平也低。尽管彼此之间的收入差距不大，但不能认为这时已经接近了收入分配协调。收入分配协调，只有在按效益分配条件下，生产要素供给者各自得到了合理的收入，而彼此之间的收入差距也是合理的时候，才能实现。在普遍低收入的条件下，无论怎样进行分配，也不可能做到收入分配的协调。

在人们谈到收入分配协调还是不协调的时候，通常既指个人收入分配的协调，又指地区收入分配的协调。后者是从另一个角度提出的收入分配协调的含义。我们应当看到，个人收入分配的协调问题尽管也会遇到一些困难，但相对于地区收入分配协调问题而言，仍然比较容易解决。这是因为，个人收入分配协调与否同个人收入分配是否合理直接有关。只要把个人收入分配是否合理问题弄清楚了（虽然这也有一定的难度，关于这一点，下面还要展开讨论），那么个人收入分配协调与否也就较易于作出判断。然而，地区收入分配协调与否的判断却要困难得多。理由是：

第一，个人收入分配的合理性是以个人作为生产要素供给者按生产要素供给的效益取得收入为标准的，但地区收入分配的合理性却很难按照同样的标准来处理。要知道，个人收入是指个人提供生产要素所得到的收入。因为只有这样，才能说明这种收入是否合理。但地区收入的含义却不明确。它可能是指地区的国民生产总值和国民收入。如果地区收入是指这些，那么就难以说明它们是否

judge the rationality of regional GNP or regional income. If regional income equals the average income that individuals make as production-factor suppliers, it is still hard to decide whether it is rational or not, because the average income conceals the differences in efficiency between production-factor suppliers. Given the difficulties in evaluating regional income rationality in its first meaning, it is likewise impossible to judge whether regional income distribution is well coordinated or not.

Second, rationality of income distribution in its second meaning (i.e., rationality of income disparity) is based on income distribution rationality in its first meaning. This should be the case with both individual and regional income distribution rationality. Since income distribution rationality in its first meaning does not apply to regional income distribution as described previously, there is no way to judge the rationality of regional income distribution. The most we can say is that the income disparity between coastal and inland regions is so glaring that something has to be done to reduce it. However, we cannot decide, due to the lack of empirical evidence, how little the disparity should be to put income distribution between the two regions on a rational footing.

Thus it can be said that even though the rationality of regional income distribution and of income disparity calls for in-depth theoretical study, it is better to focus on individual income distribution proportionality. We may as well leave regional income distribution proportionality for the future as a theoretical research topic. Of course, this does not mean we cannot use in general the term "promoting proportionality in regional income distribution," which is meant mainly to keep regional income disparity from growing out of control.

Efficiency or equality, which should come first? The answer will become clearer by treating individuals, rather than regions, as production-factor suppliers. This is because changes in efficiency—which is about effective use and allocation of resources—are relevant to the changes in the effectiveness of the production factors provided by suppliers. Equality—which refers to well-coordinated income distribution in the principle of equal opportunities—applies to individual income distribution and the income disparity arising from it, but not to regional income distribution and the income disparity resulting from

合理，从而地区收入的合理性就缺乏判断的依据。假定把地区收入理解为地区的各个生产要素供给者个人提供生产要素所得到的平均收入，那么这种平均收入同样缺乏判断其合理与否的依据。因为平均收入掩盖了各个不同的生产要素供给者的效益的差别，从而掩盖了各个不同的生产要素供给者的收入的合理性。既然地区收入的合理性缺乏依据，那么上述第一种意义上的收入分配合理与否就判断不了，于是对于地区收入分配的协调与否也是无法判断的。

第二，上述第二种意义上的收入合理分配（即收入分配差距的合理），是以第一种意义上的收入合理分配为前提的。对于个人收入分配合理与否的判断是如此，对于地区收入分配合理与否的判断也应如此。然而，正如前面所指出的，上述第一种意义上的收入合理分配对于地区收入分配是不适用的。既然如此，地区之间收入分配是否合理也就无法判断。人们至多只能说沿海地区的收入与内陆地区的收入差距过大，应当缩小这种收入差距；但却不能判断究竟两个地区之间多大的收入差距才是合理的差距，因为缺乏判断的依据。

由此看来，虽然地区收入分配的合理性和收入分配差距的合理性问题都可以从理论上进行深入的探讨，但在考察收入分配协调问题时，还是以考察个人收入分配协调为宜。至于地区收入分配协调的判断问题，则不妨作为进一步探讨的理论课题，留待今后去研究、解决。当然，这也并不妨碍我们笼统地使用“促进地区收入分配协调”这样的概念，这主要是指要避免地区收入差距过大而言。

再说，在考察效率与公平的顺序排列时，把个人作为生产要素供给者来对待，要比把地区作为生产要素供给区域来对待，更为清晰。因为效率是指资源的有效使用与有效配置；效率的变化，主要与生产要素供给者所提供的生产要素的效率变化有关。而公平，是指机会均等条件下收入分配的协调。这也只适用于对个人之间收入分配及其差距的考察，而不适用于对地区之间收入分配及其差距的

that, because, as to income distribution rationality of a certain region or income disparity rationality among regions, there are no well defined criteria from which to make such a judgment.

III. Differences in economic and social senses of income disparity rationality

Although we cannot but set individual income distribution as the focus for our study of income distribution rationality and proportionality, we must still answer the questions: What is on earth rational disparity in individual income distribution? And why does the economic sense of income disparity rationality not tally completely with its social sense?

From an economic perspective, let us imagine that production-factor suppliers are given the same opportunity to participate in market activity but end up with unequal income. This inequality in income distribution is an outcome of distribution on the basis of production efficiency in compliance with the principle of equal opportunities. Therefore income disparity rationality in an economic sense can exist under two conditions: First, all production-factor suppliers are given equal opportunities so that they can join market activity from the same starting point; and second, these suppliers earn their income according to their production efficiency. Needless to say, irrational income disparity in an economic sense stems either from unequal opportunities (meaning they are not at the same starting point) or from failing to follow the principle of distribution according to efficiency, or from both. In a purely economic sense, income disparity stemming from either or both of the two factors is irrational, and is a manifestation of poorly coordinated income distribution, whether such a disparity is glaring or not. Such irrational income distribution should be remedied through redistribution by government. In other words, in an economic sense, as long as income distribution is the result of all production-factor suppliers having equal opportunities in market activity, with each supplier getting his pay in the principle of distributing according to efficiency, the income disparity, big or small, should be regarded as a sign of rational income distribution, or proportionate income distribution.

To define whether income disparity is rational or irrational in a social sense is more difficult than in an economic sense. Why? This can be answered in two ways.

考察，因为地区收入合理与否，以及地区之间收入差距合理与否的判断标准无法确定。

三、经济意义上与社会意义上收入分配差距合理性的区别

尽管我们不得不把收入分配合理性问题和收入分配协调问题的讨论集中到个人收入分配方面来，但是我们必须承认，在这方面还有一个难题有待于分析。这就是前面已经指出的，究竟什么是个人收入分配的合理差距，以及经济意义上的收入分配差距的合理性与社会意义上的收入分配差距的合理性为什么不完全一致。

从经济上说，假定生产要素供给者都是在同一条起跑线上参与市场经济活动的，竞争的结果使他们的收入有一定的差距，这种收入分配差距是机会均等条件下按效益分配原则起作用的产物。因此，经济意义上的收入分配差距的合理性存在的条件有二：一是生产要素供给者的机会均等，他们之间参与市场经济活动的出发点是相同的；二是生产要素供给者按效益分配原则取得各自的收入。不言而喻，经济意义上收入分配的不合理差距，或者来自生产要素供给者之间机会的不均等，即他们在参与市场经济活动时并非站在同一条起跑线上；或者来自生产要素供给者并非都按效益分配原则取得收入；或者两种情况兼而有之。单纯从经济上进行分析，只要收入分配差距来自上述两个原因（或其中任何一个原因），那么不管收入分配差距是大还是小，都是收入分配的不合理差距，都是收入分配不协调的表现。于是都要政府进行第二次分配来予以协调。换言之，从经济上说，只要收入分配是机会均等条件下生产要素供给者参与市场经济活动的结果，并且各个生产要素供给者都按照效益分配原则取得了收入，那么不管收入分配差距是大还是小，都属于收入的合理分配，也就是收入分配协调的表现。

社会意义上的收入分配差距合理或不合理的界定，比经济意义上的收入分配差距合理或不合理的界定困难得多。为什么这么说？可以从以下两方面来说明：

On the one hand, to judge whether income disparity is economically rational or not, the conclusion should be strictly based on whether market activity opportunities are equal and whether income is distributed among production-factor suppliers according to their production efficiency. Yet in judging the rationality of income disparity in a social sense, it is impossible to find a criterion as strict as that for income disparity rationality in an economic sense. If the criteria used to measure the rationality of income disparity in an economic sense are the same as those for the rationality of income disparity in a social sense, then income disparity rationality would be the same in both senses. If so, isn't it unnecessary to separate the economic sense of income disparity rationality from its social sense? It seems the criterion for judging income disparity rationality in a social sense should not be limited to whether participants have equal opportunities in market activity and whether the principle of distribution according to efficiency is followed when income is distributed among production-factor suppliers. A new criterion should be set, but it is not easy to find out exactly what it should be.

On the other hand, the results of rational income disparity in an economic sense will be eventually reflected economically in efficiency improvement, productivity growth, and per capita income rise no matter how great the disparity is. Thus it is safe to say that the presence of a rational income disparity in an economic sense can yield positive results which can be felt in the immediate future. However, if income disparity is too big in a social sense, it will cause social unrest whether it is economically rational or not. Moreover, social unrest caused by a large income disparity in a social sense cannot be felt immediately—it takes time for problems to crop up and conflicts to brew to the point where social turmoil breaks out. So it is not easy either to judge income disparity rationality from its aftermath in a social sense.

Given the differences between the economic and social senses of income disparity rationality, and the difficulty to define income distribution rationality in its social sense, we cannot but ask: Is it necessary to define such rationality in a social sense apart from defining it in an economic sense? We ought to say the necessity is warranted. If income disparity is rational economically, it would be ideal if it is rational

一方面，在判断经济意义上的收入分配差距合理与否时，是严格地按照是否在机会均等条件下参与市场经济活动和生产要素供给者是否根据按效益分配原则取得了各自的收入来得出结论。而在判断社会意义上的收入分配差距合理与否时，却找不到像判断经济意义上收入分配差距合理与否那样严格的标准。如果采取同判断经济意义上的收入分配差距合理与否的相同的标准，岂不是等于说社会意义上收入分配差距合理与否就是经济意义上收入分配差距合理与否？那样一来，又有什么必要把社会意义上收入分配差距的合理性问题单列出来呢？看来，社会意义上的收入分配差距合理与否的判断标准不能仅限于机会均等条件下的对市场经济活动的参与和生产要素供给者按效益取得收入这样两项，而必须另外寻找。但这个问题却不易解决。

另一方面，经济意义上收入分配的差距，只要是合理的差距，那么不管差距多大，在经济上所反映出来的结果将是效率的增长、生产力的发展、人均收入水平的提高。于是可以认为，经济意义上收入分配合理差距的存在将带来积极的后果。这一积极的后果在近期内就可以被观察到。然而，社会意义上收入分配的差距，如果差距偏大，却会导致社会的不安定，不管这种差距在经济意义上是否合理。加之，由于社会意义上收入分配差距偏大而引起的社会不安定，不一定是近期内就可以被观察到的，这往往需要经过一段时间。问题越积越多，矛盾越来越尖锐时，才会爆发出来。这就表明：要从所产生的后果方面来判断社会意义上收入分配差距的合理性，同样不是一件容易的事情。

既然经济意义上与社会意义上收入分配差距的合理性有上述区别，而社会意义上的收入分配合理性的界定要远远难于经济意义上的收入分配合理性的界定。那么我们不禁要问：是否有必要在界定经济意义上的收入分配差距的合理性之外，再去界定社会意义上的收入分配差距的合理性呢？应当说，这种必要性是存在的。经济意义上收入分配差距合理了，如果从社会意义上说收入分配差距也合理，

socially as well. However, things may turn out like this in reality: An income disparity deemed rational economically is irrational socially; whereas an income disparity deemed irrational economically may turn out to be irrational socially, or ironically rational socially. For this reason, it is necessary to explore income disparity rationality in its social sense despite the difficulties involved. The exploration may bring us closer to solving the problem.

IV. Income disparity rationality in a social sense

As mentioned above, whether opportunities are equal or not for all production-factor suppliers in the market is one of the criteria for assessing income disparity rationality in both economic and social senses. The other criterion is whether income is distributed according to efficiency. The two criteria are necessary conditions for income disparity to be economically rational. However, they are not sufficient conditions for judging an income disparity to be rational in the social sense. It is not easy to find the missing pieces, but we are not helpless either.

Irrational income distribution disparity, manifested in a social sense by income disparity among people, can lead to social instability. Social instability holds back economic development, and causes improvements in production efficiency to slow down, stagnate, or decline, thereby reducing the per capita income level, or inhibiting its growth. Therefore, we can say income distribution disparity is rational in its social sense if social stability is not affected by income disparity among people, if the economy continues to grow in a sustained way, if production efficiency grows as usual, and if per capita income keeps rising steadily. Thus whether or not income distribution disparity leads to social instability can be adopted as a third criterion for judging whether income disparity is rational or not. At least it is a sensible criterion at the current stage of Chinese economic development.

To scrutinize the issue further, at least three questions come to surface.

First, what is the signal for social stability or instability? The economic growth, efficiency, and per capita income resulting from rational income disparity in an economic sense can be reflected in statistical indicators

那当然是最理想不过的。但在实际生活中，却很可能发生这样的情况：一种收入分配差距，从经济意义上说是合理的，而从社会意义上说，却不合理；或者，从经济意义上说是不合理的，而从社会意义上说，既可能也是不合理的，也可能反而是合理的。因此，即使对社会意义上收入分配差距的合理还是不合理的界定远为困难，但在这里作一些探讨仍是需要的。探讨，有助于使我们距离这个难题的解决更近一些。

四、社会意义上收入分配差距合理与否的判断

前面已经提到，生产要素供给者参与市场经济活动的机会均等还是不均等，是判断经济意义上与社会意义上收入分配差距合理性的共同标准之一。生产要素供给者是不是按各自的效益取得收入，是判断经济意义上与社会意义上收入分配差距合理性的另一个共同标准。要判断经济意义上的收入分配差距合理与否，有这两个标准就够了。然而，要判断社会意义上的收入分配差距合理与否，单靠这两个标准还不够（尽管它们仍是不可缺少的），而有必要另外寻找。这个问题虽然难度很大，但还不至于完全没有办法。

社会意义上的收入分配差距的不合理，表现为收入分配差距的存在使得社会上产生了不安定，而社会的不安定又会导致经济发展受阻碍，导致效率的增长缓慢、停滞或下降，导致人均收入水平的降低或难以提高。社会意义上的收入分配差距的合理，则表现为：即使收入分配存在着某种差距，但社会上并未因此而产生不安定。于是经济可以持续向前发展，效率可以依然增长，而人均收入水平也可以照常逐步提高。这样，我们就可以把收入分配差距的存在是否引起社会的不安定看成是社会意义上收入分配差距合理与否的判断标准。初步看来，这个论点是可以站得住的。

但如果再仔细推敲一下，至少有三个问题有待于明确。这三个问题是：

第一，社会安定还是不安定的标志又是什么？经济意义上收入分配差距合理性所导致的经济发展、效率增长、人均收入水平提高，

that are at once computable and comparable. What statistical indicators should be adopted to signal social stability based on rational income distribution disparity in its social sense? How can those statistics be calculated and compared?

Second, as I have said previously, whether income gap rationality or irrationality has contributed to social stability or caused social instability cannot be determined overnight. It takes a brewing period before social instability becomes keenly felt, but that period can last for a long time, which makes it harder to judge if an income gap is socially rational or not. The catch is to find out how the degree of latent social instability can be measured. When judging if an income gap is socially rational or not, how can latent social instability not be mistaken for social stability?

Third, social instability can stem from many factors, and irrational income gap is just one of them. This gives rise to the question: How should the role of irrational income gap in causing social instability be determined in a social sense, and to what degree? In particular, when the income gap is found to be rational socially, can social instability not be caused by other factors? Both questions can make it more difficult to see if the income gap is socially rational or irrational. The secret lies, firstly, in determining how to measure, in a social sense, the role of rational income gap in promoting social stability and to separate this role from the other factors that are also contributing to social stability, and secondly, in discovering how to benchmark, socially, the role of irrational income gap in causing social instability and to separate it from the other factors that are also precipitating social unrest.

I do not list these three major questions to say that we need not to probe any further because of the aforementioned snags. It is precisely because of these problems that I believe we should not and cannot lean heavily on quantitative analysis in this field of study. Rather, we had better adopt a rough-sketch type of approach. To be specific, we may use, as a benchmark, people's satisfaction with their own income and with a comparison of income with other members of society. As people's satisfaction differs in degree in both regards, the findings should be studied separately.

可以用统计指标来表示，可以计算，可以比较。社会意义上的收入分配差距合理性所导致的社会安定，或收入分配差距的不合理所导致的社会不安定，究竟用哪些指标来表示？如何计算？如何比较？

第二，正如前面已经指出的，社会意义上的收入分配差距合理还是不合理的后果表现为社会安定或社会不安定，这并不是短时期内所能观察到的。社会不安定有一个累积过程，有一个潜伏期。通常要等到问题尖锐的时候，才被人们观察到，但时间间隔是比较长的。这样就增加了判断社会意义上收入分配差距合理与否的难度。主要的困难在于：如何衡量潜伏的社会不安定程度？如何才能避免把潜伏的社会不安定当成是社会安定，从而得出社会意义上收入分配差距合理的正确论断？

第三，社会不安定的原因是很多的，社会意义上的收入分配差距不合理只是原因之一。因此，究竟怎样才能判断社会意义上收入分配差距的不合理在社会不安定形成中的作用的大小？社会不安定究竟能在多大程度上归因于社会意义上收入分配差距的不合理？特别是，在社会意义上收入分配差距合理的情况下，难道不会因其他原因而引起社会不安定吗？这些情况同样增加了判断社会意义上收入分配差距合理与否的难度。主要的困难在于：如何衡量社会意义上收入分配的合理差距在促进社会安定方面的作用，并把这种作用同促进社会安定的其他因素的作用区分开来？如何衡量社会意义上收入分配的不合理差距在导致社会不安定方面的作用，并把这种作用同导致社会不安定的其他因素的作用区分开来？

我们列举出以上三个问题，并不意味着由于这些困难的存在而不必再在这个领域内进行探讨了。而是说，正因为考虑到这些困难的存在，所以在这个领域内进行研究时不应当也不可能偏重于数量化的分析，而以比较粗线条式的研究为宜。具体地说，我们不妨以社会成员对自己的收入以及与他人的相比较的收入的满意度作为指标。社会成员对自己的收入的满意度和社会成员对于自己与他人相比较的收入的满意度是不同的，应当分别考察。

The degree of people's satisfaction with their income may be termed "an individual's absolute degree of income satisfaction." This term refers to the degree of correspondence between the income someone receives from the production factors he has supplied on the one hand, and the value of his expected income on the other. A production-factor supplier will be satisfied with his absolute income if what he earns meets his expectation. He will stay satisfied if his earning exceeds his expectation even if the two are not symmetrical. If he earns less than what he expected, he will be dissatisfied with the gap between reality and expectation. The more his actual earning falls below his expectation, the more dissatisfied he becomes, and the lower the degree of his absolute satisfaction is with his individual income.

The degree of a member of society's satisfaction with a comparison between his income and those of others can be abbreviated as the "degree of individual relative income satisfaction." This term denotes the degree of correspondence between the actual ratio of income gap between an individual and the others as production-factor suppliers and his expected ratio. He is satisfied with his relative income if the two ratios correspond with each other. He is even more satisfied if the actual ratio exceeds his expectations, even though the two factors do not correspond with each other. He is dissatisfied if the actual ratio falls below his expected ratio, that is, the two factors are ill-matched. The more the actual ratio falls short of his expected one, the more dissatisfied he becomes with his relative income, or the smaller the degree of his satisfaction is with his relative income.

Society consists of numerous members who differ in absolute or relative income satisfaction. No matter what the mode of income distribution is, there is always a gap between the degrees of the members' absolute and relative income satisfaction. However, an individual's low satisfaction with his absolute or relative income is unlikely to cause social instability. Social instability takes place only when most members of society have registered a low degree of satisfaction over individual absolute or relative income. Theoretically speaking, society's average degree of satisfaction with absolute or relative income at a given

社会成员对自己的收入的满意度可以简称为个人绝对收入满意度。个人绝对收入满意度是指个人作为生产要素供给者对于自己提供生产要素所得到的收入同期望值的对应程度。如果个人作为生产要素供给者在提供一定量的生产要素的情况下所得到的收入同期望值达到了对应，个人就对自己的绝对收入感到满意。如果个人在这种情况下所得到的收入大于期望值，尽管二者并不对应，但由于收入是大于期望值的，所以仍应认为个人对自己的绝对收入感到满意。如果个人在这种情况下所得到的收入少于期望值，表明二者不对应，个人对自己的绝对收入就感到不满意。个人在这种情况下所得到的收入越是少于期望值，个人对自己的绝对收入的不满意程度就越大，或个人绝对收入满意度就越小。

社会成员对自己与对他人相比较的收入的满意度可以简称为个人相对收入满意度。个人相对收入满意度是指个人作为生产要素供给者对于自己提供生产要素所得到的收入在同他人因提供生产要素而得到的收入的实际比率同期望比率的对应程度。如果这种实际的比率同期望的比率达到了对应，个人就对自己的相对收入感到满意。如果这种实际的比率大于期望的比率，尽管二者并不对应，但由于实际比率是大于期望比率的，所以仍应认为个人对自己的相对收入感到满意。如果这种实际的比率小于期望的比率，表明二者不对应，个人对自己的相对收入就感到不满意。实际比率越是小于期望比率，个人对自己的相对收入的不满意程度就越大，或个人相对收入满意度就越小。

社会是由众多成员所组成的。各个社会成员的个人绝对收入满意度不会一样，个人相对收入满意度也不会一样。在任何一种分配方式之下，社会成员的个人绝对收入满意度和个人相对收入满意度之间的差异总是存在的。但某一个社会成员的个人绝对收入满意度低或个人相对收入满意度低并不会造成社会的不安定，而只有在多数社会成员的个人绝对收入满意度低或个人相对收入满意度低的情况下，社会才会出现不安定。于是从理论上说，可以得到一定时点上的

moment in time can be pinpointed. Social instability happens only when this average degree of satisfaction with absolute income falls below a threshold point. The deeper it sinks below the threshold point, the greater the degree of social instability becomes. Social instability occurs when this average degree of satisfaction with relative income drops below a certain point. The more it dips below the threshold point, the greater the degree of social instability becomes.

It is worth noting that there is a difference between the degree of individual absolute income satisfaction and that of individual relative income satisfaction, with the former serving as the basis of the latter. If the degree of an individual's absolute income satisfaction is relatively high, his impact as a production-factor provider on social instability will be negligible even if his relative income satisfaction is low. If the degree of his absolute income satisfaction is low, his impact on social instability will grow even if the degree of his satisfaction with his relative income is high. The degrees of the impact of individual income satisfaction on social instability may be aligned in the following sequence:

1. A high degree of individual absolute income satisfaction alongside a high degree of individual relative income satisfaction, will have a minimum impact on social instability.

2. A high degree of individual absolute income satisfaction accompanied by a low degree of individual relative income satisfaction, will have a relatively small impact on social instability.

3. A low degree of individual absolute income satisfaction coupled with a high degree of individual relative income satisfaction, will have a relatively big impact on social instability.

4. A low degree of individual absolute income satisfaction together with a low degree of individual relative income satisfaction, will have a maximum impact on social instability.

As I have said previously, both the degree of individual absolute income satisfaction and that of individual relative income satisfaction should be indicated according to society's average degrees of absolute and relative income satisfaction. The above sequence of order in the degrees of impact of individual income satisfaction on social instability should also be expressed in the same way.

Considering that the impact of individual absolute income satisfaction on social stability is greater than individual relative income satisfaction,

社会平均绝对收入满意度和社会平均相对收入满意度。当社会平均绝对收入满意度低到某一数值（临界值）以下时，社会将出现不安定。社会平均绝对收入满意度越是低于某一数值（临界值），社会的不安定程度就越大。当社会平均相对收入满意度低于某一数值（临界值）以下时，社会将出现不安定。社会平均相对收入满意度越是低于某一数值（临界值），社会的不安定程度就越大。

要知道，个人绝对收入满意度与个人相对收入满意度是有区别的。个人绝对收入满意度是个人相对收入满意度的基础。作为生产要素供给者的个人，如果个人绝对收入满意度较好，那么即使个人相对收入满意度较差，对社会不安定的影响也不会十分突出。如果个人绝对收入满意度较差，那么即使个人相对收入满意度较好，对社会不安定的影响也会较大。可以把个人收入满意度对社会不安定的影响的轻重程度按下列顺序排列：

1. 个人绝对收入满意度较好，个人相对收入满意度较好。
……对社会不安定的影响最小
2. 个人绝对收入满意度较好，个人相对收入满意度较差。
……对社会不安定的影响较小
3. 个人绝对收入满意度较差，个人相对收入满意度较好。
……对社会不安定的影响较大
4. 个人绝对收入满意度较差，个人相对收入满意度较差。
……对社会不安定的影响最大

正如前面已经指出的，社会成员的个人绝对收入满意度和个人相对收入满意度都应当以社会平均绝对收入满意度和社会平均相对收入满意度来表示。因此，以上关于个人收入满意度对社会不安定的影响的轻重顺序排列也应以社会平均绝对收入满意度和社会平均相对收入满意度来表示。

考虑到在影响社会安定方面个人绝对收入满意度所起的作用要

when combining society's degrees of average absolute and relative income satisfaction to derive society's average degree of income satisfaction, the former should take a larger portion than the latter. Thus a threshold value can be set for society's average degree of comprehensive income satisfaction. Society's average degree of comprehensive income satisfaction and its threshold value may be applied to back up judgment of income gap rationality in a social sense of the term.

Finally, a rundown of the above discussion:

A: individual income;

B: individual's expected income;

C: the degree of correspondence between A and B, known as the degree of individual absolute income satisfaction;

D: the actual ratio between one's income and someone else's income;

E: the expected ratio between one's income and someone else's income;

F: the degree of correspondence between D and E, known as the degree of individual relative income satisfaction.

G: the average degree of social satisfaction with absolute income as derived from C;

H: the threshold value of the average degree of social satisfaction with absolute income;

I: the average degree of social satisfaction with relative income as derived from F;

J: the threshold value of the average degree of social satisfaction with relative income;

K: based on the impact of the degree of individual absolute and relative income satisfaction on social stability, to determine the portions of both factors in their combined impact on social stability;

L: to derive from G, I, and K the average degree of social comprehensive income satisfaction;

M: the threshold value of the average degree of society's comprehensive income satisfaction;

N: based on L and M, to determine, in a social sense, the degree of income gap rationality or irrationality.

大于个人相对收入满意度所起的作用，所以在把社会平均绝对收入满意度与社会平均相对收入满意度综合为一个社会平均收入满意度时，社会平均绝对收入满意度所占的比重应当大一些，社会平均相对收入满意度所占的比重应当小一些。这样就可以形成社会平均综合收入满意度，并确定社会平均综合收入满意度的临界值。社会平均综合收入满意度及其临界值，可以作为判断社会意义上收入分配差距合理与否的依据。

现在，让我们把上面所讨论的作一概述。

A：个人得到的收入；

B：个人对收入的期望值；

C：根据 A 与 B 而得出个人所得到的收入同期望值的对应程度，又称为个人绝对收入满意度；

D：个人得到的收入同他人得到的收入的实际比率；

E：个人对自己得到的收入同他人得到的收入的期望比率；

F：根据 D 与 E 而得出个人收入同他人收入的实际比率同期望比率的对应程度，又称个人相对收入满意度；

G：根据 C 而得出社会平均绝对收入满意度；

H：社会平均绝对收入满意度的临界值；

I：根据 F 而得出社会平均相对收入满意度；

J：社会平均相对收入满意度的临界值；

K：根据个人绝对收入满意度和个人相对收入满意度各自在影响社会安定方面所起作用的大小，确定二者在影响社会安定方面各自所占的比重；

L：根据 G、I、K 而得出社会平均综合收入满意度；

M：社会平均综合收入满意度的临界值；

N：根据 L 与 M 来判断社会意义上收入分配差距的合理与否以及不合理程度。

V. A further look at the relationship between income disparity and social instability

In my previous analysis, social instability is a criterion for income disparity rationality or irrationality. I have said that social instability requires a period of time to gather its momentum. Only when problems come to a head can social instability be keenly felt. Income disparity is only one of several factors that cause social instability. This being the case, we have to look deeper into the relationship between income disparity and social instability based on the previous study of the average degree of society's comprehensive income satisfaction and its threshold value.

First, consider the cumulative nature of social instability. As the old Chinese saying goes, "It takes more than one cold day for rivers to freeze three feet deep." It takes a relatively long cumulative period for social instability to amount to social upheaval. When people's absolute or relative income satisfaction begins to decline, and once it progressively reaches its threshold value, the situation can turn grim in no time. Just as the old refrain puts it, "Things can take a sudden turn for the worse, and, if mishandled, can run out of control." A possible way to prevent this situation from happening is to break the threshold value of the average degree of society's comprehensive income satisfaction into Threshold Values I and II.

When the average degree of society's comprehensive income satisfaction dives below Threshold Value I, social instability will begin to be felt—meaning such instability is relatively mild or partial.

Social instability deteriorates when the average degree of society's comprehensive income satisfaction falls further below Threshold Value II—meaning that it will soon turn into an overall social upheaval.

Thus the grey zone between Threshold Values I and II merits close government attention. Threshold Value I provides a warning sign. When the average degree of society's comprehensive income satisfaction approaches Threshold Value I, the government should be alerted and take action to avoid social upheaval by alleviating income disparity and relevant problems. If the decline in the average degree of society's comprehensive income satisfaction continues beyond Threshold Value I, the government should be further alarmed, because problems are boiling

五、对收入分配差距与社会不安定相互关系的进一步分析

前面在谈到以社会不安定作为判断社会意义上收入分配差距合理与否的依据时曾指出：社会不安定有一个累积过程，有一个潜伏期，通常要等到问题尖锐时才被人们观察到。造成社会不安定的原因较多，收入分配差距只是其中一个原因。既然如此，那么我们在考察这方面的问题时就有必要从社会平均综合收入满意度及其临界值的分析上再前进一步，对收入分配差距与社会不安定的相互关系作较为深入的研究。

先讨论社会不安定的累积问题。俗话说，冰冻三尺，非一日之寒。从社会不安定到社会的剧烈动荡的确有一个较长的累积过程。如果说人们对绝对收入的满意度的下降和对相对收入的满意度的下降都是逐步进行的话，那么一旦突破了临界值，问题很可能一下子尖锐起来。也许可以用这样的词句来形容，这就是，形势急转直下，一发不可收拾。在研究中，怎样对待这种情况呢？一个可能的解决方式是，把社会平均综合收入满意度的临界值分解为社会平均综合收入满意度临界值 I 和社会平均综合收入满意度临界值 II。

社会平均综合收入满意度临界值 I 是指：当社会平均综合收入满意度低到这一数值（临界值 I）以下时，社会将出现不安定。但这时，社会的不安定仍然是较轻的，或者带有局部性质。

社会平均综合收入满意度临界值 II 是指：社会平均综合收入满意度继续下降，当它低到这一数值（临界值 II）以下时，社会状况将急剧恶化。社会将出现严重的不安定，或称为剧烈的动荡，而且往往带有全面动荡的性质。

于是，社会平均综合收入满意度临界值 I 与社会平均综合收入满意度的临界值 II 之间的区域，是政府需要密切注意的范围。临界值 I 是路标。当社会平均综合收入满意度逐步下降而接近临界值 I 时，政府应当由此得到警告，设法缓和社会收入分配差距所产生的

over and conflicts are intensifying. Social upheaval becomes unavoidable once the average degree of society's comprehensive income satisfaction plunges below Threshold Value II. So Threshold Value II is another warning sign. It seems to me that the establishment of Threshold Values I and II can help further clarify the relationship between income disparity and social instability.

The role of income disparity in precipitating social instability, coupled its relationship with other causes of social instability, is a difficult research topic. It is oversimplifying to attribute social instability solely to income disparity. Social instability can be caused by a mixture of many factors that are affecting each other. This makes it hard to quantify the role of income disparity in causing social instability, not to mention the complex relationship between income disparity and its role in causing social instability. For instance, a small income disparity leads to low efficiency, which may result in a low average degree of society's comprehensive income satisfaction (such as in those low-income years when most members of society were disgruntled about the egalitarian practice of "everybody eating from the same big pot"), but it will have little impact on social stability. If income disparity is huge but the average degree of society's comprehensive income satisfaction is tolerable (meaning that most members of society find such an income disparity acceptable), it will not have a major impact on social stability. If income disparity is huge while the average degree of comprehensive social income satisfaction is low, its adverse impact on social instability can be felt; if the disparity grows to a certain degree and the average degree of society's comprehensive income satisfaction has also dropped below a certain threshold, the income disparity may lead to social unrest.

With the complex relationship between income disparity and social stability or instability in mind, we may handle the issue this way:

Let us take income disparity and the average degree of society's comprehensive income satisfaction as two indicators, and let income disparity be represented by the Gini Coefficient. The lower the Gini Coefficient, the smaller the disparity in income distribution. The higher

社会不满等问题，以免引起社会不安定。而临界值 II 则是另一个路标。如果社会平均综合收入满意度在降到临界值 I 之下时仍继续下降，那么尤其要引起政府的警惕。因为问题已经越积越多，矛盾已经越来越尖锐。一旦社会平均综合收入满意度再下降到临界值 II 以下时，社会的剧烈动荡将难以避免。社会平均综合收入满意度临界值分解为临界值 I 和临界值 II，看来有助于进一步说明收入分配差距与社会不安定之间的相互关系。

至于收入分配差距在造成社会不安定方面的作用，以及收入分配差距作为社会不安定的原因之一同造成社会不安定的其他原因的关系，倒是一个真正的难题。的确，把社会不安定单纯归因于收入分配差距，是过于简单的。造成社会不安定的原因很多，而且这些原因也是相互影响的，所以很不容易把收入分配差距在造成社会不安定方面的作用大小从数量上加以确定。特别困难的是，收入分配差距在造成社会不安定方面的作用，同收入分配差距之间的关系是复杂的。比如说，如果收入分配差距较小，即使社会平均综合收入满意度并不高（指社会上多数成员不满意低收入条件下“吃大锅饭”的现状），但很可能只影响经济效率的增长，而不至于影响社会的安定。如果收入分配差距较大，但社会平均综合收入满意度并不很差（指社会上多数成员认为这种收入分配差距仍然是可以接受的），那么这不会对社会的安定有较大的不利影响。如果收入分配差距较大，而社会平均综合收入满意度又比较差，这就会对社会的安定产生较大的不利影响；并且，如果收入分配差距大到一定程度，社会平均综合收入满意度也下降到一定限界之下，那么这对社会安定所产生的不利影响就会大得多，甚至可以认为这时的社会不安定、社会动荡主要是由此引起的。

了解到收入分配差距同社会安定或社会不安定之间的复杂关系，我们就可以对这个问题采取如下的处理方式：

把收入分配差距和社会平均综合收入满意度作为两项指标。收入分配差距可以用基尼系数（Gini Coefficient）代替。基尼系数越小，越接近于收入的均等化；基尼系数越大，收入分配差距

the Gini Coefficient goes, the bigger the income disparity becomes, that is, the further it drifts away from equal income distribution. Thus the relationship between income disparity and the average degree of society's comprehensive income satisfaction can be replaced with the relationship between the Gini Coefficient and the average degree of society's comprehensive income satisfaction.

Whether the average degree of society's comprehensive income satisfaction is high or low, social stability will not be considerably affected by income disparity when the Gini Coefficient is low. Let us therefore forget about this scenario for the time being.

When the average degree of society's comprehensive income satisfaction is high, income disparity will not grow to a point where it can adversely impact social stability whether the Gini Coefficient is high or low. Therefore this scenario can also be ignored as far as this study is concerned.

Thus our study is narrowed down to the scenario where the Gini Coefficient is high and society's average comprehensive income satisfaction is low. Let us set the Gini Coefficient at Levels 1, 2 and 3. The higher the Gini Coefficient, the lower its level. We may also divide society's average comprehensive income satisfaction into three tiers: Tiers 1, 2 and 3. The lower society's average comprehensive income satisfaction, the higher its tier. The three levels of the Gini Coefficient and the three tiers of society's average comprehensive income satisfaction can be paired to serve as benchmarks for judging the relationship between income disparity and social instability. Generally speaking, when the Gini Coefficient stands at Level 1, and society's average comprehensive income satisfaction at Tier 1, the adverse impact of income disparity on social stability is the highest, thereby pinpointing income disparity as the primary reason behind social instability or upheaval. When the Gini Coefficient stands at Level 3 with society's average comprehensive income satisfaction at Tier 3, social instability may be caused mainly by other factors, or a combination of factors that may or may not include income disparity, even though income disparity is also affecting social stability. Under these circumstances, it is difficult to quantify the impact of income disparity on social stability, but at least we can get a rough idea about it by studying individual cases.

越大，即距离收入均等化越远。这样，收入分配差距同社会平均综合收入满意度之间的关系，可以用基尼系数同社会平均综合收入满意度的关系来代替。

由于基尼系数小的时候，不管社会平均综合收入满意度是高还是低，社会安定都不会受到收入分配差距的较大影响，所以这种情况可以略去不讨论。

由于社会平均综合收入满意度较高时，不管基尼系数是大还是小，收入分配差距都不至于对社会安定产生较大的不利影响，所以这种情况也可以暂不讨论。

于是讨论的范围就可以限定为基尼系数大而社会平均综合收入满意度又低时的情况。可以把较大的基尼系数分为若干级。比如说，基尼系数多少为 1 级，基尼系数多少为 2 级、3 级。1 级高于 2 级，2 级高于 3 级。基尼系数越大，级别越高。把较低的社会平均综合收入满意度也分为若干级。比如说，社会平均综合收入满意度多少为 1 级，社会平均综合收入满意度多少为 2 级、3 级。同样地，1 级高于 2 级，2 级高于 3 级。社会平均综合收入满意度越低，级别越高。这样，可以把各级基尼系数同各级社会平均综合收入满意度组合在一起，根据不同的情况来判断收入分配差距同社会不安定之间的关系。一般说来，当基尼系数为 1 级，社会平均综合收入满意度为 1 级时，收入分配差距对社会安定产生的不利影响为最大。这时可以把收入分配差距看成是造成社会不安定、社会动荡的主要原因，造成社会不安定、社会动荡的其他原因相形之下退居于不重要的位置。而当基尼系数为 3 级，社会平均综合收入满意度为 3 级时，收入分配差距固然对社会安定产生了不利的影响，但这时的社会不安定也可能主要由其他因素所引起，至少由其他因素与收入分配差距共同引起。对于这种情况，目前是难以从数量上进行分析的。我们只可能通过对具体情况的具体研究来粗线条地加以说明。

VI. Conclusions

(1) "Equitable income distribution" is a vague notion that smacks of egalitarianism. "Rational income distribution" is a better term. In fact, rational income disparity denotes a reasonable gap in individual income distribution. However, it is necessary to distinguish the economic sense of income disparity rationality from its social sense. A rational income disparity in an economic sense is not necessarily the same as it is in a social sense. In the context of social stability, the government is obliged to take the social sense of income disparity rationality into consideration when intervening in income distribution.

(2) To judge if income disparity is rational or irrational in a social sense, and to decide on the degree of such rationality or irrationality, two indicators can be employed—society's average comprehensive income satisfaction and its threshold value. To maximize the effect of government regulation of income distribution, we may benchmark society's average comprehensive income satisfaction with Threshold Values I and II. In that way the government may use them as warning signs in regulating the economy.

— *Social Sciences Front* monthly, issue No. 6, 1994

小结

1.“收入分配公平”的提法是不清楚的，它容易导致平均主义分配方式的复归，所以不如改用“收入分配合理”这种提法。收入分配合理差距实际上是个人收入分配的合理差距。在这里，需要区分经济意义上的收入分配差距的合理性和社会意义上的收入分配差距的合理性。经济意义上收入分配的合理差距不一定等于社会意义上收入分配的合理差距。从社会安定的角度来看，在政府的收入调节中，不能不把社会意义上收入分配的合理差距问题考虑在内。

2. 要判断社会意义上的收入分配差距合理还是不合理，以及不合理程度究竟有多大，可以用社会平均综合收入满意度及其临界值来加以衡量。为了使政府在这方面能够发挥更好的收入调节作用，可以把社会平均综合收入满意度临界值分解为临界值 I 和临界值 II，并把它们作为两个路标，根据情况采取调节措施。

（原载《社会科学战线》，1994 年第 6 期）

MESHING FISCAL POLICY WITH MONETARY POLICY (1997)

I. Limitations of fiscal policy in an incomplete market

i. Policy effectiveness in relation to economic growth

The interaction between fiscal and monetary policies was a much debated issue between Keynesians and Monetarists. According to post-Keynesian mainstream economics, in macroeconomic regulation the government should, except in times of crisis, avoid adopting fiscal and monetary policies that are tight or loose at the same time. A better choice is to pair tight fiscal policy with loose monetary policy, or loose fiscal policy with tight monetary policy. Monetarists, in principle, are not opposed to the interaction between fiscal and monetary policies, but they maintain that fiscal policy has great limitations. For example, a loose fiscal policy may not achieve the expected goals because fiscal expansion tends to partially "crowd out" private consumption and private investment, but if fiscal policy is tight, it cuts into the economic growth rate, resulting in fiscal expenditure cutbacks that invariably bring down fiscal revenue, thereby diverting the fiscal policy from its prescribed goals. Consequently, they believe that monetary policy is more effective than fiscal policy. Such is the basic policy preference of Monetarists.

In a policy debate with Monetarists, Keynesians further argue that the coordination between fiscal and monetary policies should be discussed in combination with economic policy goals. To be specific, they argue that it is necessary to observe the effects of the coordination between these two policies from the perspective of whether it is conducive to economic stability and sustainable growth.

A loose fiscal policy is supportive of economic growth and plays a positive part in GNP growth. But can it "crowd out" private consumption and private investment? Sweeping generalizations should be avoided in answering that question. The key to the answer lies in whether the market is restrained or not, that is, whether the market can expand in time with GNP growth. If the market expands constantly, a loose fiscal policy in interaction with an equally loose monetary policy in the course of economic growth will squeeze out neither private consumption nor private investment. To put it another way, the "crowding out" effect can happen only when a loose fiscal policy interacts with a tight monetary policy. Only in that scenario can the Monetarist hypothesis make sense.

论财政政策与货币政策的配合使用（1997）

一、市场不完善条件下货币政策作用的局限性

（一）要结合经济增长来分析政策效应

货币政策与财政政策的配合，曾经是凯恩斯学派与货币学派长期争论的问题之一。根据后凯恩斯主流经济学的论述，在宏观经济调节时，除非在异常紧迫的状态中，"双紧"或"双松"都是力求避免的。需要作为政策配合所考虑和选择的是"松紧搭配"，包括松的财政政策与紧的货币政策的配合，或紧的财政政策与松的货币政策的配合。货币学派原则上并不反对货币政策与财政政策的配合，但认为财政政策本身有很大的局限性。例如在采取松的财政政策时，财政的扩张会挤出一部分私人消费与私人投资，从而财政政策不一定收到预期的效果；而在采取紧的财政政策时，经济增长率将会降低。这样，在财政支出减少的同时，财政收入也会相应地下降，从而不一定使财政政策达到预期的目标。因此货币政策的运用要比财政政策的运用更为有效，这是货币学派的基本政策主张。

凯恩斯学派在同货币学派关于政策的论战中，在货币政策与财政政策的配合问题上，进一步研究所得出的一个重要论点是，应当结合经济政策目标来讨论这种政策配合。具体地说，应当以是否有利于经济的稳定与持续增长来考察货币政策与财政政策配合的效应。

松的财政政策是支撑经济增长的，松的财政政策对国民生产总值的增长起着积极的作用。但这时是不是会挤出私人消费与私人投资呢？并不能一概而论。关键在于市场是否受限制，即市场能否随国民生产总值的增长而扩大。假定市场是一个不断扩大的市场，在经济增长过程中，松的财政政策同松的货币政策相配合，那么财政政策并不会挤出私人投资，也不会挤出私人消费。换言之，只有在松的财政政策同紧的货币政策相配合时，才有可能发生所谓的"挤出效应"。货币学派的假设在这种情况下将有效。

Nevertheless, to pair a loose fiscal policy with a loose monetary policy is bound to aggravate inflation. But this consequence can be forestalled if, on the one hand, the monetary policy is loosened only to a certain extent, and on the other, inflation is kept within bounds by boosting economic growth and aggregate supply. If this condition prevails, it broaches the topic of to what extent should monetary policy be loosened to avoid inflation resulting from increased money supply without allowing increased fiscal expenditure to suppress private consumption and private investment. Research on this topic has yet to be fully completed.

Whether the pairing is between a loose fiscal policy and a tight monetary policy or between a tight fiscal policy and a loose monetary policy, it calls for a comparison of effectiveness between the two pairings, as well as that between a tight policy and a loose one. Without such a comparison it is hard to decide how the two should be paired.

ii. Impact of market completeness on policy effectiveness

The above summary of Keynesian and Monetarist viewpoints about coordinating fiscal and monetary policies makes a valuable reference. It is hard to judge which school is correct, because it involves the margin of economic growth and the margin of growth in aggregate supply. If the economic growth rate is too low while aggregate supply grows too slowly, neither fiscal policy nor monetary policy can work whether they are tight or loose, because fiscal expenditure will crowd out private expenditure or decline along with financial revenue. In that way, coordination between fiscal and monetary policies is out of the question. The analysis of monetarists may be warranted in this case. Otherwise, the Keynesian position may sound even more reasonable.

However, the experience of China and that of some other developing nations indicate that the effectiveness of fiscal and monetary policies is associated with the degree of market completeness. To be specific, both fiscal and monetary policies work most effectively if the market is fairly complete. By comparison, a tight fiscal policy tends to meet more impediments than a tight monetary policy in the course of enforcement, and, as a result, its effectiveness will be more or less curtailed.

然而，松的财政政策与松的货币政策配合使用的结果，必然是通货膨胀的加剧。这是“双松”政策所导致的格局。但这种格局被认为是可以避免的，主要是：一方面，使货币政策的放松比较适当；另一方面，通过经济增长和社会总供给增加，使通货膨胀有一定的限度。如果这种设想可以成立，那么需要探讨的问题将是：货币政策放松到何种程度，既可以避免由于银根放松而引起通货膨胀，而又不至于使财政支出的增加挤出私人消费和私人投资。这方面的研究尚有待深入。

无论是松的财政政策与紧的货币政策相配合，还是紧的财政政策与松的货币政策相配合，既涉及财政政策与货币政策效应强弱的比较问题，也涉及松的政策与紧的政策的效应强弱的比较问题。如果不能对这些政策效应强弱的比较有所了解，那么就很难对不同政策配合使用的实际效应作出判断，从而难以对不同政策的配合方案作出选择。

（二）市场完善程度对政策效应的影响

以上有关凯恩斯学派与货币学派有关财政政策与货币政策配合问题的论述，对我们是有参考意义的。我们很难简单地作出判断，认为凯恩斯学派与货币学派之中哪一个正确，哪一个错误，因为这涉及经济增长与社会总供给增长的幅度问题。如果经济增长率过低，社会总供给增长太慢，由于财政支出会排挤私人支出，或者财政支出会同财政收入一起下降，所以松或紧的财政政策都可能起不了较大作用，从而也就谈不到财政政策与货币政策的配合。货币学派的分析这时也许是有道理的。否则，凯恩斯学派的分析似乎更有道理些。

但根据中国与一些发展中国家的经验来看，财政政策与货币政策的作用同市场的完善程度有关。具体地说，假定市场相当完善，那么无论是财政政策还是货币政策的效应，都可以比较充分地显示出来。相形之下，紧的财政政策在实行过程中所遇到的阻力要比紧的货币政策所遇到的阻力更大一些，从而其效应也就相应地受到一定的限制。

The situation will be different if the markets—capital market, securities market, foreign exchange market, property rights market, and so on—are less than complete. In this scenario, monetary policy may come across more obstacles in the course of implementation than fiscal policy, and its effectiveness may be limited to a larger extent. By the same token, a tight monetary policy may face more hindrance than a tight fiscal policy. This is because monetary policy works through the capital market, securities market, foreign exchange market, property rights market and so on, whose incompleteness can deprive the monetary policy of its transmission mechanism or make its transmission mechanism less effective.

Fiscal policy differs from monetary policy in that it impacts the commodity market directly. If the general market is incomplete, the commodity market is usually less incomplete than the other markets, while the capital, securities, foreign exchange and property rights markets tend to be most incomplete. This is exactly true of the Chinese experience, where fiscal policy works relatively more effectively even though a tight fiscal policy may still encounter a lot of obstructions.

This point may be illustrated with the effect of fiscal policy on economic growth. Because fiscal policy has a direct bearing on the commodity market and can change GNP through the extension and contraction, or ebb and flow of that market, it can either restrain or stimulate the rate of economic growth. Even if the commodity market is incomplete, fiscal policy can still act on GNP through corresponding changes in that market, which is ultimately indicated in changes of economic growth rate. This is something monetary policy cannot do, as its impact on the economic growth rate can be considerably lessened—and therefore cannot be as pronounced and direct as the impact of fiscal policy—as long as the capital, securities, foreign exchange and property rights markets remain incomplete. In China, a loosened-up fiscal policy works better than a loosened-up monetary policy in stimulating economic growth, but conversely, it is also more likely to play a larger part in aggravating inflation.

The effects of a loose policy and a tight policy are asymmetrical in an incomplete market. Given the same money market tightness benchmark, a relaxed policy is more effective than a tight policy. This is particularly

假定市场不够完善，比如说，资本市场、证券市场、外汇市场、产权交易市场等都不够完善，那么情况便有所不同。这时，货币政策在实行过程中所遇到的障碍可能大于财政政策，特别是紧的货币政策要比紧的财政政策所遇到的阻力更大一些，从而其效应也就相对地受到一定的限制。理由在于：货币政策的作用是通过资本市场、证券市场、外汇市场、产权交易市场等而发挥的，不完善的市场使货币政策缺乏相应的传导机制或使货币政策的传导机制失灵，所以货币政策不易有效地发挥作用。

财政政策与货币政策不同，财政政策主要直接作用于商品市场。如果说市场不够完善，那么商品市场的不完善程度一般要小于其他市场，而资本市场、证券市场、外汇市场、产权交易市场的不完善程度一般要大于其他市场。目前中国的情形正是如此。因此，财政政策在目前的中国较易于发挥作用，其收效程度也比较高，尽管紧的财政政策仍会遇到不少阻力。

关于这一点，不妨以对经济增长的效应为例。由于财政政策对商品市场直接发生作用，并通过商品市场的伸缩消长而使国民生产总值发生变化，于是既有可能抑制经济增长率，又有可能刺激经济增长。即使商品市场也有不够完善之处，但财政政策的放松或抽紧，依然可以通过商品市场的变化而作用于国民生产总值，并最终反映于经济增长率的变化。货币政策则不然。只要资本市场、证券市场、外汇市场、产权交易市场等是不完善的，货币政策的作用所受限制较大，从而对经济增长率变化的影响也就不那么显著，或不那么直接。在中国，要促进经济增长，松的财政政策要比松的货币政策较为有效；而在加剧通货膨胀方面，松的财政政策所起的作用也要大一些。

松的政策与紧的政策的效应，在市场不完善条件下是不对称的。一般说来，如果确定了银根松紧的标准，那么松的政策的效应

true of monetary policy in an incomplete market. This is because—under the assumption that the capital, securities, foreign exchange and property rights markets are incomplete while the monetary policy lacks a transmission mechanism—the impact of a tight money market is different than that of a loose one even though the effect of monetary policy is restricted to a certain extent. When the money market is loosened up, investors can always obtain credit from different channels, and the economy will be animated correspondingly even if the market remains incomplete. When the loose money market is tightened up, however, some investors will still act on prescribed plans, because market incompleteness has made them oblivious to the pressure of a rising interest rate or a rising reserve requirement ratio. This is because the more incomplete the market is and the bigger the informational restraints are, the more unfair competition becomes. As a result, some privileged investors can still obtain credit and make investment. They may gradually feel the pressure, but generally speaking, the effect of a tightened-up monetary policy on them always comes belatedly.

iii. Pairings of loose and tight policies in an incomplete market

This gives rise to the issue of how to pair a loose policy with a tight one in macroeconomic regulation of an incomplete market. Such pairings are different from those in a complete market in two ways.

Firstly, in a complete market, the effects of both fiscal and monetary policies are keenly felt. Even though a tight fiscal policy tends to hit more snags than a tight monetary policy, it works reasonably well, when and where necessary, to coordinate a loose fiscal policy with a tight monetary policy, or to pair a tight fiscal policy with a loose monetary policy. Yet, things are different in an incomplete market where the capital, securities, foreign exchange and property rights markets are most incomplete, through which monetary policy works. So fiscal policy is more effective than monetary policy. To meet the goal of macroeconomic regulation, fiscal policy is preferred over monetary policy, whose role can be very limited unless robustly enforced. Therefore, it is impractical to count on monetary policy in this regard. Such is one of the salient features of macroeconomic regulation under conditions of an incomplete market.

要大于紧的政策的效应，货币政策在市场不完善条件下的松或紧所产生的影响尤其这样。这是因为，假定资本市场、证券市场、外汇市场、产权交易市场等都不完善，假定缺乏完善的货币政策传导机制，虽然货币政策的效应要受到某种程度的限制，但银根松紧的效应仍是不一样的。银根放松后，即使市场还不完善，但投资者总有可能从不同的渠道获得信贷，经济便会相应地活跃起来。而在银根由松变紧之后，无论是利率上升了还是存款准备金率提高了，市场的不完善仍会使得一部分投资者并不直接感到利率上升或存款准备金率提高的压力，仍然会按照预定的投资计划进行活动。这是因为，市场越不完善，借贷中的信息约束越大，竞争中的不公平程度也越大。于是一部分居于优越地位的投资者仍能获得信贷，照常投资。也许他们以后会逐渐感受到这种压力，但总的说来，货币政策抽紧后的政策效应对投资者是滞后的。

（三）市场不完善条件下的“松紧搭配”

由此涉及在市场不完善条件下的宏观经济调节的“松紧搭配”问题。这种条件下的“松紧搭配”同市场完善条件下的“松紧搭配”是有区别的。区别大体上有两点。

第一，在市场完善条件下，由于财政政策的效应与货币政策的效应都可以显现出来，尽管紧的财政政策要比紧的货币政策所遇到的阻力更大一些，但这并不妨碍在必要时既可以用松的财政政策同紧的货币政策配合，也可以用紧的财政政策同松的货币政策配合，从而都可以收到一定成效。然而，在市场不完善条件下，情况便有所不同。由于资本市场、证券市场、外汇市场、产权交易市场等要比商品市场更加不完善，而财政政策是直接作用于商品市场的，货币政策则要通过资本市场、证券市场、外汇市场、产权交易市场等发挥作用，所以在选择财政政策与货币政策配合时，为了达到宏观经济调节的目标，财政政策使用的效果比较明显。至于货币政策，除非加大力度，否则其作用受限制较大，所以不宜对它的效应寄以不切实际的希望。这正是市场不完善条件下宏观经济调节的一个特点。

Secondly, a tight fiscal or monetary policy will strain money supply, bring down the economic growth rate, and curtail the inflation rate, whereas a relaxed fiscal or monetary policy will loosen up money supply, boost economic growth, and reduce unemployment. However, all this can happen only in a complete market. In an incomplete market, macroeconomic regulation will be slow to take effect, and worse, the results might be unexpectedly distorted. This is because the securities, foreign exchange and property rights markets are more incomplete than other markets, and therefore the transmission mechanism of monetary policy becomes even more flawed. If curtailing inflation is the goal of government policy regulation, the adoption of a tight fiscal policy can quickly cool down the economy and reduce inflation because this policy works especially well in this field when it is tightened up. However, the tight fiscal policy needs to be paired with a loose monetary policy if we are to prevent the economy from being cooled to such an extent as to thwart economic growth. Furthermore, because of the incompleteness of the market, and the flaws in monetary policy's transmission mechanism, a loosened monetary policy cannot work properly in the course of enforcing a tight fiscal policy, thereby defeating the purpose of maintaining the economy's momentum. As a result, with the tight fiscal policy having a strong effect and the loose monetary policy having a weak effect under incomplete market conditions, the economy is likely to be over cooled or even bogged down in stagnation. That echoes the saying, "It is easier to stop a car than to rev it up again."

Similarly, when raising economic growth is the goal of government policy regulation, a relaxed fiscal policy can be adopted in interaction with a tight monetary policy because this is where the relaxed fiscal policy works particularly well. Stimulated by expanded fiscal expenditure or tax reduction or exemption, the economy achieves rapid growth, but it is necessary for the relaxed fiscal policy to be accompanied by a tight monetary policy to curb inflation in this process of accelerated economic growth. However, the incompleteness of the market and the flaws in its own transmission mechanism prevent the tight monetary policy from working properly in the course of enforcing the relaxed fiscal policy, thereby failing to achieve the goal of keeping economic growth and inflation from running too high. Thus, under incomplete market conditions, the strong effects of the relaxed fiscal policy, coupled with the weak effects of the tight monetary policy, can result in excessive economic expansion, and make it hard to contain hyperinflation.

第二，市场完善条件下，当实行紧的财政政策或紧的货币政策时，银根会随之抽紧，经济增长率会下降，通货膨胀率会受到抑制。而在实行松的财政政策或松的货币政策时，银根会随之放松，经济增长率会上升，失业率也会相应地下降。但这种情况只可能出现于市场完善时。如果市场不完善，那么宏观经济调节的效应不仅不能及时显现出来，甚至其结果可能遭到扭曲，产生预料之外的结果。这是因为，在各个市场中，资本市场、证券市场、外汇市场、产权交易市场等的不完善程度较大，货币政策的传导机制更有欠缺。如果准备以抑制通货膨胀作为政策调节目标，那么在实行紧的财政政策与松的货币政策相配合时，由于紧的财政政策易于发挥作用，经济很快地冷却下来，通货膨胀可以得到抑制。但为了使经济不至于冷却过度，不至于妨碍经济增长，配合以松的货币政策是必要的。然而由于市场的不完善和货币政策传导机制的欠缺，松的货币政策在紧的财政政策实行过程中难以发挥作用，达不到使经济仍然保持活跃的目的。结果，市场不完善条件下的紧的财政政策的效应较强和松的货币政策的效应较弱，从而有可能使经济冷却过度或使经济陷于停滞状态。所谓“刹车容易启动难”正表现于此。

与此相似的是，如果准备以促进经济增长作为政策调节目标，那么在实行松的财政政策与紧的货币政策相配合时，由于松的财政政策易于发挥作用，经济受到财政支出扩张或税收减免的刺激而以较快的速度增长。但为了防止出现经济增长过程中的通货膨胀，配合以紧的货币政策是必要的。然而也正由于市场的不完善和货币政策传导机制的欠缺，紧的货币政策在松的财政政策实行过程中难以发挥作用，达不到避免经济增长率过高和通货膨胀过猛的目的。结果，市场不完善条件下的松的财政政策的效应较强和紧的货币政策的效应较弱，从而使得经济扩张过度，通货膨胀难以被抑制。

Therefore, the troubles met in the coordinated application of fiscal and monetary policies in an incomplete market are attributed to the "limping status" of both policies. In other words, the pairing of an effective policy with a less effective one makes it hard to achieve the goals.

This, however, does not preclude the combined use of fiscal policy and monetary policy in an incomplete market. Rather, it means that the forcefulness of both policies should be taken into account when pairing them up. For instance, given the strong effect of fiscal policy and the weak effect of monetary policy, we can implement the latter with more impetus than the former, so as to maximize the outcome of the combination.

iv. Conclusion: It is easier to stop a car than to rev it up again

In the previous chapters I have made a tentative study of the coordinated adoption of fiscal and monetary policies. What does this mean for the Chinese economy in the present stage of development? As I have stated in the foregoing, the effectiveness of monetary policy is considerably restrained in an incomplete market, which makes it even harder to be coordinated with fiscal policy. For this reason, I would like to draw attention to the following two points:

First, in the current stage of economic development in this nation, it is inappropriate to adopt a relaxed fiscal policy alongside a relaxed monetary policy, or a tight fiscal policy together with a tight monetary policy, because the former tends to lead to runaway inflation and the latter a stifled economy. The only option is to couple a tight fiscal policy with a relaxed monetary policy, or vice versa. Given the different attributes of the effects of the fiscal and monetary policies under incomplete market conditions, I would suggest a relatively tight fiscal policy alongside a relaxed monetary policy.

Second, under incomplete market conditions, the Chinese economy is typical of the saying, "It is easier to stop a car than to rev it up again." It is also where the asymmetrical nature of the effects of macroeconomic regulation is most pronounced. That is to say, when macroeconomic regulation tightens up, its effect is quickly felt and the economy retrenches as a result. By contrast, if macroeconomic regulation slackens only slightly, it can hardly serve the purpose, because the economy can only revive slowly or stay stagnant for a considerable time before it comes back to its own. Why? Because the economy can be dynamic, the purchasing power stays strong and the market thrives

对市场不完善条件下财政政策与货币政策的配合使用所遇到的困难，同政策的“跛足”状态有关。即两种政策的效应一强一弱，使得调节过程中不易实现预定的目标。

这并不意味着在市场不完善条件下不可能配合使用财政政策和货币政策，而是指在配合使用这些政策时应当更多在政策强度上多加考虑。比如说，考虑到财政政策的效应强而货币政策的效应弱，于是就可以减轻财政政策的强度而加重货币政策的强度，以便这两种政策在实行过程中能较有效地发挥作用。

（四）一个重要结论：要注意“刹车容易启动难”

以上，对财政政策和货币政策的配合使用问题作了一些探讨，这对于当前的中国经济有什么意义呢？正如前面所说，市场不完善使得货币政策所受到的限制更大，也使得财政政策与货币政策的配合使用更难。因此，就现阶段的中国经济而言，需要注意的是以下两点：

1. 松的财政政策与松的货币政策的配合使用，以及紧的财政政策与紧的货币政策的配合使用，对目前的中国经济都不适当。因为这样一来，要么会使通货膨胀遏制不住，要么会把整个经济搞得过死。可以考虑的只能是：财政政策与货币政策一紧一松。而根据市场不完善条件下财政政策与货币政策各自效应的特点，最好是实行稍紧的财政政策与松动的货币政策相配合。

2. 市场不完善条件下，中国经济的显著特点之一是“刹车容易启动难”。宏观调节的效应的不对称性也表现于此。这是指：宏观调节抽紧的时候，效应会迅速反映出来，经济会很快趋于紧缩。而当宏观调节放松一些的时候，调节不易达到预期的效果；经济只可能缓慢地复苏，甚至要滞后相当长的一段时间，经济才会重新活跃。理由是：要经济活跃，必须使企业与投资主体有盈利前景看好的

only when businesses and investors are optimistic about the prospects of good profits and consumers are confident in anticipation of higher income. Nevertheless, it takes time to boost optimism and confidence. Expansionary policies cannot make people sanguine about market prospects right away, while the "limping state" in which fiscal policy outplays monetary policy can land macroeconomic regulation in an impasse. It will be even harder to rev up the economy with a tight fiscal policy in the absence of a relaxed monetary policy.

Hence the foregone conclusion: At the present stage of development, China can only slightly tighten up its fiscal policy while loosening up its monetary policy a little. Otherwise, the economy can never be delivered from the dilemma in which "it is easier to stop the car than to rev it up again."

II. Be prudent with unconventional monetary policy tools

i. Three basic monetary policy tools predicated on market completeness

Monetary policy impacts GNP through its effects on the capital, securities, foreign exchange and property rights markets. If changing GNP is the policy's ultimate goal, a series of intermediary goals are needed. If changing inflation and GNP are the dual ultimate goals, they cannot be fulfilled before the intermediary goals are attained. Therefore, in our research on the impact of monetary policy on the economy, we should study this policy's transmission mechanism, and observe, through its different tools, the policy's impact on the intermediary goals, for the purpose of finding the ways and means with which to attain the ultimate goals through these intermediary ones.

Interest rate is one of the intermediary goals of monetary policy. Under complete market conditions, the central bank applies a rediscount policy to influence the interest rate. When the rediscount rate is readjusted, it will change commercial banks' cost of borrowed funds, thereby precipitating readjustments in the interest rate on the market, and compelling investors to raise or reduce their monetary demand.

Money supply thus becomes the most important of all intermediary goals that, alongside the interest rate, influences society's monetary demand, aggregate demand, and GNP. If the monetary policy's transmission mechanism is effective, it can exert its impact, through the central bank's rediscount policy, to attain both the intermediate goals and the ultimate goals. This, however, also has something to do with the economic

信心，必须使广大消费者有预期收入上升的信心。这样才能使购买力旺盛，使市场繁荣。然而，信心的增强是一个累积的过程，并不是宏观调节一放松就能积累起人们对市场前景的信心的。加之，宏观调节的"跛足状态"（即财政政策作用大于货币政策作用的状态），使得调节遇到困难。假定在实行稍紧的财政政策的同时不使货币政策松动，经济启动的困难就更大了。

结论是很清楚的：现阶段，中国的财政政策可以稍紧一些，而货币政策则应该松动一些，否则不易摆脱"刹车以后启动不了"的窘境。

二、货币政策非常规手段应当慎用

（一）货币政策三个基本手段的作用全都依存于市场完善程度

货币政策对资本市场、证券市场、外汇市场、产权交易市场等发生作用，并通过这些作用而影响国民生产总值的变化。如果以国民生产总值的变化作为最终目标的话，那么在这以前还有一系列中介目标。如果以通货膨胀率的变化和国民生产总值的变化作为双重最终目标，同样会有一系列中介目标存在。所以要研究货币政策对经济的作用，必须研究货币政策的传导机制，必须结合各种不同的货币政策手段的运用来考察货币政策对这些中介目标的影响，以及如何通过中介目标来影响最终目标。

利率是货币政策的中介目标之一。在市场完善条件下，中央银行运用再贴现政策来影响利率。当中央银行调整再贴现率时，将使得商业银行的借入资金成本发生变化，从而引起市场利率的调整，再使得投资者增加或减少对货币的需求。因此，货币供应量便是最重要的一个中介目标，它同利率水平这个中介目标一起影响着社会对货币的需求、社会总需求以及国民生产总值的变化。如果货币政策的传导机制有效，那么通过中央银行的再贴现政策可以作用于中介目标的实现，并对最终目标发生影响。然而这又同整个经济环境

environment as a whole. If the market is incomplete, rediscount policy cannot work as a monetary policy step on money demand the way it does in a complete market, nor can it work effectively for the attainment of another intermediary goal, the volume of money flow. Unless the rediscount policy is executed with government intervention, changing the rediscount rate cannot work on the increases or reductions in money flow.

We may take a further look at the impact of the rediscount rate. For the changing rate to exert a desired influence on interest rate, there need be full competition among commercial banks that are supposed to grant loans to clients strictly in line with the norms of market competition and selection, while the clients are likewise expected to compete on an equal footing. Otherwise, the impact of rediscount rate readjustments on interest rate will be much confined.

Adjusting reserve requirement ratio is another monetary policy tool to influence commercial banks' derived deposit, restrain their lending behavior, and ultimately affect money supply. Here, another intermediary goal—the volume of money supply—can be attained through adjusting the central bank's reserve requirement ratio. This, however, can materialize only when this ratio stays at a high level. Otherwise, even though the reserve requirement ratio can work as a monetary policy tool, it cannot serve the purpose of forestalling any financial crisis. Furthermore, the reserve requirement ratio cannot function as a policy tool without two preconditions. For one thing, commercial banks should set maximum profits as their goal, for without such a goal, the effectiveness of readjustments in the reserve requirement ratio and of the reserve requirement system itself will be greatly blunted. This precondition is hinged on the soundness of the commercial banking system. For another, central bank's adjustment of the reserve requirement ratio should be compulsory rather than elastic; otherwise it could defeat the purpose of this monetary policy tool to intervene in money supply.

Although the adjustment of reserve requirement ratio is not a frequent monetary policy tool, the effectiveness of its transmission mechanism still rests on the degree of market completion.

The central bank's open market operation is yet another monetary policy tool that should also be observed from an economic environment perspective. In comparison with other monetary policy tools, open

有关。假定市场不完善，再贴现作为货币政策的手段不可能像在市场完善时那样影响投资者对货币的需求，也不可能对货币供应量这一中介目标发挥有效的作用。除非再贴现政策的实行伴随着行政干预，否则货币供应量的增加或减少可能不受再贴现率变动的影响。

可以对再贴现率的作用再做些分析。如果想通过再贴现率的调整来影响市场的利率水平，那就需要有商业银行的充分竞争。并且假定商业银行完全按照市场竞争与选择规则给予客户贷款，而客户之间也存在着彼此公平竞争的关系，否则再贴现率调整对市场利率水平的影响也是不明显的。

存款准备金率的调整是另一个货币政策手段。这一手段之所以能发挥作用，是因为它的调整与使用可以影响商业银行的派生存款数额，约束商业银行的放款行为，从而影响货币供应量。在这里，货币供应量作为中介目标，可以通过中央银行存款准备金率的调整而实现。但是，除非存款准备金率很高，否则，存款准备金率作为一种货币政策手段尽管能起作用，却达不到防止金融危机的目的。此外，要让存款准备金率起作用，还需要有两个前提。一是商业银行应当以最大利润的取得作为自身的目标。如果商业银行尚不具备这样的条件，存款准备金率的调整、甚至存款准备金制度本身都不会产生多大的成效。这就同商业银行制度是否健全有关。二是中央银行的存款准备金率调整应当具有强制性而不应具有弹性，否则货币政策这一手段是难以达到影响货币供应量的目标的。由此看来，尽管存款准备金率调整并不是经常采取的一种货币政策手段，但它的传导机制是否有效仍然依赖于市场的完善程度。

至于中央银行的公开市场业务，它作为货币政策的又一手段，同样需要从经济环境上进行分析。相对于其他货币政策手段而言，

market operation calls for more stringent market conditions—a complete and mature securities market over and above a rational market interest rate and sensible investors. Pitfalls in the transmission mechanism of open market operation can not only make it hard to achieve the intermediary goal of adjusting money supply but also frustrate open market operation as a monetary policy tool.

The rediscount rate, the reserve requirement ratio, and open market operation discussed here are three essential monetary policy tools. Their transmission mechanisms are, without exception, associated with the soundness of the market and the commercial banking system. They invariably become crippled or totally ineffective under incomplete market conditions or a flawed commercial banking system.

ii. Unconventional policy tools also depend on market completeness

Now a look at two unconventional policy tools besides the three aforementioned monetary policy tools: (1) credit scale control or credit rationing; and (2) rediscount quotas and relending quotas. The central bank uses the former to control the lending scale of commercial banks, and the latter as a supplement to rediscount rate readjustments. Both are adopted under incomplete market conditions or under a flawed commercial banking system, but each uses a different transmission mechanism.

The central bank decides credit scale on the basis of its judgments of the economic situation. Differences in the grounds and perspectives for such judgment, and errors in evaluating credit scale effectiveness invariably lead to considerable arbitrariness in the central bank's credit scale control. The will of the government plays a big role therein as well. Controlled credit scale can change the money supply volume directly and rapidly, and in that sense, the transmission mechanism of the credit scale control policy is effective. However, prompt response and an effective transmission mechanism are not necessarily conducive to the attainment of the monetary policy's ultimate goal. This is mainly because resource allocation must be optimized constantly if economic growth is to be sustained and inflation is to remain low. Optimized resource allocation indicates improved efficiency. However, the effectiveness of credit scale control is a different story. The problem with credit scale control is that money supply may change the way policymakers want in the short run,

公开市场业务所要求的市场条件更为严格。它不仅要求有完善的、发育健全的证券市场，而且要求有合理的市场利率和理性的投资者。公开市场业务的传导机制有欠缺，不仅可能使货币供应量这一中介目标的调节遇到困难，还可能使公开市场业务无法顺利开展，起不到货币政策手段的作用。

以上所说的再贴现率、存款准备金率和公开市场业务是货币政策的三个基本手段。它们的传导机制全都同市场完善与商业银行制度健全有关。市场条件不完善或商业银行制度不健全，必然使得这些政策传导机制有欠缺，甚至失效。

（二）非常规的信贷手段同样依存于市场是否完善

接着，再看看这三种货币政策手段以外的两种非常规政策手段，一是信贷规模控制或信贷配额制，二是再贴现限额与再贷款限额。前者是商业银行在中央银行控制下所受到的贷款规模限制，后者被中央银行用来作为再贴现率调整的手段的补充。这两种手段一般都是在市场不完善或商业银行制度不健全的情况下被中央银行采用的。它们的传导机制各有特点。

信贷规模的大小是由中央银行根据对经济形势的判断而决定的。由于对经济形势判断的依据不一，观察问题的角度不同，以及对信贷规模效应的估计有差异，所以中央银行的信贷规模控制带有相当大程度的随意性。行政主管部门的意志在这里起着很大的作用。信贷规模受到控制，货币供应量便直接发生变化，它的效应的产生比较迅速。从这个意义上说，信贷规模控制这一手段的传导机制是有效的。但效应产生的迅速和传导机制的有效不等于效应一定有利于实现货币政策的最终目标。这主要因为，要促进经济的持续增长并使通货膨胀率保持在较低的水平，必须使资源配置不断优化。资源配置优化表明效率的增长。然而信贷规模控制的效应却是：尽管从短期来看货币供应量发生了政策决策部门所预期的变化，

but in the long run, with policymakers' will imposed on it, this monetary policy tool is detrimental to optimizing resource allocation, and will inevitably derail the monetary policy's ultimate goal.

Rediscount and relending quotas are adopted as another unconventional policy tool to make up for the limitations of rediscount rate readjustments. Rediscount quotas may enable the central bank to manipulate commercial banks' money-lending capacities by increasing or decreasing such quotas, and starting from there to further control overall money supply. The same purpose can be achieved by increasing or decreasing the relending quotas. However, the central bank's rediscount quotas and relending quotas, being arbitrarily decided by the government, are so subjective that they do not necessarily fit the reality of money supply. Therefore, whether such quotas are beneficial or detrimental to the realization of the monetary policy's ultimate goal is open to question. On the other hand, these unconventional tools may impair the optimization of resource allocation, and, in the long run, will hold back the attainment of the ultimate goal of the monetary policy.

iii. Using credit scale control and other unconventional measures with prudence

From our study of monetary policy's transmission mechanisms we may conclude that if the market is complete and the commercial banking system sound, these transmission mechanisms may work effectively. If the market is incomplete and the commercial banking system flawed, it is impossible for conventional monetary policy tools to achieve expected results. As to such unconventional monetary policy tools as credit scale control, rediscount quotas and relending quotas, although their transmission mechanisms may remain effective in such a scenario, they are, in the long run, detrimental to the optimization of resource allocation and the attainment of the monetary policy's ultimate goal.

The question at hand to be answered is: What is to be done to reactivate the economy after a period of economic retrenchment? As is noted in the previous section, the adoption of a relatively tight fiscal policy in coordination with a loosened monetary policy under these circumstances is better than the pairing of a loosened fiscal policy with a tightened monetary policy, and even better than coupling fiscal and

但只要从稍长的时间来看，这种带有行政主管部门意志的货币政策手段有损于资源的优化配置，结果不可避免地妨碍货币政策最终目标的实现。

中央银行的再贴现限额与再贷款限额作为货币政策的又一非常规手段，一般也是在市场不完善或商业银行制度不健全条件下被采用的。这主要是考虑再贴现率的调整所起的作用有限，所以要从数量上再予以限制。假定采取了再贴现限额这种做法，中央银行就有可能通过限额的增减而影响商业银行的贷款能力，进而影响货币供应量。同样的道理，中央银行也可以通过再贷款限额的增减达到同一目标。这种做法被认为有助于弥补再贷款利率调整的效力的不足。然而，无论是中央银行的再贴现限额还是再贷款限额，都是由行政主管部门随机制定的，带有较浓的主观色彩，同实际的货币供求状况不一定相符。因此对货币政策最终目标的实现究竟是有利还是不利，还难以确定。而另一方面，这些手段也会对资源优化配置产生损害，从而从较长时间来看，将会妨碍货币政策最终目标的实现。

（三）要慎重使用信贷规模控制等非常规手段

从货币政策传导机制的研究中，可以得出这样的结论：如果市场是完善的并且商业银行制度是健全的，那么传导机制可以有效地起作用。如果市场不完善，商业银行制度不健全，那么常规的货币政策手段不可能使得货币政策的最终目标实现。而诸如信贷规模控制和再贴现限额、再贷款限额之类的非常规的货币政策手段，虽然其传导机制仍然可以有效，但从较长时间来看，却不利于资源优化配置，从而不利于货币政策最终目标的实现。

现在我们所要探讨的问题是，在经历过一段时间的经济紧缩之后，怎样才能使经济再度活跃起来？在上一节中已经指出，针对这种情况，实行稍紧的财政政策与松动的货币政策的配合，要优于松动的财政政策与稍紧的货币政策的配合，更优于财政政策与货币政策

monetary policies that are both rigid or both relaxed. Our analysis of monetary policy's transmission mechanisms is further proof that this conclusion tallies with the reality of our nation.

Unconventional monetary policy tools—credit scale control, rediscount quotas, and relending quotas included—are often resorted to under incomplete market conditions. Worse, the trend is to regard these unconventional measures as conventional ones, as if the ultimate goal of the monetary policy can never be attained without doing so. In fact, this is sheer misunderstanding. Just as is discussed in the foregoing, despite being somewhat effective, these unconventional measures are harmful to optimizing resource allocation, and, corrupted by government will, cannot satisfactorily fit the money supply situation in economic operation.

To rejuvenate the economy after a period of retrenchment, it is imperative to loosen up the monetary policy more forcefully along with a relatively tight fiscal policy. Thus prudence must be applied when employing such unconventional policy measures as credit scale control, and for three reasons:

First, the transition from economic entrenchment to economic revival hinges on restoring and enhancing public confidence in market prospects, but confidence can be built up only through a cumulative process. The adoption of unconventional monetary policy tools can engender nothing but uncertainty whether they are relaxed or rigid. If the government can employ relaxed measures, it can also choose rigid ones. In either case there are no norms to go by, because things are at the mercy of those who adopt such measures. The result can be the same: People feel their confidence draining away. That being the case, little or no use should be made of unconventional measures. We would rather adopt conventional monetary policy tools that are sure to help boost people's confidence. Although incomplete market conditions may somewhat tarnish such measures' effectiveness, that can be remedied with redoubled enforcement efforts.

Second, because unconventional monetary policy tools are often misleading to investors, and thus of great disservice to optimizing resource allocation even if a relaxed monetary policy has been adopted to activate the economy, the ultimate goal still cannot be attained due to

的“双紧”或“双松”。有关货币政策传导机制的分析，进一步证实了以上的结论是符合中国当前实际情况的。

我们承认，在市场不完善条件下，非常规的货币政策手段（包括信贷规模控制、再贴现限额、再贷款限额等）经常被使用，甚至存在着把非常规的货币政策手段视为常规的货币政策手段的趋势，似乎非如此不足以实现货币政策的最终目标。其实，这纯粹是一种误解。正如前面已谈过的，非常规的货币政策手段虽然能起一定作用，但对资源的优化配置并不有利；特别是它们带有浓厚的行政主管部门意志的色彩，从而同经济运行中的货币供求状况不一定相适应。

在经历过一段时间的经济紧缩之后，要使得经济再度活跃，应在实行稍紧的财政政策的同时，使货币政策松动些，而且力度也应当加大。在这种情况下，信贷规模控制等非常规手段的使用要慎重。这主要是因为：

1. 从经济紧缩走向经济再度活跃，同人们对市场前景的信心的恢复与增强有着密切的关系，而信心的增强是一个累积的过程。假定采用非常规的货币政策手段，无论它们趋向于放松还是趋向于抽紧，都给人们一种不确定的感觉。既然行政主管部门能“放”，它们无疑也能“收”。“放”与“收”都无规律可循，都在很大程度上凭借非常规手段使用者的意志，那么人们的信心依然是不足的。在这种情况下，倒不如不使用或少使用非常规的货币政策手段，宁肯采取常规的货币政策手段，这对于信心的增强和累积反而有利些。虽然常规手段会因市场不完善而使其作用受限制，但力度加大一些，仍可弥补。

2. 由于非常规的货币政策手段的使用往往给人们以错觉，给投资主体以误导，从而不利于资源的优化配置。因此，即使依靠放松了的货币政策来活跃经济，但资源配置难以优化，实际上起不到预期的

the failure of these tools to optimize resource allocation. To rejuvenate the economy and keep it primed after a period of retrenchment, it is really important to focus on optimizing resource allocation so that production factors can be grouped and resource use efficiency increased according to market demand. In this regard, unconventional monetary policy measures compare unfavorably with conventional ones. It must be pointed out that, the restraints imposed on conventional measures by an incomplete market can always be overcome through redoubled implementation efforts.

Third, monetary policy can be loosened up a little more than usual, but this should be done on condition that commercial banks issue loans only according to the redeemability of such loans and the borrowers' fund use efficiency. Otherwise bad debts will pile up, and economic vitality will suffer. What, then, is to be done to avoid the accumulation of debts under a relaxed monetary policy? What kind of monetary policy measures—conventional or unconventional—should be employed in this regard? Obviously, unconventional monetary policy measures are susceptible to arbitrariness and government intervention, making it hard to curtail bad debts, let alone achieve the anticipated results of the relaxed monetary policy.

III. The eclipse of monetary policy's effectiveness

i. What makes monetary policy increasingly less effective

The eclipse of monetary policy's effectiveness becomes an issue when our study comes to the position and impact on objective economic regulation of such policy. This refers to the fact that after a monetary policy has been executed for some time, its positive impact on attaining the ultimate goals of economic growth and monetary stability will ebb steadily while its negative impact on the economy will increase.

The waning of a monetary policy's effectiveness may be a universal occurrence. It happens whether the market and commercial banking system are flawless or not. Naturally, the decline in policy effectiveness becomes more serious when the market is incomplete and the commercial banking system faulty.

The decreasing effectiveness of monetary policy is attributed mainly to the fact that market participants—commercial banks, other monetary institutions, and nongovernmental investors—are sensible economic

实现货币政策最终目标的作用。在经济紧缩一段时间以后，要使得经济再度活跃起来，并使这种活跃持久一些，就必须注意资源配置的优化，以便切实地按照市场需要来组合生产要素，提高资源利用效率。就这一点而论，使用非常规的货币政策手段是不如常规的货币政策手段的。至于常规手段因市场不完善而受到的限制，那就必须依靠加大力度来弥补。

3. 要松动货币政策并且松动的力度要大一点，应当以商业银行按贷款的可偿还性和贷款对象的资金使用效率发放贷款为前提，否则不良债务将增加，对经济的活跃也没有好处。那么，怎样才能防止松动之后不良债务的增加呢？是运用常规性货币政策手段更易于做到这一点，还是运用非常规的货币政策手段更易于做到这一点？显然，非常规的货币政策手段在使用中的随意性很大，行政主管机构干预的色彩很强，从而更不易防止不良债务的增加，更不易收到松动货币政策的预期效果。

三、关于货币政策效力的递减

（一）为什么货币政策的效力会递减

在研究货币政策在客观经济调节中的地位与作用时，涉及货币政策的效力递减问题。货币政策效力递减，是指货币政策在实行一段时间之后，它对经济增长与货币稳定这一最终目标的实现而言，所发生的积极影响会逐渐减弱，而其对经济的消极影响却会逐渐增大。

货币政策效力的递减可能是普遍性的，即不论是在市场完善和商业银行制度健全的条件下，还是在市场不完善和商业银行制度不健全的条件下，都会出现货币政策效力递减的情况。当然，在后一种条件下，货币政策效力的递减更加明显，也更加严重。

货币政策效力递减的主要原因在于：受到货币政策的作用的对象，包括商业银行与其他金融机构，以及社会上的投资者，是理性的

agents that react rationally to the monetary policy adopted by the central bank. Even if the market is complete and the commercial banking system healthy, these agents will take countermeasures against the changing economic landscape and policy if their overriding thought is to maximize their own interests. Such countermeasures may cause the effectiveness of a certain monetary policy measure to decrease correspondingly, or force the central bank to reconsider its policy's effectiveness and readjust it. This phenomenon is undoubtedly more pronounced under incomplete market conditions and a flawed commercial banking system.

Monetary policy's waning effectiveness has also something to do with the limitations of its transmission mechanisms. The policy attains the ultimate goal through intermediary goals. However, the economy is in a state of constant restructuring that constantly updates money demand. That is to say, the relationship between money supply and demand always changes in pace with economic restructuring. The monetary policy tools taken are, without exception, focused on changing money supply, to the neglect of the new money demand out of economic restructuring. As a matter of fact, this means the central bank's monetary policy should be designed to adapt such demand to money supply, not the other way around. Changing the money supply is an intermediary goal of monetary policy; changing the demand for money is not. To put it another way, the monetary policy of the central bank impacts directly on money supply, and indirectly on money demand by changing money supply. Thus it can be said that the monetary policy does not have a transmission mechanism that directly impacts money demand. Precisely because of this missing point in the transmission mechanism, investors in the chain of money demand inevitably seek to meet their demand for money or influence the aggregate demand for money through other channels, which are beyond the reach of policymakers. Thus the steady decline in the monetary policy's effectiveness becomes inevitable even if the market is complete and the commercial banking system perfect. The achievement of this policy's ultimate goal, observed from a monetary point of view, is predicated on changes not only in money supply but also in money demand. Only by coordinating such supply and demand can a monetary policy be effective in the attainment of the ultimate goal.

行为人。他们对于中央银行所采取的货币政策会作出理性的反应。即使市场是完善的，商业银行制度也是健全的，但只要商业银行与其他金融机构以及社会上的投资者所考虑的是本身利益的最大化，他们就会根据经济形势的变化与政策的变化，拟定自己的对策。这些对策可能使得某一项货币政策手段的效力减少，也可能迫使中央银行重新考虑政策的效应，对政策进行调整。这种情况在市场不完善和商业银行制度不健全条件下无疑会更突出。

货币政策效力递减还同货币政策传导机制本身的局限性有一定的关系。货币政策是通过中介目标而作用于最终目标的。然而经济总是处于不断的结构调整之中，这种结构调整将对货币需求量提出新的要求。也就是说，货币供应量与对货币的需求量之间的关系要随着不断的结构调整发生变化。任何一种货币政策手段，都把着重点放在货币供应量的变化方面，从而相应地忽略了结构调整对货币需求量提出的新要求。实际上，这意味着中央银行通过货币政策的实行，要让货币需求量来适应货币供应量，而不是让货币供应量去适应货币需求量。货币供应量的变化是货币政策的中介目标，对货币的需求量的变化则没有被视为货币政策的中介目标。或者可以说，中央银行的货币政策都直接作用于货币供应量，并通过货币供应量的变化间接地影响对货币的需求。因此，这些货币政策并没有直接作用于对货币需求量的传导机制。正由于货币政策传导机制有上述局限性，所以在货币政策实行过程中，经济中同货币需求有关的投资者必然设法通过不同渠道来满足自己的货币需求或影响对货币的需求量，而这是货币政策的制定者力所不及的。这样，货币政策的效力递减，即使在市场完善和商业银行制度健全的条件下，也是难以避免的。因为货币政策最终目标的实现从货币的角度来看，不仅依赖货币供应量的变动，而且依赖对货币的需求量的变动。只有货币的供给与需求两方面协调一致，才能使货币政策对最终目标的实现发生有效的作用。

ii. The eclipse of monetary policy's effectiveness under incomplete market conditions

The unstoppable ebb of a monetary policy's effectiveness under incomplete market conditions and an imperfect commercial banking system is also ascribed to the following causes that are perhaps more important than the aforementioned ones.

First, in an incomplete market and under a flawed commercial banking system, the central bank habitually resorts to unconventional monetary policy tools like credit scale control, rediscount quotas, and relending quotas. However, because the design and use of such tools smack of government intervention, the central bank is actually not in a position to make adjustments relevant to the changing economy. As a result, these tools become rigid policy measures that can only defeat the purposes. Moreover, because these policy measures are usually introduced and backed by the administration, their effectiveness is invariably whittled down because they are rejected, openly or covertly, by commercial banks and other monetary institutions.

Second, under incomplete market conditions and an unhealthy commercial banking system, the central bank's quantitative monetary control over the entire economy is limited. The more incomplete the market and the commercial banking system are, the more likely that firms and investors choose to obtain money beyond the central bank's control. Similarly, under the same conditions, the more the central bank tightens up its quantitative money control, the more firms and investors will try to dodge such control and seek money in areas beyond the reach of the central bank, resulting in a reduction in the effectiveness of the monetary policy.

Third, under incomplete market conditions and a flawed commercial banking system, the activity of the central bank and commercial banks may be interfered with by government at all levels that demand, including the demand for more loans and—in extreme cases—bank overdrafts.

This manner of government intervention inevitably cuts deeply into the monetary policy's effectiveness and makes it difficult to reach its prescribed goals. To unshackle them from such intervention, not only should the commercial banking system and the market be straightened out, but the central banking system itself should be rectified as well.

（二）市场不完善条件下货币政策效力的递减

至于在市场不完善和商业银行制度不健全的条件下货币政策效力的递减，除了上述这些原因之外，还有另一些原因。后者也许比前者更为重要。

另一些原因是：

第一，在市场不完善和商业银行制度不健全的条件下，中央银行习惯于把信贷规模控制、再贴现限额、再贷款限额等作为货币政策手段。但这些货币政策手段的制定与执行带有很大的行政管理色彩。中央银行制定了这种规模与限额后，无法根据经济情况的变化而予以调整。结果，这些货币政策手段成为脱离实际的僵硬的政策手段，达不到预定的调节目标。不仅如此，在具体操作过程中，由于这些货币政策手段是依靠行政方式来推行的，往往使商业银行和其他金融机构对中央银行的做法采取公开的或不公开的抵制，从而使得政策的效力减弱。

第二，在市场不完善和商业银行制度不健全的条件下，中央银行对整个经济中的货币数量的控制肯定是有限的。市场越不完善，商业银行制度越不健全，投资者就越有可能从中央银行控制以外的领域取得货币资金。与此相似的是，在市场不完善和商业银行制度不健全的条件下，中央银行越是想通过货币政策手段来控制货币数量，投资者就越想摆脱中央银行的控制范围，设法到中央银行控制力所达不到的领域内去寻求货币资金，其结果必然是货币政策的效力下降。

第三，在市场不完善和商业银行制度不健全的条件下，中央银行的活动以及商业银行的活动都可能受到各级政府的行政干扰，包括要求给予更多的贷款，甚至要求向银行透支。这些来自行政方面的干扰必然使货币政策难以实现预定的目标，使货币政策的效力减弱。而要摆脱这些行政干扰，除了应当健全商业银行制度和完善市场而外，还需要使中央银行制度本身健全起来，其中包括使财政部

This calls for normalizing the relationship between the Ministry of Finance and the Central Bank, and between local governments and the Central Bank's local branches.

iii. Monetary policy needs to be more loosened and forceful—judging from its eclipsed effectiveness

Now let us return to the issue of coordinating fiscal and monetary policies in the post-retrenchment years. Now that we have seen that the eclipse of a monetary policy's effectiveness is unavoidable and even more so under incomplete market conditions, we have every reason to believe that, to reactivate the economy in the wake of the retrenchment, it is necessary to adopt a slightly tightened up fiscal policy in coordination with a monetary policy that is loosened up more forcefully. Such a necessity is justified from three aspects:

First, the countermeasures taken by those under the impact of a monetary policy—commercial banks, other monetary institutions and nongovernmental investors—against the changing situation brought about by that policy can keep eroding its effectiveness. As a result, the monetary policy may not work as it should on a relaxed money market if it is not loosened up with appropriate forcefulness. Sensible investors always take countermeasures according to experience and government behavior, and are especially cautious in action after going through the retrenchment years. They will tend to hold back and bide their time, lest an ill-advised investment move put them at a disadvantage. This being the case, the monetary policy has to be relaxed a little more vigorously if its effectiveness is to stop its decline, and if its prescribed goals are to be achieved.

Second, as illustrated above, to rebuild and enhance public confidence in market and investment prospects is vital to post-retrenchment economic revival. Because this calls for a cumulative process, to loosen up the monetary policy more forcefully in coordination with a relatively tight fiscal policy is a sensible recourse for the government to prevent the monetary policy's effectiveness from diminishing endlessly and to boost people's confidence in market and investment prospects. Whether or not a consumer chooses to buy something he can do without is a conventional benchmark of his confidence or the lack of it. The consumer may make that decision on the spur of the moment, but its

与中央银行之间的关系正常化，以及地方政府同中央银行分支行之间关系的正常化等等。

（三）从货币政策效力的递减看货币政策松动以及力度加大的必要性

现在让我们回到经济紧缩之后财政政策与货币政策配合使用这个问题上来。既然我们已经懂得了货币政策效力的递减是不可避免的，以及市场不完善条件下货币政策效力的递减更是必然的现象，那么我们完全有理由认为，要让紧缩之后的经济再度活跃起来，有必要采取稍紧的财政政策与松动的货币政策的配合，而货币政策松动的力度应当大一些。下面，从三个方面来进行论述。

1. 由于受到货币政策作用的对象——包括商业银行与其他金融机构，以及社会上的投资者——是理性的行为人，他们根据形势变化与政策变化而采取的对策会使货币政策的效力递减。因此，在放松了银根的条件下，如果不适当加大放松的力度，很可能使货币政策起不到应有的作用。有理性行为的投资者总是根据以往的经验与政府的做法采取相应的对策，特别是在经历过一段时间的经济紧缩之后，他们尤其不敢轻易地采取行动，总会打一点埋伏，留一手，以免再度使自己在投资中陷于不利状态。只有货币政策放松的力度加大一些，才能在一定程度上抵消或缓解货币政策效力的递减，使货币政策的预期目标得以实现。

2. 正如以上已经指出的，在经济紧缩之后走向经济活跃的过程中，人们对市场前景和投资前景的信心的恢复与增强十分重要，而信心的增强又是一个累积的过程。因此，在政府实行稍紧的财政政策与松动的货币政策相配合的办法来推进经济活跃时，为了防止松动的货币政策的效力递减，货币政策松动的力度应当加大一些。这样才有利于人们对市场前景和投资前景的信心的增强与信心的累积。信心的充足与不足，通常表现于“可买可不买的买”与“可买可不买的不买”的不同。尽管只是一字之差，但对市场活跃程度的

impact on the market cannot be underestimated. If the monetary policy is tight, people tend not to buy things they can dispense with, and thus the hope for a revived market is dashed. That tendency will remain unchanged if the monetary policy is not loosened up enough. People will not be confident enough to buy commodities in the gray zone between necessity and nonnecessity, and the economy and market will not come back to their own unless the monetary policy is loosened up adequately.

Third, it should be noted that a booming stock market alone is not enough to put the economy back on track right after a period of retrenchment. On the contrary, if the stock market is the only thing that is thriving, it may be evidence that the economy is still in a quandary, as dim investment prospects in many other fields are channeling large sums of money into the stock market. Furthermore, a bustling stock market may most likely be built on a flimsy foundation when investment prospects are grim in other fields. Under these circumstances, we should go out of our way to boost the other investment fields, at least those industries that can bolster up the economy. In conjunction with this, the monetary policy must be loosened up more emphatically to give precedence to the indispensability of its structural nature. That is to say, the policy must not be loosened up in a disorderly fashion and regardless of the industrial and investment structures. Rather, it should be designed, in the first place, to revive selected industries that can bring the economy to life and cause a chain reaction in other industries. To loosen up the monetary policy a little more liberally for these industries helps increase effective supply to the extent where inflation will not be aggravated. Growth in effective supply means true economic growth. In addition, we have got to realize that economic growth at the present stage is not without bubbles. Of all the bubbles foaming in the economy, those in economic growth are the most obvious. To get rid of such bubbles, ineffective supply must be eradicated. This can be done by liberalizing the structural monetary policy a little more.

All in all, to shift the economy back on boom conditions in these post retrenchment years, we should not only coordinate a relatively tightened fiscal policy with a relaxed monetary policy, but also step up our effort to loosen up the latter. In the meantime, we should

影响却是不可低估的。假定货币政策仍然从紧，人们将倾向于"可买可不买的不买"，市场活跃无望。货币政策稍松动一些，但力度不够，这种倾向依然不会改变。只有货币政策松动的力度大一些，人们信心增加了，转而采取"可买可不买的买"的做法，经济的兴旺与市场的活跃才会出现。

3. 要知道，单凭股市的看好是不足以使经济紧缩之后转入再度活跃的局面的。相反地，股市一枝独秀还可能是经济尚未活跃的反映。因为其他行业的投资前景不乐观，投资渠道又窄，于是大量资金从其他投资领域流进了股市。加之，在其他行业的投资前景尚未看好的情况下，股市的上扬未免显得基础不扎实。这样，我们就应当设法启动其他行业，至少是某些能支撑经济活跃的几个行业，而在政策配合使用方面，需要让货币政策松动的力度加大一些。这实际上强调了结构性货币政策的重要性，即并非不顾行业的结构、投资的结构而让货币政策的松动无序，而是有选择地加大货币政策松动的力度，使某些能支撑经济活跃的行业先复苏，先兴旺，带动相关行业一起发展。对这些行业的货币政策松动力度大一些，将促进有效供给的增长，而不至于导致通货膨胀的加剧。有效供给增长才是名副其实的经济增长。此外，还应当注意到，现阶段的经济增长中不是没有水分的。如果说经济中确实存在着泡沫的话，那么经济增长中的水分就是最大的泡沫。要设法消除这种泡沫，那就必须消除无效供给。趋向于松动的结构性货币政策，只有力度加大一些，才能做到这一点。

总之，经济紧缩以后，要使经济转入兴旺活跃状态，根据中国的实际情况，目前我们不但需要采取稍紧的财政政策与松动的货币政策相结合，而且货币政策松动的力度要加大一些。

apply unconventional monetary policy measures with prudence, and make more use of conventional monetary policy measures. Such is the keynote of this thesis, entitled "Meshing fiscal policy with monetary policy."

— Carried in excerpts in *Asia Pacific Economic Times*, May 29, June 5 and June 12, 1997

同时，我们应当谨慎使用非常规的货币政策手段，更多地使用常规的货币政策手段。这就是《论财政政策与货币政策的配合使用》一文的中心思想。

（本文曾摘要发表于《亚太经济时报》1997 年 5 月 29 日、6 月 5 日、6 月 12 日）

THE DUAL FOUNDATIONS OF EFFICIENCY (1998)

I. The human factor in efficiency studies

In a market economy efficiency is regulated by market, as economic activity is driven by interests. To gain interest, every resource investor must group his production factors in light of supply and demand and prices, and raise his efficiency. Therefore, the mechanism behind efficiency in the market economy is none other than the interest mechanism, or market mechanism, and the investor's goal is to maximize his interest. Thus motivation for interest and the lure of goals are unified insofar as efficiency is concerned.

Where there is government regulation besides market regulation, there will be the impact of government regulation on efficiency. The lure of goals is by and large a manifestation of such impact. Government has its own goals which are multiple rather than single. To meet its goals, the government needs to influence resource investors by way of regulatory means, and compel them to choose investment fields and forms of investment in line with government goals. Efficiency is affected as a result.

Because market regulation works hand in hand with government regulation, efficiency, whether high or low, is under their combined influence. Our study of this issue, however, should not stop just here. We need to probe deeper into it, because those engaged in market activity are individual traders, each being a resource investor. Market participants are subject to government regulation, with the government itself as a resource investor. Market participants as resource investors, are concerned with both their own interests and the impact of government regulatory steps on their interests. This raises the questions: What is on the minds of resource investors? What factors are affecting their behaviors? Apart from market and government regulation, are there any other factors?

Take, for example, any normal firm. The relations in such a firm fall into two categories: relationships between people and materials, and interpersonal relationships. The relationship between people and materials finds expression mainly in the relationship between the means of production and those who use them. The condition and average

论效率的双重基础（1998年）

一、在效率问题的研究中必须考虑人的因素

在市场经济条件下，效率是受市场调节的。利益的驱动就是市场调节起作用的表现。每一个资源投入主体为了取得利益，必须根据市场上生产要素的供求状况与价格水平来组合生产要素，提高效率。因此，在市场经济中，效率背后的机制实际上就是利益机制或市场机制，资源投入主体的利益最大化就是他所追求的目标。这样，利益驱动与目标吸引在效率问题上是统一的。

假定在市场调节之外还有政府调节，那么在效率的背后必定存在着政府调节的影响，目标的吸引主要是政府调节起作用的表现。政府有自己的目标，政府目标不是单一的，而是多元的。政府为了使自己的目标得以实现，就需要通过各种调节手段对资源投入主体发生影响，使他们在资源投入领域的选择上与资源投入方式的选择上作出符合政府目标的选择，从而影响效率的变动。

由于市场调节与政府调节是共同起作用的，所以高效率或低效率的产生实际上受到市场调节与政府调节的共同影响。但对这个问题的分析不应到此为止，我们还需要作深入一层的探讨。这是因为，在市场上进行活动的是各个交易人，一个交易人就是一个资源投入主体。对市场进行调节的是政府，政府自身也是资源投入主体。受到政府调节的是市场上的交易人，他们作为资源投入主体，既要考虑自己的利益，也要考虑政府采取的调节手段对自己利益的影响。于是就出现了另外的问题：资源投入主体是怎样考虑的呢？他们的行为受哪些因素影响呢？效率除了受到市场调节与政府调节以外，是不是还受其他力量的影响呢？

让我们先以一个企业为例。一个企业内部的关系可以分为人与物之间的关系和人与人之间的关系。人与物之间的关系主要反映为生产资料使用者与生产资料之间的关系。企业的生产资料状况和平均

quantity of the means of production per worker are basic indicators of a firm's technological level, which in turn determines its efficiency level. The interpersonal relationship is a lot more complicated than the former. It can be broken up into a number of relations such as the relation between the firm's leadership and workers, between members of the leadership, between the leadership and the managerial body, between members of the managerial body and between workers. Some of these interpersonal relations are congenial, others are not. Some interpersonal relations are agreeable under one condition, but disagreeable under another. The agreeability of these interpersonal relations impacts efficiency in ways different from the impact of technology. If the technological level is low, it may be upgraded as a *sine qua non* for efficiency growth by increasing investment, adding new equipment, constructing new factory buildings, putting workers through training, or encouraging them to hone their skills with an increase in efficiency as a result. If interpersonal relations are disagreeable, can reinvestment be effective? How can it send efficiency skyrocketing?

Supposing the technological level of a company is fixed, the human factor—managers and workers included—will become so prominent as to determine the efficiency level. In this human factor, every employee's work hours, cultural attainment and skill adeptness, and how well-defined his work post responsibility is, are observable factors, but there are also unobservable factors. For one thing, people's diligence level is elusive, for it is hard to tell exactly how hardworking everyone is. For another, employees are under the effect of a certain level of inertia. Those who are less affected by it are more motivated and aggressive in work; those affected more by it are lethargic. To what extent they can overcome inertia is another unknown factor. Moreover, efficiency grows when employees' goals match their firm's goals, and drops when their goals are at odds with each other, but whether or not these two kinds of goals match each other and to what extent are anyone's guess. The impact of these unobservable factors on firm efficiency merits careful study, for it is a hard nut to crack for both market and government regulation.

Therefore the study of efficiency needs to go beyond the scope of market and government regulation. This is not to say that market

每个劳动者所使用的生产资料数量的多少，基本上反映了这个企业的技术水平，技术水平的高低影响着效率的高低。从人与人之间的关系来看，问题要比人与物之间的关系复杂些。可以把企业内部的人与人之间的关系分为若干种，例如，企业领导层同一般职工之间的关系，企业领导层内部的合作共事关系，企业领导层与各级管理人员之间的关系，各级管理人员内部的合作共事关系，一般职工相互之间的关系等等。这些人际关系中，有的协调，有的不那么协调，还有的完全不协调。有些人际关系在这种情况下比较协调，在另一种情况下却不协调。人际关系的协调程度影响着效率的高低，而且对效率的影响同技术水平对效率的影响是不一样的。如果技术水平低，企业通过增加投入，或增添新设备、修建新厂房，或进行职工培训、鼓励职工钻研技术，就可以大幅度提高技术水平，达到效率增长的要求。但如果企业内部人际关系不协调，增加投入能有多大成效？难道效率会因此而大幅度提高？

再从企业从业人员（包括各级管理人员与工人）的角度来看，在一定的技术水平之下，人的因素被摆到了显著的位置，企业的效率取决于人的因素所发挥的作用。在人的因素中，职工的工作时间、每个人已达到的文化技术等级、每个人在自己的工作岗位上的责任明确程度都是已知的。但在人的因素中，还有一些未知数。例如，职工的努力程度就是未知的，因为每个人在工作中究竟使出了多大的劲，不易确定。又如，每个人都有一定的惰性，惰性的影响小，积极性、创造性发挥得充分；反之，惰性的影响大，职工的积极性、创造性的发挥就受到阻碍。职工自身能在多大程度上克服惰性，也是一个未知数。再如，如果职工个人的目标同企业目标是协调的，效率将会增长；反之，职工个人目标同企业目标不协调，效率将会下降。但职工个人目标同企业目标究竟在何种程度上协调或不协调，同样是未知的。这些未知因素的存在对企业效率的影响，是值得研究的课题，也是市场调节或政府调节都难以解决的难点。

由此可见，对效率的研究有必要在市场调节与政府调节以外展开。

regulation and government regulation mean little to the rise and fall of efficiency. It only shows the limits of their impact, limits that, in particular, can affect our analysis of the sources of efficiency. For instance, in our research on a firm's interpersonal relationships, the impact of unobservable factors such as diligence and inertia on employees should be probed. This shows that work ethics affect human behavior and go on to affect efficiency in many ways. What is the true source of efficiency? It is the human factor. Efficiency hinges on people's motivation and innovativeness, so work ethics should never be overlooked. Efficiency improves greatly when full scope is given to people's potentials, and when they are highly motivated and innovative under the influence of work ethics.

It should be noted that the above analysis is predicated on a given technological level. Technological level, judged from the perspective of the relationship between people and the means of production, is relevant to efficiency level. If the technological level of a country, region, or firm is a lot higher than that of another country, region, or firm, it makes comparing the impact of work ethics very difficult. Only by accurately reading the impact of work ethics on efficiency at a given technological level can such comparison make sense.

II. Efficiency stems from organizational and social cohesion

As illustrated in the previous chapter, the source of efficiency at a given technological level lies in people's motivation and innovativeness. To make the most of such motivation and innovativeness, it is essential to develop rational economic operational mechanisms and agreeable interpersonal relationships.

The cohesion parameter of the agreeability of interpersonal relationship falls into two categories: cohesion of an organization, and cohesion of society. The cohesion of an organization or society hinges on the agreeability of its interpersonal relationships. Cohesion generates efficiency. Organizational cohesion delivers efficiency inside an organization, and social cohesion endows efficiency on society.

The organization in this context refers in general to businesses, institutions, communities, clubs, villages, households and others. Organizations may vary in size, but each has its own cohesion. Organizations

这并不意味着市场调节与政府调节对效率的增减不重要，这只是表明市场调节与政府调节在影响效率方面有局限性，特别是在分析效率的源泉方面有局限性。比如说，在企业内部人与人之间关系的研究中，在与人的工作努力程度、人的惰性等有关的若干未知因素对效率的影响的研究中，都需要深入到更深的层次。这就是说，道德力量在许多方面对人的行为发生作用，进而影响效率。什么是效率的真正源泉？效率的真正源泉在于人的作用的充分发挥、人的积极性与创造性的充分发挥；而要做到这一点，道德力量的作用不可忽视。在道德力量作用之下，人的作用充分发挥了，人的积极性与创造性充分发挥了，效率将会大大提高。

应当指出的是，上述分析是以技术水平既定作为前提的。技术水平的高低，从人与物之间的关系的角度来看，关系到效率的大小。比如有两个国家、两个地区或两个企业。如果一个国家、地区、企业的技术水平高出另一个国家、地区、企业很多，那么道德力量对效率发生作用后所产生的后果就难以进行比较。因此，只有把技术水平作为既定，道德力量对效率的作用才能准确地显示出来，这样的对比才有意义。

二、效率来自凝聚力：团体的凝聚力和社会的凝聚力

前面已经指出，在一定的技术水平的条件下，效率的真正源泉在于人的积极性、创造性的充分发挥。而要充分发挥人的积极性、创造性，必须有合理的经济运行机制，必须做到人际关系的协调。

凝聚力的大小是人际关系是否协调或协调到何种程度的体现。凝聚力基本上分为两类：一是团体的凝聚力，二是社会的凝聚力。团体的凝聚力以团体内部人际关系的协调为条件，社会的凝聚力则以社会中人际关系的协调为条件。凝聚力产生效率：团体的凝聚力产生团体的效率，社会的凝聚力产生社会的效率。

这里所说的团体，包括了企业、事业单位、社区、社团、村、家庭等等。团体有大有小，但各有各的凝聚力。团体的组织有松有紧，

may be structurally loose or tight. Tight structure is not synonymous with high cohesion, while loose structure does not always mean a lack of cohesion. The structural looseness or tightness of an organization is irrelevant to cohesion or the lack of it, which is directly relevant to the agreeability of the relationship between the organization and its members and between its members. If the members of an organization are given to scheming against each other or are in discord with their leaders, this organization will be devoid of cohesion no matter how close-knit its organizational structure is. By contrast, if members of a community are in an amicable relationship with one another and with their leaders and work with one mind to make progress, such a community will enjoy cohesion, and a strong cohesion at that, even if it is loosely organized.

A firm consists of workers and managers. Its cohesion is one of many kinds of organizational cohesion. To foster corporate culture helps cultivate corporate cohesion. With strong cohesion, a firm can not only improve its efficiency steadily but also overcome difficulties and tide over adversities. There is no doubt about it.

Some questions come to mind at this point of this study: How does society's cohesion come about? What is the relationship between organizational cohesion and social cohesion? How should such a relationship be handled to achieve both organizational and social cohesion?

Social cohesion is the force that rallies members of society together as one to achieve common goals. There is no lack of outstanding examples in this regard, such as the concerted effort, hard work, and self-sacrifices of people rallying against foreign invaders or natural disasters. Under such unusual circumstances, this kind of cohesion can generate high social efficiency and work wonders. Under normal circumstances, a society with harmonious interpersonal relationship and strong cohesion invariably enjoys an agreeable social environment that is a boon to the growth of efficiency.

As to the relationship between organizational cohesion and social cohesion, they may either promote or circumscribe each other, depending on what the organization's nature and goals are. There are all sorts of organizations in society that differ in nature and pursue different goals.

紧密不等于有较大的凝聚力，松散也不等于缺少凝聚力。团体组织的松散或紧密，是从组织形式上说的；团体有没有凝聚力或凝聚力有多大，则同团体与成员之间协调与否、成员与成员之间协调与否有直接的关系。比如说，某个社团有严密的组织，但成员彼此之间可能勾心斗角，难以形成一股力量；或者成员对社团的领导层离心离德，存在着强烈的离心倾向，那么不管社团的组织形式多么严密，照样没有凝聚力。反之，某个社团尽管组织形式上是比较松散的，但成员之间的关系协调，成员同社团的领导层的关系协调，成员们为社团的发展齐心协力，这样的社团不仅有凝聚力，而且凝聚力还可能是很强的。

企业是由企业工作人员组成的一个团体。企业的凝聚力是团体的凝聚力中的一种。企业文化建设有助于企业凝聚力的形成。一个企业，如果有较大的凝聚力，不仅能够促使企业效率不断提高，而且在企业遇到困难时，能够使企业克服困难，闯过难关。关于这一点，人们一般是不会产生疑问的。

需要深入探讨的问题是：社会的凝聚力如何形成？团体的凝聚力同社会的凝聚力之间存在什么样的关系？怎样正确处理这两种凝聚力之间的关系，以便既有团体的凝聚力，又有社会的凝聚力？

社会的凝聚力是指社会成员们能够团结一致，各尽所能来实现共同的目标。最显著的例子就是一个国家、一个民族在反侵略战争时期或遇到严重自然灾害时期社会成员所表现出来的齐心协力、艰苦奋斗与自我牺牲的精神。社会的这种凝聚力带来社会的高效率，会出现许多奇迹。即使在正常的情况下，如果社会上人际关系协调，社会凝聚力强，那么也会出现社会协调的环境，同样有利于效率的增长。

至于团体凝聚力与社会凝聚力之间的关系，应当认为，二者之间可能存在着相互促进的关系，也可能存在着相互制约的关系，关键在于团体的性质与团体的目标是什么样的。社会上有各种各样的

If separatism is a political organization's overriding call, then the more cohesive it is, the more destructive it becomes to society. Of course this is an extreme example that can be excluded from my discussion. Generally speaking, an organization and society can get along if they have compatible goals, and consequently the cohesion of the organization and that of society are complementary. Below let me take firms for example again.

In a market economy, maximization of interest is the primary goal of firms that function as commodity producers making their own business decisions and being accountable for their profits and losses. To meet that goal, they must beat competition by constantly adjusting their production and business directions, improving their management and enhancing their internal cohesion. Competition on a level playing field is essential to the proper handling of the relationship between firms, in which their shared interest lies in the belief that the more stable society is and the more the economy thrives, the better off the firms become. The rise of one firm does not necessarily mean the downfall of another. In an environment of social stability and economic prosperity, every firm has the opportunity to grow and convert their good intentions into reality. However, even in such a friendly environment there are still firms that have to downscale production, go bankrupt, or be annexed due to decision-making errors or failure to keep pace with technological development. These occurrences are a normal reflection of the regrouping of resources. As long as such regrouping proves salubrious to efficiency of the economy as a whole and brings new opportunities to investors, the common interest of the business world will not be hurt by the aforementioned production cuts, bankruptcies, or mergers.

Organizational cohesion and social cohesion, however, are not the same thing. Whether the former can be unified with the latter, or whether enhanced organizational cohesion can strengthen social cohesion, is determined by the substance and efficacy of advancement in culture—corporate culture, community culture, campus culture, etc.—as a major element in the promotion of organizational cohesion. Let us take the firm again. If a firm's corporate culture emphasizes not only its own goals but also the goals of society, attaches importance not only to its

团体，性质互异，目标互异。假定某个团体是政治性的组织并具有分离主义政治倾向，它的目标是要求改变现状，从一个国家分离出去。那么，这样的团体内部越有凝聚力，对社会越不利，社会的凝聚力越会受到损害。当然，这是极端的例子，我们可以把这一类团体作为特例，略去不谈。在一般情况下，团体的目标同社会的目标是相容的，也是可以协调一致的。因此，团体的凝聚力与社会的凝聚力通常有着相互促进的作用。这里仍以企业为例。

在市场经济中，企业作为自主经营、自负盈亏的商品生产者，有自己的目标，而首要的目标就是争取实现最大利益。企业之间存在着竞争的关系。为了使自己在竞争中取胜，企业不断调整生产和经营方向，也不断改进管理，增加内部凝聚力。正当竞争、合法条件下的竞争，是处理企业之间关系的前提。在这一前提下，企业之间有着共同的利益，这就是：社会越稳定，经济越繁荣，企业越能受益。一个企业的兴旺并不是必定以另一个企业的衰败为条件的。在社会稳定与经济繁荣的大环境中，企业都有发展的机遇，并且都能实现这一愿望。从现实生活中可以看到，即使在这样的大环境中，也总有一些企业由于生产经营不善，或投资决策失误，或适应不了技术迅速变化的形势，发生生产收缩、企业倒闭或被其他企业兼并等情况。但这是正常的，这只不过是资源重新组合的反映。只要资源的重新组合能给国民经济带来效率的增长，为投资者创造新的机遇，那么某些企业收缩、倒闭或被兼并不会损害企业界的共同利益。

团体的凝聚力同社会的凝聚力是两种不同类型的凝聚力。团体的凝聚力能否同社会的凝聚力统一起来，或者说，团体凝聚力的加强能否促进社会凝聚力的加强，同作为促进团体凝聚力的重要因素的文化建设（如企业文化建设、社区文化建设、校园文化建设等）的内容与成效有密切关系。不妨仍以企业为例。在一个企业中，假定企业文化不仅强调企业自身的目标，而且同样强调社会的目标；

own benefits, but to the benefits of the society as a whole, and aims not only at cultivating its own corporate spirit but also at fostering fine social mores, the achievement of such a corporate culture will be reflected in the improved cohesion of both the firm and society. The unification of corporate and social cohesion precisely embodies the social function and value of a sound corporate culture. Conversely, if a firm is bent on pursuing its own corporate and workforce interests at the expense of its corporate culture's social function and value, it will have no way of coordinating its cohesion with that of society, nor can its improved corporate cohesion result in improved social cohesion. This point should not be overlooked when analyzing the sources of efficiency.

A more nuanced understanding of the issue enables us to see that growth in national wealth is connected with society's economic prosperity and development in culture and education. A prosperous society with advanced culture and education is better endowed to promote cultural development and coordinate its own cohesion with organizational cohesion. Moral values also play an outstanding role in enhancing social and organizational cohesion, a role that cannot be superseded by market or government regulation. This is because only moral values can demonstrate to members of organizations that their own organizations' goals are in line with those of society and that the interests of individuals and organizations are, fundamentally speaking, compatible with the interests of society. That realization enables them to identify themselves completely with society's goals, thereby bolstering both organizational and social cohesion. Both organizational and social cohesion can be steadily enhanced under the impact of moral force.

Hence my conclusion: In the past, researchers of the source of efficiency have often stressed economic and technological factors to the neglect of noneconomic and nontechnological factors, emphasized the impact of interests at the expense of public goals and a sense of social responsibility, and reiterated material values regardless of human values. Under the sway of such outdated ideological and methodological approaches, researchers could neither probe into the deep-seated issue concerning changes in efficiency, nor explain that the human factor and interpersonal relations—rather than the material factor and the relationship between people and materials—are the true fountainhead for

不仅关注企业自身的利益和本企业职工的利益，而且也关注公共的利益；不仅致力于企业精神的培育，而且也致力于优良的社会风尚的培育。这样，企业文化建设的成就既表现于企业凝聚力的加强，也表现于社会凝聚力的加强，企业凝聚力与社会凝聚力是一致的。这正体现了成功的企业文化建设的社会功能与社会价值。反之，假定一个企业单纯着重企业自身利益与本企业职工利益的追求而忽略了企业文化建设的社会功能与社会价值，那么，尽管企业的凝聚力也有可能在某种程度上加强，但却无法使企业的凝聚力同社会的凝聚力协调一致，也无法使企业凝聚力的加强带来加强社会凝聚力的结果。在分析效率源泉问题时，我们不应当忽视这一点。

如果再作进一步的分析，那么可以了解到，国民财富的增加、社会的经济繁荣和文化教育事业的发展是联系在一起的。一个经济繁荣、文化教育事业发达的社会，将更有条件来进行文化建设，促进社会凝聚力与团体凝聚力共同加强。道德调节作用在促进社会凝聚力与团体凝聚力共同加强方面表现得尤为明显，道德调节的这种作用是市场调节或政府调节无法替代的。这是因为，只有运用道德力量，才能使团体的成员认识到团体目标的实现从根本上说是同社会目标一致的，个人的利益、团体的利益从根本上说是同公共利益一致的。于是团体的成员就会从内心认同社会目标，其结果将是既增强了团体的凝聚力，又增强了社会的凝聚力。团体的效率与社会的效率将在道德力量的影响下不断提高。

由此可以得出下述结论：以往在效率源泉问题的研究中，通常只着重经济因素与技术因素而忽略非经济因素与非技术因素，只注意利益的影响而不注意社会责任感与公共目标的作用，只强调物的价值实现而忽视人的价值实现。在这种传统的思想与方法的指引下，实际上研究不了效率变动的深层次问题，也揭示不了效率的真正源泉还在于人的作用以及人与人之间的关系，而不仅仅在于物的

efficiency. Organizational cohesion generates organizational efficiency, and social cohesion brings forth social efficiency. This being the case, the source of efficiency and its enhancement lies not in market mechanisms or government interventional behavior, but in the force of morality and its impact on people.

III. Where super efficiency comes from

It is generally acknowledged that efficiency rests on a material foundation. Such a foundation encompasses production equipment, raw materials, technological conditions, workers with a certain level of technical proficiency, and social infrastructure (including means of communications and transportation, telecommunications facilities, water and heat and energy utilities). The importance of the material foundation is common knowledge. Efficiency suffers when the material foundation stops improving itself.

Does efficiency have only one foundation, the material foundation? Is it true that where there is a material foundation, there will be growing efficiency? As noted previously, a material foundation alone is not enough to account for the ebb and flow in efficiency. Due consideration must be given to the other foundation—the moral foundation. Manufacturing equipment and raw materials are used by people. The efficacy of technology cannot operate without man's proficiency, motivation and creativity. In other words, workers with a certain level of proficiency are an integral part of the material foundation of efficiency. However, workers are not robots. They are human beings who think, feel, and pursue ideas and goals. They may take one attitude or another towards life, and be either devoted to or uncaring about work. In addition, they are not isolated, but interact with one another to form all sorts of interpersonal relations with varying degrees of coordination. All this constitutes the other foundation for efficiency, the moral foundation.

The material and moral foundations of efficiency exist alongside each other. Neither of them can stand alone to account for a rise or fall in efficiency. Let us imagine that two firms have the same material and technological conditions and make the same product needed by consumers: How is it that one firm is more efficient than the other? The answer can be found by comparing the differences in the moral foundation of their efficiency.

作用以及人与物之间的关系。团体凝聚力产生团体的效率，社会凝聚力产生社会的效率。在这种情况下，效率的产生与提高的原因不应当到市场机制中去寻找，也不应当到政府的调节行为中去寻找，而只能到道德力量及其对人的影响中去寻找。

三、超常规的效率是怎样产生的

效率具有物质基础，这是人们所公认的。一定的生产设备和原材料，一定的技术条件和具有一定技术水平的工作者，以及一定的社会基础设施（如交通运输设施、通讯设施、供水供热设施、能源供应设施等），构成一定的效率的物质基础。效率的物质基础的重要性已经得到了公认。不设法改善效率的物质基础，效率的提高会遇到障碍。

但是，效率是不是仅有一个基础，即物质基础呢？是不是只要具有效率的物质基础，效率就必定增长呢？从以上的论述中已经可以清楚地了解到，单有效率的物质基础是不足以充分说明效率增减的原因的。我们必须讨论效率的另一个基础，即道德基础。生产设备和原材料由人来使用，技术条件的发挥同人的素质有关，也同人的积极性、创造性有关。即以作为效率的物质基础的组成部分之一的具有一定技术水平的工作者来说，这些工作者是活生生的人，而不是机器人。他们有思想，有主张，有感情，也有目标。对待生活，他们可能持这种或那种态度；对待工作，他们可能热情，也可能冷漠。加之，他们一个个都不是孤立的人，他们同其他人交往，构成各种各样的人际关系，而这些关系的协调程度是不一样的。这一切成为效率的另一个基础，可以称之为效率的道德基础。

效率的物质基础和道德基础是并存的。单单用物质基础或道德基础都解释不了效率的增长或下降。两家企业，假定物质技术条件完全相同，生产出来的产品也相同，并且都被消费者所需要，但为什么其中一家企业的效率高而另一家企业的效率低？效率的道德基础的比较分析将会提供答案。

Thus it makes sense to say that efficiency has dual foundations, material and moral.

Organizations—as small as families, companies or villages or as large as communities or nations—cannot survive without spiritual cohesion, norms of conduct, and moral values in the same way as they cannot dispense with science and technology. In handling interpersonal relations, morality comes to assist when and where science and technology are helpless. Once interpersonal relations are finely tuned, once full scope is given to people's initiative and creativity, efficiency grows as a matter of course. This shows that efficiency does indeed have a moral foundation.

Efficiency's material foundation changes constantly with economic growth, technological advancement, and the renewal of knowledge on the part of those who use the means of production. Moreover, its changes are unstoppable. Does efficiency's moral foundation ever stop changing itself? Is there any unalterable moral principle that forms this foundation? Given that the material foundation is ever-changing, can the moral foundation stay intact alongside it? If the answer is in the positive, does the moral foundation ever change on its own or only in unison with circumstances? If it changes on its own, this refers to changes in moral values, rules of conduct, and evaluation criteria themselves. If it changes in unison with circumstances, this means that the moral foundation can adapt itself to the material foundation. However, it is difficult to distinguish between these two kinds of changes, which, in fact, are often intertwined with each other.

Now consider this question: Where does super efficiency come from? While the material foundation usually offers conventional efficiency, the moral foundation not only ensures conventional efficiency but also provides super efficiency.

The super efficiency of the immigrant societies of yore has been a topic of perennial academic interest. During the millennium-long war and turmoil following the demise of the Han dynasty (206 BC-220 AD), immigrants from central China hacked their way through brambles and throngs and settled in what are today's Guangdong and Fujian provinces, where they dredged rivers and converted barren land into fertile farmland. Beginning from the 12th century, immigrants into the

因此，正确的说法应当是：效率具有双重基础，即物质基础与道德基础。

在任何时代，小到一个家庭、一家企业、一座村庄，大到整个社会、整个国家，都需要有一种精神上的凝聚力、一种以道德规范为准则的行为引导、一种伦理观念。这些同科学技术是可以并行不悖的，而且也互不干扰。在处理人际关系时，凡是科学技术无能为力之处，就需要有道德力量来调整。人际关系融洽了，个人的积极性、创造性发挥了，效率自然会增长。这表明效率确实有自己的道德基础。

效率有双重基础，已如上述。接着要讨论的是：效率的物质基础是变化的。因为经济发展了，技术进步了，工艺改进了，使用生产资料的工作者的知识也更新了，效率的物质基础肯定发生变化，而且这种变化是不间断的。那么，效率的道德基础是不是也这样呢？难道会有一成不变的道德原则作为效率的道德基础吗？再如，既然效率具有物质基础与道德基础这样两个基础，物质基础是不断变化的，难道效率的道德基础就不会随之变化吗？如果说效率的道德基础是变化的，那么这种变化是主动的变化还是适应性的变化？所谓主动的变化，是指构成效率的道德基础的那些道德规范、行为守则、评价标准等等自身发生了变化，从而导致了效率的道德基础的变化。所谓适应性的变化，是指适应于效率的物质基础的变化而引起的效率的道德基础的变化。当然，主动变化与适应性变化有时是很难分开的。效率的道德基础的变化可能既有主动变化，又有适应性变化，二者往往交织在一起。

接着，让我们考察这样一个问题：超常规的效率究竟来自何处？物质基础通常提供的是常规效率，道德基础则不仅保证常规效率的产生，而且还能提供超常规效率。

历史上移民社会的超常规效率，一直是学术界感兴趣的课题。在中国，中原战乱期间，流民纷纷南下，在广东、福建一带披荆斩棘，排水造田，改变了当地荒芜的面貌。在西欧，从 12 世纪起，

western European region now known as the Netherlands reclaimed the land, built water conservancy projects and developed farming and animal husbandry. What these immigrants embodied was precisely a kind of super efficiency. How did they achieve such efficiency with medieval tools and limited manpower in harsh environments? There was neither market force nor government intervention during the process of immigration and the rise of the immigrant society, so what had motivated these people to toil with such high efficiency? This can only be attributed to the magical forces of morality, cohesion, and creativity. We may as well say that given the historical circumstances, these immigrants performed pioneering feats with extraordinary strength under extraordinary conditions. Even their social organizations were extraordinary. These factors combined to work miracles in human history. In the absence of a commensurate moral foundation, there could not have been such extraordinary immigrant social organizations, the immigrants could not have mustered such extraordinary strength as individuals, and such super efficiency would have been out of the question.

The achievement of super efficiency fully testifies to what potential efficiency growth can do. Such potentials can be tapped by relying on the moral foundation of efficiency. Examples in this regard are aplenty, besides the aforementioned immigrant societies. The role of morality, confidence and faith in stimulating human willpower and abilities can be seen in people's death-defying behaviors in resistance against foreign invaders, in combating natural disasters, and even in the effort of members of an organization—as small as a family or clan and as large as a nation or region—in attaining their goals or in safeguarding dignity and honor. Super efficiency arises precisely from among these people. Can the material foundation also contribute to the rise of super efficiency? Efficiency can certainly not do without its material condition. For instance, our forefathers would not have accomplished their pioneering cause without certain means of production in their possession no matter how motivated they were. We cannot combat natural adversities empty-handed. However, without the tremendous impact of morality and faith under these circumstances, material conditions can only yield mediocre efficiency. We must admit to ourselves that in the absence of a moral foundation, our efficiency may still be inadequate, low or even negative despite the provision of an efficient material foundation.

移民们就开始在尼德兰北部从事垦荒，兴修水利，发展农牧业。这些移民所表现出来的高效率，是超常规的。工具简陋，人力单薄，环境艰苦，为什么会涌现超常规的效率呢？在移民迁移过程中，甚至在移民社会形成后的较长时期内，既没有市场调节，也没有政府调节。那么，是什么力量使他们产生如此大的热情，提供如此高的效率呢？这就不能不归因于道德力量的作用、凝聚力的作用、人的创造性的作用。也许可以下这样一个结论：从历史上看，这些移民都是在超常规的客观条件下以超常规的主观力量来完成拓荒任务的，甚至移民们的社会组织也是超常规的。这些可以被看成是人类历史上的一种奇迹。如果没有相应的道德基础，就不可能有超常规的移民社会组织，也不可能有超常规的个人主观力量，从而也就不可能有超常规的效率。

超常规的效率涌现向人们充分显示：效率增长是有潜力的。效率增长潜力的发挥，主要依靠效率的道德基础的存在，依靠道德力量的作用。除了前面提到的以移民社会为例以外，还可以列举一些例证。例如，反侵略战争时期人们种种奋不顾身的行为，在抗御重大自然灾害袭击时人们作出的种种努力，甚至在为了团体（小至一个家庭、一个家族，大至一个宗教组织、一个民族或国家）的目标的实现或团体尊严、荣誉的维护方面，都可以看到道德力量、信念、信仰在激发人们的意志与能力中的作用。超常规的效率正是这样产生的。那么，效率的物质基础是不是也能为效率的超常规作出贡献呢？当然，效率的任何增长总是离不开物质条件的。例如，移民拓荒过程中，无论人的积极性多么大，总需要有一定的生产资料；抗御重大自然灾害时，也需要有一定的物质条件。但要知道，假定没有道德力量、信念、信仰等等在这些场合发生巨大的作用，依靠物质条件，人们仍然只能产生常规的效率，而不可能产生超常规的效率。不仅如此，还可以认为，假定缺少效率的道德基础，即使有效率的物质基础，完全有可能出现不充分的效率、低效率，甚至负效率。

The longstanding controversy about the conflict between the efficiency standard and the moral standard is settled through our analysis of super efficiency. The conflict between these two standards is about judging economic behavior with two criteria. One is a standard of efficiency, meaning that an economic behavior is good when it boosts efficiency, and bad when it reduces efficiency. The other is a standard of morality: Efficiency is good if it accords with the moral principle and evil if it violates it. These two standards are often in discord because rising efficiency may run counter to the moral principle, whereas efficiency that accords with the moral principle may fall. This longstanding issue cannot be settled mainly because of uncertainty about which standard to use in judging the moral good or evil of efficiency.

The efficiency standard is an issue in economics, and so is efficiency judgment. However, neither the moral standard nor moral judgment is a subject or research task for any economists. Both belong in the realm of economics where and when an economic issue touches upon the relationship between moral standard and efficiency standard, and the need arises to determine whether or not a moral judgment corresponds with an efficiency judgment. In my *Socialist Political Economics* I put it this way, "The moral judgment of economic behavior should be tested in practice, otherwise the moral principle for the economy could become elusive.... We may as well regard 'maximum workforce interests' as the moral standard for economic behavior. That is to say, an economic behavior is sound when it complies with 'maximum workforce interests', and is evil when it does not."[1] This approach to coordinating efficiency and moral standards may serve to support my judgment of certain economic behaviors.

After all, the conflict between efficiency and moral standards may still occur in evaluating some other economic behaviors, to the bewilderment of the economists of today. However, the emergence of super efficiency testifies to the accord between both standards. Extraordinary efficiency itself is evidence of an impressive boost in efficiency, and therefore, the efficiency standard is entirely applicable here. How, then, does super efficiency come about? It is directly related to the role of morality, as I have stated before. Without morality, super efficiency would have been

在学术界曾经长期引起争论的所谓效率标准与道德标准之间的冲突问题，通过对超常规效率的分析，这个问题实际上已经得到了解决。所谓效率标准与道德标准之间的冲突，通常是指：对一种经济行为，究竟如何判断，有两个标准。一是效率标准，即以效率是增长还是下降作为标准，效率增长是善，效率下降是恶；二是道德标准，即以伦理上的是非作为标准，符合伦理原则的是善，违背伦理原则的是恶。这两种标准在许多场合是不一致的，因为效率的增长很可能不符合伦理原则，而符合伦理原则的却引起效率的下降。这是一个由来已久的老问题，它之所以难以解决，主要在于伦理上的是非究竟是从什么角度来判断的。

效率标准是经济学的标准，效率判断也是经济学中的判断，而道德标准和道德判断都不是经济学的研究对象或研究任务。但是，当问题涉及道德标准同效率标准之间的关系，以及涉及道德判断同效率判断是否一致时，这些问题便进入了经济学的讨论范围。我在所著《社会主义政治经济学》中，曾对这些问题做过如下的论述："经济行为的道德判断必须和实践检验统一起来，否则经济中的伦理原则也就会变得难以捉摸……我们可以用'劳动者的最大利益'作为经济行为的伦理标准。也就是说，凡是符合'劳动者的最大利益'的，就是'是'或'善'；不符合'劳动者的最大利益'的，就是'非'或'恶'。"[1] 这是可以用来协调效率标准和道德标准的方法之一。如果采取这种方法，也许可以作为某些经济行为评价的依据。

但不管怎么说，在另一些经济行为的评价中，效率标准和道德标准的冲突仍有可能出现。这也是至今使经济学研究者感到困惑的事情。然而，单就超常规效率的产生来看，我们不难发现，效率标准和道德标准实际上已经一致了。超常规效率的产生，本身就已经表明效率的大大提高，所以效率标准在这里是完全适用的。而超常规效率是怎样产生的呢？正如前面已分析的，这与道德因素的作用直接有关。没有道德因素的作用，在移民社会中，在反侵略战争期间，

out of the question in an immigrant society or in combating foreign invaders or major natural catastrophes. Thus super efficiency that measures up to the efficiency standard is also up to the moral standard.

IV. Tapping potentials in efficiency growth

The mention of the moral foundation for efficiency brings the following question to mind: Under which condition is the potential greater for efficiency growth—the more the initiative is taken into the hands of individuals, or the less the initiative is taken into the hands of individuals while the more closely individuals are attached to their organization or society?

Why should I raise such a question? It has something to do with the moral foundation of efficiency. Given the technical nature of the means of production, given objective production conditions, and provided the cultural and technical proficiency of individuals as producers is fixed, individuals with more freedom of choice may become highly motivated and innovative, and thus have greater potential for efficiency improvement. That is to say, the larger the number is producers and workers with freedom of choice in economic activity, the more dynamic the economy becomes, the better the economy's capacity for growth is, and the easier the potentials of efficiency growth are to be tapped. Therefore, it is wrong to believe that the more autonomy is allowed for producers and workers, the more detrimental it is to the economy. On the other hand, however, given that the source of efficiency also lies in harmonious interpersonal relations and in people's compatibility with their organizations or society, it is more likely to coordinate these relations and enable individuals to adapt themselves to their organizations and society if they are subordinate to those organizations or society as a whole. Does this also point to greater potential for efficiency growth?

As a matter of fact, this question is not unanswerable. Individual autonomy and subordination to a particular organization or society can be mutually compatible instead of mutually exclusive. The moral foundation for efficiency entails not just making the most of people's enthusiasm and creativity; it also involves coordinating and harmonizing interpersonal relations. It is senseless to emphasize the former to the neglect of the latter, or vice versa. Nor can we believe that efficiency can grow continuously rather than temporarily when individuals are deprived of autonomy and lack enthusiasm and creativity as members

在重大自然灾害来临时，是不会产生超常规的效率的。因此，用道德标准来衡量，可以说明超常规效率的产生在符合效率标准的同时也符合道德标准。

四、效率增长潜力的发挥

在谈到效率的道德基础时，还有一个问题需要作进一步的探讨。这就是：是个人越有自主性，效率的增长潜力越大呢？还是个人的自主性越少，个人越是从属于某个团体、某个组织，甚至从属于整个社会，效率的增长潜力越大？

为什么会提出这个问题？这与效率的道德基础有关。在生产资料的技术性质与生产的客观条件为既定的前提下，在个人作为生产者、工作者的文化技术水平已知时，如果个人有较大的自主性，那也就会有较大的积极性和创造精神，从而效率增长的潜力较大。这就是说，经济中自主的生产者、工作者越多，经济就越具有活力，经济增长的能力就越强，效率增长的潜力就越容易发挥出来。所以，不能认为生产者、工作者的自主性越大对经济越不利。但从另一个角度来看，既然效率的源泉也在于人际关系的协调，在于人同团体或社会的适应，那么在个人从属于某个团体、某个组织，甚至从属于整个社会时，人际关系协调的可能性、人同团体或社会相适应的可能性也就越大。这岂不是表明效率增长的潜力越大吗？

其实，上述问题并不是不易弄清楚的。个人的自主性与个人对某个团体、组织、甚至社会的从属，可以相容并存；不能作出必然非此即彼、必须二者择一的结论。效率的道德基础，既包括了人的积极性、创造性的发挥，也包括了人际关系的协调与适应。只强调前一方面而忽视后一方面；或者，只强调后一方面而忽视前一方面，都是不对的。不能设想在个人从属于某个团体、组织、

of a particular organization or society, or when individuals enjoy a lot of autonomy while interpersonal relations are growing increasingly more inordinate and incompatible. Thus it is ideal to have both individual autonomy and coordinated and compatible interpersonal relations, with neither aspect neglected. This being the case, there should be individuals subordinate to organizations and society on the one side, and organizations and society holding individuals in due respect on the other—the coexistence of both conditions can keep efficiency growing steadily. In other words, individuals' subordination to organizations and society should be genuine and voluntary. Instead of being imposed upon them, their subordination should be conditioned by coordinated interpersonal relations and mutual respect, but at the same time, individuals should also conduct themselves with dignity and self-respect.

That should be the way it is in reality. People living in society are inevitably its members. A member of society invariably participates in certain organizations or institutions. The family is the smallest cell of society, and everyone belongs to a particular family. If a man is a worker, he works in a factory, where he may also be a trade union member. If he is a farmer, he may become a member of a villagers' self-governing organization, if such an organization ever exists. If he is an urban dweller, he belongs to the local community or neighborhood. If he is a private or self-employed business owner, he must belong to a certain association in which he handles interpersonal relations the best he can in order to live and work in harmony with fellow members. Meanwhile, as an individual, he should have his own wishes and demands, follow his own principles in dealing with people and daily life, and take the initiative into his own hands to stay motivated and innovative. In all, he should be a dynamic human being. Self-dependence is the prerequisite for someone to be in good interpersonal relations and get along with his organization and society. Good personal and interpersonal relations can mean nothing, and there will be no coordination and compatibility to speak of, if people are deprived of self-dependence and personal initiative. Doesn't this mean that personal initiative should be put in the first place in comparison with harmonious interpersonal relationships?

Society consists of numerous individuals, and an organization or institution comprises a certain number of individuals. If these individuals

甚至社会的同时，个人又缺乏自主性、积极性与创造性的情况下，效率会持续地、而不是暂时地增长。也不能设想在个人虽有较大的自主性，而人际关系不协调、不适应的现象却不断加剧的情况下，效率会持续增长。因此，合理的情况应当是：既有个人的自主性，又有人际关系的协调与适应，二者不可偏废。个人对某个团体、组织、甚至社会的从属，与团体、组织、社会对个人的尊重，是并存的。这种并存保证了效率的不断增长。换言之，个人对团体、组织、社会的从属应当是发自内心的，而不是强加的、被迫的；而要人际关系保持协调，人与人之间应当在各自自重的基础上相互尊重。

现实中的情况正是如此。一个人生活在社会中，他必然是社会的成员。一个人在社会中总会参加一定的团体、组织。家庭是最小的团体，一个人总属于某个家庭。如果他是职工，他会在一家企业中工作，也许他还加入工会。如果他是农民，他所在的那个村，或许有村民自治组织。如果他是城市居民，他从属于他所在的那个社区、街道。如果他是私营企业主或个体工商户，那么他有自己的协会之类的组织。总之，他既是社会的成员，又是某个团体、组织中的一员。为此，他必须尽可能地处理好人际关系，以求得相互协调，彼此适应。但与此同时，作为一个人，他有自己的愿望，自己的要求，自己待人处世的原则。他必须有自主性，然后才有积极性与创造性。换言之，他是有活力的。一个人的自主性，是他处理好人际关系的前提，也是他同团体、组织、社会协调与适应的前提。假定他连一点自主性都没有，纯粹被当作一种工具被别人所使唤、支配，他没有活力，没有生气，处理好人际关系又有什么意义？人际关系的协调、适应等等又何从谈起？这不正说明个人的自主性同人际关系的协调相比，应处于首位吗？

进一步说，社会上有无数个个人，一个团体、组织中有若干个个人。如果这些个人都有自主性，都有活力，都能发挥积极性、

enjoy self-dependence, are motivated, energetic, and innovative, and have the latitude to pursue their own goals while adapting themselves to organizational and social goals, interpersonal relations can be better handled, and efficiency can grow faster and by bigger margins. Isn't this exactly what society and organizations hope for?

Based on the above study, we know that the moral foundation of efficiency is an objective reality, but efficiency growth may either be real or potential, and the potential in efficiency growth is not necessarily tapped to capacity. To give full scope to such potential, we have to do two things: first, to respect people's self-dependence and give full scope to their motivation and innovativeness; and second, to coordinate interpersonal relations and adapt individuals to their organizations and society.

— *Journal of Peking University* (*Philosophy and Social Sciences*), issue No. 6, 1998

创造性，也都能够按自己的目标进行活动并力求同社会的目标、团体的目标相协调、相适应，那么人际关系必定处理得更好，效率的增长会更快，幅度更大。这不正是社会或团体所希望实现的吗？

以上的分析告诉我们，效率的道德基础是客观存在的。但效率的增长既有可能是现实的，也有可能是潜在的，效率增长的潜力不一定能充分发挥出来。要发挥这种潜力，一要靠对人的自主性的尊重，以便人的积极性、创造性能得到发挥；二要靠人际关系的协调，靠人同团体、组织、社会的适应。

（原载《北京大学学报（哲学社会科学版）》，1998年第6期）

POSTSCRIPT: A PROFILE OF LI YINING

I. Biographical sketch

i. Education (before 1955)

A native of Yizheng, Jiangsu province, Li Yining was born the eldest son of a family in Nanjing on November 22, 1930. When he was four, his family moved to Shanghai. Two years later, he went to the Second Elementary School Affiliated to the McTyeire School (the predecessor of the present-day Jianxiang Primary School), where he began his education as a hardworking student.

Upon graduation from elementary school, he enrolled in the Nan Yang Model High School of Shanghai. When the Japanese army sacked the city's foreign concessions after the Pacific War (1941-1945) broke out, his family fled to Yuanling, Hunan province, where Li resumed his studies in the Yali High School that had just been relocated from Changsha to avoid the war and turmoil. Shortly after the V-day of the War of Resistance against Japan (1937-1945), he returned to Nanjing to complete his high school education in the Affiliated High School of Nanking University.

Under the influence of a high school chemistry teacher, Li Yining set his mind on saving the country through industrialization, believing the root of its poverty lay in its industrial backwardness. Toward the end of 1948, while the War of Liberation (1945-1949) was still raging, Li became one of the students to be exempt from qualification exams on account of his outstanding high school academic records, and admitted to Nanking University. To live out his dream of national salvation, he chose the Department of Chemical Engineering, but victory in the war changed his plans. The founding of the People's Republic reshaped Li's outlook on China's destiny, and rekindled his hope for national prosperity and strength. Resolved to join in the construction of a new China, he preferred work over college. Thus he became an accountant with the School Stationery and Supplies Cooperative of Yuanling, Hunan province.

In his work Li found himself in dire need of knowledge. Therefore, he quit his job to prepare for college. He sat the college entrance examinations in Changsha in July 1951, and was enrolled in the Department of Economics of Peking University a month later.

后记

一、生平简述

（一）求学（1955 年以前）

厉以宁原籍江苏仪征，1930 年 11 月 22 日出生于南京，是家中的长子。在他 4 岁那年，全家从南京迁到了上海；6 岁时在距家不远的上海中西女中第二附小（现建襄小学）读书，从小就是一名勤奋好学的学生。

小学毕业后，他考进了上海南洋模范中学。太平洋战争爆发后，日军占领了上海租界，全家逃难到湖南沅陵。厉以宁转入由长沙迁到沅陵办学的雅礼中学。抗战胜利后不久，厉以宁回到南京，在南京金陵大学附中一直读到高中毕业。

在中学时代，厉以宁深受化学老师的影响，认为工业的落后是中国贫穷的根源，从而立下了实业救国的志向。1948 年底，在烽火连天的战争中，厉以宁以优异成绩从高中毕业，并被保送进入金陵大学。一心想以实业报国的厉以宁选择了化学工程系。人民解放战争的胜利改变了厉以宁一生的命运。新中国的成立，使厉以宁对中国的前途和命运改变了看法，他对中国繁荣富强的希望之火重新点燃。厉以宁决定投身于新中国建设事业，在湖南参加了工作，在湖南沅陵教育用品消费合作社担任会计。

厉以宁学生时代

Li Yining in his school days

厉以宁在工作中发现自己的知识相当贫乏。因此，1951 年，他毅然决定离职参加高考。1951 年 7 月，厉以宁在长沙应试，8 月底接到了北京大学的录取通知书，成为北京大学经济系的一名学生。

Li studied every possible moment during his college days. The eight summer and winter vacations in the four years saw him absorbed in his studies in the university library. On weekdays, he worked harder than others. Usually he had already finished his morning reading by the time his classmates began to get up; in class, he was quick to learn and able to raise insightful questions. That was the way he passed his 1,000 or so university days.

Li's wide learning, retentive memory and unflagging diligence soon shone through, and he became a top student in Peking University. As Professor Chen Zhenhan, acting dean of the Department of Economics, put it in his comment on Li Yining, "Test scores exceptionally high; definitely among the best." In July 1952, barely a year had passed since he entered college, but Li already published his essay "The new face of the Polish economy," and translated *Economic Perspectives of Herzen and Ogarev*, among other works. As the old saying goes, "A great teacher produces a brilliant student." Li owed his achievement largely to the top-notch faculty members of the Department of Economics of Peking University. Professor Luo Zhiru, the first teacher to usher Li into the study of Western economic theory, not only taught him knowledge in class, but also lent him articles copied from English books or periodicals to broaden his vision after class. A Harvard University graduate, Professor Chen Daisun's influence on him as an economics historian was at once subtle and deep. Professors Hu Daiguang, Zhou Binglin, Zhao Naichuan, Chen Zhenhan, and Xu Yuzhan also influenced Li academically in their respective ways.

ii. Getting through difficult times (1955-1980)

Li Yining joined the Peking University faculty upon graduation in 1955. During the 1955-1980 period, he plunged himself in reading, studying, contemplation and research. From the late 1950s to the early 1960s, the economic works he translated topped two million words, and the 30 issues of the *Foreign Economic Trends* journal he edited amounted to over one million words, 90% of which were compiled by himself. An avid reader of Western works on economics, Li could reel off the academic thoughts of John Maynard Keynes, Friedrich August Hayek, Alois Schumpeter, and John Richard Hicks. He was also the first Chinese economist to delve into the Western theory on economic disequilibrium.

在北京大学学习期间，厉以宁忘我地学习，他十分珍惜这四年的学习时光。大学四年的八个寒暑假，他将全部时间都留在了北大图书馆，从未回过家。平时的正常学习时间里，他比其他同学更加勤奋。在别人刚刚起床、准备投入新一天的学习时，他往往已在晨曦里完成了大量而充实的阅读工作。课堂上的厉以宁，敏锐的目光一直紧紧地追随着授课老师，他往往能比别人更早、更透彻地理解老师的讲授，并提出一些颇有见地的问题。四年里的 1000 多个日日夜夜，厉以宁从未放松过学习。

博闻强记与发奋努力结出了丰硕的成果，年轻的厉以宁很快就在北大脱颖而出，成为众所瞩目的尖子学生。当时的北大经济系代理系主任陈振汉教授对他的评语是："成绩优异，名列前茅"。1952 年 7 月，刚刚完成一年学业的厉以宁就发表了题为《波兰经济的新面貌》的论文，翻译了《赫尔岑和奥加略夫的经济观点》等专著。正所谓名师出高徒，厉以宁在大学时期的学习和研究，与当时北大经济系强大的师资力量密不可分。最早引导厉以宁钻研西方经济理论的是罗志如教授。他不仅在课堂上认真授课，而且在课下把英文书刊上的某些文章借给厉以宁阅读，使他眼界大开。陈岱孙教授毕业于美国哈佛大学，作为经济学说史研究者，他在潜移默化中影响着厉以宁。对厉以宁影响较大的老师还有胡代光、周炳琳、赵迺传、陈振汉和徐毓枬等教授。

（二）韬光养晦（1955 ~ 1980 年）

1955 年，厉以宁毕业留校任教。从 1955 年至 1980 年这一段时期，正是他潜心阅读、学习、思考和研究的时期。20 世纪 50 年代末至 60 年代初，厉以宁翻译了共约 200 多万字的经济学著作，还主办了 30 多期共 100 多万字的《国外经济学动态》，其中近 90% 的稿件是由厉以宁一人编写的。他还阅读了不少西方经济学专著，对凯恩斯、哈耶克、熊彼特和希克斯的学术思想非常熟悉。另外，他还是国内研究西方经济学非均衡理论的第一人。在如此深厚的理论基础的

Having gained a solid theoretical grounding through years of unremitting study, Li was able to come to the fore as an outstanding middle-aged scholar in Chinese academic circles at the turn of the 1970s.

Li's researches, however, were interrupted repeatedly in this 25-year period of his academic career. During the Great Leap Forward[1] of 1958, he did manual labor for a full year in west Beijing along with his colleagues. During the 1964-1965 period, he was forced to put down his books to join the "Four Clean-ups" Movement[2] in two places in rural China: Jiangling, Hubei province, from autumn 1964 to spring 1965; and Gaobeidian in Beijing's Chaoyang district from autumn 1965 to early June 1966, when the Cultural Revolution started. In October 1969, Li and other Peking University faculty members went to the Liyuzhou Farm in Jiangxi province, where he worked as a farmer until he returned to the university in 1972. In the four years that followed, Li was frequently dispatched to rural areas, where he did farm work while being "reeducated" by local farmers. It was not until early November 1976, or one month after the gang of four was incarcerated, that he was finally able to settle down in his university.

For two whole decades from the start of the struggle against the "bourgeois Rightists" in 1957 to the demise of the Cultural Revolution in 1976, Li Yining had his fill of physical and psychological trauma. The continuous trials and tribulations, however, made a mature man out of him. The grave damage done to the national economy by political movements, coupled with the poverty that reigned over the rural population, shocked his idealistic heart to the core, and smashed his belief in the traditional mode of socialism. His economic views changed dramatically, prompting him to seek a new road for the socialist economy.

支撑下，厉以宁厚积薄发，于20世纪70年代末80年代初一跃成为中国学术界引人注目的中年学者。

在这25年的时期里，厉以宁的研究也多次被打断。1958年，在大跃进浪潮中，厉以宁随北大教师队伍来到京西地区，整整劳动了一年。1964年和1965年，厉以宁再次被迫放下书本，到农村参加四清运动；1964年秋到1965年夏，在湖北江陵农村；1965年秋到1966年6月初，即“文化大革命”开始，到北京朝阳区高碑店。1969年10月，厉以宁又跟随北大教师队伍到江西鲤鱼洲农场劳动，直到1972年才回到学校。但此后4年左右，厉以宁仍一再被派往农村，边劳动，边接受再教育。直到1976年11月初，也就是“四人帮”被粉碎后一个月，才在学校里安定下来。

从1957年“反右”算起，到1976年为止，整整20年，厉以宁度过了心灵和肉体双重折磨的年代。他成熟了，是在不停的磨难中趋于成熟的。他上山下乡，亲历了国民经济遭受的严重破坏，目睹了广大农民的贫苦。他那颗充满理想主义信念的心受到了深深的震撼。他对传统社会主义模式的信念一次又一次遭到现实的无情打击，他不仅对这一传统模式产生怀疑，还进而从根本上予以否定。正是在这段时间里，厉以宁的经济观点发生了剧烈的变化，他决心自己去探寻一条研究社会主义经济的新路。

厉以宁夫妇及女儿厉放在鲤鱼洲
With wife and daughter on Liyuzhou Farm

iii. A great mind matures late (from 1980 onward)

Li Yining's twenty or so years of indefatigable toil in economics finally began to come to full fruition. From 1979 on, he had come up with a constant stream of research results. His *On Galbraith's Institutional Economics*, *A Concise Introduction to Modern Western Economics*, *The Rise and Development of Macroeconomics*, and other works on Western economics caused quite a stir in domestic economic circles the moment they came off the press. He became one of the most acclaimed teachers in Peking University shortly after his return to the lectern. His 100-seat classroom was often packed with twice as many students, and his lectures were invariably interrupted repeatedly by warm applause. His reputation spread in no time, and he eventually gained national attention as a preeminent economist.

Li Yining's academic accomplishments have everything to do with China's historic reform and opening up efforts. China was a planned economy before 1980, but has been in transition to a socialist market economy since the adoption of the policy of reform and opening up to the outside world. The transformation of such a gigantic economy is without doubt filled with uncharted dangers and fraught with uncertainties. Applying modern economic theories distilled from his near three decades of theoretical studies in Western economics, he set forth a series of reform proposals. As the initiator of the "joint-stock reform" that swept across China in the 1980s, he has since been fondly nicknamed "Li the Shareholding Guru."

In 1993, Li Yining masterminded the establishment of the Peking University Business School by merging the Department of Economics and Management and the Center of Management Science that had been established in 1985. In 1994, the Business School was renamed Guanghua School of Management after Peking University concluded, with Li as the driving force behind it, an agreement on cooperative school management with the Kwang-Hua Education Foundation of Hong Kong. Li served as the dean till 2005. Today, Guanghua is one of the best business colleges in China. A solicitous educator, Li has long been studying the peculiarly Chinese "urban-rural dual structure." He does his utmost to promote the healthy development of the private sectors of the national economy. Being attentive to the regional disparity in development, he renders great support for the development of less developed regions.

（三）大器晚成（1980 年至今）

经过 20 多年的韬光养晦，厉以宁厚积而薄发，其经济学研究结出了累累硕果。从 1979 年起，他陆续向读者展示了自己对西方经济学 20 多年的研究成果，包括《论加尔布雷思的制度经济学说》、《现代西方经济学概论》、《宏观经济学的产生和发展》等一系列著作。这些著作在当时中国经济学学术界掀起了巨大的波浪。重返讲台之后，厉以宁马上成为北京大学最受欢迎的老师之一。他在校园里的课堂上，100 人的教室，每次都能挤满 200 多人。讲课期间，掌声雷动。很快地，厉以宁在全国范围内名气大增，成为众人瞩目的经济学大师。

厉以宁的学术成就与中国改革开放的历史大潮息息相关。1980 年以前，中国实行计划经济，在改革开放后逐步向社会主义市场经济转变。如此庞大的经济体，其转型过程充满了未知和疑惑。厉以宁以其近 30 年对西方经济学的理论积淀，运用现代的经济学理论，加上其对中国现实经济的深刻理解，提出了一系列的改革主张。由于他提出并推动了 1980 年代的"股份制改革"，而被称为"厉股份"。

在这个时期，厉以宁还一手创办了北京大学光华管理学院。光华管理学院前身是 1985 年北京大学的经济管理系和管理科学中心。1993 年，厉以宁带领多名老师，在此基础上成立北京大学工商管理学院。1994 年，在厉以宁的推动下，北京大学与光华教育基金会签定合作办学协议，工商管理学院改名为光华管理学院。管理学院自成立起，厉以宁长期担任院长，直至 2005 年。目前，光华管理学院已经成为中国最好的商学院之一。厉以宁还长期研究中国特有的"城乡二元结构"，推动民营经济的健康发展，关注中国的地区发展差异和帮助贫困地区的发展。

Li Yining turned 80 in 2010. For the last three decades, he has been preeminent amongst the Chinese economics academia. Loved by his students as a teacher, and held in high esteem by the public as a scholar, he is also an economist whose influence on the nation's economic policies is keenly felt. His academic thoughts and contributions to China's reform and opening up endeavors will be elaborated in a later chapter.

iv. Family life

In Chinese mythology, there was *jian*, a one-winged lovebird. The male sported a left wing, and the female a right one. They were always flying in pairs. This couple of lovebirds is therefore likened to the union of a doting husband and his loving wife. Li and his wife, He Yuchun, are exactly such a couple who have shared weal and woe for more than five decades in conjugal bliss.

Li Yining and He Yuchun came to know each other in Yuanling, Hunan province, in the 1940s, but were not able to see each other after he went to study in Peking University in 1951 and she enrolled in the Huazhong Institute of Technology at Wuhan in 1953. It was not until February 1957 that he saw her again when he called on He Zhongyi, a former classmate who happened to be her elder brother, and whom she was visiting during a family reunion. That chance encounter kindled love between them, and before long they were talking about marriage.

They tied the knot on the lunar New Year's Eve in 1958 in a three-roomed bungalow in Haidian district, Beijing. The bridal chamber is a less than 20-square-meter property that they shared with his maternal grandmother, mother and younger brother. A few beds, a dining table, four chairs, a cupboard, and a washstand were all they had in the house. The family, nevertheless, was brimming with love and merriness.

Their wedding photo is characteristic of the era they lived in. Li, slim and bespectacled, neat and clean, is a typical intellectual dressed in a Sun Yet-sen suit. His wife, wearing a long plait tied up in a single loop with a bowknot on either side of her head, smiles meekly in a patterned woolen sweater she had knitted for herself. After a brief honeymoon the newlyweds were separated. He did manual labor in Zhaitang township, Beijing, while she became a commuter in Anshan, an industrial city in the northeastern province of Liaoning. For quite a long time, the couple lived

2010 年，厉以宁已满 80 岁。自 1980 年以来，他 30 年来一直活跃于中国经济学学术界，是学生喜爱的老师，是受社会敬重的教授，也是对经济政策具有一定影响力的经济学家。关于他的学术思想和对中国经济改革开放的贡献，后文再做详细介绍，这里不再赘述。

（四）家庭生活

中国古代传说中有一种鸟，叫鹣，雄有左翼，雌有右翼，比翼双飞。于是，人们也希望自己拥有相扶到永远的另一半，“鹣鲽情深”就成了人们对恩爱夫妻的赞美。厉以宁和他夫人何玉春，就是这样一对夫妻，患难与共，恩爱有加。

厉以宁和何玉春第一次相遇于 20 世纪 40 年代的湖南沅陵。1951 年厉以宁考取了北京大学，1953 年何玉春考取了华中工学院，两人天各一方。直至 1957 年 2 月，何玉春来京探亲，住在其兄何重义家中；厉以宁由北大来清华看望老同学何重义。两人不期而遇，从此结下一世情缘。

1958 年 2 月，正是农历除夕，厉以宁与何玉春喜结连理。新房就在北京海淀的三小间简陋平房，总面积不过 20 平方米。外祖母、母亲、弟弟都与他们住在一起。家具除了床以外，只有一张饭桌、四个板凳、一个碗柜、一个脸盆架。然而，简陋的小屋中却充溢着浓浓的甜蜜和欢笑。

两人结婚照颇具时代特点。厉以宁一身中山装，戴着眼镜，白净瘦削，显然一文静书生；何玉春穿着自织的花毛衣，两条长辫子挽上两边，一边扎一朵蝴蝶结，面带微笑。新婚后，他们在一起生活的时间很短，两人一个赴北京斋堂乡劳动，一个去辽宁鞍山上班。此后，在相当长的一段时间内，这对恩爱

厉以宁何玉春结婚照 The wedding photo

apart like so many other families at the time. In December 1970, she gave up her job and career to join him at Liyuzhou, Jiangxi province, where he was working and being reeducated with local farmers. They have since never been apart from each other.

By 2010, they had spent 52 years together as husband and wife. Their daughter, Li Fang, graduated from Monash University, Australia, with a doctor's degree. Li Wei, their son, runs his own business in Guangdong province after graduating from the Department of Chemistry of Peking University. But the Lis' happiness does not stop at the successes of their son and daughter. The era of reform and opening up gave full scope to Li Yining's talent and academic prowess, and his reputation soared as a result. In the shadow of his luminous aura stands his wife, making quiet contributions to his career. He Yuchun is a senior electrical engineer by profession, but she willingly serves as the first reader of her husband's works on economics. Li Yining said of his wife, "Whenever she spots any part of my writing that isn't succinct, lucid or readable enough, she'll demand a rewriting. I won't stop amending it until she is satisfied. If readers find my books not too difficult to read, half the credit is due my wife."

II. Academic achievements

i. Research in economic history

(i) General introduction Economic history figures prominently in Li Yining's academic studies. His first teaching assignment in Peking University in 1962 was on international economic history. In his academic career, including the last three decades that he has dedicated to the theory and practice of economic restructuring in China, he has never stopped his research in economic history, Western economic history in particular. In a sense, Li's accomplishment in economics is rooted in his scholarship in economic history. *British Economy in the 20th Century: A Study of the "British Disease," The Rise of Capitalism: A Study of Comparative Economic History* and *Roman-Byzantine Economic History*, to name just a few, are crystallizations of his wisdom and hard work in economic history.

2002 年厉以宁全家合影照
A 2002 picture of all members of the Li family

夫妻如同当时的许多家庭一样，不得不长期两地分居。直到 1970 年 12 月，夫妻分居终于熬到了头。经过长达十几年的两地相思苦煎熬之后，何玉春放弃了一切能放弃的（户口、专业、工作等），来到了江西鲤鱼洲，与厉以宁开始了一次真正不再分开的相聚。

到 2010 年，厉以宁、何玉春已相偕相伴走过了 52 个春秋。他们的女儿厉放已获得澳大利亚莫纳什大学博士学位，儿子厉伟自北京大学化学系毕业后，就南下广东创业。此时，厉以宁夫妇的幸福生活不仅体现在儿女长大成人，更体现在事业上的携手共进。在改革开放这个大舞台上，厉以宁充分施展着自己的才华，名气盛大；但在他耀眼的光环后面，是夫人何玉春默默无闻的奉献。何玉春所学并非经济学，她是电气专业的高级工程师，但她却是厉以宁经济学专著的第一读者。厉以宁说："她在阅读书稿时感到哪里还不够简明，还不易被人们看懂，我就修改，直到她满意为止。所以读者读完我的书，如果感觉到符合深入浅出的要求，那么夫人的功劳占一半。"

二、学术成就

（一）经济史研究

1．概述

经济史研究，在厉以宁的学术研究中占有重要的位置。1962 年，厉以宁第一次登上北大讲坛，讲授的就是外国经济史。在他后来几十年的学术生涯中，包括近 30 年着力研究中国经济体制改革的理论与实践问题期间，他都从未间断过对经济史、尤其是西方经济史的研究。在一定程度上可以说，厉以宁在经济学方面的建树，也来源于他在经济史方面的功力。《二十世纪的英国经济——"英国病"研究》、《资本主义的起源：比较经济史研究》以及《罗马—拜占庭经济史》等著作，都是厉以宁在经济史方面的集大成之作。

(ii) British Economy in the 20th Century: A Study of the "British Disease" Published in 1982, this book was a product of Li Yining's early research on economic history, as well as a milestone in his academic career.

The fall of the British Empire in the 20th century is a topic of heated debate in world history. While Western scholars tend to ascribe the decline of the empire to the loss of its position as a "world factory," Li is of the opinion that such a loss might be responsible for Britain's diminishing world status, but is not enough to account for its tottering economy *per se*. On the "British Disease," Li gives his own diagnosis: It was caused by a combination of factors that included the loss of that country's position as a world factory, the aftermath of its colonial expansion, the flaws of a welfare state, and the negative influence of conservatism on the economy. Through a comprehensive survey of the social, political, economic and mental landscape of twentieth-century Britain, Li arrives at a conclusion that is worlds apart from his predecessors. The first book on the economic history of twentieth-century Western countries by a contemporary Chinese economist, *British Economy in the 20th Century: A Study of the "British Disease"* is also the first study of the macroeconomic policies of the British government by a Chinese scholar.

(iii) The Rise of Capitalism: A Study of Comparative Economic History *The Rise of Capitalism: A Study of Comparative Economic History* (Commercial Press, Beijing, 2003) is Professor Li's brainchild from two decades of painstaking labor on economic history. By unremittingly exploring and contemplating the theoretical system concerning the genesis of capitalism, and by drawing on his own experience in helping draw the blueprints for the economic restructuring in China, he eventually discovered an entirely new approach to this historical question.

In the book, Li Yining divides capitalism into two types, homegrown and transplanted. The homegrown type of capitalism arose and developed in a country or region under the impact of internal factors during the disintegration of feudalism; and most West European countries belong in this category. The transplanted type of capitalism evolved during the collapse of the feudal society of a country or region under the onslaught of external forces that shook its foundation and weakened its rule; Japan and other capitalist "latecomers" in Asia, Africa, and Latin America

2.《二十世纪的英国经济——"英国病"研究》

《二十世纪的英国经济——"英国病"研究》出版于 1982 年，是厉以宁早期经济学学习研究的结晶，也是他学术生涯的一个界碑。

20 世纪大英帝国的衰落是世界史上最引人注目的话题之一。在西方一些著作中，学者们往往把大英帝国的衰落与其"世界工厂"地位的丧失等同起来。但是厉以宁对此并不完全认同。他认为，"世界工厂"地位的丧失虽然可以解释英国在世界上相对地位的下降，却解释不了为什么其经济本身陷入停停走走的状态。对于"英国病"，厉以宁给出了自己的诊断。那就是：世界工厂地位的丧失，殖民扩张的结束给国内经济带来的后果，福利国家政策所引起的问题和传统精神对经济的消极作用。在这本书中，厉以宁对英国二十世纪的社会、政治、经济和意识形态进行了综合的考察，得出了不同于前人的结论。这本书，既是中国当代经济学家撰写的第一部关于 20 世纪的西方国家的经济史，也是第一部国内学者对英国政府宏观政策进行经济分析的著作。

3.《资本主义的起源：比较经济史研究》

2003 年由商务印书馆出版的《资本主义的起源：比较经济史研究》，从策划到完稿用了二十年的时间，是厉以宁在经济史方面的呕心沥血之作。在二十年的时间中，厉以宁不断地探索、思考和完善资本主义起源的理论体系，并结合他参与中国经济改革设计的经验，最终悟出了破解资本主义起源这道历史难题的全新思路。

按照起源的不同，厉以宁将资本主义划分为原生型资本主义和非原生型的资本主义。前者是指在本国或本地区的封建社会解体的过程中，由于内部因素的作用产生和发展起来的资本主义。西欧国家大体上属于这一类型。后者是指某种外力冲击了本国或本地区的封建社会，动摇了其统治基础，削弱了其统治力量，在封建社会解体过程中产生和发展起来的资本主义。日本和其他亚洲、非洲、拉丁

are of this type. Why, then, could capitalism grow and establish itself from within feudal society in some countries while in other countries capitalism had to be midwived by external forces? Li Yining believes that it had something to do with whether the institution of a feudal society was rigid or flexible. In a feudal society with a rigid institution, the social hierarchical and identification systems were ossified, making social mobility very difficult. In a feudal society with a flexible institution, the ruler forsook stringent hierarchical and identification systems, tolerated lateral and vertical social mobility, and favored changes in power structure and flexibility in power enforcement—thereby ensuring the survival and continuity of the feudal society. The ossified power structure and enforcement in a rigid feudal society were riddled with loopholes that gave rise to dissidence. When such dissidence grew into a power center outside the feudal institution, its conflict with the established power center would eventually cause the collapse of feudalism and the birth of capitalism. By contrast, a feudal society with elastic institutions could last for a long time because it was highly maneuverable and adjustable in emergency, leaving little room for the rise of anti-establishment forces.

The rigid institution of West European feudal society looked solid and stable on the surface, but in reality it was like a worn-out cast-iron wok, too fragile to withstand any blow. The serfs, desperate for freedom, were drawn to the cities, where there were not only hopes for survival but also opportunities for the underprivileged to end their status as appendages to feudal lords and become equal members of society. The more the feudal social institution restricted social mobility, the more resolved the humble and underprivileged became to unshackle themselves from such restriction. A direct course of action for them was to rise up in arms against the serf-owners. The larger the urban population grew, the greater the cities' strength against serf-owners became. Thus feudalism in West Europe was doomed.

The Rise of Capitalism also provides vivid and original analyses of the elastic feudal system and the birth of transplanted capitalism in China. Permeating the entire book is the author's analytical approach to institutional readjustment, an approach that not only gives a convincing explanation of the origin of capitalism, but also applies to institutional adjustments under both capitalism and socialism. While dissecting

美洲的一些后发资本主义国家即属于这一类型。那么，为什么资本主义能在一些国家的封建社会内部产生、发展并最终确立下来，而在其他国家却需要外力的冲击才能确立呢？厉以宁认为，这与封建社会的不同体制有关。封建社会可以划分为刚性体制和弹性体制。在刚性体制下，社会等级制和身份制严格，社会流动不易。在弹性体制下，封建统治者未采用严格的等级制和身份制，容许纵向的和横向的社会流动；权力结构可以发生变化，权力的行使方式也灵活多样，以确保封建制度的存在和延续。在刚性体制下，由于权力结构固定，权力行使方式僵化，所以各权力之间容易出现空隙，便于体制外异己力量滋生成长；再发展壮大形成体制外的权力中心，与体制内的权力中心发生冲突，最终导致封建社会的崩溃和资本主义社会的诞生。而弹性体制下的封建制度，应变能力很强，遇到危机可以自我调整，不易产生体制外的异己力量，从而能够长期存活下来。

西欧封建社会的刚性体制看起来很坚硬、稳定，但实际上像脆弱的铁锅，经不起打击——农奴竭力想摆脱自己不自由的处境而向往城市，因为城市不但给卑贱者提供生存之路，而且提供了可以摆脱对封建主的人生依附关系和争取到平等地位的机会。社会体制越是限制社会的流动，卑贱者和等级低下的人，就越想摆脱这种限制。改变的最直接途径就是反抗。随着社会的发展，城市中聚集的人越来越多，城市的力量越来越大，形成了反对封建主的力量，最终造成了西欧封建社会的覆亡。

此书还对中国弹性的封建体制和非原生型资本主义的产生给出了生动而独到的分析。在整本书中，厉以宁关于制度调整的分析方法不但可以给资本主义的起源一个令人信服的解释，而且可以用来分析资本主义和社会主义的制度调整问题。可以说，它不仅

the genesis of capitalism, Li Yining also derives the universal norms governing transition and changes in social systems.

(iv) Roman-Byzantine Economic History A crystallization of Li Yining's years of hard work on the economic history of the Roman Republic and Byzantium, the two-volume *Roman-Byzantine Economic History* (Commercial Press, Beijing, 2006) is another major work on economic history marked by unique perspectives and profound opinions. Volume One of the book, *From the Republic to the Empire*, covers a time span of over 700 years from the heyday of the Roman Republic in the 3rd century BC to the demise of the Western Roman Empire in 476 AD. Volume Two, *Between the Oriental and the Occidental*, encompasses nearly 1,000 years from the fall of the Western Roman Empire in 476 AD to the Ottoman Empire's complete conquest of the Byzantine Empire in 1461 AD. The entire book provides a broad historical panorama of the region that stretches for thousands of miles from Britain to the Arabian Sea via the Mediterranean, and recaptures two thousand years of socioeconomic vicissitudes from the zenith of the Roman Republic to the collapse of the Byzantine Empire. In this book, Li Yining takes a series of original viewpoints on Roman-Byzantine history. For instance, he believes that the conflicts and struggles between small and big land-owners were a major factor that affected Roman society's socioeconomic life, and that the prosperity of the Roman Republic and the Roman Empire hinged on the support of yeomen in rural areas and industrialists and merchants in urban areas. He maintains that the imperial system of the Roman Empire was not transplanted from Oriental countries—it was akin to a military autocracy that retained some remnants of the Roman republican system in the early years of the empire, and absorbed more and more elements and rites of Oriental dictatorship to evolve into a quasi- or semi-Oriental imperial system.

The fall of the Western Roman Empire is a historical event of far-reaching significance. In his cause-and-effect analysis, Li Yining disagrees with those who attribute it to "class struggle" or "ethnic strife," and rejects the opinion that it was caused by the "deteriorating Roman character." "A big power, whatever it is, cannot be conquered unless it has gone through a process of self-destruction," he believes. The causes of the fall of the Western Roman Empire should be uncovered from within itself: The prosperity of both the Roman Republic and the Roman Empire stemmed from the support of the rural yeomen and the urban industrialists, who

分析了资本主义的起源，而且最终能提炼出社会制度转型和变迁的普遍规律。

4.《罗马—拜占庭经济史》

《罗马—拜占庭经济史》（上、下编）是厉以宁出版于 2006 年的一部重要经济史学著作，是厉以宁多年来研究罗马、拜占庭经济史心得的积累，也是一部见解独到、思想深邃的重要史学著作。此书共分上下两编，上编为“从共和到帝制”，时间跨度大约为 700 多年，即从公元前 3 世纪罗马共和国盛期到公元 476 年西罗马帝国灭亡。下编为“东方与西方之间”，时间跨度将近 1000 年，即从公元 476 年西罗马帝国灭亡到 1461 年拜占庭帝国全境被奥斯曼帝国征服。全书时间跨度两千年，纵横数千公里，从不列颠直到阿拉伯海，描述了围绕着地中海东西部的广阔历史画卷，对罗马共和国盛期到拜占庭帝国灭亡期间的社会经济变迁做了论述。在这本书中，厉以宁针对罗马—拜占庭的历史提出了一系列自己的观点。如，小土地所有者和大土地所有者之间的矛盾和斗争是贯穿罗马社会经济生活的主要线索；罗马共和国的兴盛和罗马帝国的兴盛所依靠的是乡村自耕农和城市工商业者的支持；罗马的帝制并不是古代东方国家的帝制的搬用。罗马帝制初期类似于军事独裁制，同时又保存了罗马共和制的一些因素。只是到了后来才吸收了越来越多的东方专制制度的内容和仪式，形成一种准东方的或半东方的帝制。

西罗马帝国的灭亡是一个影响深远的历史事件。对这一事件的原因，厉以宁既不同意“阶级斗争论”，也不同意“民族斗争论”，更不同意“罗马人素质退化论”。他认为，“任何大国在未经自我毁灭之前是不会为他国所征服的。”西罗马帝国的灭亡要从它自身寻找原因：罗马共和国和罗马帝国的兴盛所依靠的都是乡村中自耕农

provided both the Republic and the Empire with an ample supply of conscripts, a full state treasury, a booming economy, and basic social stability. However, all this changed with the demise of the Antonine Dynasty (96-192 AD). The long years of repression and deprivation that followed pushed the yeomen, industrialists, and businessmen to bankruptcy and sent them into exile. The supply of conscripts dried up, and so did the state treasury. The economy slumped, and society was in chaos. In this way, the Western Roman Empire ruined the middle class, the very social foundation it relied on for existence. At this point, what awaited the Western Roman Empire was nothing but downfall.

Li maintains that the fall of the Byzantine Empire was a replay of the tragedy of the Western Roman Empire. The Byzantine Empire did exactly what the Romans had done nearly a millennium before, tearing down the very foundation for its survival in rural small land-owners and urban industrialists and merchants, and thus losing its sources of military manpower and tax revenue. After running out of local conscripts, the empire had no alternative but to man its main military force with mercenaries. To maintain these mercenaries, it had to levy more taxes, which drove more and more urban industrialists and merchants into bankruptcy, prison, or exile. The tax revenue shrank further as a result.

Both *The Rise of Capitalism* and *Roman-Byzantine Economic History* display Li Yining's persistent passion for economic history studies over the years. This passion, coupled with a penetrating insight, is the reason why he has been able to accomplish so much in this field of academic pursuit.

ii. Study of transitional economics

(i) An overview Li Yining's theory of economic transition and development in China derives from his interpretation of transitional economics. By probing deeply into issues pertinent to the Chinese economy in transition on the basis of the theory of two categories of economic disequilibrium, he comes up with three important viewpoints:

First, ownership reform is more important than price reform; second, unemployment is more worrisome than inflation; third, analyzing economic growth is more useful than analyzing money flow. In his study of transitional economics, he also looks systematically into such major issues in the course of economic transition as government regulation, coordinated social development, and conceptual upgrading.

和城市中工商业者的支持，兵源充足、府库充实、经济繁荣、社会基本稳定。但是，安东尼王朝结束以后，长时期内自耕农和工商业者备受打击、剥夺，相继沦于破产、逃亡的困境。兵源枯竭了，府库空虚了，经济萧条了，社会动荡不安，西罗马帝国自己摧毁了赖以生存的社会基础——社会的中产阶级。所以等待它的只有覆亡。

厉以宁认为，近1000年后拜占庭帝国的灭亡则重演了西罗马帝国灭亡的悲剧：拜占庭帝国毁坏了自己赖以生存的基础，即乡村中的小土地所有者和城市中的工商业者，兵源和税源都枯竭了。兵源枯竭后，只能由外族的雇佣兵来充当军队的主力。为了供养这批外族的雇佣兵，又只能加重赋税，迫使城市中的工商业者继续破产、被捕或逃亡，税源就更加枯竭了。

《资本主义的起源》和《罗马—拜占庭经济史》这两部经济史巨著说明，厉以宁对于经济史方面的学术研究，数十年保持了一种高度的热情。正是由于有这种热情，再加上他高超的洞察力，厉以宁才能够在经济史研究方面取得如此巨大的成就。

（二）转型经济学研究

1．概述

厉以宁关于中国经济转型与经济发展理论的集中体现，是他关于转型经济学的观点。以两类经济非均衡的理论为基础，厉以宁对中国经济的转型问题做了深入的研究，并提出了三个重要的观点。第一，产权改革比价格改革更重要；第二，失业问题比通货膨胀问题更令人担心；第三，经济增长分析比货币流量分析更有用。在他的转型经济学研究中，厉以宁还系统分析了经济转型过程中的政府调节、社会协调发展以及观念更新等许多重要的问题。

(ii) The Chinese Economy in Disequilibrium In *The Chinese Economy in Disequilibrium* (Encyclopedia of China Publishing House, Beijing, 2009), Li Yining elaborates the disequilibrium theory in depth, and, basing himself on this theory, studies the current situation with the Chinese economy and goes on to propose his strategy for Chinese economic reform.

Based on Western disequilibrium theories, he divides disequilibrium in an economy into two categories. Economic disequilibrium of the first category is characterized by an incomplete market, inflexible prices, the presence of both excess demand and excess supply, and of restraints on both demand and supply, while the microeconomic agents in the market are independent commodity producers that make their own business decisions, are responsible for their own gains and losses, have the freedom to choose investment opportunities and modes of management, and bear investment and business risks on their own. Economic disequilibrium in the second category is characterized by an incomplete market and inflexible prices, the presence of both excess demand and supply and of restraints on both demand and supply. It is also marked by a market filled with microeconomic agents that, instead of being independent commodity producers making their own business decisions and taking responsibility for their own gains and losses, neither have the freedom to choose investment opportunities and management modes nor bear investment and management risks on their own. In a word, these microeconomic agents have not quit their status as government subsidiaries. Li believes that disequilibrium in a capitalist economy belongs in the first category, while disequilibrium in a socialist economy belongs in the second category because its firms are yet to end their status as government subsidiaries. For this reason, economic restructuring in China should be focused on ownership reform, that is, reform of property rights relationships. That means to energize slumping firms and enable them to make their own business decisions and take responsibility for their gains and losses. Only in this way can the Chinese economy accomplish the transition from the second category of disequilibrium to the first category, and, by continuing to improve the market mechanism, move gradually on to equilibrium.

Li Yining's theory of two categories of economic disequilibrium constitutes the starting point for his pronouncements on a series of Chinese economic issues, such as what the focus should be for economic restructuring, reconstructing the nation's microeconomic foundation through joint-stock reform, shareholding as a major form of new public ownership, and the capital market.

2.《非均衡的中国经济》

在《非均衡的中国经济》一书中，厉以宁深入阐述了非均衡理论，又以非均衡理论为基础，分析了中国的经济现状，继而提出了中国经济改革的方略。

在西方非均衡理论的基础上，厉以宁将经济中的非均衡区分为两类。第一类经济非均衡是指：市场不完善、价格不灵活、超额需求或超额供给都存在、需求约束或供给约束也都存在，但参加市场活动的微观经济单位是自主经营、自负盈亏的独立商品生产者，它们有投资机会和经营方式的自由选择权，自行承担投资风险和经营风险。第二类非均衡是指：市场不完善、价格不灵活、超额需求和超额供给都存在、需求约束或供给约束也都存在，但参加市场活动的微观经济单位并非自主经营、自负盈亏的独立商品生产者，缺乏自由选择投资机会和经营方式的自主权，也不自行承担投资风险和经营风险。微观经济单位没有摆脱行政机构附属物的地位。厉以宁认为，资本主义经济中所出现的非均衡属于第一类，而社会主义经济中的企业由于没有摆脱行政机构附属物的地位，因此属于第二类非均衡。因此，中国的经济体制改革应当以所有制改革，即产权改革为主线，使企业从缺乏活力转为具有活力，转为自主经营和自负盈亏，以便使中国经济由第二类非均衡状态过渡到第一类非均衡状态；然后继续完善市场，使中国经济由第一类非均衡状态逐渐向均衡状态靠拢。

厉以宁有关中国经济改革主线的论述，通过股份制改革重新构造微观经济基础的论述，以股份制为主要形式的新公有制的论述，以及有关资本市场的论述，都是从他的两类非均衡理论出发的。

(iii) Double-coverage theory: socialist planning and the market In *Socialist Political Economics* (Commercial Press, Beijing, 1986), Li Yining gives a systematic illustration of his double-regulation theory: on the one hand, microeconomic regulation, which, in essence, is regulation by market; and on the other, macroeconomic regulation, which, in essence, is regulation by governmental macroeconomic mechanisms. He points out that government regulation of the economy means a great deal for the eradication of disequilibrium in economic aggregates and structure caused by dissonance between micro- and macro-economies, because it can set the national economy in orbit and guarantee the fulfillment of prescribed socioeconomic development goals. Li regards market and government as the "dual mechanisms" for the socialist economy. According to him, the socialist market should be regulated, first, by the market itself, and second, at a higher level, by the government. When the government mechanism works on resource allocation, its impact invariably manifests itself in all aspects of social and economic lives through the changes in the relationship between supply and demand on the market. In that sense, government regulation works atop market regulation on the whole society. In other words, the market is subject to two layers of regulation: the market mechanism as the first layer, and government mechanism the second. Such is Li Yining's "double coverage" theory, derived from the "second regulation" and "dual regulation" theories he founded in the early stage of his academic career.

(iv) Shareholding: the target mode for ownership reform Since the 1980s Chinese economic circles had been divided on which should take the center stage of economic restructuring—price reform or corporate reform. Li Yining, a staunch supporter of the latter, believes that the Chinese economy is in the second category of disequilibrium on the ground that neither of the two prerequisites for market regulation to become effective—a relatively complete market and energetic microeconomic agents—is available in the economy, and that the fundamental problem lies at the microeconomic level, where firms have yet to quit their status as government subsidiaries. His analysis drives home the urgent significance of economic restructuring, in particular the reform to invigorate firms, for economic development. Indeed, restructuring the property rights system and standardizing the behavior of market participants are pivotal to the building of a modern market economy in this country.

3．双覆盖论：社会主义计划与市场

在 1986 年出版的《社会主义政治经济学》一书中，厉以宁系统阐述了他的两次调节论：一种调节是微观经济调节机制，实质上就是市场机制的调节；一种调节是宏观经济调节机制，实质上就是政府对宏观经济的调节。厉以宁指出，政府的经济调节对于消除由宏观、微观经济的不协调而引起的总量和结构失衡，有重大的意义。它能够保证国民经济的正常运行，使经济和社会发展达到预定目标。厉以宁将并存着的市场机制和政府调节称为社会主义经济中的二元机制，市场调节是第一次调节，政府调节是第二次调节，即高层次的调节。政府对资源配置进行调节的结果，必然使政府调节的作用通过市场供求关系的相应变化而在全社会经济的各个方面表现出来。从这个意义上讲，政府调节是覆盖于全社会的，而且政府调节对全社会的覆盖是一种再覆盖，即覆盖于市场调节之上的覆盖。作为第一次调节的市场调节是对社会经济的第一次覆盖，作为第二次调节的政府调节对社会经济的覆盖是第二次覆盖，也是第二个层次的覆盖。这就是厉以宁由早期的“第二次调节论”、“两次调节论”逐步演变而成的“双覆盖论”。

4．股份制：所有制改革的目标模式

自 20 世纪 80 年代以来，中国经济学界对中国的经济体制改革一直存在两种思路：“价格改革主线论”和“企业改革主线论”。厉以宁是后一种改革思路的坚定支持者。他认为，中国经济的非均衡属于第二类非均衡。在这种经济中，市场调节取得成效的两个条件——完善的市场环境和有活力的微观经济单位——都不具备，根本问题在于微观层面，即企业没有摆脱行政机构附属的地位。这一分析充分说明了经济体制改革、尤其是激发企业活力的改革，对经济发展具有迫切的意义。中国建设现代市场经济体制的核心问题，是产权制度的重新构造与市场主体行为的规范化。

Li further asserts that the fundamental strategy in restructuring the corporate system and defining the property rights relationship is to introduce the shareholding system that separates ownership and management in firms, and on this basis, to bring the ownership structure to near perfection. He points out that, rather than replacing public ownership with private ownership, ownership reform is meant to break through traditional state ownership and transform it into a new type of public ownership. In his view, the greatest inspiration from the rural economic restructuring in the 1980s was that the vitality of the rural economy hinged on ownership reform, in which a household contract responsibility system linking remuneration with output was introduced. Ownership reform in cities calls for the emergence of more shareholding firms, so as to restructure the microeconomic foundation for the operation of the national economy.

iii. Economic ethics and the power of morality

(i) An overview Li Yining insists all along that the study of people represents the supreme level of economic research, and that economics is meaningless without studying human beings and the quality of human life. Economic ethics and the power of morality are part and parcel of his humanity-oriented economic theory.

(ii) Exploring the issue of economic ethics Ethics in economics has always commanded Li Yining's attention as a major research topic. His achievements in this field of study find concentrated expression in his *Ethics in Economics* (SDX Joint Publishing Company, Beijing, 1995). In this book, he proceeds from social ethics to dwell on some essential socioeconomic issues that have occurred during China's transition from traditional central planning to a socialist market economy. These include the relationship between efficiency and equity, transactions in property rights, unemployment and inflation, consumption and investment by individuals, the cost of economic growth, and rational economic growth rate. By adopting normative economic approaches, setting common prosperity as the ultimate goal of socialist development, and regarding workers' maximum interests as the benchmark for truth and falsehood and good and evil in the socioeconomic realm, *Ethics in Economics* provides an array of incisive viewpoints from the perspective of ethics and morality.

(iii) The role of moral power in the economy Through many years of contemplation, Li Yining arrives at the conclusion that economics is

厉以宁进而认为，进行企业制度的重新构造、明确财产关系的根本出路在于对企业实行所有权与经营权分离的股份制，并在此基础上完善所有制改革。他指出，所有制改革不是将公有制改为私有制，而是突破传统的全民所有制形式，把传统的公有制改造成为新型的公有制。他认为，20 世纪 80 年代中国农村经济体制改革给人们的最大启示是：农村活力的源泉来自所有制改革，即家庭联产承包责任制的推广。城市的所有制改革则需要以建立更多的股份制企业为基础，以重新构造经济运行的微观基础。

（三）经济伦理与道德力量

1．概述

厉以宁一直坚持认为，人的研究，是经济学研究的最高层次。离开了对人的研究、对生活质量的研究，经济学会变得没有意义。对经济伦理与道德力量的研究，则是厉以宁经济学人本理论的重要组成部分。

2．经济伦理问题的探讨

经济学的伦理问题，一直是厉以宁关注的一个重要课题。他在这方面研究心得的集中体现，是出版于 1995 年的《经济学的伦理问题》一书。在这本书中，厉以宁从社会伦理的角度，讨论了中国由传统计划经济体制向社会主义市场经济体制转轨的过程中经济社会的一些焦点问题，如效率与公平的关系问题、产权交易的问题、失业与通货膨胀、个人消费问题、个人投资问题、经济增长的代价、合理的经济增长率等。厉以宁采用规范经济学的方法，把共同富裕作为社会主义发展的根本性目标，以劳动者的最大利益作为评价经济社会中是非善恶的标准，从伦理和道德的角度，提出了很多精辟的观点。

3．道德力量在经济中的作用

厉以宁经过长期的思考，认为经济学是研究资源配置及其机制的

a discipline of resource allocation and its mechanisms, and that market regulation and government regulation are two different mechanisms for resource allocation. Besides these, he says, there is a third mechanism: custom and morality, which combine to be the only regulatory mechanism for resource allocation prior to the advent of market and government mechanisms, and is still the only mechanism that can work in areas beyond the reach of market and government. Therefore, it is necessary to study morality as a regulation mechanism apart from market and government mechanisms, and emphasize the role of morality in regulating resource allocation.

On that basis Li has also studied what constitutes the foundations for efficiency. To him, efficiency rests on dual foundations—first, materials and technology, and second, morality. While the material and technological foundation guarantees conventional efficiency, morality not only ensures conventional efficiency but also provides extraordinary efficiency. The potentials for higher efficiency can be tapped mainly by relying on efficiency's moral foundation and on the role of moral force.

iv. Educational economics

Li Yining published his paper "Technology education and capitalist industrialization: a study of the rise of technological power in Western Europe and America" in the *Social Sciences Front* journal, issue No. 4, 1978. Since then, educational economics has become another main field in his researches. Based on a series of papers that he had written on that subject, he published the book *Educational Economics* (Beijing Publishing House, Beijing, 1984). With its wealth of ground-breaking academic findings, it was hailed as "the first exclusive work on educational economics in contemporary China."

In *Educational Economics*, Li spells out the role of education in economic growth and socioeconomic development in China, what is entailed in the economic returns of intellectual investment, benchmark options, and approaches to enhancing the economic returns of such investment. His all-around dissection of the mechanisms by which investment in education boosts labor productivity brings to light the relationship between education investment and labor productivity. In this book he points out that the economic returns of educational or intellectual investment are both macroeconomic and microeconomic, and follows up with a discussion on the quantifiability of each category of returns. Moreover, the book also covers such issues as the time-lag in the commercialization of technological knowledge, and the potentials in the development of school graduates.

科学。市场调节和政府调节是两种不同的资源配置方式。此外，还存在第三种调节方式，那就是习惯和道德调节。习惯和道德调节是市场调节与政府调节出现以前唯一起调节作用的经济调节方式，也是市场力量与政府力量达不到的领域内唯一起调节作用的经济调节方式。因此，在中国经济改革与发展中，有必要对市场调节与政府调节以外的道德调节进行研究，并加强道德调节的作用。

在此基础上，厉以宁还研究了效率的基础问题。他认为，效率有两个基础，一个是物质技术基础，一个是道德基础。物质技术基础通常提供的是常规效率，道德基础则不仅保证常规效率的产生，而且还提供超常规效率。效率增长潜力的发挥，主要依靠效率的道德基础的存在，依靠道德力量的作用。

（四）教育经济学

1978 年，厉以宁在《社会科学战线》上发表《技术教育与资本主义工业化》一文。从那时起，厉以宁一直将教育经济学作为自己的研究重点。在随后的一系列学术论文的基础上，厉以宁在 1984 年出版了《教育经济学》一书。该书提出了许多富有开创性的学术观点，是“中国当代第一部教育经济学专著”。

厉以宁阐明了教育在中国经济增长以及经济和社会发展中的作用，阐明了智力投资的经济效果的含义、指标的选择和提高智力投资经济效果的途径。他对教育投资促进劳动生产率的机理进行了全面的剖析，揭示了教育投资和劳动生产率之间的关系。他指出，教育或智力投资的经济效果可以分为宏观经济效果和微观经济效果，并分别讨论了效果的可计量性。厉以宁还研究了知识转化滞后以及毕业生发展潜力等问题。

III. Social contributions

i. Promoting the shareholding system

Reference has already been made to the division, from 1986 onward, in Chinese economic circles between two opinions on what should take the lead in the nation's economic restructuring, price reform or corporate reform. Li Yining is a proponent of corporate reform. Although price reform, or price decentralization, has dominated national policy decision-making since 1984, the controversy remains unresolved to this day.

Unlike those who put price reform above anything else, Li Yining believes that precedence should be given to corporate reform when shaping the general principle for economic restructuring. His reason: Because commodity prices are based on the prices of production factors, which are in turn predicated on ownership, prices are ultimately the prerequisites of transactions for ownership between market participants. Without an efficient ownership structure, there will be no effective restraints on the property rights relationship between firms and consumers, still less a truly reasonable price system. In addition, in the presence of large numbers of quotas in a shortage economy like ours, the impact of price regulation on the restoration of economic equilibrium is negligible. Chinese firms are yet to become free legal entities of commodity producers in the true sense of the term. To decentralize prices can only exacerbate economic disorder when there are shortages in various fields, and fail to achieve what postwar West Germany and Japan did in price reform. So Li Yining proposes that before anything else, the property rights relationships should be straightened out and firms demutualized over a period of about eight years. During this period, it is necessary to link the reform of corporate management mechanisms with the reform of the property rights relationship and to link nonstandard contractual management with standard property rights reform. In this eight-year span, the weight of corporate reform should be gradually shifted from a contractual system to a shareholding system, and from low-level management mechanisms and property rights relationships to high-level ones.

His proposal was adopted, and shareholding reform came under way all over the land. The *Decision of the Party Central Committee on Issues Concerning the Establishment of a Socialist Market Economic Structure*, adopted at the Third Plenary Session of the Fourteenth Party Central Committee in November 1993, sets the goal for the transformation of

三、社会贡献

（一）推动股份制改革

自 1986 年开始，中国经济学界对中国未来经济体制改革一直存在两种不同的思路。后来人们把两种不同主张分别称为“价格改革主线论”和“企业改革主线论”。厉以宁一直是后一主张的代表。1984 年以来，价格改革先行、放开物价曾经成为影响国策的指导思想，但两种主张的争论一直没有停止过。

与“价格改革主线论”者将价格改革放在首位不同，厉以宁认为，在设计中国经济体制改革的总体思路时应该把企业制度的改革放在首位。他的理由是：商品价格以生产要素价格为基础，生产要素价格又以所有权为基础，所以价格说到底是市场当事人之间转让所有权的交易条件。没有有效的所有权结构，就不可能有对企业和消费者有效的财产权力关系的约束，也就不可能有真正合理的价格体系。而且我国是短缺经济，存在较多的数量配额的情况下，价格和价格水平的调整对经济恢复均衡的作用是微乎其微的。中国的企业不具有真正商品生产者法人的自由度，放开价格只能加剧短缺条件下的经济混乱，而不能收到二战后西德和日本价格改革带来的效果。因此，厉以宁提出，改革的首要任务是用八年左右时间明确企业产权关系，实现企业的公司化。应把企业经营机制的改革与企业产权关系的改革联系起来，把非规范化的承包与规范化的产权改革联系起来。在八年的时间里，企业改革的重点应逐渐由承包制向股份制过渡，由低层次的经营机制与产权关系的改革向高层次的经营机制与产权关系的改革过渡。

厉以宁的主张随后被采纳，波澜壮阔的股份制改革在全中国推行。1993 年 11 月，中共十四届三中全会通过了《中共中央关于建立社会主义市场经济体制若干问题的决定》，明确指出，我国国有

state firms to establish a modern corporate system that "conforms to the requirements of the market economy and large-scale production, with well-defined property rights, rights and responsibilities, separates government and management, and is under scientific management." The document also sets the requirement to turn firms, through the establishment of such a modern corporate system, into legal entities and market competitors that make their own business decisions, bear the responsibility for their own gains and losses, seek their own development, and regulate themselves. Following Li Yining's thoughts, the goal of the reform of state-owned firms to establish a modern corporate system has been gradually clarified, the strategic regrouping of state-owned firms and the restructuring of the state sector of the national economy have been making steady headway, and a capital market has started from scratch to achieve healthy and sustained development. It can be said that China's economic miracle over the past three decades has everything to do with the decision to introduce the shareholding system. As an advocator and practitioner of the theory on this system, Li has made no small contribution to the nation's economic reforms. Hence his nickname, in Chinese, "Li the Shareholding Guru."

ii. Promoting a nonpublic economy

Coined during the reform and opening-up process, the concept of "nonpublic economy" encompasses self-employed industrial and commercial businesses and private firms, but is not limited to these entities. Since the adoption of the policy of reform and opening up to the outside world in 1978, the nonpublic economy has started from nothing and grown into the foremost sector of the national economy.

The development of the nonpublic economy, however, is not without its problems, those concerning state policy in particular. Reports on these policy-associated problems came flooding in from various provinces and municipalities, and eventually came to the attention of the National Committee of the Chinese People's Political Consultative Conference.

In the latter half of 2003, the CPPCC Economic Committee set up a panel for a survey of the nonpublic economy. Li Yining, who had already received complaints from many entrepreneurs about the snags they had encountered in developing the nonpublic economy, was appointed as head of the panel. From the facts collected by a series of surveys and discussion meetings in Liaoning, Guangdong, Jilin, Hebei, Jiangsu, Zhejiang, and Fujian provinces, he was able to see that the problems were real. For example, nonpublic firms were allowed a much narrower

企业的改革方向是建立"适应市场经济和社会化大生产要求的、产权清晰、权责明确、政企分开和管理科学"的现代企业制度，要求通过建立现代企业制度，使企业成为自主经营、自负盈亏、自我发展、自我约束的法人实体和市场竞争主体。按照厉以宁的思路，中国国企改革逐步明确建立现代企业制度的目标，国有企业战略性改组与国有经济布局调整稳步推进，资本市场从无到有持续健康发展。可以说，中国过去 30 年取得的经济奇迹，与选择股份制改革的道路是密不可分的。作为"股份制改革"理论的倡导者和实践者，厉以宁对中国股份制改革作出了巨大贡献，被公众以及媒体尊称为"厉股份"。

（二）促进民营经济发展

民营经济这个概念是中国改革开放过程中的一大创造，它包括个体工商户和私营企业在内，但又不限于个体工商户和私营企业。自改革开放以来，民营经济从无到有，从小到大，至今已经成为国民经济最重要的力量。

然而，民营经济的发展并不是一帆风顺，尤其是政策方面的问题。各省市根据实践，把民营经济发展的政策问题反映上来，从而引起了全国政协的高度重视。2003 年下半年，全国政协经济委员会成立了非公有制经济专题组，厉以宁任专题组组长。专题组到辽宁、广东两省的一些城市进行调研，还在吉林、河北、江苏、浙江、福建等省召开了调研会、座谈会。调研前和调研期间，厉以宁收集到很多民营企业家的反映，表示他们在发展中遇到了一些障碍。厉以宁经过调研发现民营企业家反映的情况是存在的。比如准入限制，民营企业进入的领域还不如外商；政府在融资、税收、

business access than foreign investors, and were held back by government discrimination in financing, tax, land use, and foreign trade. Public opinion was prejudiced against them as well.

Toward the end of 2003, the CPPCC Economic Committee submitted a survey report by Li Yining's panel to the State Council. It drew the attention of Premier Wen Jiabao, who instructed in February 2004 that, in order to comply with the spirit of the Third Plenary Session of the Sixteenth Party Central Committee and promote the nonpublic economy, it was necessary to take the overall situation into consideration and draft a document to provide guidelines on relevant policy issues. The premier entrusted the State Council Research Office and the State Development and Reform Commission to take the lead in drafting the document. The draft was discussed at meetings of the Economic Committee, and amended by taking the suggestions of Li Yining and other members into consideration. On February 24, 2005, the State Council promulgated the *Opinions on Encouraging, Supporting and Guiding the Development of the Nonpublic Economy*, known as *36 Regulations on the Nonpublic Economy*. The promulgation of the document ushered the nonpublic economy in China into a new period of development. The *36 Regulations* is hailed as a "comprehensive and systematic policy document for promoting the nonpublic sectors." Its implementation marks a breakthrough in the development of this sector of the national economy. For his immense contributions to the *36 Regulations*, Li Yining has been dubbed, in Chinese, "Li the Nonpublic Economist."

iii. Helping impoverished areas

Poverty is one of the sternest challenges confronting humanity. Eradication of poverty has become a global concern. In China, a huge part of the population still lives in absolute poverty. With his personal experience of such poverty in the 1960s and 1970s, Li Yining has made painstaking efforts for the development of the nation's less developed regions. While persisting in exploring ways and means to hasten economic growth in these regions, he has also devoted personal time, energy and wealth to the effort of improving the lot of his countrymen there.

- November 2005. He became dean of the Peking University Institute of Poverty Research that he initiated.
- March-April 2006. He organized five investigative teams on fact-finding tours in five types of poverty-stricken areas—Bijie county

土地使用、对外贸易等方面，对民营企业都有不公平的地方；舆论环境对民营经济也不好等等。

2003 年年底，以厉以宁为组长的调研组形成了一份报告，经全国政协经济委员会讨论后，由全国政协报送国务院。温家宝总理很重视，在 2004 年 2 月作了批示。批示指出：要落实中共十六届三中全会精神，促进非公有制经济发展，似应有一个通盘考虑，着手研究一些重大的政策性问题，最好能够形成一个指导性文件。温家宝让国务院研究室和发改委牵头起草文件。在文件起草过程中，初稿曾拿到全国政协经济委员会讨论，厉以宁和委员会提了一些修改意见。最终，文件在 2005 年 2 月出台。2005 年 2 月 24 日，国务院下发了《关于鼓励支持和引导个体私营等非公有制经济发展的若干意见》(民间称之为“非公经济 36 条”)。从此，中国民营经济的发展进入了一个新的阶段。“非公经济 36 条”被社会上认为“是改革开放以来中国最全面、最系统的一部关于促进非公有制经济发展的政策性文件”，其发布实施是中国非公经济发展的一项突破。厉以宁也因为其推动“非公经济 36 条”的巨大贡献，被媒体称为“厉民营”。

（三）帮助贫困地区

贫困是人类社会面临的最严峻挑战之一，消除贫困是当今世界共同的课题。中国目前的绝对贫困人口数量仍然庞大。由于对中国 1960 和 1970 年代贫困的亲身体验，厉以宁对中国贫困地区的发展倾注了许多心血，不仅持续研究如何促进贫困地区的发展，而且身体力行地以时间、精力和物质支持贫困地区的发展。

——2005 年 11 月，发起成立了北京大学贫困地区发展研究院，并出任院长；

——2006 年 3 ~ 4 月，组织五个调研组，分赴贵州省毕节县、

in Guizhou province, Huaihua and Youxian counties in Hunan province, Dingxi county in Gansu province, and Mentougou district of Beijing.

- May 2006. He initiated the first session of the China Forum on Strategies for Sustainable Development of Less Developed Areas in Tianjin.
- September 2008. He chaired the second session of the China Forum on Strategies for Sustainable Development of Less Developed Areas in Bijie county, Guizhou province.
- July 2004. He donated his 3-million-yen (equivalent to 200,500 yuan) Fukuoka Asian Culture Prize to Bijie, Guizhou, for the construction of the Zonglin Primary School.
- October 2006. He donated over 400,000 yuan to the Eryou Miao Autonomous Township, Yuanling county, Hunan province, for the construction of another Zonglin Primary School.
- December 2008. He collected 1.26 million yuan from two charity auctions of the paintings of his wife He Yuchun with his own inscriptions, donating one million yuan for the medical treatment of senior cataract patients in impoverished mountain areas, and 260,000 yuan for the construction of libraries in those areas.

  ...

This incomplete record is enough to bear out Li Yining's devotion and contribution to underprivileged people and underdeveloped areas.

In March 2004, Li Yining ran his first training class for government officials in Bijie, Guizhou, shortly after he was appointed to head a panel of experts and advisors for the Bijie Experimental Area under the Central Task Force for Intellectual Support of Peripheral Regions. Since then he has made it an annual routine to visit the experimental area and train local officials.

厉以宁在贫困地区考察 Visiting an impoverished village

湖南省怀化县和攸县、甘肃省定西县、北京门头沟五种类型的贫困地区进行实地调查；

——2006 年 5 月，发起举办了首届中国贫困地区可持续发展战略论坛（在天津召开）；

——2008 年 9 月，举办了第二届中国贫困地区可持续发展战略论坛（在贵州毕节召开）；

——2004 年 7 月，将日本福冈亚洲文化奖奖金 300 万日元（合人民币 20.05 万元）全部捐出，在贵州毕节地区毕节市捐建宗琳小学；

——2006 年 10 月，出资 40 余万元，在湖南省沅陵县二酉苗族自治乡捐建宗琳学校；

——2008 年 12 月，由厉以宁夫人何玉春作画、厉以宁题词，举行义卖，两次共卖得 126 万元；其中 100 万元用于山区贫困农民老年白内障治疗，26 万元用作捐建山区农村图书室。

……

以上这份纪录并不完整，但已足以展现厉以宁对贫困地区、对弱势群体、对欠发达地区的热忱与奉献。

2004 年 3 月，厉以宁出任中央智力支边小组毕节实验区专家顾问组组长，并为毕节的干部做了脱贫致富的第一次培训。从那时开始，厉以宁开始了扶贫解困的深入实践。此后，他每年去一次贵州毕节，并在当地组织培训讲座。

China today is on the threshold of the Twelfth Five-Year Plan Period (2011-2015), which is pivotal to the nation's poverty eradication efforts. Li Yining has adopted a two-fold research approach accordingly: first, case studies on specific areas or groups of people, which will help him make specific poverty alleviation proposals; second, policy theory studies that enable him to observe the actual effects of national aid-the-poor policies, and, on this basis, to make improvement proposals that will help these policies achieve enduring effects. That is the way Li Yining makes his voice heard once again when national development enters a crucial period.

IV. Li Yining the poet

i. Double identity

Li Yining is not just a towering figure in economics. He is an accomplished poet as well. He has been composing lyric poems for the last 50 or more years since his senior middle school days. Even the chaos of the Cultural Revolution could not prevent him from jotting down his thoughts and feelings in verse whenever the mood hit him. Poetry is instrumental in voicing his musings on society, history and economic development; it also showcases his profound attainment in the humanities. Seemingly irrelevant to economic research, this attainment actually reflects his prolific imagination and incisive acumen, without which he would not have become the erudite scholar he is today.

Li Yining's verse is lucid and natural, without the least affectation. In one of his seven-character quatrains, he says poetry is the natural revelation of his innermost feelings and thoughts, and that you will never come up with good poems if you are doing someone's bidding. It is this crystal-clear frame of mind that enables him to imbue his verse with genuine passion, economic insight, philosophical wisdom, and penetrating observations of reality.

ii. Expressing economic thoughts in verse

Most of the hundreds of poems he has written over the decades are about personal experience, family life, teacher-student emotional ties, and camaraderie between school friends. Some of them portray scenes and sights, and places of historical and humanistic interest. Upon a closer perusal, however, his economic thoughts are discernible between the lines of some of his poems. In other words, his ruminations on economics

当前正值我国即将进入第十二个五年规划时期，这是我国根除贫困的关键时期。厉以宁定位了两条研究思路。一方面进行实地考察案例研究，以某一特定地区或者特定群体为对象，提出有针对性的缓解贫困的方案；一方面进行政策理论研究，以扶贫政策本身为研究对象，通过历史数据考察既有政策的实施效果，提出改进方向，使之具有可持续的效果。这就是厉以宁在中国发展的关键时期又一次发出的声音。

四、诗人与经济学家

（一）双重身份

厉以宁不但在经济学研究方面成就卓越，而且在诗词创作方面也有独到的建树。厉以宁从 1947 年读高中时便开始填词，至今 50 多年，从未间断。即使在“文化大革命”期间，只要有感触，他就会情不自禁地用诗词写下自己的所思所想。诗词不但以特殊的方式承担了厉以宁对社会、对历史、对经济发展的思考，而且也显示了厉以宁在人文方面的修养。这种修养看似和经济学研究没有关系，但实际上显示了厉以宁丰沛的想象力和敏锐的感受力。他能成为学问大家，与此是密不可分的。

厉以宁的诗作清新自然，丝毫没有矫饰做作之态。他曾在一首七绝中表示，诗词是感情和思想的自然流露，奉命作诗，是不会有好作品的。厉以宁就是怀着这样纯朴的想法在写诗。厉以宁的诗词总是充溢着真情实感，反映的也都是他对现实的观察，很多诗都具有浓郁的感情，并且蕴藏着他的经济学思想以及深刻的人生哲理。

（二）诗词中的经济思想

厉以宁几十年来所写的数百首诗词，绝大多数都是谈个人的生活经历、家庭亲情、师生和同学之谊，以及所到之处的自然风光或人文景观。但是，如果仔细品味，会发现某些诗词也反映了他的经济思想，或者说，他的经济思想也能在这些诗词中有意无意地流露

often reveal themselves consciously or unconsciously in his verse.

In a poem written during a 1998 inspection tour of Longyan, Fujian province, he cites Hakka history to drive home the role of morality in economic development, a role that he has always cherished in his academic studies. In ancient times, clan after clan of the Hakkas' ancestors fled the war and turmoil of central China, and settled down in south China despite its harsh natural environment. The land of what is the present-day city of Longyan, is clustered with more than ten thousand dwelling complexes, in which several hundred Hakka people lived under the same roof. According to Li Yining, the extraordinary efficiency of such an immigrant society was made possible precisely because of the regulatory role of morality.

Attending a round-table conference on labor, wage and economic restructuring co-sponsored by the Research Office of the Secretariat of the Party Central Committee and the State Labor Bureau in April and May 1980, Li Yining composed a seven-character quatrain to voice his opinions about economic restructuring. At the time, he was under fire for some of his reform proposals that people found unacceptable. Convinced that outmoded conventions and customs would give way sooner or later, in that poem he indicates that one should not haggle over personal honor or disgrace, gains or losses, and that a person's merits and demerits should be left to the judgment of time and posterity.

In 1981, when the reform and opening-up policy was still in its infancy, Li Yining attended the first annual meeting of the Society of History of Foreign Economic Thoughts in Chengdu, Sichuan province. That gave him the opportunity to visit the nearby Qingcheng Mountain, a famous Taoist domain studded with caves in which Taoist priests of yore practiced alchemy. Inspired by the mountain's ancient Taoist alchemical tradition, he improvised a lyric poem to the tune of *Partridge Sky*, in which he says that immortality and truth can be attained not with wonder drugs but often in a flash of inspired thought. Extending that idea to the philosophy of state governance, he argues that reform should advance progressively and social problems can be addressed only through patient persuasion and proper guidance. With the current situation in mind, he suggests in this poem that the economy should be regulated,

出来。如同上文提到的，厉以宁非常重视道德力量在经济发展中的作用，他有一些诗词，就是反映这个思想的。

1998 年，厉以宁在福建龙岩市考察时写下的一首诗，以客家人发展的历史为例，说明了道德调节在社会发展中的作用。客家人的祖先原在中原，历朝动乱时期，以家族为单位陆续南迁到了南方，在蛮荒之地恶劣的自然环境中扎下根来。福建省龙岩市约有一万多座客家的土楼，每座土楼中都有几百户客家人共同生活在一起。厉以宁认为，移民社会之所以能有这种超常的效率，恰恰是由于道德调节的作用。

1980 年 4 ~ 5 月，厉以宁参加了中共中央书记处研究室和国家劳动总局联合召开的劳动工资座谈会，讨论经济体制改革问题。在会议期间，厉以宁写了一首七绝，反映了他对经济体制改革的看法。厉以宁曾提出许多关于改革的建议，某些建议在开始时不能被人们所理解，甚至遭到批评。但他始终坚信陈规陋习是迟早要改变的，人不应该计较荣辱得失，而是要让时间来检验一切，让后人评价自己的功过是非。

1981 年，改革开放之初，厉以宁到成都参加外国经济学说史研究会首届年会，并到青城山一游。青城山是道教名山，洞穴甚多，都是历代道士炼丹之处。厉以宁在这里填了一首《鹧鸪天》。这首词由古代中国道士的炼丹传统生发开来，说明要想悟道、得到真理，并不能依赖神丹仙药，而往往在于是非一念之间。在这首词中，厉以宁还引申到了治国的

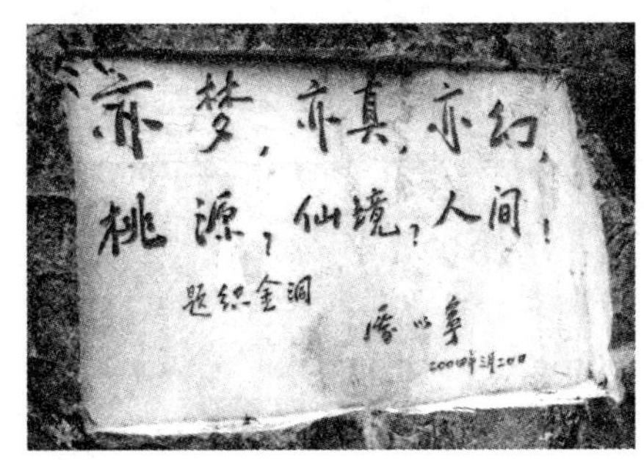

厉以宁的题词 An inscription by Li Yining

and social resources allocated, with an "invisible hand." According to him, only when the market is activated can people's living standards be raised and social stability achieved.

iii. Versifying a philosophy of life

In 1963, Li Yining acquired quite a following with a poem he wrote on a tour of the Tanzhe Temple in Beijing. In it he likens a person's peace of mind to the tranquil water in that temple's Dragon Pool, indicating that one can resist the interference of the outside world if he has done enough in self-edification. In traditional Chinese culture, such self-edification is deemed a major part of one's character and wisdom. According to the poet, we may not be able to control the environment around us, but we can adapt to it through self-cultivation. "Whether the wind moves or not is beyond my control," Li says, "but my mind can remain in peace come what may. By the same token, whether it is hot or not is beyond us, but we can stay cool as long as we maintain a peaceful frame of mind. Such is the state of mind we can strive for."

During the Cultural Revolution, Li Yining, like so many people around him, was denounced and manhandled at public meetings, his house was ransacked, and his research work interrupted by long years of physical labor. Nevertheless, he could always overcome these disturbances, and keep his economic studies and poetic composition going uninterrupted. In these reform and opening-up years, he has taken up more and more public positions, which has vastly increased his workload and social activities. But he never gives up writing, and his new ideas and books come in a constant stream. His exuberant creativity is intimately associated with his tranquil mindset.

Visiting Taoyuan county in Hunan province on a fact-finding tour in 1988, he composed a profoundly philosophical poem on the name of the county meaning "peach blossom spring." In the imagination of our ancestors, the Peach-blossom Spring is the Chinese translation of Shangri-la, where people are free from the chaos of the mundane world and live in peace and bliss. In that poem Li points out that the Peach-blossom Spring is a utopian ideal, but it is possible to carve out

理念：改革需要渐进，处理社会问题则重在疏导。在当时的形势下，厉以宁用诗词语言表达了自己的想法：要用“看不见的手”来调节经济，进行社会资源的配置。市场活跃了，人民生活水平提高了，社会自然就安定了。

（三）诗词中的人生哲理

厉以宁1963年游览北京的潭柘寺时曾写过一首诗，这首诗受到了很多人的喜爱。在这首诗中，厉以宁以潭柘寺中的龙潭水作比喻，指出一个人如果有足够的修养，便可以抵挡外界的干扰。这在中国的传统文化中，也被视为一种重要的修养和智慧。在现实中，我们对于客观的把握常常无能为力，但我们可以通过自身修养来提高适应客观环境的能力。风动不动我把握不了，但我可以心不动。天热不热我无可奈何，但我可以心静自然凉。这是人生的一种境界。

厉以宁在“文革”期间，和周围的许多人一样，被批斗、抄家、长期从事体力劳动，正常的研究工作无法进行。但他总是能抵挡外界的干扰，无论是经济学研究，还是诗词创作，都从未中断。改革开放以来，厉以宁担任的社会职务越来越越多，工作日益繁重，社会活动也异常频繁；但他依然能笔耕不辍，不断有新的观点和新的著作问世。这种旺盛的创造力，和他心灵的沉静是分不开的。

1988年，厉以宁到湖南桃源考察，写了一首咏诗，其中蕴含了深刻的哲理。桃花源在中国古代人的想象中，是一方远离乱世干扰、人人享受平静幸福生活的净土，寄托了饱受战乱之苦的人们

厉以宁在题词 Writing a calligraphic inscription

such a wonderland in our heart. We can be bathed in the serenity of this wonderland anytime we want it, provided we stay magnanimous and optimistic. As one line in Li Yining's poem goes, "For those who are open-minded, the Peach-blossom Spring is everywhere."

Philosophical meditation is the ultimate way of thinking. In this sense, Li Yining, the accomplished economist, is also a philosopher with a penetrating eye. (*Translated by Peng Lin, Ren Xiaomei and Zhong Zhilan*)

Bibliography

Fu, Xu. *A Poetic Life of Li Yining*. Beijing: Economic Science Press, 2003.

Li, Yining. *Mountains Should Be Viewed Sideways*. Beijing: Peking University Press, 2003.

Li, Qingyun and Bao Shoubai eds. *An Introduction to Economics Writings by Li Yining*. Beijing: Economic Science Press, 2005.

Liu, Yuming and Liu Wei. *Listening to Professor Li Yining's Lecture on Poetry*. Beijing: Jinghua Press, 2005.

Lu, Hao. *Academic Biographies of Modern Chinese Economists: Li Yining*. Xi'an: Shaanxi Normal University Press, 2006.

一种美好的愿望。厉以宁在这首诗中提到，这种美好的愿望只能是一种愿望，世界上并不存在真正的“世外桃源”。但是，人们的心中却可以有这样一片美好的乐土，只要人心胸宽广、豁达、乐观，便可以随时享受桃源的怡然之美。这就是“心宽无处不桃源”。

哲学的思考是最终极的思考。从这个意义上来说，厉以宁不仅是一位造诣深厚的经济学家，也是一个洞悉世间百态的哲人。

参考书目：

《当代中国经济学家学术评传——厉以宁》，陆昊著，陕西师范大学出版社

《厉以宁经济学著作导读》，李庆云、鲍寿柏主编，经济科学出版社

《厉以宁的诗意人生》，傅旭著，经济科学出版社

《山景总须横侧看》，厉以宁，北京大学出版社

《听厉以宁教授讲诗词》，刘玉铭、刘伟，京华出版社

GLOSSARY 专有名词表

I. Personal names

阿歇尔（美）	Usher, Abbott Payson, American economic historian
艾希利（英）	Ashley, William James, British economic historian
贝纳西（法）	Benassy, Jean Pascal, French economist
毕歇尔（德）	Bücher, Karl Wilhelm, German economist
波士坦（英）	Postan, Michael Moissey, British economic historian
布莱克（美）	Black, Cyril Edwin, American historian
道布希（奥）	Dopsch, Alfons, Austrian economist
登巴（美）	Dunbar, Charles Franklin, American economist
恩格尔曼（美）	Engerman, Stanley Lewis, American economic historian
法尔南（美）	Farnam, Henry Walcott, American economist
福格尔（美）	Fogel, Robert William, American economic historian and scientist
格罗斯（美）	Gross, Gerald C., American economist
格辛克隆（美）	Gerschenkron, Alexander, American economic historian
赫尔希曼（美）	Hirschman, Alber Otto, American economist
赫克歇尔（瑞典）	Heckscher, Eli Filip, Swedish political economist, economic historian
亨利·瑟(法）	Sée, Henri, French historian
吉宾斯（英）	Gibbins, Henry de Beltgens, British historian
凯恩斯（英）	Keynes, John Maynard, British economist
科尔内（匈）	Kornai, János, Hungarian economist
克拉潘（英）	Clapham, John Harold, British economic historian
克劳威尔（美）	Clower, Robert Wayne, American economist
库兹涅茨（美）	Kuznets, Simon Smith, Russian-American economist
莱恩（美）	Lane, Frederic C., American historian
莱荣霍夫德（瑞典）	Leijonhufvud, Alex, Swedish economist
勒瓦瑟尔（法）	Levasseur, Emile, French economist
罗宾逊（英）	Robinson, Joan, British economist
罗伯特·索洛（美）	Solow, Robert M., American economist
罗杰斯（英）	Rogers, James Edwin Thorold, British economist

罗斯托（美）	Rostow, Walt Whitman, American economist and political theorist
罗斯托夫采夫（美）	Rostovtzeff, Mikhail Ivanovich, American historian
马克斯·韦伯（德）	Weber, Max, German political economist, sociologist
梅洛蒂（意）	Melotti, Umberto, Italian political sociologist
纳克斯（美）	Nurkse, Ragnar, American economist, policy maker
诺思（美）	North, Douglass Cecil, American economist
皮朗（比）	Pirenne, Henri, Belgian economist
桑巴特（德）	Sombart, Werner, German economist and sociologist
施本格勒（德）	Spengler, Oswald, German historian, philosopher
施莫勒（德）	Schmoller, Gustav von, German economist
汤普逊（美）	Thompson, James Walter, American pioneer of advertising techniques
汤因比（英）	Toynbee, Arnold, British historian
托马斯（美）	Thomas, Robert Paul, American economist
托尼（英）	Tawney, Richard Henry, British economic historian
瓦尔拉（法）	Walras, Léon, French mathematical economist
瓦格曼（德）	Wagemann, Ernst, German economist
悉尼·波拉德（英）	Pollard, Sidney, British historian
谢夫莱（德）	Schaffle, Albert Eberhard Fridrich, German economist
熊彼特（美）	Schumpeter, Joseph Alois, American economist, political scientist
伊利（美）	Ely, Richard Theodore, American economist
约翰·希克斯（英）	Hicks, John, British economist

II. Journals and economic works

北京大学学报（哲学社会科学版）	*Journal of Peking University (Philosophy and Social Sciences)*
财贸经济	*Finance & Trade Economics*
短缺经济学	*Economics of Shortage*
反均衡	*Anti-Equilibrium*
非均衡的中国经济	*Disequilibrium in the Chinese Economy*
工业化与欧洲经济	"Industrialization and the European Economy"
宏观经济学：非瓦尔拉分析方法导论	*Macroeconomics: An Introduction to the Non-Walrasian Approach*

宏观经济学与非均衡理论	*Macroeconomics and Imperfect Competition*
货币理论的微观基础的再考虑	*A Reconsideration of the Microfoundations of Monetary Theory*
技术教育和资本主义工业化：西欧和美国技术力量形成问题	"Technology education and capitalist industria-lization: a study of the rise of technological power in Western Europe and America"
经济史理论	*A Theory of Economic History*
经济史评论	*Economic History Review*
经济文化	*Economics & Culture*
经济学展望	*Journal of Economic Perspectives*
经济研究参考资料	*Economic Reference*
经济周期理论	*A Contribution to the Theory of the Trade Cycle*
就业、利息和货币通论	*The General Theory of Employment, Interest, and Money*
凯恩斯经济学的危机	*Crisis in Keynesian Economics*
凯恩斯派反革命：理论上的再评价	*The Keynesian Counter-Revolution: A Theoretical Appraisal*
历史研究	*A Study of History*
利率理论	*The Theory of Interest Rates*
论凯恩斯派经济学和凯恩斯的经济学	*On Keynesian Economics and the Economics of Keynes*
论资本密集型经济和劳动密集型经济在发展中国家现代化过程中的作用	"On the roles of capital-intensive and labor-intensive economies in the modernization process of developing nations"
美国经济评论	*American Economic Review*
美国经济史的重新解释	*The Reinterpretation of American Economic History*
日本和俄国的现代化	*The Modernization of Japan and Russia*
社会科学战线	*Social Sciences Front*
社会主义政治经济学	*Socialist Political Economics*
世界经济	*World Economy*
市场非均衡经济学	*The Economics of Market Disequilibrium*
数量经济技术经济研究	*Quantitative & Technical Economics*
西方的没落	*The Decline of the West*
西方经济学杂志	*Western Economic Journal*
亚太经济时报	*Asia Pacific Economic Times*

增长、短缺与效率	*Growth, Shortage and Efficiency*
政府在近代初期经济增长中所起的作用	"The role of government in economic growth in early modern times"
中国社会科学	*Social Sciences in China*
走向繁荣的战略选择	*Strategic Choice for Prosperity*

III. Economic terms

安置费	relocation grant
按劳分配	distribution according to work done; distributing to each according to one's work
北京大学"五四"科学讨论会	Peking University "May Fourth" Symposium
比较经济史	comparative economic history
变量	variable
补偿	compensation
不充分补偿	inadequate compensation
不等价交换	unequal exchange of value
不等价交换制度	system of unequal exchange
不合理投资	irrational investment
不良债务	bad debt
不完全竞争的价格	price from imperfect competition
部分补偿	partial compensation
财政拨款	fiscal appropriation; fiscal funding
财政赤字	fiscal deficit
财政平衡	fiscal balance; financial balance
财政收入	fiscal revenue
财政收支	fiscal revenue and expenditure
财政政策	fiscal policy
参与制	participatory system
仓储设备	storage facilities
产出增长率	output growth rate
产品经济	commodity economy
产权改革	reform of property rights
产权关系不明确	ambiguous property rights
产权交易市场	property rights market

产业结构	industrial structure
产业结构调整	industrial restructuring
产值	output value
长波理论	theory on the Long Wave
长期经济效益	long-term economic benefit
超常规效率	super efficiency
成本—收益分析方法	cost-benefit analysis
成本下降率	cost reduction rate
成本与收益之比	cost-benefit ratio
承包	contract; subcontract
承包经营	contracted management
城市“大集体”企业	urban collective enterprise
乘数—加速原理分析	Multiplier-Accelerator model
持股公司	holding company
充分补偿	full compensation; compensate in full
重复建设	repetitious construction; redundant construction
初级产品	primary product
传导机制	transmission mechanism
次优选择	second-best choice
存款准备金率	reserve requirement ratio
大规模商品经济	large-scale commodity economy
贷款的可偿还性	redeemability of loans
单一的所有制	monomorphic ownership structure
道德标准	moral standard
道德判断	moral judgment
低收入家庭生活补助	allowances for low-income family
抵押	mortgage
地下的市场价格	black market price
第二次分配	redistribution
第二警戒线	second alert line
第一警戒线	first alert line
动力机制	impetus mechanism
短边原则	law of the shortest side

短缺	shortage; shortfall
短缺资源的渗漏现象	resale of scarce resources
短缺资源的自发分配	spontaneous distribution of scarce resources
短线（短边）	shortest side
短线决定原则	wooden barrel principle
短线顽症	shortest-side syndrome
多线发展模式	multi-linear mode of growth
二元机制	dual mechanism
发展经济学	development economics
“发疹”假设	“red spots” hypothesis
反事实度量法	counterfactual analysis
房地产市场（房产市场）	real estate market
非公有制	nonpublic ownership
非均衡	disequilibrium
非均衡理论	disequilibrium theory
非零失业率	nonzero unemployment rate
非零通货膨胀率	nonzero inflation rate
非贸易项目的国际收入	international revenue from nontrade item
非熟练劳动力	unskilled worker; unskilled laborer
非熟练劳动密集型	unskilled-labor-intensive
非瓦尔拉均衡	non-Walrasian equilibrium
非物质生产部门	nonmaterial production sector
非正常波动	abnormal fluctuation
非正常短缺度	abnormal shortage
分期补偿（多次补偿）	payment in installments
负值经济效益	negative economic returns
高层次的调节作用	high-level regulating role
个人经济效益	individual’s economic returns
个人绝对收入满意度	individual’s absolute degree of income satisfaction
个人相对收入满意度	individual relative income satisfaction
个人消费基金的结余部分	surplus of personal consumption fund
个人职业选择性	individual occupation selectivity
个体劳动者	self-employed worker

个体所有制	private ownership
各尽所能，按劳分配	from each according to his ability, to each according to his work
工资成本	wage cost
工资刚性	wage rigidity
公方	public owner
公股持有者	public shareholder
公积金	public accumulation fund
公开的市场价格	open market price
公开失业率	registered unemployment rate
公开市场业务	open market operation
公开通货膨胀率	registered inflation rate
公司财团（企业财团）	enterprise consortium
公益金	public welfare fund
公有制	public ownership
供给价格弹性	price elasticity in supply
供给约束	restraint on supply
供销社	supply and marketing cooperative
购买主体	purchaser
古典经济学	classical economics
股份合作制	joint-stock cooperative system
股份化	shareholding system; demutualization
股份经济	shareholding economy
股份企业	shareholding company
股份制	shareholding (system)
股票经纪人	(stock) broker
股权	equity
关键性产品	key commodity
官倒	official smuggling
规范方法	normative approach
规范经济学	normative economics
规模效益	economies of scale
国际贸易	international trade
国际收支	international payment

国际收支逆差	balance of payments deficit
国际收支平衡	balance of international payments
国际资本市场	world capital market
国民财富	national assets
国民生产总值	GNP
国民生产总值或国民收入的年变动率	annual rate of changes in GNP or national income
国民收入	national income
国民收入均衡公式	equilibrium equation for national income
国有企业	state firm; state enterprise
过度扩张	excessive expansion
过度收缩	excessive recession
哈罗德—多马模型	Harrod-Domar model
合理投资	rational investment
合作企业	cooperative firm
合作制	cooperative system
横向经济联系	lateral ties in the economy
宏观经济调节措施	macroeconomic regulatory step
宏观经济管理体制的改革	macroeconomic administrative reform
宏观经济效果	macroeconomic effectiveness
后发性劣势	disadvantages of a latecomer
后发性优势	advantages of a latecomer
后凯恩斯经济学派	post-Keynesian theorists
环境保护经济学	economics of environmental protection
环境经济学	environmental economics
环境破坏	environmental damage
环境治理	environmental treatment
环境治理费用	environmental treatment cost
混合经济型企业	mixed-ownership company
混合企业	company under mixed ownership
活劳动部分	living labor
货币供应量	money supply; amount of currency in circulation
货币回笼	withdraw money from circulation

货币流通量增长率	growth rate of the amount of currency in circulation
货币市场	money market
货币学派	Monetarists
货币政策	monetary policy
货币资金	monetary fund
货源缺口	supply shortfall
积累率	saving rate; accumulation rate
基础性的调节作用	basic regulating role
基尼系数	Gini Coefficient
集体股	collective share
集体所有制	collective ownership
集体所有制企业	collective firm
挤出效应	crowding-out effect
计划管理	planned management
计划价格	planned price
计划经济体制	planned economic system
计量经济史学	econometric history
技术创新理论	theory on technological innovation
技术创新史	history of technological innovation
技术改造	technical renovation
技术结构	technological structure
技术市场	technology market
家庭财产存量	household wealth
家庭承包	household responsibility system
价格刚性	price rigidity
价格伸缩	price flexibility
价格限制	price limit
价格信号	price signal
间接补偿	indirect compensation
减产	reduce output
交易成本	trading cost
交易人	trader
金本位制度	gold standard system

紧缩投资	tighten up investment
紧缩需求	reduce demand
紧缩政策	retrenchment policy
近似值	approximate value
经济波动	economic fluctuation
经济波动论	theory of economic fluctuations
经济的不平衡增长	imbalanced economic growth; uneven economic growth
经济的横向联系	lateral economic tie
经济的平衡增长	balanced economic growth
经济调节	economic regulation
经济管理体制	economic administration
经济核算	financial auditing
经济计量学	econometrics
经济结构	economic structure
经济紧缩	economic austerity
经济联合体	economic conglomerate
经济史学	economic history
经济体制改革	economic restructuring
经济效率	economic efficiency
经济效益	economic returns
经济行为规范	economic norm
经济运行机制	economic operational mechanism
经济增长（正值增长、零增长或负增长）	economic growth (positive, zero or negative)
经济增长率	economic growth rate
经济增长主体	principal of economic growth
经济周期史	historiography of business cycles
经济资源	economic resources
经济组织形式	economic organizational form
警戒线	alert line
净产值	net output value
净收益	net returns
纠偏	rectification
就业结构	employment structure

就业问题的“结构性”	“structural” nature of the employment problem
均衡价格	equilibrium price
均衡经济学	theory based on equilibrium
凯恩斯学派	Keynesians
控股制	controlling shareholder system
亏损	in the red
劳动管理体制	labor administration
劳动力	workforce
劳动力的结构	labor structure
劳动力流动状况	labor mobility
劳动力市场	labor market
劳动力总资源	aggregate volume of labor resources
劳动密集型经济	labor-intensive economy
劳动生产率	workforce productivity; labor productivity
劳务	labor services; labor and services
劳务市场	service market
累进制的个人所得税税率	private income tax rate within the framework of a progressive tax system
累进制的所得税	progressive income tax
历史比例原则	principle of historical ratios
历史计量学	cliometrics
利率	interest rate
利益刚性	rigidity of interest; rigidity in interest
利益机制	interest mechanism
利益主体	master of one’s own interests; interest principal
联产承包责任制	household responsibility system
联合经营组织	voluntary economic cooperative
临界值	threshold value
零短缺度	no shortage
零失业率	zero unemployment
零通货膨胀率	zero inflation
流通	circulation
每小时工资购买力	hourly wage’s purchasing power

每小时工资收入与耐用消费品的交换比率	exchange ratio between hourly wage and durable consumption goods
名义生产能力	nominal production capacity
目标机制	goals mechanism
目标吸引	lure of goals
目标原则	goals principle
内部积累机制	internal accumulation mechanism
内在约束机制	self-restraint mechanism
农村产业结构	rural economic structure
农业合作化	Movement of Agricultural Collectivization
农业生产率	productivity in agriculture
排除干扰机制	interference elimination mechanism
排他性	cliquishness
配额均衡	balance of government quotas; rationed equilibrium
“平等”和效率的交替	trade-off between “equality” and efficiency
平均国民收入	per capita national income
平均技术熟练水平	average skill proficiency
平均原则	principle of averages
破产法	bankruptcy law
企业保留资金	business reserve fund
企业股	corporate share
企业家精神	entrepreneurship
企业控股制	corporate stock-holding system
企业体制	corporate system
企业运行机制	corporate operational mechanism
企业制度的改革	corporate institutional reform
企业资产存量	corporate capital stock
潜在的生产要素	latent production factor
清产核资	liquidate the assets and check the accounts
全民所有制	state ownership
全民所有制企业	state firm; public company
缺口	gap
人口增长率	population growth rate
人力投资	investment in human capital

人力资本理论	theory on human capital
人民公社化	Movement of the People's Communes
人员的水平流动、垂直流动	labor's lateral and vertical mobility
商品经济	commodity economy
商品市场	commodity market
设备更新	equipment upgrading
社会补偿	social compensation
社会补偿基金	social compensation fund
社会化大生产	society's large-scale production
社会经济发展目标	socioeconomic development goal
社会平均绝对收入满意度	average absolute income satisfaction in the society
社会平均相对收入满意度	average relative income satisfaction in the society
社会平均综合收入满意度	average degree of society's comprehensive income satisfaction
社会效益	social returns
社会效益的变动幅度	magnitude of changes in positive or negative social returns
社会主义经济制度	socialist economy
社会总产品	aggregate social product
社会总产品增长率	growth rate of aggregate social product
生产成本	production cost
生产方法	means of production; tools of production
生产管理体制	administration and management of production
生产过剩	overproduction
生产和再生产	production and reproduction
生产力水平	labor productivity
生产能力	production capacity
生产设备	production equipment
生产型投资	productive investment
生产要素	production factor
生产要素的流动	flow of production factors
生产资料	means of production; capital goods

生产资料的社会主义公有制	socialist public ownership of capital goods
生产资料公有制	public ownership of capital goods
生产资料所有权	capital goods ownership; proprietorship over capital goods
生产资料投入量	capital goods input in production
生产资料资本主义私有制	private ownership of capital goods under capitalism
生产组织形式	organizational form of production
生活津贴	living allowance
剩余	surplus
实际生产能力	real production capacity
实证方法	positive approach
食物支出	food expense
使用价值	use value
市场单一定价制	sole market price
市场的优先原则、垄断原则	market principles of priority and monopoly
市场调节	market regulation
市场机制	market mechanism
市场经济体制	market economy system
市场缺口	demand shortfall
市场条件	marketability; market condition
适者生存	survival of the fittest
收入分配协调	income distribution; coordination of income distribution; equitable income distribution
收益分配	income distribution
收益增长率	profit growth rate
熟练劳动力	skilled worker
熟练劳动密集型	skilled-labor-intensive
数量配额	quantity quota
数量限制	quantity constraint
双轨价格	double-track price system
双轨经济体制	dual-track economic system
税后利润	after-tax profit
私倒	nonofficial smuggling

私营企业	private enterprise; private firm
所有制的多元化	ownership diversity
所有制改革	ownership reform
所有制体系（所有制形式）	ownership structure
体制改革	institutional reform
调节税	income-adjustment tax
贴现	discount for cash
贴现率	depreciation rate
停产	stop production
通货膨胀	inflation
投入	investment
投入产出分析方法	input-output analysis
投资 · 储蓄—流动偏好 · 货币供给分析	IS-LM (investment · savings—liquidity preference · money supply) model
投资的自我约束机制	self-restraint in investment
投资回收期	investment-recouping period
投资率	rate of investment
投资增量	reinvestment
投资主体	investment principal
瓦尔拉均衡	Walrasian equilibrium
外汇储备	foreign exchange reserve
外汇市场	foreign exchange market
外汇收入	foreign exchange earnings
外贸平衡	balance of foreign trade
外资企业	foreign-invested company
完全竞争	perfect competition
微观经济单位	microeconomic agent
文化经济学	cultural economics
无效供给	ineffective supply
无效投资	ineffective investment
物化劳动	materialized labor
物化形态	in the form of physical commodity
物质生产部门	material production sector

物质生产领域	material production
物质资源	material resources
现有资金	available capital
乡镇企业	rural firm
乡镇企业合作制	cooperative system for rural enterprises
消费基金	consumption fund
消费基金发放主体	consumption fund issuer
消费结构	consumer-goods structure; consumption composition; consumption structure
消费品市场	consumer goods market
消费早熟	premature consumption
销售收入	sales income
小生产者	small-time producer
小型合作企业	small cooperative
效力递减	eclipse of effectiveness
效率标准	efficiency standard
效率判断	efficiency judgment
效率增长潜力	potential in efficiency growth
新公有制	new public ownership
新古典模型	Neo-classical model
新剑桥模型	Neo-Cambridge model
新经济史学	new economic history
信贷规模控制	credit scale control
信贷配额制	credit rationing
信贷平衡	credit market equilibrium
信贷条件	credit condition
行政改革	administrative reform
需求价格弹性	price elasticity in demand
需求约束	restraint on demand
需求主体	demander
亚西亚生产方式	Asian mode of production
一人一票制	"one man, one vote" decision-making system
遗产税	inheritance tax
抑制性通货膨胀	repressed inflation

银根	money supply
银行信贷	bank credit
银行信贷膨胀	bank credit expansion
隐蔽失业	concealed unemployment; disguised unemployment
隐蔽失业率	disguised unemployment rate
隐蔽通货膨胀率	disguised inflation rate
盈亏的对称性	symmetrical treatment of gains and losses
赢利性	profitability
有限市场的自发分割	spontaneous division of a limited market
有效投资	effective investment
预期	expectation
预算软约束	soft budget constraint
预算硬约束	hard budget constraint
原材料消耗	consumption of raw materials
运输手段	means of transportation
运行机制	operational mechanism
再补偿	double compensation; twofold compensation; recompensation
再贷款限额	relending quota
再贴现率	rediscount rate
再贴现限额	rediscount quota
再贴现政策	rediscount policy
再投入	reinvestment
债务链	debt chain
折股到户	distribute the stock to every member household
折旧费	depreciation expenses
正常波动	normal fluctuation
正常短缺度	normal shortage
正值经济效益	positive economic returns
证券市场	securities market
政府的平均原则、目标原则、历史原则	government's principles of egalitarianism, goals, and history
政府调节	government regulation
政企不分	government-business collusion; government administration intermixed with business management

政企分开	detach government administration from business management; separate government administration from business management
政治市场与公共选择理论	theory on the political market and public choices
政治周期理论	theory on political cycles
知识密集型经济	knowledge-intensive economy
直接补偿	direct compensation
职位空缺	job vacancy
职业歧视	workplace discrimination
职业世袭制	hereditary tenure
指标	indicator
指导性计划	guidance planning; central planning; mandatory planning
制度创新理论	theory on institutional innovation
制度创新史	history of institutional innovation
滞销	unsalability
滞销积压	overstocked and unsalable
滞胀	stagflation
中间购买者	intermediate buyer
中世纪庄园制	Western European medieval manorial system
中外合资企业	joint venture with Chinese and foreign investment
重商主义	mercantilism
主导产业政策	industry-prioritizing policy
专业银行	specialized banks
资本市场	capital market
资本主义雇佣劳动制度	capitalist hired-labor system
资本主义垄断阶段	monopolist stage of capitalism
资本主义所有制	capitalist ownership of capital goods
资产重估	assets reevaluation
资金存量折股	convert capital stock into stock share
资金使用效率	capital utilization efficiency
资金市场	capital market
资金周转	fund turnover rate

资源存量	stock of resources
资源分配比例	distribution ratio
资源利用效率	resource use efficiency
资源配置	resource allocation
资源配置不当	improper resource allocation
资源配置机制	resource allocation mechanism
资源投入和组合	resource input and combination
资源增量的变动	incremental changes in resources
自负盈亏	take responsibility for one's own gains and losses; function as an independent accounting unit; liable for one's own gains and losses
自然单位的劳动投入量	labor and capital goods inputs in production by natural physical units
自我制约	self-restrain
自行调节功能	self-regulatory function
自由价格	free price
自主经营	make one's own business decisions
自主经营权	decision-making autonomy
总供给	aggregate demand
总需求	aggregate supply
租赁	lease
租赁经营	leased management
最大效益原则	maximum gains at a certain expense
最小成本原则	minimum expense in return for a certain amount of gain

NOTES 注释

FOREWORD

1 For an excellent critical review on market socialism in general and its manifestation in the 1980s in particular, see Kornai, János (1992), *The Socialist System*, Princeton: Princeton University Press. For a leading essay on market socialism for China, see Sun, Yefang (1982), "Some theoretical issues in socialist economies," originally published in Chinese in the period 1958-1961, in Fung, K. K. (ed.), *Social Needs versus Economic Efficiency in China*, Armonk, N.Y.: M. E. Sharp. For an influential essay which promotes comprehensive price reform in China, see Wu, Jinglian and Reynolds, Bruce L. (1987), "Choosing a strategy for China's economic reform," *American Economic Review*, Vol. 78, No. 2, pp. 461-466.

2 See Kornai, János (1990), *The Road to a Free Economy*, New York and London: W. W. Norton & Company.

3 For more detailed and systematic discussions on multiple property rights and ownership reform by Professor Li, see Li, Yining (1986), *Political Economy of Socialism*, Beijing: Commercial Press; Li, Yining (1987), *An Exploratory Study of Economic System Reform*, Beijing: People's Daily Press; and Li, Yining (1989), *Thoughts on China's Economic Reform*, Beijing: Zhongguo Zhanwang Press. All these three books are in Chinese.

4 Granick, David (1990), *Chinese State Enterprises: A Regional Property Rights Analysis*, Chicago: University of Chicago Press.

5 Also see, for example, Li, Yining (2003), *The Rise of Capitalism: A Study of Comparative Economic History*, Beijing: Commercial Press; Li, Yining (2006), *The Economic History of Rome-Byzantine Empire*, Beijing: Commercial Press. Both books are in Chinese.

6 More detailed and systematic analysis on this topic is presented in Li, Yining (1990), *Chinese Economy in Disequilibrium*, Beijing: Beijing Daily Press. This book is in Chinese.

7 An important parallel research on the viability issue of SOEs in China (and other transitional economies) has been conducted by Professor Justin Yifu Lin. Lin employs the analytical perspective of comparative advantage and argues that the firms in heavy industries prioritized by the government in transitional centrally planned economies are not viable in open, competitive markets because their activities are inconsistent with the economy's comparative advantage. This viability problem is another root of the soft budget constraint (SBC) syndrome. If the viability problem is not solved, the SBC syndrome will not be eliminated even

though the socialist government is overthrown and all firms are privatized. See, Lin, Justin Y. (2003), "Development strategy, viability and economic convergence," *Economic Development and Cultural Change*, Vol. 53, pp. 277-308; Lin, Justin Y. (2005), "Viability, economic transition and reflection on neoclassical economics," *Kyklos*, Vol. 58, No. 2, pp. 239-264.

THE ROLE OF EDUCATION IN ECONOMIC GROWTH (1980)

1 This speech was delivered at Peking University 1978 "May Fourth" Symposium and carried in *Social Sciences Front*, issue No. 4, 1978.

2 Referring to individuals who know that no suitable jobs are available but choose not to register as being employed, even though they would prefer to have a job. (*Translator*)

LAYING A SOLID FOUNDATION FOR NEW CULTURE (1989)

1 Narrowly speaking, the May Fourth Movement refers to the Chinese student demonstrations in Beijing on May 4, 1919, in protest against the government's yielding to the pressure of Western countries in signing the Treaty of Versailles. These demonstrations sparked national debates on why China was economically and politically weak and the role of traditional Chinese culture. The movement triggered the New Culture Movement of 1915-1921, in which intellectuals criticized Confucianism and advocated Western-style liberty, democracy and science. The May Fourth Movement Spirit is anti-tradition, anti-feudalism, and pro-new culture. (*Translator*)

2 The Tian'anmen Incident of 1976 took place in Beijing on April 5, 1976, when thousands of citizens gathered at Tian'anmen Square to honor the memory of the late Premier Zhou Enlai, and voice their burning indignation against the Gang of Four. (*Translator*)

COMPARATIVE ECONOMIC HISTORY AND THE MODERNIZATION OF CHINA (1993)

1 Fogel, Robert William and Stanley Lewis Engerman (eds.) (1971), *The Reinterpretation of American Economic History*, New York: Harper and Row, p. 8.
福格尔和恩格尔曼：《美国经济史的重新解释》，纽约，1971 年，第 8 页。

2 Li, Yining (1989), "John Hicks's research on economic history," *Reading*, issue No. 5, pp. 29-34.
厉以宁：《希克斯的经济史研究》，载《读书》1989 年第 5 期，第 29～34 页。

3 Hicks, John Richard (1969), *A Theory of Economic History*, Oxford: Clarendon Press, p. 2.
希克斯：《经济史理论》中译本，商务印书馆 1987 年版，第 5 页。

4 Pollard, Sidney (1973), "Industrialization and the European Economy," *The Economic History Review*, New Series, Vol. 26, No. 4, p. 647.
波拉德：《工业化与欧洲经济》，载英国《经济史评论》，1973 年 11 月，第 647 页。

5 Solow, Robert M. (1985), "Economic History and Economics," *American Economic Review*, Vol. 75, No. 2, Papers and Proceedings of the Ninety-seventh Annual Meeting of the American Economic Association (May 1985), p. 328.
《美国经济评论》，1985 年 5 月号。

6 Ibid, p. 331.
同上。

7 North, Douglass C. and Robert Paul Thomas (1975), "The Tasks of Economic History," *The Journal of Economic History*, Vol. 35, No. 1, p. 19.
莱恩的论文和诺思、托马斯的评论文章均载于美国《经济史杂志》，1975 年 3 月号。

GROWTH AND FLUCTUATIONS IN ECONOMIC DISEQUILIBRIUM (1993)

1 Hahn, F. H. and F. P. R. Brechling (eds.) (1965), *The Theory of Interest Rates*, London: Macmillan.

2 *Western Economic Journal*, issue No. 6, 1967.

3 Leijonhufvud, Axel (1968), *On Keynesian Economics and the Economics of Keynes: A Study in Monetary Theory*, New York: Oxford University Press.

4 Benassy, Jean-Pascal (1982), *The Economics of Market Disequilibrium*, New York: Academic Press; (1986), *Macroeconomics and Imperfect Competition*, Paris; (1986), *Macroeconomics: An Introduction to the Non-Walrasian Approach*, New York: Academic Press.

5 Kornai, János (1971), *Anti-Equilibrium: On Economic Systems Theory and the Tasks of Research*, Amsterdam: North-Holland Pub. Co.; (1980), *Economics of Shortage*, Amsterdam: North-Holland Pub. Co.; (1982), *Growth, Shortage and Efficiency*, Oxford: Basil Blackwell.

6 Li, Yining (1990), *Disequilibrium in the Chinese Economy*, Beijing: Economic Daily Press.

7 Li, Yining et al (1991), *Strategic Choice for Prosperity*, Beijing: Economic Daily Press, p. 204.
厉以宁等：《走向繁荣的战略选择》，经济日报出版社 1991 年版，第 204 页。

8 Ibid, pp. 204-205.
同上，第 204～205 页。

9 Li, Yining (1990), *Disequilibrium in Chinese Economy*, Beijing: Economic Daily Press, pp. 70-71.
厉以宁：《非均衡的中国经济》，经济日报出版社 1990 年版，第 70～71 页。

PROPERTY RIGHTS REFORM OF RURAL ENTERPRISES (1994)

1 Large urban collective, a term dating back to the Great Leap Forward of 1958, referring to firms in which capital is owned collectively while workers are accorded the same wages and welfare benefits as state enterprise employees. (*Translator*)

THE DUAL FOUNDATIONS OF EFFICIENCY (1998)

1 Li, Yining (1986), *Socialist Political Economics*, Beijing: Commercial Press, pp. 438-439.
厉以宁：《社会主义政治经济学》，商务印书馆 1986 年版，第 438～439 页。

POSTSCRIPT: A PROFILE OF LI YINING

1 A socialist movement designed to mobilize the nation's abundant labor force to accomplish a "leap" in industry and agriculture (1958-1960). It failed due to the fact that "Comrade Mao Zedong and many leading comrades, both at the center and in the localities, had become smug about their successes, were impatient for quick results and overestimated the role of man's subjective will and efforts," according to the *Resolution on Certain Questions in the History of Our Party since the Founding of the People's Republic of China*, 1981. (*Translator*)

2 A national movement to clean things up in the fields of politics, economy, organization and ideology (1963-1966). (*Translator*)